COMMUNISM, FASCISM, AND DEMOCRACY

THE THEORETICAL FOUNDATIONS

COMMUNISM, FASCISM, AND DEMOCRACY

THE THEORETICAL FOUNDATIONS

THIRD EDITION

Edited by

Carl Cohen
The University of Michigan

THE MCGRAW-HILL COMPANIES, INC.

New York   St. Louis   San Francisco   Auckland   Bogotá   Caracas   Lisbon
London   Madrid   Mexico City   Milan   Montreal   New Delhi
San Juan   Singapore   Sydney   Tokyo   Toronto

This book was set in Times Roman by The Clarinda Company.
The editors were Sarah Moyers and John M. Morriss;
The production supervisor was Paula Keller.
The cover was designed by Wanda Lubelska.
Project supervision was done by Tage Publishing Service, Inc.
R. R. Donnelley & Sons Company was printer and binder.

McGraw-Hill

A Division of The **McGraw·Hill** Companies

COMMUNISM, FASCISM, AND DEMOCRACY

This book is printed on acid-free paper.

1 2 3 4 5 6 7 8 9 0   DOC   DOC   909876

ISBN 0-07-011609-1

Library of Congress Cataloging-in-Publication Data
Communism, fascism, and democracy : the theoretical foundations /
    edited by Carl Cohen. — 3rd ed.
        p.   cm.
    Includes index.
    ISBN 0-07-011609-1
    1. Communism.   2. Fascism.   3. Democracy.   I. Cohen, Carl, (date)
JC348.C63   1997
320.5—dc20   96-21812

ABOUT
THE AUTHOR

CARL COHEN is Professor of Philosophy at The University of Michigan where he has taught political philosophy, ethics, and logic since 1955. He received an A.B. from the University of Miami, an M.A. from the University of Illinois, a Ph.D. from the University of California at Los Angeles, and an honorary L.D. from Ripon College. He was one of the founders of the Residential College at The University of Michigan in which he remains active. He has served as Chairman of the Faculty Senate of The University of Michigan, as Chairman of the American Civil Liberties Union of Michigan, and as a member of the National Board of Directors of the ACLU. He serves as a labor/management arbitrator for the American Arbitration Association and for the Michigan Employment Relations Commission. He has taught as a visiting professor at universities in Peru, Israel, Hong Kong, Singapore, and New Zealand, at the Universities of Illinois and Miami, and at Davidson College in North Carolina.

Professor Cohen has published widely in learned journals (*Ethics, The Journal of Philosophy, The New England Journal of Medicine,* and others) and frequently in journals of political and literary opinion (*The Nation, Commentary, The Yale Review,* and others). He is the author of *Civil Disobedience* (Columbia University Press), *Democracy* (The Free Press/Macmillan), *Four Systems* (Random House), and most recently *Naked Racial Preference* (Madison Books, 1995). With Irving M. Copi he is co-author of *Introduction to Logic*, 9th Edition (Macmillan/Prentice Hall).

Carl Cohen lives in Ann Arbor with his wife, Jan, their two young children, Jaclyn and Noah, and their dog, Charlie.

v

This book is dedicated to the
memory of my mother and
father, to my wife, Jan, and to
my children, Jaclyn and Noah

CONTENTS

PREFACE

This third edition of *Communism, Fascism, and Democracy: The Theoretical Foundations* retains the general structure and spirit of earlier editions, although it has been much revised. Philosohical writings most influential in the development of these three great political philosophies appear as they did; the central ideas in these works are again presented using original texts. Most important, the central intellectual themes of these great philosophies have been put into intelligible order, partly chronological and partly substantive, that is true to the spirit of the systems themselves.

Major historical developments and some adjustments in approach have required substantial revisions in the selections used. Those new to the book, as well as those familiar with its earlier editions, may be helped by a brief review of the changes incorporated in this new edition.

Part One, Communism, has been amended somewhat. The development of Marxist thought has been carried from the early utopian socialists through to the 20th century, as earlier had been done—but passages that chiefly reflect phases of the history of Soviet and Chinese communism have been eliminated. The account of the theory of dialectical and historical materialism has been expanded by the inclusion of more from Marx's economic writings—notably the passage from *Das Kapital* on the "Fetishism of Commodities." Overall, the main elements of Part One have remained much as they were.

Part Two, Fascism, has been changed little. Some minor additions have been made to the background materials. But the central passages from leading Italian and German fascists, not readily accessible elsewhere, and found exceedingly useful by very many past users, have not been reduced. The order of their presentation, however, has been adjusted somewhat to exhibit more clearly the relation between the early theoretical defenses of irrationalism and nationalism, and manifestations of these themes in the politics of fascist Italy and Germany.

Part Three, Democracy, has been very greatly changed, its structure as well as its content rebuilt. Many selections have been added, come classical and some contemporary. The great works in the history of democratic thought have been retained, but their placement is more *systematic*. The first section of this part now begins with accounts of the *nature* of democracy; the second section encompasses the arguments, classical and modern, presented to *justify* democracy—first as a deduction from laws of nature, then as a system believed most likely to achieve good consequences. The third section addresses the issues encountered when, selecting some decision-making rule and some representative system, we seek to make democracy *effective*.

The final long section of the third part deals with the *ideals* of democracy—fraternity, liberty, equality, and autonomy in turn. *Fraternity* is viewed from an American perspective, as the ideal of a union to be preserved so that the people can govern themselves; *autonomy* is viewed from a universal perspective, as the ideal of a system of rules genuinely self-imposed in any democratic community. Of ideal *liberty* two families are distinguished: the liberties of speech and expression on the one hand, and liberties in the realm of economics on the other. To the ideal of *equality*, two approaches are presented: those explaining the deep meanings of human equality, and those (made concrete in American Constitutional history) in which the ideal of equality is brought to bear on everyday life.

This more systematic approach to the philosophy of democracy has required the partial sacrifice of historical order in the appearance of classical arguments. The nature of democracy is presented first both in ancient and in very modern terms; the classical defenses of democracy by Locke, Mill, de Tocqueville and others follow those formulations. Later, in the exploration of representation and its complications, contemporary arguments have been presented, preceding some classical accounts of the ideals of democracy that appear in the final section. The movement back and forth in time is designed to support the intellectual understanding of the whole, to make the relations of the theoretical parts of the system as clear as they can be made.

Balance in the presentation of views has been a primary consideration throughout. On controversial matters like the suitability of proportional representation in a democracy, or the role of socialism or capitalism in supporting democracy, every effort has been made to present the several positions fairly, through their most distinguished representatives. The *integrity* of more complicated arguments has been protected, so far as space permitted, by retaining long passages from some major works, *The Second Treatise of Government, On Liberty*, and others. But it has also been necessary to catch the essence of certain critical arguments, to rely, in places, upon short excerpts from the writings of the most notable exponents of those views.

Contemporary issues within democratic theory have been given a much greater role than formerly, illuminated by selections from landmark cases before the U.S. Supreme Court. For example, the limits that may be rightly placed upon free speech are explored with passages from notable decisions and dissents; and the ideal of equality, likewise, is given content with some outstanding judicial opinions of recent date, and with the writings of some international heroes of democracy in the late 20th century.

In all, the account of the philosophical foundations of democracy has been enriched and strengthened, and the account of the foundations of all three systems updated and refined. Thoughtful readers are likely to think of great philosophical passages that they judge ought not to have been omitted, or to judge unsatisfying some passages that have been included. Such differences of view are obviously inevitable. But taken as a whole the selections chosen will serve, I submit, as a full and provocative presentation of the theoretical foundations of communism, fascism, and democracy.

I acknowledge, with heartfelt thanks, the thoughtful criticisms and helpful suggestions of countless users of this book over the years. Naming all these persons here would be tedious and counterproductive. I report the awareness of my debt, and my earnest hope that the expectations of my colleagues for this new edition will have been substantially fulfilled.

When *Communism, Fascism, and Democracy* was first published its Introduction began with this passage from the *Politics* of Aristotle:

> If all communities aim at some good, the state, or political community, which is the highest of all, and which embraces all the rest, aims at good in a greater degree than any other, and at the highest good.

Through the study of conflicting accounts of the nature of the state and its proper aims, and through reflection upon the philosophical foundations of the different systems of government, we can participate in the pursuit of that great good.

Carl Cohen

Ann Arbor

INTRODUCTION

At the time of the Second World War some half a century ago, Marxism-Leninism was mighty in the Union of Soviet Socialist Republics, and fascism in Germany, Italy, Spain, and Japan dominated Europe and much of Asia. Democratic nations, soon to be victorious in war, nevertheless felt beleaguered and under ideological attack.

Today democracy is more widely practiced and more deeply rooted. Nazism is everywhere despised. Communism as an international movement appears to have failed. Everywhere there is a lust for the material prosperity that market economies have recently enjoyed.

But democracy is far from secure. Is it *the* right form of government, the one form best for human communities? If so, why? And how may it best succeed? The philosophical issues raised by communists in the 19th century, and by fascists in the early 20th century, confront us perennially: What is the national state, and how did it come to be? Will it one day be replaced? What duties are owed by individual citizens to their country, or to their class, and why?

Fascism, or its legacy, is very much alive. Irrational political enthusiasms engendering bloody war are rampant around the globe. Rascism, anti-Semitism, ethnic hatreds are widespread. Dictatorships, although disavowed, are common in fact. There are more people ready to march for some variety of national glory now than there have been since the Allies invaded Europe in 1944.

Marxism is very much alive. The Union of Soviet Socialist Republics came to an end on the 25th of December, 1991. The end of the cold war, the reunification of Germany, the collapse of the international communist movement, all followed with remarkable speed. But the Marxist philosophy that had inspired and sustained that communist movement continues to thrive, not merely as intellectual history, but as a fruitful mode of historical interpretation. For some it remains the intellectual framework for future revolution. Karl Marx was a great philosopher. His vision of ideal human communities, his dialectical account of world history, and the system he and his followers developed based upon that account, remain rich with insight. Many who today call themselves Marxists are delighted to be burdened no longer with the expectation that their humanism must somehow be brought into accord with corrupt Soviet tyranny that had, in their view, undermined genuine Marxist ideals.

Democracy as a set of ideals is professed almost everywhere today, as it has been for decades. But it is practiced concretely and effectively only in some countries, and it is realized fully in none. How democracy is rightly to be understood, what institutions are consistent with it, how its principles ought to be applied in practice, are all matters of continuing bitter controversy.

The philosophical underpinnings of communism, fascism, and democracy are still neither widely enough nor well enough understood. Lip service is easily given to a name or a slogan, to the "class struggle of the proletariat" or the "democratic way of life." But we are not well served by the careless use of expressions which, through thoughtless repetition, have lost much of their original significance. Whether our object be to defend or to oppose communism, or fascism, or democracy, we cannot do so intelligently or effectively without a full understanding of the theory and practice of each, of the works and the aims of its advocates. It is reasonable to conclude that the study of the philosophical foundations of communism, and fascism, and democracy was never more timely or more important than it is now.

These philosophical foundations are presented here chiefly in the original words of their classical and contemporary proponents. Each of the three systems is developed in turn, with selections arranged in an order that is in part chronological and in part systematic. The aim throughout is to make the essential principles of each system clearly understandable, and to preserve so far as possible the intellectual integrity of each without prejudice.

The arrangement of authors and works—especially their inclusion under the general headings of communism, fascism, and democracy—should certainly not be constructed as a labeling of individual philosophers. Hegel, for example, appears here (however much he would have winced at the thought) as a contributor to the foundations of both communism and fascism, and can himself be classified as neither. Hobbes and Bodin are no more properly called fascists than Feuerbach is properly called a communist. The structure of the volume has been designed to exhibit the historical development and the intellectual wholeness of political philosophies, not to encourage the classification of philosophers.

Brief comment about the format in which the selections appear may prove helpful. A short prefatory note begins each part and section. These notes are intended neither as summaries nor as interpretations; their chief purpose is to set the scene for the selections that follow, to orient the reader by disclosing something of the character and substance of the philosophical views to be presented. Within the several sections each selection is headed by an introductory paragraph or two, whose purpose is to identify the author and the work, and to orient the reader with reference to the coming passage. The headings interspersed within the selections themselves are often taken from the original texts; but in many cases, when needed for purposes of clarification, headings have been supplied (and bracketed) by the editor.

Communism, fascism, and democracy have been, and remain, the ruling political philosophies of our time. The interplay of theory and practice, the impact of philosophical speculation upon the course of human life, is nowhere clearer than in the realm of political realities they dominate. Upon our understanding of these political forms and their philosophical foundations, and our ability to judge them intelligently, depend not only the just disposition of our present affairs, but the wise preparation for our future.

PART ONE

COMMUNISM

The term "communism" remains charged with emotive content. For many decades the name has aroused strong feelings of reverence and enthusiasm, or uneasy concern, or condemnation and hatred. But, its name, like "fascism" and "democracy," has a primary cognitive meaning that must be understood if we are to pass wise judgment.

Of course the term "communism" can refer to any system in which goods are held in common. As the term has been most commonly used, however, it refers to a particular kind of communal organization—one that claims to arise out of the revolutionary movement begun by Karl Marx and Friedrich Engels in the nineteenth century. In the middle decades of the twentieth century that movement achieved great successes in the Union of Soviet Socialist Republics, and in other socialist nations of Eastern Europe and Asia. In the late years of the twentieth century most communist governments collapsed.

But the collapse of Marxist regimes in the Soviet Union and Eastern Europe has certainly not destroyed the ideals and aspirations of many contemporary Marxists. The collapse of Soviet Communism (they believe) was a consequence of its betrayal of sound communist theory and genuine communist ideals. Indeed, many of Marx's views have been absorbed by many democratic thinkers, and no longer even seem revolutionary. But revolutionary Communism remains, even where it is no longer in power, the foundation of a deep critique of capitalism, and the motivating theoretical force behind a great many dissident movements around the globe.

A rational evaluation of the Marxist critique requires that we first answer the following questions: What *is* communism? What *claims* does it make about the individual and the state? What *changes* does it demand, and why? And what are the underlying methodological and metaphysical principles upon which it rests? In this objective spirit we will turn later in this book to the theoretical foundations of fascism and democracy as well.

The philosophical method of Marxist communism is *dialectics;* its metaphysical principles are grounded in a strict *materialism;* the view as a whole is therefore properly described as *dialectical materialism.* Although Marxists consider theirs to be a scientific approach to social development, their professed ideals are far-reaching and humane, owing much to the yearnings of the utopian socialists who preceded them. The selections in this Part of the book trace the development of Marxist communism from the speculations of Marx's predecessors, through the full development of communist theory by Marx and his contemporaries, to the later applications of Marxism by their successors.

1

UTOPIAN SOCIALISM

Socialism in the modern world began in earnest in the last quarter of the eighteenth century, a time of great revolutions. We think first of the American Revolution, which did much to advance the cause of self-government—but the French Revolution was far more cataclysmic, and the recurring upheavals to which it led disclosed chronic ailments in European civilization. More fundamental than these political convulsions, however, was the Industrial Revolution, rapidly sweeping over Europe, whose impact was painfully felt but only dimly understood.

The growth of modern industry, the development of powerful new instruments of production and distribution, had profound and far-reaching consequences in the lives and work of ordinary people. Many of these consequences were delayed, but one early result of the intense competition of unregulated capitalist enterprises was human degradation, the cruel exploitation of newly created masses of industrial workers. By the middle decades of the nineteenth century the living and working conditions of laborers—women and men and children—in the industrial centers of Europe were so bad as to be almost beyond belief.

This great and widespread distress among working men and women gave rise to many moving humanitarian complaints. Among the most effective critics of this period were those thinkers, chiefly French and English, who came to be known as utopian socialists. Witnessing extremes of poverty and misery on the one hand, and leisure and luxury on the other, they concluded that the only possible remedy lay in a total reorganization of the structure of society, and a thorough reapportionment of its wealth. The schemes these utopians put forward varied greatly, but

3

they had in common the demand for a totally new order, one in which everyone would work, goods would be owned in common, and each person would receive an equitable share of the wealth produced.

The proposals of most of the utopian socialists were far-fetched, impractical, in some cases verging upon the absurd. But they did manifest great human sympathy, a keen critical spirit, and vivid imagination. Their speculations constitute the background of social striving out of which modern communism arose. In articulating the plight of the exploited, they opened a path that Marx and Engels were soon to follow, and their condemnation of the greed and excess of the existing order contributed extensively to Marx's later critique of capitalism.

Karl Marx himself expressed disdain for the foolishness and impracticality of these early socialists, their outright utopianism. Yet when others attacked them, he came to their defense, holding that because of their place in history it was not possible for them to have supplied a true solution to the problems they had correctly identified; they did the best they could. In spite of their naive optimism and wild dreams these thinkers, Marx and Engels later said, were among the greatest social philosophers in history. But their socialism was regrettably *utopian;* what was needed, Marx thought, was a socialist theory of society that would be truly *scientific.* That contribution, he believed, was destined to be his own.

The spirit of utopianism remains alive. Widespread misery and distress continue to provoke the quest for a happy human future in a new order enhanced perhaps by coming revolutions in biology or communication or fields of study not yet well formed. But all social visionaries, including Marx, must carry a debt to the insight and imagination of these early utopian socialists who redesigned society in their heads.

1
Friedrich Engels

Friedrich Engels (1820–1895) was Karl Marx's lifelong friend and frequent
collaborator; their names are linked as the founders of modern communism. The
work from which the following selection is taken is made up of three chapters
from a larger work, by Engels alone, *Herr Eugen Dühring's Revolution in Science*
(known as the Anti-Dühring), first published in 1878. These three chapters (the
second and third of which appear later in this volume) provide one of the clearest
statements of communist theory. In this first chapter Engels acknowledges his
great debt to the utopian socialists and discusses the relation of their theories to
the newer communism developed by Marx and himself.

SOCIALISM, UTOPIAN AND SCIENTIFIC: PART I*

[The Utopians]

Modern socialism is, in its essence, the direct product of the recognition, on the one
hand, of the class antagonisms, existing in the society of today, between proprietors
and non-proprietors, between capitalists and wage workers; on the other hand, of
the anarchy existing in production. But, in its theoretical form, modern socialism
originally appears ostensibly as a more logical extension of the principles laid down
by the great French philosophers of the eighteenth century. Like every new theory,
modern socialism had, at first, to connect itself with the intellectual stock-in-trade
ready to its hand, however deeply its roots lay in material economic facts.

The great men, who in France prepared men's minds for the coming revolution,
were themselves extreme revolutionists. They recognized no external authority of
any kind whatever. Religion, natural science, society, political institutions, everything, was subjected to the most unsparing criticism: everything must justify its
existence before the judgment seat of reason, or give up existence. Reason became
the sole measure of everything. It was the time when, as Hegel says, the world
stood upon its head;† first, in the sense that the human head, and the principles
arrived at by its thought, claimed to be the basis of all human action and associa-

---

*From F. Engels, *Socialism, Utopian and Scientific,* Swan Sonnenschein and Co., London, 1892.
†This is the passage on the French Revolution: "Thought, the concept of law, all at once made itself felt,
and against this the old scaffolding of wrong could make no stand. In this conception of law, therefore, a
constitution has now been established, and henceforth everything must be based upon this. Since the sun had
been in the firmament, and the planets circled round him, the sight had never been seen of man standing
upon his head—i.e., on the idea—and building reality after this image. Anaxagoras first said that the *Nous,*
reason, rules the world; but now, for the first time, had man come to recognize that the Idea must rule the
mental reality. And this was a magnificent sunrise. All thinking beings have participated in celebrating this
holy day. A sublime emotion swayed men at that time, an enthusiasm of reason pervaded the world, as if
now had come the reconciliation of the Divine Principle with the world." [Hegel: *Philosophy of History,*
1840, p. 535.] Is it not high time to set the Anti-Socialist Law in action against such teachings, subversive
and to the common danger, by the late Professor Hegel?

tion; but by and by, also, in the wider sense that the reality which was in contradiction to these principles had, in fact, to be turned upside down. Every form of society and government then existing, every old traditional notion was flung into the lumber room as irrational; the world had hitherto allowed itself to be led solely by prejudices; everything in the past deserved only pity and contempt. Now, for the first time, appeared the light of day, the kingdom of reason; henceforth superstition, injustice, privilege, oppression, were to be superseded by eternal truth, eternal right, equality based on nature and the inalienable rights of man.

We know today that this kingdom of reason was nothing more than the idealized kingdom of the bourgeoisie; that this eternal right found its realization in bourgeois justice; that this equality reduced itself to bourgeois equality before the law; that bourgeois property was proclaimed as one of the essential rights of man; and that the government of reason, the *Contrat Social* of Rousseau, came into being, and only could come into being, as a democratic bourgeois republic. The great thinkers of the eighteenth century could, no more than their predecessors, go beyond the limits imposed upon them by their epoch.

But, side by side with the antagonism of the feudal nobility and the burghers, who claimed to represent all the rest of society, was the general antagonism of exploiters and exploited, of rich idlers and poor workers. It was this very circumstance that made it possible for the representatives of the bourgeoisie to put themselves forward as representing not one special class, but the whole of suffering humanity. Still further. From its origin, the bourgeoisie was saddled with its antithesis: capitalists cannot exist without wage workers, and, in the same proportion as the mediaeval burgher of the guild developed into the modern bourgeois, the guild journeyman and the day laborer, outside the guilds, developed into the proletarian. And although, upon the whole, the bourgeoisie, in their struggle with the nobility, could claim to represent at the same time the interests of the different working classes of that period, yet in every great bourgeois movement there were independent outbursts of that class which was the forerunner, more or less developed, of the modern proletariat. For example, at the time of the German reformation and the peasants' war, the Anabaptists and Thomas Münzer; in the great English Revolution, the Levellers; in the great French Revolution, Babeuf.

There were theoretical enunciations corresponding with these revolutionary uprisings of a class not yet developed; in the sixteenth and seventeenth centuries, utopian pictures of ideal social conditions; in the eighteenth, actual communistic theories (Morelly and Mably). The demand for equality was no longer limited to political rights; it was extended also to the social conditions of individuals. It was not simply class privileges that were to be abolished, but class distinctions themselves. A communism, ascetic, denouncing all the pleasures of life, Spartan, was the first form of the new teaching. Then came the three great Utopians: Saint Simon, to whom the middle class movement, side by side with the proletarian, still had a certain significance; Fourier; and Owen, who in the country where capitalist production was most developed, and under the influence of the antagonisms begotten of this, worked out his proposals for the removal of class distinction systematically and in direct relation to French materialism.

One thing is common to all three. Not one of them appears as a representative of the interests of that proletariat, which historical development had in the meantime produced. Like the French philosophers, they do not claim to emancipate a particular class to begin with, but all humanity at once. Like them, they wish to bring in the kingdom of reason and eternal justice, but this kingdom, as they see it, is as far as heaven from earth from that of the French philosophers.

For, to our three social reformers, the bourgeois world, based upon the principles of these philosophers, is quite as irrational and unjust, and, therefore, finds its way to the dust hole quite as readily as feudalism and all the earlier stages of society. If pure reason and justice have not, hitherto, ruled the world, this has been the case only because men have not rightly understood them. What was wanted was the individual man of genius, who has now arisen and who understands the truth. That he has now arisen, that the truth has now been clearly understood, is not an inevitable event, following of necessity in the chain of historical development, but a mere happy accident. He might just as well have been born 500 years earlier, and might then have spared humanity 500 years of error, strife and suffering.

We saw how the French philosophers of the eighteenth century, the forerunners of the revolution, appealed to reason as the sole judge of all that is. A rational government, rational society, were to be founded; everything that ran counter to eternal reason was to be remorselessly done away with. We saw also that this eternal reason was in reality nothing but the idealized understanding of the eighteenth century citizen, just then evolving into the bourgeois. The French Revolution had realized this rational society and government.

But the new order of things, rational enough as compared with earlier conditions, turned out to be by no means absolutely rational. The state based upon reason completely collapsed. Rousseau's *Contrat Social* had found its realization in the Reign of Terror, from which bourgeoisie, who had lost confidence in their own political capacity, had taken refuge first in the corruption of the Directorate, and, finally, under the wing of the Napoleonic despotism. The promised eternal peace was turned into an endless war of conquest. The society based upon reason had fared no better. The antagonism between rich and poor, instead of dissolving into general prosperity, had become intensified by the removal of the guild and other privileges, which had to some extent bridged it over, and by the removal of the charitable institutions of the Church. The "freedom of property" from feudal fetters, now veritably accomplished, turned out to be, for the small capitalists and small proprietors, the freedom to sell their small property, crushed under the overmastering competition of the large capitalists and landlords, to these great lords, and thus, as far as the small capitalists and peasant proprietors were concerned, became "freedom *from* property." The development of industry upon a capitalistic basis made poverty and misery of the working masses conditions of existence of society. Cash payment became more and more, in Carlyle's phrase, the sole nexus between man and man. The number of crimes increased from year to year. Formerly, the feudal vices had openly stalked about in broad daylight; though not eradicated, they were now at any rate thrust into the background. In their stead, the bourgeois vices, hitherto practiced in secret, began to blossom all the more luxuriantly. Trade became to a greater and greater extent cheating. The "fraternity" of the revolutionary motto was realized in the chicanery and rivalries of the battle of competition. Oppression by force was replaced by corruption; the sword, as the first social lever, by gold. The right of the first night was transferred from the feudal lords to the bourgeois manufacturers. Prostitution increased to an extent never heard of. Marriage itself remained, as before, the legally recognized form, the official cloak of prostitution, and, moreover, was supplemented by rich crops of adultery.

In a word, compared with the splendid promises of the philosophers, the social and political institutions born of the "triumph of reason" were bitterly disappointing caricatures. All that was wanting was the men to formulate this disappointment, and they came with the turn of the century. In 1802 Saint Simon's Geneva Letters appeared; in 1808 appeared Fourier's first work, although the groundwork of his theory dated from 1799; on January 1, 1800, Robert Owen undertook the direction of New Lanark.

At this time, however, the capitalist mode of production, and with it the antagonism between the bourgeoisie and the proletariat, was still very incompletely developed. Modern industry, which had just arisen in England, was still unknown in France. But modern industry develops, on the one hand, the conflicts which make absolutely necessary a revolution in the mode of production and the doing away with its capitalistic character—conflicts not only between the classes begotten of it, but also between the very productive forces and the forms of exchange created by it. And, on the other hand, it develops, in these very gigantic productive forces, the means of ending these conflicts. If, therefore, about the year 1800, the conflicts arising from the new social order were only just beginning to take shape, this holds still more fully as to the means of ending them. The "have-nothing" masses of Paris, during the Reign of Terror, were able for a moment to gain the mastery, and thus to lead the bourgeois revolution to victory in spite of the bourgeoisie themselves. But, in doing so, they only proved how impossible it was for their domination to last under the conditions then obtaining. The proletariat, which then for the first time evolved itself from these "have-nothing" masses as the nucleus of a new class, as yet quite incapable of independent political action, appeared as an oppressed, suffering order, to whom, in its incapacity to help itself, help could, at best, be brought in from without or down from above.

This historical situation also dominated the founders of socialism. To the crude conditions of capitalistic production and the crude class conditions corresponded crude theories. The solution of the social problems, which as yet lay hidden in undeveloped economic conditions, the utopians attempted to evolve out of the human brain. Society presented nothing but wrongs; to remove these was the task of reason. It was necessary, then, to discover a new and more perfect system of social order and to impose this upon society from without by propaganda, and, wherever it was possible, by the example of model experiments. These new social systems were foredoomed as utopian; the more completely they were worked out in detail, the more they could not avoid drifting off into pure fantasies.

These facts once established, we need not dwell a moment longer upon this side of the question, now wholly belonging to the past. We can leave it to the literary small fry to solemnly quibble over these fantasies, which today only make us smile, and to crow over the superiority of their own bald reasoning, as compared with such "insanity." For ourselves, we delight in the stupendously grand thoughts and germs of thought that everywhere break out through their fantastic covering, and to which these philistines are blind.

Saint Simon was a son of the great French Revolution, at the outbreak of which he was not yet thirty. The revolution was the victory of the third estate, i.e., of the great masses of the nation, *working* in production and in trade over the privileged *idle* classes, the nobles and the priests. But the victory of the third estate soon revealed itself as exclusively the victory of a small part of this "estate," as the conquest of political power by the socially privileged section of it, i.e., the propertied bourgeoisie. And the bourgeoisie had certainly developed rapidly during the revolution, partly by speculation in the lands of the nobility and of the Church, confiscated and afterwards put up for sale, and partly by frauds upon the nation by means of army contracts. It was the domination of these swindlers that, under the Directorate, brought France to the verge of ruin, and thus gave Napoleon the pretext for his *coup d'état.*

Hence, to Saint Simon the antagonism between the third estate and the privileged classes took the form of an antagonism between "workers" and "idlers." The idlers were not merely the old privileged classes, but also all who, without taking any part in production or distribution, lived on their incomes. And the workers were not only the wage workers, but also the manufacturers, the merchants, the bankers. That the idlers had lost the capacity for intellectual leadership and political supremacy had been proved, and was by the revolution finally settled. That the non-possessing classes had not this capacity seemed to Saint Simon proved by the experiences of the Reign of Terror. Then, who was to lead and command? According to Saint Simon, science and industry, both united by a new religious bond, destined to restore that unity of religious ideas which had been lost since the time of the Reformation—a necessarily mystic and rigidly hierarchic "new Christianity." But science, that was the scholars; and industry, that was, in the first place, the working bourgeois, manufacturers, merchants, bankers. These bourgeoisie were, certainly, intended by Saint Simon to transform themselves into a kind of public officials, or social trustees; but they were still to hold, vis-á-vis of the workers, a commanding and economically privileged position. The bankers especially were to be called upon to direct the whole of social production by the regulation of credit. This conception was in exact keeping with a time in which modern industry in France and, with it, the chasm between bourgeoisie and proletariat was only just coming into existence. But what Saint Simon especially lays stress upon is this: what interests him first, and above all other things, is the lot of the class that is the most numerous and the most poor (*"la classe la plus nombreuse et la plus pauvre"*).

Already, in his Geneva Letters, Saint Simon lays down the proposition that "all men ought to work." In the same work he recognizes also that the Reign of Terror was the reign of the non-possessing masses. "See," says he to them, "what happened in France at the time when your comrades held sway there; they brought about a famine." But to recognize the French Revolution as a class war, and not simply one between nobility and bourgeoisie, but between nobility, bourgeoisie and the non-possessors, was, in the year 1802, a most pregnant discovery. In 1816 he declares that politics is the science of production, and foretells the complete absorption of politics by economics. The knowledge that economic conditions are the basis of political institutions appears here only in embryo. Yet what is here already very plainly expressed is the idea of the future conversion of political rule over men into an administration of things and a direction of processes of production—that is to say, the "abolition of the state," about which recently there has been so much noise.

Saint Simon shows the same superiority over his contemporaries, when in 1814, immediately after the entry of the allies into Paris, and again in 1815, during the Hundred Days' War, he proclaims the alliance of France with England, and then of both these countries with Germany, as the only guarantee for the prosperous development and peace of Europe. To preach to the French in 1815 an alliance with the victors of Waterloo required as much courage as historical foresight.

If in Saint Simon we find a comprehensive breadth of view, by virtue of which almost all the ideas of later socialists, that are not strictly economic, are found in him in embryo, we find in Fourier a criticism of the existing conditions of society, genuinely French and witty, but not upon that account any the less thorough. Fourier takes the bourgeoisie, their inspired prophets before the revolution, and their interested eulogists after it, at their own word. He lays bare remorselessly the material and moral misery of the bourgeois world. He confronts it with the earlier philosophers' dazzling promises of a society in which reason alone should reign, of a civilization in which happiness should be universal, of an illimitable human perfectibility, and with the rose-colored phraseology of the bourgeois ideologists of his time. He points out how everywhere the most pitiful reality corresponds with the most high-sounding phrases, and he overwhelms this hopeless fiasco of phrases with his mordant sarcasm.

Fourier is not only a critic; his imperturbably serene nature makes him a satirist and assuredly one of the greatest satirists of all time. He depicts, with equal power and charm, the swindling speculations that blossomed out upon the downfall of the revolution, and the shopkeeping spirit prevalent in, and characteristic of, French commerce at that time. Still more masterly is his criticism of the bourgeois form of the relations between the sexes, and the position of woman in bourgeois society. He was the first to declare that in any given society the degree of woman's emancipation is the natural measure of the general emancipation.

But Fourier is at his greatest in his conception of the history of society. He divides its whole course, thus far, into four stages of evolution—savagery, barbarism, the patriarchate, civilization. This last is identical with the so-called civil, or bourgeois society of today—i.e., with the social order that came in with the sixteenth century. He proves "that the civilized stage raises every vice practiced by barbarism in a simple fashion, into a form of existence, complex, ambiguous,

equivocal, hypocritical"—that civilization moves in "a vicious circle," in contradictions which it constantly reproduces without being able to solve them; hence it
constantly arrives at the very opposite to that which it wants to attain, or pretends
to want to attain, so that, e.g., "under civilization poverty is born of superabundance itself."

Fourier, as we see, uses the dialectic method in the same masterly way as his
contemporary, Hegel. Using these same dialectics, he argues against the talk about
illimitable human perfectibility that every historical phase has its period of ascent
and also its period of descent, and he applies this observation to the future of the
whole human race. As Kant introduced into natural science the idea of the ultimate
destruction of the earth, Fourier introduced into historical science that of the ultimate destruction of the human race.

While in France the hurricane of the revolution swept over the land, in England
a quieter, but not on that account less tremendous, revolution was going on. Steam
and the new tool-making machinery were transforming manufacture into modern
industry, and thus revolutionizing the whole foundation of bourgeois society. The
sluggish march of development of the manufacturing period changed into a veritable storm and stress period of production. With constantly increasing swiftness
the splitting-up of society into large capitalists and non-possessing proletarians
went on. Between these, instead of the former stable middle class, an unstable
mass of artisans and small shopkeepers, the most fluctuating portion of the population, now led a precarious existence.

The new mode of production was, as yet, only at the beginning of its period of
ascent; as yet it was the normal, regular method of production—the only one possible under existing conditions. Nevertheless, even then it was producing crying
social abuses—the herding together of a homeless population in the worst quarters
of the large town; the loosening of all traditional moral bonds, of patriarchal subordination, of family relations; overwork, especially of women and children, to a
frightful extent; complete demoralization of the working class, suddenly flung into
altogether new conditions, from the country into the town, from agriculture into
modern industry, from stable conditions of existence into insecure ones that
changed from day to day.

At this juncture there came forward as a reformer a manufacturer 29 years
old—a man of almost sublime, childlike simplicity of character, and at the same
time one of the few born leaders of men. Robert Owen had adopted the teaching
of the materialistic philosophers: that man's character is the product, on the one
hand, of heredity, on the other, of the environment of the individual during his lifetime, and especially during his period of development. In the industrial revolution
most of his class saw only chaos and confusion, and the opportunity of fishing in
these troubled waters and making large fortunes quickly. He saw in it the opportunity of putting into practice his favorite theory, and so of bringing order out of
chaos. He had already tried it with success, as superintendent of more than five
hundred men in a Manchester factory. From 1800 to 1829, he directed the great
cotton mill at New Lanark, in Scotland, as managing partner, along the same lines,
but with greater freedom of action and with a success that made him a European

reputation. A population, originally consisting of the most diverse and, for the most part, very demoralized elements, a population that gradually grew to 2,500, he turned into a model colony, in which drunkenness, police, magistrates, lawsuits, poor laws, charity were unknown. And all this simply by placing the people in conditions worthy of human beings, and especially by carefully bringing up the rising generation. He was the founder of infant schools, and introduced them first at New Lanark. At the age of two the children came to school, where they enjoyed themselves so much that they could scarcely be got home again. While his competitors worked their people thirteen or fourteen hours a day, in New Lanark the working day was only ten and a half hours. When a crisis in cotton stopped work for four months, his workers received their full wages all the time. And with all this the business more than doubled in value, and to the last yielded large profits to its proprietors.

In spite of all this, Owen was not content. The existence which he secured for his workers was, in his eyes, still far from being worthy of human beings. "The people were slaves at my mercy." The relatively favorable conditions in which he had placed them were still far from allowing a rational development of the character and of the intellect in all directions, much less of the free exercise of all their faculties. "And yet, the working part of this population of 2,500 persons was daily producing as much real wealth for society as, less than half a century before, it would have required the working part of a population of 600,000 to create. I asked myself, what became of the difference between the wealth consumed by 2,500 persons and that which would have been consumed by 600,000?"*

The answer was clear. It had been used to pay the proprietors of the establishment 5 per cent on the capital they had laid out, in addition to over £300,000 clear profit. And that which held for New Lanark held to a still greater extent for all the factories in England. "If this new wealth had not been created by machinery, imperfectly as it has been applied, the wars of Europe, in opposition to Napoleon, and to support the aristocratic principles of society, could not have been maintained. And yet this new power was the creation of the working classes."† To them, therefore, the fruits of this new power belonged. The newly-created, gigantic productive forces, hitherto used only to enrich individuals and to enslave the masses, offered to Owen the foundations for a reconstruction of society; they were destined, as the common property of all, to be worked for the common good of all.

Owen's communism was based upon this purely business foundation, the outcome, so to say, of commercial calculation. Throughout, it maintained this practical character. Thus, in 1823, Owen proposed the relief of the distress in Ireland by communist colonies, and drew up complete estimates of costs of founding them, yearly expenditure and probable revenue. And in his definite plan for the future, the technical working out of details is managed with such practical knowledge—ground plan, front and side and bird's-eye views all included—that the Owen

---

*From *The Revolution in Mind and Practice,* p. 21, a memorial addressed to all the "red republicans, communists and socialists of Europe," and sent to the provisional government of France, 1848, and also "to Queen Victoria and her responsible advisers."
†*Ibid.*

method of social reform once accepted, there is from the practical point of view little to be said against the actual arrangement of details.

His advance in the direction of communism was the turning-point in Owen's life. As long as he was simply a philanthropist, he was rewarded with nothing but wealth, applause, honor and glory. He was the most popular man in Europe. Not only men of his own class, but statesmen and princes listened to him approvingly. But when he came out with his communist theories, that was quite another thing. Three great obstacles seemed to him especially to block the path to social reform: private property, religion, the present form of marriage. He knew what confronted him if he attacked these—outlawry, excommunication from official society, the loss of his whole social position. But nothing of this prevented him from attacking them without fear of consequences, and what he had foreseen happened. Banished from official society, with a conspiracy of silence against him in the press, ruined by his unsuccessful communist experiments in America, in which he sacrificed all his fortune, he turned directly to the working class and continued working in their midst for thirty years. Every social movement, every real advance in England on behalf of the workers links itself on to the name of Robert Owen. He forced through in 1819, after five years' fighting, the first law limiting the hours of labor of women and children in factories. He was president of the first congress at which all the trade unions of England united in a single great trade association. He introduced as transition measures to the complete communistic organization of society, on the one hand, cooperative societies for retail trade and production. These have since that time, at least, given practical proof that the merchant and the manufacturer are socially quite unnecessary. On the other hand, he introduced labor bazaars for the exchange of the products of labor through the medium of labor notes, whose unit was a single hour of work; institutions necessarily doomed to failure, but completely anticipating Proudhon's bank of exchange of a much later period, and differing entirely from this in that it did not claim to be the panacea for all social ills, but only a first step towards a much more radical revolution of society.

The Utopians' mode of thought has for a long time governed the socialist ideas of the nineteenth century, and still governs some of them. Until very recently all French and English socialists did homage to it. The earlier German communism, including that of Weitling, was of the same school. To all these, socialism is the expression of absolute truth, reason and justice, and has only to be discovered to conquer all the world by virtue of its own power. And as absolute truth is independent of time, space, and of the historical development of man, it is a mere accident when and where it is discovered. With all this, absolute truth, reason and justice are different with the founder of each different school. And as each one's special kind of absolute truth, reason and justice is again conditioned by his subjective understanding, his conditions of existence, the measure of his knowledge and his intellectual training, there is no other ending possible in this conflict of absolute truths than that they shall be mutually exclusive one of the other. Hence, from this nothing could come but a kind of eclectic, average socialism, which, as a matter of fact, has up to the present time dominated the minds of most of the socialist workers in France and England. Hence, a mish-mash allowing of the most manifold shades of opinion; a mish-mash of such critical statements, economic theories, pictures of future society by the founders of different sects, as excite a minimum of opposition; a mish-mash which is the more easily brewed the more the definite sharp edges of the individual constituents are rubbed down in the stream of debate, like rounded pebbles in a brook.

To make a science of socialism, it had first to be placed upon a real basis.

2
Henri Comte de Saint-Simon

Henri de Saint-Simon (1760–1825) was a typical and influential representative of the utopian socialists. Although his schemes were unrealistic and grandiose and his manner overweening, he was insistent upon the need for a science of social development (of which he conceived himself as founder) and placed great stress on the need to improve the lot of the poor. The new order that he proposed would, he believed, revive a genuine Christianity and establish a golden age.

THE NEW CHRISTIANITY*

I conclude this first dialogue by declaring frankly what I think of the Christian revelation. We are certainly superior to our ancestors in the particular, applied sciences. It is only since the fifteenth century, and chiefly since the beginning of the last century, that we have made considerable progress in mathematics, physics, chemistry and physiology. But there is a science much more important for the community than physical and mathematical science—the science on which society is founded, namely ethics, the development of which has been completely different from that of the physical and mathematical sciences. It is more than eighteen centuries since its fundamental principle has been produced, and since then none of the researches of the men of the greatest genius has been able to discover a principle superior in universality or precision to that formulated by the Founder of Christianity. I will go further and say that when society has lost sight of this principle, and ceased to use it as a guide to its conduct, it has promptly relapsed under the despotism of Caesar, and the rule of brute force, which this principle of Christianity had subordinated to the rule of reason.

I therefore put the question whether the intelligence which produced, eighteen centuries ago, the governing principle of the human race, and produced it fifteen centuries before any important progress was made in the physical and mathemati-

---

*From *New Christianity,* 1825. This and the following passages are taken from *Selected Writings* of Henri Comte de Saint-Simon, translated and edited by F. M. H. Markham, 1952. Reprinted by permission of the publisher, Basil Blackwell, Oxford.

cal sciences, must not obviously be superhuman in character, and whether there can be any greater proof of the divine revelation of Christianity.

Yes, I believe that Christianity is divinely instituted, and I am persuaded that God extends a special protection to those who strive to subordinate all human institutions to the fundamental principle of this sublime doctrine. I am convinced that I am fulfilling a divine mission in recalling nations and kings to the true spirit of Christianity. Fully confident of the divine protection specially given me in my tasks, I feel emboldened to criticize the kings of Europe who are allied under the sacred name of the Holy Alliance. I address them directly, daring to say to them:

Princes,

What is the nature and character, in the eyes of God and of Christians, of the power which you wield?

What is the basis of the social system which you endeavor to establish? What measures have you taken to improve the moral and physical condition of the poor?

You call yourselves Christians, and yet you base your power on material force; you are still the successors of Caesar, and you forget that true Christians have as the final goal of their efforts the abolition of the power of the sword, the power of Caesar, which by its nature is essentially transitory.

. . .

Princes,

Hearken to the voice of God which speaks through me. Return to the path of Christianity; no longer regard mercenary armies, the nobility, the heretical priests and perverse judges, as your principal support, but, united in the name of Christianity, understand how to carry out the duties which Christianity imposes on those who possess power. Remember that Christianity commands you to use all your powers to increase as rapidly as possible the social welfare of the poor!

[A WORLD UPSIDE DOWN]*

Suppose that France suddenly lost fifty of her best physicists, chemists, physiologists, mathematicians, poets, painters, sculptors, musicians, writers; fifty of her best mechanical engineers, civil and military engineers, artillery experts, architects, doctors, surgeons, apothecaries, seamen, clockmakers; fifty of her best bankers, two hundred of her best business men, two hundred of her best farmers, fifty of her best ironmasters, arms manufacturers, tanners, dyers, miners, cloth-makers, cotton manufacturers, silk-makers, linen-makers, manufacturers of hardware, of pottery and china, of crystal and glass, ship chandlers, carriers, printers, engravers, goldsmiths, and other metal-workers; her fifty best masons, carpenters, joiners, farriers, locksmiths, cutlers, smelters, and a hundred other persons of various unspecified occupations, eminent in the sciences, fine

*From Henri de Saint-Simon, *The Organizer,* 1819.

arts, and professions; making in all the three thousand leading scientists, artists, and artisans of France.

These men are the Frenchmen who are the most essential producers, those who make the most important products, those who direct the enterprises most useful to the nation, those who contribute to its achievements in the sciences, fine arts and professions. They are in the most real sense the flower of French society; they are, above all Frenchmen, the most useful to their country, contribute most to its glory, increasing its civilization and prosperity. The nation would become a lifeless corpse as soon as it lost them. It would immediately fall into a position of inferiority compared with the nations which it now rivals, and would continue to be inferior until this loss had been replaced, until it had grown another head. It would require at least a generation for France to repair this misfortune; for men who are distinguished in work of positive ability are exceptions, and nature is not prodigal of exceptions, particularly in this species.

Let us pass on to another assumption. Suppose that France preserves all the men of genius that she possesses in the sciences, fine arts and professions, but has the misfortune to lose in the same day Monsieur the King's brother, Monseigneur le duc d'Angoulême, Monseigneur le duc de Berry, Monseigneur le duc d'Orléans, Monseigneur le duc de Bourbon, Madame la duchesse d'Angoulême, Madame la duchesse de Berry, Madame la duchesse d'Orléans, Madame la duchesse de Bourbon, and Mademoiselle de Condé. Suppose that France loses at the same time all the great officers of the royal household, all the ministers (with or without portfolio), all the councillors of state, all the chief magistrates, marshals, cardinals, archbishops, bishops, vicars-general, and canons, all the prefects and sub-prefects, all the civil servants, and judges, and, in addition, ten thousand of the richest proprietors who live in the style of nobles.

This mischance would certainly distress the French, because they are kind-hearted, and could not see with indifference the sudden disappearance of such a large number of their compatriots. But this loss of thirty-thousand individuals, considered to be the most important in the State, would only grieve them for purely sentimental reasons and would result in no political evil for the State.

In the first place, it would be very easy to fill the vacancies which would be made available. There are plenty of Frenchmen who could fill the function of the King's brother as well as can Monsieur; plenty who could take the place of a Prince as appropriately as Monseigneur le duc d'Angoulême, or Monseigneur le duc d'Orléans, or Monseigneur le duc de Bourbon. There are plenty of Frenchwomen who would be as good princesses as Madame la duchesse d'Angoulême, or Madame la duchesse de Berry, or Mesdames d'Orléans, de Bourbon, and de Condé.

The ante-chambers of the palace are full of courtiers ready to take the place of the great household officials. The army has plenty of soldiers who would be as good leaders as our present Marshals. How many clerks there are who are as good as our ministers? How many administrators who are capable of managing the affairs of the departments better than the existing prefects and sub-prefects? How many barristers who are as good lawyers as our judges? How many vicars as expert as our cardinals, archbishops, bishops, vicars-general, and canons? As for the ten thousand aristocratic landowners, their heirs could need no apprenticeship to do the honors of their drawing-rooms as well as they.

The prosperity of France can only exist through the effects of the progress of the sciences, fine arts and professions. The Princes, the great household officials, the Bishops, Marshals of France, prefects and idle landowners contribute nothing directly to the progress of the sciences, fine arts and professions. Far from contributing they only hinder, since they strive to prolong the supremacy existing to this day of conjectural ideas over positive science. They inevitably harm the prosperity of the nation by depriving, as they do, the scientists, artists, and artisans of the high esteem to which they are properly entitled. They are harmful because they expend their wealth in a way which is of no direct use to the sciences, fine arts, and professions: they are harmful because they are a charge on the national taxation, to the amount of three or four hundred millions under the heading of appointments, pensions, gifts, compensations, for the upkeep of their activities which are useless to the nation.

These suppositions underline the most important fact of present politics: they provide a point of view from which we can see this fact in a flash in all its extent; they show clearly, though indirectly, that our social organization is seriously defective: that men still allow themselves to be governed by violence and ruse, and that the human race (politically speaking) is still sunk in immorality.

The scientists, artists, and artisans, the only men whose work is of positive utility to society, and cost it practically nothing, are kept down by the princes and other rulers who are simply more or less incapable bureaucrats. Those who control honors and other national awards owe, in general, the supremacy they enjoy, to the accident of birth, to flattery, intrigue and other dubious methods.

Those who control public affairs share between them every year one half of the taxes, and they do not even use a third of what they do not pocket personally in a way which benefits the citizen.

These suppositions show that society is a world which is upside down.

The nation holds as a fundamental principle that the poor should be generous to the rich, and that therefore the poorer classes should daily deprive themselves of necessities in order to increase the superfluous luxury of the rich.

The most guilty men, the robbers on a grand scale, who oppress the mass of the citizens, and extract from them three or four hundred millions a year, are given the responsibility of punishing minor offenses against society.

Ignorance, superstition, idleness and costly dissipation are the privilege of the leaders of society, and men of ability, hard-working and thrifty, are employed only as inferiors and instruments.

To sum up, in every sphere men of greater ability are subject to the control of men who are incapable. From the point of view of morality, the most immoral men have the responsibility of leading the citizens toward virtue; from the point of view of distributive justice, the most guilty men are appointed to punish minor delinquents.

[THE PLAN OF A NEW SOCIETY]*

Let us return to the plan which I propose. If you adopt it and maintain it, you will place permanently in the hands of the twenty-one most enlightened men the two great weapons of domination—prestige and wealth. The consequence will be, for many reasons, rapid progress in the sciences. It is a fact that, with every advance in the sciences, discovery becomes easier; so that those who, like yourselves, can only devote little time to your education, will be able to learn more, and, as you become more educated, you will diminish the domination gained by the rich. You will soon see, my friends, excellent results. But I cannot spend more time on matters which are comparatively remote consequences of a course of action on which you have not yet embarked. Let us talk of what is immediately in view. You give your respect, that is to say, you voluntarily concede a degree of domination to men who perform services which you consider useful to you. The mistake which you make, in common with the whole of humanity, is in not distinguishing clearly enough between the immediate and more lasting benefits, between those of local and more general interest, between those which benefit a part of humanity at the expense of the rest, and those which promote the happiness of the whole of humanity. In short, you have not yet realized that there is but one interest common to the whole of humanity, the progress of the sciences.

. . .

Here is an idea which seems to me sound. The elementary needs of life are the most imperative. The have-nots can only satisfy them inadequately. A physiologist can see clearly that their most constant desire must be to reduce taxation, or to increase wages, which comes to the same thing. I believe that all classes of society would benefit from an organization on these lines: the spiritual power in the hands of the scientists, the temporal power in the hands of the property-owners; the power to nominate those who should perform the functions of the leaders of humanity, in the hands of all; the reward of the rulers, esteem.

[THE GOLDEN AGE]†

I have tried in this work to prove that the establishment of a political system in conformity with the present state of enlightenment, and the creation of a common power possessing force enough to repress the ambitions of peoples and kings, is the only means of producing a stable and peaceful order in Europe. In this respect the actual plan of organization which I have suggested is of secondary importance; if it were refuted, if it were found to be essentially faulty, I would still have done what I set out to do, provided some other plan were adopted.

. . .

. . . There will come a time, without doubt, when all the peoples of Europe will feel that questions of common interest must be dealt with before coming down to national interests; then evils will begin to lessen, troubles abate, wars die out. That

---

*From Henri de Saint-Simon, *Letters from an Inhabitant of Geneva,* 1803.
†From Henri de Saint-Simon, *The Reorganization of the European Community,* 1814.

is the ultimate direction in which we are steadily progressing; it is there that the progress of the human mind will carry us. But which is more worthy of man's prudence—to hasten towards it, or to let ourselves be dragged there?

Poetic imagination has put the Golden Age in the cradle of the human race, amid the ignorance and brutishness of primitive times; it is rather the Iron Age which should be put there. The Golden Age of the human race is not behind us but before us; it lies in the perfection of the social order. Our ancestors never saw it; our children will one day arrive there; it is for us to clear the way.

3
F. M. Charles Fourier

Charles Fourier (1772–1837) was a typically eccentric and unrealistic social thinker of this period. While he emphasized the fundamental importance of industry, which he called "the primordial function," and demanded its regulation in the new society, he is most famous for the utopian communities that he proposed. He described in meticulous detail the buildings, grounds, organization, and circumstances of life in the self-sufficient socialist societies, called phalanxes, which he conceived as being founded upon totally new principles of organization. Individualism, he contended, had led to general misery; only true social harmony, properly realized in the phalanx, holds promise of relief.

[OF ASSOCIATION]*

It has been vaguely formulated as a principle that men are made for SOCIETY: it has not been noted that society may be of two orders, the *scattered or disjointed (morcelé)* and the *combined,* the nonassociative and the associative condition. The difference between the one and the other is the difference between truth and falsehood, between riches and poverty, between light and darkness, between a comet and a planet, between a butterfly and a caterpillar.

The present age, with its presentiments of association, has pursued a hesitating advance; it has been afraid to trust to its inspirations which opened up hopes of a great discovery. It has dreamed of social union without daring to undertake the investigation of the means; it has never thought of speculating upon the following alternatives:

There can be but two methods in the exercise of industry, namely: the disjointed order or that of isolated families, such as we see, or the associative order.

---

*From C. Fourier, *The Theory of Universal Unity,* 1822. This and the following passages are from *Selections from the Works of Fourier,* translated by Julia Franklin, published by Swan Sonnenschein and Co., London, 1901.

God can choose for the prosecution of human labor only between GROUPS and INDI-VIDUALS; *associative and combined* action, and *incoherent and disjointed* action.

As a wise dispenser, he could not have speculated upon the employment of iso-lated couples, working without union, according to the civilized method; for indi-vidual action carries within itself seven germs of disorganization, of which each one by itself would engender a multitude of disorders. We may judge by a list of these evils whether God could for an instant have hesitated to proscribe disjointed labor which engenders them all.

[EVILS OF INDIVIDUAL ACTION IN INDUSTRY]*

Wage labor, indirect servitude.
1 Death of the functionary.
2 Personal inconstancy.
3 Contrast between the characters of the father and son.
4 Absence of mechanical economy.
5 Fraud, theft, and general mistrust.
6 Intermission of industry on account of lack of means.
7 Conflict of contradictory enterprises.
Opposition of individual and collective interest.
Absence of unity in plans and execution.

God would have adopted all these evils as a basis of the social system had he fixed upon the philosophic method or disjointed labor; can we suspect the Creator of such unreason? . . .

All the sophists agree in declaring that *man is made for society:* according to this principle ought man to aim for the smallest or the largest society possible? It is beyond doubt that it is in the largest that all the mechanical and economical advantages will be found: and since we have only attained the infinitely small, "family-labor" *("travail familial"),* is any other indication required to verify the fact that civilization is the antipodes of destiny as well as of truth? . . .

To sum up, all our reformers feel and proclaim the necessity of uniting the working classes into masses or social phalanxes, but they do not wish to acknowledge that the associative process belongs to a science of which the economists have no conception, and of which I alone have formulated a regu-lar theory, ample and without gaps, attacking, and solving all problems, boldly presenting those before which all economists have recoiled, such as the equi-librium of population, industry attractive and guaranteeing the good morals of the people.

*From C. Fourier, *The Mistakes of Industry,* 1836.

4
Robert Owen

Robert Owen (1771–1858) is the most extraordinary and inspiring of the utopian socialists. From humble origins he rose to the position of an immensely successful industrialist and entrepreneur. In his own mills and plants in Scotland and England he proved that the reform of the living and working conditions of the laborer was not only feasible but could be made highly profitable for all. His later attempts to incorporate these reforms into utopian communities, however (as in New Harmony, Indiana), proved abysmal failures. Highly critical of an economic order in which men were "merely trained to buy cheap and sell dear," he envisioned a wholly rational society in which, through the power of intelligence and education, a new and superior type of human character might be developed, and a new moral world brought into being.

[TO THE NATIONS OF THE WORLD]*

You are now in the midst of a conflict which involves the deepest and dearest interest of every individual of the human race; and upon its result depends the misery or happiness of the present and future generations.

It is a contest between those who believe, that it is for their individual interest and happiness that man should continue to be kept in ignorance, and be governed, as heretofore, by force and fraud; and those who are convinced, that for his happiness, he should be henceforward governed by truth and justice only.

. . . For the experienced know, that all nations might, now, easily adopt arrangements to produce more of all kinds of wealth, essential to human happiness, than would satisfy all to the full extent of their desire, and also establish new institutions, in which the natural faculties and powers of each, might be cultivated from birth, to be greatly superior to any character ever formed, or that can be formed under any of the old institutions of the world. This vital change in the condition and character of the human race, may now be effected with only light, healthy, beneficial, and agreeable manual labour, combined with the most desirable and pleasant mental exercise: and this change may be effected in peace, with universal consent, without injury to the mind, body, or estate, of a single individual, in any rank or country.

This is the revolution which the progress of knowledge now requires from those who have hitherto ruled the destinies of nations; a revolution in the fundamental principles, and in the arrangement of society, which will essentially promote the interest, and secure the progressive happiness of all, from the highest to the lowest.

*Robert Owen, "An Address from the Association of All Classes of All Nations to the Governments and People of All Nations." This and the following selections are from *The Book of the New Moral World*, published by H. Robinson and Co., Glasgow, 1837.

We undertake to explain the principles of nature, and to unfold the practical measures consequent upon them, by which this great revolution in human affairs, may be now effected, without disorder, or evil of any kind, not even disturbing existing private properties.

We proceed one step further; and consequently state, that the progress of knowledge now renders this revolution, in the general character of mankind, so irresistible, that no earthly power can prevent, or much retard its course; and it will be effected either by reason, or by violence forced upon society by the mental degradation of all, and the extreme misery of the many. We, therefore, as the disinterested friends of all Classes of all Nations, recommend to all Governments and People, that the old prejudices of the world, for or against class, sect, party, country, sex, and color, derived solely from ignorance, should be now allowed, by the common consent of all, to die their natural death; that standing armies of all nations should be disbanded, in order that the men may be employed in producing instead of destroying wealth; that the rising generation should be educated from birth to become superior, in character and conduct, to all past generations; that all should be trained to have as much enjoyment, in producing as in using or consuming wealth, which, through the progress of science, can be easily effected; that all should freely partake of it; and that, thus, the reign of peace, intelligence, and universal sympathy, or affection, may, for ever, supersede the reign of ignorance and oppression.

[FROM THE OLD WORLD TO THE NEW]

The religious, moral, political, and commercial arrangements of society, throughout the world, have been based, from the commencement of history, upon an error respecting the nature of man; an error so grievous in its consequences, that it has deranged all the proceedings of society, made man irrational in his thoughts, feelings, and actions, and, consequently, more inconsistent, and perhaps more miserable, than any other animal.

This work is written to explain, first—the cause of this universal error, which has produced the derangement, degradation, and misery of the human race; and secondly—open to the present generation, a NEW MORAL WORLD founded on principles opposed to this error; and in which, the causes producing it will cease. In this NEW WORLD, the inhabitants will attain a state of existence, in which a spirit of charity and affection will pervade the whole human race, man will become spiritualized, and happy amidst a race of superior beings.

The knowledge which he will thus acquire of himself and of nature, will induce and enable him through his self-interest, or desire for happiness, to form such superior external arrangements as will place him within a terrestrial paradise.

As in this New World, all will know, that far more happiness can be obtained by union, than by disunion, all opposition and contention between man and man, and nation and nation, for individual or national advantages, of any kind, will cease.

The overwhelming power, which, through the progress of knowledge, may be now obtained by the external circumstances under the control of society, to form the general character of the human race, will become evident to all, and in consequence, no child will be permitted to grow up in ignorance, in superstition, or with inferior dispositions or habits; or without a knowledge of his own organization, of its laws, of the laws of nature generally, of the useful sciences, and of the practical arts of life.

The degradation, therefore, of mind and body, hitherto produced by a general training in error, regarding the organization or natural powers of man, and the innumerable errors thence arising, will be altogether unknown.

The evils, also, which are now produced by the desire ignorantly created to obtain individual superiority in wealth, privileges, and honours will not exist; but advantages much superior to these, will be secured to all, and feelings of a higher character than individual distinctions can create, will be universally experienced.

Scientific arrangements will be formed to make wealth everywhere, and at all times superabound beyond the wants or wishes of the human race, and all desire for individual accumulation, or any inequality of condition, will consequently cease.

The necessity for a never-ceasing supply of wealth for the use and enjoyment of all, and the right of each to produce and to enjoy his fair share of it, will be obvious and admitted. It will be equally evident that the unwrought materials to produce manufactured wealth, exist in superfluity, and that scientific aids may now be constructed to procure and work up these materials without any disagreeable, unhealthy, or premature manual labour, into every variety of the most useful and valuable productions.

With means thus ample to procure wealth with ease and pleasure to all, none will be so unwise as to desire to have the trouble and care of individual property. To divide riches among individuals in unequal proportions, or to hoard it for individual purposes, will be perceived to be as useless and as injurious as it would be to divide water or air into unequal quantities for different individuals, or that they should hoard them for their future use.

As more wealth will be produced through scientific aid, by healthy exercise, and as a gratifying amusement, than the population of the earth can require or advantageously use, no anxious thoughts, or care for a continued supply will perplex the mind, or injuriously occupy the time of any one. And as sufficient wealth will be so easily produced by scientific arrangements to effect whatever riches and knowledge can accomplish by the union of mankind, a far better education than any which has ever yet been proposed or conceived in the old world, will be given from birth to every one. In consequence of the ease with which wealth and scientific knowledge will be obtained, and made abundant for the most ample use and gratification of all, the inferior existing circumstances will be abandoned, and man will no longer live in crowded cities, or in seclusion from enlightened and superior society; but other arrangements will be formed to enable all, as soon as they shall be made rational, to live in superior habitations surrounded by gardens, pleasure-grounds, and scenery, far better designed and executed than any yet possessed by the monarchs of the most powerful, wealthy, and extended empires. The human race will also be surrounded by other very superior circumstances, which, now, by the progress of knowledge, can be placed for the first time under the control of man; circumstances of a far higher character than any which have yet existed in any part of the globe.

Ignorance therefore, and poverty, or the fear of it, now the fruitful causes of crime and misery, will no longer disunite man, and be the bane of his happiness. These evils will be known only in the history of the past, or of the irrational period of human existence.

Money, which has hitherto been the root, if not of *all* evil of great injustice, oppression and misery to the human race, making some slavish producers of wealth, and others its wasteful consumers or destroyers, will be no longer required to carry on the business of life: for as wealth of all kinds will be so delightfully created in greater abundance than will ever be required, no money price will be known, for happiness will not be purchaseable, except by a reciprocity of good actions and kind feelings.

Consequently, the present classification of society will be not only useless, but it will be discovered to be unjust and productive of every kind of evil; necessarily destructive of sincerity, honesty, and of all the finest feelings, and most valuable sympathies of our nature. This artificial and most injurious classification will be superseded by one derived immediately from nature—one that shall insure sincerity and honesty; that shall cultivate, foster, and encourage the finest feelings, and best sympathies, and continually calling into action the higher qualities of our nature, and that shall insure to every one the full amount of happiness that his original constitution, under the most favourable circumstances, shall be capable of receiving. These effects can be obtained, only, by a natural classification into employments according to age and capacity. All, at the same period of life, will pursue the same general occupations, for the public benefit, for which all, by their superior training and education, will be made more than competent; and all will have a large portion of each day to employ according to their peculiar capacities and individual inclinations, without interfering with the happiness of others.

By these arrangements, and this classification, all will become superior, physically, intellectually, and morally; each will know all the duties of life, and will have the greatest desire to execute them in the best manner. In this classification, however, none will be trained to teach incongruities or mysteries, which must derange the mental faculties and disorder all the transactions of mankind—none will be engaged in devising or administering laws in opposition to the laws of nature; or, in adjudging artificial rewards and punishments to counteract those of nature, which are all wise and efficient. It will be obvious, even to children, thus rationally educated, that all human laws must be either unnecessary, or in opposition to Nature's laws, they must create disunion, produce crime incessantly, and involve all transactions in inextricable confusion. None will be trained in idleness and uselessness to waste extravagantly the productions of others, to which no just law can give them a shadow of right or title; and no unjust law will be admitted into the code of the NEW MORAL WORLD. None will be trained and set apart to attack, plunder, and murder their fellow-men; this conduct will be known to be irrational, and the very essence of wickedness; nor, yet, will any be trained to bargain with, or even to attempt to take advantage of another, or to desire individual privileges or distinctions of any kind. The individual who is trained to buy cheap, sell dear, and seek for individual benefits above his fellows, is thereby degraded—is unfitted to acquire superior qualities—is deprived of the finest feelings of our nature, and rendered totally incompetent to experience the highest enjoyments of human existence. Nor will any be permitted, by society, to be trained in an *inferior manner,* or for *inferior purposes;* because one such example will be injurious to every one—but all will have the original powers and faculties of their nature directed and cultivated, in such a manner, as shall make it unavoidable, that each shall become, at maturity, superior in mind, manner, and conduct.

In this NEW WORLD, the sympathies of human nature will be rightly directed from infancy, and will engender a spirit of benevolence, confidence, and affection, which will pervade mankind.

The impurities of the present system, arising from human laws opposed to nature's laws, will be unknown. The immense mass of degradation of character, and of heart-rending suffering, experienced by both sexes, but especially by women, will be altogether prevented—and the characters of all women will, by a superior, yet natural training, be elevated to become lovely, good, and intellectual. Of this state of purity and felicity few of the present generation have been trained to form any correct or rational conception.

In this *New World,* founded on universal and everlasting truths, no attempt will be made to falsify any of our physical or mental feelings; they will be known to be instincts given, as necessary parts of our nature, to be beneficially exercised and enjoyed.

Thus will be attained perfect truth, the great desideratum of human life, to prepare it for the enjoyment of happiness—truth, which, in this *New World,* will be, upon every subject, the sole language of man to the full extent of his knowledge.

There will, therefore, be an undeviating unity between all the thoughts, feelings, language, and actions of the human race. It will be distinctly perceived, that falsehood necessarily produces misery, and that truth necessarily produces happiness; consequently, no motives will arise among beings rationally educated, and possessing a knowledge of their own nature, to induce any one even to imagine a falsehood.

In this regenerated state of human existence, all will be trained from birth to attain physically, mentally, and morally, very superior qualities, and to have them regularly exercised up to the point of temperance, according to the constitution of each.

Thus will the well-being, the well-doing, and the happiness of each be insured, and permanently maintained.

It must now be evident, that the *New Moral World,* will have little in common with the old, excepting humanity as it comes into existence at birth, and the simple materials of nature; and even these will be made to receive forms and qualities so superior to those which have hitherto been given to them, that the inexperienced would scarcely believe their natures to be the same.

In this book the difference between the two states of existence, and also the mode by which the change from the one to the other will be effected, without injury to person or property, will be made so plain as easily to be understood.

The first part contains an explanation of the Constitution of Human Nature, and the Moral Science of Man, in order that a solid foundation may be laid at the commencement. In the succeeding parts of this book the Conditions requisite to insure the happiness of man, will be stated, with the reason for each Condition. Having considered what individual man is by nature, and what is necessary to the happiness of a being so constituted, an Explanation will be given of the arrangements which are necessary for his social condition, which will lead to the consideration of the best mode to *Produce and Distribute wealth—to Form the Character, and to Govern men in the aggregate, so as to insure their happiness.* The Religion and Morals of the NEW WORLD will then be explained, and their superiority shown over the mysteries and inconsistencies of the religions and morals of the old world. The principles on which to found a rational government for mankind will next follow, with its laws, the reasons for each law, and the consequences of such a government to the population of the world. To these will succeed an explanation of the practical arrangements by which *all* the conditions requisite to happiness may be obtained for, and *permanently* insured to, the human race; together with the mode of effecting the change from the Old to the New World.

[THE DEVELOPMENT OF SUPERIOR HUMAN CHARACTER]

A superior human being, or any one approaching a character deserving the name of rational, has not yet been known among mankind. A man intelligent and yet consistent in his feelings, thoughts, and actions, does not now exist even in the most civilized part of the world. . . .

Before a truly superior character can be formed among men, a new arrangement of external circumstances must be combined, all of which must be in unison with human nature, and calculated to produce rational impressions only upon the human organization. Every external circumstance, too, must be superior of its kind; and there must be also the absence of slavery and servitude, that no inferior impressions may be made upon any of our faculties.

Before this character can be given to the human race, a great change must occur in the whole proceedings of mankind; their feelings, thoughts, and actions must arise from principles altogether different from the vague and fanciful notions by which the mental part of the character of man has been hitherto formed; the whole external circumstances relative to the production and distribution of wealth, the formation of character, and the government of men, must be changed; the whole of these parts must be re-modeled and united into one system, in which each part shall contribute to the perfection of the whole; nothing must be left to the ignorance or inexperience of individuals or of individual families, whose apparent interests are made to oppose those of their fellows and neighbours; a false interest which diffuses a spirit of jealousy and competition among the members of every class, sect, and party, in every nation, city, town, and village, and too often in families.

No! a rational and superior character can be formed only by changing the whole of the existing irrational circumstances, now everywhere prevalent in the domestic, commercial, political, literary, and religious arrangements of mankind, for an entirely new and scientific combination of all these separate parts into one entire whole; and this so simplified and arranged, that all may be trained, even at an early period of life, to comprehend it, and also the reason for the formation of each part of this new and scientific machine of society. But this change can never be effected during the continuance of the laws, institutions, and customs of the world, which have arisen from the belief that the character of the individual is formed *by* himself; that he possesses within himself the power to form his own will, and the inclination or motives which induce him to act. These *errors* of the imagination have produced the most lamentable consequences. . . .

[THE IRRATIONAL SOCIETY]

These facts and laws make it evident that human nature is a compound of qualities, different from that which it has hitherto appeared to be; that these qualities have been misconceived, and that the true nature of man has been, to the present time, hidden from the human race; that this want of all knowledge of himself from which man has hitherto suffered, is now the great, and almost sole cause of all crime and misery. He has mistaken the most important instincts of his nature for the creations of his will, whereas facts now prove that his will is created by these instincts. This fundamental error respecting the qualities of the material of human nature, has, of necessity, deranged all the proceedings of mankind, and prevented the whole race from becoming rational. Man has imagined that he has been formed to believe and to feel as he likes, by the power of his will, and to be to a great extent, independent of external nature. All past society has been founded on these erroneous assumptions, and, in consequence, the human mind has been a chaos of perplexing inconsistencies, and all human affairs a compound of the most irrational transactions, individually, nationally, and universally.

The stronger members of every association have tyrannized over the weaker, and by open force or by fraud, made them their slaves—such is the state of society over the world at this moment. But tyrants and slaves are never rational; nor can such a condition of society ever produce intelligence, wealth, union, virtue, and happiness among mankind; or place man in a condition of permanent progressive improvement.

This division into tyrants and slaves, has produced a classification of society, which, however necessary in its early stages, is now creating every kind of evil over the earth, and prevents the possibility of any one attaining that high degree of excellence and happiness which, otherwise, might be so easily secured to the whole of the human race; a classification which must be destroyed before injustice and oppression—vice and misery, can be removed. For while men shall be divided into castes of employers and employee—masters and servants, sovereign and subject, tyrant and slave—ignorance, poverty, and disunion must pervade the world, and there must be an alternate advance and retrogression in all nations. The division of the inhabitants of the earth into tyrants and slaves has produced, not only the general classification which has been mentioned, but others subdividing these into Emperors, Kings, and Princes, into Legislators and Professors of divinity, law, medicine and arms; into producers and nonproducers of wealth and knowledge; into buyers and sellers of each other's powers, faculties, and products, and into the respective servants of all these divisions. Thus making a heterogeneous mass of contending interests among the whole human race, which, while these opposing feelings shall be created, must sever man from man, and nation from nation, to the incalculable injury of every individual of all nations.

It is now, therefore, evident that man has committed the same mistake from the beginning, respecting the power and faculties of his own nature, as he did for so long a period in relation to the laws of motion which govern the solar system; and from the same cause—the want of a sufficient number of facts accurately observed and systematically arranged to enable him to draw sound deductions, and discover the truth. It is equally evident, that while these fundamental errors respecting the powers and faculties of human nature shall be entertained by, and shall control the conduct of those who govern the nations of the world, the same confusion of ideas, in the conception and direction of human affairs, must prevail, as existed in all minds respecting the solar system, when it was generally believed that the earth was the centre of the universe, and that the sun, stars, and planets moved round it.

.   .   .

[THE NEW MORAL WORLD]

These facts and laws of nature, whenever they shall be fully understood and generally adopted in practice, will become the means of forming a new character for the human race. Instead of being made irrational, as they have hitherto been, they will be made rational, they will be formed to become of necessity, CHARITABLE to their fellow-men of every clime, color, language, sentiment, and feeling; and KIND to all that has life. When a knowledge of these facts and laws shall be taught to all from infancy, they will know that the clime, color, language, opinions, and feelings, are the necessary effects of causes over which the individuals, subject to their influence, have no control; they will not, therefore, be angry with their fellow-men for experiencing influences which are unavoidable. These different effects will be considered varieties of nature, useful for observation and reflection, for instruction and amusement. Such varieties in the character of man, as now produce opposing feelings and interests, and thence anger, violence, wars, and disunion, and all manner of oppression and injustice, crimes and misery, will, on the contrary, elicit knowledge, friendship, and pleasure. Hence characters the most opposite by nature will seek each other, unite and form intimate associations, in order that the most extended knowledge of human nature, and of nature generally, may be acquired, one interest formed, and affection made everywhere to abound.

The necessary result of unions of opposite varieties of character, will be, speedily to remove prejudices of every description, to dispel ignorance, root out all evil passions, destroy the very germs of disunion, and make men wise to their own happiness. Thus there will be no opposing interests or feelings among men in any part of the globe: the spirit of the world will be changed, and the selfishness of ignorance will be superseded by the self-interest, or, which is the same, the benevolence of intelligence.

The individuality of man, unavoidable by his nature, which is, now, through ignorance, a cause of so much of the disunion of the human race, will become the cause of the more intimate union, and of the increase of pleasure and enjoyment. Contrasts of feelings and opinions which have been hitherto causes of anger, hatred, and repulsion, will become sources of attraction, as being the most easy and direct mode to acquire an extended knowledge of our nature, and of the laws which govern it. The causes which produce these differences will be examined with affection by the parties, and solely with a view to discover the truth; for all will be lovers of truth, and no one will feel, or think of being ashamed of truth.

. . . When truth, in every department of human knowledge, shall supersede error and falsehood; when, by common consent, from conviction of the injury produced, men shall abandon falsehood, and speak the language of truth only, throughout all nations, then, indeed, will some conception be acquired of what human nature is, and what are its powers and capacities for improvement and enjoyment.

Under this change, man will appear to be a new-created being. The powers, capacities, and dispositions cultivated under a system of falsehood, arising from ignorance of the laws of his nature, will assume another character, when cultivated from infancy under a system of truth—a character so different in manner and spirit, that, could they now be seen in juxtaposition, they would appear to belong to opposite natures; the one irrational, actively engaged in measures to defeat its own happiness, and in making the earth a Pandemonium; the other rational, daily occupied in measures to promote and secure the happiness of all around, and in making the earth a paradise.

Thus will the present irrational arrangements of society give place to those which are rational. The existing classification of the population of the world will cease. One portion of mankind will not, as now, be trained and placed to oppress, by force or fraud, another portion, to the great disadvantage of both; neither will one portion be trained in idleness, to live in luxury on the industry of those whom they oppress, while the latter are made to labor daily and to live in poverty. Nor yet will some be trained to force falsehood into the human mind, and be paid extravagantly for so doing, while other parties are prevented from teaching the truth, or severely punished if they make the attempt. There will be no arrangements to give knowledge to a few, and to withhold it from the many; but, on the contrary, all will be taught to acquire knowledge of themselves, of nature generally, and of the principles and practice of society, in all its departments, which knowledge will be easily made familiar to every one. The whole business of life will be so simplified, that each will understand it, and will delight in its varied practice.

Thus, will the effects upon society, of a knowledge of these facts and laws, remove the causes of all evil, and establish the reign of good over the world.

2

DIALECTICS

The utopian socialists provided a critical background for Marxism, but the positive character of communist thought has far more complex and abstruse philosophical roots. Central among the ideas that Marx borrowed from earlier philosophers and incorporated into his own system was the concept of dialectical method, which virtually all Marxian communists have accepted as the only truly scientific approach to the course of history and the process of social development.

Dialectics, although part of a venerable philosophic tradition, does not become a paramount theme until its appearance in the philosophical and historical treatises of the German thinker, Georg Hegel. Marx became an active social critic and revolutionary, but he began adult life as a serious student of academic philosophy, and of the philosophy of Hegel especially. Eventually Marx came to reject some of the principal elements of the Hegelian system, but he accepted and retained as fundamental the dialectical interpretation of history that Hegel had emphasized. Contemporary Marxists, like Marx himself, hold that it is the dialectic of history that makes inevitable the coming of the classless society to which they look forward.

The dialectical method is not easy to describe or to understand. Put oversimply, it views the logical and historical process of events as constituted by opposing or conflicting elements or phases, each conflict eventually overcome by reconciliation within some higher or more perfect union, or synthesis. Out of each new synthesis, which may be a concept or an event or even an epoch, its own opposite arises in turn, and a new dialectical conflict emerges, which must lead to yet another synthesis, and so on. Only with the correct understanding of this inexorable, spiral-like development (the dialectician contends) can the course of past and present world events become fully intelligible.

In the following selections from Engels, Hegel and Marx, the nature of dialectics and the application of the dialectic to history are presented in the writings of its most celebrated practitioners.

5
Friedrich Engels

This, the second chapter of *Socialism, Utopian and Scientific* (the first chapter appears in the preceding section), is the clearest description yet written of the communist conception of dialectical thinking and the relation of communist philosophy to the Hegelian system. The dialectic of Hegel, Engels argues, while profound and powerful and correct in essence, was not at first correctly applied. Its correct application, he later held, was one of Marx's great achievements and makes possible a truly scientific socialism.

SOCIALISM, UTOPIAN AND SCIENTIFIC: PART II*

[Dialectical Philosophy]

In the meantime, along with and after the French philosophy of the eighteenth century had arisen the new German philosophy, culminating in Hegel. Its greatest merit was the taking up again of dialectics as the highest form of reasoning. The old Greek philosophers were all natural born dialecticians, and Aristotle, the most encyclopedic intellect of them, had already analyzed the most essential forms of dialectic thought. The newer philosophy, on the other hand, although in it also dialectics had brilliant exponents (e.g. Descartes and Spinoza), had, especially through English influence, become more and more rigidly fixed in the so-called metaphysical mode of reasoning, by which also the French of the eighteenth century were almost wholly dominated, at all events in their special philosophical work. Outside philosophy in the restricted sense, the French nevertheless produced masterpieces of dialectic. We need only call to mind Diderot's *Le Neveu de Rameau,* and Rousseau's *Discours sur l'origine et les fondements de l'inégalité parmi les hommes.* We give here, in brief, the essential character of these two modes of thought.

When we consider and reflect upon nature at large, or the history of mankind, or our own intellectual activity, at first we see the picture of an endless entanglement of relations and reactions, permutations and combinations, in which nothing remains what, where, and as it was, but everything moves, changes, comes into being and passes away. We see, therefore, at first the picture as a whole, with its individual parts still more or less kept in the background; we observe the movements, transitions, connections, rather than the things that move, combine, and are connected. This primitive, naïve, but intrinsically correct conception of the world is that of ancient Greek philosophy, and was first clearly formulated by Heraclitus: everything is and is not, for everything is fluid, is constantly changing, constantly coming into being and passing away.

But this conception, correctly as it expresses the general character of the picture of appearances as a whole, does not suffice to explain the details of which this pic-

---

*From F. Engels, *Socialism, Utopian and Scientific,* Swan Sonnenschein and Co., London, 1892.

ture is made up, and so long as we do not understand these, we have not a clear idea of the whole picture. In order to understand these details we must detach them from their natural or historical connection and examine each one separately, its nature, special causes, effects, etc. This is, primarily, the task of natural science and historical research; branches of science which the Greeks of classical times, on very good grounds, relegated to a subordinate position, because they had first of all to collect materials for these sciences to work upon. A certain amount of natural and historical material must be collected before there can be any critical analysis, comparison and arrangement in classes, orders and species. The foundations of the exact natural sciences were, therefore, first worked out by the Greeks of the Alexandrian period, and later, in the Middle Ages, by the Arabs. Real natural science dates from the second half of the fifteenth century, and thence onward it has advanced with constantly increasing rapidity. The analysis of nature into its individual parts, the grouping of the different natural processes and objects in definite classes, the study of the internal anatomy of organized bodies in their manifold forms—these were the fundamental conditions of the gigantic strides in our knowledge of nature that have been made during the last four hundred years. But this method of work has also left us as legacy the habit of observing natural objects and processes in isolation, apart from their connection with the vast whole; of observing them in repose, not in motion; as constants, not as essentially variables; in their death, not in their life. And when this way of looking at things was transferred by Bacon and Locke from natural science to philosophy, it begot the narrow, metaphysical mode of thought peculiar to the last century.

To the metaphysician, things and their mental reflexes, ideas, are isolated, are to be considered one after the other and apart from each other, are objects of investigation fixed, rigid, given once for all. He thinks in absolutely irreconcilable antitheses. "His communication is 'yea, yea; nay, nay'; for whatsoever is more than these cometh of evil." For him a thing either exists or does not exist; a thing cannot at the same time be itself and something else. Positive and negative absolutely exclude one another; cause and effect stand in a rigid antithesis one to the other.

At first sight this mode of thinking seems to us very luminous, because it is that so-called sound common sense. Only sound common sense, respectable fellow that he is, in the homely realm of his own four walls, has very wonderful adventures directly he ventures out into the wide world of research. And the metaphysical mode of thought, justifiable and necessary as it is in a number of domains whose extent varies according to the nature of the particular object of investigation, sooner or later reaches a limit, beyond which it becomes one-sided, restricted, abstract, lost in insoluble contradictions. In the contemplation of individual things, it forgets the connection between them; in the contemplation of their existence, it forgets the beginning and end of that existence; of their repose, it forgets their motion. It cannot see the wood for the trees.

For everyday purposes we know and can say, e.g., whether an animal is alive or not. But, upon closer inquiry, we find that this is, in many cases, a very complex question, as the jurists know very well. They have cudgeled their brains in vain to discover a rational limit beyond which the killing of the child in its mother's womb is murder. It is just as impossible to determine absolutely the moment of death, for physiology proves that death is not an instantaneous, momentary phenomenon, but a very protracted process.

In like manner, every organized being is every moment the same and not the same; every moment it assimilates matter supplied from without, and gets rid of other matter; every moment some cells of its body die and others build themselves anew; in a longer or shorter time the matter of its body is completely renewed, and is replaced by other molecules of matter, so that every organized being is always itself, and yet something other than itself.

Further, we find upon closer investigation that the two poles of an antithesis, positive and negative, e.g., are as inseparable as they are opposed, and that despite all their opposition, they mutually interpenetrate. And we find, in like manner, that cause and effect are conceptions which only hold good in their application to individual cases; but as soon as we consider the individual cases in their general connection with the universe as a whole, they run into each other, and they become confounded when we contemplate that universal action and reaction in which causes and effects are eternally changing places, so that what is effect here and now will be cause there and then, and vice versa.

None of these processes and modes of thought enters into the framework of metaphysical reasoning. Dialectics, on the other hand, comprehends things and their representations, ideas, in their essential connection, concatenation, motion, origin and ending. Such processes as those mentioned above are, therefore, so many corroborations of its own method of procedure.

Nature is the proof of dialectics, and it must be said for modern science that it has furnished this proof with very rich materials increasing daily, and thus has shown that, in the last resort, nature works dialectically and not metaphysically; that she does not move in the eternal oneness of a perpetually recurring circle, but goes through a real historical evolution. In this connection Darwin must be named before all others. He dealt the metaphysical conception of nature the heaviest blow by his proof that all organic beings, plants, animals and man himself, are the products of a process of evolution going on through millions of years. But the naturalists who have learned to think dialectically are few and far between, and this conflict of the results of discovery with preconceived modes of thinking explains the endless confusion now reigning in theoretical natural science, the despair of teachers as well as learners, of authors and readers alike.

An exact representation of the universe, of its evolution, of the development of mankind, and of the reflection of this evolution in the minds of men, can therefore only be obtained by the methods of dialectics, with its constant regard to the innumerable actions and reactions of life and death, of progressive or retrogressive changes. And in this spirit the new German philosophy has worked. Kant began his career by resolving the stable solar system of Newton and its eternal duration, after the famous initial impulse had once been given, into the result of a historic process, the formation of the sun and all the planets out of a rotating nebulous mass. From this he at the same time drew the conclusion that, given this origin of the solar system, its future death followed of necessity. His theory half a century later was established mathematically by Laplace, and half a century after that the spectroscope proved the existence in space of such incandescent masses of gas in various stages of condensation.

This new German philosophy culminated in the Hegelian system. In this system—and herein is its great merit—for the first time the whole world, natural, historical, intellectual, is represented as a process, i.e., as in constant motion, change, transformation, development; and the attempt is made to trace out the internal connection that makes a continuous whole of all this movement and development. From this point of view the history of mankind no longer appeared as a wild whirl of senseless deeds of violence, all equally condemnable at the judgment seat of mature philosophic reason, and which are best forgotten as quickly as possible, but as the process of evolution of man himself. It was now the task of the intellect to follow the gradual march of this process through all its devious ways, and to trace out the inner law running through all its apparently accidental phenomena.

That the Hegelian system did not solve the problem it propounded is here immaterial. Its epoch-making merit was that it propounded the problem. This problem is one that no single individual will ever be able to solve. Although Hegel was—with Saint Simon—the most encyclopedic mind of his time, yet he was limited, first by the necessarily limited extent of his own knowledge, and, second, by the limited extent and depth of the knowledge and conceptions of his age. To these limits a third must be added. Hegel was an idealist. To him the thoughts within his brain were not the more or less abstract pictures of actual things and processes, but, conversely, things and their evolution were only the realized pictures of the "Idea," existing somewhere from eternity before the world was. This way of thinking turned everything upside down, and completely reversed the actual connection of things in the world. Correctly and ingeniously as many individual groups of facts were grasped by Hegel, yet, for the reasons just given, there is much that is botched, artificial, labored, in a word, wrong in point of detail. The Hegelian system, in itself, was a colossal miscarriage—but it was also the last of its kind. It was suffering, in fact, from an internal and incurable contradiction. Upon the one hand, its essential proposition was the conception that human history is a process of evolution, which, by its very nature, cannot find its intellectual final term in the discovery of any so-called absolute truth. But, on the other hand, it laid claim to being the very essence of this absolute truth. A system of natural and historical knowledge embracing everything, and final for all time, is a contradiction to the fundamental law of dialectic reasoning. This law, indeed, by no means excludes, but, on the contrary, includes the idea that the systematic knowledge of the external universe can make giant strides from age to age.

The perception of the fundamental contradiction in German idealism led necessarily back to materialism, but *nota bene,* not to the simply metaphysical, exclusively mechanical materialism of the eighteenth century. Old materialism looked upon all previous history as a crude heap of irrationality and violence; modern materialism sees in it the process of evolution of humanity, and aims at discovering the laws thereof. With the French of the eighteenth century, and even with Hegel, the conception obtained of nature as a whole, moving in narrow circles, and forever immutable, with its eternal celestial bodies, as Newton, and unalterable organic species, as Linnaeus, taught. Modern materialism embraces the more recent discoveries of natural science according to which nature also has its history in time, the celestial bodies, like the organic species that, under favorable conditions, people them, being born and perishing. And even if nature, as a whole, must still be said to move in recurrent cycles, these cycles assume infinitely larger dimensions. In both aspects, modern materialism is essentially dialectic, and no longer requires the assistance of that sort of philosophy which, queen-like, pretended to rule the remaining mob of sciences. As soon as each special science is bound to make clear its position in the great totality of things and of our knowledge of things, a special science dealing with this totality is superfluous or unnecessary. That which still survives of all earlier philosophy is the science of thought and its laws—formal logic and dialectics. Everything else is subsumed in the positive science of nature and history.

While, however, the revolution in the conception of nature could only be made in proportion to the corresponding positive materials furnished by research, already much earlier certain historical facts had occurred which led to a decisive change in the conception of history. In 1831, the first working class rising took place in Lyons; between 1838 and 1842, the first national working class movement, that of the English Chartists, reached its height. The class struggle between proletariat and bourgeoisie came to the front in the history of the most advanced countries in Europe, in proportion to the development, upon the one hand, of modern industry, upon the other, of the newly-acquired political supremacy of the bourgeoisie. Facts more and more strenuously gave the lie to the teachings of bourgeois economy as to the identity of the interests of capital and labor, as to the universal harmony and universal prosperity that would be the consequence of unbridled competition. All these things could no longer be ignored, any more than the French and English socialism, which was their theoretical, though very imperfect, expression. But the old idealist conception of history, which was not yet dislodged, knew nothing of class struggles based upon economic interests, knew nothing of economic interests; production and all economic relations appeared in it only as incidental, subordinate elements in the "history of civilization."

The new facts made imperative a new examination of all past history. Then it was seen that *all* past history, with the exception of its primitive stages, was the history of class struggles; that these warring classes of society are always the products of the modes of production and of exchange—in a word, of the *economic* conditions of their time; that the economic structure of society always furnishes the real basis, starting from which we can alone work out the ultimate explanation of the whole superstructure of juridical and political institutions as well as of the religious, philosophical and other ideas of a given historical period. Hegel had freed history from metaphysics—he had made it dialectic; but his conception of history was essentially idealistic. But now idealism was driven from its last refuge, the philosophy of history; now a materialistic treatment of history was propounded, and a method found of explaining man's "knowing" by his "being," instead of, as heretofore, his "being" by his "knowing."

From that time forward socialism was no longer an accidental discovery of this or that ingenious brain, but the necessary outcome of the struggle between two historically developed classes—the proletariat and the bourgeoisie. Its task was no longer to manufacture a system of society as perfect as possible, but to examine the historico-economic succession of events from which these classes and their antagonisms had of necessity sprung, and to discover in the economic conditions thus created the means of ending the conflict. But the socialism of earlier days was as incompatible with this materialistic conception as the conception of nature of the French materialists was with dialectics and modern natural science. The socialism of earlier days certainly criticized the existing capitalistic mode of production and its consequences. But it could not explain them, and, therefore, could not get the mastery of them. It could only simply reject them as bad. The more strongly this earlier socialism denounced the exploitation of the working class, inevitable under capitalism, the less able was it clearly to show in what this exploitation consisted and how it arose. But for this it was necessary—(1) to present the capitalistic method of production in its historical connection and its inevitableness during a particular historical period, and therefore, also, to present its inevitable downfall; and (2) to lay bare its essential character, which was still a secret. This was done by the discovery of *surplus value.* It was shown that the appropriation of unpaid labor is the basis of the capitalist mode of production and of the exploitation of the worker that occurs under it; that even if the capitalist buys the labor power of his laborer at its full value as a commodity on the market, he yet extracts more value from it than he paid for; and that in the ultimate analysis this surplus value forms those sums of value from which are heaped up the constantly increasing masses of capital in the hands of the possessing classes. The genesis of capitalist production and the production of capital were both explained.

These two great discoveries, the materialistic conception of history and the revelation of the secret of capitalistic production through surplus value, we owe to Marx. With these discoveries socialism became a science. The next thing was to work out all its details and relations.

6
Georg Wilhelm Friedrich Hegel

Georg Hegel (1770–1831) was one of the great philosophers of all time. He had not only an encyclopedic mind, as Engels said, but a grand synoptic vision, and he has exerted a powerful influence upon philosophers of every description. Except in communist circles, his philosophical method is no longer commonly held in high repute; yet his contributions to the political philosophies of both extreme left and extreme right have been very great. He is a difficult, puzzling, and gigantic figure in the history of thought. The following selection, from *The Philosophy of History,* illustrates the complexity of Hegel's views and the way in which the dialectic serves him as an instrument of interpretation and comprehension. The whole of world history is to be understood, he claims, as the dialectical development of Spirit in time.

[DIALECTICAL HISTORY]*

Universal history—as already demonstrated—shows the development of the consciousness of Freedom on the part of Spirit, and of the consequent realization of that Freedom. This development implies a gradation—a series of increasingly adequate expressions or manifestations of Freedom, which result from its Idea. The logical, and—as still more prominent—the *dialectical* nature of the Idea in general, viz. that it is self-determined—that it assumes successive forms which it successively transcends; and by this very process of transcending its earlier stages, gains an affirmative, and, in fact, a richer and more concrete shape—this necessity of its nature, and the necessary series of pure abstract forms which the Idea successively assumes—is exhibited in the department of *Logic.* Here we need adopt only one of its results, viz. that every step in the process, as differing from any other, has its determinate peculiar principle. In history this principle is idiosyncrasy of Spirit—peculiar National Genius. It is within the limitations of this idiosyncrasy that the spirit of the nation, concretely manifested, expresses every aspect of its consciousness and will—the whole cycle of its realization. Its religion, its polity, its ethics, its legislation, and even its science, art, and mechanical skill, all bear its stamp. These special peculiarities find their key in that common peculiarity—the particular principle that characterizes a people; as, on the other hand, in the facts which History presents in detail, that common characteristic principle may be detected. That such or such a specific quality constitutes the peculiar genius of a people, is the element of our inquiry which must be derived from experience, and historically proved. To accomplish this, pre-supposes not only a disciplined faculty of abstraction, but an intimate acquaintance with the Idea. The investigator must be familiar *à priori* (if we like to call it so), with the whole cir-

---

*From G. W. F. Hegel, *Lectures on the Philosophy of History.* These passages are from a translation by J. Sibree, published by Henry G. Bohn, London, 1861.

cle of conceptions to which the principles in question belong—just as Kepler (to name the most illustrious example in this mode of philosophizing) must have been familiar *à priori* with ellipses, with cubes and squares, and with ideas of their relations, before he could discover, from the empirical data, those immortal "Laws" of his, which are none other than forms of thought pertaining to those classes of conceptions. He who is unfamiliar with the science that embraces these abstract elementary conceptions, is as little capable—though he may have gazed on the firmament and the motions of the celestial bodies for a lifetime—of *understanding* those Laws, as of *discovering* them. From this want of acquaintance with the ideas that relate to the development of Freedom, proceed a part of those objections which are brought against the philosophical consideration of a science usually regarded as one of mere experience; the so-called *à priori* method, and the attempt to insinuate ideas into the empirical data of history, being the chief points in the indictment. Where this deficiency exists, such conceptions appear alien—not lying within the object of investigation. To minds whose training has been narrow and merely subjective—which have not an acquaintance and familiarity with ideas— they are something strange—not embraced in the notion and conception of the subject which their limited intellect forms. Hence the statement that Philosophy does not understand such sciences. It must, indeed, allow that it has not that kind of understanding which is the prevailing one in the domain of those sciences, that it does not proceed according to the categories of such Understanding, but according to the categories of *Reason*—though at the same time recognizing that Understanding, and its true value and position. It must be observed that in this very process of scientific *Understanding,* it is of importance that the essential should be distinguished and brought into relief in contrast with the so-called nonessential. But in order to render this possible, we must know what is *essential;* and that is— in view of the History of the World in general—the Consciousness of Freedom, and the phases which this consciousness assumes in developing itself. . . .

History in general is therefore the development of Spirit in *Time,* as Nature is the development of the Idea in *Space.*

If then we cast a glance over the World's-History generally, we see a vast picture of changes and transactions; of infinitely manifold forms of peoples, states, individuals, in unresting succession. Everything that can enter into and interest the soul of man—all our sensibility to *goodness, beauty, and greatness*—is called into play. On every hand aims are adopted and pursued, which we recognize, whose accomplishment we desire—we hope and fear for them. In all these occurrences and changes we behold human action and suffering predominant; everywhere something akin to ourselves, and therefore everywhere something that excites our interest for or against. Sometimes it attracts us by beauty, freedom, and rich variety, sometimes by energy such as enables even vice to make itself interesting. Sometimes we see the more comprehensive mass of some general interest advancing with comparative slowness, and subsequently sacrificed to an infinite complication of trifling circumstances, and so dissipated into atoms. Then, again, with a vast expenditure of power a trivial result is produced; while from what appears unimportant a tremendous issue proceeds. On every hand there is the motliest throng of events drawing us within the circle of its interest, and when one combination vanishes another immediately appears in its place.

The general thought—the category which first presents itself in this restless mutation of individuals and peoples, existing for a time and then vanishing—is that of *change* at large. The sight of the ruins of some ancient sovereignty directly leads us to contemplate this thought of change in its negative aspect. What traveler among the ruins of Carthage, of Palmyra, Persepolis, or Rome, has not been stimulated to reflections on the transiency of kingdoms and men, and to sadness at the thought of a vigorous and rich life now departed—a sadness which does not expend itself on personal losses and the uncertainty of one's own undertakings, but is a disinterested sorrow at the decay of a splendid and highly cultured national life! But the next consideration which allies itself with that of change, is, that change while it imports dissolution, involves at the same time the rise of a *new life*—that while death is the issue of life, life is also the issue of death. This is a grand conception; one which the Oriental thinkers attained, and which is perhaps the highest in their metaphysics. In the idea of *Metempsychosis* we find it evolved in its relation to individual existence; but a myth more generally known, is that of the *Phoenix* as a type of the Life of *Nature;* eternally preparing for itself its funeral pile, and consuming itself upon it; but so that from its ashes is produced the new, renovated, fresh life. But this image is also Asiatic; oriental not occidental. Spirit—consuming the envelope of its existence—does not merely pass into another envelope, nor rise rejuvenescent from the ashes of its previous form; it comes forth exalted, glorified, a purer spirit. It certainly makes war upon itself—consumes its own existence; but in this very destruction it works up that existence into a new form, and each successive phase becomes in its turn a material, working on which it exalts itself to a new grade.

If we consider Spirit in this aspect—regarding its changes not merely as rejuvenescent transitions, i.e., returns to the same form, but rather as manipulations of itself, by which it multiplies the material for future endeavors—we see it exerting itself in a variety of modes and directions; developing its powers and gratifying its desires in a variety which is inexhaustible; because every one of its creations, in which it has already found gratification, meets it anew as material, and is a new stimulus to plastic activity. The abstract conception of mere change gives place to the thought of spirit manifesting, developing, and perfecting its powers in every direction which its manifold nature can follow. What powers it inherently possesses we learn from the variety of products and formations which it originates. In this pleasurable activity, it has to do only with itself. As involved with the conditions of mere nature—internal and external—it will indeed meet in these not only opposition and hindrance, but will often see its endeavors thereby fail; often sink under the complications in which it is entangled either by Nature or by itself. But in such case it perishes in fulfilling its own destiny and proper function, and even thus exhibits the spectacle of self-demonstration as spiritual activity.

The very essence of Spirit is activity; it realizes its potentiality—makes itself its own deed, its own work—and thus it becomes an object to itself; contemplates itself as an objective existence. Thus is it with the Spirit of a people: it is a Spirit having strictly defined characteristics, which erects itself into an objective world, that exists and persists in a particular religious form of worship, customs, constitution, and political laws—in the whole complex of its institutions—in the events and transactions that make up its history. That is its work—that is what this particular Nation *is*. Nations are what their deeds are. Every Englishman will say: We are the men who navigate the ocean, and have the commerce of the world; to whom the East Indies belong and their riches; who have a parliament, juries, etc.—The relation of the individual to that Spirit is that he appropriates to himself this substantial existence; that it becomes his character and capability, enabling him to have a definite place in the world—to be *something*. For he finds the being of the people to which he belongs an already established, firm world—objectively present to him—with which he has to incorporate himself. In this its work, therefore—its world—the Spirit of the people enjoys its existence and finds its satisfaction.—A Nation is moral—virtuous—vigorous—while it is engaged in realizing its grand objects, and defends its work against external violence during the process of giving to its purposes an objective existence. The contradiction between its potential, subjective being—its inner aim and life—and its *actual* being is removed; it has attained full reality, has itself objectively present to it. But this having been attained, the activity displayed by the Spirit of the people in question is no longer needed; it has its desire. The Nation can still accomplish much in war and peace at home and abroad; but the living substantial soul itself may be said to have ceased its activity. The essential, supreme interest has consequently vanished from its life, for interest is present only where there is opposition. The nation lives the same kind of life as the individual when passing from maturity to old age—in the enjoyment of itself—in the satisfaction of being exactly what it desired and was able to attain. Although its imagination might have transcended that limit, it nevertheless abandoned any such aspirations as objects of *actual endeavor,* if the real world was less than favorable to their attainment—and restricted its aim by the conditions thus imposed. This mere *customary life* (the watch wound up and going on of itself) is that which brings on natural death. Custom is activity without opposition, for which there remains only a formal duration; in which the fulness and zest that originally characterized the aim of life are out of the question— a merely external sensuous existence which has ceased to throw itself enthusiastically into its object. Thus perish individuals, thus perish peoples by a natural death; and though the latter may continue in being, it is an existence without intellect or vitality; having no need of its institutions, because the need for them is satisfied—a political nullity and tedium. In order that a truly universal interest may arise, the Spirit of a People must advance to the adoption of some new purpose; but whence can this new purpose originate? It would be a higher, more comprehensive conception of itself—a transcending of its principle—but this very act would involve a principle of a new order, a new National Spirit.

Such a new principle does in fact enter into the Spirit of a people that has arrived at full development and self-realization; it dies not a simply natural death—for it is not a mere single individual, but a spiritual, generic life; in its case natural death appears to imply destruction through its own agency. The reason of this difference from the single natural individual, is that the Spirit of a people exists as a *genus,* and consequently carries within it its own negation, in the very generality which characterizes it. A people can only die a violent death when it has become naturally dead in itself, as, e.g., the German Imperial Cities, the German Imperial Constitution.

It is not of the nature of all-pervading Spirit to die this merely natural death; it does not simply sink into the senile life of mere custom, but—as being a National Spirit belonging to Universal History—attains to the consciousness of what its work is; it attains to a conception of itself. In fact it is world-historical only in so far as a *universal principle* has lain in its fundamental element—in its grand aim: only so far is the work which such a spirit produces, a moral, political organization. If it be mere desires that impel nations to activity, such deeds pass over without leaving a trace; or their traces are only ruin and destruction. Thus, it was first Chronos— Time—that ruled; the Golden Age, without moral products; and what was pro- duced—the offspring of that Chronos—was devoured by it. It was Jupiter—from whose head Minerva sprang, and to whose circle of divinities belong Apollo and the Muses—that first put a constraint upon Time, and set a bound to its principle of decadence. He is the Political god, who produced a moral work—the State.

In the very element of an achievement the quality of generality, of thought, is contained; without thought it has no objectivity; that is its basis. The highest point in the development of a people is this—to have gained a conception of its life and condition—to have reduced its laws, its ideas of justice and morality to a science; for in this unity [of the objective and subjective] lies the most intimate unity that Spirit can attain to in and with itself. In its work it is employed in rendering itself an object of its own contemplation; but it cannot develop itself objectively in its essential nature, except in *thinking* itself.

At this point, then, Spirit is acquainted with its principles—the general charac- ter of its acts. But at the same time, in virtue of its very generality, this work of thought is different in point of form from the actual achievements of the national genius, and from the vital agency by which those achievements have been per- formed. We have then before us a *real* and an *ideal* existence of the Spirit of the Nation. If we wish to gain the general idea and conception of what the Greeks were, we find it in Sophocles and Aristophanes, in Thucydides and Plato. In these individuals the Greek spirit conceived and thought itself. This is the profounder kind of satisfaction which the Spirit of a people attains; but it is "ideal," and dis- tinct from its "real" activity.

At such a time, therefore, we are sure to see a people finding satisfaction in the *idea* of virtue; putting *talk* about virtue partly side by side with actual virtue, but partly in the place of it. On the other hand pure, universal thought, since its nature is universality, is apt to bring the Special and Spontaneous—Belief, Trust, Cus- tomary Morality—to reflect upon itself, and its primitive simplicity; to show up the limitation with which it is fettered—partly suggesting reasons for renouncing duties, partly itself *demanding reasons,* and the connection of such requirements with Universal Thought; and not finding that connection, seeking to impeach the authority of duty generally, as destitute of a sound foundation.

At the same time the isolation of individuals from each other and from the Whole makes its appearance; their aggressive selfishness and vanity; their seeking personal advantage and consulting this at the expense of the State at large. That inward principle in transcending its outward manifestations is subjective also in *form*—viz., selfishness and corruption in the unbound passions and egotistic interests of men.

Zeus, therefore, who is represented as having put a limit to the devouring agency of Time, and stayed this transiency by having established something inherently and independently durable—Zeus and his race are themselves swallowed up, and that by the very power that produced them—the principle of thought, perception, reasoning, insight derived from rational grounds, and the requirement of such grounds.

Time is the negative element in the sensuous world. Thought is the same negativity, but it is the deepest, the infinite form of it, in which therefore all existence generally is dissolved; first *finite* existence—*determinate,* limited form: but existence *generally,* in its objective character, is limited; it appears therefore as a mere datum—something immediate—authority—and is either intrinsically finite and limited, or presents itself as a limit for the thinking subject, and its infinite reflection on itself [unlimited abstraction].

But first we must observe how the life which proceeds from death, is itself, on the other hand, only individual life; so that, regarding the species as the real and substantial in this vicissitude, the perishing of the individual is a regress of the species into individuality. The perpetuation of the race is, therefore, none other than the monotonous repetition of the same kind of existence. Further, we must remark how perception—the comprehension of being by thought—is the source and birthplace of a new, and in fact higher form, in a principle which while it preserves, dignifies its material. For Thought is that *Universal*—that *Species* which is immortal, which preserves identity with itself. The particular form of Spirit not merely passes away in the world by natural causes in Time, but is annulled in the automatic self-mirroring activity of consciousness. Because this annulling is an activity of thought, it is at the same time conservative and elevating in its operation. While then, on the one side, Spirit annuls the reality, the permanence of that which it *is,* it gains on the other side, the essence, the Thought, the Universal element of that which *it only was* [its transient conditions]. Its principle is no longer that immediate import and aim which it was previously, but the *essence* of that import and aim.

The result of this process is then that Spirit, in rendering itself objective and making this its being an object of thought, on the one hand destroys the determinate form of its being, on the other hand gains a comprehension of the universal element which it involves, and thereby gives a new form to its inherent principle. In virtue of this, the substantial character of the National Spirit has been altered—that is, its principle has risen into another, and in fact a higher principle.

It is of the highest importance in apprehending and comprehending History to have and to understand the thought involved in this transition. The individual traverses as a unity various grades of development, and remains the same individual;

in like manner also does a people, till the Spirit which it embodies reaches the grade of universality. In this point lies the fundamental, the Ideal necessity of transition. This is the soul—the essential consideration—of the philosophical comprehension of History.

Spirit is essentially the result of its own activity: its activity is the transcending of immediate, simple, unreflected existence—the negation of that existence, and the returning into itself. We may compare it with the seed; for with this the plant begins, yet it is also the result of the plant's entire life. But the weak side of life is exhibited in the fact that the commencement and the result are disjoined from each other. Thus also is it in the life of individuals and peoples. The life of a people ripens a certain fruit; its activity aims at the complete manifestation of the principle which it embodies. But this fruit does not fall back into the bosom of the people that produced and matured it; on the contrary, it becomes a poison-draught to it. That poison-draught it cannot let alone, for it has an insatiable thirst for it: the taste of the draught is its annihilation, though at the same time the rise of a new principle.

We have already discussed the final aim of this progression. The principles of the successive phases of Spirit that animate the Nations in a necessitated gradation, are themselves only steps in the development of the one universal Spirit, which through them elevates and completes itself to a self-comprehending *totality*.

While we are thus concerned exclusively with the Idea of Spirit, and in the History of the World regard everything as only its manifestation, we have, in traversing the past—however extensive its periods—only to do with what is *present;* for philosophy, as occupying itself with the True, has to do with the *eternally present.* Nothing in the past is lost for it, for the Idea is ever present; Spirit is immortal; with it there is no past, no future, but an essential *now.* This necessarily implies that the present form of Spirit comprehends within it all earlier steps. These have indeed unfolded themselves in succession independently; but what Spirit is it has always been essentially; distinctions are only the development of this essential nature. The life of the ever present Spirit is a circle of progressive embodiments, which looked at in one aspect still exist beside each other, and only as looked at from another point of view appear as past. The grades which Spirit seems to have left behind it, it still possesses in the depths of its present.

7
Friedrich Engels

The following brief letter, written to give assistance in reading Hegel, is also valuable in presenting the essential character of the Hegelian dialectic, as Engels understood it.

ENGELS TO CONRAD SCHMIDT*

(London, 1 November 1891)

[On Understanding Hegel]

It is impossible, of course, to dispense with Hegel and the man also takes some time to digest. The shorter *Logic* in the Encyclopedia makes quite a good beginning. But you must take the edition in the sixth volume of the *Works,* not the separate edition by Rosenkranz (1845), because there are far more explanatory additions from the lectures in the former, even if that ass Henning has often not understood them himself.

In the Introduction you have the criticism, first (par. 26, etc.) of Wolf's version of Leibnitz (metaphysics *in the historical sense*), then of English-French empiricism (par. 37, etc.) then Kant (par. 40, seq.) and finally (par. 61) of Jacoby's mysticism. In the first section (Being) do not spend too long over Being and Nothing; the last paragraphs on Quality and then Quantity and Measure are much finer, but the theory of Essence is the main thing: the resolution of the abstract contradictions into their own instability, where one no sooner tries to hold on to one side alone than it is transformed unnoticed into the other, etc. At the same time you can always make the thing clear to yourself by concrete examples; for instance, you, as a bridegroom, have a striking example of the inseparability of identity and difference in yourself and your bride. It is absolutely impossible to decide whether sexual love is pleasure in the identity in difference or in the difference in identity. Take away the difference (in this case of sex) or the identity (the human nature of both) and what have you got left? I remember how much this very inseparability of identity and difference worried me at first, although we can never take a step without stumbling upon it.

But you ought on no account to read Hegel as Herr Barth has done, namely in order to discover the bad syllogisms and rotten dodges which served him as levers in construction. That is pure schoolboy's work. It is much more important to discover the truth and the genius which lie beneath the false form and within the artificial connections. Thus the transitions from one category or from one contradiction to the next are nearly always arbitrary—often made through a pun, as when Positive and Negative (par. 120) *"zugrunde gehen"* [perish] in order that Hegel

---

*From *Selected Correspondence of Marx and Engels,* 1942. Reprinted by permission of International Publishers, New York.

may arrive at the category of *"Grund"* [reason, ground]. To ponder over this much is waste of time.

Since with Hegel every category represents a stage in the history of philosophy (as he generally indicates), you would do well to compare the lectures on the history of philosophy (one of his most brilliant works). As relaxation, I can recommend the Aesthetic. When you have worked yourself into that a bit you will be amazed.

Hegel's dialectic is upside down because it is supposed to be the "self-development of thought," of which the dialectic of facts therefore is only a reflection, whereas really the dialectic in our heads is only the reflection of the actual development which is fulfilled in the world of nature and of human history in obedience to dialectical forms.

If you just compare the development of the commodity into capital in Marx with the development from Being to Essence in Hegel, you will get quite a good parallel for the concrete development which results from facts; there you have the abstract construction, in which the most brilliant ideas and often very important transmutations, like that of quality into quantity and vice versa, are reduced to the apparent self-development of one concept from another—one could have manufactured a dozen more of the same kind. . . .

8
Karl Marx

Karl Marx (1818–1883) is the most important single figure in the development of modern communism, and one of the most influential thinkers of all time. His profound creativity, keen critical powers, and humane vision enabled him to produce the theoretical base for more than a century of revolution and reconstruction. Marxist governments are now few, but Marx himself remains an intellectual hero to millions around the globe. The *Economic and Philosophical Manuscripts* (1844), never published in his lifetime, he wrote when 26, much under the influence of the Hegelian dialectic, with whose terminology the work abounds. Applying the dialectic to human labor and to social needs, he probes here the deep philosophical faults—as he thought them—of the system of "political economy," the classical capitalism of his day. His passionate, often sarcastic criticisms of capitalism led him to envision a wholly different frame for human life. This work, although obscure in parts, provides the best picture of Marx's genuine humanism—an aspect of his philosophy now much emphasized by contemporary Marxists. Although never completed and never polished, these manuscripts, from which the following selections come, are Marx's finest philosophical work.

ALIENATED LABOR*

We have begun from the presuppositions of political economy. We have accepted its terminology and its laws. We presupposed private property, the separation of labor, capital and land, as also of wages, profit and rent, the division of labor, competition, the concept of exchange value, etc. From political economy itself, in its own words, we have shown that the worker sinks to the level of a commodity, and to a most miserable commodity; that the misery of the worker increases with the power and volume of his production; that the necessary result of competition is the accumulation of capital in a few hands, and thus a restoration of monopoly in a more terrible form; and finally that the distinction between capitalist and landlord, and between agricultural laborer and industrial worker, must disappear and the whole of society divide into the two classes of property *owners* and propertyless *workers*. . . .

. . . we have now to grasp the real connection between this whole system of alienation—private property, acquisitiveness, the separation of labor, capital and land, exchange and competition, value and the devaluation of man, monopoly and competition—and the system of *money*. . . .

We shall begin from a *contemporary* economic fact. The worker becomes poorer the more wealth he produces and the more his production increases in power and extent. The worker becomes an ever cheaper commodity the more goods he creates. The *devaluation* of the human world increases in direct relation with the *increase in value* of the world of things. Labor does not only create goods; it also produces itself and the worker as a *commodity,* and indeed in the same proportion as it produces goods.

This fact simply implies that the object produced by labor, its product, now stands opposed to it as an *alien being,* as a *power independent* of the producer. The product of labor is labor which has been embodied in an object and turned into a physical thing; this product is an *objectification* of labor. The performance of work is at the same time its objectification. The performance of work appears in the sphere of political economy as a *vitiation* of the worker, objectification as a *loss* and as *servitude to the object,* and appropriation as *alienation.*

So much does the performance of work appear as vitiation that the worker is vitiated to the point of starvation. So much does objectification appear as loss of the object that the worker is deprived of the most essential things not only of life but also of work. Labor itself becomes an object which he can acquire only by the greatest effort and with unpredictable interruptions. So much does the appropriation of the object appear as alienation that the more objects the worker produces the fewer he can possess and the more he falls under the domination of his product, of capital.

All these consequences follow from the fact that the worker is related to the *product of his labor* as to an *alien* object. For it is clear on this presupposition that the more the worker expends himself in work the more powerful becomes

*This and the following selections are from Karl Marx, *Early Writings,* translated by T. B. Bottomore, C. A. Watts, London 1963, and reprinted in Erich Fromm, *Marx's Concept of Man,* 1961, Frederick Ungar Publishing Co., New York. They are reprinted here by permission of Pitman Publishing, London.

the world of objects which he creates in face of himself, the poorer he becomes in his inner life, and the less he belongs to himself. It is just the same as in religion. The more of himself man attributes to God the less he has left in himself. The worker puts his life into the object, and his life then belongs no longer to himself but to the object. The greater his activity, therefore, the less he possesses. What is embodied in the product of his labor is no longer his own. The greater this product is, therefore, the more he is diminished. The *alienation* of the worker in his product means not only that his labor becomes an object, assumes an *external* existence, but that it exists independently, *outside himself,* and alien to him, and that it stands opposed to him as an autonomous power. The life which he has given to the object sets itself against him as an alien and hostile force.

Let us now examine more closely the phenomenon of *objectification,* the worker's production and the *alienation* and *loss* of the object it produces, which is involved in it. The worker can create nothing without *nature,* without the *sensuous external world.* The latter is the material in which his labor is realized, in which it is active, out of which and through which it produces things.

But just as nature affords the *means of existence* of labor in the sense that labor cannot *live* without objects upon which it can be exercised, so also it provides the *means of existence* in a narrower sense; namely the means of physical existence for the *worker* himself. Thus, the more the worker *appropriates* the external world of sensuous nature by his labor the more he deprives himself of *means of existence,* in two respects: first, that the sensuous external world becomes progressively less an object belonging to his labor or a means of existence of his labor, and secondly, that it becomes progressively less a means of existence in the direct sense, a means for the physical subsistence of the worker.

In both respects, therefore, the worker becomes a slave of the object; first, in that he receives an *object of work,* i.e., receives *work,* and secondly that he receives *means of subsistence.* Thus the object enables him to exist, first as a *worker* and secondly, as a *physical subject.* The culmination of this enslavement is that he can only maintain himself as a *physical subject* so far as he is a *worker,* and that it is only as a *physical subject* that he is a worker.

(The alienation of the worker in his object is expressed as follows in the laws of political economy: the more the worker produces the less he has to consume; the more value he creates the more worthless he becomes; the more refined his product the more crude and misshapen the worker; the more civilized the product the more barbarous the worker; the more powerful the work the more feeble the worker; the more the work manifests intelligence the more the worker declines in intelligence and becomes a slave of nature.)

Political economy conceals the alienation in the nature of labor insofar as it does not examine the direct relationship between the worker (work) and production. Labor certainly produces marvels for the rich but it produces privation for the worker. It produces palaces, but hovels for the worker. It produces beauty, but deformity for the worker. It replaces labor by machinery, but it casts some of the workers back into a barbarous kind of work and turns the others into machines. It produces intelligence, but also stupidity and cretinism for the workers.

The direct relationship of labor to its products is the relationship of the worker to the objects of his production. The relationship of property owners to the objects of production and to production itself is merely a *consequence* of this first relationship and confirms it. We shall consider this second aspect later.

Thus, when we ask what is the important relationship of labor, we are concerned with the relationship of the *worker* to production.

So far we have considered the alienation of the worker only from one aspect; namely, *his relationship with the products of his labor.* However, alienation appears not only in the result, but also in the *process,* of *production,* within *productive activity* itself. How could the worker stand in an alien relationship to the product of his activity if he did not alienate himself in the act of production itself? The product is indeed only the *résumé* of activity, of production. Consequently, if the product of labor is alienation, production itself must be active alienation—the alienation of activity and the activity of alienation. The alienation of the object of labor merely summarizes the alienation in the work activity itself.

What constitutes the alienation of labor? First, that the work is *external* to the worker, that it is not part of his nature; and that, consequently, he does not fulfill himself in his work but denies himself, has a feeling of misery rather than well being, does not develop freely his mental and physical energies but is physically exhausted and mentally debased. The worker therefore feels himself at home only during his leisure time, whereas at work he feels homeless. His work is not voluntary but imposed, *forced labor.* It is not the satisfaction of a need, but only a *means* for satisfying other needs. Its alien character is clearly shown by the fact that as soon as there is no physical or other compulsion it is avoided like the plague. External labor, labor in which man alienates himself, is a labor of self-sacrifice, of mortification. Finally, the external character of work for the worker is shown by the fact that it is not his own work but work for someone else, that in work he does not belong to himself but to another person.

Just as in religion the spontaneous activity of human fantasy, of the human brain and heart, reacts independently as an alien activity of gods or devils upon the individual, so the activity of the worker is not his own spontaneous activity. It is another's activity and a loss of his own spontaneity.

We arrive at the result that man (the worker) feels himself to be freely active only in his animal functions—eating, drinking and procreating, or at most also in his dwelling and in personal adornment—while in his human functions he is reduced to an animal. The animal becomes human and the human becomes animal.

Eating, drinking and procreating are of course also genuine human functions. But abstractly considered, apart from the environment of other human activities, and turned into final and sole ends, they are animal functions.

We have now considered the act of alienation of practical human activity, labor, from two aspects:

(1) the relationship of the worker to the *product of labor* as an alien object which dominates him. This relationship is at the same time the relationship to the sensuous external world, to natural objects, as an alien and hostile world.

(2) the relationship of labor to the *act of production within labor.* This is the relationship of the worker to his own activity as something alien and not belonging to him, activity as suffering (passivity), strength as powerlessness, creation as emasculation, the *personal* physical and mental energy of the worker, his personal life (for what is life but activity?) as an activity which is directed against himself, independent of him and not belonging to him. This is *self-alienation* as against the above-mentioned alienation of the *thing*.

We have now to infer a third characteristic of *alienated labor* from the two we have considered.

Man is a species-being* not only in the sense that he makes the community (his own as well as those of other things) his object both practically and theoretically, but also (and this is simply another expression for the same thing) in the sense that he treats himself as the present, living species, as a *universal* and consequently free being.

Species-life, for man as for animals, has its physical basis in the fact that man (like animals) lives from inorganic nature, and since man is more universal than an animal so the range of inorganic nature from which he lives is more universal. Plants, animals, minerals, air, light, etc. constitute, from the theoretical aspect, a part of human consciousness as objects of natural science and art; they are man's spiritual inorganic nature, his intellectual means of life, which he must first prepare for enjoyment and perpetuation. So also, from the practical aspect they form a part of human life and activity. In practice man lives only from these natural products, whether in the form of food, heating, clothing, housing, etc. The universality of man appears in practice in the universality which makes the whole of nature into his inorganic body: (1) as a direct means of life; and equally (2) as the material object and instrument of his life activity. Nature is the *inorganic body* of man; that is to say, nature excluding the human body itself. To say that man *lives* from nature means that nature is his *body* with which he must remain in a continuous interchange in order not to die. The statement that the physical and mental life of man, and nature, are interdependent means simply that nature is interdependent with itself, for man is a part of nature.

Since alienated labor: (1) alienates nature from man; and (2) alienates man from himself, from his own active function, his life activity; so it alienates him from the species. It makes *species-life* into a means of individual life. In the first place it alienates species-life and individual life, and secondly, it turns the latter, as an abstraction, into the purpose of the former, also in its abstract and alienated form.

For labor, *life activity, productive life,* now appear to man only as *means* for the satisfaction of a need, the need to maintain his physical existence. Productive

---

*The term "species-being" is taken from Feuerbach's *Das Wesen des Christentums (The Essence of Christianity).* Feuerbach used the notion in making a distinction between consciousness in man and animals. Man is conscious not merely of himself as an individual but of the human species or "human essence."—*Tr. Note*

life is, however, species-life. It is life creating life. In the type of life activity resides the whole character of a species, its species-character; and free, conscious activity is the species-character of human beings. Life itself appears only as a *means of life.*

The animal is one with its life activity. It does not distinguish the activity from itself. It is *its activity.* But man makes his life activity itself an object of his will and consciousness. He has a conscious life activity. It is not a determination with which he is completely identified. Conscious life activity distinguishes man from the life activity of animals. Only for this reason is he a species-being. Or rather, he is only a self-conscious being, i.e. his own life is an object for him, because he is a species-being. Only for this reason is his activity free activity. Alienated labor reverses the relationship, in that man because he is a self-conscious being makes his life activity, his *being,* only a means for his *existence.*

The practical construction of an *objective world,* the *manipulation* of inorganic nature, is the confirmation of man as a conscious species-being, i.e. a being who treats the species as his own being or himself as a species-being. Of course, animals also produce. They construct nests, dwellings, as in the case of bees, beavers, ants, etc. But they only produce what is strictly necessary for themselves or their young. They produce only in a single direction, while man produces universally. They produce only under the compulsion of direct physical need, while man produces when he is free from physical need and only truly produces in freedom from such need. Animals produce only themselves, while man reproduces the whole of nature. The products of animal production belong directly to their physical bodies, while man is free in face of his product. Animals construct only in accordance with the standards and needs of the species to which they belong, while man knows how to produce in accordance with the standards of every species and knows how to apply the appropriate standard to the object. Thus man constructs also in accordance with the laws of beauty.

It is just in his work upon the objective world that man really proves himself as a *species-being.* This production is his active species life. By means of it nature appears as *his* work and his reality. The object of labor is, therefore, the *objectification of man's species life;* for he no longer reproduces himself merely intellectually, as in consciousness, but actively and in a real sense, and he sees his own reflection in a world which he has constructed. While, therefore, alienated labor takes away the object of production from man, it also takes away his *species life,* his real objectivity as a species-being, and changes his advantage over animals into a disadvantage in so far as his inorganic body, nature, is taken from him.

Just as alienated labor transforms free and self-directed activity into a means, so it transforms the species life of man into a means of physical existence.

Consciousness, which man has from his species, is transformed through alienation so that species life becomes only a means for him.

(3) Thus alienated labor turns the *species life of man,* and also nature as his mental species-property, into an *alien* being and into a *means* for his *individual existence.* It alienates from man his own body, external nature, his mental life and his *human* life.

(4) A direct consequence of the alienation of man from the product of his labor, from his life activity and from his species life is that *man* is *alienated* from other *men.* When man confronts himself he also confronts *other* men. What is true of man's relationship to his work, to the product of his work and to himself, is also true of his relationship to other men, to their labor and to the objects of their labor.

In general, the statement that man is alienated from his species life means that each man is alienated from others, and that each of the others is likewise alienated from human life.

Human alienation, and above all the relation of man to himself, is first realized and expressed in the relationship between each man and other men. Thus in the relationship of alienated labor every man regards other men according to the standards and relationships in which he finds himself placed as a worker.

.   .   .

We began with an economic fact, the alienation of the worker and his production. We have expressed this fact in conceptual terms as *alienated labor,* and in analyzing the concept we have merely analyzed an economic fact.

Let us now examine further how this concept of alienated labor must express and reveal itself in reality. If the product of labor is alien to me and confronts me as an alien power, to whom does it belong? If my own activity does not belong to me but is an alien, forced activity, to whom does it belong? To a being *other* than myself. And who is this being? The *gods?* It is apparent in the earliest stages of advanced production, e.g., temple building, etc. in Egypt, India, Mexico, and in the service rendered to gods, that the product belonged to the gods. But the gods alone were never the lords of labor. And no more was *nature.* What a contradiction it would be if the more man subjugates nature by his labor, and the more the marvels of the gods are rendered superfluous by the marvels of industry, he should abstain from his joy in producing and his enjoyment of the product for love of these powers.

The *alien* being to whom labor and the product of labor belong, to whose service labor is devoted, and to whose enjoyment the product of labor goes, can only be *man* himself. If the product of labor does not belong to the worker, but confronts him as an alien power, this can only be because it belongs to *a man other than the worker.* If his activity is a torment to him it must be a source of enjoyment and pleasure to another. Not the gods, nor nature, but only man himself can be this alien power over men.

Consider the earlier statement that the relation of man to himself is first realized, objectified, through his relation to other men. If therefore he is related to the product of his labor, his objectified labor, as to an *alien,* hostile, powerful and independent object, he is related in such a way that another alien, hostile, powerful and independent man is the lord of this object. If he is related to his own activity as to unfree activity, then he is related to it as activity in the service, and under the domination, coercion and yoke, of another man.

.   .   .

Thus, through alienated labor the worker creates the relation of another man, who does not work and is outside the work process, to this labor. The relation of the worker to work also produces the relation of the capitalist (or whatever one likes to call the lord of labor) to work. *Private property* is therefore the product, the necessary result, of *alienated labor,* of the external relation of the worker to nature and to himself.

Private property is thus derived from the analysis of the concept of *alienated labor;* that is, alienated man, alienated labor, alienated life, and estranged man.

We have, of course, derived the concept of *alienated labor (alienated life)* from political economy, from an analysis of the *movement of private property.* But the analysis of this concept shows that although private property appears to be the basis and cause of alienated labor, it is rather a consequence of the latter, just as the gods are *fundamentally* not the cause but the product of confusions of human reason. At a later stage, however, there is a reciprocal influence.

Only in the final stage of the development of private property is its secret revealed, namely, that it is on one hand the *product* of alienated labor, and on the other hand the *means* by which labor is alienated, the *realization of this alienation.*

. . .

[COMMUNISM: CRUDE AND REFINED]

. . . *communism* is the *positive* expression of the abolition of private property, and in the first place of universal private property. In taking this relation in its *universal aspect* communism is (1) in its first form, only the generalization and fulfilment of the relation. As such it appears in a double form; the domination of material property looms so large that it aims to destroy everything which is incapable of being possessed by everyone as private property. It wishes to eliminate talent, etc. by *force.* Immediate physical possession seems to it the unique goal of life and existence. The role of *worker* is not abolished, but is extended to all men. The relation of private property remains the relation of the community to the world of things. Finally, this tendency to oppose general private property to private property is expressed in an animal form; *marriage* (which is incontestably a form of *exclusive private property*) is contrasted with the community of women, in which women become communal and common property. One may say that this idea of the *community of women* is the *open secret* of this entirely crude and unreflective communism. Just as women are to pass from marriage to universal prostitution, so the whole world of wealth (i.e., the objective being of man) is to pass from the relation of exclusive marriage with the private owner to the relation of universal prostitution with the community. This communism, which negates the *personality* of man in every sphere, is only the logical expression of private property, which is this negation. Universal *envy* setting itself up as a power is only a camouflaged form of cupidity which re-establishes itself and satisfies itself in a different way. The thoughts of every individual private property are *at least* directed against any *wealthier* private property, in the form of envy and the desire to reduce everything to a common level; so that this envy and leveling in fact constitute the essence of competition. Crude communism is only the culmination of such envy and leveling-down on the basis of a *preconceived* minimum. How little this abolition of private property represents a genuine appropriation is shown by the abstract negation of the whole world of culture and civilization, and the regression to the *unnatural* simplicity of the poor and wantless individual who has not only not surpassed private property but has not yet even attained to it.

The community is only a community of *work* and of *equality of wages* paid out by the communal capital, by the *community* as universal capitalist. The two sides of the relation are raised to a *supposed* universality; *labor* as a condition in which everyone is placed, and *capital* as the acknowledged universality and power of the community.

In the relationship with *woman,* as the prey and the handmaid of communal lust, is expressed the infinite degradation in which man exists for himself; for the secret of this relationship finds its *unequivocal,* incontestable, *open* and revealed expression in the relation of man to woman and in the way in which the *direct* and *natural species* relationship is conceived. The immediate, natural and necessary relation of human being to human being is also the *relation* of *man* to *woman.* In this *natural* species relationship man's relation to nature is directly his relation to man, and his relation to man is directly his relation to nature, to his own *natural* function. Thus, in this relation is *sensuously revealed,* reduced to an observable *fact,* the extent to which human nature has become nature for man and to which nature has become human nature for him. From this relationship man's whole level of development can be assessed. It follows from the character of this relationship how far *man* has become, and has understood himself as, a *species-being,* a *human being.* The relation of man to woman is the *most natural* relation of human being to human being. It indicates, therefore, how far man's *natural* behavior has become *human,* and how far his *human* essence has become a *natural* essence for him, how far his *human nature* has become *nature for him.* It also shows how far man's *needs* have become *human* needs, and consequently how far the other person, as a person, has become one of his needs, and to what extent he is in his individual existence at the same time a social being. The first positive annulment of private property, crude communism, is therefore only a *phenomenal form* of the infamy of private property representing itself as positive community.

(2) Communism (a) still political in nature, democratic or despotic; (b) with the abolition of the state, yet still incomplete and influenced by private property, that is, by the alienation of man. In both forms communism is already aware of being the reintegration of man, his return to himself, the supersession of man's self-alienation. But since it has not yet grasped the positive nature of private property, or the *human* nature of needs, it is still captured and contaminated by private property. It has well understood the concept, but not the essence.

(3) *Communism* is the *positive* abolition of *private property,* of *human self-alienation,* and thus the real *appropriation* of *human* nature through and for man. It is, therefore, the return of man himself as a *social,* i.e., really human, being, a complete and conscious return which assimilates all the wealth of previous development. Communism as a fully-developed naturalism is humanism and as a fully-developed humanism is naturalism. It is the *definitive* resolution of the antagonism between man and nature, and between man and man. It is the true solution of the

conflict between existence and essence, between objectification and self-affirmation, between freedom and necessity, between individual and species. It is the solution of the riddle of history and knows itself to be this solution.

[THE SUPERSESSION OF PRIVATE PROPERTY]

Just as *private property* is only the sensuous expression of the fact that man is at the same time an *objective* fact for himself and becomes an alien and non-human object for himself; just as his manifestation of life is also his alienation of life and his self-realization a loss of reality, the emergence of an *alien* reality; so the positive supersession of private property, i.e., the *sensuous* appropriation of the human essence and of human life, of objective man and of human *creations,* by and for man, should not be taken only in the sense of *immediate,* exclusive *enjoyment,* or only in the sense of *possession* or *having.* Man appropriates his manifold being in an all-inclusive way, and thus as a whole man. All his *human* relations to the world—seeing, hearing, smelling, tasting, touching, thinking, observing, feeling, desiring, acting, loving—in short all the organs of his individuality, like the organs which are directly communal in form . . . are, in their objective action (their *action in relation to the object*) the appropriation of this object, the appropriation of human reality. The way in which they react to the object is the confirmation of *human reality.** It is human effectiveness and human *suffering,* for suffering humanly considered is an enjoyment of the self for man.

Private property has made us so stupid and partial that an object is only *ours* when we have it, when it exists for us as capital or when it is directly eaten, drunk, worn, inhabited, etc., in short, *utilized* in some way; although private property itself only conceives these various forms of possession as *means of life,* and the life for which they serve as means is the *life* of *private property*—labor and creation of capital.

Thus *all* the physical and intellectual senses have been replaced by the simple alienation of *all* these senses; the sense of *having.* The human being had to be reduced to this absolute poverty in order to be able to give birth to all his inner wealth. (On the category of *having* see Hess in *Einundzwanzig Bogen.*)

The supersession of private property is therefore the complete *emancipation* of all the human qualities and senses. It is this emancipation because these qualities and senses have become *human,* from the subjective as well as the objective point of view. The eye has become a *human* eye when its *object* has become a *human,* social object, created by man and destined for him. The senses have therefore become directly theoreticians in practice. They relate themselves to the thing for the sake of the thing, but the thing itself is an *objective human* relation to itself and to man, and vice versa.[†] Need and enjoyment have thus lost their *egoistic* character, and nature has lost its mere *utility* by the fact that its utilization has become *human* utilization.

---

*It is therefore just as varied as the determinations of human nature and activities are diverse.

[†]In practice I can only relate myself in a human way to a thing when the thing is related in a human way to man.

NEEDS, PRODUCTION, AND DIVISION OF LABOR

We have seen what importance should be attributed, in a socialist perspective, to the *wealth* of human needs, and consequently also to a *new mode of production* and to a new *object* of production. A new manifestation of *human* powers and a new enrichment of the human being. Within the system of private property it has the opposite meaning. Every man speculates upon creating a *new* need in another in order to force him to a new sacrifice, to place him in a new dependence, and to entice him into a new kind of pleasure and thereby into economic ruin. Everyone tries to establish over others an *alien* power in order to find there satisfaction of his own egoistic need. With the mass of objects, therefore, there also increases the realm of alien entities to which man is subjected. Every new product is a new *potentiality* of mutual deceit and robbery. Man becomes increasingly poor as a man; he has increasing need of *money* in order to take possession of the hostile being. The power of his *money* diminishes directly with the growth of the quantity of production, i.e., his need increases with the increasing *power* of money. The need for money is therefore the real need created by the modern economy, and the only need which it creates. The *quantity* of money becomes increasingly its only important quality. Just as it reduces every entity to its abstraction, so it reduces itself in its own development to a *quantitative* entity. Excess and immoderation become its true standard. This is shown subjectively, partly in the fact that the expansion of production and of needs becomes an *ingenious* and always *calculating* subservience to inhuman, depraved, unnatural, and *imaginary* appetites. Private property does not know how to change crude need into *human* need; its *idealism* is *fantasy, caprice* and *fancy*. No eunuch flatters his tyrant more shamefully or seeks by more infamous means to stimulate his jaded appetite, in order to gain some favor, than does the eunuch of industry, the entrepreneur, in order to acquire a few silver coins or to charm the gold from the purse of his dearly beloved neighbor. (Every product is a bait by means of which the individual tries to entice the essence of the other person, his money. Every real or potential need is a weakness which will draw the bird into the lime. Universal exploitation of human communal life. As every imperfection of man is a bond with heaven, a point from which his heart is accessible to the priest, so every want is an opportunity for approaching one's neighbor, with an air of friendship, and saying, "Dear friend, I will give you what you need, but you know the *conditio sine qua non*. You know what ink you must use in signing yourself over to me. I shall swindle you while providing your enjoyment.") The entrepreneur accedes to the most depraved fancies of his neighbor, plays the role of pander between him and his needs, awakens unhealthy appetites in him, and watches for every weakness in order, later, to claim the remuneration for this labor of love.

   This alienation is shown in part by the fact that the refinement of needs and of the means to satisfy them produces as its counterpart a bestial savagery, a complete, primitive and abstract simplicity of needs; or rather, that it simply reproduces itself in its opposite sense. For the worker even the need for fresh air ceases to be a need. Man returns to the cave dwelling again, but it is now poisoned by the pestilential breath of civilization. The worker has only a *precarious* right to inhabit it, for it has become an alien dwelling which may suddenly not be available, or from which he may be evicted if he does not pay the rent. He has to *pay* for this mortuary. The dwelling full of light which Prometheus, in Aeschylus, indicates as one of the great gifts by which he has changed savages into men, ceases to exist for the worker. Light, air, and the simplest *animal* cleanliness cease to be human needs. *Filth,* this corruption and putrefaction which runs in the *sewers* of civilization (this is to be taken literally) becomes the *element in which man lives.* Total and *unnatural* neglect, putrified nature, becomes the *element in which he lives.* None of his senses exist any longer, either in a human form, or even in a *non-human,* animal form. The crudest *methods* (and *instruments*) of human labor reappear; thus the *tread-mill* of the Roman slaves has become the mode of production and mode of existence of many English workers. It is not enough that man should lose his human needs; even animal needs disappear. The Irish no longer have any need but that of *eating—eating potatoes,* and then only the worst kind, *mouldy potatoes.* But France and England already possess in every industrial town a *little* Ireland. Savages and animals have at least the need for hunting, exercise and companionship. But the simplification of machinery and of work is used to make workers out of those who are just growing up, who are still immature, *children,* while the worker himself has become a child deprived of all care. Machinery is adapted to the weakness of the human being, in order to turn the weak human being into a machine.

The fact that the growth of needs and of the means to satisfy them results in a lack of needs and of means is demonstrated in several ways by the economist (and by the capitalist; in fact, it is always *empirical* businessmen we refer to when we speak of economists, who are their *scientific* self-revelation and existence). First, by reducing the needs of the worker to the miserable necessities required for the maintenance of his physical existence, and by reducing his activity to the most abstract mechanical movements, the economist asserts that man has no needs, for activity or enjoyment, beyond that; and yet he declares that this kind of life is a *human* way of life. Secondly, by reckoning as the general standard of life (general because it is applicable to the mass of men) the *most impoverished* life conceivable, he turns the worker into a being who has neither senses nor needs, just as he turns his activity into a pure abstraction from all activity. Thus all working class *luxury* seems to him blameworthy, and everything which goes beyond the most abstract need (whether it be a passive enjoyment or a manifestation of personal activity) is regarded as a *luxury.* Political economy, the science of *wealth,* is therefore, at the same time, the science of renunciation, of privation and of saving, which actually succeeds in depriving man of fresh *air* and of physical *activity.* This science of a marvelous industry is at the same time the science of *asceticism.* Its true ideal is the *ascetic* but *usurious* miser and the *ascetic* but *productive* slave. Its moral ideal is the *worker* who takes a part of his wages to the savings bank. It has even found a servile art to embody this favorite idea, which has been produced in a sentimental manner on the stage. Thus, despite its worldly and pleasure-seeking appearance, it is a truly moral science, the most moral of all sciences. Its principal thesis is the renunciation of life and of human needs. The less you eat, drink, buy books, go to the theatre or to balls, or the public house, and the less you think, love, theorize, sing, paint, fence, etc., the more you will be able to save and the *greater* will become your treasure which neither moth nor rust will corrupt—your *capital.* The less you *are,* the less you express your life, the more you *have,* the greater is your *alienated* life and the greater is the saving of your alienated being. Everything which the economist takes from you in the way of life and humanity, he restores to you in the form of *money* and *wealth.* And everything which you are unable to do, your money can do for you; it can eat, drink, go to the ball and to the theatre. It can acquire art, learning, historical treasures, political power; and it can travel. It *can* appropriate all these things for you, can purchase everything; it is the true *opulence.* But although it can do all this, it only *desires* to create itself, and to buy itself, for everything else is subservient to it. When one owns the master, one also owns the servant, and one has no need of the master's servant. Thus all passions and activities must be submerged in *avarice.* The worker must have just what is necessary for him to want to live, and he must want to live only in order to have this.

MONEY

. . . the meaning of private property—released from its alienation—is the *existence of essential objects* for man, as objects of enjoyment and activity.

Money, since it has the property of purchasing everything, of appropriating objects to itself, is therefore the *object par excellence.* The universal character of this *property* corresponds to the omnipotence of money, which is regarded as an omnipotent being . . . money is the *pander* between need and object, between human life and the means of subsistence. But *that which* mediates *my* life mediates also the existence of other men for me. It is for me the *other* person.

. . .

That which exists for me through the medium of *money,* that which I can pay for (i.e., which money can buy), that *I am,* the possessor of the money. My own power is as great as the power of money. The properties of money are my own (the possessor's) properties and faculties. What I *am* and *can* do is, therefore, not at all determined by my individuality. I *am* ugly, but I can buy the *most beautiful* woman for myself. Consequently, I am not *ugly,* for the effect of *ugliness,* its power to repel, is annulled by money. As an individual I am *lame,* but money provides me with twenty-four legs. Therefore, I am not lame. I am a detestable, dishonorable, unscrupulous and stupid man but money is honored and so also is its possessor. Money is the highest good, and so its possessor is good. Besides, money saves me the trouble of being dishonest; therefore, I am presumed honest. I am *stupid,* but since money is the *real mind* of all things, how should its possessor be stupid? Moreover, he can buy talented people for himself, and is not he who has power over the talented more talented than they? I who can have, through the power of money, *everything* for which the human heart longs, do I not possess all human abilities? Does not my money, therefore, transform all my incapacities into their opposites?

If *money* is the bond which binds me to *human* life, and society to me, and which links me with nature and man, is it not the bond of all *bonds?* Is it not, therefore also the universal agent of separation? It is the real means of both *separation* and *union,* the galvano-*chemical* power of society.

. . . Two properties of money:

1 it is the visible deity, the transformation of all human and natural qualities into their opposites, the universal confusion and inversion of things; it brings incompatibles into fraternity;

2 it is the universal whore, the universal pander between men and nations.

The power to confuse and invert all human and natural qualities, to bring about fraternization of incompatibles, the *divine* power of money, resides in its *character* as the alienated and self-alienating species-life of man. It is the alienated *power* of *humanity.*

What I as a *man* am unable to do, and thus what all my individual faculties are unable to do, is made possible for me by *money.* Money, therefore, turns each of these faculties into something which it is not, into its *opposite.*

If I long for a meal, or wish to take the mail coach because I am not strong enough to go on foot, money provides the meal and the mail coach; i.e., it transforms my desires from representations into *realities,* from imaginary being into *real being.* In mediating thus, money is a *genuinely creative* power.

Demand also exists for the individual who has no money, but his demand is a mere creature of the imagination which has no effect, no existence for me . . . and which thus remains *unreal* and *without object.* The difference between effective demand, supported by money, and ineffective demand, based upon my need, my passion, my desire, etc. is the difference between *being* and *thought,* between the merely *inner* representation and the representation which exists outside myself as a *real object.*

If I have no money for travel I have no *need*—no real and self-realizing need—for travel. If I have a *vocation* for study but no money for it, then I have *no* vocation, i.e., no *effective, genuine* vocation. Conversely, if I really have *no* vocation for study, but have money and the urge for it, then I have an *effective* vocation. *Money* is the external, universal *means* and *power* (not derived from man as man or from human society as society) to change *representation* into *reality* and *reality* into *mere representation.* It transforms *real human and natural faculties* into mere abstract representations, i.e., *imperfections* and tormenting chimeras; and on the other hand, it transforms *real imperfections and fancies,* faculties which are really impotent and which exist only in the individual's imagination, into *real faculties and powers.* In this respect, therefore, money is the general inversion of *individualities,* turning them into their opposites and associating contradictory qualities with their qualities.

Money, then, appears as a *disruptive* power for the individual and for the social bonds, which claim to be self-subsistent *entities.* It changes fidelity into infidelity, love into hate, hate into love, virtue into vice, and vice into virtue, servant into master, stupidity into intelligence and intelligence into stupidity.

Since money, as the existing and active concept of value, confounds and exchanges everything, it is the universal *confusion and transposition* of all things, the inverted world, the confusion and transposition of all natural and human qualities.

He who can purchase bravery is brave, though a coward. Money is not exchanged for a particular quality, a particular thing, or a specific human faculty, but for the whole objective world of man and nature. Thus, from the standpoint of its possessor, it exchanges every quality and object for every other, even though they are contradictory. It is the fraternization of incompatibles; it forces contraries to embrace.

Let us assume *man* to be *man,* and his relation to the world to be a human one. Then love can only be exchanged for love, trust for trust, etc. If you wish to enjoy art you must be an artistically cultivated person; if you wish to influence other people you must be a person who really has a stimulating and encouraging effect upon others. Every one of your relations to man and to nature must be a *specific expression,* corresponding to the object of your will, of your *real individual* life. If you love without evoking love in return, i.e., if you are not able, by the *manifestation* of yourself as a loving person, to make yourself a *beloved person,* then your love is impotent and a misfortune.

3

MATERIALISM

Earlier philosophers, Marx believed—even those who had grasped the powers of the dialectic—had erred in applying it only in the realm of pure thought. It was essential, he argued, that it be applied correctly. The dialectic had to be applied to the concrete concerns of human beings, to human needs and wants—in a word, to *matter.* Philosophical materialism was therefore the only correct starting point for Marx and Engels, and in expressing this conviction they acknowledged their debt to the German materialist Ludwig Feuerbach. But their materialism was new and more true and more powerful than his, they believed, because theirs was the first to view the world not only as constituted by matter but as matter organized dialectically. Only with this dialectical underpinning could materialism become truly scientific. And only on these materialist premises, Marx and Engels claimed, could the dialectic be properly utilized and world history understood.

Because Marx and Engels were thoroughgoing materialists, they rejected all beliefs and principles based upon supernatural powers or the accounts of miracles and the like. They rejected theism; they rejoiced in Feuerbach's atheistic account of the essence of Christianity. Learned in Greek language and culture, Marx chose Prometheus as his favorite myth—one who brought fire and light to mankind, was punished by being bound to a great rock, and yet remained defiant of the gods. Their materialist convictions have led communists since Marx to condemn all organized religion as no better than superstition, and to deny the truth of ethical or religious principles founded on claims of divine or supernatural authority.

9
Karl Marx and Friedrich Engels

Marx and Engels often collaborated productively in their philosophical work. *The German Ideology* (1846) was an early product of this collaboration, written after Marx's *Economic and Philosophic Manuscripts* but before their philosophical system had developed fully. The great and pervasive failing of Hegelian philosophy (the "German ideology") was here identified as its mistaken philosophic idealism, its primary reliance upon pure concepts, its dearth of concreteness, and its resulting practical irrelevance. "In contrast to German philosophy," Marx and Engels wrote derisively, "which descends from heaven to earth, here we ascend from earth to heaven."

[THE PREMISES OF MATERIALISM]*

The premises from which we begin are not arbitrary ones, not dogmas, but real premises from which abstraction can only be made in the imagination. They are the real individuals, their activity and the material conditions under which they live, both those which they find already existing and those produced by their activity. These premises can thus be verified in a purely empirical way.

The first premise of all human history is, of course, the existence of living human individuals. Thus the first fact to be established is the physical organization of these individuals and their consequent relation to the rest of nature. . . .

The fact is, therefore, that definite individuals who are productively active in a definite way enter into these definite social and political relations. Empirical observation must in each separate instance bring out empirically, and without any mystification and speculation, the connection of the social and political structure with production. The social structure and the state are continually evolving out of the life process of definite individuals, but of individuals not as they may appear in their own or other people's imagination, but as they really are, i.e., as they are effective, produce materially, and are active under definite material limits, presuppositions, and conditions independent of their will.

The production of ideas, of conceptions, of consciousness is at first directly interwoven with the material activity and the material intercourse of men, the language of real life. Conceiving, thinking, the mental intercourse of men appear at this stage as the direct efflux of their material behavior. The same applies to mental production as expressed in the language of the politics, laws, morality, religion, metaphysics of a people. Men are the producers of their conceptions, ideas, etc.— real, active men, as they are conditioned by a definite development of their productive forces and of the intercourse corresponding to these, up to its furthest forms. Consciousness can never be anything else than conscious existence, and the

---

*From K. Marx and F. Engels, *The German Ideology*. Written in 1845–46, this work was first published almost a century later. These passages are reprinted by permission of International Publishers, New York.

existence of men is their actual life process. If in all ideology men and their circumstances appear upside down, as in a *camera obscura,* this phenomenon arises just as much from their historical life process as the inversion of objects on the retina does from their physical life process.

In direct contrast to German philosophy, which descends from heaven to earth, here we ascend from earth to heaven. That is to say, we do not set out from what men say, imagine, conceive, nor from men as narrated, thought of, imagined, conceived, in order to arrive at men in the flesh. We set out from real, active men, and on the basis of their real life process we demonstrate the development of the ideological reflexes and echoes of this life process. The phantoms formed in the human brain are also, necessarily, sublimates of their material life process, which is empirically verifiable and bound to material premises. Morality, religion, metaphysics, all the rest of ideology and their corresponding forms of consciousness, thus no longer retain the semblance of independence. They have no history, no development; but men, developing their material production and their material intercourse, alter, along with this, their real existence, their thinking, and the products of their thinking. Life is not determined by consciousness, but consciousness by life. In the first method of approach the starting point is consciousness taken as the living individual; in the second it is the real, living individuals themselves, as they are in actual life, and consciousness is considered solely as *their* consciousness.

This method of approach is not devoid of premises. It starts out from the real premises, and does not abandon them for a moment. Its premises are men, not in any fantastic isolation or abstract definition, but in their actual, empirically perceptible process of development under definite conditions. As soon as this active life process is described, history ceases to be a collection of dead facts, as it is with the empiricists (themselves still abstract), or an imagined activity of imagined subjects, as with the idealists.

Where speculation ends—in real life—there real, positive science begins: the representation of the practical activity, of the practical process of development of men. Empty talk about consciousness ceases, and real knowledge has to take its place. When reality is depicted, philosophy as an independent branch of activity loses its medium of existence. At best, its place can be taken only by a summing up of the most general results, abstractions which arise from the observation of the historical development of men. Viewed apart from real history, these abstractions have in themselves no value whatsoever. They can only serve to facilitate the arrangement of historical material, to indicate the sequence of its separate strata. But they by no means afford a recipe or schema, as does philosophy, for neatly trimming the epochs of history. On the contrary, our difficulties begin only when we set about the observation and the arrangement—the real depiction—of our historical material, whether of a past epoch or of the present. The removal of these difficulties is governed by premises which it is quite impossible to state here, but which only the study of the actual life process and the activity of the individuals of each epoch will make evident. We shall select here some of these abstractions, which we use to refute the ideologists, and shall illustrate them by historical examples.

10
Friedrich Engels

Marx and Engels were greatly influenced by the hard-headed philosophic materialism of Ludwig Feuerbach, their younger contemporary. This debt was gratefully acknowledged by Engels, late in his life, with a small volume entitled: *Ludwig Feuerbach and the End of Classical German Philosophy*. In this work is to be found the most powerful statement of the Marxist conception of the opposition of idealism and materialism, and a concise recapitulation of the materialistic presuppositions of the communist philosophy.

[FEUERBACH AND HEGEL]*

. . . One can imagine what a tremendous effect this Hegelian system must have produced in the philosophy-tinged atmosphere of Germany. It was a triumphal procession which lasted for decades and which by no means came to a standstill on the death of Hegel. On the contrary, it was precisely from 1830 to 1840 that "Hegelianism" reigned most exclusively and, to a greater or lesser extent, infected even its opponents. It was precisely in this period that Hegelian views, consciously or unconsciously, most extensively penetrated the most diversified sciences and leavened even popular literature and the daily press, from which the average "educated consciousness" derives its mental pabulum. But this victory along the whole front was only the prelude to an internal struggle.

As we have seen, the doctrine of Hegel, taken as a whole, left plenty of room for giving shelter to the most diverse practical party views. And in the theoretical Germany of that time two things above all were practical: religion and politics. Whoever placed the chief emphasis on the Hegelian *system* could be fairly conservative in both spheres; whoever regarded the dialectical *method* as the main thing could belong to the most extreme opposition, both in politics and religion. Hegel himself, despite the fairly frequent outbursts of revolutionary wrath in his works, seemed on the whole to be more inclined to the conservative side. . . .

We will not go further into . . . the decomposition process of the Hegelian school. More important for us is the following: the main body of the most determined Young Hegelians was, by the practical necessities of its fight against positive religion, driven back to Anglo-French materialism. This brought them into conflict with their school system. While materialism conceives nature as the sole reality, nature in the Hegelian system represents merely the "alienation" of the Absolute Idea, so to say, a degradation of the Idea. At all events, thinking and its thought product, the Idea, is here the primary, nature the derivative, which exists

*From F. Engels, *Ludwig Feuerbach and the End of Classical German Philosophy*. These passages are reprinted from *Basic Writings on Politics and Philosophy* by Marx and Engels, edited by L. S. Feuer, Doubleday and Company, Anchor Books, New York, 1959.

at all only by the condescension of the Idea. And in this contradiction they floun-
dered as well or as ill as they could.

Then came Feuerbach's *Essence of Christianity.* With one blow it pulverized
the contradiction, in that without circumlocutions it placed materialism on the
throne again. Nature exists independently of all philosophy. It is the foundation
upon which we human beings, ourselves products of nature, have grown up. Nothing exists outside nature and man, and the higher beings our religious fantasies
have created are only the fantastic reflection of our own essence. The spell was
broken, the "system" was exploded and cast aside, and the contradiction, shown to
exist only in our imagination, was dissolved. One must himself have experienced
the liberating effect of this book to get an idea of it. Enthusiasm was general; we
all became at once Feuerbachians. How enthusiastically Marx greeted the new
conception and how much—in spite of all critical reservations—he was influenced
by it, one may read in *The Holy Family.* . . .

The Hegelian school disintegrated, but Hegelian philosophy was not overcome
through criticism. . . . Feuerbach broke through the system and simply discarded
it. But a philosophy is not disposed of by the mere assertion that it is false. And so
powerful a work as Hegelian philosophy, which had exercised so enormous an
influence on the intellectual development of the nation, could not be disposed of
by simply being ignored. It had to be "sublated" in its own sense, that is, in the
sense that while its form had to be annihilated through criticism, the new content
which had been won through it had to be saved. How this was brought about we
shall see below.

[IDEALISM AND MATERIALISM]

The great basic question of all philosophy, especially of more recent philosophy,
is that concerning the relation of thinking and being. From the very early times
when men, still completely ignorant of the structure of their own bodies, under the
stimulus of dream apparitions came to believe that their thinking and sensation
were not activities of their bodies, but of a distinct soul which inhabits the body
and leaves it at death—from this time men have been driven to reflect about the
relation between this soul and the outside world. If upon death it took leave of the
body and lived on, there was no occasion to invent yet another distinct death for
it. Thus arose the idea of its immortality, which at that stage of development
appeared not at all as a consolation, but as a fate against which it was no use fighting, and often enough, as among the Greeks, as a positive misfortune. Not religious desire for consolation, but the quandary arising from the common universal
ignorance of what to do with this soul, once its existence had been accepted, after
the death of the body led in a general way to the tedious notion of personal immortality. In an exactly similar manner the first gods arose through the personification
of natural forces. And these gods in the further development of religions assumed
more and more an extra-mundane form, until finally by a process of abstraction, I
might almost say of distillation, occurring naturally in the course of man's intel-

lectual development, out of the many more or less limited and mutually limiting gods there arose in the minds of men the idea of the one exclusive God of the monotheistic religions.

Thus the question of the relation of thinking to being, the relation of the spirit to nature—the paramount question of the whole of philosophy—has, no less than all religion, its roots in the narrowminded and ignorant notions of savagery. But this question could for the first time be put forward in its whole acuteness, could achieve its full significance, only after humanity in Europe had awakened from the long hibernation of the Christian Middle Ages. The question of the position of thinking in relation to being, a question which, by the way, had played a great part also in the scholasticism of the Middle Ages, the question: Which is primary, spirit or nature?—that question, in relation to the Church, was sharpened into this: Did God create the world or has the world been in existence eternally?

The answers which the philosophers gave to this question split them into two great camps. Those who asserted the primacy of spirit to nature and, therefore, in the last instance, assumed world creation in some form or other—and among the philosophers, Hegel, for example, this creation often becomes still more intricate and impossible than in Christianity—comprised the camp of idealism. The others, who regarded nature as primary, belong to the various schools of materialism.

These two expressions, idealism and materialism, originally signify nothing else but this; and here, too, they are not used in any other sense. What confusion arises when some other meaning is put into them will be seen below.

But the question of the relation of thinking and being has yet another side: In what relation do our thoughts about the world surrounding us stand to this world itself? Is our thinking capable of the cognition of the real world? Are we able in our ideas and notions of the real world to produce a correct reflection of reality? In philosophical language this question is called the question of the identity of thinking and being, and the overwhelming majority of philosophers give an affirmative answer to this question. With Hegel, for example, its affirmation is self-evident; for what we cognize in the real world is precisely its thought content—that which makes the world a gradual realization of the Absolute Idea, which Absolute Idea has existed somewhere from eternity, independent of the world and before the world. But it is manifest without further proof that thought can know a content which is from the outset a thought content. It is equally manifest that what is to be proved here is already tacitly contained in the premises. But that in no way prevents Hegel from drawing the further conclusion from his proof of the identity of thinking and being that his philosophy, because it is correct for his thinking, is therefore the only correct one, and that the identity of thinking and being must prove its validity by mankind immediately translating his philosophy from theory into practice and transforming the whole world according to Hegelian principles. This is an illusion which he shares with well-nigh all philosophers.

In addition there is yet a set of different philosophers—those who question the possibility of any cognition, or at least of an exhaustive cognition, of the world. To them, among the more modern ones, belong Hume and Kant, and they have played a very important role in philosophical development. What is decisive in the refutation of this view has already been said by Hegel, in so far as this was possible from an idealist standpoint. The materialistic additions made by Feuerbach are more ingenious than profound. The most telling refutation of this, as of all other philosophical crotchets, is practice, namely, experiment and industry. If we are able to prove the correctness of our conception of a natural process by making it ourselves, bringing it into being out of its conditions and making it serve our own purposes into the bargain, then there is an end to the Kantian ungraspable "thing-in-itself." The chemical substances produced in the bodies of plants and animals remained just such things-in-themselves until organic chemistry began to produce them one after another, whereupon the thing-in-itself became a thing for us, as, for instance, alizarin, the coloring matter of the madder, which we no longer trouble to grow in the madder roots in the field, but produce much more cheaply and simply from coal tar. For three hundred years the Copernican solar system was a hypothesis with a hundred, a thousand, or ten thousand chances to one in its favor, but still always a hypothesis. But when Leverrier, by means of the data provided by this system, not only deduced the necessity of the existence of an unknown planet, but also calculated the position in the heavens which this planet must necessarily occupy, and when Galle really found this planet the Copernican system was proved. If, nevertheless, the Neo-Kantians are attempting to resurrect the Kantian conception in Germany and the agnostics that of Hume in England (where in fact it never became extinct), this is, in view of their theoretical and practical refutation, accomplished long ago, scientifically a regression and practically merely a shamefaced way of surreptitiously accepting materialism while denying it before the world.

But during this long period from Descartes to Hegel and from Hobbes to Feuerbach the philosophers were by no means impelled, as they thought they were, solely by the force of pure reason. On the contrary, what really pushed them forward most was the powerful and ever more rapidly onrushing progress of natural science and industry. Among the materialists this was plain on the surface, but the idealist systems also filled themselves more and more with a materialist content, and attempted pantheistically to reconcile the antithesis between mind and matter. Thus, ultimately, the Hegelian system represents merely a materialism idealistically turned upside down in method and content. . . .

The course of evolution of Feuerbach is that of a Hegelian—a never quite orthodox Hegelian, it is true—into a materialist, an evolution which at a definite stage necessitates a complete rupture with the idealist system of his predecessor. With irresistible force Feuerbach is finally driven to the realization that the Hegelian premundane existence of the Absolute Idea, the "pre-existence of the logical categories" before the world existed, is nothing more than the fantastic survival of the belief in the existence of an extramundane creator; that the material, sensuously perceptible world to which we ourselves belong is the only reality; and that our consciousness and thinking, however suprasensuous they may seem, are the product of a material, bodily organ, the brain. Matter is not a product of mind, but mind itself is merely the highest product of matter. This is, of course, pure materialism. . . .

. . . But just as idealism underwent a series of stages of development, so also did materialism. With each epoch-making discovery even in the sphere of natural science it has to change its form, and after history also was subjected to materialistic treatment a new avenue of development has opened here, too.

The materialism of the last century was predominantly mechanical . . . [Its] specific limitation . . . lay in its inability to comprehend the universe as a process, as matter undergoing uninterrupted historical development. This was in accordance with the level of the natural science of that time, and with the metaphysical, that is, anti-dialectical, manner of philosophizing connected with it. Nature—so much was known—was in eternal motion. But according to the ideas of that time, this motion turned, also eternally, in a circle and therefore never moved from the spot; it produced the same results over and over again. This conception was at that time inevitable. The Kantian theory of the origin of the solar system had been put forward but recently, and was still regarded merely as a curiosity. The history of the development of the earth, geology, was still totally unknown, and the conception that the animate natural beings of today are the result of a long sequence of development from the simple to the complex could not at that time scientifically be put forward at all. The unhistorical view of nature was therefore inevitable.

. . .

It is therefore not Feuerbach's fault that the historical conception of nature, which had now become possible and which removed all the one-sidedness of French materialism, remained inaccessible to him.

. . . Feuerbach is quite correct in asserting that exclusively natural-scientific materialism is indeed "the foundation of the edifice of human knowledge, but not the edifice itself." For we live not only in nature but also in human society, and this also no less than nature has its history of development and its science. It was therefore a question of bringing the science of society, that is, the sum total of the so-called historical and philosophical sciences, into harmony with the materialist foundation, and of reconstructing it thereupon. But it did not fall to Feuerbach's lot to do this. . . .

11
Ludwig Andreas Feuerbach

Ludwig Feuerbach (1804–1872) was a popular German philosopher whose materialism was expressed in the famous epigram: Man is what he eats. *(Der Mensch ist was er isst.)* In *The Essence of Christianity,* from the preface to which the following passage is taken, Feuerbach denies that God exists, except as an idealized object of human consciousness. "Let it be remembered," he remarks, "that atheism is the secret of religion itself."

[MATERIALISM AND ATHEISM]*

The clamor excited by the present work has not surprised me and hence it has not in the least moved me from my position. On the contrary, I have once more, in all calmness, subjected my work to the severest scrutiny, both historical and philosophical; I have, as far as possible, freed it from its defects of form, and enriched it with new developments, illustrations and historical testimonies—testimonies in the highest degree striking and irrefragable. Now that I have thus verified by analysis by historical proofs, it is to be hoped that readers whose eyes are not sealed will be convinced and will admit, even though reluctantly, that my work contains a faithful, correct translation of the Christian religion out of the oriental language of imagery into plain speech. And it has no pretension to be anything more than a close translation, or, to speak literally, an empirical or historico-philosophical analysis, a solution of the enigma of the Christian religion. The general propositions which I premise in the Introduction are no *à priori,* excogitated propositions, no products of speculation; they have arisen out of the analysis of religion; they are only, as indeed are all the fundamental ideas of the work, generalizations from the known manifestations of human nature, and in particular of the religious consciousness—facts converted into thoughts, i.e., expressed in general terms, and thus made the property of the understanding. The ideas of my work are only conclusions, *consequences,* drawn from premises which are not themselves mere ideas, but objective facts either actual or historical—facts which had not their place in my head simply in virtue of their ponderous existence in folio. I unconditionally repudiate *absolute,* immaterial, self-sufficing speculation—that speculation which draws its material from within. I differ *toto coelo* from those philosophers who pluck out their eyes that they may see better; for *my* thought I require the senses, especially sight; I found my ideas on materials which can be appropriated only through the activity of the senses. I do not generate the object from the thought, but the thought from the object; and I hold *that* alone to be an object which has an existence beyond one's own brain. I am an idealist only in the region of *practical* philosophy, that is, I do not regard the limits of the past and present as the limits of humanity, of the future; on the contrary, I firmly believe that many things—yes, many things—which with the short-sighted, pusillanimous practical men of today, pass for flights of imagination, for ideas never to be realized, for mere chimeras, will tomorrow, i.e., in the next century—centuries in individual life are days in the life of humanity—exist in full reality. Briefly, the "Idea" is to me only faith in the historical future, in the triumph of truth and virtue; it has for me only a political and moral significance: for in the sphere of strictly theoretical philosophy, I attach myself, in direct opposition to the Hegelian philosophy, only to *realism,* to materialism in the sense above indicated. The maxim hitherto adopted by speculative philosophy: all that is mine I carry with me, the old *omnia mea mecum porto,* I cannot, alas! appropriate. I have many things outside myself,

*From *The Essence of Christianity,* translated by Marian Evans. Published by John Chapman, London, 1854.

which I cannot convey either in my pocket or my head, but which nevertheless I look upon as belonging to me, not indeed as a mere man—a view not now in question—but as a philosopher. I am nothing but a *natural philosopher in the domain of mind;* and the natural philosopher can do nothing without instruments, without material means. In this character I have written the present work, which consequently contains nothing else than the principle of a new philosophy verified practically, i.e., *in concreto,* in application to a special object, but an object which has a universal significance: namely, to religion, in which this principle is exhibited, *developed* and thoroughly carried out. This philosophy is essentially distinguished from the systems hitherto prevalent, in that it corresponds to the real, complete nature of man; but for that very reason it is antagonistic to minds perverted and crippled by a super-human, i.e., anti-human, anti-natural religion and speculation. It does not, as I have already said elsewhere, regard the *pen* as the only fit organ for the revelation of truth, but the eye and ear, the hand and foot; it does not identify the idea of the fact with the fact itself, so as to reduce real existence to an existence on paper, but it separates the two, and precisely by this separation attains to the *fact itself;* it recognizes as the true thing, not the thing as it is an object of the abstract reason, but as it is an object of the real, complete man, and hence as it is itself a real, complete thing. This philosophy does not rest on an understanding *per se,* on an absolute, nameless understanding, belonging one knows not to whom, but on the understanding of man—though not, I grant, on that of man enervated by speculation and dogma—and it speaks the language of men, not an empty, unknown tongue. Yes, both in substance and in speech, it places philosophy in *the negation of philosophy,* i.e., it declares *that* alone to be the true philosophy which is converted *in succum et sanguinem,* which is incarnate in Man; and hence it finds its highest triumph in the fact that to all dull and pedantic minds, which place the *essence* of philosophy in the *show* of philosophy, it appears to be no philosophy at all.

This philosophy has for its principle, not the Substance of Spinoza, not the *ego* of Kant and Fichte, not the Absolute Identity of Schelling, not the Absolute Mind of Hegel, in short, no abstract, merely conceptional being, but a *real* being, the true *Ens realissimum*—man; its principle, therefore, is in the highest degree positive and real. It generates thought from the *opposite* of thought, from Matter, from existence, from the senses; it has relation to its object first through the senses, i.e., passively, before defining it in thought. Hence my work, as a specimen of this philosophy, so far from being a production to be placed in the category of Speculation—although in another point of view it is the true, the incarnate result of prior philosophical systems—is the direct opposite of speculation, nay, puts an end to it by explaining it. Speculation makes religion say only what it has *itself* thought, and expressed far better than religion; it assigns a meaning to religion without any reference to the *actual* meaning of religion; it does not look beyond itself. I, on the contrary, let religion itself speak; I constitute myself only its listener and interpreter, not its prompter. Not to invent, but to discover, "to unveil existence," has been my sole object; to *see* correctly, my sole endeavor. It is not I, but religion that worships man, although religion, or rather theology, denies this; it is not I, an insignificant individual, but religion itself that says: God is man, man is God; it is not I, but religion that denies the God who is *not* man, but only an *ens rationis*—since it makes God become man, and then constitutes this God, not distinguished from man, having a human form, human feelings and human thoughts, the object of its worship and veneration. I have only found the key to the cipher of the Christian religion, only extricated its true meaning from the web of contradictions and delusions called theology—but in doing so I have certainly committed a sacrilege. If therefore my work is negative, irreligious, atheistic, let it be remembered that atheism—at least in the sense of this work—is the secret of religion itself; that religion itself, not indeed on the surface, but fundamentally, not in intention or according to its own supposition, but in its heart, in its essence, believes in nothing else than the truth and divinity of human nature. . . .

12
Karl Marx

In the spring of 1845 Marx jotted down some notes on the philosophy of Ludwig Feuerbach, observations intended for his own use which were soon forgotten and came to light only many years later. Called the *Theses on Feuerbach,* these notes exhibit Marx's eagerness to put philosophy to work in human life, as well as the revolutionary direction of his thought. Among these jottings was an incisive aphorism destined to become famous: "The philosophers have only *interpreted* the world, in various ways; the point, however, is to *change* it."

THESES ON FEUERBACH*

I

The chief defect of all hitherto existing materialism—that of Feuerbach included—is that the thing [*Gegenstand*], reality, sensuousness, is conceived only in the form of the *object* [*Objekt*] or of *contemplation* [*Anschauung*], but not as *human sensuous activity, practice,* not subjectively. Hence it happened that the *active* side, in contradistinction to materialism, was developed by idealism—but only abstractly, since, of course, idealism does not know real, sensuous activity as such. Feuerbach wants sensuous objects really differentiated from the thought objects, but he does not conceive human activity itself as *objective* [*gegenständliche*] activity. Hence, in the *Essence of Christianity,* he regards the theoretical attitude as the only genuinely human attitude, while practice is conceived and fixed only in its dirty-judaical form of appearance. Hence he does not grasp the significance of "revolutionary," of "practical-critical," activity.

---

*Reprinted from *Basic Writings on Politics and Philosophy,* by Marx and Engels, edited by L. S. Feuer, Doubleday and Company, Anchor Books, New York, 1959.

II

The question whether objective [*gegenständliche*] truth can be attributed to human thinking is not a question of theory, but is a *practical* question. In practice man must prove the truth, that is, the reality and power, the this-sidedness [*Diesseit-igkeit*] of his thinking. The dispute over the reality or non-reality of thinking which is isolated from practice is a purely *scholastic* question.

III

The materialist doctrine that men are products of circumstances and upbringing, and that, therefore, changed men are products of other circumstances and changed upbringing, forgets that it is men that change circumstances, and that the educator himself needs educating. Hence this doctrine necessarily arrives at dividing society into two parts, of which one is superior to society (in Robert Owen, for example).

The coincidence of the changing of circumstances and of human activity can be conceived and rationally understood only as *revolutionizing practice.*

IV

Feuerbach starts out from the fact of religious self-alienation, the duplication of the world into a religious, imaginary world and a real one. His work consists in the dissolution of the religious world into its secular basis. He overlooks the fact that after completing this work, the chief thing still remains to be done. For the fact that the secular foundation detaches itself from itself and establishes itself in the clouds as an independent realm is really to be explained only by the self-cleavage and self-contradictoriness of this secular basis. The latter must itself, therefore, first be understood in its contradiction and then, by the removal of the contradiction, revolutionized in practice. Thus, for instance, once the earthly family is discovered to be the secret of the holy family, the former must then itself be criticized in theory and revolutionized in practice. . . .

VII

Feuerbach, consequently, does not see that the "religious sentiment" is itself a *social product,* and that the abstract individual whom he analyzes belongs in reality to a particular form of society.

VIII

Social life is essentially *practical.* All mysteries which mislead theory to mysticism find their rational solution in human practice and in the comprehension of this practice.

IX

The highest point attained by *contemplative* materialism, that is, materialism which does not understand sensuousness as practical activity, is the contemplation of single individuals in "civil society."

X

The standpoint of the old materialism is *"civil"* society; the standpoint of the new is *human* society, or socialized humanity.

XI

The philosophers have only *interpreted* the world, in various ways; the point, however, is to *change* it.

4

THE THEORY OF DIALECTICAL AND HISTORICAL MATERIALISM

The dialectic applied to matter—sound philosophic method put to work on the real stuff of the world—provides the skeleton of dialectical materialism. Much flesh upon those bones would be needed to prove the theory true. By combining philosophical analysis and economic research, Marx and Engels sought tirelessly to provide that proof. Only one correct result, they believed, could emerge from the correct application of dialectical materialism to all world events. The account of human history they thus derived was called *historical materialism.*

Historical materialism asserts that history can be correctly understood only as the development of human societies attempting, in their several ways, to satisfy the material needs of conflicting economic classes. Economic considerations are always paramount in this view, always controlling—and therefore social classes must struggle endlessly for control of the production and distribution of goods, and of the entire economic order. These bitter class struggles will succeed one another in a great dialectical progression, each dominant class necessarily giving birth to its own economic antithesis, and thus promoting a new conflict that must lead to the next higher synthesis and the domination of a new class. That is the way it has always been, and until a society without classes comes into being, that is the way it must be. "The history of all hitherto existing society," *The Communist Manifesto* begins, "is the history of class struggles."

The detailed account of historical materialism, which Marx and his associates were seeking constantly to improve and perfect, will disclose the precise dialectical role of the present stage in the series of class struggles. Under the current capitalist system, they believed, dialectical conflict is concentrated in the clash of two great classes: the bourgeoisie, which now controls the means of production and distribution, and the proletariat, or mass of exploited industrial workers, which is inevitably created by the bourgeoisie and must come ultimately to oppose and overcome it.

The selections in this section are taken from core treatises in communist philosophy. They present the Marxist account of the development and the essential nature of this nearly climactic stage of world history, as well as the general character of the events that Marxists contend are destined to succeed it. Capitalism, Marx held, is but the latest of a long series of phases through which the dialectic of history inevitably moves. It too will pass. The theory was early outlined with broad strokes in *The Communist Manifesto,* later greatly enriched by Engels's systematic account of "scientific socialism." In *Capital,* Marx's detailed critique of political economy, the real character of the capitalist system is analyzed and (as he believed) exposed, the essential contradictions contained within it at last revealed. These internal contradictions, Marx concluded, laid bare by dialectical materialism, inevitably result in the downfall of the capitalist system and its eventual replacement by a new and higher synthesis. For Marx and Engels, the exposition and defense of historical materialism was the great project of their lives.

13
Karl Marx and Friedrich Engels

In 1847 Marx and Engels prepared—for a small group, meeting in London, calling itself the International Communist League—a general statement of policy, which came to be known as *The Communist Manifesto.* In this, their most famous and most influential work, Marx and Engels consciously apply the principles of materialism and dialectical method to social and economic problems. Into a pamphlet of only thirty-five pages they compress a general theory of history, an analysis of the ills of European society, a program for revolutionary action, and a vision of the post-capitalist future. Yet the *Manifesto* is more than a program, more than an analysis or an argument; it is an impassioned plea for the solidarity of the laboring classes. "Let the ruling classes tremble at a Communist revolution. The proletarians have nothing to lose but their chains. They have a world to win. Workingmen of all countries, unite!"

MANIFESTO OF THE COMMUNIST PARTY*

A specter is haunting Europe—the specter of Communism. All the powers of old Europe have entered into a holy alliance to exorcise this specter: Pope and Czar, Metternich and Guizot, French Radicals and German police-spies.

Where is the party in opposition that has not been decried as communistic by its opponents in power? Where the Opposition that has not hurled back the branding reproach of Communism, against the more advanced opposition parties, as well as against its reactionary adversaries?

Two things result from this fact:

1 Communism is already acknowledged by all European powers to be itself a power.

2 It is high time that Communists should openly, in the face of the whole world, publish their views, their aims, their tendencies, and meet this nursery tale of the specter of Communism with a manifesto of the party itself.

To this end, Communists of various nationalities have assembled in London, and sketched the following manifesto, to be published in the English, French, German, Italian, Flemish and Danish languages.

I Bourgeois and Proletarians

The history of all hitherto existing society is the history of class struggles.

Freeman and slave, patrician and plebeian, lord and serf, guild-master and journeyman, in a word, oppressor and oppressed, stood in constant opposition to one

---

*Reprinted here in its entirety, with the exception of Part III, a short polemic against certain socialist groups of their time with whom Marx and Engels sharply disagreed.

another, carried on an uninterrupted, now hidden, now open fight, a fight that each time ended, either in a revolutionary reconstitution of society at large, or in the common ruin of the contending classes.

In the earlier epochs of history, we find almost everywhere a complicated arrangement of society into various orders, a manifold gradation of social rank. In ancient Rome we have patricians, knights, plebeians, slaves; in the Middle Ages, feudal lords, vassals, guild-masters, journeymen, apprentices, serfs; in almost all of these classes, again, subordinate gradations.

The modern bourgeois society that has sprouted from the ruins of feudal society, has not done away with class antagonisms. It has but established new classes, new conditions of oppression, new forms of struggle in place of the old ones.

Our epoch, the epoch of the bourgeoisie, possesses, however, this distinctive feature: It has simplified the class antagonisms. Society as a whole is more and more splitting up into two great hostile camps, into two great classes directly facing each other—bourgeoisie and proletariat.

From the serfs of the Middle Ages sprang the chartered burghers of the earliest towns. From these burgesses the first elements of the bourgeoisie were developed.

The discovery of America, the rounding of the Cape, opened up fresh ground for the rising bourgeoisie. The East-Indian and Chinese markets, the colonization of America, trade with the colonies, the increase in the means of exchange and in commodities generally, gave to commerce, to navigation, to industry, an impulse never before known, and thereby, to the revolutionary element in the tottering feudal society, a rapid development.

The feudal system of industry, in which industrial production was monopolized by closed guilds, now no longer sufficed for the growing wants of the new markets. The manufacturing system took its place. The guild-masters were pushed aside by the manufacturing middle class; division of labor between the different corporate guilds vanished in the face of division of labor in each single workshop.

Meantime the markets kept ever growing, the demand ever rising. Even manufacture no longer sufficed. Thereupon, steam and machinery revolutionized industrial production. The place of manufacture was taken by the giant, modern industry, the place of the industrial middle class, by industrial millionaires—the leaders of whole industrial armies, the modern bourgeois.

Modern industry has established the world market, for which the discovery of America paved the way. This market has given an immense development to commerce, to navigation, to communication by land. This development has, in its turn, reacted on the extension of industry; and in proportion as industry, commerce, navigation, railways extended, in the same proportion the bourgeoisie developed, increased its capital, and pushed into the background every class handed down from the Middle Ages.

We see, therefore, how the modern bourgeoisie is itself the product of a long course of development, of a series of revolutions in the modes of production and of exchange.

Each step in the development of the bourgeoisie was accompanied by a corresponding political advance of that class. An oppressed class under the sway of the feudal nobility, it became an armed and self-governing association in the medieval commune; here independent urban republic (as in Italy and Germany), there taxable "third estate" of the monarchy (as in France); afterwards, in the period of manufacture proper, serving either the semi-feudal or the absolute monarchy as a counterpoise against the nobility, and, in fact, corner-stone of the great monarchies in general—the bourgeoisie has at last, since the establishment of modern industry and of the world market, conquered for itself, in the modern representative state, exclusive political sway. The executive of the modern state is but a committee for managing the common affairs of the whole bourgeoisie.

The bourgeoisie has played a most revolutionary rôle in history.

The bourgeoisie, wherever it has got the upper hand, has put an end to all feudal, patriarchal, idyllic relations. It has pitilessly torn asunder the motley feudal ties that bound man to his "natural superiors," and has left no other bond between man and man than naked self-interest, than callous "cash payment." It has drowned the most heavenly ecstasies of religious fervor, of chivalrous enthusiasm, of philistine sentimentalism, in the icy water of egotistical calculation. It has resolved personal worth into exchange value, and in place of the numberless indefeasible chartered freedoms, has set up that single, unconscionable freedom—Free Trade. In one word, for exploitation, veiled by religious and political illusions, it has substituted naked, shameless, direct, brutal exploitation.

The bourgeoisie has stripped of its halo every occupation hitherto honored and looked up to with reverent awe. It has converted the physician, the lawyer, the priest, the poet, the man of science, into its paid wage-laborers.

The bourgeoisie has torn away from the family its sentimental veil, and has reduced the family relation to a mere money relation.

The bourgeoisie has disclosed how it came to pass that the brutal display of vigor in the Middle Ages, which reactionaries so much admire, found its fitting complement in the most slothful indolence. It has been the first to show what man's activity can bring about. It has accomplished wonders far surpassing Egyptian pyramids, Roman aqueducts, and Gothic cathedrals; it has conducted expeditions that put in the shade all former migrations of nations and crusades.

The bourgeoisie cannot exist without constantly revolutionizing the instruments of production, and thereby the relations of production, and with them the whole relations of society. Conservation of the old modes of production in unaltered form, was, on the contrary, the first condition of existence for all earlier industrial classes. Constant revolutionizing of production, uninterrupted disturbance of all social conditions, everlasting uncertainty and agitation distinguish the bourgeois epoch from all earlier ones. All fixed, fast-frozen relations, with their train of ancient and venerable prejudices and opinions, are swept away, all new-formed ones become antiquated before they can ossify. All that is solid melts into air, all that is holy is profaned, and man is at last compelled to face with sober senses his real conditions of life and his relations with his kind.

The need of a constantly expanding market for its products chases the bourgeoisie over the whole surface of the globe. It must nestle everywhere, settle everywhere, establish connections everywhere.

The bourgeoisie has through its exploitation of the world market given a cosmopolitan character to production and consumption in every country. To the great chagrin of reactionaries, it has drawn from under the feet of industry the national ground on which it stood. All old-established national industries have been destroyed or are daily being destroyed. They are dislodged by new industries, whose introduction becomes a life and death question for all civilized nations, by industries that no longer work up indigenous raw material, but raw material drawn from the remotest zones; industries whose products are consumed, not only at home, but in every quarter of the globe. In place of the old wants, satisfied by the production of the country, we find new wants, requiring for their satisfaction the products of distant lands and climes. In place of the old local and national seclusion and self-sufficiency, we have intercourse in every direction, universal interdependence of nations. And as in material, so also in intellectual production. The intellectual creations of individual nations become common property. National one-sidedness and narrow-mindedness become more and more impossible, and from the numerous national and local literatures there arises a world literature.

The bourgeoisie, by the rapid improvement of all instruments of production, by the immensely facilitated means of communication, draws all nations, even the most barbarian, into civilization. The cheap prices of its commodities are the heavy artillery with which it batters down all Chinese walls, with which it forces the barbarians' intensely obstinate hatred of foreigners to capitulate. It compels all nations, on pain of extinction, to adopt the bourgeois mode of production; it compels them to introduce what it calls civilization into their midst, i.e., to become bourgeois themselves. In a word, it creates a world after its own image.

The bourgeoisie has subjected the country to the rules of the towns. It has created enormous cities, has greatly increased the urban population as compared with the rural, and has thus rescued a considerable part of the population from the idiocy of rural life. Just as it has made the country dependent on the towns, so it has made barbarian and semi-barbarian countries dependent on the civilized ones, nations of peasants on nations of bourgeois, the East on the West.

More and more the bourgeoisie keeps doing away with the scattered state of the population, of the means of production, and of property. It has agglomerated population, centralized means of production, and has concentrated property in a few hands. The necessary consequence of this was political centralization. Independent, or but loosely connected provinces, with separate interests, laws, governments and systems of taxation, became lumped together into one nation, with one government, one code of laws, one national class interest, one frontier and one customs tariff.

The bourgeoisie, during its rule of scarce one hundred years, has created more massive and more colossal productive forces than have all preceding generations together. Subjection of nature's forces to man, machinery, application of chemistry to industry and agriculture, steam-navigation, railways, electric telegraphs, clearing of whole continents for cultivation, canalization of rivers, whole populations conjured out of the ground—what earlier century had even a presentiment that such productive forces slumbered in the lap of social labor?

We see then that the means of production and of exchange, which served as the foundation for the growth of the bourgeoisie, were generated in feudal society. At a certain stage in the development of these means of production and of exchange, the conditions under which feudal society produced and exchanged, the feudal organization of agriculture and manufacturing industry, in a word, the feudal relations of property became no longer compatible with the already developed productive forces; they became so many fetters. They had to be burst asunder; they were burst asunder.

Into their place stepped free competition, accompanied by a social and political constitution adapted to it, and by the economic and political sway of the bourgeois class.

A similar movement is going on before our own eyes. Modern bourgeois society with its relations of production, of exchange and of property, a society that has conjured up such gigantic means of production and of exchange, is like the sorcerer who is no longer able to control the powers of the nether world whom he has called up by his spells. For many a decade past the history of industry and commerce is but the history of the revolt of modern productive forces against modern conditions of production, against the property relations that are the conditions for the existence of the bourgeoisie and of its rule. It is enough to mention the commercial crises that by their periodical return put the existence of the entire bourgeois society on trial, each time more threateningly. In these crises a great part not only of the existing products, but also of the previously created productive forces, are periodically destroyed. In these crises there breaks out an epidemic that, in all earlier epochs, would have seemed an absurdity—the epidemic of over-production. Society suddenly finds itself put back into a state of momentary barbarism; it appears as if a famine, a universal war of devastation had cut off the supply of every means of subsistence; industry and commerce seem to be destroyed. And why? Because there is too much civilization, too much means of subsistence, too much industry, too much commerce. The productive forces at the disposal of society no longer tend to further the development of the conditions of bourgeois property; on the contrary, they have become too powerful for these conditions, by which they are fettered, and no sooner do they overcome these fetters than they bring disorder into the whole of bourgeois society, endanger the existence of bourgeois property. The conditions of bourgeois society are too narrow to comprise the wealth created by them. And how does the bourgeoisie get over these crises? On the one hand by enforced destruction of a mass of productive forces; on the other, by the conquest of new markets, and by the more thorough exploitation of the old ones. That is to say, by paving the way for more extensive and more destructive crises, and by diminishing the means whereby crises are prevented.

The weapons with which the bourgeoisie felled feudalism to the ground are now turned against the bourgeoisie itself.

But not only has the bourgeoisie forged the weapons that bring death to itself; it has also called into existence the men who are to wield those weapons—the modern working class—the proletarians.

In proportion as the bourgeoisie, i.e., capital, is developed, in the same propor-tion is the proletariat, the modern working class, developed—a class of laborers, who live only so long as they find work, and who find work only so long as their labor increases capital. These laborers, who must sell themselves piecemeal, are a commodity, like every other article of commerce, and are consequently exposed to all the vicissitudes of competition, to all the fluctuations of the market.

Owing to the extensive use of machinery and to division of labor, the work of the proletarians has lost all individual character, and, consequently, all charm for the workman. He becomes an appendage of the machine, and it is only the most simple, most monotonous, and most easily acquired knack, that is required of him. Hence, the cost of production of a workman is restricted, almost entirely, to the means of subsistence that he requires for his maintenance, and for the propagation of his race. But the price of a commodity, and therefore also of labor, is equal to its cost of production. In proportion, therefore, as the repulsiveness of the work increases, the wage decreases. Nay more, in proportion as the use of machinery and division of labor increases, in the same proportion the burden of toil also increases, whether by prolongation of the working hours, by increase of the work exacted in a given time, or by increased speed of the machinery, etc.

Modern industry has converted the little workshop of the patriarchal master into the great factory of the industrial capitalist. Masses of laborers, crowded into the factory, are organized like soldiers. As privates of the industrial army they are placed under the command of a perfect hierarchy of officers and sergeants. Not only are they slaves of the bourgeois class, and of the bourgeois state; they are daily and hourly enslaved by the machine, by the over-looker, and, above all, by the individual bourgeois manufacturer himself. The more openly this despotism proclaims gain to be its end and aim, the more petty, the more hateful and the more embittering it is.

The less the skill and exertion of strength implied in manual labor, in other words, the more modern industry develops, the more is the labor of men super-seded by that of women. Differences of age and sex have no longer any distinctive social validity for the working class. All are instruments of labor, more or less expensive to use, according to their age and sex.

No sooner has the laborer received his wages in cash, for the moment escaping exploitation by the manufacturer, than he is set upon by the other portions of the bourgeoisie, the landlord, the shopkeeper, the pawnbroker, etc.

The lower strata of the middle class—the small tradespeople, shopkeepers, and retired tradesmen generally, the handicraftsmen and peasants—all these sink grad-ually into the proletariat, partly because their diminutive capital does not suffice for the scale on which modern industry is carried on, and is swamped in the com-petition with the large capitalists, partly because their specialized skill is rendered worthless by new methods of production. Thus the proletariat is recruited from all classes of the population.

The proletariat goes through various stages of development. With its birth begins its struggle with the bourgeoisie. At first the contest is carried on by indi-vidual laborers, then by the work people of a factory, then by the operatives of one trade, in one locality, against the individual bourgeois who directly exploits them. They direct their attacks not against the bourgeois conditions of production, but against the instruments of production themselves; they destroy imported wares that compete with their labor, they smash machinery to pieces, they set factories ablaze, they seek to restore by force the vanished status of the workman of the Middle Ages.

At this stage the laborers still form an incoherent mass scattered over the whole country, and broken up by their mutual competition. If anywhere they unite to form more compact bodies, this is not yet the consequence of their own active union, but of the union of the bourgeoisie, which class, in order to attain its own political ends, is compelled to set the whole proletariat in motion, and is moreover still able to do so for a time. At this stage, therefore, the proletarians do not fight their enemies, but the enemies of their enemies, the remnants of absolute monarchy, the landowners, the non-industrial bourgeois, the petty bourgeoisie. Thus the whole historical movement is concentrated in the hands of the bourgeoisie; every victory so obtained is a victory for the bourgeoisie.

But with the development of industry the proletariat not only increases in number; it becomes concentrated in greater masses, its strength grows, and it feels that strength more. The various interests and conditions of life within the ranks of the proletariat are more and more equalized, in proportion as machinery obliterates all distinctions of labor and nearly everywhere reduces wages to the same low level. The growing competition among the bourgeois, and the resulting commercial crises, make the wages of the workers ever more fluctuating. The unceasing improvement of machinery, ever more rapidly developing, makes their livelihood more and more precarious; the collisions between individual workmen and individual bourgeois take more and more the character of collisions between two classes. Thereupon the workers begin to form combinations (trade unions) against the bourgeoisie; they club together in order to keep up the rate of wages; they found permanent associations in order to make provision beforehand for these occasional revolts. Here and there the contest breaks out into riots.

Now and then the workers are victorious, but only for a time. The real fruit of their battles lies, not in the immediate result, but in the ever expanding union of the workers. This union is furthered by the improved means of communication which are created by modern industry, and which place the workers of different localities in contact with one another. It was just this contact that was needed to centralize the numerous local struggles, all of the same character, into one national struggle between classes. But every class struggle is a political struggle. And that union, to attain which the burghers of the Middle Ages, with their miserable highways, required centuries, the modern proletarians, thanks to railways, achieve in a few years.

This organization of the proletarians into a class, and consequently into a political party, is continually being upset again by the competition between the workers themselves. But it ever rises up again, stronger, firmer, mightier. It compels legislative recognition of particular interests of the workers, by taking advantage of the divisions among the bourgeoisie itself. Thus the ten-hour bill in England was carried.

Altogether, collisions between the classes of the old society further the course of development of the proletariat in many ways. The bourgeoisie finds itself involved in a constant battle. At first with the aristocracy; later on, with those portions of the bourgeoisie itself whose interests have become antagonistic to the progress of industry; at all times with the bourgeoisie of foreign countries. In all these battles it sees itself compelled to appeal to the proletariat, to ask for its help, and thus, to drag it into the political arena. The bourgeoisie itself, therefore, supplies the proletariat with its own elements of political and general education, in other words, it furnishes the proletariat with weapons for fighting the bourgeoisie.

Further, as we have already seen, entire sections of the ruling classes are, by the advance of industry, precipitated into the proletariat, or are at least threatened in their conditions of existence. These also supply the proletariat with fresh elements of enlightenment and progress.

Finally, in times when the class struggle nears the decisive hour, the process of dissolution going on within the ruling class, in fact within the whole range of old society, assumes such a violent, glaring character, that a small section of the ruling class cuts itself adrift, and joins the revolutionary class, the class that holds the future in its hands. Just as, therefore, at an earlier period, a section of the nobility went over to the bourgeoisie, so now a portion of the bourgeoisie goes over to the proletariat, and in particular, a portion of the bourgeois ideologists, who have raised themselves to the level of comprehending theoretically the historical movement as a whole.

Of all the classes that stand face to face with the bourgeoisie today, the proletariat alone is a really revolutionary class. The other classes decay and finally disappear in the face of modern industry; the proletariat is its special and essential product.

The lower middle class, the small manufacturer, the shopkeeper, the artisan, the peasant, all these fight against the bourgeoisie, to save from extinction their existence as fractions of the middle class. They are therefore not revolutionary, but conservative. Nay more, they are reactionary, for they try to roll back the wheel of history. If by chance they are revolutionary, they are so only in view of their impending transfer into the proletariat; they thus defend not their present, but their future interests; they desert their own standpoint to adopt that of the proletariat.

The "dangerous class," the social scum *(Lumpenproletariat),* that passively rotting mass thrown off by the lowest layers of old society, may, here and there, be swept into the movement by a proletarian revolution; its conditions of life, however, prepare it far more for the part of a bribed tool of reactionary intrigue.

The social conditions of the old society no longer exist for the proletariat. The proletarian is without property; his relation to his wife and children has no longer anything in common with bourgeois family relations; modern industrial labor, modern subjection to capital, the same in England as in France, in America as in Germany, has stripped him of every trace of national character. Law, morality, religion, are to him so many bourgeois prejudices, behind which lurk in ambush just as many bourgeois interests.

All the preceding classes that got the upper hand, sought to fortify their already acquired status by subjecting society at large to their conditions of appropriation. The proletarians cannot become masters of the productive forces of society, except by abolishing their own previous mode of appropriation, and thereby also every other previous mode of appropriation. They have nothing of their own to secure and to fortify; their mission is to destroy all previous securities for, and insurances of, individual property.

All previous historical movements were movements of minorities, or in the interest of minorities. The proletarian movement is the self-conscious, independent movement of the immense majority, in the interest of the immense majority. The proletariat, the lowest stratum of our present society, cannot stir, cannot raise itself up, without the whole superincumbent strata of official society being sprung into the air.

Though not in substance, yet in form, the struggle of the proletariat with the bourgeoisie is at first a national struggle. The proletariat of each country must, of course, first of all settle matters with its own bourgeoisie.

In depicting the most general phases of the development of the proletariat, we traced the more or less veiled civil war, raging within existing society, up to the point where that war breaks out into open revolution, and where the violent over-throw of the bourgeoisie lays the foundation for the sway of the proletariat.

Hitherto, every form of society has been based, as we have already seen, on the antagonism of oppressing and oppressed classes. But in order to oppress a class, certain conditions must be assured to it under which it can, at least, con-tinue its slavish existence. The serf, in the period of serfdom, raised himself to membership in the commune, just as the petty bourgeois, under the yoke of feudal absolutism, managed to develop into a bourgeois. The modern laborer, on the contrary, instead of rising with the progress of industry, sinks deeper and deeper below the conditions of existence of his own class. He becomes a pau-per, and pauperism develops more rapidly than population and wealth. And here it becomes evident, that the bourgeoisie is unfit any longer to be the ruling class in society, and to impose its conditions of existence upon society as an over-riding law. It is unfit to rule because it is incompetent to assure an exis-tence to its slave within his slavery, because it cannot help letting him sink into such a state, that it has to feed him, instead of being fed by him. Society can no longer live under this bourgeoisie, in other words, its existence is no longer compatible with society.

The essential condition for the existence and sway of the bourgeois class, is the formation and augmentation of capital; the condition for capital is wage-labor. Wage-labor rests exclusively on competition between the laborers. The advance of industry, whose involuntary promoter is the bourgeoisie, replaces the isolation of the laborers, due to competition, by their revolutionary combination, due to asso-ciation. The development of modern industry, therefore, cuts from under its feet the very foundation on which the bourgeoisie produces and appropriates products.

What the bourgeoisie therefore produces, above all, are its own grave-diggers. Its fall and the victory of the proletariat are equally inevitable.

II Proletarians and Communists

In what relation do the Communists stand to the proletarians as a whole?

The Communists do not form a separate party opposed to other working class parties.

They have no interests separate and apart from those of the proletariat as a whole.

They do not set up any sectarian principles of their own, by which to shape and mold the proletarian movement.

The Communists are distinguished from the other working class parties by this only: 1. In the national struggles of the proletarians of the different countries, they point out and bring to the front the common interests of the entire proletariat, independently of all nationality. 2. In the various stages of development which the struggle of the working class against the bourgeoisie has to pass through, they always and everywhere represent the interests of the movement as a whole.

The Communists, therefore, are on the one hand, practically, the most advanced and resolute section of the working class parties of every country, that section which pushes forward all others; on the other hand, theoretically, they have over the great mass of the proletariat the advantage of clearly understanding the line of march, the conditions, and the ultimate general results of the proletarian movement.

The immediate aim of the Communists is the same as that of all the other proletarian parties: Formation of the proletariat into a class, overthrow of bourgeois supremacy, conquest of political power by the proletariat.

The theoretical conclusions of the Communists are in no way based on ideas or principles that have been invented, or discovered, by this or that would-be universal reformer.

They merely express, in general terms, actual relations springing from an existing class struggle, from a historical movement going on under our very eyes. The abolition of existing property relations is not at all a distinctive feature of Communism.

All property relations in the past have continually been subject to historical change consequent upon the change in historical conditions.

The French Revolution, for example, abolished feudal property in favor of bourgeois property.

The distinguishing feature of Communism is not the abolition of property generally, but the abolition of bourgeois property. But modern bourgeois private property is the final and most complete expression of the system of producing and appropriating products that is based on class antagonisms, on the exploitation of the many by the few.

In this sense, the theory of the Communists may be summed up in the single sentence: Abolition of private property.

We Communists have been reproached with the desire of abolishing the right of personally acquiring property as the fruit of a man's own labor, which property is alleged to be the groundwork of all personal freedom, activity and independence.

Hard-won, self-acquired, self-earned property! Do you mean the property of the petty artisan and of the small peasant, a form of property that preceded the bourgeois form? There is no need to abolish that; the development of industry has to a great extent already destroyed it, and is still destroying it daily.

Or do you mean modern bourgeois private property?

But does wage-labor create any property for the laborer? Not a bit. It creates capital, i.e., that kind of property which exploits wage-labor, and which cannot increase except upon condition of begetting a new supply of wage-labor for fresh exploitation. Property, in its present form, is based on the antagonism of capital and wage-labor. Let us examine both sides of this antagonism.

To be a capitalist, is to have not only a purely personal, but a social *status* in production. Capital is a collective product, and only by the united action of many members, nay, in the last resort, only by the united action of all members of society, can it be set in motion.

Capital is therefore not a personal, it is a social, power.

When, therefore, capital is converted into common property, into the property of all members of society, personal property is not thereby transformed into social property. It is only the social character of the property that is changed. It loses its class character.

Let us now take wage-labor.

The average price of wage-labor is the minimum wage, i.e., that quantum of the means of subsistence which is absolutely requisite to keep the laborer in bare existence as a laborer. What, therefore, the wage-laborer appropriates by means of his labor, merely suffices to prolong and reproduce a bare existence. We by no means intend to abolish this personal appropriation of the products of labor, an appropriation that is made for the maintenance and reproduction of human life, and that leaves no surplus wherewith to command the labor of others. All that we want to do away with is the miserable character of this appropriation, under which the laborer lives merely to increase capital, and is allowed to live only insofar as the interest of the ruling class requires it.

In bourgeois society, living labor is but a means to increase accumulated labor. In Communist society, accumulated labor is but a means to widen, to enrich, to promote the existence of the laborer.

In bourgeois society, therefore, the past dominates the present; in Communist society, the present dominates the past. In bourgeois society capital is independent and has individuality, while the living person is dependent and has no individuality.

And the abolition of this state of things is called by the bourgeois, abolition of individuality and freedom! And rightly so. The abolition of bourgeois individuality, bourgeois independence, and bourgeois freedom is undoubtedly aimed at.

By freedom is meant, under the present bourgeois conditions of production, free trade, free selling and buying.

But if selling and buying disappears, free selling and buying disappears also. This talk about free selling and buying, and all the other "brave words" of our bourgeoisie about freedom in general, have a meaning, if any, only in contrast with restricted selling and buying, with the fettered traders of the Middle Ages, but have no meaning when opposed to the Communist abolition of buying and selling, of the bourgeois conditions of production, and of the bourgeoisie itself.

You are horrified at our intending to do away with private property. But in your existing society, private property is already done away with for nine-tenths of the population; its existence for the few is solely due to its non-existence in the hands of those nine-tenths. You reproach us, therefore, with intending to do away with a form of property, the necessary condition for whose existence is the non-existence of any property for the immense majority of society.

In a word, you reproach us with intending to do away with your property. Precisely so; that is just what we intend.

From the moment when labor can no longer be converted into capital, money, or rent, into a social power capable of being monopolized, i.e., from the moment when individual property can no longer be transformed into bourgeois property, into capital, from that moment, you say, individuality vanishes.

You must, therefore, confess that by "individual" you mean no other person than the bourgeois, than the middle class owner of property. This person must, indeed, be swept out of the way, and made impossible.

Communism deprives no man of the power to appropriate the products of society; all that it does is to deprive him of the power to subjugate the labor of others by means of such appropriation.

It has been objected, that upon the abolition of private property all work will cease, and universal laziness will overtake us.

According to this, bourgeois society ought long ago to have gone to the dogs through sheer idleness; for those of its members who work, acquire nothing, and those who acquire anything, do not work. The whole of this objection is but another expression of the tautology: There can no longer be any wage-labor when there is no longer any capital.

All objections urged against the Communist mode of producing and appropriating material products, have, in the same way, been urged against the Communist modes of producing and appropriating intellectual products. Just as, to the bourgeois, the disappearance of class property is the disappearance of production itself, so the disappearance of class culture is to him identical with the disappearance of all culture.

That culture, the loss of which he laments is, for the enormous majority, a mere training to act as a machine.

But don't wrangle with us so long as you apply, to our intended abolition of bourgeois property, the standard of your bourgeois notions of freedom, culture, law, etc. Your very ideas are but the outgrowth of the conditions of your bourgeois production and bourgeois property, just as your jurisprudence is but the will of your class made into a law for all, a will whose essential character and direction are determined by the economic conditions of existence of your class.

The selfish misconception that induces you to transform into eternal laws of nature and of reason, the social forms springing from your present mode of production and form of property—historical relations that rise and disappear in the progress of production—this misconception you share with every ruling class that has preceded you. What you see clearly in the case of ancient property, what you admit in the case of feudal property, you are of course forbidden to admit in the case of your own bourgeois form of property.

Abolition of the family! Even the most radical flare up at this infamous proposal of the Communists.

On what foundation is the present family, the bourgeois family, based? On capital, on private gain. In its completely developed form this family exists only among the bourgeoisie. But this state of things finds its complement in the practical absence of the family among the proletarians, and in public prostitution.

The bourgeois family will vanish as a matter of course when its complement vanishes, and both will vanish with the vanishing of capital.

Do you charge us with wanting to stop the exploitation of children by their parents? To this crime we plead guilty.

But, you will say, we destroy the most hallowed of relations, when we replace home education by social.

And your education! Is not that also social, and determined by the social conditions under which you educate, by the intervention of society, direct or indirect, by means of schools, etc.? The Communists have not invented the intervention of society in education; they do but seek to alter the character of that intervention, and to rescue education from the influence of the ruling class.

The bourgeois claptrap about the family and education, about the hallowed co-relation of parent and child, becomes all the more disgusting, the more, by the action of modern industry, all family ties among the proletarians are torn asunder, and their children transformed into simple articles of commerce and instruments of labor.

But you Communists would introduce community of women, screams the whole bourgeoisie in chorus.

The bourgeois sees in his wife a mere instrument of production. He hears that the instruments of production are to be exploited in common, and, naturally, can come to no other conclusion than that the lot of being common to all will likewise fall to the women.

He has not even a suspicion that the real point aimed at is to do away with the status of women as mere instruments of production.

For the rest, nothing is more ridiculous than the virtuous indignation of our bourgeois at the community of women which, they pretend, is to be openly and officially established by the Communists. The Communists have no need to introduce community of women; it has existed almost from time immemorial.

Our bourgeois, not content with having the wives and daughters of their proletarians at their disposal, not to speak of common prostitutes, take the greatest pleasure in seducing each other's wives.

Bourgeois marriage is in reality a system of wives in common and thus, at the most, what the Communists might possibly be reproached with is that they desire to introduce, in substitution for a hypocritically concealed, an openly legalized community of women. For the rest, it is self-evident, that the abolition of the present system of production must bring with it the abolition of the community of women springing from that system, i.e., of prostitution both public and private.

The Communists are further reproached with desiring to abolish countries and nationality.

The workingmen have no country. We cannot take from them what they have not got. Since the proletariat must first of all acquire political supremacy, must rise to be the leading class of the nation, must constitute itself *the* nation, it is, so far, itself national, though not in the bourgeois sense of the word.

National differences and antagonisms between peoples are vanishing gradually from day to day, owing to the development of the bourgeoisie, to freedom of commerce, to the world market, to uniformity in the mode of production and in the conditions of life corresponding thereto.

The supremacy of the proletariat will cause them to vanish still faster. United action, of the leading civilized countries at least, is one of the first conditions for the emancipation of the proletariat.

In proportion as the exploitation of one individual by another is put an end to, the exploitation of one nation by another will also be put an end to. In proportion as the antagonism between classes within the nation vanishes, the hostility of one nation to another will come to an end.

The charges against Communism made from a religious, a philosophical, and, generally, from an ideological standpoint, are not deserving of serious examination.

Does it require deep intuition to comprehend that man's ideas, views, and conceptions, in one word, man's consciousness, changes with every change in the conditions of his material existence, in his social relations and in his social life?

What else does the history of ideas prove, than that intellectual production changes its character in proportion as material production is changed? The ruling ideas of each age have ever been the ideas of its ruling class.

When people speak of ideas that revolutionize society, they do but express the fact that within the old society the elements of a new one have been created, and that the dissolution of the old ideas keeps even pace with the dissolution of the old conditions of existence.

When the ancient world was in its last throes, the ancient religions were overcome by Christianity. When Christian ideas succumbed in the 18th century to rationalist ideas, feudal society fought its death-battle with the then revolutionary bourgeoisie. The ideas of religious liberty and freedom of conscience, merely gave expression to the sway of free competition within the domain of knowledge.

"Undoubtedly," it will be said, "religion, moral, philosophical and juridical ideas have been modified in the course of historical development. But religion, morality, philosophy, political science, and law, constantly survived this change.

"There are, besides, eternal truths, such as Freedom, Justice, etc., that are common to all states of society. But Communism abolishes eternal truths, it abolishes all religion, and all morality, instead of constituting them on a new basis; it therefore acts in contradiction to all past historical experience."

What does this accusation reduce itself to? The history of all past society has consisted in the development of class antagonisms, antagonisms that assumed different forms at different epochs.

But whatever form they may have taken, one fact is common to all past ages, viz., the exploitation of one part of society by the other. No wonder, then, that the social consciousness of past ages, despite all the multiplicity and variety it displays, moves within certain common forms, or general ideas, which cannot completely vanish except with the total disappearance of class antagonisms.

The Communist revolution is the most radical rupture with traditional property relations; no wonder that its development involves the most radical rupture with traditional ideas.

But let us have done with the bourgeois objections to Communism.

We have seen above, that the first step in the revolution by the working class, is to raise the proletariat to the position of ruling class, to establish democracy.

The proletariat will use its political supremacy to wrest, by degrees, all capital from the bourgeoisie, to centralize all instruments of production in the hands of the state, i.e., of the proletariat organized as the ruling class; and to increase the total of productive forces as rapidly as possible.

Of course, in the beginning, this cannot be effected except by means of despotic inroads on the rights of property, and on the conditions of bourgeois production; by means of measures, therefore, which appear economically insufficient and untenable, but which, in the course of the movement, outstrip themselves, necessitate further inroads upon the old social order, and are unavoidable as a means of entirely revolutionizing the mode of production.

These measures will of course be different in different countries.

Nevertheless in the most advanced countries, the following will be pretty generally applicable.

1 Abolition of property in land and application of all rents of land to public purposes.

2 A heavy progressive or graduated income tax.

3 Abolition of all right of inheritance.

4 Confiscation of the property of all emigrants and rebels.

5 Centralization of credit in the hands of the state, by means of a national bank with state capital and an exclusive monopoly.

6 Centralization of the means of communication and transport in the hands of the state.

7 Extension of factories and instruments of production owned by the state; the bringing into cultivation of waste lands, and the improvement of the soil generally in accordance with a common plan.

8 Equal obligation of all to work. Establishment of industrial armies, especially for agriculture.

9 Combination of agriculture with manufacturing industries; gradual abolition of the distinction between town and country, by a more equable distribution of the population over the country.

10 Free education for all children in public schools. Abolition of child factory labor in its present form. Combination of education with industrial production, etc.

When, in the course of development, class distinctions have disappeared, and all production has been concentrated in the hands of a vast association of the whole nation, the public power will lose its political character. Political power, properly so called, is merely the organized power of one class for oppressing another. If the proletariat during its contest with the bourgeoisie is compelled, by the force of circumstances, to organize itself as a class; if, by means of a revolution, it makes itself the ruling class, and, as such sweeps away by force the old conditions of production, then it will, along with these conditions, have swept away the conditions for the existence of class antagonisms, and of classes generally, and will thereby have abolished its own supremacy as a class.

In place of the old bourgeois society, with its classes and class antagonisms, we shall have an association, in which the free development of each is the condition for the free development of all.

.   .   .

IV. Position of the Communists in Relation to the Various Existing Opposition Parties

Section II has made clear the relations of the Communists to the existing working class parties, such as the Chartists in England and the Agrarian Reformers in America.

The Communists fight for the attainment of the immediate aims, for the enforcement of the momentary interests of the working class; but in the movement of the present, they also represent and take care of the future of that movement. In France the Communists ally themselves with the Social-Democrats, against the conservative and radical bourgeoisie, reserving, however, the right to take up a critical position in regard to phrases and illusions traditionally handed down from the great Revolution.

In Switzerland they support the Radicals, without losing sight of the fact that this party consists of antagonistic elements, partly of Democratic Socialists, in the French sense, partly of radical bourgeois.

In Poland they support the party that insists on an agrarian revolution as the prime condition for national emancipation, that party which fomented the insurrection of Cracow in 1846.

In Germany they fight with the bourgeoisie whenever it acts in a revolutionary way, against the absolute monarchy, the feudal squirearchy, and the petty bourgeoisie.

But they never cease, for a single instant, to instill into the working class the clearest possible recognition of the hostile antagonism between bourgeoisie and proletariat, in order that the German workers may straightway use, as so many weapons against the bourgeoisie, the social and political conditions that the bourgeoisie must necessarily introduce along with its supremacy, and in order that, after the fall of the reactionary classes in Germany, the fight against the bourgeoisie itself may immediately begin.

The Communists turn their attention chiefly to Germany, because that country is on the eve of a bourgeois revolution that is bound to be carried out under more advanced conditions of European civilization and with a much more developed proletariat than what existed in England in the 17th and in France in the 18th century, and because the bourgeois revolution in Germany will be but the prelude to an immediately following proletarian revolution.

In short, the Communists everywhere support every revolutionary movement against the existing social and political order of things.

In all these movements they bring to the front, as the leading question in each case, the property question, no matter what its degree of development at the time.

Finally, they labor everywhere for the union and agreement of the democratic parties of all countries.

The Communists disdain to conceal their views and aims. They openly declare that their ends can be attained only by the forcible overthrow of all existing social conditions. Let the ruling classes tremble at a Communist revolution. The proletarians have nothing to lose but their chains. They have a world to win.

Workingmen of all countries, unite!

14
Vladimir I. Lenin*

V. I. Lenin (1870–1924) was one of the greatest figures of modern communism. Leader of the successful communist revolution in Russia in 1917, he became the principal founder and charismatic hero of The Union of Soviet Socialist Republics, seeking to apply Marx's principles (within the Soviet Union and around the globe) during what was thought to be the transition from capitalism to the new world order. The Communist Party of the Soviet Union, which was the real governing authority in that country, ceased to exist (and the Soviet Union itself dissolved into its constituent republics) in 1991, after a painful communist experiment lasting seventy-four years. Whether the policies and conduct of the Soviet Union, and other communist governments now defunct, did truly represent an experiment in the application of Marxist theory to modern life remains a highly controversial question.

*Lenin's original name was Vladimir Ilyich Ulyanov, although he later came to be known as Nikolai Lenin. Following the most usual practice, however, he will be referred to here as Vladimir I. Lenin.—*Ed.*

There is no doubt, however, that Lenin himself was a learned and vigorous thinker, and a sincerely dedicated Marxist revolutionary whose writings (some appearing later in this volume) made substantial contributions to communist philosophy. *The Teachings of Karl Marx,* from which the following selection is taken, sought to make Marx's theory (as Lenin understood it) more widely accessible. Here Lenin presents a straightforward explanation of the concepts of value and surplus value, which play a central role in Marx's economic theory.

MARX'S ECONOMIC DOCTRINE*

"It is the ultimate aim of this work to reveal the economic law of motion of modern society" (that is to say, capitalist, bourgeois society), writes Marx in the preface to the first volume of *Capital.* The study of the production relationships in a given, historically determinate society, in their genesis, their development, and their decay—such is the content of Marx's economic teaching. In capitalist society the dominant feature is the production of *commodities,* and Marx's analysis therefore begins with an analysis of a commodity.

Value

A commodity is, firstly, something that satisfies a human need; and, secondly, it is something that is exchanged for something else. The utility of a thing gives it *use-value.* Exchange-value (or simply, value) presents itself first of all as the proportion, the ratio, in which a certain number of use-values of one kind are exchanged for a certain number of use-values of another kind. Daily experience shows us that by millions upon millions of such exchanges, all and sundry use-values in themselves very different and not comparable one with another, are equated to one another. Now, what is common in these various things which are constantly weighed one against another in a definite system of social relationships? That which is common to them is that they are *products of labor.* In exchanging products, people equate to one another most diverse kinds of labor. The production of commodities is a system of social relationships in which different producers produce various products (the social division of labor), and in which all these products are equated to one another in exchange. Consequently, the element common to all commodities is not concrete labor in a definite branch of production, not labor of one particular kind, but *abstract* human labor—human labor in general. All the labor power of a given society, represented in the sum total of values of all commodities, is one and the same human labor power. Millions upon millions of acts of exchange prove this. Consequently, each particular commodity represents only a certain part of *socially necessary* labor time. The magnitude of the value is determined by the amount of socially necessary labor, or by the labor time that is

---

*This and the following passages are from *The Teachings of Karl Marx.* Reprinted by permission of the Foreign Languages Publishing House, Moscow.

socially requisite for the production of the given commodity of the given use-value. ". . . Exchanging labor products of different kinds one for another, they equate the values of the exchanged products; and in doing so they equate the different kinds of labor expended in production, treating them as homogeneous human labor. They do not know that they are doing this, but they do it." As one of the earlier economists said, value is a relationship between two persons, only he should have added that it is a relationship hidden beneath a material wrapping. We can only understand what value is when we consider it from the point of view of a system of social production relationships in one particular historical type of society; and, moreover, of relationships which present themselves in a mass form, the phenomenon of exchange repeating itself millions upon millions of times. "As values, all commodities are only definite quantities of congealed labor time." Having made a detailed analysis of the twofold character of the labor incorporated in commodities, Marx goes on to analyze the *form of value and of money.* His main task, then, is to study the *origin* of the money form of value, to study the *historical process* of the development of exchange, beginning with isolated and casual acts of exchange ("simple, isolated, or casual value form," in which a given quantity of one commodity is exchanged for a given quantity of another), passing on to the universal form of value, in which a number of different commodities are exchanged for one and the same particular commodity, and ending with the money form of value, when gold becomes this particular commodity, the universal equivalent. Being the highest product of the development of exchange and of commodity production, money masks the social character of individual labor, and hides the social tie between the various producers who come together in the market. Marx analyzes in great detail the various functions of money; and it is essential to note that here (as generally in the opening chapters of *Capital*) what appears to be an abstract and at times purely deductive mode of exposition in reality reproduces a gigantic collection of facts concerning the history of the development of exchange and commodity production.

> Money . . . presupposes a definite level of commodity exchange. The various forms of money (simple commodity equivalent or means of circulation, or means of payment, treasure, or international money) indicate, according to the different extent to which this or that function is put into application, and according to the comparative predominance of one or other of them, very different grades of the social process of production. [*Capital,* Vol. I.]

Surplus Value

At a particular stage in the development of commodity production, money becomes transformed into capital. The formula of commodity circulation was C-M-C (commodity—money—commodity); the sale of one commodity for the purpose of buying another. But the general formula of capital, on the contrary, is M-C-M (money—commodity—money); purchase for the purpose of selling—at a profit. The designation "surplus value" is given by Marx to the increase over the original value of money that is put into circulation. The fact of this "growth" of money in capitalist society is well known. Indeed, it is this "growth" which transforms money into *capital* as a special, historically defined, social relationship of production. Surplus value cannot arise out of the circulation of commodities, for this represents nothing more than the exchange of equivalents; it cannot arise out of an advance in prices, for the mutual losses and gains of buyers and sellers would equalize one another; and we are concerned here, not with what happens to individuals, but with a mass or average or social phenomenon. In order that he may be able to receive surplus value, "Moneybags must . . . find in the market a commodity whose use-value has the peculiar quality of being a source of value"— a commodity, the actual process of whose use is at the same time the process of the creation of value. Such a commodity exists. It is human labor power. Its use is labor, and labor creates value. The owner of money buys labor power at its value, which is determined, like the value of every other commodity, by the socially necessary labor time requisite for its production (that is to say, the cost of maintaining the worker and his family). Having bought labor power, the owner of money is entitled to use it, that is to set it to work for the whole day—twelve hours, let us suppose. Meanwhile, in the course of six hours ("necessary" labor time) the laborer produces sufficient to pay back the cost of his own maintenance; and in the course of the next six hours ("surplus" labor time), he produces a "surplus" product for which the capitalist does not pay him—surplus product or surplus value. In capital, therefore, from the viewpoint of the process of production, we have to distinguish between two parts: first, constant capital, expended for the means of production (machinery, tools, raw materials, etc.), the value of this being (all at once or part by part) transferred, unchanged, to the finished product; and, secondly, variable capital, expended for labor power. The value of this latter capital is not constant, but grows in the labor process, creating surplus value. To express the degree of exploitation of labor power by capital, we must therefore compare the surplus value, not with the whole capital, but only with the variable capital. Thus, in the example just given, the rate of surplus value, as Marx calls this relationship, will be 6:6, i.e., 100%.

There are two historical prerequisites to the genesis of capital: first, accumulation of a considerable sum of money in the hands of individuals living under conditions in which there is a comparatively high development of commodity production. Second, the existence of workers who are "free" in a double sense of the term: free from any constraint or restriction as regards the sale of their labor power; free from any bondage to the soil or to the means of production in general—i.e., of propertyless workers, of "proletarians" who cannot maintain their existence except by the sale of their labor power.

There are two fundamental ways in which surplus value can be increased: by an increase in the working day ("absolute surplus value"); and by a reduction in the necessary working day ("relative surplus value"). Analyzing the former method, Marx gives an impressive picture of the struggle of the working class for shorter hours and of government interference, first (from the fourteenth century to the seventeenth) in order to lengthen the working day, and subsequently (factory legislation of the nineteenth century) to shorten it. Since the appearance of *Capital,* the history of the working-class movement in all lands provides a wealth of new facts to amplify this picture. . . .

Of extreme importance and originality is Marx's analysis of the *accumulation of capital,* that is to say, the transformation of a portion of surplus value into capital and the applying of this portion to additional production, instead of using it to supply the personal needs or to gratify the whims of the capitalist. Marx pointed out the mistake made by earlier classical political economy (from Adam Smith on), which assumed that all the surplus value which was transformed into capital became variable capital. In actual fact, it is divided into *means of production* plus variable capital. The more rapid growth of constant capital as compared with variable capital in the sum total of capital is of immense importance in the process of development of capitalism and in that of the transformation of capitalism into Socialism.

The accumulation of capital, accelerating the replacement of workers by machinery, creating wealth at the one pole and poverty at the other, gives birth to the so-called "reserve army of labor," to a "relative overabundance" of workers or to "capitalist over-population." This assumes the most diversified forms, and gives capital the possibility of expanding production at an exceptionally rapid rate. This possibility, in conjunction with enhanced facilities for credit and with the accumulation of capital in the means of production, furnishes, among other things the key to the understanding of the *crises* of overproduction that occur periodically in capitalist countries—first about every ten years, on an average, but subsequently in a more continuous form and with a less definite periodicity. From accumulation of capital upon a capitalist foundation we must distinguish the so-called "primitive accumulation": the forcible severance of the worker from the means of production, the driving of the peasants off the land, the stealing of the communal lands, the system of colonies and national debts, of protective tariffs, and the like. "Primitive accumulation" creates, at one pole, the "free" proletarian: at the other, the owner of money, the capitalist. . . .

15
Karl Marx

The last years of Marx's life were devoted to a laborious effort to provide the definitive account of the principles, excesses, and contradictions of the capitalist economy. The result, never completed, was *Capital (Das Capital),* one of the most influential economic treatises ever written. The following passages are from the first volume of *Capital.* In the first passage below (from Part I on Commodities and Money) Marx explains how the rule of capitalism perverts human life (as he believed) by subjecting creative human beings to the mindless rule of things and markets. Commodities, material objects, become a nearly universal human fetish. In the later passages (from Part VII on The Accumulation of Capital) Marx identifies and explains several of what he believed to be scientific laws governing the behavior of capital, and describes some of the degrading effects of their inexorable operation. In *Capital,* unlike most economic textbooks, technical analyses are suffused with the unashamed moral condemnation of a system Marx thought brutally inhumane.

THE FETISHISM OF COMMODITIES AND THE SECRET THEREOF*

A commodity appears, at first sight, a very trivial thing, and easily understood. Its analysis shows that it is, in reality, a very queer thing, abounding in metaphysical subtleties and theological niceties. So far as it is a value in use, there is nothing mysterious about it, whether we consider it from the point of view that by its properties it is capable of satisfying human wants, or from the point that those properties are the product of human labour. It is as clear as noon-day, that man, by his industry, changes the forms of the materials furnished by Nature, in such a way as to make them useful to him. The form of wood, for instance, is altered, by making a table out of it. Yet, for all that, the table continues to be that common, every-day thing, wood. But, so soon as it steps forth as a commodity, it is changed into something transcendent. It not only stands with its feet on the ground, but, in relation to all other commodities, it stands on its head, and evolves out of its wooden brain grotesque ideas, far more wonderful than "table-turning" ever was.

The mystical character of commodities does not originate, therefore, in their use-value. Just as little does it proceed from the nature of the determining factors of value. For, in the first place, however varied the useful kinds of labour, or productive activities, may be, it is a physiological fact, that they are functions of the human organism, and that each such function, whatever may be its nature or form, is essentially the expenditure of human brain, nerves, muscles, &c. Secondly, with regard to that which forms the ground-work for the quantitative determination of value, namely, the duration of that expenditure, or the quantity of labour, it is quite clear that there is a palpable difference between its quantity and quality. In all states of society, the labour-time that it costs to produce the means of subsistence, must necessarily be an object of interest to mankind, though not of equal interest in different stages of development.[†] And lastly, from the moment that men in any way work for one another, their labour assumes a social form.

Whence, then, arises the enigmatical character of the product of labour, so soon as it assumes the form of commodities? Clearly from this form itself. The equality of all sorts of human labour is expressed objectively by their products all being

---

*From K. Marx, *Capital.* This and the following selections are reprinted from the original English translation by Samuel Moore and Edward Aveling, edited by Friedrich Engels, and published by Swan Sonnenschein, Lowery, and Co., London, 1887.

[†]Among the ancient Germans the unit for measuring land was what could be harvested in a day, and was called Tagwerk, Tagwanne (jurnale, or terra jurnalis, or diornalis). Mannsmaad, &c.

equally values; the measure of the expenditure of labour-power by the duration of that expenditure, takes the form of the quantity of value of the products of labour; and finally, the mutual relations of the producers, within which the social character of their labour affirms itself, take the form of a social relation between the products.

A commodity is therefore a mysterious thing, simply because in it the social character of men's labour appears to them as an objective character stamped upon the product of that labour; because the relation of the producers to the sum total of their own labour is presented to them as a social relation, existing not between themselves, but between the products of their labour. This is the reason why the products of labour become commodities, social things whose qualities are at the same time perceptible and imperceptible by the senses. In the same way the light from an object is perceived by us not as the subjective excitation of our optic nerve, but as the objective form of something outside the eye itself. But, in the act of seeing, there is at all events, an actual passage of light from one thing to another, from the external object to the eye. There is a physical relation between physical things. But it is different with commodities. There, the existence of the things _quâ_ commodities, and the value-relation between the products of labour which stamps them as commodities, have absolutely no connexion with their physical properties and with the material relations arising therefrom. There it is a definite social relation between men, that assumes, in their eyes, the fantastic form of a relation between things. In order, therefore, to find an analogy, we must have recourse to the mist-enveloped regions of the religious world. In that world the productions of the human brain appear as independent beings endowed with life, and entering into relation both with one another and the human race. So it is in the world of commodities with the products of men's hands. This I call the Fetishism which attaches itself to the products of labour, so soon as they are produced as commodities, and which is therefore inseparable from the production of commodities.

This Fetishism of commodities has its origin, as the foregoing analysis has already shown, in the peculiar social character of the labour that produces them.

As a general rule, articles of utility become commodities, only because they are products of the labour of private individuals or groups of individuals who carry on their work independently of each other. The sum total of the labour of all these private individuals forms the aggregate labour of society. Since the producers do not come into social contact with each other until they exchange their products, the specific social character of each producer's labour does not show itself except in the act of exchange. In other words, the labour of the individual asserts itself as a part of the labour of society, only by means of the relations which the act of exchange establishes directly between the products, and indirectly, through them, between the producers. To the latter, therefore, the relations connecting the labour of one individual with that of the rest appear, not as direct social relations between individuals at work, but as what they really are, material relations between persons and social relations between things. It is only by being exchanged that the products of labour acquire, as values, one uniform social status, distinct from their var-icd forms of existence as objects of utility. This division of a product into a useful thing and a value becomes practically important, only when exchange has acquired such an extension that useful articles are produced for the purpose of being exchanged, and their character as values has therefore to be taken into account, beforehand, during production. From this moment the labour of the individual producer acquires socially a two-fold character. On the one hand, it must, as a definite useful kind of labour, satisfy a definite social want, and thus hold its place as part and parcel of the collective labour of all, as a branch of a social division of labour that has sprung up spontaneously. On the other hand, it can satisfy the manifold wants of the individual producer himself, only in so far as the mutual exchange-ability of all kinds of useful private labour is an established social fact, and therefore the private useful labour of each producer ranks on an equality with that of all others. The equalisation of the most different kinds of labour can be the result only of an abstraction from their inequalities, or of reducing them to their common denominator, viz., expenditure of human labour-power or human labour in the abstract. The two-fold social character of the labour of the individual appears to him, when reflected in his brain, only under those forms which are impressed upon that labour in every-day practice by the exchange of products. In this way, the character that his own labour possesses of being socially useful takes the form of the condition, that the product must be not only useful, but useful for others, and the social character that his particular labour has of being the equal of all other particular kinds of labour, takes the form that all the physically different articles that are the products of labour, have one common quality, viz., that of having value.

Hence, when we bring the products of our labour into relation with each other as values, it is not because we see in these articles the material receptacles of homogeneous human labour. Quite the contrary: whenever, by an exchange, we equate as values our different products, by that very act, we also equate, as human labour, the different kinds of labour expended upon them. We are not aware of this, nevertheless we do it. Value, therefore, does not stalk about with a label describing what it is. It is value, rather, that converts every product into a social hieroglyphic. Later on, we try to decipher the hieroglyphic, to get behind the secret of our own social products; for to stamp an object of utility as a value, is just as much a social product as language. The recent scientific discovery, that the products of labour, so far as they are values, are but material expressions of the human labour spent in their production, marks, indeed, an epoch in the history of the development of the human race, but, by no means, dissipates the mist through which the social character of labour appears to us to be an objective character of the products themselves. The fact, that in the particular form of production with which we are dealing, viz., the production of commodities, the specific social character of private labour carried on independently, consists in the equality of every kind of that labour, by virtue of its being human labour, which character, therefore, assumes in the product the form of value—this fact appears to the producers, notwithstanding the discovery above referred to, to be just as real and final, as the fact, that, after the discovery by science of the component gases of air, the atmosphere itself remained unaltered.

What, first of all, practically concerns producers when they make an exchange, is the question, how much of some other product they get for their own? in what proportions the products are exchangeable? When these proportions have, by custom, attained a certain stability, they appear to result from the nature of the products, so that, for instance, one ton of iron and two ounces of gold appear as naturally to be of equal value as a pound of gold and a pound of iron in spite of their different physical and chemical qualities appear to be of equal weight. The character of having value, when once impressed upon products, obtains fixity only by reason of their acting and re-acting upon each other as quantities of value. These quantities vary continually, independently of the will, foresight and action of the producers. To them, their own social action takes the form of the action of objects, which rule the producers instead of being ruled by them. It requires a fully developed production of commodities before, from accumulated experience alone, the scientific conviction springs up, that all the different kinds of private labour, which are carried on independently of each other, and yet as spontaneously developed branches of the social division of labour, are continually being reduced to the quantitative proportions in which society requires them. And why? Because, in the midst of all the accidental and ever fluctuating exchange-relations between the products, the labour-time socially necessary for their production forcibly asserts itself like an over-riding law of Nature. The law of gravity thus asserts itself when a house falls about our ears.* The determination of the magnitude of value by labour-time is therefore a secret, hidden under the apparent fluctuations in the relative values of commodities. Its discovery, while removing all appearance of mere accidentality from the determination of the magnitude of the values of products, yet in no way alters the mode in which that determination takes place.

Man's reflections on the forms of social life, and consequently, also, his scientific analysis of those forms, take a course directly opposite to that of their actual historical development. He begins, post festum, with the results of the process of development ready to hand before him. The characters that stamp products as commodities, and whose establishment is a necessary preliminary to the circulation of commodities, have already acquired the stability of natural, self-understood forms of social life, before man seeks to decipher, not their historical character, for in his eyes they are immutable, but their meaning. Consequently it was the analysis of the prices of commodities that alone led to the determination of the magnitude of value, and it was the common expression of all commodities in money that alone led to the establishment of their characters as values. It is, however, just this ultimate money-form of the world of commodities that actually conceals, instead of disclosing, the social character of private labour, and the social relations between the individual producers. When I state that coats or boots stand in a relation to linen, because it is the universal incarnation of abstract human labour, the

*"What are we to think of a law that asserts itself only by periodical revolutions? It is just nothing but a law of Nature founded on the want of knowledge of those whose action is the subject of it." (Friedrich Engels: "Umrisse zu einer Kritik der Nationalökonomie," in the "Deutsch-Französische Jahrbücher," edited by Arnold Ruge and Karl Marx. Paris, 1844.)

absurdity of the statement is self-evident. Nevertheless, when the producers of coats and boots compare those articles with linen, or, what is the same thing, with gold or silver, as the universal equivalent, they express the relation between their own private labour and the collective labour of society in the same absurd form.

The categories of bourgeois economy consist of such like forms. They are forms of thought expressing with social validity the conditions and relations of a definite, historically determined mode of production, viz., the production of commodities. The whole mystery of commodities, all the magic and necromancy that surrounds the products of labour as long as they take the form of commodities, vanishes therefore, so soon as we come to other forms of production.

Since Robinson Crusoe's experiences are a favourite theme with political economists, let us take a look at him on his island. Moderate though he be, yet some few wants he has to satisfy, and must therefore do a little useful work of various sorts, such as making tools and furniture, taming goats, fishing and hunting. Of his prayers and the like we take no account, since they are a source of pleasure to him, and he looks upon them as so much recreation. In spite of the variety of his work, he knows that his labour, whatever its form, is but the activity of one and the same Robinson, and consequently, that it consists of nothing but different modes of human labour. Necessity itself compels him to apportion his time accurately between his different kinds of work. Whether one kind occupies a greater space in his general activity than another, depends on the difficulties, greater or less as the case may be, to be overcome in attaining the useful effect aimed at. This our friend Robinson soon learns by experience, and having rescued a watch, ledger, and pen and ink from the wreck, commences, like a true-born Briton, to keep a set of books. His stock-book contains a list of the objects of utility that belong to him, of the operations necessary for their production; and lastly, of the labour-time that definite quantities of those objects have, on an average, cost him. All the relations between Robinson and the objects that form this wealth of his own creation, are here so simple and clear as to be intelligible without exertion, even to Mr. Sedley Taylor. And yet those relations contain all that is essential to the determination of value.

Let us now transport ourselves from Robinson's island bathed in light to the European middle ages shrouded in darkness. Here, instead of the independent man, we find everyone dependent, serfs and lords, vassals and suzerains, laymen and clergy. Personal dependence here characterises the social relations of production just as much as it does the other spheres of life organised on the basis of that production. But for the very reason that personal dependence forms the groundwork of society, there is no necessity for labour and its products to assume a fantastic form different from their reality. They take the shape, in the transactions of society, of services in kind and payments in kind. Here the particular and natural form of labour, and not, as in a society based on production of commodities, its general abstract form is the immediate social form of labour. Compulsory labour is just as properly measured by time, as commodity-producing labour; but every serf knows that what he expends in the service of his lord, is a definite quantity of his own personal labour-power. The tithe to be rendered to the priest is more matter of fact than his blessing. No matter, then, what we may think of the parts played by the different classes of people themselves in this society, the social relations between individuals in the performance of their labour, appear at all events as their own mutual personal relations, and are not disguised under the shape of social relations between the products of labour.

For an example of labour in common or directly associated labour, we have no occasion to go back to that spontaneously developed form which we find on the threshold of the history of all civilised races.* We have one close at hand in the patriarchal industries of a peasant family, that produces corn, cattle, yarn, linen, and clothing for home use. These different articles are, as regards the family, so many products of its labour, but as between themselves, they are not commodities. The different kinds of labour, such as tillage, cattle tending, spinning, weaving and making clothes, which result in the various products, are in themselves, and such as they are, direct social functions, because functions of the family, which, just as much as a society based on the production of commodities, possesses a spontaneously developed system of division of labour. The distribution of the work within the family, and the regulation of the labour-time of the several members, depend as well upon differences of age and sex as upon natural conditions varying with the seasons. The labour-power of each individual, by its very nature, operates in this case merely as a definite portion of the whole labour-power of the family, and therefore, the measure of the expenditure of individual labour-power by its duration, appears here by its very nature as a social character of their labour.

Let us now picture to ourselves, by way of change, a community of free individuals, carrying on their work with the means of production in common, in which the labour-power of all the different individuals is consciously applied as the combined labour-power of the community. All the characteristics of Robinson's labour are here repeated, but with this difference, that they are social, instead of individual. Everything produced by him was exclusively the result of his own personal labour, and therefore simply an object of use for himself. The total product of our community is a social product. One portion serves as fresh means of production and remains social. But another portion is consumed by the members as means of subsistence. A distribution of this portion amongst them is consequently necessary. The mode of this distribution will vary with the productive organisation of the community, and the degree of historical development attained by the producers. We will assume, but merely for the sake of a parallel with the production of commodities, that the share of each individual producer in the means of subsistence is

---

*"A ridiculous presumption has latterly got abroad that common property in its primitive form is specifically a Slavonian, or even exclusively Russian form. It is the primitive form that we can prove to have existed amongst Romans, Teutons, and Celts, and even to this day we find numerous examples, ruins though they be, in India. A more exhaustive study of Asiatic, and especially of Indian forms of common property, would show how from the different forms of primitive common property, different forms of its dissolution have been developed. Thus, for instance, the various original types of Roman and Teutonic private property are deducible from different forms of Indian common property." (Karl Marx, "Zur Kritik, &c.," p. 10.)

determined by his labour-time. Labour-time would, in that case, play a double part. Its apportionment in accordance with a definite social plan maintains the proper proportion between the different kinds of work to be done and the various wants of the community. On the other hand, it also serves as a measure of the portion of the common labour borne by each individual, and of his share in the part of the total product destined for individual consumption. The social relations of the individual producers, with regard both to their labour and to its products, are in this case perfectly simple and intelligible, and that with regard not only to production but also to distribution.

The religious world is but the reflex of the real world. And for a society based upon the production of commodities, in which the producers in general enter into social relations with one another by treating their products as commodities and values, whereby they reduce their individual private labour to the standard of homogeneous human labour—for such a society, Christianity with its *cultus* of abstract man, more especially in its bourgeois developments, Protestantism, Deism, &c., is the most fitting form of religion. In the ancient Asiatic and other ancient modes of production, we find that the conversion of products into commodities, and therefore the conversion of men into producers of commodities, holds a subordinate place, which, however, increases in importance as the primitive communities approach nearer and nearer to their dissolution. Trading nations, properly so called, exist in the ancient world only in its interstices, like the gods of Epicurus in the Intermundia, or like Jews in the pores of Polish society. Those ancient social organisms of production are, as compared with bourgeois society, extremely simple and transparent. But they are founded either on the immature development of man individually, who has not yet severed the umbilical cord that unites him with his fellowmen in a primitive tribal community, or upon direct relations of subjection. They can arise and exist only when the development of the productive power of labour has not risen beyond a low stage, and when, therefore, the social relations within the sphere of material life, between man and man, and between man and Nature, are correspondingly narrow. This narrowness is reflected in the ancient worship of Nature, and in the other elements of the popular religions. The religious reflex of the real world can, in any case, only then finally vanish, when the practical relations of every-day life offer to man none but perfectly intelligible and reasonable relations with regard to his fellowmen and to Nature.

The life-process of society, which is based on the process of material production, does not strip off its mystical veil until it is treated as production by freely associated men, and is consciously regulated by them in accordance with a settled plan. This, however, demands for society a certain material ground-work or set of conditions of existence which in their turn are the spontaneous product of a long and painful process of development.

Political Economy has indeed analysed, however incompletely, value and its magnitude, and has discovered what lies beneath these forms. But it has never once asked the question why labour is represented by the value of its product and labour-time by the magnitude of that value.* These formulae, which bear it stamped upon them in unmistakeable letters that they belong to a state of society, in which the process of production has the mastery over man, instead of being controlled by him, such formulae appear to the bourgeois intellect to be as much a self-evident necessity imposed by Nature as productive labour itself. Hence forms of social production that preceded the bourgeois form, are treated by the bourgeoisie in much the same way as the Fathers of the Church treated pre-Christian religions.[†]

To what extent some economists are misled by the Fetishism inherent in commodities, or by the objective appearance of the social characteristics of labour, is shown, amongst other ways, by the dull and tedious quarrel over the part played by Nature in the formation of exchange-value. Since exchange-value is a definite social manner of expressing the amount of labour bestowed upon an object, Nature has no more to do with it, than it has in fixing the course of exchange.

---

*It is one of the chief failings of classical economy that it has never succeeded, by means of its analysis of commodities, and, in particular, of their value, in discovering that form under which value becomes exchange-value. Even Adam Smith and Ricardo, the best representatives of the school, treat the form of value as a thing of no importance, as having no connexion with the inherent nature of commodities. The reason for this is not solely because their attention is entirely absorbed in the analysis of the magnitude of value. It lies deeper. The value-form of the product of labour is not only the most abstract, but is also the most universal form, taken by the product in bourgeois production, and stamps that production as a particular species of social production, and thereby gives it its special historical character. If then we treat this mode of production as one eternally fixed by Nature for every state of society, we necessarily overlook that which is the differentia specifica of the value-form, and consequently of the commodity-form, and of its further developments, money-form, capital-form, &c. We consequently find that economists, who are thoroughly agreed as to labour-time being the measure of the magnitude of value, have the most strange and contradictory ideas of money, the perfected form of the general equivalent. This is seen in a striking manner when they treat of banking, where the commonplace definitions of money will no longer hold water. This led to the rise of a restored mercantile system (Ganilh, &c.), which sees in value nothing but a social form, or rather the unsubstantial ghost of that form. Once for all I may here state, that by classical Political Economy, I understand that economy which, since the time of W. Petty, has investigated the real relations of production in bourgeois society, in contradistinction to vulgar economy, which deals with appearances only, ruminates without ceasing on the materials long since provided by scientific economy, and there seeks plausible explanations of the most obtrusive phenomena, for bourgeois daily use, but for the rest, confines itself to systematising in a pedantic way, and proclaiming for everlasting truths, the trite ideas held by the self-complacent bourgeoisie with regard to their own world, to them the best of all possible worlds.

[†]I seize this opportunity of shortly answering an objection taken by a German paper in America, to my work, "Zur Kritik der Pol. Oekonomie, 1859." In the estimation of that paper, my view that each special mode of production and the social relations corresponding to it, in short, that the economic structure of society, is the real basis on which the juridical and political superstructure is raised, and to which definite social forms of thought correspond; that the mode of production determines the character of the social, political, and intellectual life generally, all this is very true for our own times, in which material interests preponderate, but not for the middle ages, in which Catholicism, nor for Athens and Rome, where politics, reigned supreme. In the first place it strikes one as an odd thing for any one to suppose that these well-worn phrases about the middle ages and the ancient world are unknown to anyone else. This much, however, is clear, that the middle ages could not live on Catholicism, nor the ancient world on politics. On the contrary, it is the mode in which they gained a livelihood that explains why here politics, and there Catholicism, played the chief part. For the rest, it requires but a slight acquaintance with the history of the Roman republic, for example, to be aware that its secret history is the history of its landed property. On the other hand, Don Quixote long ago paid the penalty for wrongly imagining that knight errantry was compatible with all economic forms of society.

The mode of production in which the product takes the form of a commodity, or is produced directly for exchange, is the most general and most embryonic form of bourgeois production. It therefore makes its appearance at an early date in history, though not in the same predominating and characteristic manner as now-a-days. Hence its Fetish character is comparatively easy to be seen through. But when we come to more concrete forms, even this appearance of simplicity vanishes. Whence arose the illusions of the monetary system? To it gold and silver, when serving as money, did not represent a social relation between producers, but were natural objects with strange social properties. And modern economy, which looks down with such disdain on the monetary system, does not its superstition come out as clear as noon-day, whenever it treats of capital? How long is it since economy discarded the physiocratic illusion, that rents grow out of the soil and not out of society?

But not to anticipate, we will content ourselves with yet another example relating to the commodity-form. Could commodities themselves speak, they would say: Our use-value may be a thing that interests men. It is no part of us as objects. What, however, does belong to us as objects, is our value. Our natural intercourse as commodities proves it. In the eyes of each other we are nothing but exchange-values. Now listen how those commodities speak through the mouth of the economist. "Value"—(*i.e.,* exchange-value) "is a property of things, riches"—(*i.e.,* use-value) "of man. Value, in this sense, necessarily implies exchanges, riches do not."* "Riches" (use-value) "are the attribute of men, value is the attribute of commodities. A man or a community is rich, a pearl or a diamond is valuable . . . A pearl or a diamond is valuable" as a pearl or diamond.† So far no chemist has ever discovered exchange-value either in a pearl or a diamond. The economic discoverers of this chemical element, who by-the-by lay special claim to critical acumen, find however that the use-value of objects belongs to them independently of their material properties, while their value, on the other hand, forms a part of them as objects. What confirms them in this view, is the peculiar circumstance that the use-value of objects is realised without exchange, by means of a direct relation between the objects and man, while, on the other hand, their value is realised only by exchange, that is, by means of a social process. Who fails here to call to mind our good friend, Dogberry, who informs neighbour Seacoal, that, "To be a well-favoured man is the gift of fortune; but reading and writing comes by Nature."‡

---

*"Observations on certain verbal disputes in Pol. Econ., particularly relating to value and to demand and supply." Lond., 1821, p. 16.

†S. Bailey, l. c., p. 165.

‡The author of "Observations" and S. Bailey accuse Ricardo of converting exchange-value from something relative into something absolute. The opposite is the fact. He has explained the apparent relation between objects, such as diamonds and pearls, in which relation they appear as exchange-values, and disclosed the true relation hidden behind the appearances, namely, their relation to each other as mere expressions of human labour. If the followers of Ricardo answer Bailey somewhat rudely, and by no means convincingly, the reason is to be sought in this, that they were unable to find in Ricardo's own works any key to the hidden relations existing between value and its form, exchange-value.

[THE COMPOSITION OF CAPITAL]

In this chapter we consider the influence of the growth of capital on the lot of the laboring class. The most important factor in this inquiry, is the composition of capital and the changes it undergoes in the course of the process of accumulation.

The composition of capital is to be understood in a two-fold sense. On the side of value, it is determined by the proportion in which it is divided into constant capital or value of the means of production, and variable capital or value of labor-power, the sum total of wages. On the side of material, as it functions in the process of production, all capital is divided into means of production and living labor-power. This latter composition is determined by the relation between the mass of the means of production employed, on the one hand, and the mass of labor necessary for their employment on the other. I call the former the *value composition,* the latter the *technical composition* of capital. Between the two there is a strict correlation. To express this, I call the value-composition of capital, insofar as it is determined by its technical composition and mirrors the changes of the latter, the *organic composition* of capital. Wherever I refer to the composition of capital, without further qualification, its organic composition is always understood.

The many individual capitals invested in a particular branch of production have, one with another, more or less different compositions. The average of their individual compositions gives us the composition of the total capital in this branch of production. Lastly, the average of these averages, in all branches of production, gives us the composition of the total social capital of a country, and with this alone are we, in the last resort, concerned in the following investigation.

[THE LAW OF CAPITALIST ACCUMULATION]

Growth of capital involves growth of its variable constituent or of the part invested in labor-power. A part of the surplus-value turned into additional capital must always be retransformed into variable capital, or additional labor-fund. If we suppose that, all other circumstances remaining the same, the composition of capital also remains constant (i.e., that a definite mass of means of production constantly needs the same mass of labor-power to set in motion), then the demand for labor and the subsistence-fund of the laborers clearly increase in the same proportion as the capital, and the more rapidly, the more rapidly the capital increases. . . . As simple reproduction constantly reproduces the capital-relation itself, i.e., the relation of capitalists on the one hand, and wage-workers on the other, so reproduction on a progressive scale, i.e., accumulation, reproduces the capital relation on a progressive scale, more capitalists or larger capitalists at this pole, more wage-workers at that. The reproduction of a mass of labor-power, which must incessantly reincorporate itself with capital for that capital's self-expansion; which cannot get free from capital, and whose enslavement to capital is only concealed by the variety of individual capitalists to whom it sells itself, this reproduction of labor-power forms, in fact, an essential of the reproduction of capital itself. Accumulation of capital is, therefore, increase of the proletariat. . . .

The law of capitalist production, that is at the bottom of the pretended "natural law of population," reduces itself simply to this: The correlation between accumulation of capital and rate of wages is nothing else than the correlation between the unpaid labor transformed into capital, and the additional paid labor necessary for the setting in motion of this additional capital. It is therefore in no way a relation between two magnitudes, independent one of the other: on the one hand, the magnitude of the capital; on the other, the number of the laboring population; it is rather, at bottom, only the relation between the unpaid and the paid labor of the same laboring population. If the quantity of unpaid labor supplied by the working-class, and accumulated by the capitalist class, increases so rapidly that its conversion into capital requires an extraordinary addition of paid labor, then wages rise, and, all other circumstances remaining equal, the unpaid labor diminishes in proportion. But as soon as this diminution touches the point at which the surplus-labor that nourishes capital is no longer supplied in normal quantity, a reaction sets in: a smaller part of revenue is capitalized, accumulation lags, and the movement of rise in wages receives a check. The rise of wages therefore is confined within limits that not only leave intact the foundations of the capitalistic system, but also secure its reproduction on a progressive scale. The law of capitalistic accumulation, metamorphosed by economists into a pretended law of nature, in reality merely states that the very nature of accumulation excludes every diminution in the degree of exploitation of labor, and every rise in the price of labor, which could seriously imperil the continual reproduction, on an ever enlarging scale, of the capitalistic relation. It cannot be otherwise in a mode of production in which the laborer exists to satisfy the needs of self-expansion of existing values, instead of on the contrary, material wealth existing to satisfy the needs of development on the part of the laborer. As, in religion, man is governed by the products of his own brain, so in capitalistic production, he is governed by the products of his own hand.

In Part IV it was shown, how the development of the productiveness of social labor presupposes co-operation on a large scale; how it is only upon this supposition that division and combination of labor can be organized, and the means of production economized by concentration on a vast scale; how instruments of labor which, from their very nature, are only fit for use in common, such as a system of machinery, can be called into being; how huge natural forces can be pressed into the service of production; and how the transformation can be effected of the process of production into a technological application of science.* On the basis of the production of commodities, where the means of production are the property of private persons, and where the artisan therefore either produces commodities, isolated from and independent of others, or sells his labor-power as a commodity, because he lacks the means for independent industry, co-operation on a large scale

---

*In Part IV, Marx explains that surplus value may be increased not only by increasing the length of the working day, but also by increasing the productivity of the worker. This reduces the time required for the laborer to produce the value needed for his own subsistence. By increasing productivity, therefore, the capitalist is enabled to take a larger *proportion* of the value created during the working day. This Marx calls "the production of relative surplus value."—*Ed.*

can realize itself only in the increase of individual capitals, only in proportion as the means of social production and the means of subsistence are transformed into the private property of capitalists. The basis of the production of commodities can admit of production on a large scale in the capitalistic form alone. A certain accumulation of capital, in the hands of individual producers of commodities, forms therefore the necessary preliminary of the specifically capitalistic mode of production. We had, therefore, to assume that this occurs during the transition from handicraft to capitalistic industry. It may be called primitive accumulation, because it is the historic basis, instead of the historic result of specifically capitalist production. How it itself originates, we need not here inquire as yet. It is enough that it forms the starting point. But all methods for raising the social productive power of labor that are developed on this basis, are at the same time methods for the increased production of surplus-value or surplus-product, which in its turn is the formative element of accumulation. They are, therefore, at the same time methods of the production of capital by capital, or methods of its accelerated accumulation. The continual retransformation of surplus-value into capital now appears in the shape of the increasing magnitude of the capital that enters into the process of production. This in turn is the basis of an extended scale of production, of the methods for raising the productive power of labor that accompany it, and of accelerated production of surplus-value. If, therefore, a certain degree of accumulation of capital appears as a condition of the specifically capitalist mode of production, the latter causes conversely an accelerated accumulation of capital. With the accumulation of capital, therefore, the specifically capitalistic mode of production develops, and with the capitalist mode of production the accumulation of capital. Both these economic factors bring about, in the compound ratio of the impulses they reciprocally give one another, that change in the technical composition of capital by which the variable constituent becomes always smaller and smaller as compared with the constant. . . .

[THE LAW OF THE CONCENTRATION OF CAPITAL]

Every individual capital is a larger or smaller concentration of means of production, with a corresponding command over a larger or smaller labor-army. Every accumulation becomes the means of new accumulation. With the increasing mass of wealth which functions as capital, accumulation increases the concentration of that wealth in the hands of individual capitalists, and thereby widens the basis of production on a large scale and of the specific methods of capitalist production. The growth of social capital is effected by the growth of many individual capitals. All other circumstances remaining the same, individual capitals, and with them the concentration of the means of production, increase in such proportion as they form aliquot parts of the total social capital. At the same time portions of the original capitals disengage themselves and function as new independent capitals. Besides other causes, the division of property, within capitalist families, plays a great part in this. With the accumulation of capital, therefore, the number of capitalists grows to a greater or lesser extent. Two points characterize this kind of concentration which grows directly out of, or rather is identical with, accumulation. First: The increasing concentration of the social means of production in the hands of individual capitalists is, other things remaining equal, limited by the degree of increase of social wealth. Second: The part of social capital domiciled in each particular sphere of production is divided among many capitalists who face one another as independent commodity-producers competing with each other. Accumulation and the concentration accompanying it are, therefore, not only scattered over many points, but the increase of each functioning capital is thwarted by the formation of new and the subdivision of old capitals. Accumulation, therefore, presents itself on the one hand as increasing concentration of the means of production, and of the command over labor; on the other, as repulsion of many individual capitals one from another.

This splitting-up of the total social capital into many individual capitals or the repulsion of its fractions one from another, is counteracted by their attraction. This last does not mean that simple concentration of the means of production and of the command over labor, which is identical with accumulation. It is concentration of capitals already formed, destruction of their individual independence, expropriation of capitalist by capitalist, transformation of many small into few large capitals. This process differs from the former in this, that it only presupposes a change in the distribution of capital already to hand, and functioning; its field of action is therefore not limited by the absolute growth of social wealth, by the absolute limits of accumulation. Capital grows in one place to a huge mass in a single hand, because it has in another place been lost by many. This is centralization proper, as distinct from accumulation and concentration.

The laws of this centralization of capitals, or of the attraction of capital by capital, cannot be developed here. A brief hint at a few facts must suffice. The battle of competition is fought by cheapening of commodities. The cheapness of commodities depends, *cæteris paribus,* on the productiveness of labor, and this again on the scale of production. Therefore, the larger capitals beat the smaller. It will further be remembered that, with the development of the capitalist mode of production, there is an increase in the minimum amount of individual capital necessary to carry on a business under its normal conditions. The smaller capitals, therefore, crowd into spheres of production which modern industry has only sporadically or incompletely got hold of. Here competition rages in direct proportion to the number, and in inverse proportion to the magnitudes, of the antagonistic capitals. It always ends in the ruin of many small capitalists, whose capitals partly pass into the hand of their conquerors, partly vanish. Apart from this, with capitalist production an altogether new force comes into play—the credit system. Not only is this itself a new and mighty weapon in the battle of competition. By unseen threads it, moreover, draws the disposable money, scattered in larger or smaller masses over the surface of society, into the hands of individual or associated capitalists. It is the specific machine for the centralization of capitals.

The centralization of capitals or the process of their attraction becomes more intense, in proportion as the specifically capitalist mode of production develops along with accumulation. In its turn, centralization becomes one of the greatest levers of this development. It shortens and quickens the transformation of separate processes of production into processes socially combined and carried out on a large scale.

The increasing bulk of individual masses of capital becomes the material basis of an uninterrupted revolution in the mode of production itself. Continually the capitalist mode of production conquers branches of industry not yet wholly, or only sporadically, or only formally, subjugated by it. At the same time there grow up on its soil new branches of industry, such as could not exist without it. Finally, in the branches of industry already carried on upon the capitalist basis, the productiveness of labor is made to ripen, as if in a hothouse. In all these cases, the number of laborers falls in proportion to the mass of the means of production worked up by them. An ever increasing part of the capital is turned into means of production, an ever decreasing one into labor-power. With the extent, the concentration and the technical efficiency of the means of production, the degree lessens progressively, in which the latter are means of employment for laborers. A steam plow is an incomparably more efficient means of production than an ordinary plow, but the capital-value laid out in it is an incomparably smaller means for employing men than if it were laid out in ordinary plows. At first, it is the mere adding of new capital to old, which allows of the expansion and technical revolution of the material conditions of the process of production. But soon the change of composition and the technical transformation get more or less completely hold of all old capital that has reached the term of its reproduction, and therefore has to be replaced. This metamorphosis of old capital is independent, to a certain extent, of the absolute growth of social capital, in the same way as its centralization. But this centralization which only redistributes the social capital already to hand, and melts into one a number of old capitals, works in its turn as a powerful agent in this metamorphosis of old capital.

On the one hand, therefore, the additional capital formed in the course of accumulation attracts fewer and fewer laborers in proportion to its magnitude. On the other hand, the old capital periodically reproduced with change of composition, repels more and more of the laborers formerly employed by it.

[THE LAW OF INCREASING MISERY]

The greater the social wealth, the functioning capital, the extent and energy of its growth, and, therefore, also the absolute mass of the proletariat and the productiveness of its labor, the greater is the industrial reserve-army. The same causes which develop the expansive power of capital, develops also the labor-power at its disposal. The relative mass of the industrial reserve-army increases therefore with the potential energy of wealth. But the greater this reserve-army in proportion to the active labor-army, the greater is the mass of a consolidated surplus population, whose misery is in inverse ratio to its torment of labor. The more extensive, finally, the Lazarus-layers of the working-class, and the industrial reserve-army, the greater is official pauperism. *This is the absolute general law of capitalist accumulation.* Like all other laws it is modified in its working by many circumstances, the analysis of which does not concern us here.

The folly is now patent of the economic wisdom that preaches to the laborers the accommodation of their number to the requirements of capital. The mechanism of capitalist production and accumulation constantly effects this adjustment. The first word of this adaptation is the creation of a relative surplus population, or industrial reserve-army. Its last word is the misery of constantly extending strata of the active army of labor, and the dead weight of pauperism.

The law by which a constantly increasing quantity of means of production, thanks to the advance in the productiveness of social labor, may be set in movement by a progressively diminishing expenditure of human power, this law, in a capitalist society—where the laborer does not employ the means of production, but the means of production employ the laborer—undergoes a complete inversion and is expressed thus: the higher the productiveness of labor, the greater is the pressure of the laborers on the means of employment, the more precarious, therefore, becomes their condition of existence, viz., the sale of their own labor-power for the increasing of another's wealth, or for the self-expansion of capital. The fact that the means of production, and the productiveness of labor, increase more rapidly than the productive population, expresses itself, therefore, capitalistically in the inverse form that the laboring population always increases more rapidly than the conditions under which capital can employ this increase for its own self-expansion.

We saw in Part IV, when analyzing the production of relative surplus value: within the capitalist system all methods for raising the social productiveness of labor are brought about at the cost of the individual laborer; all means for the development of production transform themselves into means of domination over, and exploitation of, the producers; they mutilate the laborer into a fragment of a man, degrade him to the level of an appendage of a machine, destroy every remnant of charm in his work and turn it into a hated toil; they estrange from him the intellectual potentialities of the labor-process in the same proportion as science is incorporated in it as an independent power; they distort the conditions under which he works, subject him during the labor-process to a despotism the more hateful for its meanness; they transform his lifetime into working time, and drag his wife and child beneath the wheels of the juggernaut of capital. But all methods for the production of surplus value are at the same time methods of accumulation; and every extension of accumulation becomes again a means for the development of those methods. It follows therefore that in proportion as capital accumulates, the lot of the laborer, be his payment high or low, must grow worse. The law, finally, that always equilibrates the relative surplus population, or industrial reserve-army, to the extent and energy of accumulation, this law rivets the laborer to capital more firmly than the wedges of Vulcan did Prometheus to the rock. It establishes an accumulation of misery, corresponding with accumulation of capital. Accumulation of wealth at one pole is, therefore, at the same time accumulation of misery, agony of toil, slavery, ignorance, brutality, mental degradation, at the opposite pole, i.e., on the side of the class that produces its own product in the form of capital.

16
Friedrich Engels

The following selection is the third chapter of Engels' *Socialism, Utopian and Scientific,* of which the two earlier chapters have been included in Sections I and II of this first Part. The general theory of historical materialism is given orderly restatement in this passage, but because this was written late in the nineteenth century, Engels could use Marx's analysis of commodities in *Capital* (appearing in the immediately preceding selection) to buttress his explanation of the contradictions of capitalism which (he argues) will lead to capitalism's internal collapse and overthrow, the withering away of the state as the instrument of oppression, and the emergence of a new society without classes. This is probably the best single short statement of the communist world view.

[SCIENTIFIC SOCIALISM]*

The materialist conception of history starts from the proposition that the production of the means to support human life and, next to production, the exchange of things produced, is the basis of all social structure; that in every society that has appeared in history, the manner in which wealth is distributed and society divided into classes or orders is dependent upon what is produced, how it is produced, and how the products are exchanged. From this point of view the final causes of all social changes and political revolutions are to be sought, not in men's brains, not in man's better insight into eternal truth and justice, but in changes in the modes of production and exchange. They are to be sought, not in the *philosophy,* but in the *economics* of each particular epoch. The growing perception that existing social institutions are unreasonable and unjust, that reason has become unreason, and right wrong, is only proof that in the modes of production and exchange changes have silently taken place, with which the social order, adapted to earlier economic conditions, is no longer in keeping. From this it also follows that the means of getting rid of the incongruities that have been brought to light must also be present, in a more or less developed condition, within the changed modes of production themselves. These means are not to be invented by deduction from fundamental principles, but are to be discovered in the stubborn facts of the existing system of production.

What is, then, the position of modern socialism in this connection?

The present structure of society—this is now pretty generally conceded—is the creation of the ruling class of today, of the bourgeoisie. The mode of production peculiar to the bourgeoisie, known, since Marx, as the capitalist mode of production, was incompatible with the feudal system, with the privileges it conferred upon individuals, entire social ranks and local corporations, as well as with the hereditary ties of subordination which constituted the framework of its social orga-

*From F. Engels, *Socialism, Utopian and Scientific,* Swan Sonnenschein and Co., London, 1892.

nization. The bourgeoisie broke up the feudal system and built upon its ruins the capitalist order of society, the kingdom of free competition, of personal liberty, of equality before the law of all commodity owners, and of all the rest of the capitalist blessings. Thenceforward the capitalist mode of production could develop in freedom. Since steam, machinery and the making of machines by machinery transformed the older manufacture into modern industry, the productive forces evolved under the guidance of the bourgeoisie developed with a rapidity and in a degree unheard of before. But just as the older manufacture, in its time, and handicraft, becoming more developed under its influence, had come into collision with the feudal trammels of the guilds, so now modern industry, in its more complete development, comes into collision with the bounds within which the capitalistic mode of production holds it confined. The new productive forces have already outgrown the capitalistic mode of using them. And this conflict between productive forces and modes of production is not a conflict engendered in the mind of man, like that between original sin and divine justice. It exists, in fact, objectively, outside us, independently of the will and actions even of the men that have brought it on. Modern socialism is nothing but the reflex, in thought, of this conflict in fact; its ideal reflection in the minds, first, of the class directly suffering under it, the working class.

Now, in what does this conflict consist?

Before capitalistic production, i.e., in the Middle Ages, the system of petty industry obtained generally, based upon the private property of the laborers in their means of production; in the country, the agriculture of the small peasant, freeman or serf; in the towns, the handicrafts organized in guilds. The instruments of labor—land, agricultural implements, the workshop, the tool—were the instruments of labor of single individuals, adapted for the use of one worker, and, therefore, of necessity, small, dwarfish, circumscribed. But for this very reason they belonged, as a rule, to the producer himself. To concentrate these scattered, limited means of production, to enlarge them, to turn them into the powerful levers of production of the present day—this was precisely the historic rôle of capitalist production and of its upholder, the bourgeoisie. In Part IV of *Capital* Marx has explained in detail, how since the fifteenth century this has been historically worked out through the three phases of simple cooperation, manufacture and modern industry. But the bourgeoisie, as is also shown there, could not transform these puny means of production into mighty productive forces, without transforming them, at the same time, from means of production of the individual into *social* means of production only workable by a collectivity of men. The spinning-wheel, the hand-loom, the blacksmith's hammer were replaced by the spinning machine, the power-loom, the steam-hammer; the individual workshop, by the factory, implying the co-operation of hundreds and thousands of workmen. In like manner, production itself changed from a series of individual into a series of social acts, and the products from individual to social products. The yarn, the cloth, the metal articles that now came out of the factory were the joint product of many workers, through whose hands they had successively to pass before they were ready. No one person could say of them: "I made that; this is *my* product."

But where, in a given society, the fundamental form of production is that spontaneous division of labor which creeps in gradually and not upon any preconceived plan, there the products take on the form of *commodities,* whose mutual exchange, buying and selling, enable the individual producers to satisfy their manifold wants. And this was the case in the Middle Ages. The peasant, e.g., sold to the artisan agricultural products and bought from him the products of handicraft. Into this society of individual producers, of commodity producers, the new mode of production thrust itself. In the midst of the old division of labor, grown up spontaneously and upon *no definite plan,* which had governed the whole of society, now arose division of labor upon a *definite plan,* as organized in the factory; side by side with *individual* production appeared *social* production. The products of both were sold in the same market, and, therefore, at prices at least approximately equal. But organization upon a definite plan was stronger than spontaneous division of labor. The factories working with the combined social forces of a collectivity of individuals produced their commodities far more cheaply than the individual small producers. Individual production succumbed in one department after another. Socialized production revolutionized all the old methods of production. But its revolutionary character was, at the same time, so little recognized, that it was, on the contrary, introduced as a means of increasing and developing the production of commodities. When it arose, it found ready-made, and made liberal use of, certain machinery for the production and exchange of commodities; merchants' capital, handicraft, wage labor. Socialized production thus introducing itself as a new form of the production of commodities, it was a matter of course that under it the old forms of appropriation remained in full swing, and were applied to its products as well.

In the medieval stage of evolution of the production of commodities, the question as to the owner of the product of labor could not arise. The individual producer, as a rule, had, from raw material belonging to himself, and generally his own handiwork, produced it with his own tools, by the labor of his own hands or of his family. There was no need for him to appropriate the new product. It belonged wholly to him, as a matter of course. His property in the product was, therefore, based *upon his own labor.* Even where external help was used, this was, as a rule, of little importance, and very generally was compensated by something other than wages. The apprentices and journeymen of the guilds worked less for board and wages than for education, in order that they might become master craftsmen themselves.

Then came the concentration of the means of production and of the producers in large workshops and manufactories, their transformation into actual socialized means of production and socialized producers. But the socialized producers and means of production and their products were still treated, after this change, just as they had been before, i.e., as the means of production and the products of individuals. Hitherto, the owner of the instruments of labor had himself appropriated the product, because as a rule it was his own product and the assistance of others was the exception. Now the owner of the instruments of labor always appropriated to himself the product, although it was no longer *his* product but exclusively the product of the *labor of others*. Thus, the products now produced socially were not appropriated by those who had actually set in motion the means of production and actually produced the commodities, but by the *capitalists*. The means of production, and production itself, had become in essence socialized. But they were subjected to a form of appropriation which presupposes the private production of individuals, under which, therefore, everyone owns his own product and brings it to market. The mode of production is subjected to this form of appropriation, although it abolishes the conditions upon which the latter rests.*

This contradiction, which gives to the new mode of production its capitalistic character, *contains the germ of the whole of the social antagonisms of today*. The greater the mastery obtained by the new mode of production over all important fields of production and in all manufacturing countries, the more it reduced individual production to an insignificant residuum, *the more clearly was brought out the incompatibility of socialized production with capitalistic appropriation*.

The first capitalists found, as we have said, alongside of other forms of labor, wage labor ready-made for them in the market. But it was exceptional, complimentary, necessary, transitory wage labor. The agricultural laborer, though, upon occasion, he hired himself out by the day, had a few acres of his own land on which he could at all events live at a pinch. The guilds were so organized that the journeyman of today became the master of tomorrow. But all this changed, as soon as the means of production became socialized and concentrated in the hands of capitalists. The means of production, as well as the product of the individual producer became more and more worthless; there was nothing left for him but to turn wage worker under the capitalist. Wage labor, aforetime the exception and accessory, now became the rule and basis of all production; aforetime complementary, it now became the sole remaining function of the worker. The wage worker for a time became a wage worker for life. The number of these permanent wage workers was further enormously increased by the breaking up of the feudal system that occurred at the same time, by the disbanding of the retainers of the feudal lords, the eviction of the peasants from their homesteads, etc. The separation was made complete between the means of production concentrated in the hands of the capitalists on the one side, and the producers, possessing nothing but their labor power, on the other. *The contradiction between socialized production and capitalistic appropriation manifested itself as the antagonism of proletariat and bourgeoisie.*

We have seen that the capitalistic mode of production thrust its way into a society of commodity producers, of individual producers, whose social bond was the exchange of their products. But every society, based upon the production of com-

---

*It is hardly necessary in this connection to point out, that, even if the form of appropriation remains the same, the *character* of the appropriation is just as much revolutionized as production is by the changes described above. It is, of course, a very different matter whether I appropriate to myself my own product or that of another. Note in passing that wage labor, which contains the whole capitalistic mode of production in embryo, is very ancient; in a sporadic, scattered form it existed for centuries alongside of slave labor. But the embryo could duly develop into the capitalistic mode of production only when the necessary historical pre-conditions had been furnished.

modities, has this peculiarity: that the producers have lost control over their own social interrelations. Each man produces for himself with such means of production as he may happen to have, and for such exchange as he may require to satisfy his remaining wants. No one knows how much of his particular article is coming on the market, nor how much of it will be wanted. No one knows whether his individual product will meet an actual demand, whether he will be able to make good his cost of production or even to sell his commodity at all. Anarchy reigns in socialized production.

But the production of commodities, like every other form of production, has its peculiar inherent laws inseparable from it; and these laws work, despite anarchy, in and through anarchy. They reveal themselves in the only persistent form of social inter-relations, i.e., in exchange, and here they affect the individual producers as compulsory laws of competition. They are, at first, unknown to these producers themselves, and have to be discovered by them gradually and as the result of experience. They work themselves out, therefore, independently of the producers, and in antagonism to them, as inexorable natural laws of their particular form of production. The product governs the producers.

In medieval society, especially in the earlier centuries, production was essentially directed towards satisfying the wants of the individual. It satisfied, in the main, only the wants of the producer and his family. Where relations of personal dependence existed, as in the country, it also helped to satisfy the wants of the feudal lord. In all this there was, therefore, no exchange; the products, consequently, did not assume the character of commodities. The family of the peasant produced almost everything they wanted: clothes and furniture, as well as means of subsistence. Only when it began to produce more than was sufficient to supply its own wants and the payments in kind to the feudal lord, only then did it also produce commodities. This surplus, thrown into socialized exchange and offered for sale, became commodities.

The artisans of the towns, it is true, had from the first to produce for exchange. But they, also, themselves supplied the greatest part of their own individual wants. They had gardens and plots of land. They turned their cattle out into the communal forest, which, also, yielded them timber and firing. The women spun flax, wool, and so forth. Production for the purpose of exchange, production of commodities was only in its infancy. Hence, exchange was restricted, the market narrow, the methods of production stable; there was local exclusiveness without, local unity within; the mark in the country, in the town, the guild.

But with the extension of the production of commodities, and especially with the introduction of the capitalist mode of production, the laws of commodity production, hitherto latent, came into action more openly and with greater force. The old bonds were loosened, the old exclusive limits broken through, the producers were more and more turned into independent, isolated producers of commodities. It became apparent that the production of society at large was ruled by absence of plan, by accident, by anarchy; and this anarchy grew to greater and greater height. But the chief means by aid of which the capitalist mode of production intensified this anarchy of socialized production was the exact opposite of anarchy. It was the increasing organization of production, upon a social basis, in every individual productive establishment. By this, the old, peaceful, stable condition of things was ended. Wherever this organization of production was introduced into a branch of industry, it brooked no other method of production by its side. The field of labor became a battle ground. The great geographical discoveries, and the colonization following upon them, multiplied markets and quickened the transformation of handicraft into manufacture. The war did not simply break out between the individual producers of particular localities. The local struggles begat in their turn national conflicts, the commercial wars of the seventeenth and the eighteenth centuries.

Finally, modern industry and the opening of the world market made the struggle universal, and at the same time gave it an unheard-of virulence. Advantages in natural or artificial conditions of production now decide the existence or non-existence of individual capitalists, as well as of whole industries and countries. He that falls is remorselessly cast aside. It is the Darwinian struggle of the individual for existence transferred from nature to society with intensified violence. The conditions of existence natural to the animal appear as the final term of human development. The contradiction between socialized production and capitalistic appropriation now presents itself as *an antagonism between the organization of production in the individual workshop and the anarchy of production in society generally.*

The capitalistic mode of production moves in these two forms of the antagonism immanent to it from its very origin. It is never able to get out of that "vicious circle," which Fourier had already discovered. What Fourier could not, indeed, see in his time is: that this circle is gradually narrowing; that the movement becomes more and more a spiral, and must come to an end, like the movement of the planets, by collision with the center. It is the compelling force of anarchy in the production of society at large that more and more completely turns the great majority of men into proletarians; and it is the masses of the proletariat again who will finally put an end to anarchy in production. It is the compelling force of anarchy in social production that turns the limitless perfectibility of machinery under modern industry into a compulsory law by which every individual industrial capitalist must perfect his machinery more and more, under penalty of ruin.

But the perfecting of machinery is making human labor superfluous. If the introduction and increase of machinery means the displacement of millions of manual, by a few machine workers, improvement in machinery means the displacement of more and more of the machine workers themselves. It means, in the last instance, the production of a number of available wage workers in excess of the average needs of capital, the formation of a complete industrial reserve army, as I called it in 1845,* available at the times when industry is working at high pressure, to be cast out upon the street when the inevitable crash comes, a constant dead weight upon the limbs of the working class in its struggle for existence with capital, a regulator for the keeping of wages down to the low level that suits the

*The Condition of the Working Class in England, Sonnenschein and Co., p. 84.

interests of capital. Thus it comes about, to quote Marx, that machinery becomes the most powerful weapon in the war of capital against the working class; that the instruments of labor constantly tear the means of subsistence out of the hands of the laborer; that the very product of the worker is turned into an instrument for his subjugation. Thus it comes about that the economizing of the instruments of labor becomes at the same time, from the outset, the most reckless waste of labor power, and robbery based upon the normal conditions under which labor functions; that machinery, "the most powerful instrument for shortening labor time, becomes the most unfailing means for placing every moment of the laborer's time and that of his family at the disposal of the capitalist for the purpose of expanding the value of his capital." (*Capital,* p. 406) Thus it comes about that overwork of some becomes the preliminary condition for the idleness of others, and that modern industry, which hunts after new consumers over the whole world, forces the consumption of the masses at home down to a starvation minimum, and in doing thus destroys its own home market. "The law that always equilibrates the relative surplus population, or industrial reserve army, to the extent and energy of accumulation, this law rivets the laborer to capital more firmly than the wedges of Vulcan did Prometheus to the rock. It establishes an accumulation of misery, corresponding with accumulation of capital. Accumulation of wealth at one pole is, therefore, at the same time, accumulation of misery, agony of toil, slavery, ignorance, brutality, mental degradation, at the opposite pole, i.e., on the side of the class that produces *its own product in the form of capital.*" (Marx, *Capital,* p. 661) And to expect any other division of the products from the capitalistic mode of production is the same as expecting the electrodes of a battery not to decompose acidulated water, not to liberate oxygen at the positive, hydrogen at the negative pole, so long as they are connected with the battery.

We have seen that the ever-increasing perfectibility of modern machinery is, by the anarchy of social production, turned into a compulsory law that forces the individual industrial capitalist always to improve his machinery, always to increase its productive force. The bare possibility of extending the field of production is transformed for him into a similar compulsory law. The enormous expansive force of modern industry, compared with which that of gases is mere child's play, appears to us now as a *necessity* for expansion, both qualitative and quantitative, that laughs at all resistance. Such resistance is offered by consumption, by sales, by the markets for the products of modern industry. But the capacity for extension, extensive and intensive, of the markets is primarily governed by quite different laws, that work much less energetically. The extension of the markets cannot keep pace with the extension of production. The collision becomes inevitable, and as this cannot produce any real solution so long as it does not break in pieces the capitalist mode of production, the collisions become periodic. Capitalist production has begotten another "vicious circle."

As a matter of fact, since 1825, when the first general crisis broke out, the whole industrial and commercial world, production and exchange among all civilized peoples and their more or less barbaric hangers-on, are thrown out of joint about once every ten years. Commerce is at a standstill, the markets are glutted, products accumulate, as multitudinous as they are unsalable, hard cash disappears, credit vanishes, factories are closed, the mass of the workers are in want of the means of subsistence, because they have produced too much of the means of subsistence; bankruptcy follows upon bankruptcy, execution upon execution. The stagnation lasts for years; productive forces and products are wasted and destroyed wholesale, until the accumulated mass of commodities finally filter off, more or less depreciated in value, until production and exchange gradually begin to move again. Little by little the pace quickens. It becomes a trot. The industrial trot breaks into a canter, the canter in turn grows into the headlong gallop of a perfect steeplechase of industry, commercial credit and speculation, which finally, after breakneck leaps, ends where it began—in the ditch of a crisis. And so over and over again. We have now, since the year 1825, gone through this five times, and at the present moment (1877) we are going through it for the sixth time. And the character of these crises is so clearly defined that Fourier hit all of them off when he described the first as *"crise pléthorique,"* a crisis from plethora.

In these crises, the contradiction between socialized production and capitalist appropriation ends in a violent explosion. The circulation of commodities is, for the time being, stopped. Money, the means of circulation, becomes a hindrance to circulation. All the laws of production and circulation of commodities are turned upside down. The economic collision has reached its apogee. *The mode of production is in rebellion against the mode of exchange.*

The fact that the socialized organization of production within the factory has developed so far that it has become incompatible with the anarchy of production in society, which exists side by side with and dominates it, is brought home to the capitalists themselves by the violent concentration of capital that occurs during crises, through the ruin of many large, and a still greater number of small, capitalists. The whole mechanism of the capitalist mode of production breaks down under the pressure of the productive forces, its own creations. It is no longer able to turn all this mass of means of production into capital. They lie fallow, and for that very reason the industrial reserve army must also lie fallow. Means of production, means of subsistence, available laborers, all the elements of production and of general wealth, are present in abundance. But "abundance becomes the source of distress and want" (Fourier), because it is the very thing that prevents the transformation of the means of production and subsistence into capital. For in capitalistic society the means of production can only function when they have undergone a preliminary transformation into capital, into the means of exploiting human labor power. The necessity of this transformation into capital of the means of production and subsistence stands like a ghost between these and the workers. It alone prevents the coming together of the material and personal levers of production; it alone forbids the means of production to function, the workers to work and live. On the one hand, therefore, the capitalistic mode of production stands convicted of its own incapacity to further direct these productive forces. On the other, these productive forces themselves, with increasing energy, press forward to the removal of the existing contradiction, to the abolition of their quality as capital, to the *practical recognition of their character as social productive forces.*

This rebellion of the productive forces, as they grow more and more powerful, against their quality as capital, this stronger and stronger command that their social character shall be recognized, forces the capitalist class itself to treat them more and more as social productive forces, so far as this is possible under capitalist conditions. The period of industrial high pressure, with its unbounded inflation of credit, not less than the crash itself, by the collapse of great capitalist establishments, tends to bring about that form of the socialism of great masses of means of production, which we meet with in the different kinds of joint-stock companies. Many of these means of production and of distribution are, from the outset, so colossal, that, like the railroads, they exclude all other forms of capitalistic exploitation. At a further stage of evolution this form also becomes insufficient. The producers on a large scale in a particular branch of industry in a particular country unite in a "trust," a union for the purpose of regulating production. They determine the total amount to be produced, parcel it out among themselves, and thus enforce the selling price fixed beforehand. But trusts of this kind, as soon as business becomes bad, are generally liable to break up, and, on this very account, compel a yet greater concentration of association. The whole of the particular industry is turned into one gigantic joint-stock company; internal competition gives place to the internal monopoly of this one company. This has happened in 1890 with the English *alkali* production, which is now, after the fusion of 48 large works, in the hands of one company, conducted upon a single plan, and with a capital of £6,000,000.

In the trusts, freedom of competition changes into its very opposite—into monopoly; and the production without any definite plan of capitalistic society capitulates to the production upon a definite plan of the invading socialistic society. Certainly this is so far still to the benefit and advantage of the capitalists. But in this case the exploitation is so palpable that it must break down. No nation will put up with production conducted by trusts, with so barefaced an exploitation of the community by a small band of dividend mongers.

In any case, with trusts or without, the official representative of capitalist society—the state—will ultimately have to undertake the direction of production.*

---

*I say "have to." For only when the means of production and distribution have *actually* outgrown the form of management by joint-stock companies, and when, therefore, the taking them over by the state has become *economically* inevitable, only then—even if it is the state of today that effects this—is there an economic advance, the attainment of another step preliminary to the taking over of all productive forces by society itself. But of late, since Bismarck went in for state ownership of industrial establishments, a kind of spurious socialism has arisen, degenerating, now and again, into something of flunkeyism, that without more ado declares *all* state ownership, even of the Bismarckian sort, to be socialistic. Certainly, if the taking over by the state of the tobacco industry is socialistic, then Napoleon and Metternich must be numbered among the founders of socialism. If the Belgian state, for quite ordinary political and financial reasons, itself constructed its chief railway lines; if Bismarck, not under any economic compulsion, took over for the state the chief Prussian lines, simply to be the better able to have them in hand in case of war, to bring up the railway employees as voting cattle for the government, and especially to create for himself a new source of income independent of parliamentary votes—this was, in no sense, a socialistic measure, directly or indirectly, consciously or unconsciously. Otherwise, the Royal Maritime Company, the Royal porcelain manufacture, and even the regimental tailor of the army would also be socialistic institutions, or even, as seriously proposed by a sly dog in Frederick William III's reign, the taking over by the state of the brothels.

This necessity of conversion into state property is felt first in the great institutions for intercourse and communication—the post-office, the telegraphs, the railways.

If the crises demonstrate the incapacity of the bourgeoisie for managing any longer modern productive forces, the transformation of the great establishments for production and distribution into joint-stock companies, trusts and state property, show how unnecessary the bourgeoisie are for that purpose. All the social functions of the capitalist are now performed by salaried employees. The capitalist has no further social function than that of pocketing dividends, tearing off coupons, and gambling on the Stock Exchange, where the different capitalists despoil one another of their capital. At first the capitalistic mode of production forces out the workers. Now it forces out the capitalists, and reduces them, just as it reduced the workers, to the ranks of the surplus population, although not immediately into those of the industrial reserve army.

But the transformation, either into joint-stock companies and trusts, or into state ownership, does not do away with the capitalistic nature of the productive forces. In the joint-stock companies and trusts this is obvious. And the modern state again, is only the organization that bourgeois society takes on in order to support the external conditions of the capitalist mode of production against the encroachments, as well of the workers as of individual capitalists. The modern state, no matter what its form, is essentially a capitalist machine, the state of the capitalists, the ideal personification of the total national capital. The more it proceeds to the taking over of productive forces, the more does it actually become the national capitalist, the more citizens does it exploit. The workers remain wage workers—proletarians. The capitalist relation is not done away with. It is rather brought to a head. But, brought to a head, it topples over. State ownership of the productive forces is not the solution of the conflict, but concealed within it are the technical conditions that form the elements of that solution.

This solution can only consist in the practical recognition of the social nature of the modern forces of production, and therefore in the harmonizing of the modes of production, appropriation and exchange with the socialized character of the means of production. And this can only come about by society openly and directly taking possession of the productive forces which have outgrown all control except that of society as a whole. The social character of the means of production and of the products today reacts against the producers, periodically disrupts all production and exchange, acts only like a law of nature working blindly, forcibly, destructively. But with the taking over by society of the productive forces, the social character of the means of production and of the products will be utilized by the producers with a perfect understanding of its nature, and instead of being a source of disturbance and periodical collapse, will become the most powerful lever of production itself.

Active social forces work exactly like natural forces; blindly, forcibly, destructively, so long as we do not understand and reckon with them. But when once we understand them, when once we grasp their action, their direction, their effects, it depends only upon ourselves to subject them more and more to our own will, and by means of them to reach our own ends. And this holds quite especially of the mighty productive forces of today. As long as we obstinately refuse to understand the nature of the character of these social means of action—and this understanding goes against the grain of the capitalist mode of production and its defenders—so long these forces are at work in spite of us, in opposition to us, so long they master us, as we have shown above in detail.

But when once their nature is understood, they can, in the hands of the producers working together, be transformed from master demons into willing servants. The difference is as that between the destructive force of electricity in the lightning of the storm, and electricity under command in the telegraph and the voltaic arc; the difference between a conflagration, and fire working in the service of man. With this recognition at last of the real nature of the productive forces of today, the social anarchy of production gives place to a social regulation of production upon a definite plan, according to the needs of the community and of each individual. Then the capitalist mode of appropriation, in which the product enslaves first the producer and then the appropriator, is replaced by the mode of appropriation of the products that is based upon the nature of the modern means of production; upon the one hand, direct social appropriation, as means to the maintenance and extension of production—on the other, direct individual appropriation, as means of subsistence and of enjoyment.

Whilst the capitalist mode of production more and more completely transforms the great majority of the population into proletarians, it creates the power which, under penalty of its own destruction, is forced to accomplish this revolution. Whilst it forces on more and more the transformation of the vast means of production, already socialized, into state property, it shows itself the way to accomplishing this revolution. *The proletariat seizes political power and turns the means of production into state property.*

But, in doing this, it abolishes itself as proletariat, abolishes all class distinctions and class antagonisms, abolishes also the state as state. Society thus far, based upon class antagonisms, had need of the state. That is, of an organization of the particular class which was *pro tempore* the exploiting class, an organization for the purpose of preventing any interference from without with the existing conditions of production, and therefore, especially, for the purpose of forcibly keeping the exploited classes in the condition of oppression corresponding with the given mode of production (slavery, serfdom, wage labor). The state was the official representative of society as a whole; the gathering of it together into a visible embodiment. But it was this only in so far as it was the state of that class which itself represented, for the time being, society as a whole; in ancient times, the state of slave-owning citizens; in the Middle Ages, the feudal lords; in our own time, the bourgeoisie. When at last it becomes the real representative of the whole of society, it renders itself unnecessary. As soon as there is no longer any social class to be held in subjection; as soon as class rule and the individual struggle for existence based upon our present anarchy in production, with the collisions and excesses arising from these, are removed, nothing more remains to be repressed, and a special repressive force, a state, is no longer necessary. The first act by virtue of which the state really constitutes itself the representative of the whole of society—the taking possession of the means of production in the name of society—this is, at the same time, its last independent act as a state. State interference in social relations becomes, in one domain after another, superfluous, and then dies out of itself; the government of persons is replaced by the administration of things, and by the conduct of processes of production. The state is not "abolished." *It dies out.** This gives the measure of the value of the phrase "a free state," both as to its justifiable use at times by agitators, and as to its ultimate scientific insufficiency; and also of the demands of the so-called anarchists for the abolition of the state out of hand.

Since the historical appearance of the capitalist mode of production, the appropriation by society of all the means of production has often been dreamed of, more or less vaguely, by individuals, as well as by sects, as the ideal of the future. But it could become possible, could become a historical necessity, only when the actual conditions for its realization were there. Like every other social advance, it becomes practicable, not by men understanding that the existence of classes is in contradiction to justice, equality, etc., not by the mere willingness to abolish these classes, but by virtue of certain new economic conditions. The separation of society into an exploiting and an exploited class, a ruling and an oppressed class, was the necessary consequence of the deficient and restricted development of production in former times. So long as the total social labor only yields a produce which but slightly exceeds that barely necessary for the existence of all; so long, therefore, as labor engages all or almost all the time of the great majority of the members of society—so long, of necessity, this society is divided into classes. Side by side with the great majority, exclusively bond slaves to labor, arises a class freed from directly productive labor, which looks after the general affairs of society, the direction of labor, state business, law, science, art, etc. It is, therefore, the law of division of labor that lies at the basis of the division into classes. But this does not prevent this division into classes from being carried out by means of violence and robbery, trickery and fraud. It does not prevent the ruling class, once having the upper hand, from consolidating its power at the expense of the working class, from turning their social leadership into an intensified exploitation of the masses.

But if, upon this showing, division into classes has a certain historical justification, it has this only for a given period, only under given social conditions. It was based upon the insufficiency of production. It will be swept away by the complete development of modern productive forces. And, in fact, the abolition of classes in society presupposes a degree of historical evolution, at which the existence, not simply of this or that particular ruling class, but of any ruling class at all, and, therefore, the existence of class distinction itself has become an obsolete anachronism. It presupposes, therefore, the development of production carried out to a degree at which appropriation of the means of production and of the products, and, with this, of political domination, of the monopoly of culture, and of intellectual leadership by a particular class of society, has become not only superfluous, but economically, politically, intellectually a hindrance to development.

Editor's note: This key sentence, later to become the source of much controversy, has also been translated thus: *"It withers away."*

This point is now reached. Their political and intellectual bankruptcy is scarcely any longer a secret to the bourgeoisie themselves. Their economic bankruptcy recurs regularly every ten years. In every crisis, society is suffocated beneath the weight of its own productive forces and products, which it cannot use, and stands helpless, face to face with the absurd contradiction that the producers have nothing to consume, because consumers are wanting. The expansive force of the means of production bursts the bonds that the capitalist mode of production had imposed upon them. Their deliverance from these bonds is the one precondition for an unbroken, constantly accelerated development of the productive forces, and therewith for a practically unlimited increase of production itself. Nor is this all. The socialized appropriation of the means of production does away not only with the present artificial restrictions upon production, but also with the positive waste and devastation of productive forces and products that are at the present time the inevitable concomitants of production, and that reach their height in the crises. Further, it sets free for the community at large a mass of means of production and of products, by doing away with the senseless extravagance of the ruling classes of today, and their political representatives. The possibility of securing for every member of society, by means of socialized production, an existence not only fully sufficient materially, and becoming day by day more full, but an existence guaranteeing to all the free development and exercise of their physical and mental faculties—this possibility is now for the first time here, but *it is here.*

With the seizing of the means of production by society, production of commodities is done away with, and, simultaneously, the mastery of the product over the producer. Anarchy in social production is replaced by systematic definite organization. The struggle for individual existence disappears. Then for the first time, man, in a certain sense, is finally marked off from the rest of the animal kingdom, and emerges from mere animal conditions of existence into really human ones. The whole sphere of the conditions of life which environ man, and which have hitherto ruled man, now comes under the dominion and control of man, who for the first time becomes the real, conscious lord of nature, because he has now become master of his own social organization. The laws of his own social action, hitherto standing face to face with man as laws of nature foreign to and dominating him, will then be used with full understanding, and so mastered by him. Man's own social organization, hitherto confronting him as a necessity imposed by nature and history, now becomes the result of his own free action. The extraneous objective forces that have hitherto governed history pass under the control of himself. Only from that time will man himself, more and more consciously, make his own history—only from that time will the social causes set in movement by him have, in the main and in a constantly growing measure, the results intended by him. It is the ascent of man from the kingdom of necessity to the kingdom of freedom.

Let us briefly sum up our sketch of historical evolution.

I Medieval Society   Individual production on a small scale. Means of production adapted for individual use; hence primitive, ungainly, petty, dwarfed in action. Production for immediate consumption, either of the producer himself or of his feudal lords. Only where an excess of production over this consumption occurs is such excess offered for sale, enters into exchange. Production of commodities therefore, is only in its infancy. But already it contains within itself, in embryo, *anarchy in the production of society at large.*

II Capitalist Revolution Transformation of industry, at first by means of simple co-operation and manufacture. Concentration of the means of production, hitherto scattered, into great workshops. As a consequence, their transformation from individual to social means of production—a transformation which does not, on the whole, affect the form of exchange. The old forms of appropriation remain in force. The capitalist appears. In his capacity as owner of the means of production, he also appropriates the products and turns them into commodities. Production has become a *social* act. Exchange and appropriation continue to be *individual* acts, the acts of individuals. *The social product is appropriated by the individual capitalist.* Fundamental contradiction, whence arise all the contradictions in which our present day society moves, and which modern industry brings to light.

A. Severance of the producer from the means of production. Condemnation of the worker to wage labor for life. *Antagonism between the proletariat and the bourgeoisie.*

B. Growing predominance and increasing effectiveness of the laws governing the production of commodities. Unbridled competition. *Contradiction between socialized organization in the individual factory and social anarchy in production as a whole.*

C. On the one hand, perfecting of machinery, made by competition compulsory for each individual manufacturer, and complemented by a constantly growing displacement of laborers. *Industrial reserve army.* On the other hand, unlimited extension of production, also compulsory under competition, for every manufacturer. On both sides, unheard of development of productive forces, excess of supply over demand, overproduction, glutting of the markets, crises every ten years, the vicious circle: excess here, of means of production and products—excess there, of laborers, without employment and without means of existence. But these two levers of production and of social well-being are unable to work together because the capitalist form of production prevents the productive forces from working and the products from circulating, unless they are first turned into capital—which their very superabundance prevents. The contradiction has grown into an absurdity. *The mode of production rises in rebellion against the form of exchange.* The bourgeoisie are convicted of incapacity further to manage their own social productive forces.

D. Partial recognition of the social character of the productive forces forced upon the capitalists themselves. Taking over of the great institutions for production and communication, first by joint-stock companies, later on by trusts, then by the state. The bourgeoisie demonstrated to be a superfluous class. All its social functions are now performed by salaried employees.

III Proletarian Revolution Solution of the contradictions. The proletariat seizes the public power, and by means of this transforms the socialized means of production, slipping from the hands of the bourgeoisie, into public property. By this act, the proletariat frees the means of production from the character of capital they have thus far borne, and gives their socialized character complete freedom to work itself out. Socialized production upon a predetermined plan becomes henceforth possible. The development of production makes the existence of different classes of society thenceforth an anachronism. In proportion as anarchy in social production vanishes, the political authority of the state dies out. Man, at last the master of his own form of social organization, becomes at the same time the lord over nature, his own master—free.

To accomplish this act of universal emancipation is the historical mission of the modern proletariat. To thoroughly comprehend the historical conditions and thus the very nature of this act, to impart to the now oppressed proletarian class a full knowledge of the conditions and of the meaning of the momentous act it is called upon to accomplish, this is the task of the theoretical expression of the proletarian movement, scientific socialism.

5

IMPERIALISM

Communist theory views world history as a series of dialectical stages, of which the period of capitalist domination is but one. Marxists had (and have) no doubt that capitalism would eventually collapse, and be superseded. But when? And where? Two large theoretical questions were left unanswered at Marx's death: How, *concretely,* would the excesses of capitalism lead to its demise? And, since the industrial capitalism of which Marx had written was largely a European and North American phenomenon, how explain its replacement by a new *global* order?

Marx's intellectual heirs—especially V. I. Lenin in Russia—set themselves to answer these questions. The key to these answers, Lenin argued, lay in understanding the stages of capitalism itself, its growth and its inevitable expansion over the face of the entire planet. The internal dynamic of the capitalist system requires that it grow unceasingly; it is internally compelled always to find more markets for its goods, new proletarians for its rapacious exploitation. Imperialism, driven by these inexorable capitalist appetites, was well-advanced by the late nineteenth century, and would (they held) reach its apogee in the early decades of the twentieth century. The entire surface of the globe had finally been marked off, on Lenin's account, by the major capitalist regimes: Great Britain, France, Germany, The United States. Among these capitalist giants there could be no harmonious division of the spoils when their economic interests collided, as inevitably they must. Economic conflict would bring global chaos, and global war. This was the Marxist explanation Lenin gave of the cause of the First World War, whose tumult led, in part, to the success of the communist revolution in Russia in 1917.

Imperialism was the key to the accounts given also by later communist leaders of their roles in the dialectic of history. Josef Stalin, Lenin's successor as the leader of Soviet communism, and Mao Tse-tung, Lenin's younger contemporary who led the successful communist revolution in China, repeatedly used allegations of imperialism to justify their own policies, and to explain the inevitable conflict between what they believed to be the reactionary forces of international capitalism, and the progressive forces of revolutionary communism guided by the theories of Marx and Lenin. Imperialism would take many forms, they insisted, and even when the formalities of imperial rule were largely ended after the Second World War, the reality of capitalist control and exploitation of "the third world" would continue through the insidious devices of neo-colonialism, until the capitalist order was finally overthrown.

17
Josef Stalin*

Josef Stalin (1879–1953) became the leader of the Communist Party, and the autocratic ruler of the Soviet Union, upon Lenin's death in 1924. Shortly thereafter he gave a series of lectures—published in book form as *The Foundations of Leninism*—aiming to explain Lenin's interpretation and application of Marx's theories. Stalin's absolute power in the Soviet Union for nearly thirty years gave his theoretical views supreme authority there; here follows his account of how Marxism-Leninism is to be understood.

[WHAT IS LENINISM?]†

And so, what is Leninism?

Some say that Leninism is the application of Marxism to the peculiar conditions of the situation in Russia. This definition contains a particle of truth, but not the whole truth by any means. Lenin, indeed, applied Marxism to Russian conditions, and applied it in a masterly way. But if Leninism were only the application of Marxism to the peculiar situation in Russia it would be a purely national and only a national, a purely Russian and only a Russian phenomenon. We know, however, that Leninism is not merely a Russian, but an international phenomenon rooted in the whole of international development. That is why I think this definition suffers from onesidedness.

Others say that Leninism is the revival of the revolutionary elements of Marxism of the forties of the nineteenth century, as distinct from the Marxism of subsequent years, when, it is alleged, it became moderate, non-revolutionary. If we disregard this foolish and vulgar division of the teachings of Marx into two parts, revolutionary and moderate, we must admit that even this totally inadequate and unsatisfactory definition contains a particle of truth. That particle of truth is that Lenin did indeed restore the revolutionary content of Marxism, which had been immured by the opportunists of the Second International. Still, that is but a particle of the truth. The whole truth about Leninism is that Leninism not only restored Marxism, but also took a step forward, developing Marxism further under the new conditions of capitalism and of the class struggle of the proletariat.

What, then, in the last analysis, is Leninism?

Leninism is Marxism of the era of imperialism and of the proletarian revolution. To be more exact, Leninism is the theory and tactics of the proletarian revolution in general, the theory and tactics of the dictatorship of the proletariat in particular. Marx and Engels pursued their activities in the pre-revolutionary period (we have the proletarian revolution in mind), when developed imperialism did not

*Stalin's original name was Iosif Viassarionovich Dzhugashvili.
†From J. Stalin's *The Foundations of Leninism,* 1924. Reprinted by permission of the Foreign Languages Publishing House, Moscow.

yet exist, in the period of the proletarians' preparation for a revolution, in the period when the proletarian revolution was not yet a direct, practical inevitability. Lenin, however, the disciple of Marx and Engels, pursued his activities in the period of developed imperialism, in the period of the unfolding proletarian revolution, when the proletarian revolution had already triumphed in one country, had smashed bourgeois democracy and had ushered in the era of proletarian democracy, the era of the Soviets.

That is why Leninism is the further development of Marxism.

18
V. I. Lenin

Imperialism, The Highest Stage of Capitalism, one of Lenin's most important contributions to communist theory, was completed in Switzerland in 1916, where Lenin was in exile. The First World War was in progress; it had been caused, he believed, by the life-and-death struggles of capitalist economies against one another. Free competition had been transformed into international super-monopolies; the export of goods had been transformed into the export of capital. But with the imperialistic division of the world by the capitalists completed, it was no longer possible for capitalism to grow, and without growth it could not survive. The end of the road had been reached. Imperialism may therefore be understood as the final stage in the history of the capitalist epoch, culminating in a colossal bloodbath that would open the path to a new economic order.

CONCENTRATION OF PRODUCTION AND MONOPOLIES*

Fifty years ago, when Marx was writing *Capital,* free competition appeared to most economists to be a "natural law." Official science tried, by a conspiracy of silence, to kill the works of Marx, which by a theoretical and historical analysis of capitalism showed that free competition gives rise to the concentration of production, which, in turn, at a certain stage of development, leads to monopoly. Today, monopoly has become a fact. The economists are writing mountains of books in which they describe the diverse manifestations of monopoly, and continue to declare in chorus that "Marxism is refuted." But facts are stubborn things, as the English proverb says, and they have to be reckoned with, whether we like it or not. The facts show that differences between capitalist countries, e.g., in the manner of protection or free trade, only give rise to insignificant variations in the form of monopolies or in the moment of their appearance; and that the rise of monopolies,

*This and the following passages are from V. I. Lenin, *Imperialism: The Highest Stage of Capitalism,* 1916. Reprinted by permission of the Foreign Languages Publishing House, Moscow.

as the result of the concentration of production, is a general and fundamental law of the present stage of development of capitalism.

For Europe, the time when the new capitalism *definitely* superseded the old can be established with fair precision: it was the beginning of the twentieth century. . . .

Thus, the principal stages in the history of monopolies are the following: (1) 1860–70, the highest stage, the apex of development of free competition; monopoly is in the barely discernible embryonic stage. (2) After the crisis of 1873, a wide zone of development of cartels; but they are still the exception. They are not yet durable. They are still a transitory phenomenon. (3) The boom at the end of the nineteenth century and the crisis of 1900–03. Cartels become one of the foundations of the whole of economic life. Capitalism has been transformed into imperialism.

Cartels come to an agreement on the conditions of sale, terms of payment, etc. They divide the markets among themselves. They fix the quantity of goods to be produced. They fix prices. They divide the profits among the various enterprises, etc. . . .

Competition becomes transformed into monopoly. The result is immense progress in the socialization of production. In particular, the process of technical invention and improvement becomes socialized.

This is no longer the old type of free competition between manufacturers, scattered and out of touch with one another, and producing for an unknown market. Concentration has reached the point at which it is possible to make an approximate estimate of all sources of raw materials (for example, the iron ore deposits) of a country and even, as we shall see, of several countries, or of the whole world. Not only are such estimates made, but these sources are captured by gigantic monopolist combines. An approximate estimate of the capacity of markets is also made, and the combines divide them up amongst themselves by agreement. Skilled labor is monopolized, the best engineers are engaged; the means of transport are captured; railways in America, shipping companies in Europe and America. Capitalism in its imperialist stage arrives at the threshold of the most complete socialization of production. In spite of themselves, the capitalists are dragged, as it were, into a new social order, a transitional social order from complete free competition to complete socialization.

Production becomes social, but appropriation remains private. The social means of production remain the private property of a few. The general framework of formally recognized free competition remains, but the yoke of a few monopolists on the rest of the population becomes a hundred times heavier, more burdensome and intolerable. . . .

Translated into ordinary human language this means that the development of capitalism has arrived at a stage when, although commodity production still "reigns" and continues to be regarded as the basis of economic life, it has in reality been undermined and the big profits go to the "geniuses" of financial manipulation. At the basis of these swindles and manipulations lies socialized production; but the immense progress of humanity, which achieved this socialization, goes to benefit the speculators. We shall see later how "on these grounds" reactionary, petty-bourgeois critics of capitalist imperialism dream of going *back* to "free," "peaceful" and "honest" competition. . . .

The statement that cartels can abolish crises is a fable spread by bourgeois economists who at all costs desire to place capitalism in a favorable light. On the contrary, when monopoly appears in *certain* branches of industry, it increases and intensifies the anarchy inherent in capitalist production *as a whole*. The disparity between the development of agriculture and that of industry, which is characteristic of capitalism, is increased. The privileged position of the most highly cartelized industry, so-called *heavy* industry, especially coal and iron, causes "a still greater lack of concerted organization" in other branches of production—as Jeidels, the author of one of the best works on the relationship of the German big banks to industry, puts it.*

"The more developed an economic system is," writes Liefmann, one of the most unblushing apologists of capitalism, "the more it resorts to risky enterprises, or enterprises abroad, to those which need a great deal of time to develop, or finally, to those which are only of local importance."[†]

The increased risk is connected in the long run with the prodigious increase of capital, which overflows the brim, as it were, flows abroad, etc. At the same time the extremely rapid rate of technical progress gives rise more and more to disturbances in the co-ordination between the various spheres of national economy, to anarchy and crisis. . . .

Crises of every kind—economic crises more frequently, but not only these—in their turn increase very considerably the tendency towards concentration and monopoly. . . .

Monopoly! This is the last word in the "latest phase of capitalist development." But we shall only have a very insufficient, incomplete, and poor notion of the real power and the significance of modern monopolies if we do not take into consideration the part played by the banks.

THE EXPORT OF CAPITAL

Under the old capitalism, when free competition prevailed, the export of *goods* was the most typical feature. Under modern capitalism, when monopolies prevail, the export of *capital* has become the typical feature.

Capitalism is commodity production at the highest stage of development, when labor power itself becomes a commodity. The growth of internal exchange, and particularly of international exchange, is the characteristic distinguishing feature of capitalism. The uneven and spasmodic character of the development of individual enterprises, of individual branches of industry and individual countries, is inevitable under the capitalist system. England became a capitalist country before any other, and in the middle of the nineteenth century, having adopted free trade,

---

*Otto Jeidels, *The Relationship of the German Big Banks to Industry,* Leipzig, 1905, p. 271.
[†]Robert Liefmann, *Holding and Finance Companies,* p. 434.

claimed to be the "workshop of the world," the great purveyor of manufactured goods to all countries, which in exchange were to keep her supplied with raw materials. But in the last quarter of the nineteenth century, *this* monopoly was already undermined. Other countries, protecting themselves by tariff walls, had developed into independent capitalist states. On the threshold of the twentieth century, we see a new type of monopoly coming into existence. Firstly, there are monopolist capitalist combines in all advanced capitalist countries; secondly, a few rich countries, in which the accumulation of capital reaches gigantic proportions, occupy a monopolist position. An enormous "superabundance of capital" has accumulated in the advanced countries.

It goes without saying that if capitalism could develop agriculture, which today lags far behind industry everywhere, if it could raise the standard of living of the masses, who are everywhere still poverty-stricken and underfed, in spite of the amazing advance in technical knowledge, there could be no talk of a superabundance of capital. This "argument" the petty-bourgeois critics of capitalism advance on every occasion. But if capitalism did these things it would not be capitalism; for uneven development and wretched conditions of the masses are fundamental and inevitable conditions and premises of this mode of production. As long as capitalism remains what it is, surplus capital will never be utilized for the purpose of raising the standard of living of the masses in a given country, for this would mean a decline in profits for the capitalists; it will be used for the purpose of increasing those profits by exporting capital abroad to the backward countries. In these backward countries profits are usually high, for capital is scarce, the price of land is relatively low, wages are low, raw materials are cheap. The possibility of exporting capital is created by the fact that numerous backward countries have been drawn into international capitalist intercourse; main railways have either been built or are being built there; the elementary conditions for industrial development have been created, etc. The necessity for exporting capital arises from the fact that in a few countries capitalism has become "over-ripe" and (owing to the backward state of agriculture and the impoverished state of the masses) capital cannot find "profitable" investment. . . .

The export of capital greatly affects and accelerates the development of capitalism in those countries to which it is exported. While, therefore, the export of capital may tend to a certain extent to arrest development in the countries exporting capital, it can only do so by expanding and deepening the further development of capitalism throughout the world.

The countries which export capital are nearly always able to obtain "advantages."

. . .

Finance capital has created the epoch of monopolies, and monopolies introduce everywhere monopolist methods: the utilization of "connections" for profitable transactions takes the place of competition on the open market. The most usual thing is to stipulate that part of the loan that is granted shall be spent on purchases in the country of issue, particularly on orders for war materials, or for ships, etc. . . .

Thus, finance capital, almost literally, one might say, spreads its net over all countries of the world. . . .

The capital exporting countries have divided the world among themselves in the figurative sense of the term. But finance capital has also led to the *actual* division of the world.

THE DIVISION OF THE WORLD AMONG CAPITALIST COMBINES

Monopolist capitalist combines—cartels, syndicates, trusts—divide among themselves, first of all, the whole internal market of a country, and impose their control, more or less completely, upon the industry of that country. But under capitalism the home market is inevitably bound up with the foreign market. Capitalism long ago created a world market. As the export of capital increased, and as the foreign and colonial relations and the "spheres of influence" of the big monopolist combines expanded, things "naturally" gravitated towards an international agreement among these combines, and towards the formation of international cartels.

This is a new stage of world concentration of capital and production, incomparably higher than the preceding stages. Let us see how this super-monopoly develops. . . .

Certain bourgeois writers (with whom K. Kautsky, who has completely abandoned the Marxist position he held, for example, in 1909, has now associated himself) express the opinion that international cartels are the most striking expressions of the internationalization of capital, and, therefore, give the hope of peace among nations under capitalism. Theoretically, this opinion is absurd, while in practice it is sophistry and a dishonest defense of the worst opportunism. International cartels show to what point capitalist monopolies have developed, and they *reveal the object* of the struggle between the various capitalist groups. This last circumstance is the most important; it alone shows us the historico-economic significance of events; for the *forms* of the struggle may and do constantly change in accordance with varying, relatively particular, and temporary causes, but the *essence* of the struggle, its class *content, cannot* change while classes exist. . . . The capitalists divide the world, not out of any particular malice, but because the degree of concentration which has been reached forces them to adopt this method in order to get profits. And they divide it in proportion to "capital," in proportion to "strength," because there cannot be any other system of division under commodity production and capitalism. But strength varies with the degree of economic and political development. In order to understand what takes place, it is necessary to know what questions are settled by this change of forces. The question as to whether these changes are "purely" economic or *non*-economic (e.g., military) is a secondary one, which does not in the least affect the fundamental view on the latest epoch of capitalism. To substitute for the question of the *content* of the struggle and agreements between capitalist combines the question of the *form* of these struggles and agreements (today peaceful, tomorrow war-like, the next day war-like again) is to sink to the role of a sophist.

The epoch of modern capitalism shows us that certain relations are established between capitalist alliances, *based* on the economic division of the world; while parallel with this fact and in connection with it, certain relations are established between political alliances, between states, on the basis of the territorial division of the world, of the struggle for colonies, of the "struggle for economic territory."

.   .   .

IMPERIALISM AS A SPECIAL STAGE OF CAPITALISM

We must now try to sum up and put together what has been said above on the subject of imperialism. Imperialism emerged as the development and direct continuation of the fundamental attributes of capitalism in general. But capitalism only became capitalist imperialism at a definite and very high stage of its development, when certain of its fundamental attributes began to be transformed into their opposites, when the features of a period of transition from capitalism to a higher social and economic system began to take shape and reveal themselves all along the line. Economically, the main thing in this process is the substitution of capitalist monopolies for capitalist free competition. Free competition is the fundamental attribute of capitalism, and of commodity production generally. Monopoly is exactly the opposite of free competition; but we have seen the latter being transformed into monopoly before our very eyes, creating large-scale industry and eliminating small industry, replacing large-scale industry by still larger-scale industry, finally leading to such a concentration of production and capital that monopoly has been and is the result: cartels, syndicates and trusts, and merging with them, the capital of a dozen or so banks manipulating thousands of millions. At the same time monopoly, which has grown out of free competition, does not abolish the latter, but exists over it and alongside of it, and thereby gives rise to a number of very acute, intense antagonisms, friction and conflicts. Monopoly is the transition from capitalism to a higher system.

If it were necessary to give the briefest possible definition of imperialism we should have to say that imperialism is the monopoly stage of capitalism. Such a definition would include what is most important, for, on the one hand, finance capital is the bank capital of a few big monopolist banks, merged with the capital of the monopolist combines of manufacturers; and, on the other hand, the division of the world is the transition from a colonial policy which has extended without hindrance to territories unoccupied by any capitalist power, to a colonial policy of monopolistic possession of the territory of the world which has been completely divided up.

But very brief definitions, although convenient, for they sum up the main points, are nevertheless inadequate, because very important features of the phenomenon that has to be defined have to be specially deduced. And so, without forgetting the conditional and relative value of all definitions, which can never include all the concatenations of a phenomenon in its complete development, we must give a definition of imperialism that will embrace the following five essential features:

1 The concentration of production and capital developed to such a high stage that it created monopolies which play a decisive role in economic life.

2 The merging of bank capital with industrial capital, and the creation, on the basis of this "finance capital," of a "financial oligarchy."

3 The export of capital, which has become extremely important, as distinguished from the export of commodities.

4 The formation of international capitalist monopolies which share the world among themselves.

5 The territorial division of the whole world among the greatest capitalist powers is completed.

Imperialism is capitalism in that stage of development in which the dominance of monopolies and finance capital has established itself; in which the export of capital has acquired pronounced importance; in which the division of the world among the international trusts has begun; in which the division of all territories of the globe among the great capitalist powers has been completed.

We shall see later that imperialism can and must be defined differently if consideration is to be given, not only to the basic, purely economic factors—to which the above definition is limited—but also to the historical place of this stage of capitalism in relation to capitalism in general, or to the relations between imperialism and the two main trends in the working class movement. The point to be noted just now is that imperialism, as interpreted above, undoubtedly represents a special stage in the development of capitalism. In order to enable the reader to obtain as well grounded an idea of imperialism as possible, we deliberately quoted largely from *bourgeois* economists who are obliged to admit the particularly incontrovertible facts regarding modern capitalist economy. With the same object in view, we have produced detailed statistics which reveal the extent to which bank capital, etc., has developed, showing how the transformation of quantity into quality, of developed capitalism into imperialism, has expressed itself. Needless to say, all boundaries in nature and in society are conditional and changeable, and, consequently, it would be absurd to discuss the exact year or the decade in which imperialism "definitely" became established.

. . .

THE PLACE OF IMPERIALISM IN HISTORY

We have seen that the economic quintessence of imperialism is monopoly capitalism. This very fact determines its place in history, for monopoly that grew up on the basis of free competition, and precisely out of free competition, is the transition from the capitalist system to a higher social-economic order. We must take special note of the four principal forms of monopoly, or the four principal manifestations of monopoly capitalism, which are characteristic of the epoch under review.

Firstly, monopoly arose out of the concentration of production at a very advanced stage of development. This refers to the monopolist capitalist combines, cartels, syndicates and trusts. We have seen the important part that these play in modern economic life. At the beginning of the twentieth century, monopolies acquired complete supremacy in the advanced countries. And although the first steps towards the formation of the cartels were first taken by countries enjoying the protection of high tariffs (Germany, America), Great Britain, with her system of free trade, was not far behind in revealing the same basic phenomenon, namely, the birth of monopoly out of the concentration of production.

Secondly, monopolies have accelerated the capture of the most important sources of raw materials, especially for the coal and iron industries, which are the basic and most highly cartelized industries in capitalist society. The monopoly of the most important sources of raw materials has enormously increased the power of big capital, and has sharpened the antagonism between cartelized and non-cartelized industry.

Thirdly, monopoly has sprung from the banks. The banks have developed from modest intermediary enterprises into the monopolists of finance capital. Some three or five of the biggest banks in each of the foremost capitalist countries have achieved the "personal union" of industrial and bank capital, and have concentrated in their hands the disposal of thousands upon thousands of millions which form the greater part of the capital and income of entire countries. A financial oligarchy, which throws a close net of relations of dependence over all the economic and political institutions of contemporary bourgeois society without exception—such is the most striking manifestation of this monopoly.

Fourthly, monopoly has grown out of colonial policy. To the numerous "old" motives of colonial policy, finance capital has added the struggle for the sources of raw materials, for the export of capital, for "spheres of influence," i.e., for spheres for profitable deals, concessions, monopolist profits and so on; in fine, for economic territory in general. . . .

The extent to which monopolist capital has intensified all the contradictions of capitalism is generally known. It is sufficient to mention the high cost of living and the oppression of the cartels. This intensification of contradictions constitutes the most powerful driving force of the transitional period of history, which began from the time of the definite victory of world finance capital.

Monopolies, oligarchy, the striving for domination instead of the striving for liberty, the exploitation of an increasing number of small or weak nations by an extremely small group of the richest or most powerful nations—all these have given birth to those distinctive characteristics of imperialism which compel us to define it as parasitic or decaying capitalism. More and more prominently there emerges, as one of the tendencies of imperialism, the creation of the "bondholding" (rentier) state, the usurer state, in which the bourgeoisie lives on the proceeds of capital exports and by "clipping coupons." It would be a mistake to believe that this tendency to decay precludes the possibility of the rapid growth of capitalism. It does not. In the epoch of imperialism, certain branches of industry, certain strata of the bourgeoisie and certain countries betray, to a more or less degree, one or other of these tendencies. On the whole, capitalism is growing far more rapidly than before. But this growth is not only becoming more and more uneven in general; its unevenness also manifests itself, in particular, in the decay of the countries which are richest in capital.

. . .

From all that has been said in this book on the economic nature of imperialism, it follows that we must define it as capitalism in transition, or, more precisely, as moribund capitalism. It is very instructive in this respect to note that the bourgeois economists, in describing modern capitalism, frequently employ terms like "interlocking," "absence of isolation," etc.; "in conformity with their functions and course of development," banks are "not purely private business enterprises; they are more and more outgrowing the sphere of purely private business regulation." And this very Riesser, who uttered the words just quoted, declares with all seriousness that the "prophecy" of the Marxists concerning "socialization" has "not come true"!

What then does this word "interlocking" express? It merely expresses the most striking feature of the process going on before our eyes. It shows that the observer counts the separate trees, but cannot see the wood. It slavishly copies the superficial, the fortuitous, the chaotic. It reveals the observer as one who is overwhelmed by the mass of raw material and is utterly incapable of appreciating its meaning and importance. Ownership of shares and relations between owners of private property "interlock in a haphazard way." But the underlying factor of this interlocking, its very base, is the changing social relations of production. When a big enterprise assumes gigantic proportions, and, on the basis of exact computation of mass data, organizes according to plan the supply of primary raw materials to the extent of two-thirds, or three-fourths of all that is necessary for tens of millions of people; when the raw materials are transported to the most suitable place of production, sometimes hundreds or thousands of miles away, in a systematic and organized manner; when a single center directs all the successive stages of work right up to the manufacture of numerous varieties of finished articles; when these products are distributed according to a single plan among tens and hundreds of millions of consumers (as in the case of the distribution of oil in America and Germany by the American "oil trust")—then it becomes evident that we have socialization of production, and not mere "interlocking"; that private economic relations and private property relations constitute a shell which is no longer suitable for its contents, a shell which must inevitably begin to decay if its destruction be delayed by artificial means; a shell which may continue in a state of decay for a fairly long period (particularly if the cure of the opportunist abscess is protracted), but which will inevitably be removed.

19
Mao Tse-tung

Mao Tse-tung (1893–1976) was one of the twelve founders of the Communist Party of China in 1921. The son of a peasant, he organized and led a communist guerrilla army in China for a quarter of a century, a struggle culminated by the success of the Chinese communist revolution in 1949. That year he wrote *On People's Democratic Dictatorship,* restating the Marxist foundations of the revolutionary regime he was to control. Until his death in 1976 Mao remained Chairman of the Communist Party of China and the unquestioned leader of his country, "Supreme Commander of the Whole Nation and the Whole Army." In China today he is still viewed by many as the symbol of a glorious national rebirth—and he is despised by many as the architect of an oppressive totalitarian system. He remains the greatest figure of Chinese Marxism, a hero of the international communist movement, and for some a source of personal inspiration.

The exploiting imperialists are doomed, Mao thought, but their final eradication would require long and arduous labor. This could be accomplished only with rule that must sometimes be harsh. In *On People's Democratic Dictatorship* the imperialism of the first half of the twentieth century is seen through the lens of Mao's Chinese Marxism.

[WESTERN BOURGEOIS CIVILIZATION IS BANKRUPT]*

Our Party has already run a course of twenty-eight years. As we all know, the course has not been a peaceful one, but beset with difficulties. We have had to fight foreign and domestic enemies, as well as enemies inside and outside the Party. We are indebted to Marx, Engels, Lenin, and Stalin for our weapon. This weapon is not a machine gun, but Marxism-Leninism. . . .

It was through the Russians that the Chinese were introduced to Marxism. Before the October Revolution, the Chinese were not only unaware of Lenin and Stalin but did not even know of Marx or Engels. The salvos of the October Revolution awoke us to Marxism-Leninism. The October Revolution helped the progressives of China and of the whole world to adopt the proletarian world outlook as an instrument for foreseeing a nation's future and considering anew one's own problems. "Follow the path of the Russians" was the conclusion.

In 1919, the May Fourth Movement took place in China. In 1921, the Communist Party of China was founded. Sun Yat-sen, then in the depths of despair, encountered the October Revolution and the Chinese Communist Party. He welcomed the October Revolution, welcomed Russian aid to the Chinese, and welcomed the co-operation of the Chinese Communist Party.

Sun Yat-sen died and Chiang Kai-shek rose to power. In the course of the long period of twenty-two years, Chiang Kai-shek dragged China into helpless straits.

---

*From Mao Tse-tung, *On People's Democratic Dictatorship,* 1949. These passages are from an official translation, published by the Foreign Languages Press, Peking, as the revised fifth edition, 1952.

Within this period there occurred the anti-fascist Second World War, with the Soviet Union as its main force. This resulted in the downfall of three great imperialist powers and the weakening of two others. Only one great imperialist power came out unscathed, the United States. However, the domestic crisis in the United States is very grave; she wants to enslave the world, and by supplying Chiang Kai-shek with arms, has helped slaughter several million Chinese. Under the leadership of the Chinese Communist Party, the Chinese people, after driving out Japanese imperialism, have carried on the War of Liberation for three years and have basically gained victory.

That is how it happened that Western bourgeois civilization, bourgeois democracy, and the bourgeois pattern of republic all went bankrupt in the eyes of the Chinese people. Bourgeois democracy gives way to the people's democracy under the leadership of the working class, and the bourgeois republic gives way to the people's republic. This creates the possibility of passing through a people's republic to Socialism and Communism, to the disappearance of classes and the attainment of universal harmony. . . .

Internationally we belong to the side of the anti-imperialist front, headed by the Soviet Union. We can only turn to this side for genuine and friendly help, not to the side of the imperialist front.

Imperialism and All Reactionaries are Paper Tigers

Just as there is not a single thing in the world without a dual nature (this is the law of the unity of opposites), so imperialism and all reactionaries have a dual nature—they are real tigers and paper tigers at the same time. . . . On the one hand, they were real tigers; they devoured people, devoured people by the millions and tens of millions. The cause of the people's struggle went through a period of difficulties and hardships, and along the path there were many twists and turns. To destroy the rule of imperialism, feudalism and bureaucrat-capitalism in China took the Chinese people more than a hundred years and cost them tens of millions of lives before the victory in 1949. Look! Were these not living tigers, iron tigers, real tigers? But in the end they changed into paper tigers, dead tigers, bean-curd tigers. These are historical facts. Have people not seen or heard about these facts? There have indeed been thousands and tens of thousands of them! Thousands and tens of thousands! Hence, imperialism and all reactionaries, looked at in essence, from a long-term point of view, from a strategic point of view, must be seen for what they are—paper tigers. On this we should build our strategic thinking. On the other hand, they are also living tigers, iron tigers, real tigers which can devour people. On this we should build our tactical thinking.

> Speech at the Wuchang Meeting of the Political Bureau of the Central
> Committee of the Communist Party of China (December 1, 1958), quoted
> in the explanatory note to "Talk with the American Correspondent Anna
> Louise Strong," *Selected Works,* Vol. IV, pp. 98–99.

We must despise the enemy with respect to the whole, but we must take him seriously with respect to each and every concrete question. If we do not despise the enemy with respect to the whole, we shall be committing the error of opportunism. Marx and Engels were only two individuals, and yet in those early days they already declared that capitalism would be overthrown throughout the world. But in dealing with concrete problems and particular enemies we shall be committing the error of adventurism unless we take them seriously.

Speech at the Moscow Meeting of Communists
and Workers' Parties (November 18, 1957).

The Mass Line

The people, and the people alone, are the motive force in the making of world history.

"On Coalition Government" (April 24, 1945), *Selected Works,* Vol. III, p. 257.

20
Kwame Nkrumah

Kwame Nkrumah (1909–1972) was the first President of the Republic of Ghana and long an active leader of resurgent African nationalism and the movement for Pan-African unity. He studied politics and economics in England and the United States, and served as Prime Minister of the Gold Coast under British rule; his judgments of neo-colonialism arose from practical experience as well as theoretical reflections. Between the great powers and the minor powers, Nkrumah believed, relations are always those of economic exploitation, as Marx had argued long before. Old-fashioned colonialism, with its attendant humiliation and subordination, is eventually replaced, he argued, by "neo-colonialism"— economic exploitation that is less blatant but more insidious. Neo-colonialism corrupts not only the exploited, Nkrumah contended, but the exploiters as well. Lenin had predicted that capitalism would collapse when it passed through imperialism, its "highest stage." Nkrumah extended this account by describing neo-colonialism as "the last stage of imperialism."

NEO-COLONIALISM*

The neo-colonialism of today represents imperialism in its final and perhaps its most dangerous stage. In the past it was possible to convert a country upon which a neo-colonial regime had been imposed—Egypt in the nineteenth century is an example—into a colonial territory. Today this process is no longer feasible. Old-fashioned colonialism is by no means entirely abolished. It still constitutes an African problem, but it is everywhere on the retreat. Once a territory has become

*Reprinted from Kwame Nkrumah, *Neo-Colonialism: The Last Stage of Imperialism,* 1966, with permission of International Publishers, New York.

nominally independent it is no longer possible, as it was in the last century, to reverse the process. Existing colonies may linger on, but no new colonies will be created. In place of colonialism as the main instrument of imperialism we have today neo-colonialism.

The essence of neo-colonialism is that the State which is subject to it is, in theory, independent and has all the outward trappings of international sovereignty. In reality its economic system and thus its political policy is directed from outside.

The methods and form of this direction can take various shapes. For example, in an extreme case the troops of the imperial power may garrison the territory of the neo-colonial State and control the government of it. More often, however, neo-colonialist control is exercised through economic or monetary means. The neo-colonial State may be obliged to take the manufactured products of the imperialist power to the exclusion of competing products from elsewhere. Control over government policy in the neo-colonial State may be secured by payments towards the cost of running the State, by the provision of civil servants in positions where they can dictate policy, and by monetary control over foreign exchange through the imposition of a banking system controlled by the imperial power.

Where neo-colonialism exists the power exercising control is often the State which formerly ruled the territory in question, but this is not necessarily so. For example, in the case of South Vietnam the former imperial power was France, but neo-colonial control of the State has now gone to the United States. It is possible that neo-colonial control may be exercised by a consortium of financial interests which are not specifically identifiable with any particular State. The control of the Congo by great international financial concerns is a case in point.

The result of neo-colonialism is that foreign capital is used for the exploitation rather than for the development of the less developed parts of the world. Investment under neo-colonialism increases rather than decreases the gap between the rich and the poor countries of the world.

The struggle against neo-colonialism is not aimed at excluding the capital of the developed world from operating in less developed countries. It is aimed at preventing the financial power of the developed countries being used in such a way as to impoverish the less developed. . . .

Neo-colonialism is also the worst form of imperialism. For those who practise it, it means power without responsibility and for those who suffer from it, it means exploitation without redress. In the days of old-fashioned colonialism, the imperial power had at least to explain and justify at home the actions it was taking abroad. In the colony those who served the ruling imperial power could at least look to its protection against any violent move by their opponents. With neo-colonialism neither is the case.

Above all, neo-colonialism, like colonialism before it, postpones the facing of the social issues which will have to be faced by the fully developed sector of the world before the danger of world war can be eliminated or the problem of world poverty resolved.

Neo-colonialism, like colonialism, is an attempt to export the social conflicts of the capitalist countries. The temporary success of this policy can be seen in the ever widening gap between the richer and the poorer nations of the world. But the internal contradictions and conflicts of neo-colonialism make it certain that it cannot endure as a permanent world policy. How it should be brought to an end is a problem that should be studied, above all, by the developed nations of the world, because it is they who will feel the full impact of the ultimate failure. The longer it continues the more certain it is that its inevitable collapse will destroy the social system of which they have made it a foundation. . . .

Neo-colonialism is based upon the principle of breaking up former large united colonial territories into a number of small non-viable States which are incapable of independent development and must rely upon the former imperial power for defence and even internal security. Their economic and financial systems are linked, as in colonial days, with those of the former colonial ruler.

At first sight the scheme would appear to have many advantages for the developed countries of the world. All the profits of neo-colonialism can be secured if, in any given area, a reasonable proportion of the States have a neo-colonialist system. It is not necessary that they *all* should have one. Unless small States can combine they must be compelled to sell their primary products at prices dictated by the developed nations and buy their manufactured goods at the prices fixed by them. So long as neo-colonialism can prevent political and economic conditions for optimum development, the developing countries, whether they are under neo-colonialist control or not, will be unable to create a large enough market to support industrialisation. In the same way they will lack the financial strength to force the developed countries to accept their primary products at a fair price.

In the neo-colonialist territories, since the former colonial power has in theory relinquished political control, if the social conditions occasioned by neo-colonialism cause a revolt the local neo-colonialist government can be sacrificed and another equally subservient one substituted in its place. On the other hand, in any continent where neo-colonialism exists on a wide scale the same social pressures which can produce revolts in neo-colonial territories will also affect those States which have refused to accept the system and therefore neo-colonialist nations have a ready-made weapon with which they can threaten their opponents if they appear successfully to be challenging the system.

These advantages, which seem at first sight so obvious, are, however, on examination, illusory because they fail to take into consideration the facts of the world today.

The introduction of neo-colonialism increases the rivalry between the great powers which was provoked by the old-style colonialism. However little real power the government of a neo-colonialist State may possess, it must have, from the very fact of its nominal independence, a certain area of manoeuvre. It may not be able to exist without a neo-colonialist master but it may still have the ability to change masters.

The ideal neo-colonialist State would be one which was wholly subservient to neo-colonialist interests but the existence of the socialist nations makes it impossible to enforce the full rigour of the neo-colonialist system. The existence of an alternative system is itself a challenge to the neo-colonialist regime. Warnings about "the dangers of Communist subversion" are likely to be two-edged since they bring to the notice of those living under a neo-colonialist system the possibility of a change of regime. In fact neo-colonialism is the victim of its own contradictions. In order to make it attractive to those upon whom it is practised it must be shown as capable of raising their living standards, but the economic object of neo-colonialism is to keep those standards depressed in the interest of the developed countries. It is only when this contradiction is understood that the failure of innumerable "aid" programmes, many of them well intentioned, can be explained.

In the first place, the rulers of neo-colonial States derive their authority to govern, not from the will of the people, but from the support which they obtain from their neo-colonialist masters. They have therefore little interest in developing education, strengthening the bargaining power of their workers employed by expatriate firms, or indeed of taking any step which would challenge the colonial pattern of commerce and industry, which it is the object of neo-colonialism to preserve. "Aid," therefore, to a neo-colonial State is merely a revolving credit, paid by the neo-colonial master, passing through the neo-colonial State and returning to the neo-colonial master in the form of increased profits.

Secondly, it is in the field of "aid" that the rivalry of individual developed States first manifests itself. So long as neo-colonialism persists, so long will spheres of interest persist, and this makes multilateral aid—which is in fact the only effective form of aid—impossible.

Once multilateral aid begins the neo-colonialist masters are faced by the hostility of the vested interests in their own country. Their manufacturers naturally object to any attempt to raise the price of the raw materials which they obtain from the neo-colonialist territory in question, or to the establishment there of manufacturing industries which might compete directly or indirectly with their own exports to the territory. Even education is suspect as likely to produce a student movement and it is, of course, true that in many less developed countries the students have been in the vanguard of the fight against neo-colonialism.

In the end the situation arises that the only type of aid which the neo-colonialist masters consider as safe is "military aid."

Once a neo-colonialist territory is brought to such a state of economic chaos and misery that revolt actually breaks out then, and only then, is there no limit to the generosity of the neo-colonial overlord, provided, of course, that the funds supplied are utilised exclusively for military purposes.

Military aid in fact marks the last stage of neo-colonialism and its effect is self-destructive. Sooner or later the weapons supplied pass into the hands of the opponents of the neo-colonialist regime and the war itself increases the social misery which originally provoked it.

Neo-colonialism is a mill-stone around the necks of the developed countries which practise it. Unless they can rid themselves of it, it will drown them. . . .

6

REVOLUTION

The downfall of capitalism was absolutely inevitable, according to Marxist theory. When the internal contradictions of capitalism reached a critical point, the exploited proletariat would certainly rise up in revolution. But the timing and the character of that inevitable revolution remained a matter of bitter controversy among Marxist thinkers. A number of issues divided them:

1 What objective features of the capitalist system would indicate that the situation was ripe for revolution?

2 Are these objective circumstances now realized? If not, when are they likely to arise, and how will they be identified?

3 The revolution must surely be worldwide; the *Internationale* was its anthem. But would it explode in all parts of the globe at once? Or would it spread gradually, consolidating its gains first in one country or in a few countries?

4 If the revolution would come first in one country, or had done so as most Soviet Marxists believed, how explain the fact that the worldwide revolution began in Russia, an industrially backward country, and seemed to be spreading chiefly to the underdeveloped nations, rather than to those (as Marx's theory seemed to suggest likely) in which capitalism had passed through its mature stages?

5 The character of the revolution itself, and the tactics that might lead to its speedy success, were also matters of dispute. Would it need to be a violent overthrow of tenacious capitalist regimes, or might it be a democratic transition—radical but not brutal—in which civilized leaders gradually came to recognize the need to replace capitalism with new forms of production and distribution, thus peacefully ushering in a new age?

Communist theorists almost invariably sought to reconcile their answers to such questions with the writings of Marx and Engels, and with the views of Lenin, the great tactician. But in the writings of the masters there were apparent gaps and inconsistencies. Engels had written that the state would "wither away." What does that mean? Does the inevitability of the revolution reduce the need to sustain political agitation? What role must be played by the Communist Party and its leaders in extirpating bourgeois power and culture?

All through the twentieth century communist thinkers faced the frustrating and never ending task of reconciling the actual course of world affairs with a nineteenth-century theory whose flexibility was often strained. Lasting success eluded them.

21
V. I. Lenin

In *State and Revolution* Lenin presents what became the orthodox communist view of the nature of the state, its inevitable downfall, and its replacement by the dictatorship of the proletariat. Every state, Lenin argues, is in essence an instrument of oppression and exploitation; as capitalism collapses and is replaced by new collective institutions, therefore, the state will come to be recognized as theoretically obsolete, at first a necessary evil, and then not necessary at all.

After the proletarian revolution, however, the socialist state remains. The correct theoretical account of the transition from capitalism to communism therefore must involve several stages. The first stage is the uprising of the proletariat that will overthrow the capitalist state; this revolution, Lenin held, will be inescapably violent. Once the proletariat holds power, states will be needed only to control the residue of the bourgeoisie; eventually (but only after an extended transitional period) states will be no longer needed and will wither away.

The circumstances under which the first proletarian uprising will take place may come with surprising suddenness. Lenin was writing this most influential pamphlet while in exile in Switzerland in September of 1917; he did not complete it because the sudden collapse of the regime in Russia invited the October revolution of 1917, which Lenin went to St. Petersburg to lead. His success, and the success of the Marxist revolution in China under Mao Tse-tung, who played an analogous role decades later, were among the greatest moments of communism in the twentieth century.

THE STATE AS THE PRODUCT OF THE IRRECONCILABILITY OF CLASS ANTAGONISMS*

What is now happening to Marx's doctrine has, in the course of history, often happened to the doctrines of other revolutionary thinkers and leaders of oppressed classes struggling for emancipation. During the lifetime of great revolutionaries, the oppressing classes have visited relentless persecution on them and received their teaching with the most savage hostility, the most furious hatred, the most ruthless campaign of lies and slanders. After their death, attempts are made to turn them into harmless icons, canonize them, and surround their *names* with a certain halo for the "consolation" of the oppressed classes and with the object of duping them, while at the same time emasculating and vulgarizing the *real essence* of their revolutionary theories and blunting their revolutionary edge. At the present time, the bourgeoisie and the opportunists within the labor movement are co-operating in this work of adulterating Marxism. They omit, obliterate, and distort the

*This and the following passages are from V. I. Lenin, *State and Revolution,*1917. Reprinted by permission of the Foreign Languages Publishing House, Moscow.

revolutionary side of its teaching, its revolutionary soul. They push to the foreground and extol what is, or seems, acceptable to the bourgeoisie. . . .

In such circumstances, the distortion of Marxism being so widespread, it is our first task to *resuscitate* the real teachings of Marx on the state. For this purpose it will be necessary to quote at length from the works of Marx and Engels themselves. . . .

Summarizing his historical analysis Engels says:

> The state is therefore by no means a power imposed on society from the outside; just as little is it "the reality of the moral idea," "the image and reality of reason," as Hegel asserted. Rather, it is a product of society at a certain stage of development; it is the admission that this society has become entangled in an insoluble contradiction with itself, that it is cleft into irreconcilable antagonisms which it is powerless to dispel. But in order that these antagonisms, classes with conflicting economic interests, may not consume themselves and society in sterile struggle, a power apparently standing above society becomes necessary, whose purpose is to moderate the conflict and keep it within the bounds of "order"; and this power arising out of society, but placing itself above it, and increasingly separating itself from it, is the state.*

Here we have, expressed in all its clearness, the basic idea of Marxism on the question of the historical rôle and meaning of the state. The state is the product and the manifestation of the *irreconcilability* of class antagonisms. The state arises when, where, and to the extent that the class antagonisms *cannot* be objectively reconciled. And conversely, the existence of the state proves that the class antagonisms *are* irreconcilable.

THE STATE AS A RELIC OF ANTIQUITY

A general summary of his views is given by Engels in the most popular of his works in the following words:

> The state, therefore, has not existed from all eternity. There have been societies which managed without it, which had no conception of the state and state power. At a certain stage of economic development, which was necessarily bound up with the cleavage of society into classes, the state became a necessity owing to this cleavage. We are now rapidly approaching a stage in the development of production at which the existence of these classes has not only ceased to be a necessity, but is becoming a positive hindrance to production. They will disappear as inevitably as they arose at an earlier stage. Along with them, the state will inevitably disappear. The society that organizes production anew on the basis of a free and equal association of the producers will put the whole state machine where it will then belong: in the museum of antiquities, side by side with the spinning wheel and the bronze ax.†

It is not often that we find this passage quoted in the propaganda and agitation literature of contemporary Social-Democracy. But even when we do come across it, it is generally quoted in the same manner as one bows before an icon, i.e., it is

---

*Friedrich Engels, *The Origin of the Family, Private Property, and the State.*—Ed.
†*Ibid.*—Ed.

done merely to show official respect for Engels, without any attempt to gauge the breadth and depth of revolutionary action presupposed by his relegating of "the whole state machine . . . to the museum of antiquities." In most cases we do not even find an understanding of what Engels calls the state machine.

THE "WITHERING AWAY" OF THE STATE AND VIOLENT REVOLUTION

Engels' words regarding the "withering away" of the state enjoy such popularity, they are so often quoted, and they show so clearly the essence of the usual adulteration by means of which Marxism is made to look like opportunism, that we must dwell on them in detail. Let us quote the whole passage from which they are taken. [Editor's Note: Lenin here quotes that long paragraph from Engels' *Socialism, Utopian and Scientific,* which appears in this volume on pp. 122-123.]

. . .

Without fear of committing an error, it may be said that of this argument by Engels so singularly rich in ideas, only one point has become an integral part of Socialist thought among modern Socialist parties, namely, that, unlike the Anarchist doctrine of the "abolition" of the state, according to Marx the state "withers away." To emasculate Marxism in such a manner is to reduce it to opportunism, for such an "interpretation" only leaves the hazy conception of a slow, even, gradual change, free from leaps and storms, free from revolution. The current popular conception, if one may say so, of the "withering away" of the state undoubtedly means a slurring over, if not a negation, of revolution.

Yet, such an "interpretation" is the crudest distortion of Marxism, which is advantageous only to the bourgeoisie; in point of theory, it is based on a disregard for the most important circumstances and considerations pointed out in the very passage summarizing Engels' ideas, which we have just quoted in full.

In the first place, Engels at the very outset of his argument says that, in assuming state power, the proletariat by that very act "puts an end to the state as the state." One is "not accustomed" to reflect on what this really means. Generally, it is either ignored altogether, or it is considered as a piece of "Hegelian weakness" on Engels' part. As a matter of fact, however, these words express succinctly the experience of one of the greatest proletarian revolutions—the Paris Commune of 1871, of which we shall speak in greater detail in its proper place. As a matter of fact, Engels speaks here of the destruction of the bourgeois state by the proletarian revolution, while the words about its withering away refer to the remains of *proletarian* statehood *after* the Socialist revolution. The bourgeois state does not "wither away," according to Engels, but is "put an end to" by the proletariat in the course of the revolution. What withers away after the revolution is the proletarian state or semi-state.

Secondly, the state is a "special repressive force." This splendid and extremely profound definition of Engels' is given by him here with complete lucidity. It follows from this that the "special repressive force" of the bourgeoisie for the suppression of the proletariat, of the millions of workers by a handful of the rich, must be replaced by a "special repressive force" of the proletariat for the suppression of the bourgeoisie (the dictatorship of the proletariat). It is just this that constitutes the destruction of "the state as the state." It is just this that constitutes the "act" of "the seizure of the means of production in the name of society." And it is obvious that such a substitution of one (proletarian) "special repressive force" for another (bourgeois) "special repressive force" can in no way take place in the form of a "withering away."

Thirdly, as to the "withering away" or, more expressively and colorfully, as to the state "becoming dormant," Engels refers quite clearly and definitely to the period *after* "the seizure of the means of production [by the state] in the name of society," that is, *after* the Socialist revolution. We all know that the political form of the "state" at that time is complete democracy. But it never enters the head of any of the opportunists who shamelessly distort Marx that when Engels speaks here of the state "withering away," or "becoming dormant," he speaks of *democracy.* At first sight this seems very strange. But it is "unintelligible" only to one who has not reflected on the fact that democracy is *also* a state and that, consequently, democracy will *also* disappear when the state disappears. The bourgeois state can only be "put an end to" by a revolution. The state in general, i.e., most complete democracy, can only "wither away."

Fourthly, having formulated his famous proposition that "the state withers away," Engels at once explains concretely that this proposition is directed equally against the opportunists and the Anarchists. In doing this, however, Engels puts in the first place that conclusion from his proposition about the "withering away" of the state which is directed against the opportunists. . . .

Fifthly, in the same work of Engels, from which everyone remembers his argument on the "withering away" of the state, there is also a disquisition on the significance of a violent revolution. The historical analysis of its rôle becomes, with Engels, a veritable panegyric on violent revolution. This, of course, "no one remembers"; to talk or even to think of the importance of this idea is not considered good form by contemporary Socialist parties, and in the daily propaganda and agitation among the masses it plays no part whatever. Yet it is indissolubly bound up with the "withering away" of the state in one harmonious whole.

Here is Engels' argument:

> . . . That force, however, plays another role (other than that of a diabolical power) in history, a revolutionary role; that, in the words of Marx, it is the midwife of every old society which is pregnant with the new; that it is the instrument with whose aid social movement forces its way through and shatters the dead, fossilized political forms—of this there is not a word in Herr Dühring. It is only with sighs and groans that he admits the possibility that force will perhaps be necessary for the overthrow of the economic system of exploitation—unfortunately! because all use of force, forsooth, demoralizes the person who uses it. And this in spite of the immense moral and spiritual impetus which has resulted from every victorious revolution! And this in Germany, where a violent collision—which indeed may be forced on the people—would at least have the advantage of wiping out the servility which has permeated the national consciousness as a result of the humiliation of the Thirty Years' War. And this parson's mode of thought—lifeless, insipid and impotent—claims to impose itself on the most revolutionary party which history has known?*

---

*Ibid. This passage appears in a portion of the *Anti-Dühring* which is not included within *Socialism, Utopian and Scientific.—Ed.*

How can this panegyric on violent revolution, which Engels insistently brought to the attention of the German Social-Democrats between 1878 and 1894, i.e., right to the time of his death, be combined with the theory of the "withering away" of the state to form one doctrine?

Usually the two views are combined by means of eclecticism, by an unprincipled, sophistic, arbitrary selection (to oblige the powers that be) of either one or the other arguments, and in ninety-nine cases out of a hundred (if not more often), it is the idea of the "withering away" that is specially emphasized. Eclecticism is substituted for dialectics—this is the most usual, the most widespread phenomenon to be met with in the official Social-Democratic literature of our day in relation to Marxism. Such a substitution is, of course, nothing new; it may be observed even in the history of classic Greek philosophy. When Marxism is adulterated to become opportunism, the substitution of eclecticism for dialectics is the best method of deceiving masses; it gives an illusory satisfaction; it seems to take into account all sides of the process, all the tendencies of development, all the contradictory factors and so forth, whereas in reality it offers no consistent and revolutionary view of the process of social development at all.

We have already said above and shall show more fully later that the teaching of Marx and Engels regarding the inevitability of a violent revolution refers to the bourgeois state. It *cannot* be replaced by the proletarian state (the dictatorship of the proletariat) through "withering away," but, as a general rule, only through a violent revolution. The panegyric sung in its honor by Engels and fully corresponding to the repeated declarations of Marx (remember the concluding passages of the *Poverty of Philosophy* and the *Communist Manifesto,* with its proud and open declaration of the inevitability of a violent revolution; remember Marx's *Critique of the Gotha Programme* of 1875 in which, almost thirty years later, he mercilessly castigates the opportunist character of that programme)—this praise is by no means a mere "impulse," a mere declamation, or a polemical sally. The necessity of systematically fostering among the masses *this* and just this point of view about violent revolution lies at the root of the *whole* of Marx's and Engels' teaching. The neglect of such propaganda and agitation by both the present predominant social-chauvinist and the Kautskyist currents brings their betrayal of Marx's and Engels' teaching into prominent relief.

The replacement of the bourgeois by the proletarian state is impossible without a violent revolution. The abolition of the proletarian state, i.e., of all states, is only possible through "withering away."

22
Eduard Bernstein

Eduard Bernstein (1850–1932) was a leader among the small group of early
Marxist thinkers, having worked closely with Engels, and later serving as one of
Marx's literary executors. But he differed from mainstream Marxists by insisting
that the coming revolution should not and would not be violent. Communism will
be achieved, he held, only as the result of an extended evolutionary process. He
was distressed by the dictatorial tendencies in the Communist Party, and was
bitterly attacked by Lenin as a traitor and "revisionist." But Bernstein remained
convinced that socialist goals could be achieved through the democratic,
parliamentary pursuit of fundamental change.

[DOGMATISM AND SCIENTIFIC SOCIALISM]*

A dualism runs through the whole monumental work of Marx . . .—a dualism
which consists in this, that the work aims at being a scientific inquiry and also at
proving a theory laid down long before its drafting; a formula lies at the basis of
it in which the result to which the exposition should lead is fixed beforehand. The
return to the *Communist Manifesto* points here to a real residue of Utopianism in
the Marxist system. Marx had accepted the solution of the Utopians in essentials,
but had recognised their means and proofs as inadequate. He therefore undertook
a revision of them, and this with the zeal, the critical acuteness, and love of truth
of a scientific genius. He suppressed no important fact, he also forebore belittling
artificially the importance of these facts as long as the object of the inquiry had no
immediate reference to the final aim of the formula to be proved. To that point his
work is free of every tendency necessarily interfering with the scientific method.

For the general sympathy with the strivings for emancipation of the working
classes does not in itself stand in the way of the scientific method. But, as Marx
approaches a point when that final aim enters seriously into the question, he
becomes uncertain and unreliable. Such contradictions then appear as were shown
in the book under consideration, for instance, in the section on the movement of
incomes in modern society. It thus appears that this great scientific spirit was, in
the end, a slave to a doctrine. To express it figuratively, he has raised a mighty
building within the framework of a scaffolding he found existing, and in its erec-
tion he kept strictly to the laws of scientific architecture as long as they did not
collide with the conditions which the construction of the scaffolding prescribed,
but he neglected or evaded them when the scaffolding did not allow of their observance. Where the scaffolding put limits in the way of the building, instead of
destroying the scaffolding, he changed the building itself at the cost of its right
proportions and so made it all the more dependent on the scaffolding. Was it the

---

*These passages are from E. Bernstein, *Evolutionary Socialism,* E. C. Harvey, tr. (New York: B. W.
Huebsch Co., 1909).

consciousness of this irrational relation which caused him continually to pass from completing his work to amending special parts of it? However that may be, my conviction is that wherever that dualism shows itself the scaffolding must fall if the building is to grow in its right proportions. In the latter, and not in the former, is found what is worthy to live in Marx.

Nothing confirms me more in this conception than the anxiety with which some persons seek to maintain certain statements in *Capital,* which are falsified by facts. It is just some of the more deeply devoted followers of Marx who have not been able to separate themselves from the dialectical form of the work—that is the scaffolding alluded to—who do this. At least, that is only how I can explain the words of a man, otherwise so amenable to facts as Kautsky, who, when I observed in Stuttgart that the number of wealthy people for many years had increased, not decreased, answered: "If that were true then the date of our victory would not only be very long postponed, but we should never attain our goal. If it be capitalists who increase and not those with no possessions, then we are going even further from our goal the more evolution progresses, then capitalism grows stronger, not socialism."

That the number of the wealthy increases and does not diminish is not an invention of bourgeois "harmony economists," but a fact established by the boards of assessment for taxes, often to the chagrin of those concerned, a fact which can no longer be disputed. But what is the significance of this fact as regards the victory of socialism? Why should the realisation of socialism depend on its refutation? Well, simply for this reason: because the dialectical scheme seems so to prescribe it; because a post threatens to fall out of the scaffolding if one admits that the social surplus product is appropriated by an increasing instead of a decreasing number of possessors. But it is only the speculative theory that is affected by this matter; it does not at all affect the actual movement. Neither the struggle of the workers for democracy in politics nor their struggle for democracy in industry is touched by it. The prospects of this struggle do not depend on the theory of concentration of capital in the hands of a diminishing number of magnates, nor on the whole dialectical scaffolding of which this is a plank, but on the growth of social wealth and of the social productive forces, in conjunction with general social progress, and, particularly, in conjunction with the intellectual and moral advance of the working classes themselves.

Suppose the victory of socialism depended on the constant shrinkage in the number of capitalist magnates, social democracy, if it wanted to act logically, either would have to support the heaping up of capital in ever fewer hands, or at least to give no support to anything that would stop this shrinkage. As a matter of fact it often enough does neither the one nor the other. These considerations, for instance, do not govern its votes on questions of taxation. From the standpoint of the catastrophic theory a great part of this practical activity of the working classes is an undoing of work that ought to be allowed to be done. It is not social democracy which is wrong in this respect. The fault lies in the doctrine which assumes that progress depends on the deterioration of social conditions.

.   .   .

[LEGISLATION VERSUS REVOLUTION]

. . . I hold a whole series of objections raised by opponents against certain items in Marx's theory as unrefuted, some as irrefutable. And I can do this all the more easily as these objections are quite irrelevant to the strivings of social democracy. . . .

Marxism preached . . . political action as the most important duty of the movement. But it was thereby involved in great contradictions. It also recognised, and separated itself thereby from the demagogic parties, that the working classes had not yet attained the required maturity for their emancipation, and also that the economic preliminary conditions for such were not present. But in spite of that it turned again and again to tactics which supposed both preliminary conditions as almost fulfilled. We come across passages in its publications where the immaturity of the workers is emphasised with an acuteness which differs very little from the doctrinairism of the early Utopian socialists, and soon afterwards we come across passages according to which we should assume that all culture, all intelligence, all virtue, is only to be found among the working classes—passages which make it incomprehensible why the most extreme social revolutionaries and physical force anarchists should not be right. Corresponding with that, political action is ever directed towards a revolutionary convulsion expected in an imminent future, in the face of which legislative work for a long time appears only as a *pis aller*—a merely temporary device. And we look in vain for any systematic investigation of the question of what can be expected from legal, and what from revolutionary action.

It is evident at the first glance that great differences exist in the latter respect. But they are usually found to be this: that law, or the path of legislative reform, is the slower way, and revolutionary force the quicker and more radical. But that only is true in a restricted sense. Whether the legislative or the revolutionary method is the more promising depends entirely on the nature of the measures and on their relation to different classes and customs of the people.

In general, one may say here that the revolutionary way (always in the sense of revolution by violence) does quicker work as far as it deals with removal of obstacles which a privileged minority places in the path of social progress: that its strength lies on its negative side.

Constitutional legislation works more slowly in this respect as a rule. Its path is usually that of compromise, not the prohibition, but the buying out of acquired rights. But it is stronger than the revolution scheme where prejudice and the limited horizon of the great mass of the people appear as hindrances to social progress, and it offers greater advantages where it is a question of the creation of permanent economic arrangements capable of lasting; in other words, it is best adapted to positive social-political work.

In legislation, intellect dominates over emotion in quiet times; during a revolution emotion dominates over intellect. But if emotion is often an imperfect leader, the intellect is a slow motive force. Where a revolution sins by over haste, the every-day legislator sins by procrastination. Legislation works as a systematic force, revolution as an elementary force.

As soon as a nation has attained a position where the rights of the propertied minority have ceased to be a serious obstacle to social progress, where the negative tasks of political action are less pressing than the positive, then the appeal to a revolution by force becomes a meaningless phrase. One can overturn a government or a privileged minority, but not a nation. . . .

23
Josef Stalin

Josef Stalin was one of Lenin's closest associates, becoming paramount leader of the Soviet Union after Lenin's death in 1924—the same year in which he published *The Foundations of Leninism,* from which the following passages are taken. "Leninism," said Stalin, is "Marxism of the era of imperialism and of the proletarian revolution."

But the fact that the proletarian revolution had first taken place in a country, Russia, that had not experienced the full maturation of capitalism was problematic for many Marxists. This surprising turn of events was nevertheless in accord with Marxist theory, Stalin insisted, if one sees international capitalist imperialism as a great chain, of which Russia was the weakest link. The scope of the proletarian revolution was also very bitterly disputed. Can a revolution that is essentially international be successful if limited to one country, as the Russian revolution was? Yes, Stalin answered, it must be consolidated in one country as the first of many steps, for only in that way may the early gains of the proletariat be made secure.

REVOLUTION WHERE?*

Formerly, the analysis of the conditions for the proletarian revolution was usually approached from the point of view of the economic state of individual countries. Now, this approach is no longer adequate. Now the matter must be approached from the point of view of the economic state of all or the majority of countries, from the point of view of the state of world economy; for individual countries and individual national economies have ceased to be self-sufficient units, have become links in a single chain called world economy; for the old "cultured" capitalism has evolved into imperialism, and imperialism is a world system of financial enslavement and colonial oppression of the vast majority of the population of the earth by a handful of "advanced" countries.

Formerly, it was the accepted thing to speak of the existence or absence of objective conditions for the proletarian revolution in individual countries, or, to be more precise, in one or another developed country. Now this point of view is no longer adequate. Now we must speak of the existence of objective conditions for the revolution in the entire system of world imperialist economy as an integral

*This and the following passages are from J. Stalin's *The Foundations of Leninism,* 1924. Reprinted by permission of the Foreign Languages Publishing House, Moscow.

unit; the existence within this system of some countries that are not sufficiently developed industrially cannot serve as an insurmountable obstacle to the revolution, *if* the system as a whole, or, more correctly, *because* the system as a whole is already ripe for revolution.

Formerly it was the accepted thing to speak of the proletarian revolution in one or another developed country as of something separate and self-sufficient, facing a separate national front of capital as its opposite. Now this point of view is no longer adequate. Now we must speak of the world proletarian revolution; for the separate national fronts of capital have become links in a single chain called the world front of imperialism, which must be opposed by a common front of the revolutionary movement in all countries.

Formerly, the proletarian revolution was regarded exclusively as the result of the internal development of a given country. Now this point of view is no longer adequate. Now the proletarian revolution must be regarded primarily as the result of the development of the contradictions within the world system of imperialism, as the result of the snapping of the chain of the imperialist world front in one country or another.

Where will the revolution begin? Where, in what country, can the front of capital be pierced first?

Where industry is more developed, where the proletariat constitutes the majority, where there is more culture, where there is more democracy—that was the reply usually given formerly.

No, objects the Leninist theory of revolution; *not necessarily where industry is more developed,* and so forth. The front of capital will be pierced where the chain of imperialism is weakest, for the proletarian revolution is the result of the breaking of the chain of the world imperialist front at its weakest link; and it may turn out that the country which has started the revolution, which has made a breach in the front of capital, is less developed in a capitalist sense than other, more developed, countries, which have, however, remained within the framework of capitalism.

In 1917 the chain of the imperialist world front proved to be weaker in Russia than in the other countries. It was there that the chain gave way and provided an outlet for the proletarian revolution. Why? Because in Russia a great popular revolution was unfolding, and at its head marched the revolutionary proletariat, which had such an important ally as the vast mass of the peasantry who were oppressed and exploited by the landlords. Because the revolution there was opposed by such a hideous representative of imperialism as tsarism, which lacked all moral prestige and was deservedly hated by the whole population. The chain proved to be weaker in Russia, although that country was less developed in a capitalist sense than, say, France or Germany, England or America.

Where will the chain break in the near future? Again, where it is weakest. It is not precluded that the chain may break, say, in India. Why? Because that country has a young, militant, revolutionary proletariat, which has such an ally as the national liberation movement—an undoubtedly powerful and undoubtedly important ally. Because there the revolution is opposed by such a well-known foe as foreign imperialism, which lacks all moral credit and is deservedly hated by the oppressed and exploited masses of India. . . .

Briefly, the chain of the imperialist front must, as a rule, give way where the links are weaker and, at all events, not necessarily where capitalism is more developed, where there is such and such a percentage of proletarians and such and such a percentage of peasants, and so on.

This is why in deciding the question of proletarian revolution statistical calculations of the percentage of the proletarian population in a given country lose the exceptional importance so eagerly attached to them by the pedants of the Second International, who have not understood imperialism and who fear revolution like the plague.

[REVOLUTION IN ONE COUNTRY]

To proceed. Formerly, the victory of the revolution in one country was considered impossible, on the assumption that it would require the combined action of the proletarians of all or at least of a majority of the advanced countries to achieve victory over the bourgeoisie. Now this point of view no longer accords with the facts. Now we must proceed from the possibility of such a victory, for the uneven and spasmodic character of the development of the various capitalist countries under the conditions of imperialism, the development, within imperialism, of catastrophic contradictions leading to inevitable wars, the growth of the revolutionary movement in all countries of the world—all this leads, not only to the possibility, but also to the necessity of the victory of the proletariat in individual countries. The history of the Russian revolution is direct proof of this. At the same time, however, it must be borne in mind that the overthrow of the bourgeoisie can be successfully accomplished only when certain absolutely necessary conditions exist, in the absence of which there can be even no question of the proletariat taking power.

Here is what Lenin says about these conditions in his pamphlet *"Left-Wing" Communism: An Infantile Disorder:*

> The fundamental law of revolution, which has been confirmed by all revolutions, and particularly by all three Russian revolutions in the twentieth century, consists in the following: it is not enough for revolution that the exploited and oppressed masses should understand the impossibility of living in the old way and demand changes; for revolution it is necessary that the exploiters should not be able to live and rule in the old way. Only when the "lower classes" *do not want* the old way, and when the "upper classes" *cannot carry on in the old way*—only then can revolution triumph. This truth may be expressed in other words: *Revolution is impossible without a nationwide crisis (affecting both the exploited and the exploiters)*. It follows that for revolution it is essential, first, that a majority of the workers (or at least a majority of the class conscious, thinking, politically active workers) should fully understand the necessity for revolution and be ready to sacrifice their lives for it; secondly, that the ruling classes should be passing through a governmental crisis which would draw even the most backward masses into politics . . . weaken the government and make it possible for the revolutionaries to overthrow it rapidly. (*Selected Works,* Vol. X, p. 127.)

But the overthrow of the power of the bourgeoisie and establishment of the power of the proletariat in one country still does not mean that the complete victory of socialism has been ensured. After consolidating its power and taking the peasantry in tow, the proletariat of the victorious country can and must build up a socialist society. But does this mean that it will thereby achieve the complete and final victory of socialism, i.e., does it mean that with the forces of only one country it can finally consolidate socialism and fully guarantee that country against intervention and, consequently, also against restoration? No, it does not. For this the victory of the revolution in at least several countries is needed. Therefore, the development and support of revolution in other countries is an essential task of the victorious revolution. Therefore, the revolution in the victorious country must regard itself not as a self-sufficient entity but as an aid, as a means of hastening the victory of the proletariat in other countries.

24
Leon Trotsky*

Leon Trotsky (1879–1940) was one of the leaders of the Russian Revolution, founder of the Red Army, commissar of foreign affairs and of war in early Soviet governments, and Stalin's chief antagonist and critic. The revolution might indeed begin in Russia, he contended, but it must not be contained or stymied there. The revolution, having many phases, must be constantly developing and expanding, in depth and breadth, until it becomes truly global. Only then will the classless society be achieved. This theoretical account of the passage to communism, presented in the *The Permanent Revolution* from which the following selections are taken, was Trotsky's chief contribution to Marxist thought, and was indeed rooted in Marx's sketchy treatment of this aspect of communist theory.

Although losing the internal struggle for power to Stalin, Trotsky remained a hero and guide to many dissident Marxists. He was forced to flee the Soviet Union; in 1940, in Mexico, he was assassinated.

WHAT IS THE PERMANENT REVOLUTION?[†]

Fundamental Theses

I hope that the reader will not object if, to end up this book, I attempt, without fear of repetition, to formulate briefly the most fundamental conclusions.

1 The theory of the permanent revolution now demands the greatest attention of every Marxist, for the course of the ideological and class struggle has finally and conclusively raised this question from the realm of reminiscences over the old differences of opinion among Russian Marxists and converted it into a question of the character, the inner coherence and the methods of the international revolution in general.

2 With regard to the countries with a belated bourgeois development, especially the colonial and semi-colonial countries, the theory of the permanent revo-

---

*Trotsky's original name was Lev Davidovich Bronstein.
†From L. Trotsky, *The Permanent Revolution,* Max Shachtman, tr. (New York: Pioneer Publishers), 1931.

lution signifies that the complete and genuine solution of their tasks, *democratic and national emancipation,* is conceivable only through the dictatorship of the proletariat as the leader of the subjugated nation, above all of its peasant masses.

3 Not only the agrarian, but also the national question, assigns to the peasantry, the overwhelming majority of the population of the backward countries, an important place in the democratic revolution. Without an alliance of the proletariat with the peasantry, the tasks of the democratic revolution cannot be solved, nor even seriously posed. But the alliance of these two classes can be realized in no other way than through an intransigeant struggle against the influence of the national liberal bourgeoisie.

4 No matter how the first episodic stages of the revolution may be in the individual countries, the realization of the revolutionary alliance between the proletariat and the peasantry is conceivable only under the political direction of the proletarian vanguard, organized in the Communist Party. This in turn means that the victory of the democratic revolution is conceivable only through the dictatorship of the proletariat which bases itself upon the alliance with the peasantry and first solves the problems of the democratic revolution.

5 The old slogan of Bolshevism—"the democratic dictatorship of the proletariat and peasantry" expresses precisely the above characterized relationship of the proletariat, the peasantry and the liberal bourgeoisie. . . . The peasant follows either the worker or the bourgeois. This means that the "democratic dictatorship of the proletariat and peasantry" is only conceivable as a *dictatorship of the proletariat that leads the peasant masses behind it.*

.   .   .

8 The dictatorship of the proletariat which has risen to power as the leader of the democratic revolution is inevitably and very quickly placed before tasks that are bound up with deep inroads into the rights of bourgeois property. The democratic revolution grows over immediately into the socialist, and thereby becomes a *permanent* revolution.

9 The conquest of power by the proletariat does not terminate the revolution, but only opens it. Socialist construction is conceivable only on the foundation of the class struggle, on a national and international scale. This struggle, under the conditions of an overwhelming predominance of capitalist relationships on the world arena, will inevitably lead to explosions, that is, internally to civil wars, and externally to revolutionary wars. Therein lies the permanent character of the socialist revolution as such, regardless of whether it is a backward country that is involved, which only yesterday accomplished its democratic revolution, or an old capitalist country, which already has behind it a long epoch of democracy and parliamentarism.

10 The completion of the socialist revolution within national limits is unthinkable. One of the basic reasons for the crisis in bourgeois society is the fact that the productive forces created by it conflict with the framework of the national state. From this follow, on the one hand, imperialist wars, and on the other, the utopia of the bourgeois United States of Europe. The socialist revolution commences on the

national arena, is developed further on the inter-state and finally on the world arena. Thus, the socialist revolution becomes a permanent revolution in a newer and broader sense of the word; it attains completion only in the final victory of the new society on our entire planet.

11 The above outlined schema of the development of the world revolution eliminates the question of the countries that are "mature" or "immature" for socialism in the spirit of that pedantic, lifeless classification given by the present program of the Comintern. In so far as capitalism has created the world market, the division of labor and productive forces throughout the world, it has also prepared world economy for socialist transformation.

The various countries will go through this process at different tempos. Backward countries, under certain conditions, can arrive at the dictatorship of the proletariat sooner than the advanced countries, but they come later than the latter to socialism.

A backward colonial or semi-colonial country, whose proletariat is insufficiently prepared to unite the peasantry and seize power, is thereby incapable of bringing the democratic revolution to its conclusion. On the contrary, in a country where the proletariat has power in its hands as the result of the democratic revolution, the subsequent fate of the dictatorship and socialism is not only and not so much dependent in the final analysis upon the national productive forces, as it is upon the development of the international socialist revolution.

12 The theory of socialism in one country which rose on the yeast of the reaction against October is the only theory that consistently, and to the very end, opposes the theory of the permanent revolution.

The attempt of the epigones, under the blows of our criticism, to confine the application of the theory of socialism in one country exclusively to Russia, because of its specific characteristics (its extensiveness and its natural resources) does not improve matters but only makes them worse. The break with the international position always leads to a national messianism, that is, to attribute special prerogatives and peculiarities to one's own country, which would permit it to play a rôle that other countries cannot attain.

The world division of labor, the dependence of Soviet industry upon foreign technique, the dependence of the productive forces of the advanced countries of Europe upon Asiatic raw materials, etc., etc., make the construction of a socialist society in any single country impossible.

13 The theory of Stalin-Bucharin not only contrasts the democratic revolution quite mechanically to the socialist revolution, but also tears the national revolution from the international path.

This theory sets the revolution in the backward countries the task of establishing an unrealizable régime of the democratic dictatorship, it contrasts this régime to the dictatorship of the proletariat, thus introducing illusion and fiction into politics, paralyzing the struggle for power of the proletariat in the East, and hampering the victory of the colonial revolution. . . .

14 The program of the Comintern created by Bucharin is thoroughly eclectic. It makes the hopeless attempt to reconcile the theory of socialism in one country with Marxian internationalism, which is, however, inseparable from the permanent character of the world revolution. The struggle of the Communist Left Opposition for a correct policy and a healthy régime in the Communist International is inseparably combined with a struggle for a Marxian program. The question of the program in turn is inseparable from the question of the two mutually exclusive theories: the theory of permanent revolution and the theory of socialism in one country. The problem of the permanent revolution has long ago outgrown the episodic differences of opinion between Lenin and Trotsky, which were completely exhausted by history. The struggle is between the basic ideas of Marx and Lenin on the one side and the eclectics of the Centrists on the other.

Constantinople, *November 30, 1929*

25
Mao Tse-tung

Chairman Mao was one of the world's most successful revolutionaries; his pithy remarks about revolution appear in *Quotations from Chairman Mao Tse-tung*—a miniature volume compiling epigrams, arguments, and observations that present the core of Mao's philosophical and political thought. Millions upon millions of copies of this "Little Red Book" were distributed; it became an ideological scripture in China during the years of Mao's absolute supremacy, to be studied, memorized, quoted, and applied. Citizens were expected to carry the little book with them everywhere—and at mass gatherings all would wave their copies as a symbol of their loyalty to the Communist Party, to Chairman Mao, and to the revolution.

[REVOLUTION IS MADE BY A DISCIPLINED REVOLUTIONARY PARTY]*

If there is to be revolution, there must be a revolutionary party. Without a revolutionary party, without a party built on the Marxist-Leninist revolutionary theory and in the Marxist-Leninist revolutionary style, it is impossible to lead the working class and the broad masses of the people in defeating imperialism and its running dogs.

"Revolutionary Forces of the World Unite, Fight Against Imperialist Aggression!" (November 1948), *Selected Works,* Vol. IV, p. 284.

A well-disciplined Party armed with the theory of Marxism-Leninism, using the method of self-criticism and linked with the masses of the people; an army under the leadership of such a Party; a united front of all revolutionary classes and all revolutionary groups under the leadership of such a Party—these are the three main weapons with which we have defeated the enemy.

"On the People's Democratic Dictatorship" (June 30, 1949), *Selected Works,* Vol. IV, p. 422.

*Selections are from *Quotations from Chairman Mao Tse-tung* (Beijing, Foreign Languages Press, 1966.)

We must have faith in the masses and we must have faith in the Party. These are two cardinal principles. If we doubt these principles, we shall accomplish nothing.

On the Question of Agricultural Co-operation (July 31, 1955), 3rd ed., p. 7.

Patriotism and Internationalism

Can a Communist, who is an internationalist, at the same time be a patriot? We hold that he not only can be but must be. The specific content of patriotism is determined by historical conditions. . . . We are at once internationalists and patriots, and our slogan is, "Fight to defend the motherland against the aggressors." . . . Thus in wars of national liberation patriotism is applied internationalism.

"The Role of the Chinese Communist Party in the National War"
(October 1938), *Selected Works,* Vol. II, p. 196.

War and Peace

Revolutions and revolutionary wars are inevitable in class society and without them, it is impossible to accomplish any leap in social development and to overthrow the reactionary ruling classes and therefore impossible for the people to win political power.

"On Contradiction" (August 1937), *Selected Works,*Vol. I, p. 344.

Revolutionary war is an antitoxin which not only eliminates the enemy's poison but also purges us of our own filth. Every just, revolutionary war is endowed with tremendous power and can transform many things or clear the way for their transformation.

"On Protracted War" (May 1938), *Selected Works,*Vol. II, p. 131.

The seizure of power by armed force, the settlement of the issue by war, is the central task and the highest form of revolution. This Marxist-Leninist principle of revolution holds good universally, for China and for all other countries.

Ibid., p. 219.

We are advocates of the abolition of war, we do not want war; but war can only be abolished through war, and in order to get rid of the gun it is necessary to take up the gun.

Ibid.

Classes and Class Struggle

Classes struggle, some classes triumph, others are eliminated. Such is history, such is the history of civilization for thousands of years. To interpret history from this viewpoint is historical materialism; standing in opposition to this viewpoint is historical idealism.

"Cast Away Illusions, Prepare for Struggle" (August 14, 1949),
*Selected Works,*Vol. IV, p. 428.

In class society everyone lives as a member of a particular class, and every kind of thinking, without exception, is stamped with the brand of a class.

"On Practice" (July 1937), *Selected Works,* Vol. I, p. 296.

Changes in society are due chiefly to the development of the internal contradictions in society, that is, the contradiction between the productive forces and the relations of production, the contradiction between classes and the contradiction between the old and the new; it is the development of these contradictions that pushes society forward and gives the impetus for the supersession of the old society by the new.

"On Contradiction" (August 1937), *Selected Works,* Vol. I, p. 314.

A revolution is not a dinner party, or writing an essay, or painting a picture, or doing embroidery; it cannot be so refined, so leisurely and gentle, so temperate, kind, courteous, restrained and magnanimous. A revolution is an insurrection, an act of violence by which one class overthrows another.

"Report on an Investigation of the Peasant Movement in Hunan" (March 1927), *Selected Works,* Vol. I, p. 28.

26
W. E. B. DuBois

William Edward Burghardt DuBois (1868–1963) was one of the founders of the National Association for the Advancement of Colored People (NAACP) in the United States, and a life-long defender of equal rights for all. A scholar passionately interested in the revival of African ethnic values, he became convinced that the best hope for such values lay in the defeat of capitalism, the success of an international communist revolution, and the achievement of genuine unity for all of Africa. His intellectual spirit was that of Lenin in *Imperialism;* his rhetorical style was that of Marx in the *Manifesto.*

PAN AFRICA*

Fellow Africans: About 1735, my great-great grandfather was kidnapped on this coast of West Africa and taken by the Dutch to the Colony of New York in America, where he was sold in slavery. About the same time a French Huguenot, Jacques DuBois migrated from France to America and his great-grandson, born in the West Indies and with Negro blood, married the great-great-granddaughter of my black ancestor. I am the son of this couple, born in 1868, hence my French name and my African loyalty.

*From "Pan Africa, 1919–1958" a speech by W. E. B. DuBois, delivered at the All-African People's Conference, Accra, Ghana, December 1958, and published in the *News Bulletin* (Vol. 1, No. 3) of that conference. Reprinted by permission of Mrs. W. E. B. DuBois.

. . . this meeting now in Accra is the sixth effort to bring this great [Pan-African] movement before the world and to translate its experience into ACTION. My only role in this meeting is one of advice from one who has lived long, who has studied Africa and has seen the modern world.

. . . let us mince no words. We face triumph or tragedy without alternative. Africa, ancient Africa has been called by the world and has lifted up her hands! Which way shall Africa go? First, I would emphasize the fact that today Africa has no choice between private Capitalism and Socialism. The whole world, including capitalist countries, is moving toward socialism, inevitably inexorably. You can choose between blocs of military alliance, you can choose between groups of political union, you cannot choose between Socialism and Private Capitalism because Private Capitalism is doomed!

But what is Socialism? It is disciplined economy and political organisation in which the first duty of a citizen is to serve the state; and the state is not a selected aristocracy, or a group of self-seeking oligarchs who have seized wealth and power. No! The mass of workers with hand and brain are the ones whose collective destiny is the chief object of all effort. Gradually, every state is coming to this concept of its aim. The great Communist states like the Soviet Union and China have surrendered completely to this idea. The Scandinavian states have yielded partially; Britain has yielded in some respects, France in part and even the United States adopted the New Deal which was largely socialism! Though today further American socialism is held at bay by sixty great groups of corporations who control individual capitalists and the trade union leaders.

On the other hand, the African tribe, whence all of you sprung, was communistic in its very beginnings. No tribesman was free. All were servants of the tribe of whom the chief was father and voice. Read of the West Coast trade as described by Casely-Hayford. There is no trace of private enterprise or individual initiative. It was the tribe which carried on trade and the chief was mouthpiece of the common will.

When now, with a certain suddenness, Africa is whirled by the bitter struggle of dying private Capitalism into the last great battle-ground of its death throes, you are being tempted to adopt at least a passing private capitalism as a step to some partial socialism. This would be a grave mistake. For four hundred years Europe and North America have built their civilization and comfort on theft of coloured labour and the land and materials which rightly belong to those colonial peoples. They are still today determined to make most of the world's people work for the comfort of the few: this is today true in London, Paris and New York. The dominant exploiting nations are willing to yield more to the demands of the mass of men than were their fathers. But their yielding takes the form of sharing the loot—not of stopping the looting. It takes the form of stopping socialism by force and not of surrendering the fatal mistakes of private capitalism. Either capital belongs to all or power is denied all.

Here then, my Brothers, you face your great decision: Will you for temporary advantage—for automobiles, refrigerators and Paris gowns—spend your income in paying interest on borrowed funds, or will you sacrifice your present comfort and the chance to shine before your neighbours, in order to educate your children, develop such industry as best serves the great mass of people and makes your country strong in ability, self-support and self-defence? Such union of effort for strength calls for sacrifice and self-denial, while the capital offered you at high price by the colonial powers like France, Britain, Holland, Belgium and the United States, will prolong fatal colonial imperialism, from which you have suffered slavery, serfdom and colonialism. You are not helpless. You are the buyers; and to continue existence as sellers of capital, these great nations, former owners of the world, must sell or face bankruptcy. You are not compelled to buy all they offer now. You can wait. You can starve a while longer rather than sell your great heritage for a mess of western capitalistic pottage. You can not only beat down the price of capital as offered by the united and monopolized western private capitalists, but at last today you can compare their offers with those of socialist countries like the Soviet Union and China, which with infinite sacrifice and pouring out of blood and tears, are at last able to offer weak nations needed capital on better terms than the west. The supply which socialist nations can at present spare is small as compared with that of the bloated monopolies of the west, but it is large and rapidly growing. Its acceptance involves no bonds which a free Africa may not safely assume. It certainly does not involve slavery and colonial control which is the price which the west has demanded and still demands. Today she offers a compromise, but one of which you must beware: She offers to let some of your smarter and less scrupulous leaders become fellow capitalists with the white exploiters if in turn they induce the nation's masses to pay the awful cost. This has happened in the West Indies and in South America. This may yet happen in the Middle East and Eastern Asia.

Strive against it with every fibre of your bodies and souls. A body of local private capitalists, even if they are black, can never free Africa; they will simply sell it into new slavery to old masters overseas.

As I have said, this is a call for sacrifice. Great Goethe sang, "*Entbehren sollst du, sollst entbehren*"—"Thou shalt forego, Shalt do without." If Africa unites it will be because each part, each nation, each tribe gives up a part of its heritage for the good of the whole. That is what union means; that is what Pan-Africa means: When the child is born into the tribe the price of his growing up is to give over a part of his freedom to the tribe. This he soon learns or dies. When the tribe becomes a union of tribes, the individual tribe surrenders some part of its freedom to the paramount tribe.

When the nation arises, the constituent tribes, clans and groups must each yield power and some freedom to the demands of the nation or the nation dies before it is born. Your local tribal, much-loved languages must yield to the few world tongues which serve the largest numbers of people and promote understanding and world literature. This is the great dilemma which faces Africans today; faces one and all: Give up individual rights for the needs of Mother Africa; give up tribal independence for the needs of the nation. Forget nothing but set everything in its rightful place; the glory of the six Ashanti Wars against Britain: the wisdom of the Fanti

Confederation; the growth of Nigeria; the song of the Songhay and Hausa; the rebellion of the Mahdi and the hands of Ethiopia; the greatness of the Basuto and the fighting of Chaka; the revenge of Mutessi, and many other happenings and men; but above all—Africa, Mother of Men. Your nearest friends and neighbours are the coloured people of China and India, the rest of Asia, the Middle East and the sea isles, once close bound to the heart of Africa and now long severed by the greed of Europe. Your bond is not mere colour of skin but the deeper experience of wage slavery and contempt. So too, your bond with the white world is closest to those who support and defend China and help India and not those who exploit the Middle East and South America.

Awake, awake, put on thy strength, O Zion; reject the weakness of missionaries who teach neither love nor brotherhood, but chiefly the virtues of private profit from capital, stolen from your land and labour. Africa awake, put on the beautiful robes of Pan-African Socialism!

> You have nothing to lose but your Chains!
> You have a continent to regain!
> You have freedom and human dignity to attain!!

27
Nikita S. Khrushchev

Nikita Sergeyevich Khrushchev (1894–1971) was Stalin's eventual successor (in 1957) as First Secretary of the Communist Party and paramount leader of the USSR. In the autumn of 1959, during a visit to the United States for talks with President Eisenhower, he gave a press conference in which he reaffirmed Soviet dedication to the orthodox dialectical principles of Marx and Engels. But the eventual revolution, he allowed, might take a more gradual course than earlier Marxists had believed. Whether speedily or slowly, however, Khrushchev had no doubt that the success of the international communist revolution was inevitable. To his American audience he said bluntly: "We will bury you."

"WE WILL BURY YOU"*

Mr. Lawrence: A number of questions reflect a great interest in another remark once attributed to you, Mr. Khrushchev, to a diplomat at a reception, that you would bury us.

If you didn't say it, say so, and if you did say it, could you explain what you meant?

---

*From replies to questions at a press conference at the National Press Club, Washington, D.C., as reported by *The Washington Post,* September 17, 1959. Reprinted by permission of *The Washington Post.*

Premier Khrushchev: Present here is only a very small portion of the American people. But if I were to start to try to bury even this group, one life would not be enough. I believe I did use that expression once, and if I did, I will try to explain why and what it means. To put it more precisely, the expression I used was distorted, and on purpose, because what was meant was not the physical burial of any people but the question of the historical force of development.

It is well known that at the present time no one social or economic system is dominant throughout the world, but that there are different systems, social systems in different countries. And those systems change. At one time the most widespread system of society in the world was feudalism.

Then capitalism took its place. Why was that? Because capitalism was a more progressive kind of a system than was feudalism.

As compared to feudalism capitalism provided better opportunities to develop the productive forces of society. We believe that now capitalism has developed so far that it has given birth to certain fundamental differences within itself, and each society gives birth to the kind of society that will follow it. We believe that Karl Marx, Engels and Lenin gave scientific proof of the fact that the system, the social system of socialism would take the place of capitalism.

We believe in that. You do not, not all of you. I am sure there are people, many people under your form, system of society, who believe in that, and that is why I said that looking at the matter from the historical point of view, socialism, communism, would take the place of capitalism and capitalism thereby would be, so to speak, buried. You will say that that cannot be. But it will be recalled that in the ages past, feudals used to burn people who said that feudalism would disappear. Yet capitalism came to take the place of feudalism.

Now, capitalism is struggling, fighting against communism. I personally am convinced that communism will be victorious, as a system of society which provides better possibilities for the development of a country's productive forces; which enables every person to develop his capacities best; and insures full freedom of a person in that society. Many of you will not agree with that, but that means that I cannot agree with you either.

What is to be done? Let us each of us live under the system which we prefer, you under capitalism, and we will continue to build under communism.

All that is not progressive will die away someday, because if capitalism, the capitalist society, is a better form of society and gives better opportunities to develop a country's productive forces, then certainly it will win. But we think that the short history of the existence of our state does not speak in your favor. What place did our country hold in economics before the revolution, and in the development in the world? It was an illiterate country. Today the rate of literacy in our country is higher than anywhere else. We now have 160,000 engineers graduate from our universities each year, which is three times more than this country. Some say that the more scientists we have, the sooner will communism collapse. Then we seem to be working to our own end, but that is not the case. We regard communism as a science.

Thank you, ladies and gentlemen.

28
Daniel and Gabriel Cohn-Bendit

Daniel Cohn-Bendit (1945–)—Danny the Red—was a leader of the radical
student movement in Europe during the 1960s. In his book, *Obsolete
Communism,* he suggests that university uprisings—in Berkeley, New York,
Berlin, Tokyo, Paris—may serve as models for the socialist revolution. "A spectre
is haunting Europe," he writes, "the spectre of student revolt." He rejects the
bureaucracy and hierarchy of the Leninist tradition, but not its reliance upon
violence. In any case, the revolution cannot be brought to pass by corrupt
"leaders," but must arise spontaneously from the masses—all acting freely in
their own best interests. *"C'est pour toi que tu fais la revolution."*

[IT IS FOR YOURSELF THAT YOU MAKE THE REVOLUTION]*

Lenin tried to show that the party can only overcome the class enemy by turning
itself into a professional revolutionary body in which everyone is allocated a fixed
task. Certain of its infallibility, a Party appoints itself the natural spokesman and
sole defender of the interests of the working class, and as such wields power on
their behalf—i.e. acts as a bureaucracy.

   We take quite a different view: far from having to teach the masses, the revolutionary's job is to try to understand and express their common aspirations; far
from being Lenin's 'tribune of the people who uses every manifestation of tyranny
and oppression . . . to explain his Socialist convictions and his Social Democratic
demands,' the real militant must encourage the workers to struggle on their own
behalf, and show how their every struggle can be used to drive a wedge into capitalist society. If he does so, the militant acts as an agent of the people and no
longer as their leader.

   The setting up of any party inevitably reduces freedom of the people to freedom
to agree with the party.

   In other words, democracy is not suborned by bad leadership but by the very
existence of leadership. Democracy cannot even exist within the Party, because the
Party itself is not a democratic organization, i.e. it is based upon authority and not
on representation. Lenin realized full well that the Party is an artificial creation,
that it was imposed upon the working class "from without." Moral scruples have
been swept aside: the Party is "right" if it can impose its views upon the masses
and wrong if it fails to do so. For Lenin, the whole matter ends there. In his *State
and Revolution,* Lenin did not even raise the problem of the relationship between
the people and the party. Revolutionary power was a matter of fact, based upon
people who are prepared to fight for it; the paradox is that the party's programme,

   *These passages are reprinted from Daniel and Gabriel Cohn-Bendit, *Obsolete Communism: The Left
Wing Alternative.* Copyright © 1968. English translation by Andre Deutsch, Ltd. Used with permission of
McGraw-Hill Book Company and Andre Deutsch, Ltd., London.

endorsed by these people, was precisely: All power to the Soviets! But whatever its programme, in retrospect we can see that the Party, because of its basic conception, is bound to bring in privilege and bureaucracy, and we must wash our hands of all organizations of this sort. To try and pretend that the Bolshevk Party is truly democratic is to deceive oneself, and this, at least, is an error that Lenin himself never committed.

What then is our conception of the role of the revolutionary? To begin with, we are convinced that the revolutionary cannot and must not be a leader. Revolutionaries are a militant minority drawn from various social strata, people who band together because they share an ideology, and who pledge themselves to struggle against oppression, to dispel the mystification of the ruling classes and the bureaucrats, to proclaim that the workers can only defend themselves and build a socialist society by taking their fate into their own hands, believing that political maturity comes only from revolutionary struggle and direct action.

By their action, militant minorities can do no more than support, encourage, and clarify the struggle. They must always guard against any tendency to become a pressure group outside the revolutionary movement of the masses. When they act, it must always be with the masses, and not as a faction.

. . . militant students whose dynamic theories emerged from their practice, were imitated by others, who developed new forms of action appropriate to their own situation. The result was a mass movement unencumbered by the usual chains of command. By challenging the repressive nature of their own institution—the university—the revolutionary students forced the state to show its hand, and the brutality with which it did so caused a general revulsion and led to the occupation of the factories and the general strike. The mass intervention of the working class was the greatest achievement of our struggle; it was the first step on the path to a better society, a path that, alas, was not followed to the end. The militant minorities failed to get the masses to follow their example: to take collective charge of the running of society. We do not believe for a single moment that the workers are incapable of taking the next logical step beyond occupying the factories—which is to run them on their own. We are sure that they can do what we ourselves have done in the universities. The militant minorities must continue to wage their revolutionary struggle, to show the workers what their trade unions try to make them forget: their own gigantic strength. The distribution of petrol by the workers in the refineries and the local strike committees shows clearly what the working class is capable of doing once it puts its mind to it.

During the recent struggle, many student militants became hero-worshippers of the working class, forgetting that every group has its own part to play in defending its own interests, and that, during a period of total confrontation, these interests converge.

The student movement must follow its own road—only thus can it contribute to the growth of militant minorities in the factories and workshops. We do not pretend that we can be leaders in the struggle, but it is a fact that small revolutionary groups can, at the right time and place, rupture the system decisively and irreversibly.

. . . It is absurd and romantic to speak of revolution with a capital R and to think of it as resulting from a single, decisive action. The revolutionary process grows and is strengthened daily not only in revolt against the boredom of a system that prevents people from seeing the "beach under the paving stones" but also in our determination to make the beach open to all.

If a revolutionary movement is to succeed, no form of organization whatever must be allowed to dam its spontaneous flow. It must evolve its own forms and structures.

. . . we can get some idea of the form that the movement of the future must take. Every small action committee, no less than every mass movement which seeks to improve the lives of all men must resolve:

1 to respect and guarantee the plurality and diversity of political currents within the revolutionary mainstream. It must accordingly grant minority groups the right of independent action—only if the plurality of ideas is allowed *to express itself in social practice* does this idea have any real meaning;

2 to ensure that all delegates are accountable to, and subject to immediate recall by, those who have elected them, and to oppose the introduction of specialists and specialization at every step by widening the skill and knowledge of all;

3 to ensure a continuous exchange of ideas, and to oppose any control of information and knowledge;

4 to struggle against the formation of any kind of hierarchy;

5 to abolish all artificial distinctions within labour, in particular between manual and intellectual work, and discrimination on grounds of sex;

6 to ensure that all factories and businesses are run by those who work in them;

7 to rid ourselves, in practice, of the Judaeo-Christian ethic, with its call for renunciation and sacrifice. There is only one reason for being a revolutionary— because it is the best way to live.

Reaction, which is bound to become more and more violent as the revolutionary movement increases its impact on society, forces us to look to our defences. But our main task is to keep on challenging the traditional bureaucratic structures both in the government and also in the working-class movements.

How can anyone represent anyone else? All we can do is to involve them. We can try and get a few movements going, inject politics into all the structures of society, into the Youth Clubs, Youth Hostels, the YMCA and the Saturday Night dance, get out on to the streets, out on to all the streets of all the towns. To bring real politics into everyday life is to get rid of the politicians. We must pass from a critique of the university to the anti-university, open to all. Our challenge of the collective control of knowledge by the bourgeoisie must be radical and intransigent.

The multiplication of nuclei of confrontation decentralizes political life and neutralizes the repressive influence of the radio, television and party politics. Every time we beat back intimidation on the spot, we are striking a blow for freedom. To break out from isolation, we must carry the struggle to every market place and not create Messianic organizations to do the job for us. We reject the policy committee and the editorial board.

. . .

Effective revolutionary action does not spring from "individual" or "external" needs—it can only occur when the two coincide so that the distinction itself breaks down. Every group must find its own form, take its own action, and speak its own language. When all have learnt to express themselves, in harmony with the rest, we shall have a free society.

Reader, you have come to the end of this book, a book that wants to say only one thing: between us we can change this rotten society. Now, put on your coat and make for the nearest cinema. Look at their deadly love-making on the screen. Isn't it better in real life? Make up your mind to learn to love. Then, during the interval, when the first advertisements come on, pick up your tomatoes or, if you prefer, your eggs, and chuck them. Then get out into the street, and peel off all the latest government proclamations until underneath you discover the message of the days of May and June.

Stay awhile in the street. Look at the passers-by and remind yourself: the last word has not yet been said. Then act. Act with others, not for them. Make the revolution here and now. It is your own. *C'est pour toi que tu fais la révolution.*

29
Fidel Castro

Fidel Castro (1927–), scholar, lawyer, and guerrilla leader, was the first to succeed in directing a communist revolution in the Western Hemisphere. His strong, charismatic leadership has met with wide support in Cuba and intense opposition from the most powerful governments of the hemisphere. Although his theoretical position has wavered over the years, Castro has given many strong statements of his Marxist principles and of his conviction that, in and out of Cuba, there is a continuing communist revolution, difficult and dangerous, to be fought and won.

THOSE WHO ARE NOT REVOLUTIONARY FIGHTERS CANNOT BE CALLED COMMUNISTS*

. . . To us the international communist movement is in the first place just that, a movement of communists, of revolutionary fighters. And those who are not revolutionary fighters cannot be called communists!

We conceive of Marxism as revolutionary thinking and action. Those who do not possess a truly revolutionary spirit cannot be called communists.

*These passages are from *Those Who Are Not Revolutionary Fighters Cannot Be Called Communists* (New York: Merit Publishers, 1968). They were originally delivered as a speech at the University of Havana, March 13, 1967.

There Are Some Who Call Themselves Revolutionaries Who Are Not Revolutionaries at All

Anyone can give himself the name of "eagle" without having a single feather on his back. (Laughter.) In the same way, there are people who call themselves communists without having a communist hair on their head. The international communist movement, to our way of thinking, is not a church, it is not a religious sect or a Masonic lodge that obliges us to hallow any weakness, any deviation, that obliges us to follow the policy of a mutual admiration society with all kinds of reformists and pseudo-revolutionaries.

Our stand regarding communist parties will be based on strictly revolutionary principles. The parties that have a line without hesitations and capitulationism, the parties that in our opinion, have a consistent revolutionary line, will receive our support in all circumstances; but the parties that entrench themselves behind the name of communists or Marxists and believe themselves to have a monopoly on revolutionary sentiment—what they really monopolize is reformism—will not be treated by us as revolutionary parties.

And if in any country those who call themselves communists do not know how to fulfill their duty, we will support those who, without calling themselves communists, conduct themselves like real communists in action and in struggle. For every true revolutionary, who bears within him the revolutionary spirit, revolutionary vocation, will always come to Marxism! It is impossible for a man, traveling the road of revolution, not to arrive at Marxism! And every revolutionary on the continent who is deserving of the name will arrive at the Marxist conception of society! What is important are the revolutionaries, those who are capable of making revolutions and developing themselves in revolutionary theory.

Many times practice comes first and then theory. Our people too are an example of that. Many, the immense majority of those who today proudly call themselves Marxist-Leninists, arrived at Marxism-Leninism by way of the revolutionary struggle. To exclude, to deny, to reject a priori all those who from the beginning did not call themselves communists is an act of dogmatism and unqualified sectarianism. Whoever denies that it is the road of revolution which leads the people to Marxism is no Marxist although he may call himself a communist.

This will be our line of conduct. It is the line that has guided our conduct in relations with the revolutionary movements.

This Revolution Will Follow Its Own Ideological Line and Will Never Be Anybody's Puppet

We proclaim it to the world: This Revolution will hold true to its path, this Revolution will follow its own line, this Revolution will never be anybody's satellite or yes-man. It will never ask anybody's permission to maintain its own position either in matters of ideology, or on domestic or foreign affairs; proudly and courageously our people are ready to face the future, whatever that future may hold.

Today we work with feverish enthusiasm, with more enthusiasm than ever before; and we are advancing in our national development, in the development of our economy more impetuously than at any other time in the past eight years. Great ideological battles are being won on all fronts, in all respects; and we will confidently hold true to our ideological path, with the confidence of true revolutionaries, with confidence in our people and in our masses.

Perhaps, if it had not been necessary to deal with the subjects I have been concerned with tonight, it would have been necessary to talk about this profound, incredible revolution that is taking place in the awareness of our people. We look to the future serenely and confidently, as we face any eventuality. We are aware that this struggle will not and cannot be easy, that we live on a continent in full revolutionary ferment, in the midst of a score of peoples who are waking up to reality, who are already fighting or are getting ready to do so. We realize that threats of all kinds will be hurled at us, and conspiracies will be organized against us, and possibly even aggressions by the dozens will be launched against us. Very well, from this very moment, we declare ourselves invincible.

7

THE DICTATORSHIP OF THE PROLETARIAT

It was evident that the overthrow of capitalist regimes could not result in the immediate achievement of the classless society; all the profound social changes that had been envisaged by communist thinkers would certainly have to await the completion of a transitional period, during which the remnants of the old order would be cleared away, and the foundations for the new order laid down.

But the stages of this transition, and the form of government during these stages, became matters of intense dispute among communist theoreticians. Lenin, of course, was the principal master; as architect of the first successful proletarian revolution, and leader of the most powerful socialist state, his views concerning the forms and methods of governing during the transition were the starting point for almost all communists.

Lenin, a man of very strong will, insisted that although the state was destined to wither away (as Engels had written) it could not do so while bourgeois power remained a serious threat to the Union of Soviet Socialist Republics from within and from without. The response of the Soviet state—very far from having withered away—must be iron-fisted. A dictatorship was called for: the dictatorship of the proletariat.

Not all Marxists accepted the need for absolute autocracy during the transition to communism. Karl Kautsky, Eduard Bernstein, and others remained hopeful that democratic institutions could be retained, even strengthened as Marxism progressed. That was not to be. Communist governments, from the time of Lenin's first accession to power in 1917 until the general collapse of the communist governments in Europe in 1991, remained rigidly hierarchical. Most communist regimes were totalitarian and avowedly dictatorial. The movement that Marx had begun with the hope that human exploitation might finally be eradicated was consummated not in the humane and creative society of which he had dreamed, but in the brutality of the dictatorship of the proletariat.

30
V. I. Lenin

In *State and Revolution* Lenin dealt extensively with the transition from capitalism to communism. There must be socialist states during this period, of course, and like all states they must be repressive—but their repression will be directed against the residue of bourgeois power, and they will serve to protect the achievements of the now-ruling proletariat. The minority of exploiters who had long suppressed others will now taste suppression themselves. There will be stages in the advance toward the classless society, of course—but the length of time these stages will require, and the forms that the withering away of state power will take, are matters that must be left completely open. Lenin is forthright in promising a government that will rule with a heavy hand.

THE TRANSITION FROM CAPITALISM TO COMMUNISM*

It is clear that there can be no question of defining the exact moment of the *future* withering away—the more so as it must obviously be a rather lengthy process. . . .

The whole theory of Marx is an application of the theory of evolution—in its most consistent, complete, well considered and fruitful form—to modern capitalism. It was natural for Marx to raise the question of applying this theory both to the *coming* collapse of capitalism and to the *future* evolution of *future* Communism.

On the basis of what *data* can the future evolution of future Communism be considered?

On the basis of the fact that *it has its origin* in capitalism, that it develops historically from capitalism, that it is the result of the action of a social force to which capitalism *has given birth*. There is no shadow of an attempt on Marx's part to conjure up a Utopia, to make idle guesses about that which cannot be known. Marx treats the question of Communism in the same way as a naturalist would treat the question of the evolution of, say, a new biological species, if he knew that such and such was its origin, and such and such the direction in which it changed.

Marx, first of all, brushes aside the confusion the Gotha Programme brings into the question of the interrelation between state and society.

Contemporary society" is the capitalist society—he writes—which exists in all civilized countries, more or less free of medieval admixture, more or less modified by each country's particular historical development, more or less developed. In contrast with this, the "contemporary state" varies with every state boundary. It is different in the Prusso-German Empire from what it is in Switzerland, and different in England from what it is in the United States. The "contemporary state" is therefore a fiction.

Nevertheless, in spite of the motley variety of their forms, the different states of the various civilized countries all have this in common: they are all based on modern bour-

*This and the following passages are from V. I. Lenin, *State and Revolution*, 1917. Reprinted by permission of the Foreign Languages Publishing House, Moscow.

geois society, only a little more or less capitalistically developed. Consequently, they also have certain essential characteristics in common. In this sense, it is possible to speak of the "contemporary state" in contrast to the future, when its present root, bourgeois society, will have perished.

Then the question arises: what transformation will the state undergo in a Communist society? In other words, what social functions analogous to the present functions of the state will then still survive? This question can only be answered scientifically, and however many thousand times the word people is combined with the word state, we get not a flea-jump closer to the problem. . . .*

Having thus ridiculed all talk about a "people's state," Marx formulates the question and warns us, as it were, that to arrive at a scientific answer one must rely only on firmly established scientific data.

The first fact that has been established with complete exactness by the whole theory of evolution, by science as a whole—a fact which the Utopians forgot, and which is forgotten by the present-day opportunists who are afraid of the Socialist revolution—is that, historically, there must undoubtedly be a special stage or epoch of *transition* from capitalism to Communism. . . .

Between capitalist and Communist society—Marx continues—lies the period of the revolutionary transformation of the former into the latter. To this also corresponds a political transition period, in which the state can be no other than *the revolutionary dictatorship of the proletariat.*†

This conclusion Marx bases on an analysis of the role played by the proletariat in modern capitalist society, on the data concerning the evolution of this society, and on the irreconcilability of the opposing interests of the proletariat and the bourgeoisie.

Earlier the question was put thus: to attain its emancipation, the proletariat must overthrow the bourgeoisie, conquer political power and establish its own revolutionary dictatorship.

Now the question is put somewhat differently: the transition from capitalist society, developing towards Communism, towards a Communist society, is impossible without a "political transition period," and the state in this period can only be the revolutionary dictatorship of the proletariat.

What, then, is the relation of this dictatorship to democracy?

We have seen that the *Communist Manifesto* simply places side by side the two ideas: the "transformation of the proletariat into the ruling class" and the "establishment of democracy." On the basis of all that has been said above, one can define more exactly how democracy changes in the transition from capitalism to Communism.

In capitalist society, under the conditions most favorable to its development, we have more or less complete democracy in the democratic republic. But this democracy is always bound by the narrow framework of capitalist exploitation, and con-

---

*K. Marx, *Critique of the Gotha Programme.—Ed.*
†*Ibid.—Ed.*

sequently always remains, in reality, a democracy for the minority, only for the possessing classes, only for the rich. Freedom in capitalist society always remains just about the same as it was in the ancient Greek republics: freedom for the slave-owners. The modern wage-slaves, owing to the conditions of capitalist exploitation, are so much crushed by want and poverty that "democracy is nothing to them," "politics is nothing to them"; that, in the ordinary peaceful course of events, the majority of the population is debarred from participating in social and political life. . . .

Democracy for an insignificant minority, democracy for the rich—that is the democracy of capitalist society. If we look more closely into the mechanism of capitalist democracy, everywhere, both in the "petty"—so-called petty—details of the suffrage (residential qualification, exclusion of women, etc.), and in the technique of the representative institutions, in the actual obstacles to the right of assembly (public buildings are not for "beggars"!), in the purely capitalist organization of the daily press, etc., etc.—on all sides we see restriction after restriction upon democracy. These restrictions, exceptions, exclusions, obstacles for the poor, seem slight, especially in the eyes of one who has himself never known want and has never been in close contact with the oppressed classes in their mass life (and nine-tenths, if not ninety-nine hundredths, of the bourgeois publicists and politicians are of this class), but in their sum total these restrictions exclude and squeeze out the poor from politics and from an active share in democracy.

Marx splendidly grasped this *essence* of capitalist democracy, when, in analyzing the experience of the Commune, he said that the oppressed were allowed, once every few years, to decide which particular representatives of the oppressing class should be in parliament to represent and repress them!

But from this capitalist democracy—inevitably narrow, subtly rejecting the poor, and therefore hypocritical and false to the core—progress does not march onward, simply, smoothly, and directly, to "greater and greater democracy," as the liberal professors and petty-bourgeois opportunists would have us believe. No, progress marches onward, i.e., towards Communism, through the dictatorship of the proletariat; it cannot do otherwise, for there is no one else and no other way to *break the resistance* of the capitalist exploiters.

But the dictatorship of the proletariat—i.e., the organization of the vanguard of the oppressed as the ruling class for the purpose of crushing the oppressors—cannot produce merely an expansion of democracy. *Together* with an immense expansion of democracy which *for the first time* becomes democracy for the poor, democracy for the people, and not democracy for the rich folk, the dictatorship of the proletariat produces a series of restrictions of liberty in the case of the oppressors, the exploiters, the capitalists. We must crush them in order to free humanity from wage-slavery; their resistance must be broken by force; it is clear that where there is suppression there is also violence, there is no liberty, no democracy.

Engels expressed this splendidly in his letter to Bebel when he said, as the reader will remember, that "as long as the proletariat still *needs* the state, it needs it not in the interests of freedom, but for the purpose of crushing its antagonists; and as soon as it becomes possible to speak of freedom, then the state, as such, ceases to exist."

Democracy for the vast majority of the people, and suppression by force, i.e., exclusion from democracy, of the exploiters and oppressors of the people—this is the modification of democracy during the *transition* from capitalism to Communism.

Only in Communist society, when the resistance of the capitalists has been completely broken, when the capitalists have disappeared, when there are no classes (i.e., there is no difference between the members of society in their relation to the social means of production), *only then* "the state ceases to exist," and *"it becomes possible to speak of freedom."* Only then a really full democracy, a democracy without any exceptions, will be possible and will be realized. And only then will democracy itself begin to *wither away* due to the simple fact that, freed from capitalist slavery, from the untold horrors, savagery, absurdities and infamies of capitalist exploitation, people will gradually *become accustomed* to the observance of the elementary rules of social life that have been known for centuries and repeated for thousands of years in all school books; they will become accustomed to observing them without force, without compulsion, without subordination, without the *special apparatus* for compulsion which is called the state.

The expression "the state *withers away,"* is very well chosen, for it indicates both the gradual and the elemental nature of the process. Only habit can, and undoubtedly will, have such an effect; for we see around us millions of times how readily people get accustomed to observe the necessary rules of life in common, if there is no exploitation, if there is nothing that causes indignation, that calls forth protest and revolt and has to be *suppressed.*

Thus, in capitalist society, we have a democracy that is curtailed, poor, false; a democracy only for the rich, for the minority. The dictatorship of the proletariat, the period of transition to Communism, will, for the first time, produce democracy for the people, for the majority, side by side with the necessary suppression of the minority—the exploiters. Communism alone is capable of giving a really complete democracy, and the more complete it is the more quickly will it become unnecessary and wither away of itself.

In other words: under capitalism we have a state in the proper sense of the word, that is, special machinery for the suppression of one class by another, and of the majority by the minority at that. Naturally, for the successful discharge of such a task as the systematic suppression by the exploiting minority of the exploited majority, the greatest ferocity and savagery of suppression are required, seas of blood are required, through which mankind is marching in slavery, serfdom, and wage-labor.

Again, during the *transition* from capitalism to Communism, suppression is *still* necessary; but it is the suppression of the minority of exploiters by the majority of exploited. A special apparatus, special machinery for suppression, the "state," is *still* necessary, but this is now a transitional state, no longer a state in the usual sense, for the suppression of the minority of exploiters, by the majority of the wage slaves of *yesterday,* is a matter comparatively so easy, simple and natural that it will cost far less bloodshed than the suppression of the risings of slaves, serfs or wage laborers, and will cost mankind far less. This is compatible with the diffusion of democracy among such an overwhelming majority of the population, that the need for *special machinery* of suppression will begin to disappear. The exploiters are, naturally, unable to suppress the people without a most complex machinery for performing this task; but *the people* can suppress the exploiters even with very simple "machinery," almost without any "machinery," without any special apparatus, by the simple *organization of the armed masses* (such as the Soviets of Workers' and Soldiers' Deputies, we may remark, anticipating a little).

Finally, only Communism renders the state absolutely unnecessary, for there is *no one* to be suppressed—"no one" in the sense of a *class,* in the sense of a systematic struggle with a definite section of the population. We are not Utopians, and we do not in the least deny the possibility and inevitability of excesses on the part of *individual persons,* nor the need to suppress *such* excesses. But, in the first place, no special machinery, no special apparatus of repression is needed for this; this will be done by the armed people itself, as simply and as readily as any crowd of civilized people, even in modern society, parts a pair of combatants or does not allow a woman to be outraged. And, secondly, we know that the fundamental social cause of excesses which consist in violating the rules of social life is the exploitation of the masses, their want and their poverty. With the removal of this chief cause, excesses will inevitably begin to *"wither away."* We do not know how quickly and in what succession, but we know that they will wither away. With their withering away, the state will also *wither away.*

Without going into Utopias, Marx defined more fully what can *now* be defined regarding this future, namely, the difference between the lower and higher phases (degrees, stages) of Communist society.

FIRST PHASE OF COMMUNIST SOCIETY

. . . Marx gives a sober estimate of exactly how a Socialist society will have to manage its affairs. Marx undertakes a *concrete* analysis of the conditions of life of a society in which there is no capitalism, and says:

> What we are dealing with here [analyzing the programme of the party] is not a Communist society which has *developed* on its own foundations, but, on the contrary, one which is just *emerging* from capitalist society, and which therefore in all respects—economic, moral and intellectual—still bears the birthmarks of the old society from whose womb it sprung.*

And it is this Communist society—a society which has just come into the world out of the womb of capitalism, and which, in all respects, bears the stamp of the old society—that Marx terms the "first," or lower, phase of Communist society.

The means of production are no longer the private property of individuals. The means of production belong to the whole of society. Every member of society, performing a certain part of socially-necessary work, receives a certificate from society to the effect that he has done such and such a quantity of work. According to this certificate, he receives from the public warehouses, where articles of consumption are stored, a corresponding quantity of products. Deducting that propor-

*Ibid.—Ed.

tion of labor which goes to the public fund, every worker, therefore, receives from society as much as he has given it.

"Equality" seems to reign supreme.

. . .

"Equal right," says Marx, we indeed have here; but it is *still* a "bourgeois right," which, like every right, *presupposes inequality.* Every right is an application of the *same* measure to *different* people who, in fact, are not the same and are not equal to one another; this is why "equal right" is really a violation of equality, and an injustice. In effect, every man having done as much social labor as every other, receives an equal share of the social products (with the above-mentioned deductions).

But different people are not alike: one is strong, another is weak; one is married, the other is not; one has more children, another has less, and so on.

> . . . With equal labor—Marx concludes—and therefore an equal share in the social consumption fund, one man in fact receives more than the other, one is richer than the other, and so forth. In order to avoid all these defects, rights, instead of being equal, must be unequal.*

The first phase of Communism, therefore, still cannot produce justice and equality; differences, and unjust differences, in wealth will still exist, but the *exploitation* of man by man will have become impossible, because it will be impossible to seize as private property the *means of production,* the factories, machines, land, and so on. In tearing down Lassalle's petty-bourgeois, confused phrase about "equality" and "justice" *in general,* Marx shows the *course of development* of Communist society, which is forced at first to destroy *only* the "injustice" that consists in the means of production having been seized by private individuals, and which *is not capable* of destroying at once the further injustice consisting in the distribution of the articles of consumption "according to work performed" (and not according to need).

The vulgar economists, including the bourgeois professors and also "our" Tugan-Baranovsky, constantly reproach the Socialists with forgetting the inequality of people and with "dreaming" of destroying this inequality. Such a reproach, as we see, only proves the extreme ignorance of the gentlemen propounding bourgeois ideology.

Marx not only takes into account with the greatest accuracy the inevitable inequality of men; he also takes into account the fact that the mere conversion of the means of production into the common property of the whole of society ("Socialism" in the generally accepted sense of the word) *does not remove* the defects of distribution and the inequality of "bourgeois right" which *continue to rule* as long as the products are divided "according to work performed."

> But these defects—Marx continues—are unavoidable in the first phase of Communist society, when, after long travail, it first emerges from capitalist society. Justice can never rise superior to the economic conditions of society and the cultural development conditioned by them.†

Ibid.—Ed.
†*Ibid.—Ed.*

And so, in the first phase of Communist society (generally called Socialism) "bourgeois right" is *not* abolished in its entirety, but only in part, only in respect of the means of production. "Bourgeois right" recognizes them as the private property of separate individuals. Socialism converts them into common property. *To that extent,* and to that extent alone, does "bourgeois right" disappear.

However, it continues to exist as far as its other part is concerned; it remains in the capacity of regulator (determining factor) distributing the products and allotting labor among the members of society. "He who does not work, shall not eat"— this Socialist principle is *already* realized; "for an equal quantity of labor, an equal quantity of products"—this Socialist principle is also *already* realized. However, this is not yet Communism, and this does not abolish "bourgeois right," which gives to unequal individuals, in return for an unequal (in reality unequal) amount of work, an equal quantity of products.

This is a "defect," says Marx, but it is unavoidable during the first phase of Communism; for, if we are not to fall into Utopianism, we cannot imagine that, having overthrown capitalism, people will at once learn to work for society *without any standards of right;* indeed, the abolition of capitalism *does not immediately lay* the economic foundations for *such* a change.

And there is no other standard yet than that of "bourgeois right." To this extent, therefore, a form of state is still necessary, which, while maintaining public ownership of the means of production, would preserve the equality of labor and equality in the distribution of products.

The state is withering away in so far as there are no longer any capitalists, any classes, and, consequently, no *class* can be suppressed.

But the state has not yet altogether withered away, since there still remains the protection of "bourgeois right" which sanctifies actual inequality. For the complete extinction of the state, complete Communism is necessary.

HIGHER PHASE OF COMMUNIST SOCIETY

Marx continues:

> In a higher phase of Communist society, when the enslaving subordination of individuals in the division of labor has disappeared, and with it also the antagonism between mental and physical labor; when labor has become not only a means of living, but itself the first necessity of life; when, along with the all-round development of individuals, the productive forces too have grown, and all the springs of social wealth are flowing more freely—it is only at that stage that it will be possible to pass completely beyond the narrow horizon of bourgeois rights, and for society to inscribe on its banners: from each according to his ability; to each according to his needs!*

Only now can we appreciate the full correctness of Engels' remarks in which he mercilessly ridiculed all the absurdity of combining the words "freedom" and "state." While the state exists there is no freedom. When there is freedom, there will be no state.

*Ibid.—Ed.

The economic basis for the complete withering away of the state is that high stage of development of Communism when the antagonism between mental and physical labor disappears, that is to say, when one of the principal sources of modern *social* inequality disappears—a source, moreover, which it is impossible to remove immediately by the mere conversion of the means of production into public property, by the mere expropriation of the capitalists.

This expropriation will make a gigantic development of the productive forces *possible.* And seeing how incredibly, even now, capitalism *retards* this development, how much progress could be made even on the basis of modern technique at the level it has reached, we have a right to say, with the fullest confidence, that the expropriation of the capitalists will inevitably result in a gigantic development of the productive forces of human society. But how rapidly this development will go forward, how soon it will reach the point of breaking away from the division of labor, of removing the antagonism between mental and physical labor, of transforming work into the "first necessity of life"—this we do not and *cannot* know.

Consequently, we have a right to speak solely of the inevitable withering away of the state, emphasizing the protracted nature of this process and its dependence upon the rapidity of development of the *higher phase* of Communism; leaving quite open the question of lengths of time, or the concrete forms of withering away, since material for the solution of such questions is *not available.*

The state will be able to wither away completely when society has realized the rule: "From each according to his ability; to each according to his needs," i.e., when people have become accustomed to observe the fundamental rules of social life, and their labor is so productive, that they voluntarily work *according to their ability.* "The narrow horizon of bourgeois rights," which compels one to calculate, with the hard-heartedness of a Shylock, whether he has not worked half an hour more than another, whether he is not getting less pay than another—this narrow horizon will then be left behind. There will then be no need for any exact calculation by society of the quantity of products to be distributed to each of its members; each will take freely "according to his needs."

From the bourgeois point of view, it is easy to declare such a social order "a pure Utopia," and to sneer at the Socialists for promising each the right to receive from society, without any control of the labor of the individual citizen, any quantity of truffles, automobiles, pianos, etc. Even now, most bourgeois "savants" deliver themselves of such sneers, thereby displaying at once their ignorance and their self-seeking defense of capitalism.

Ignorance—for it has never entered the head of any Socialist to "promise" that the highest phase of Communism will arrive; while the great Socialists, in *foreseeing* its arrival, presupposed both a productivity of labor unlike the present and a person not like the present man in the street, capable of spoiling, without reflection, like the seminary students in Pomyalovsky's book, the stores of social wealth, and of demanding the impossible.

Until the "higher" phase of Communism arrives, the Socialists demand the *strictest* control, *by society and by the state,* of the quantity of labor and the quantity of consumption; only this control must *start* with the expropriation of the capitalists, with the control of the workers over the capitalists, and must be carried out, not by a state of bureaucrats, but by a state of *armed workers.*

. . .

And here we come to that question of the scientific difference between Socialism and Communism, upon which Engels touched in his above-quoted discussion on the incorrectness of the name "Social-Democrat." The political difference between the first, or lower, and the higher phase of Communism will in time, no doubt, be tremendous; but it would be ridiculous to emphasize it now, under capitalism, and only, perhaps, some isolated Anarchist could invest it with primary importance. . . .

But the scientific difference between Socialism and Communism is clear. What is generally called Socialism was termed by Marx the "first" or lower phase of Communist society. In so far as the means of production become *public* property, the word "Communism" is also applicable here, providing we do not forget that it is *not* full Communism. The great significance of Marx's elucidations consists in this: that here, too, he consistently applies materialist dialectics, the doctrine of evolution, looking upon Communism as something which evolves *out of* capitalism. Instead of artificial, "elaborate," scholastic definitions and profitless disquisitions on the meaning of words (what Socialism is, what Communism is), Marx gives an analysis of what may be called stages in the economic ripeness of Communism.

In its first phase or first stage Communism *cannot* as yet be economically ripe and entirely free of all tradition and of all taint of capitalism. Hence the interesting phenomenon of Communism retaining, in its first phase, "the narrow horizon of bourgeois rights." Bourgeois rights, with respect to distribution of articles of *consumption,* inevitably presupposes, of course, the existence of the *bourgeois state,* for rights are nothing without an apparatus capable of *enforcing* the observance of the rights.

Consequently, for a certain time not only bourgeois rights, but even the bourgeois state remains under Communism, without the bourgeoisie!

This may look like a paradox, or simply a dialectical puzzle for which Marxism is often blamed by people who would not make the least effort to study its extraordinarily profound content.

But, as a matter of fact, the old surviving in the new confronts us in life at every step, in nature as well as in society. Marx did not smuggle a scrap of "bourgeois" rights into Communism of his own accord; he indicated what is economically and politically inevitable in a society issuing *from the womb* of capitalism.

Democracy is of great importance for the working class in its struggle for freedom against the capitalists. But democracy is by no means a limit one may not overstep; it is only one of the stages in the course of development from feudalism to capitalism, and from capitalism to Communism.

Democracy means equality. The great significance of the struggle of the proletariat for equality, and the significance of equality as a slogan, are apparent, if we correctly interpret it as meaning the abolition of *classes.* But democracy means only *formal* equality. Immediately after the attainment of equality for all members of society in *respect of* the ownership of the means of production, that is, of equality of labor and equality of wages, there will inevitably arise before humanity the question of going further from formal equality to real equality, i.e., to realizing the rule, "From each according to his ability; to each according to his needs." By what stages, by means of what practical measures humanity will proceed to this higher aim—this we do not and cannot know. But it is important to realize how infinitely mendacious is the usual bourgeois presentation of Socialism as something lifeless, petrified, fixed once for all, whereas in reality, it is *only* with Socialism that there will commence a rapid, genuine, real mass advance, in which first the *majority* and then the whole of the population will take part—an advance in all domains of social and individual life.

Democracy is a form of the state—one of its varieties. Consequently, like every state, it consists in organized, systematic application of force against human beings. This on the one hand. On the other hand, however, it signifies the formal recognition of the equality of all citizens, the equal right of all to determine the structure and administration of the state. This, in turn, is connected with the fact that, at a certain stage in the development of democracy, it first rallies the proletariat as a revolutionary class against capitalism, and gives it an opportunity to crush, to smash to bits, to wipe off the face of the earth the bourgeois state machinery—even its republican variety: the standing army, the police, and bureaucracy; then it substitutes for all this a *more* democratic, but still a state machinery in the shape of armed masses of workers, which becomes transformed into universal participation of the people in the militia.

Here "quantity turns into quality": *such* a degree of democracy is bound up with the abandonment of the framework of bourgeois society, and the beginning of its Socialist reconstruction. If *everyone* really takes part in the administration of the state, capitalism cannot retain its hold. In its turn, capitalism, as it develops, itself creates *prerequisites* for "everyone" *to be able* really to take part in the administration of the state. Among such prerequisites are: universal literacy, already realized in most of the advanced capitalist countries, then the "training and disciplining" of millions of workers by the huge, complex, and socialized apparatus of the post-office, the railways, the big factories, large-scale commerce, banking, etc., etc.

With such *economic* prerequisites it is perfectly possible, immediately, within twenty-four hours after the overthrow of the capitalists and bureaucrats, to replace them, in the control of production and distribution, in the business of *control* of labor and products, by the armed workers, by the whole people in arms. (The question of control and accounting must not be confused with the question of the scientifically educated staff of engineers, agronomists and so on. These gentlemen work today, obeying the capitalists; they will work even better tomorrow, obeying the armed workers.)

Accounting and control—these are the *chief* things necessary for the organizing and correct functioning of the *first phase* of Communist society. *All* citizens are here transformed into hired employees of the state, which is made up of the armed workers. *All* citizens become employees and workers of *one* national state "syndicate." All that is required is that they should work equally, should regularly do their share of work, and should receive equal pay. The accounting and control necessary for this have been *simplified* by capitalism to the utmost, till they have become the extraordinarily simple operations of watching, recording and issuing receipts, within the reach of anybody who can read and write and knows the first four rules of arithmetic.*

When the *majority* of the people begin everywhere to keep such accounts and maintain such control over the capitalists (now converted into employees) and over the intellectual gentry, who still retain capitalist habits, this control will really become universal, general, national; and there will be no way of getting away from it, there will be "nowhere to go."

The whole of society will have become one office and one factory, with equal work and equal pay.

But this "factory" discipline, which the proletariat will extend to the whole of society after the defeat of the capitalists and the overthrow of the exploiters, is by no means our ideal, or our final aim. It is but a *foothold* necessary for the radical cleansing of society of all the hideousness and foulness of capitalist exploitation, *in order to advance further.*

From the moment when all members of society, or even only the overwhelming majority, have learned how to govern the state *themselves,* have taken this business into their own hands, have "established" control over the insignificant minority of capitalists, over the gentry with capitalist leanings, and the workers thoroughly demoralized by capitalism—from this moment the need for any government begins to disappear. The more complete the democracy, the nearer the moment when it begins to be unnecessary. The more democratic the "state" consisting of armed workers, which is "no longer a state in the proper sense of the word," the more rapidly does *every* state begin to wither away.

For when *all* have learned to manage, and independently are actually managing by themselves social production, keeping accounts, controlling the idlers, the gentlefolk, the swindlers and similar "guardians of capitalist traditions," then the escape from this national accounting and control will inevitably become so increasingly difficult, such a rare exception, and will probably be accompanied by such swift and severe punishment (for the armed workers are men of practical life, not sentimental intellectuals, and they will scarcely allow anyone to trifle with them), that very soon the *necessity* of observing the simple, fundamental rules of everyday social life in common will have become a *habit.*

The door will then be wide open for the transition from the first phase of Communist society to its higher phase, and along with it to the complete withering away of the state.

---

*When most of the functions of the state are reduced to this accounting and control by the workers themselves, then it ceases to be a "political state," and the "public functions will lose their political character and be transformed into simple administrative functions" [Engels, *Neue Zeit,* 1913, Vol. 32, p. 39—*Ed.*]

31
V. I. Lenin

Three years after the establishment of the Union of Soviet Socialist Republics, in which Lenin himself (as General Secretary of the Communist Party) had become the supreme authority, he published *"Left Wing" Communism: An Infantile Disorder.* Having overcome his enemies on the right, and now faced with the practical problems of state leadership, he was infuriated by unsophisticated Marxists who did not understand the steps he thought required to protect and advance the revolution in other states, especially in the Western "democracies." These doctrinaire "left wing" communists did not appreciate how essential it was to infiltrate the trade unions, to win elections to bourgeois parliaments—and above all, to *compromise* when doing so was tactically advantageous.

How are communist parties to be structured? They must maintain rigid internal discipline, combined with the utmost flexibility in external affairs. The dictatorship of the proletariat in the U.S.S.R. must support the advance of communism around the world; working classes everywhere must be instructed, inspired, their class-consciousness raised. Marxist theory is true and vital, thought Lenin—but it must be applied concretely with intelligent revolutionary tactics.

"LEFT WING" COMMUNISM*

Certainly nearly everyone now realizes that the Bolsheviks could not have maintained themselves in power for two and a half months, let alone for two and a half years, unless the strictest, truly iron discipline prevailed in our Party, and unless the latter had been rendered the fullest and unreserved support of the whole mass of the working class, that is, of all its thinking, honest, self-sacrificing and influential elements who are capable of leading or of attracting the backward strata.

The dictatorship of the proletariat is a most determined and most ruthless war waged by the new class against a *more powerful* enemy, the bourgeoisie, whose resistance is increased *tenfold* by its overthrow (even if only in one country), and whose power lies not only in the strength of international capital, in the strength and durability of the international connections of the bourgeoisie, but also in the *force of habit,* in the strength of *small production.* For, unfortunately, small production is still very, very widespread in the world, and small production *engenders* capitalism and the bourgeoisie continuously, daily, hourly, spontaneously, and on a mass scale. For all these reasons the dictatorship of the proletariat is essential, and victory over the bourgeoisie is impossible without a long, stubborn and desperate war of life and death, a war demanding perseverance, discipline, firmness, indomitableness and unity of will. . . .

*This and the following passages are from V. I. Lenin, *"Left Wing" Communism: An Infantile Disorder,* 1920. Reprinted by permission of the Foreign Languages Publishing House, Moscow.

. . . the question arises: how is the discipline of the revolutionary party of the proletariat maintained? How is it tested? How is it reinforced? First, by the class consciousness of the proletarian vanguard and by its devotion to the revolution, by its perseverance, self-sacrifice and heroism. Secondly, by its ability to link itself, to keep in close touch with, and to a certain extent, if you like, to merge itself with the broadest masses of the toilers—primarily with the proletarian, *but also with the non-proletarian* toiling masses. Thirdly, by the correctness of the political leadership exercised by this vanguard and of its political strategy and tactics, provided that the broadest masses have been convinced *by their own experiences* that they are correct. Without these conditions, discipline in a revolutionary party that is really capable of being a party of the advanced class, whose mission it is to overthrow the bourgeoisie and transform the whole of society, cannot be achieved. Without these conditions, all attempts to establish discipline inevitably fall flat and end in phrasemongering and grimacing. On the other hand, these conditions cannot arise all at once. They are created only by prolonged effort and hard-won experience. Their creation is facilitated by correct revolutionary theory, which, in its turn, is not a dogma but assumes final shape only in close connection with the practical activity of a truly mass and truly revolutionary movement.

[COMPROMISES]

. . . The conclusion to be drawn is clear: to reject compromises "on principle," to reject the admissibility of compromises in general, no matter of what kind, is childishness which it is difficult even to take seriously. A political leader who desires to be useful to the revolutionary proletariat must know how to single out *concrete* cases of such compromises as are inadmissible, as express opportunism and *treachery,* and direct all the force of his criticism, the edge of his merciless exposure and relentless war, against *those concrete* compromises, and not allow the highly experienced "practical" Socialists and parliamentary Jesuits to dodge and wriggle out of responsibility by resorting to arguments about "compromises in general." It is precisely in this way that Messieurs the "leaders" of the British trade unions, as well as of the Fabian Society and the "Independent" Labour Party, dodge responsibility *for the treachery they have perpetrated,* for the commission of a compromise that *really* expresses the worst kind of opportunism, treachery and betrayal.

There are compromises and compromises. One must be able to analyze the situation and the concrete conditions of each compromise, or of each variety of compromise. One must learn to distinguish between a man who gave the bandits money and firearms in order to lessen the evil committed by them and to facilitate the task of getting them captured and shot, and a man who gives bandits money and firearms in order to share in the loot. In politics this is not always as easy as in this childishly simple example. But anyone who set out to invent a recipe for the workers that would provide ready-made solutions for all cases in life, or who promised that the politics of the revolutionary proletariat would never encounter difficult or intricate situations, would be simply a charlatan. . . .

. . . Of course, to very young and inexperienced revolutionaries, as well as to petty-bourgeois revolutionaries of even a very respectable age and very experienced, it seems exceedingly "dangerous," incomprehensible and incorrect to "allow compromises." And many sophists (being super-experienced or excessively "experienced" politicians) reason exactly in the same way as the British leaders of opportunism mentioned by Comrade Lansbury: "If it is permissible for the Bolsheviks to make such and such a compromise, then why should we not be allowed to make any compromise?" But proletarians schooled in numerous strikes (to take only this manifestation of the class struggle) usually understand quite well the very profound (philosophical, historical, political, and psychological) truth expounded by Engels. Every proletarian has been through strikes and has experienced "compromises" with the hated oppressors and exploiters, when the workers had to go back to work either without having achieved anything or consenting to a partial satisfaction of their demands. Every proletarian—owing to the conditions of the mass struggle and the sharp intensification of class antagonisms in which he lives—notices the difference between a compromise enforced by objective conditions (such as lack of strike funds, no outside support, extreme hunger and exhaustion), a compromise which in no way diminishes the revolutionary devotion and readiness for further struggle on the part of the workers who have agreed to such a compromise, and a compromise by traitors who try to ascribe to outside causes their own selfishness (strikebreakers also effect "compromises"!), cowardice, desire to toady to the capitalists and readiness to yield to intimidation, sometimes to persuasion, sometimes to sops, and sometimes to flattery on the part of the capitalists. (Such cases of traitors' compromises by trade union leaders are particularly plentiful in the history of the British labor movement; but in one form or another nearly all workers in all countries have witnessed the same sort of thing.)

Of course, individual cases of exceptional difficulty and intricacy occur when it is possible to determine the real character of this or that "compromise" only with the greatest difficulty; just as there are cases of homicide where it is very difficult to decide whether the homicide was fully justified and even essential (as, for example, legitimate self-defense), or due to unpardonable negligence, or even to a cunningly executed plan. Of course, in politics, in which extremely complicated—national and international—relations between classes and parties have sometimes to be dealt with, very many cases will arise that will be much more difficult than a legitimate "compromise" during a strike, or the treacherous "compromise" of a strikebreaker, or of a treacherous leader, etc. It would be absurd to concoct a recipe or general rule ("No Compromise!") to serve all cases. One must have the brains to analyze the situation in each separate case. Incidentally, the significance of a party organization and of party leaders worthy of the name lies precisely in the fact that they help by means of the prolonged, persistent, varied and all-round efforts of all thinking representatives of the given class, in the acquisition of the necessary knowledge, the necessary experience and—apart from knowledge and experience—the necessary political instinct for the speedy and correct solution of intricate political problems.

Naïve and utterly inexperienced people imagine that it is sufficient to admit the permissibility of compromises *in general* in order to obliterate the dividing line between opportunism, against which we wage and must wage an irreconcilable struggle, and revolutionary Marxism, or Communism. But if such people do not yet know that *all* dividing lines in nature and in society are mutable and to a certain extent conventional—they cannot be assisted otherwise than by a long process of training, education, enlightenment, and by political and everyday experience. It is important to single out from the practical questions of the politics of each separate or specific historical moment those which reveal the principal type of impermissible, treacherous compromises embodying the opportunism that is fatal to the revolutionary class, and to exert all efforts to explain them and combat them. . . .

". . . to reject most emphatically all compromises with other parties . . . all policy of maneuvering and compromise," write the German "Lefts" in the Frankfurt pamphlet.

It is a wonder that, holding such views, these "Lefts" do not emphatically condemn Bolshevism! For, the German "Lefts" must know that the whole history of Bolshevism, both before and after the October Revolution, is *full* of instances of maneuvering, temporizing and compromising with other parties, bourgeois parties included!

To carry on a war for the overthrow of the international bourgeoisie, a war which is a hundred times more difficult, prolonged and complicated than the most stubborn of ordinary wars between states, and to refuse beforehand to maneuver, to utilize the conflict of interests (even though temporary) among one's enemies, to refuse to temporize and compromise with possible (even though transitory, unstable, vacillating and conditional) allies—is not this ridiculous in the extreme? Is it not as though, when making a difficult ascent of an unexplored and hitherto inaccessible mountain, we were to refuse beforehand ever to move in zigzags, ever to retrace our steps, ever to abandon the course once selected to try others? . . .

[COMMUNISM AND TRADE UNIONS]

And we cannot but regard as equally ridiculous and childish nonsense the ponderous, very learned, and frightfully revolutionary disquisitions of the German Lefts to the effect that Communists cannot and should not work in reactionary trade unions, that it is permissible to refuse to do such work, that it is necessary to leave the trade unions and to create an absolutely brand-new, immaculate "Workers Union" invented by very nice (and for the most part, probably, very youthful) Communists, etc., etc.

Capitalism inevitably bequeaths to Socialism, on the one hand, old trade and craft distinctions among the workers, distinctions evolved in the course of centuries, and, on the other, trade unions which only very slowly, in the course of years and years, can and will develop into broader, industrial unions with less of the craft union about them (embracing whole industries, and not only crafts, trades and occupations), and later proceed, through these industrial unions, to the abolition of the division of labor among people, to the education, schooling and training of people with *an all-round development and an all-round* training, people *able to do everything*. Communism is marching and must march towards this goal, and *will reach it,* but only after very many years. To attempt in practice today to anticipate this future result of a fully developed, fully stabilized and formed, fully expanded and mature Communism would be like trying to teach higher mathematics to a four year old child.

We can (and must) begin to build Socialism not with imaginary human material, not with human material invented by us, but with the human material bequeathed to us by capitalism. That is very "difficult," it goes without saying, but no other approach to this task is serious enough to warrant discussion.

The trade unions were a tremendous progressive step for the working class at the beginning of the development of capitalism, inasmuch as they represented a transition from the disunity and helplessness of the workers to the *rudiments* of class organization. When the *highest* form of proletarian class organization began to arise, viz., the *revolutionary part of the proletariat* (which will not deserve the name until it learns to bind the leaders with the class and the masses into one single indissoluble whole), the trade unions inevitably began to reveal *certain* reactionary features, a certain craft narrowness, a certain tendency to be non-political, a certain inertness, etc. But the development of the proletariat did not, and could not, proceed anywhere in the world otherwise than through the trade unions, through their interaction with the party of the working class. The conquest of political power by the proletariat is a gigantic forward step for the proletariat as a class, and the Party must more than ever, and not merely in the old way but in a new way, educate and guide the trade unions, at the same time not forgetting that they are and will long remain an indispensable "school of Communism" and a preparatory school for training the proletarians to exercise their dictatorship, an indispensable organization of the workers for the gradual transfer of the management of the whole economic life of the country to the working *class* (and not to the separate trades), and later to all the toilers.

A *certain* amount of "reactionariness" in trade unions, in the sense mentioned, is *inevitable* under the dictatorship of the proletariat. He who does not understand this utterly fails to understand the fundamental conditions of the *transition* from capitalism to Socialism. To fear *this* "reactionariness," to try to *avoid* it, to skip it, would be the greatest folly, for it would mean fearing that function of the proletarian vanguard which consists in training, educating, enlightening and drawing into the new life the most backward strata and masses of the working class and the peasantry. On the other hand, to postpone the achievement of the dictatorship of the proletariat until a time when not a single worker with a narrow craft outlook, not a single worker with craft and craft-union prejudices is left, would be a still greater mistake. The art of politics (and the Communist's correct understanding of his tasks) lies in correctly gauging the conditions and the moment when the vanguard of the proletariat can successfully seize power, when it is able, during and after the seizure of power, to obtain adequate support from adequately broad strata of the working class and of the non-proletarian toiling masses, and when it is able thereafter to maintain, consolidate and extend its rule by educating, training and attracting ever broader masses of the toilers. . . .

But we wage the struggle against the "labor aristocracy" in the name of the masses of the workers and in order to attract them to our side; we wage the strug-

gle against the opportunist and social-chauvinist leaders in order to attract the working class to our side. To forget this most elementary and self-evident truth would be
stupid. But it is just this stupidity the German "Left" Communists are guilty of
when, *because* of the reactionary and counter-revolutionary character of the *heads*
of the trade unions, they jump to the conclusion that . . . we must leave the trade
unions!! that we must refuse to work in them!! that we must create new and *artificial* forms of labor organization!! This is such an unpardonable blunder as to be
equivalent to the greatest service the Communists could render the bourgeoisie. . . .
To refuse to work in the reactionary trade unions means leaving the insufficiently
developed or backward masses of the workers under the influence of the reactionary
leaders, the agents of the bourgeoisie, the labor aristocrats, or the workers who have
"become completely bourgeois" (*cf.* Engels' letter to Marx in 1852 on the British
workers) [*Selected Correspondence* of Marx and Engels, p. 60].

It is just this absurd "theory" that the Communists must not belong to reactionary trade unions that most clearly shows how frivolous is the attitude of the
"Left" Communists towards the question of influencing "the masses," and how
they abuse their vociferations about "the masses." If you want to help "the
masses" and to win the sympathy, confidence and support of "the masses," you
must not fear difficulties, you must not fear the pin-pricks, chicanery, insults and
persecution of the "leaders" (who, being opportunists and social-chauvinist, are in
most cases directly or indirectly connected with the bourgeoisie and the police),
but must imperatively *work wherever the masses are to be found.* You must be
capable of every sacrifice, of overcoming the greatest obstacles in order to carry
on agitation and propaganda systematically, perserveringly, persistently and
patiently precisely in those institutions, societies and associations—even the most
reactionary—in which proletarian or semi-proletarian masses are to be found. And
the trade unions and workers' cooperatives (the latter at least sometimes) are precisely the organizations where the masses are to be found. . . .

There can be no doubt that people like Gompers, Henderson, Jouhaux and
Legien are very grateful to "Left" revolutionaries who, like the German opposition "on principle" (heaven preserve us from such "principles"!) or like some of
the revolutionaries in the American Industrial Workers of the World, advocate
leaving the reactionary trade unions and refusing to work in them. There can be
no doubt that those gentlemen, the "leaders" of opportunism, will resort to every
trick of bourgeois diplomacy, to the aid of bourgeois governments, the priests,
the police and the courts, to prevent Communists joining the trade unions, to
force them out by every means, to make their work in the trade unions as
unpleasant as possible, to insult, bait and persecute them. We must be able to
withstand all this, to agree to any sacrifice, and even—if need be—to resort to all
sorts of stratagems, artifices, illegal methods, to evasions and subterfuges, only
so as to get into the trade unions, to remain in them, and to carry on Communist
work within them at all costs. . . . Of course, in Western Europe, where legal-
istic, constitutionalist, bourgeois-democratic prejudices are very deeply ingrained,
it is more difficult to carry on such work. But it can and should be carried on,
and carried on systematically. . . .

[COMMUNISM AND PARLIAMENTS]

On German "Left" Communists, with the greatest contempt—and with the greatest frivolity—reply to the question [of a parliament] in the negative. Their arguments? . . .

> . . . One must emphatically reject . . . all reversion to parliamentary forms of struggle, which have become historically and politically obsolete. . . .

This is said with absurd pretentiousness, and is obviously incorrect. "Reversion" to parliamentarism! Perhaps there is already a Soviet republic in Germany? It does not look like it! How, then, is it possible to speak of "reversion"? Is it not an empty phrase?

Parliamentarism has become "historically obsolete." That is true as regards propaganda. But everyone knows that this is still a long way from overcoming it *practically.* Capitalism could have been declared, and quite rightly, to be "historically obsolete" many decades ago, but that does not at all remove the need for a very long and very persistent struggle *on the soil* of capitalism. Parliamentarism is "historically obsolete" from the standpoint of *world history,* that is to say, the *epoch* of bourgeois parliamentarism has come to an end and the *epoch* of the proletarian dictatorship has *begun.* That is incontestable. But when dealing with world *history* one counts in decades. Ten or twenty years sooner or later makes no difference when measured by the scale of world history; from the standpoint of world history it is a trifle that cannot be calculated even approximately. But that is precisely why it is a howling theoretical blunder to measure questions of practical politics with the scale of world history.

Is parliamentarism "politically obsolete"? That is quite another matter. . . . How can one say that "parliamentarism is politically obsolete," when "millions" and "legions" of *proletarians* are not only still in favour of parliamentarism in general, but are downright "counter-revolutionary"!? Clearly, parliamentarism in Germany is *not yet* politically obsolete. Clearly, the "Lefts" in Germany have mistaken *their desire,* their ideological-political attitude, for actual fact. That is the most dangerous mistake revolutionaries can make. In Russia—where the extremely fierce and savage yoke of tsardom for a very long time and in very varied forms produced revolutionaries of diverse shades, revolutionaries who displayed astonishing devotion, enthusiasm, heroism and strength of will—we observed this mistake of the revolutionaries very closely, we studied it very attentively and are very well acquainted with it, and we can therefore notice it very clearly in others. Parliamentarism, of course, is "politically obsolete" for the Communists in Germany; but—and that is the whole point—we must not regard what is obsolete *for us* as being obsolete *for the class,* as being obsolete *for the masses.* Here again we find that the "Lefts" do not know how to reason, do not know how to conduct themselves as the party of the *class,* as the party of the *masses.* You must not sink to the level of the masses, to the level of the backward strata of the class. That is incontestable. You must tell them the bitter truth. You must call their bourgeois-democratic and parliamentary prejudices—prejudices. But at the same time you must *soberly* observe the *actual* state of class consciousness and preparedness of the whole class (not only of its Communist vanguard), of all the toiling *masses* (not only of its advanced elements). . . .

[THE TASK OF THE COMMUNIST PARTIES]

. . . As long as national and state differences exist among peoples and countries—and these differences will continue to exist for a very long time even after the dictatorship of the proletariat has been established on a world scale—the unity of international tactics of the Communist working class movement of all countries demands, not the elimination of variety, not the abolition of national differences (that is a foolish dream at the present moment), but such an application of the *fundamental* principles of Communism (Soviet power and the dictatorship of the proletariat) as will *correctly modify* these principles in *certain particulars,* correctly adapt and apply them to national and national-state differences. The main task of the historical period through which all the advanced countries (and not only the advanced countries) are now passing is to investigate, study, seek, divine, grasp that which is peculiarly national, specifically national in the *concrete manner* in which each country *approaches* the fulfillment of the *single* international task, the victory over opportunism and "Left" doctrinairism within the working class movement, the overthrow of the bourgeoisie, and the establishment of a Soviet republic and a proletarian dictatorship. The main thing—not everything by a very long way, of course, but the main thing—has already been achieved in that the vanguard of the working class has been won over, in that it has ranged itself on the side of the Soviet power against parliamentarism, on the side of the dictatorship of the proletariat against bourgeois democracy. Now all efforts, all attention, must be concentrated on the *next* step—which seems, and from a certain standpoint really is, less fundamental, but which, on the other hand, is actually much closer to the practical carrying out of the task—namely, on seeking the forms of *transition* or *approach* to the proletarian revolution.

The proletarian vanguard has been ideologically won over. That is the main thing. Without it not even the first step towards victory can be made. But it is still a fairly long way from victory. Victory cannot be won with the vanguard alone. To throw the vanguard alone into the decisive battle, before the whole class, before the broad masses have taken up a position either of direct support of the vanguard, or at least of benevolent neutrality towards it and one in which they cannot possibly support the enemy, would be not merely folly but a crime. And in order that actually the whole class, that actually the broad masses of toilers and those oppressed by capital may take up such a position, propaganda and agitation alone are not enough. For this the masses must have their own political experience. Such is the fundamental law of all great revolutions. . . .

The immediate task that confronts the class-conscious vanguard of the international labor movement, i.e., the Communist Parties, groups and trends, is to be able to *lead* the broad masses (now, for the most part, slumbering, apathetic, hidebound, inert and dormant) to their new position, or, rather, to be able to lead *not only* their own party, but also these masses in their approach, their transition to the new position. While the first historical task (viz., that of winning over the class-conscious vanguard of the proletariat to the side of the Soviet power and the dictatorship of the working class) could not be accomplished without a complete ideological and political victory over opportunism and social-chauvinism, the second task, which now becomes the immediate task, and which consists in being able to lead *the masses* to the new position that will ensure the victory of the vanguard in the revolution. . . .

The Communists in Western Europe and America must learn to create a new, unusual, non-opportunist, non-careerist parliamentarism; the Communist Parties must issue their slogans; real proletarians, with the help of the unorganized and downtrodden poor, should scatter and distribute leaflets, canvass workers' houses and the cottages of the rural proletarians and peasants in the remote villages (fortunately there are not nearly so many remote villages in Europe as there are in Russia, and in England there are very few); they should go into the most common taverns, penetrate into the unions, societies and casual meetings where the common people gather, and talk to the people, not in scientific (and not in very parliamentary) language, they should not at all strive to "get seats" in parliament, but should everywhere strive to rouse the minds of the masses and to draw them into the struggle, to catch the bourgeois on their own statements, to utilize the apparatus they have set up, the elections they have appointed, the appeals to the country they have made, and to tell the people what Bolshevism is in a way that has never been possible (under bourgeois rule) outside of election times (not counting, of course, times of big strikes, when, in Russia, a *similar* apparatus for widespread popular agitation worked even more intensively). It is very difficult to do this in Western Europe and America, very, very difficult; but it can and must be done, because the tasks of Communism cannot be fulfilled without effort; and every effort must be made to fulfill *practical* tasks, ever more varied, ever more closely connected with all branches of social life, *winning* branch after branch and sphere after sphere *from the bourgeoisie.*

.   .   .

But in all cases and in all countries Communism is becoming steeled and is growing; its roots are so deep that persecution does not weaken it, does not debilitate it, but strengthens it. Only one thing is lacking to enable us to march forward more confidently and firmly to victory, namely, the universal and thoroughly thought-out appreciation by all Communists in all countries of the necessity of displaying the utmost *flexibility* in their tactics. . . .

[ON COMMUNIST MORALITY]*

[Morality, like all else in the social world, is determined (according to Lenin's view) by class interest and class struggle. The proletarian repudiation of morality, therefore, is the rejection of the moral standards and ideals of the capitalist class and leads to the development of its own, practical, class-oriented ethic. Ed.]

---

*From *The Tasks of the Youth Leagues,* an address delivered to the Third All-Russian Congress of the Russian Young Communist League, October 2, 1920. Reprinted from *The Strategy and Tactics of World Communism,* Supplement I, United States Government Printing Office, Washington, 1948.

. . . This brings me to the question of how we should teach Communism and what are the specific features of our methods.

Here, first of all, I will deal with the question of Communist ethics.

You must train yourselves to become Communists. The task of the Young Communist League is to organize its practical activities in such a way that, in learning, organizing, uniting and fighting, it shall train its members and all those who look upon it as their leader, train them to become Communists. The whole object of the training, education and tuition of the youth of today should be to imbue them with Communist ethics.

But is there such a thing as Communist ethics? Is there such a thing as Communist morality? Of course there is. Often it is made to appear that we have no ethics of our own; and very often the bourgeoisie accuse us Communists of repudiating all ethics. This is a method of shuffling concepts, of throwing dust in the eyes of the workers and peasants.

In what sense do we repudiate ethics and morality?

In the sense that they were preached by the bourgeoisie, who declared that ethics were God's commandments. We, of course, say that we do not believe in God, and that we know perfectly well that the clergy, the landlords and the bourgeoisie spoke in the name of God in order to pursue their own exploiters' interests. Or, instead of deducing these ethics from the commandments of morality, from the commandments of God, they deduced them from idealistic or semi-idealistic phrases, which were always very similar to God's commandments.

We repudiate all mortality that is taken outside of human, class concepts. We say that this is deception, a fraud, which clogs the brains of the workers and peasants in the interests of the landlords and capitalists.

We say that our morality is entirely subordinated to the interests of the class struggle of the proletariat. Our mortality is deduced from the class struggle of the proletariat.

The old society was based on the oppression of all the workers and peasants by the landlords and capitalists. We had to destroy this, we had to overthrow this; but for this we had to create unity. God will not create such unity.

This unity could be created only by the factories and works, only by the proletariat, trained, and roused from its age-long slumber; only when that class was formed did the mass movement begin which led to what we see now—the victory of the proletariat revolution in one of the weakest countries in the world, a country which for three years has repelled the attacks of the bourgeoisie of the whole world. And we see that the proletarian revolution is growing all over the world. We now say, on the basis of experience, that the proletariat alone could create the compact force that could take the lead of the disunited and scattered peasantry, that could withstand all the attacks of the exploiters. This class alone can help the toiling masses to unite, to rally and completely withstand all attacks upon, completely consolidate and completely build up, Communist society.

That is why we say that for us there is no such thing as morality taken outside of human society; such a morality is a fraud. For us, morality is subordinated to the interests of the class struggle of the proletariat.

32
Josef Stalin

It was Marx who originated the phrase "the dictatorship of the proletariat"; the elaboration of the phrase and its first realization were the work of Lenin. But it was Josef Stalin who turned that dictatorship into an extended national nightmare. How can one justify continuing rule with an iron fist in a Marxist society? Stalin's claim was that only by force could the revolution be protected, the nation preserved. He also claimed that oppressive measures would be directed only against the remnants of the bourgeoisie, yet millions of those oppressed by that dictatorship were Russian workers and peasants. Dictator for nearly thirty years, Stalin was greatly feared and widely hated. Shortly after his death in 1953 he and his "cult of personality" were condemned by his successors. But as an interpreter and expositor of Leninism, Stalin remains prominent. The dominant branch of orthodox Marxism-Leninism that he represented continued as a dictatorship almost until the collapse of the U.S.S.R. in 1991.

THE DICTATORSHIP OF THE PROLETARIAT AS THE INSTRUMENT OF THE PROLETARIAN REVOLUTION*

The question of the proletarian dictatorship is above all a question of the main content of the proletarian revolution. The proletarian revolution, its movement, its scope and its achievements acquire flesh and blood only through the dictatorship of the proletariat. The dictatorship of the proletariat is the instrument of the proletarian revolution, its organ, its most important mainstay, brought into being for the purpose of, firstly, crushing the resistance of the overthrown exploiters and consolidating the achievements of the proletarian revolution, and, secondly, carrying the proletarian revolution to its completion, carrying the revolution to the complete victory of socialism. The revolution can vanquish the bourgeoisie, can overthrow its power, without the dictatorship of the proletariat. But the revolution will be unable to crush the resistance of the bourgeoisie, to maintain its victory and to push forward to the final victory of socialism unless, at a certain stage in its development, it creates a special organ in the form of the dictatorship of the proletariat as its principal mainstay.

"The fundamental question of revolution is the question of power." (*Lenin.*) Does this mean that all that is required is to assume power, to seize it? No, it does not mean that. The seizure of power is only the beginning. For many reasons the bourgeoisie that is overthrown in one country remains for a long time stronger than the proletariat which has overthrown it. Therefore, the whole point is to retain power, to consolidate it, to make it invincible. What is needed to attain this? To attain this it is necessary to carry out at least the three main tasks that confront the dictatorship of the proletariat "on the morrow" of victory:

*This and the following passages are from J. Stalin's *The Foundations of Leninism,* 1924. Reprinted by permission of the Foreign Languages Publishing House, Moscow.

(a) to break the resistance of the landlords and capitalists who have been over-thrown and expropriated by the revolution, to liquidate every attempt on their part to restore the power of capital;

(b) to organize construction in such a way as to rally all the laboring people around the proletariat, and to carry on this work along the lines of preparing for the liquidation, the abolition of classes;

(c) to arm the revolution, to organize the army of the revolution for the strug-gle against foreign enemies, for the struggle against imperialism.

The dictatorship of the proletariat is needed to carry out, to fulfil these tasks.

.   .   .

That is why Lenin says:

> The dictatorship of the proletariat is a most determined and most ruthless war waged by the new class against a *more powerful* enemy, the bourgeoisie, whose resistance is increased *tenfold* by its overthrow, [that] the dictatorship of the proletariat is a persistent struggle—sanguinary and bloodless, violent and peaceful, military and economic, edu-cational and administrative—against the forces and traditions of the old society. (*Selected Works,* Vol. X, pp. 60, 84.)

It need hardly be proved that there is not the slightest possibility of carrying out these tasks in a short period, of doing all this in a few years. Therefore, the dictatorship of the proletariat, the transition from capitalism to communism, must not be regarded as a fleeting period of "super-revolutionary" acts and decrees, but as an entire historical era, replete with civil wars and external conflicts, with persistent organizational work and economic construction, with advances and retreats, victories and defeats. This historical era is needed not only to create the economic and cultural prerequisites for the complete victory of socialism, but also to enable the proletariat, first, to educate itself and become steeled as a force capable of governing the country, and, secondly, to re-educate and remold the petty-bourgeois strata along such lines as will assure the organization of socialist production.

.   .   .

THE DICTATORSHIP OF THE PROLETARIAT AS THE DOMINATION OF THE PROLETARIAT OVER THE BOURGEOISIE

From the foregoing it is evident that the dictatorship of the proletariat is not a mere change of personalities in the government, a change of "cabinet," etc., leav-ing the old economic and political order intact. The Mensheviks and opportunists of all countries, who fear dictatorship like fire and in their fright substitute the concept "conquest of power" for the concept "dictatorship of the proletariat," usually reduce the meaning of "conquest of power" to a change of "cabinet," to the accession to power of a new ministry made up of people like Scheidemann and Noske, MacDonald and Henderson. It is hardly necessary to explain that these and similar cabinet changes have nothing in common with the dictatorship of the proletariat, with the conquest of real power by the real proletariat. The

MacDonalds and Scheidemanns in power, while the old bourgeois order is allowed to remain, their so-called governments cannot be anything else than an apparatus serving the bourgeoisie, a screen to hide the ulcers of imperialism, a weapon in the hands of the bourgeoisie against the revolutionary movement of the oppressed and exploited masses. Capital needs such governments as a screen when it finds it inconvenient, unprofitable, difficult to oppress and exploit the masses without the aid of a screen. Of course, the appearance of such governments is a symptom that "over there" (i.e., in the capitalist camp) "all is not quiet at the Shipka Pass"; nevertheless, governments of this kind necessarily remain governments of capital in disguise. The government of a MacDonald or a Scheidemann is as far removed from the conquest of power by the proletariat as the sky from the earth. The dictatorship of the proletariat is not a mere change of government, but a new state, with new organs of power, both central and local; it is the state of the proletariat, which has arisen on the ruins of the old state, the state of the bourgeoisie.

The dictatorship of the proletariat arises not on the basis of the bourgeois order, but in the process of the breaking up of this order after the overthrow of the bourgeoisie, in the process of the expropriation of the landlords and capitalists, in the principal instruments and means of production, in the process of violent proletarian revolution. The dictatorship of the proletariat is a revolutionary power based on the use of force against the bourgeoisie.

The state is a machine in the hands of the ruling class for suppressing the resistance of its class enemies. *In this respect* the dictatorship of the proletariat does not differ essentially from the dictatorship of any other class, for the proletarian state is a machine for the suppression of the bourgeoisie. But there is one *substantial* difference. This difference consists in the fact that all hitherto existing class states have been dictatorships of an exploiting minority over the exploited majority, whereas the dictatorship of the proletariat is the dictatorship of the exploited majority over the exploiting minority.

Briefly: *the dictatorship of the proletariat is the rule—unrestricted by law and based on force—of the proletariat over the bourgeoisie, a rule enjoying the sympathy and support of the laboring and exploited masses.* (State and Revolution.)

From this follow two main conclusions:

First Conclusion   The dictatorship of the proletariat cannot be "complete" democracy, democracy for *all,* for the rich as well as for the poor; the dictatorship of the proletariat "must be a state that is democratic *in a new way—for** the proletarians and the propertyless in general—and dictatorial *in a new way—against** the bourgeoisie. . . ." (Lenin, *Selected Works,* Vol. VII, p. 34.) The talk of Kautsky and Co. about universal equality, about "pure" democracy, about "perfect" democracy, and the like, is but a bourgeois screen to conceal the indubitable fact that equality between exploited and exploiters is impossible. The theory of "pure" democracy is the theory of the upper stratum of the working class, which has been

*My italics.—*J.S.*

broken in and is being fed by the imperialist robbers. It was brought into being for the purpose of concealing the ulcers of capitalism, of touching up imperialism and lending it moral strength in the struggle against the exploited masses. Under capitalism there are no real "liberties" for the exploited, nor can there be, if for no other reason than that the premises, printing plants, paper supplies, etc., indispensable for the actual enjoyment of "liberties" are the privilege of the exploiters. Under capitalism the exploited masses do not, nor can they, really participate in the administration of the country, if for no other reason than that, even under the most democratic regime, governments, under the conditions of capitalism, are not set up by the people but by the Rothschilds and Stinneses, the Rockefellers and Morgans. Democracy under capitalism is *capitalist* democracy, the democracy of the exploiting minority, based on the restriction of the rights of the exploited majority and directed against this majority. Only under the dictatorship of the proletariat are real "liberties" for the exploited and real participation in the administration of the country by the proletarians and peasants possible. Under the dictatorship of the proletariat, democracy is *proletarian* democracy, the democracy of the exploited majority, based upon the restriction of the rights of the exploiting minority and directed against this minority.

Second Conclusion   The dictatorship of the proletariat cannot arise as the result of the peaceful development of bourgeois society and of bourgeois democracy; it can arise only as the result of the smashing of the bourgeois state machine, the bourgeois army, the bourgeois bureaucratic machine, the bourgeois police.

In a preface to *The Communist Manifesto* Marx and Engels wrote, quoting from *The Civil War in France:*

> The working class cannot simply lay hold of the ready-made state machine and wield it for its own purposes. (Marx, *Selected Works,* Vol. I, p. 190.)

In a letter to Kugelmann (1871) Marx wrote that the task of the proletarian revolution is

> no longer as before, to transfer the bureaucratic military machine from one hand to another, but to *smash* it, and that is a preliminary condition for every real people's revolution on the Continent. (Marx, *Selected Works,* Vol. II, p. 528.)

Marx's qualifying phrase about the Continent gave the opportunists and Mensheviks of all countries a pretext for proclaiming that Marx had thus conceded the possibility of the peaceful evolution of bourgeois democracy into a proletarian democracy, at least in certain countries outside the European continent (England, America). Marx did in fact concede that possibility, and he had good grounds for conceding it in regard to England and America in the 'seventies of the last century, when monopoly capitalism, and imperialism did not yet exist, and when these countries, owing to the special conditions of their development, had as yet no developed militarism and bureaucracy. That was the situation before the appearance of developed imperialism. But later, after a lapse of thirty or forty years, when the situation in these countries had radically changed, when imperialism had developed and had embraced all capitalist countries without exception, when militarism and bureaucracy had appeared in England and America also, when the special conditions for peaceful development in England and the United States had disappeared—then the qualification in regard to these countries necessarily could no longer hold good.

> Today [said Lenin], in 1917, in the epoch of the first great imperialist war, this qualification made by Marx is no longer valid. Both England and America, the greatest and the last representatives—in the whole world—of Anglo-Saxon "liberty," in the sense that militarism and bureaucracy were absent, have slid down entirely into the all-European, filthy, bloody morass of military-bureaucratic institutions to which everything is subordinated and which trample everything underfoot. Today, both in England and in America, the "preliminary condition for every real people's revolution" is the smashing, the *destruction* of the "ready-made state machine" (brought in those countries, between 1914 and 1917, to general "European" imperialist perfection). (*Selected Works,* Vol. VII, p. 37.)

In other words, the law of violent proletarian revolution, the law of the smashing of the bourgeois state machine as a preliminary condition for such a revolution, is an inevitable law of the revolutionary movement in the imperialist countries of the world.

Of course, in the remote future, if the proletariat is victorious in the most important capitalist countries, and if the present capitalist encirclement is replaced by a socialist encirclement, a "peaceful" path of development is quite possible for certain capitalist countries, whose capitalists, in view of the "unfavorable" international situation, will consider it expedient "voluntarily" to make substantial concessions to the proletariat. But this supposition applies only to a remote and possible future. With regard to the immediate future, there is no ground whatsoever for this supposition.

Therefore, Lenin is right in saying:

> The proletarian revolution is impossible without the forcible destruction of the bourgeois state machine and the substitution for it of a *new one*. . . . (*Selected Works,* Vol. VII, p. 124.)

33
Mao Tse-tung

Chairman Mao made no bones about the fact that his was a dictatorial regime. He was forthright in saying that repression would at times be essential if communist goals were to be achieved. His thoughts on the Communist Party, on dialectical analysis, and on the role of the arts during the transitional period are spelled out in *The Little Red Book*. In all his writings Mao emphasized the need for *discipline* in a highly centralized proletarian democracy—the dictatorship of the proletariat.

[THE PEOPLE'S DEMOCRATIC DICTATORSHIP]*

"You are dictatorial." My dear sirs, just as you say. That is just what we are. All the experiences of the Chinese people, accumulated in the course of several decades, tell us to put into effect a people's democratic dictatorship. This means that the reactionaries must be deprived of the right to voice their opinions; only the people have that right.

Who are the "people"? At the present stage in China, they are the working class, the peasantry, the petty bourgeoisie, and the national bourgeoisie.

Under the leadership of the working class and the Communist Party these classes unite to create their own state and elect their own government so as to enforce their dictatorship over the henchmen of imperialism—the landlord class and bureaucratic capitalist class, as well as the reactionary clique of the Kuomintang, which represents these classes, and their accomplices. The people's government will suppress such individuals. It will only tolerate them if they behave themselves, but not if they prove intractable in speech or action. If they are intractable, they will be instantly curbed and punished. Within the ranks of the people, the democratic system is carried out by giving freedom of speech, assembly, and association. The right to vote is given only to the people, not to the reactionaries.

These two aspects, democracy for the people and dictatorship for the reactionaries, when combined, constitute the people's democratic dictatorship.

Why must things be done in this way? Everyone is clear on this point. If things were not done in this way, the revolution would fail, the people would suffer, and the state would perish.

"Don't you want to abolish state power?" Yes, we do, but not at the present time. We cannot yet afford to. Why not? Because imperialism still exists, and within our country reactionaries and classes still exist.

Our present task is to strengthen the people's state machine—meaning principally the people's army, the people's police, and the people's courts—so that national defense can be made secure and the people's interests protected. Given these conditions, China, under the leadership of the working class and the Communist Party, can develop steadily from an agricultural into an industrial country and from a New Democratic into a Socialist and, eventually, a Communist society, when all classes will disappear and universal harmony become a reality. . . .

Summarizing our experiences and putting them in a nutshell: the people's democratic dictatorship is led by the working class through the Communist Party

*From Mao Tse-tung, *On People's Democratic Dictatorship*, 1949. The passage is from an official translation, published by the Foreign Languages Press, Peking, as the revised fifth edition, 1952.

and based upon the alliance of the workers and peasants. This dictatorship must unite with all international revolutionary forces. Such then is our formula, our main experience, our main program. . . .

The Communist Party*

The force at the core leading our cause forward is the Chinese Communist Party. The theoretical basis guiding our thinking is Marxism-Leninism.

> Opening address at the First Session of the First National People's Congress of the People's Republic of China (September 15, 1954).

. . . If we actually forget the Party's general line and general policy, then we shall be blind, half-baked, muddle-headed revolutionaries, and when we carry out a specific line for work and a specific policy, we shall lose our bearings and vacillate now to the left and now to the right, and the work will suffer.

> "Speech at a Conference of Cadres in the Shansi-Suiyuan Liberated Area" (April 1, 1948), *Selected Works*, Vol. IV, p. 238.

Socialism and Communism

Communism is at once a complete system of proletarian ideology and a new social system. It is different from any other ideological and social system, and is the most complete, progressive, revolutionary and rational system in human history. . . . The communist ideological and social system alone is full of youth and vitality, sweeping the world with the momentum of an avalanche and the force of a thunderbolt.

> "On New Democracy" (January 1940), *Selected Works*, Vol. II, pp. 360–61.

The socialist system will eventually replace the capitalist system; this is an objective law independent of man's will. However much the reactionaries try to hold back the wheel of history, sooner or later revolution will take place and will inevitably triumph.

> "Speech at the Meeting of the Supreme Soviet of the U.S.S.R. in Celebration of the 40th Anniversary of the Great October Socialist Revolution" (November 6, 1957).

The Correct Handling of Contradictions Among the People

We are confronted by two types of social contradictions—those between ourselves and the enemy and those among the people themselves. The two are totally different in their nature.

> *On the Correct Handling of Contradictions Among the People* (February 27, 1957), 1st pocket ed., p. 2.

*This and the following selections are from *Quotations from Chairman Mao Tse-tung* (Peking: Foreign Language Press, 1966).

The contradictions between ourselves and the enemy are antagonistic contradictions. Within the ranks of the people, the contradictions among the working people are non-antagonistic, while those between the exploited and the exploiting classes have a non-antagonistic aspect in addition to an antagonistic aspect.

Ibid., p. 3.

Qualitatively different contradictions can only be resolved by qualitatively different methods. For instance, the contradiction between the proletariat and the bourgeoisie is resolved by the method of socialist revolution; the contradiction between the great masses of the people and the feudal system is resolved by the method of democratic revolution; the contradiction between the colonies and imperialism is resolved by the method of national revolutionary war; the contradiction between the working class and the peasant class in socialist society is resolved by the method of collectivization and mechanization in agriculture; contradiction within the Communist Party is resolved by the method of criticism and self-criticism; the contradiction between society and nature is resolved by the method of developing the productive forces. . . . The principle of using different methods to resolve different contradictions is one which Marxist-Leninists must strictly observe.

"On Contradiction" (August 1937), *Selected Works,* Vol. I, pp. 321–22.

Contradiction and struggle are universal and absolute, but the methods of resolving contradictions, that is, the forms of struggle, differ according to the differences in the nature of the contradictions. . . .

"On Contradiction" (August 1937), *Selected Works,* Vol. I, p. 344.

Methods of Thinking and Methods of Work

The Marxst philosophy of dialectical materialism has two outstanding characteristics. One is its class nature: it openly avows that dialectical materialism is in the service of the proletariat. The other is its practicality: it emphasizes the dependence of theory on practice, emphasizes that theory is based on practice and in turn serves practice.

"On Practice" (July 1937), *Selected Works,* Vol. 1, p. 297.

Where do correct ideas come from? Do they drop from the skies? No. Are they innate in the mind? No. They come from social practice, and from it alone; they come from three kinds of social practice, the struggle for production, the class struggle and scientific experiment.

Where Do Correct Ideas Come From? (May 1963), 1st pocket ed., p. 1.

Often, correct knowledge can be arrived at only after many repetitions of the process leading from matter to consciousness and then back to matter, that is, leading from practice to knowledge and then back to practice. Such is the Marxist theory of knowledge, the dialectical materialist theory of knowledge.

Ibid., p. 3.

The fundamental cause of the development of a thing is not external but internal; it lies in the contradictoriness within the thing. This internal contradiction exists in every single thing, hence its motion and development. Contradictoriness within a thing is the fundamental cause of its development, while its interrelations and interactions with other things are secondary causes.

"On Contradiction" (August 1937), *Selected Works,* Vol. I, p. 313.

Marxist philosophy holds that the law of the unity of opposites is the fundamental law of the universe. This law operates universally, whether in the natural world, in human society, or in man's thinking. Between the opposites in a contradiction there is at once unity and struggle, and it is this that impels things to move and change. Contradictions exist everywhere, but they differ in accordance with the different nature of different things. In any given phenomenon or thing, the unity of opposites is conditional, temporary and transitory, and hence relative, whereas the struggle of opposites is absolute.

On the Correct Handling of Contradictions Among the People
(February 27, 1957), 1st pocket ed., p. 18.

The analytical method is dialectical. By analysis, we mean analysing the contradictions in things. And sound analysis is impossible without intimate knowledge of life and without real understanding of the pertinent contradictions.

*Speech at the Chinese Communist Party's National Conference
on Propaganda Work* (March 12, 1957), 1st pocket ed., p. 20.

Discipline

Within the ranks of the people, democracy is correlative with centralism and freedom with discipline. They are the two opposites of a single entity, contradictory as well as united, and we should not one-sidedly emphasize one to the denial of the other. Within the ranks of the people, we cannot do without freedom, nor can we do without discipline; we cannot do without democracy, nor can we do without centralism. This unity of democracy and centralism, of freedom and discipline, constitutes our democratic centralism. Under this system, the people enjoy extensive democracy and freedom, but at the same time they have to keep within the bounds of socialist discipline.

On the Correct Handling of Contradictions Among the People
(February 27, 1957), 1st pocket ed., pp. 10–11.

We must affirm anew the discipline of the Party, namely:

1 the individual is subordinate to the organization;
2 the minority is subordinate to the majority;
3 the lower level is subordinate to the higher level; and
4 the entire membership is subordinate to the Central Committee.

Whoever violates these articles of discipline disrupts Party unity.

> "The Role of the Chinese Communist Party in the National War"
> (October 1938), *Selected Works,* Vol. II, pp. 203–04.

The Communist Party does not fear criticism because we are Marxists, the truth is on our side, and the basic masses, the workers and peasants, are on our side.

> *Speech at the Chinese Communist Party's National Conference
> on Propaganda Work* (March 12, 1957), 1st pocket ed., p. 14.

Culture and Art

In the world today all culture, all literature and art belong to definite classes and are geared to definite political lines. There is in fact no such thing as art for art's sake, art that stands above classes, art that is detached from or independent of politics. Proletarian literature and art are part of the whole proletarian revolutionary cause; they are, as Lenin said, cogs and wheels in the whole revolutionary machine.

> "Talks at the Yenan Forum on Literature and Art"
> (May 1942), *Selected Works,* Vol. III, p. 86.

All our literature and art are for the masses of the people, and in the first place for the workers, peasants and soldiers; they are created for the workers, peasants and soldiers and are for their use.

> "Talks at the Yenan Forum on Literature and Art"
> (May 1942), *Selected Works,* Vol. III, p. 84.

[Our purpose is] to ensure that literature and art fit well into the whole revolutionary machine as a component part, that they operate as powerful weapons for uniting and educating the people and for attacking and destroying the enemy, and that they help the people fight the enemy with one heart and one mind.

> *Ibid.,* p. 70.

In literary and art criticism there are two criteria, the political and the artistic. . . .
. . . What we demand is the unity of politics and art, the unity of content and form, the unity of revolutionary political content and the highest possible perfection of artistic form. Works of art which lack artistic quality have no force, however progressive they are politically. Therefore, we oppose both works of art with a wrong political viewpoint and the tendency towards the "poster and slogan style" which is correct in political viewpoint but lacking in artistic power. On questions of literature and art we must carry on a struggle on two fronts.

> *Ibid.,* pp. 88–90.

Study

The theory of Marx, Engels, Lenin and Stalin is universally applicable. We should regard it not as a dogma, but as a guide to action. Studying it is not merely a matter of learning terms and phrases but of learning Marxism-Leninism as the science of revolution.

> "The Role of the Chinese Communist Party in the National War"
> (October 1938), *Selected Works,* Vol. II, pp. 208–09.

[CENTRALIZED DEMOCRACY]

In the sphere of organization, ensure democracy under centralized guidance. It should be done on the following lines:

1 The leading bodies of the Party must give a correct line of guidance and find solutions when problems arise, in order to establish themselves as centres of leadership.

2 The higher bodies must be familiar with the situation in the lower bodies and with the life of the masses so as to have an objective basis for correct guidance.

3 No Party organization at any level should make casual decisions in solving problems. Once a decision is reached, it must be firmly carried out.

4 All decisions of any importance made by the Party's higher bodies must be promptly transmitted to the lower bodies and the Party rank and file. . . .

5 The lower bodies of the Party and the Party rank and file must discuss the higher bodies' directives in detail in order to understand their meaning thoroughly and decide on the methods of carrying them out.

> "On Correcting Mistaken Ideas in the Party" (December 1929),
> *Selected Works,* Vol. I, p. 109.

Education in democracy must be carried on within the Party so that members can understand the meaning of democratic life, the meaning of the relationship between democracy and centralism, and the way in which democratic centralism should be put into practice. Only in this way can we really extend democracy within the Party and at the same time avoid ultra-democracy and the *laissez-faire* which destroys discipline.

> "The Role of the Chinese Communist Party in the National
> War" (October 1938), *Selected Works,* Vol. II, p. 205.

In the sphere of theory, destroy the roots of ultra-democracy. First, it should be pointed out that the danger of ultra-democracy lies in the fact that it damages or even completely wrecks the Party organization and weakens or even completely undermines the Party's fighting capacity, rendering the Party incapable of fulfilling its fighting tasks and thereby causing the defeat of the revolution. Next, it should be pointed out that the source of ultra-democracy consists in the petty bourgeoisie's individualistic aversion to discipline. When this characteristic is brought

into the Party, it develops into ultra-democratic ideas politically and organization-
ally. These ideas are utterly incompatible with the fighting tasks of the proletariat.

"On Correcting Mistaken Ideas in the Party" December 1929),
Selected Works, Vol. I, p. 108.

Our state is a people's democratic dictatorship led by the working class and
based on the worker-peasant alliance. What is this dictatorship for? Its first function is to suppress the reactionary classes and elements and those exploiters in our
country who resist the socialist revolution, to suppress those who try to wreck our
socialist construction, or in other words, to resolve the internal contradictions
between ourselves and the enemy. For instance, to arrest, try and sentence certain
counter-revolutionaries, and to deprive landlords and bureaucrat-capitalists of their
right to vote and their freedom of speech for a specified period of time—all this
comes within the scope of our dictatorship. To maintain public order and safeguard the interests of the people, it is likewise necessary to exercise dictatorship
over embezzlers, swindlers, arsonists, murderers, criminal gangs and other
scoundrels who seriously disrupt public order. The second function of this dictatorship is to protect our country from subversion and possible aggression by external enemies. In that event, it is the task of this dictatorship to resolve the external
contradiction between ourselves and the enemy. The aim of this dictatorship is to
protect all our people so that they can devote themselves to peaceful labour and
build China into a socialist country with a modern industry, agriculture, science
and culture.

On the Correct Handling of Contradictions Among the People
(February 27, 1957), 1st pocket ed., pp. 6–7.

The people's democratic dictatorship uses two methods. Towards the enemy, it
uses the method of dictatorship, that is, for as long a period of time as is necessary
it does not let them take part in political activities and compels them to obey the
law of the People's Government and to engage in labour and, through labour,
transform themselves into new men. Towards the people, on the contrary, it uses
the method not of compulsion but of democracy, that is, it must necessarily let
them take part in political activities and does not compel them to do this or that,
but uses the method of democracy in educating and persuading them.

Closing speech at the Second Session of the First National Committee of the
Chinese People's Political Consultative Conference (June 23, 1950).

34
Karl Kautsky

Karl Kautsky (1854–1938) was an Austrian socialist and activist and Marx's loyal friend. After Marx died in 1883, Kautsky served as editor of his uncompleted economic and philosophical works. He was deeply worried by Lenin's abandonment of democratic process; he was horrified when, after the success of the revolution in 1917, Lenin instituted a rigid, dictatorial regime in Russia. In *The Dictatorship of the Proletariat,* a sharp rejection of Leninist elitism and heavy-handedness written in 1918, Kautsky argued that communist revolution need not be dictatorial, that it can prosper with general participation and the retention of individual civil liberties. Lenin and Stalin, whose bitter animosity he provoked, thereafter referred to him always as "the renegade Kautsky."

[DEMOCRACY AND THE DICTATORSHIP OF THE PROLETARIAT]*

These democratic institutions [freedom of combination and of the press and universal suffrage] have been called the safety valve of society. It is quite false to say that the proletariat in a democracy ceases to be revolutionary, that it is contented with giving public expression to its indignation and its sufferings, and renounces the idea of social and political revolution. Democracy cannot remove the class antagonisms of capitalist society, nor prevent the overthrow of that society, which is their inevitable outcome. But if it cannot prevent the Revolution, it can avoid many reckless and premature attempts at revolution, and render many revolutionary movements unnecessary. It gives a clear indication of the relative strength of classes and parties; it does not do away with their antagonism, nor does it avoid the ultimate outcome of their struggle, but it serves to prevent the rising classes from attempting tasks to which they are not equal, and it also restrains the ruling classes from refusing concessions when they no longer have the strength to maintain such refusal. The direction of evolution is not thereby altered, but the pace is made more even and steady. The coming to the front of the proletariat in a State with some measure of democratic government will not be marked by such a striking victory as attended the middle classes in their revolutionary period, nor will it be exposed to a violent overthrow. . . .

The proletarian-democratic method of conducting the struggle may seem to be a slower affair than the revolutionary period of the middle class; it is certainly less dramatic and striking, but it also exacts a smaller measure of sacrifice. This may be quite indifferent to the finely endowed literary people who find in Socialism an interesting pastime, but not to those who really carry on the fight.

This so-called peaceful method of the class struggle, which is confined to non-militant methods, Parliamentarism, strikes, demonstrations, the Press, and similar

*From K. Kautsky, *The Dictatorship of the Proletariat,* H. J. Stenning, tr. (Manchester: The National Labour Press, Ltd., 1924).

means of pressure, will retain its importance in every country according to the effectiveness of the democratic institutions which prevail there, the degree of political and economic enlightenment, and the self-mastery of the people.

On these grounds, I anticipate that the social revolution of the proletariat will assume quite other forms than that of the middle class, and that it will be possible to carry it out by peaceful economic, legal and moral means, instead of by physical force, in all places where democracy has been established.

. . . [E]verywhere the class-conscious proletariat and their representatives fight for the realisation of democracy, and many of them have shed their life's blood for it.

They know that without democracy nothing can be done. The stimulating results of the struggle with a despotism are confined to a handful, and do not touch the masses. On the other hand, the degenerating influence of democracy on the proletariat need not be exaggerated. Often is it the consequence of the lack of leisure from which the proletariat suffers, not of democracy itself.

It would be indeed extraordinary if the possession of freedom necessarily made men more narrow and trivial than its absence. The more democracy tends to shorten the working day, the greater the sum of leisure at the disposal of the proletariat, the more it is enabled to combine devotion to large problems with attention to necessary detail. And the impulse thereto is not lacking. For whatever democracy may be able to accomplish it cannot resolve the antagonisms inherent in a capitalist system of production, so long as it refrains from altering this system. On the contrary, the antagonisms in capitalist society become more acute and tend to provoke bigger conflicts, in this way forcing great problems on the attention of the proletariat, and taking its mind off routine and detail work.

Under democracy this moral elevation is no longer confined to a handful, but is shared in by the whole of the people, who are at the same time gradually accustomed to self-government by the daily performance of routine work.

Again, under democracy, the proletariat does not always think and talk of revolution, as under despotism. It may for years, and even decades, be immersed in detail work, but everywhere situations must arise which will kindle in it revolutionary thought and aspirations.

When the people are roused to action under a democracy, there is less danger than under despotism that they have been prematurely provoked, or will waste their energy in futile efforts. When victory is achieved, it will not be lost, but successfully maintained. And that is better in the end than the mere nervous excitement of a fresh revolutionary drama.

35
Programme of the Communist International

The Marxist goal was and remains worldwide revolution—in Russia, in China, in the United States, in Africa, in Latin America—wherever the bourgeoisie is dominant and the working class oppressed. The Third Communist International (or Comintern), cofounded by Lenin and Trotsky in 1919, adopted (at its Sixth World Congress in 1928) a "programme"—never altered—crisply presenting the agenda and the intermediate objectives of international communism. From the earliest days of the movement Communists have differed greatly among themselves about revolutionary means that would be appropriate or necessary. But their ultimate objective—the replacement of capitalism everywhere by a world communist system—has not changed. That goal seemed very distant when the twentieth century began; as the twentieth century comes to a close it seems very little closer.

THE ULTIMATE AIM OF THE COMMUNIST INTERNATIONAL— WORLD COMMUNISM*

The ultimate aim of the Communist International is to replace world capitalist economy by a world system of Communism. Communist society, the basis for which has been prepared by the whole course of historical development, is mankind's only way out, for it alone can abolish the contradictions of the capitalist system which threaten to degrade and destroy the human race.

Communist society will abolish the class division of society, i.e., simultaneously with the abolition of anarchy in production, it will abolish all forces of exploitation and oppression of man by man. Society will no longer consist of antagonistic classes in conflict with each other, but will represent a united commonwealth of labor. For the first time in its history mankind will take its fate into its own hands. Instead of destroying innumerable human lives and incalculable wealth in struggles between classes and nations, mankind will devote all its energy to the struggle against the forces of nature, to the development and strengthening of its own collective might.

After abolishing private ownership in the means of production and converting them into social property, the world system of Communism will replace the elemental forces of the world market, of competition and the blind process of social production, by consciously organized and planned production for the purpose of satisfying rapidly growing social needs. With the abolition of competition and anarchy in production, devastating crises and still more devastating wars will dis-

---

*From *The Programme of the Communist International,* 1928. Reprinted from *The Strategy and Tactics of World Communism,* Supplement I, United States Government Printing Office, Washington, 1948.

appear. Instead of colossal waste of productive forces and spasmodic development of society—there will be planned utilization of all material resources and painless economic development on the basis of unrestricted, smooth and rapid development of productive forces.

The abolition of private property and the disappearance of classes will do away with the exploitation of man by man. Work will cease to be toiling for the benefit of a class enemy: instead of being merely a means of livelihood it will become a necessity of life: want and economic inequality, the misery of enslaved classes, and a wretched standard of life generally will disappear; the hierarchy created in the division of labor system will be abolished together with the antagonism between mental and manual labor; and the last vestige of the social inequality of sexes will be removed. At the same time, the organs of class domination, and the State in the first place, will disappear also. The State, being the embodiment of class domination, will die out insofar as classes die out, and with it all measures of coercion will expire.

With the disappearance of classes the monopoly of education in every form will be abolished. Culture will become the acquirement of all and the class ideologies of the past will give place to scientific materialist philosophy. Under such circumstances the domination of man over man, in any form, becomes impossible, and a great field will be opened for the social selection and the harmonious development of all the talents inherent in humanity.

In Communist society no social restrictions will be imposed upon the growth of the forces of production. Private ownership in the means of production, the selfish lust for profits, the artificial retention of the masses in a state of ignorance, poverty—which retards technical progress in capitalist society, and unproductive expenditures will have no place in a Communist society. The most expedient utilization of the forces of nature and of the natural conditions of production in the various parts of the world; the removal of the antagonism between town and country, that under capitalism results from the low technical level of agriculture and its systematic lagging behind industry; the closest possible cooperation between science and technics; the utmost encouragement of research work and the practical application of its results on the widest possible social scale; planned organization of scientific work; the application of the most perfect methods of statistical accounting and planned regulation of economy; the rapidly growing social need, which is the most powerful internal driving force of the whole system—all these will secure the maximum productivity of social labor, which in turn will release human energy for the powerful development of science and art.

The development of the productive forces of world Communist society will make it possible to raise the well-being of the whole of humanity and to reduce to a minimum the time devoted to material production and, consequently, will enable culture to flourish as never before in history. This new culture of a humanity that is united for the first time in history, and has abolished all State boundaries, will, unlike capitalist culture, be based upon clear and transparent human relationships. Hence, it will bury forever all mysticism, religion, prejudice and superstition and will give a powerful impetus to the development of all-conquering scientific knowledge.

This higher stage of Communism, the stage in which Communist society has already developed on its own foundation, in which an enormous growth of social productive forces has accompanied the manifold development of man, in which humanity has already inscribed on its banner: "From each according to his abilities to each according to his needs!"—presupposes, as an historical condition precedent, a lower stage of development, the stage of Socialism. At this lower stage, Communist society only just emerges from capitalist society and bears all the economic, ethical and intellectual birthmarks it has inherited from the society from whose womb it is just emerging. The productive forces of Socialism are not yet sufficiently developed to assure a distribution of the products of labor according to needs: these are distributed according to the amount of labor expended. Division of labor, i.e., the system whereby certain groups perform certain labor functions, and especially the distinction between mental and manual labor, still exists. Although classes are abolished, traces of the old class division of society and, consequently, remnants of the Proletarian State power, coercion, laws, still exist. Consequently, certain traces of inequality, which have not yet managed to die out altogether, still remain. The antagonism between town and country has not yet been entirely removed. But none of these survivals of former society is protected or defended by any social force. Being the product of a definite level of development of productive forces, they will disappear as rapidly as mankind, freed from the fetters of the capitalist system, subjugates the forces of nature, re-educates itself in the spirit of Communism, and passes from Socialism to complete Communism.

PART **TWO**

FASCISM

"Fascism" is the twentieth-century version of a very old tradition in political philosophy, revised to fit modern circumstances, reformulated using concepts recently developed, and presented as the justification of some powerful modern governments. The English word "fascism" comes, through the Italian, from an ancient Roman tradition: the *fasces* were bundles of thin rods bound together with an ax among them, and carried before the highest magistrates of imperial Rome as a symbol of authority and of the strength that a tightly unified community may enjoy. The old themes of organic unity and disciplined power were re-woven, with flair and efficiency, by the fascist philosophers of the twentieth century.

But as a political philosophy, fascism is not easy to define or to explicate. Fascist thinkers have borrowed freely from both ancients and moderns, and they have delighted in deliberate irrationality. As realized in actual modern governments, fascism has been a potpourri of doctrine impossible to present as a fully coherent theory. In this Part are presented selections from zealous leaders of fascist nations, but also selections from philosophers—Machiavelli, Hobbes, and Nietzsche, for example—who were not fascists but who did provide intellectual materials of which recent and contemporary fascists have made much use.

Within this mixture of old and new, of principles and dogmas and expedients, three main streams of thought may be distinguished. Fascism may perhaps be best understood as a contemporary blend of these three philosophical traditions.

The first is the *absolutist* tradition. On this view, the powers of government must lie entirely in the hands of one powerful and intelligent leader—the prince or sovereign, *Il Duce* or *Der Führer.* Such absolutism has many ramifications. It largely determines the principles of organization within the state, which are authoritarian and generally patterned on military lines. All authority exercised by or in behalf of the state stems from the leader, and rights enjoyed in every sphere are owed to him; while on every subordinate echelon the principal duties are those of obedience and responsibility to superiors. Again, since the leader is the source of the law, he himself is above the law. The standards of conduct that apply to him, therefore, are not those that apply to the private citizen; he may be judged, as leader, only by his success in maintaining and extending his power and the power of his state. The result is rightly called Machiavellianism, for fascist dictators have generally acted under Machiavelli's principle that "if the act accuse him, the result will excuse him."

The second leading element in fascism is *organicism.* According to this theory a nation is properly understood to be an organic unity, like a human being, but of greater import, having many separate organs that contribute to the general welfare, and a larger interest, or general will, that is necessarily superior to the interest or will of any particular member or members. There is some plausibility to this organic approach to human communities, and fascists are not the only theorists who have developed it. When carried to extremes, however, organicism can lead to the conclusion that the state has not only an organic reality but a super-reality, so awesome that its apparent will is the true will of subordinate citizens, whether they think so or not. Nothing may then obstruct this state, or super-organism, from liquidating those elements within it that interfere with the achievement of its objectives. Some have gone so far as to elevate the state to an object of worship or to view it as a reality having supernatural or divine attributes. Hegel said: "The March of God in the world, that is what the State is." One serious problem for this theory is that of determining what the will of the state really is and how it is to be known. This problem is resolved, sometimes painfully, when the theories of organicism and absolutism are combined. The general will of the state is then identified with the will of its leader, whose character and physical person is taken to represent the essence of the nation. This identification is one of the distinguishing marks of twentieth-century fascism, especially as manifested in Italy and Germany.

Serving as catalyst in combining the two elements already mentioned is a third, no less important element: deliberate *irrationalism.* Sometimes an attitude, sometimes a manipulative device, sometimes a seriously proposed methodology, the express denial of the competence of reason to guide human life opens the door to acts and claims immune to effective criticism. Many varieties of philosophic irrationalism have achieved great popularity, from that of the early Christians (said Tertullian: *"Credo, quia impossibile"*—"I believe it because it is impossible") through its more sophisticated versions in Schopenhauer and Bergson and some contemporary existentialists. The deliberate manufacture of racial and social myths, the inculcation of those myths in public sentiment and then their implementation in national policy—culminating in horrors almost beyond belief—were the fruits of this irrationalism as applied to politics.

Fascism may be described—oversimply but not mistakenly—as the commingling of these traditions of absolutism, organicism, and irrationalism. Its roots go very deep, but its full realization came only in the twentieth century.

1

ABSOLUTISM

The belief that absolute power in the hands of the sovereign is essential—necessary both for the internal good order of any state as well as for its survival as a state—is very old. In the tyrannies of classical Greece and Rome, as in ancient Oriental empires, the absolute rule of the sovereign was largely taken for granted. The philosophical justification of such authority—the theoretical account of sovereign power—was given only much later, with the rise of modern absolutism in Europe during the fifteenth and sixteenth centuries.

During that period the national state was becoming the typical and paramount political institution in Western Europe. The monarch was coming to be viewed as the supreme earthly power, divinely instituted as ruler, and representing in his person the will and interest of the state. Actual political tensions most frequently took the form of conflicts between the governing power of the sovereign, on the one side, and the several individuals and institutions within the nation, on the other. In France, England, and Spain, this process of national unification, and the triumph of monarchy, came at a relatively early date. Italy and Germany, on the other hand, were not to experience full unity under one powerful leader for some centuries.

The political philosophers represented in this section all belong to this period of early modern European history. Each, in his way, was presenting the case for national unity and the placement of absolute power in the hands of the monarch. But these early modern thinkers would not likely have been defenders of the fascist regimes their works were later used to support. Each had views that were, in important respects, inconsistent with modern fascism. Nevertheless, the theoretical foundations for unrestricted sovereign power were formulated and refined by modern absolutists, and in doing this they contributed substantially to what became the philosophy of fascism. Modern fascists greatly admired these sophisticated absolutists, and borrowed freely from them.

36
Niccolo Machiavelli

Niccolo Machiavelli (1469–1527) was one of the most remarkable and influential
political philosophers of early modern Europe. A patriot who wished above all for
the unity and glory of the Italian state, he was at the same time a practical man
and an honest observer of the political circumstances of his time. Although his
ideals were sometimes noble, he had no illusions about the immediate needs of
Italy, in which unity could be achieved and maintained, he believed, only through
the vigorous and ruthless rule of a strong man—The Prince—after whom he
named his most famous work. Cruelty, bad faith, deception, and other modes of
conduct that are clearly vicious when practiced by private citizens may be essential
for the security of his rule, Machiavelli argued, and if their use does result in
the stability and prosperity of his reign and the greater well-being of his subjects,
then the Prince is deeply justified in resorting to such practices. *The Prince*,
(1515)from which the following passages come, was dedicated to Lorenzo de Medici
of Florence and may be read as a manual for the successful despot.

Concerning the Things for which Men, and Especially Princes, are Praised or
Blamed.*

It remains now to see what ought to be the rules of conduct for a prince towards
subject and friends. . . .
. . . It is necessary for a prince wishing to hold his own to know how to do
wrong, and to make use of it or not according to necessity. . . . It is necessary for
him to be sufficiently prudent that he may know how to avoid the reproach of
those vices which would lose him his state; and also to keep himself, if it be possible, from those which would not lose him it; but this not being possible, he may
with less hesitation abandon himself to them. And again, he need not make himself uneasy at incurring a reproach for those vices without which the state can only
be saved with difficulty, for if everything is considered carefully, it will be found
that something which looks like virtue, if followed, would be his ruin; while something else, which looks like vice, yet followed brings him security and prosperity.

Concerning Cruelty and Clemency, and Whether it is Better to be Loved than
Feared

. . . Every prince ought to desire to be considered clement and not cruel. Nevertheless he ought to take care not to misuse this clemency. Cesare Borgia was

---

*From *The Prince* by Niccolo Machiavelli. Trans. by W. K. Marriott. Everyman's Library edition. Published by E. P. Dutton & Co., Inc. and used with their permission and that of J. M. Dent and Sons, Ltd., London.

considered cruel; notwithstanding, his cruelty reconciled the Romagna, unified it, and restored it to peace and loyalty. And if this be rightly considered, he will be seen to have been much more merciful than the Florentine people, who, to avoid a reputation for cruelty, permitted Pistoia to be destroyed. Therefore a prince, so long as he keeps his subjects united and loyal, ought not to mind the reproach of cruelty; because with a few examples he will be more merciful than those who, through too much mercy, allow disorders to arise, from which follow murder or robbery; for these are wont to injure the whole people, while those executions which originate with a prince offend the individual only.

And of all princes, it is impossible for the new prince to avoid the imputation of cruelty, owing to new states being full of dangers. . . . Nevertheless he ought to be slow to believe and to act, nor should he himself show fear, but proceed in a temperate manner with prudence and humanity, so that too much confidence may not make him incautious and too much distrust render him intolerable.

Upon this a question arises: whether it be better to be loved than feared or feared than loved? It may be answered that one should wish to be both, but, because it is difficult to unite them in one person, it is much safer to be feared than loved, when, of the two, either must be dispensed with. Because this is to be asserted in general of men, that they are ungrateful, fickle, false, cowards, covetous, and as long as you succeed they are yours entirely; they will offer you their blood, property, life, and children, as is said above, when the need is far distant; but when it approaches they turn against you. And that prince who, relying entirely on their promises, has neglected other precautions, is ruined; because friendships that are obtained by payments, and not by greatness or nobility of mind, may indeed be earned, but they are not secured, and in time of need cannot be relied upon; and men have less scruple in offending one who is beloved than one who is feared, for love is preserved by the link of obligation which, owing to the baseness of men, is broken at every opportunity for their advantage; but fear preserves you by a dread of punishment which never fails.

Nevertheless a prince ought to inspire fear in such a way that, if he does not win love, he avoids hatred; because he can endure very well being feared while he is not hated, which will always be as long as he abstains from the property of his citizens and subjects and from their women. But when it is necessary for him to proceed against the life of someone, he must do it on proper justification and for manifest cause, but above all things he must keep his hands off the property of others, because men more quickly forget the death of their father than the loss of their patrimony. Besides, pretexts for taking away the property are never wanting; for he who has once begun to live by robbery will always find pretexts for seizing what belongs to others; but reasons for taking life, on the contrary, are more difficult to find and sooner lapse. But when a prince is with his army, and has under control a multitude of soldiers, then it is quite necessary for him to disregard the reputation of cruelty, for without it he would never hold his army united or disposed to its duties.

Among the wonderful deeds of Hannibal this one is enumerated: that having led an enormous army, composed of many various races of men, to fight in foreign lands, no dissensions arose either among them or against the prince, whether in his bad or in his good fortune. This arose from nothing else than his inhuman cruelty, which, with his boundless valor, made him revered and terrible in the sight of his soldiers, but without that cruelty, his other virtues were not sufficient to produce this effect. And short-sighted writers admire his deeds from one point of view and from another condemn the principal cause of them. . . .

Returning to the question of being feared or loved, I come to the conclusion that, men loving according to their own will and fearing according to that of the prince, a wise prince should establish himself on that which is in his own control and not in that of others; he must endeavor only to avoid hatred, as is noted.

Concerning the Way in which Princes Should Keep Faith

Every one admits how praiseworthy it is in a prince to keep faith, and to live with integrity and not with craft. Nevertheless our experience has been that those princes who have done great things have held good faith of little account, and have known how to circumvent the intellect of men by craft, and in the end have overcome those who have relied on their word. You must know there are two ways of contesting, the one by the law, the other by force; the first method is proper to men, the second to beasts; but because the first is frequently not suffi-cient, it is necessary to have recourse to the second. Therefore it is necessary for a prince to understand how to avail himself of the beast and the man. This has been figuratively taught to princes by ancient writers, who describe how Achilles and many other princes of old were given to the Centaur Chiron to nurse, who brought them up in his discipline; which means solely that, as they had for a teacher one who was half beast and half man, so it is necessary for a prince to know how to make use of both natures, and that one without the other is not durable. A prince, therefore, being compelled knowingly to adopt the beast, ought to choose the fox and the lion; because the lion cannot defend himself against snares and the fox cannot defend himself against wolves. Therefore, it is necessary to be a fox to discover the snares and a lion to terrify the wolves. Those who rely simply on the lion do not understand what they are about. There-fore a wise lord cannot, nor ought he to, keep faith when such observance may be turned against him, and when the reasons that caused him to pledge it exist no longer. If men were entirely good this precept would not hold, but because they are bad, and will not keep faith with you, you too are not bound to observe it with them. Nor will there ever be wanting to a prince legitimate reasons to excuse this non-observance. Of this endless modern examples could be given, showing how many treaties and engagements have been made void and of no effect through the faithlessness of princes; and he who has known best how to employ the fox has succeeded best.

But it is necessary to know well how to disguise this characteristic, and to be a great pretender and dissembler; and men are so simple, and so subject to present necessities, that he who seeks to deceive will always find someone who will allow himself to be deceived. One recent example I cannot pass over in silence. Alexander the Sixth did nothing else but deceive men, nor ever thought of doing otherwise, and he always found victims; for there never was a man who had greater power in asserting, or who with greater oaths would affirm a thing, yet would observe it less; nevertheless his deceits always succeeded according to his wishes, because he well understood this side of mankind.

Therefore it is unnecessary for a prince to have all the good qualities I have enumerated, but it is very necessary to appear to have them. And I shall dare to say this also, that to have them and always to observe them is injurious, and that to appear to have them is useful; to appear merciful, faithful, humane, religious, upright, and to be so, but with a mind so framed that should you require not to be so, you may be able and know how to change to the opposite.

And you have to understand this, that a prince, especially a new one, cannot observe all those things for which men are esteemed, being often forced, in order to maintain the state, to act contrary to fidelity, friendship, humanity, and religion. Therefore it is necessary for him to have a mind ready to turn itself accordingly as the winds and variations of fortune force it, yet, as I have said above, not to diverge from the good if he can avoid doing so, but, if compelled, then to know how to set about it.

For this reason a prince ought to take care that he never lets anything slip from his lips that is not replete with the above-named five qualities, that he may appear to him who sees and hears him altogether merciful, faithful, humane, upright, and religious. There is nothing more necessary to appear to have than this last quality, inasmuch as men judge generally more by the eye than by the hand, because it belongs to everybody to see you, to few to come in touch with you. Everyone sees what you appear to be, few really know what you are, and those few dare not oppose themselves to the opinion of the many, who have the majesty of the state to defend them; and in the actions of all men, and especially of princes, which it is not prudent to challenge, one judges by the result.

For that reason, let a prince have the credit of conquering and holding his state, the means will always be considered honest, and he will be praised by everybody; because the vulgar are always taken by what a thing seems to be and by what comes of it; and in the world there are only the vulgar, for the few find a place there only when the many have no ground to rest on.

One prince of the present time, whom it is not well to name, never preaches anything else but peace and good faith, and to both he is most hostile, and either, if he had kept it, would have deprived him of reputation and kingdom many a time.

That One Should Avoid Being Despised and Hated

. . . The prince must consider, as has been in part said before, how to avoid those things which will make him hated or contemptible; and as often as he shall have succeeded he will have fulfilled his part, and he need not fear any danger in other reproaches.

It makes him hated above all things, as I have said, to be rapacious, and to be a violator of the property and women of his subjects, from both of which he must abstain. And when neither their property nor honor is touched, the majority of men live content, and he has only to contend with the ambition of a few, whom he can curb with ease in many ways.

It makes him contemptible to be considered fickle, frivolous, effeminate, mean-spirited, irresolute, from all of which a prince should guard himself as from a rock; and he should endeavour to show in his actions greatness, courage, gravity, and fortitude; and in his private dealings with his subjects let him show that his judgments are irrevocable, and maintain himself in such reputation that no one can hope either to deceive him or to get round him.

That prince is highly esteemed who conveys this impression of himself, and he who is highly esteemed is not easily conspired against; for, provided it is well known that he is an excellent man and revered by his people, he can only be attacked with difficulty. For this reason a prince ought to have two fears, one from within, on account of his subjects, the other from without, on account of external powers. From the latter he is defended by being well armed and having good allies, and if he is well armed he will have good friends, and affairs will always remain quiet within when they are quiet without, unless they should have been already disturbed by conspiracy; and even should affairs outside be disturbed, if he has carried out his preparations and has lived as I have said, as long as he does not despair, he will resist every attack, as I said Nabis the Spartan did.

But concerning his subjects, when affairs outside are disturbed he has only to fear that they will conspire secretly, from which a prince can easily secure himself by avoiding being hated and despised, and by keeping the people satisfied with him, which it is most necessary for him to accomplish, as I said above at length. And one of the most efficacious remedies that a prince can have against conspiracies is not to be hated and despised by the people, for he who conspires against a prince always expects to please them by his removal; but when the conspirator can only look forward to offending them, he will not have the courage to take such a course, for the difficulties that confront a conspirator are infinite. And as experience shows, many have been the conspiracies, but few have been successful; because he who conspires cannot act alone, nor can he take a companion except from those whom he believes to be malcontents, and as soon as you have opened your mind to a malcontent you have given him the material with which to content himself, for by denouncing you he can look for every advantage; so that, seeing the gain from this course to be assured, and seeing the other to be doubtful and full of dangers, he must be a very rare friend, or a thoroughly obstinate enemy of the prince, to keep faith with you. . . .

For this reason I consider that a prince ought to reckon conspiracies of little account when his people hold him in esteem; but when it is hostile to him, and bears hatred towards him, he ought to fear everything and everybody. And well-ordered states and wise princes have taken every care not to drive the nobles to desperation, and to keep the people satisfied and contented, for this is one of the most important objects a prince can have.

The Art of War

A prince ought to have no other aim or thought, nor select anything else for his study, than war and its rules and discipline; for this is the sole art that belongs to him who rules, and it is of such force that it not only upholds those who are born princes, but it often enables men to rise from a private station to that rank. And, on the contrary, it is seen that when princes have thought more of ease than of arms they have lost their states. And the first cause of your losing it is to neglect this art; and what enables you to acquire a state is to be master of the art. Francesco Sforza, through being martial, from a private person became Duke of Milan; and the sons, through avoiding the hardships and troubles of arms, from dukes became private persons. For among other evils which being unarmed brings you, it causes you to be despised, and this is one of those ignominies against which a prince ought to guard himself, as is shown later on. Because there is nothing proportionate between the armed and the unarmed; and it is not reasonable that he who is armed should yield obedience willingly to him who is unarmed, or that the unarmed man should be secure among armed servants. Because, there being in the one disdain and in the other suspicion, it is not possible for them to work well together. And therefore a prince who does not understand the art of war, over and above the other misfortunes already mentioned, cannot be respected by his soldiers, nor can he rely on them. He ought never, therefore, to have out of his thoughts this subject of war, and in peace he should addict himself more to its exercise than in war. . . .

An Exhortation to Liberate Italy from the Barbarians

. . . If, as I said, it was necessary that the people of Israel should be captive so as to make manifest the ability of Moses; that the Persians should be oppressed by the Medes so as to discover the greatness of the soul of Cyrus; and that the Athenians should be dispersed to illustrate the capabilities of Theseus: then at the present time, in order to discover the virtue of an Italian spirit, it was necessary that Italy should be reduced to the extremity she is now in, that she should be more enslaved than the Hebrews, more oppressed than the Persians, more scattered than the Athenians; without head, without order, beaten, despoiled, torn, overrun; and to have endured every kind of desolation.

. . . Italy, left as without life, waits for him who shall yet heal her wounds and put an end to the ravaging and plundering of Lombardy, to the swindling and taxing of the Kingdom and of Tuscany, and cleanse those sores that for long have festered. It is seen how she entreats God to send some one who shall deliver her from these wrongs and barbarous insolencies. It is seen also that she is ready and willing to follow a banner if only someone will raise it.

Nor is there to be seen at present one in whom she can place more hope than in your illustrious house,* with its valor and fortune, favored by God and by the

*Machiavelli is referring here to the powerful Medici family. —*Ed.*

Church of which it is now the chief, and which could be made the head of this redemption. This will not be difficult if you will recall to yourself the actions and lives of the men I have named. And although they were great and wonderful men, yet they were men, and each one of them had no more opportunity than the present offers, for their enterprises were neither more just nor easier than this, nor was God more their friend than He is yours.

With us there is great justice, because that war is just which is necessary, and arms are hallowed when there is no other hope but in them. Here there is the greatest willingness, and where the willingness is great the difficulties cannot be great if you will only follow those men to whom I have directed your attention. Further than this, how extraordinarily the ways of God have been manifested beyond example: the sea is divided, a cloud has led the way, the rock has poured forth water, it has rained manna, everything has contributed to your greatness; you ought to do the rest. God is not willing to do everything, and thus take away our free will and that share of glory which belongs to us.

Here [in Italy] there is great valor in the limbs while it fails in the head. Look attentively at the duels and the hand-to-hand combats, how superior the Italians are in strength, dexterity, and subtlety. But when it comes to armies they do not bear comparison, and this springs entirely from the insufficiency of the leaders, since those who are capable are not obedient, and each one seems to himself to know, there having never been anyone so distinguished above the rest, either by valor or fortune, that others would yield to him. Hence it is that for so long a time, and during so much fighting in the past twenty years, whenever there has been an army wholly Italian, it has always given a poor account of itself.

This opportunity, therefore, ought not to be allowed to pass for letting Italy at last see her liberator appear. Nor can one express the love with which he would be received in all those provinces which have suffered so much from these foreign scourings, with what thirst for revenge, with what stubborn faith, with what devotion, with what tears. What door would be closed to him? Who would refuse obedience to him? What envy would hinder him? What Italian would refuse him homage? To all of us this barbarous dominion stinks. Let, therefore, your illustrious house take up this charge with that courage and hope with which all just enterprises are undertaken, so that under its standard our native country may be ennobled, and under its auspices may be verified that saying of Petrarch:

Virtue against violence will take up arms;
    And be the combat quickly sped!
For the ancient valor of Italian hearts
    Is not yet dead.

37
Jean Bodin

Jean Bodin (1530–1596) wrote the *Six Books of the Commonwealth* with the specific intention of strengthening the authority of the French monarch. In it he undertook a complete discussion of politics and the state; but the most influential part of the work was its philosophical treatment of sovereignty—"power supreme and perpetual, absolute, and subject to no law"—and all its necessary attributes. It is, he claims, that majesty which alone can be "the distinguishing mark of a state."

[CONCERNING SOVEREIGNTY]*

Sovereignty is that absolute and perpetual power vested in a commonwealth which in Latin is termed *majestas*. . . . The term needs careful definition, because although it is the distinguishing mark of a commonwealth, and an understanding of its nature fundamental to any treatment of politics, no jurist or political philosopher has in fact attempted to define it. . . .

I have described it as *perpetual* because one can give absolute power to a person or group of persons for a period of time, but that time expired they become subjects once more. Therefore even while they enjoy power, they cannot properly be regarded as sovereign rulers, but only as the lieutenants and agents of the sovereign ruler, till the moment comes when it pleases the prince or the people to revoke the gift. The true sovereign remains always seized of his power. Just as a feudal lord who grants lands to another retains his eminent domain over them, so the ruler who delegates authority to judge and command, whether it be for a short period, or during pleasure, remains seized of those rights of jurisdiction actually exercised by another in the form of a revocable grant, or precarious tenancy. For this reason the law requires the governor of a province, or the prince's lieutenant, to make a formal surrender of the authority committed to him, at the expiration of his term of office. In this respect there is no difference between the highest officer of state and his humblest subordinate. If it were otherwise, and the absolute authority delegated by the prince to a lieutenant was regarded as itself sovereign power, the latter could use it against his prince who would thereby forfeit his eminence, and the subject could command his lord, the servant his master. This is a manifest absurdity, considering that the sovereign is always excepted personally, as a matter of right, in all delegations of authority, however extensive. However much he gives there always remains a reserve of right in his own person, whereby he may command, or intervene by way of prevention, confirmation, evocation, or any other way he thinks fit, in all matters delegated to a subject, whether in virtue of an office or a commission. Any authority exercised in virtue of an office or a commission can be revoked, or made tenable for as long or short a period as the sovereign wills. . . .

*From J. Bodin, *Six Books of the Commonwealth,* 1576. These passages are from a translation by M. J. Tooley, reprinted by permission of the publisher. Basil Blackwell, Oxford, 1955.

But supposing the king grants absolute power to a lieutenant for the term of his life, is not that a perpetual sovereign power? For if one confines *perpetual* to that which has no termination whatever, then sovereignty cannot subsist save in aristocracies and popular states, which never die. If one is to include monarchy too, sovereignty must be vested not in the king alone, but in the king and the heirs of his body, which supposes a strictly hereditary monarchy. In that case there can be very few sovereign kings, since there are only a very few strictly hereditary monarchies. Those especially who come to the throne by election could not be included.

A perpetual authority therefore must be understood to mean one that lasts for the lifetime of him who exercises it. If a sovereign magistrate is given office for one year, or for any other predetermined period, and continues to exercise the authority bestowed on him after the conclusion of his term, he does so either by consent or by force and violence. If he does so by force, it is manifest tyranny. The tyrant is a true sovereign for all that. The robber's possession by violence is true and natural possession although contrary to the law, for those who were formerly in possession have been disseized. But if the magistrate continues in office by consent, he is not a sovereign prince, seeing that he only exercises power on sufferance. Still less is he a sovereign if the term of his office is not fixed, for in that case he has no more than a precarious commission. . . .

What bearing have these considerations on the case of the man to whom the people has given absolute power for the term of his natural life? One must distinguish. If such absolute power is given him simply and unconditionally, and not in virtue of some office or commission, nor in the form of a revocable grant, the recipient certainly is, and should be acknowledged to be, a sovereign. The people has renounced and alienated its sovereign power in order to invest him with it and put him in possession, and it thereby transfers to him all its powers, authority, and sovereign rights, just as does the man who gives to another possessory and proprietary rights over what he formerly owned. The civil law expresses this in the phrase "all power is conveyed to him and vested in him."*

But if the people gives such power for the term of his natural life to anyone as its official or lieutenant, or only gives the exercise of such power, in such a case he is not a sovereign, but simply an officer, lieutenant, regent, governor, or agent, and as such has the exercise only of a power inhering in another. When a magistrate institutes a perpetual lieutenant, even if he abandons all his rights of jurisdiction and leaves their exercise entirely to his lieutenant, the authority to command and to judge nevertheless does not reside in the lieutenant, nor the action and force of the law derive from him. If he exceeds his authority his acts have no validity, unless approved and confirmed by him from whom he draws his authority. For this reason King John, after his return from captivity in England, solemnly ratified all the acts of his son Charles, who had acted in his name as regent, in order, as was necessary, to regularize the position.

Ei et in eum omnem potestatem contulit.

Whether then one exercises the power of another by commission, by institution, or by delegation, or whether such exercise is for a set term, or in perpetuity, such a power is not a sovereign power, even if there is no mention of such words as representative, lieutenant, governor, or regent, in the letters of appointment, or even if such powers are a consequence of the normal working of the laws of the country. In ancient times in Scotland, for instance, the law vested the entire governance of the realm in the next of kin, if the king should be a minor, on condition that everything that was done, was done in the king's name. But this law was later altered because of its inconvenient consequences.

Let us now turn to the other term of our definition and consider the force of the word *absolute*. The people or the magnates of a commonwealth can bestow simply and unconditionally upon someone of their choice a sovereign and perpetual power to dispose of their property and persons, to govern the state as he thinks fit, and to order the succession, in the same way that any proprietor, out of his liberality, can freely and unconditionally make a gift of his property to another. Such a form of gift, not being qualified in any way, is the only true gift, being at once unconditional and irrevocable. Gifts burdened with obligations and hedged with conditions are not true gifts. Similarly sovereign power given to a prince charged with conditions is neither properly sovereign, nor absolute, unless the conditions of appointment are only such as are inherent in the laws of God and of nature. . . .

On the other hand it is the distinguishing mark of the sovereign that he cannot in any way be subject to the commands of another, for it is he who makes law for the subject, abrogates law already made, and amends obsolete law. No one who is subject either to the law or to some other person can do this. That is why it is laid down in the civil law that the prince is above the law, for the word *law* in Latin implies the command of him who is invested with sovereign power. Therefore we find in all statutes the phrase "notwithstanding all edicts and ordinances to the contrary that we have infringed, or do infringe by these present." This clause applies both to former acts of the prince himself, and to those of his predecessors. For all laws, ordinances, letters patent, privileges, and grants whatsoever issued by the prince, have force only during his own lifetime, and must be expressly, or at least tacitly, confirmed by the reigning prince who has cognizance of them. . . . In proof of which, it is the custom of this realm for all corporations and corporate bodies to ask for the confirmation of their privileges, rights, and jurisdictions, on the accession of a new king. Even Parlements and high courts do this, as well as individual officers of the crown.

If the prince is not bound by the laws of his predecessors, still less can he be bound by his own laws. One may be subject to laws made by another, but it is impossible to bind oneself in any matter which is the subject of one's own free exercise of will. As the law says, "there can be no obligation in any matter which proceeds from the free will of the undertaker."* It follows of necessity that the king cannot be subject to his own laws. Just as, according to the canonists, the Pope can never tie his own hands, so the sovereign prince cannot bind himself, even if he

---

Nulla obligatio consistere potest, quae a voluntate promittentis statum capit.

wishes. For this reason edicts and ordinances conclude with the formula "for such is our good pleasure," thus intimating that the laws of a sovereign prince, even when founded on truth and right reason, proceed simply from his own will. . . .

From all this it is clear that the principal mark of sovereign majesty and absolute power is the right to impose laws generally on all subjects regardless of their consent. . . . And if it is expedient that if he is to govern his state well, a sovereign prince must be above the law, it is even more expedient that the ruling class in an aristocracy should be so, and inevitable in a popular state. A monarch in a kingdom is set apart from his subjects, and the ruling class from the people in an aristocracy. There are therefore in each case two parties, those that rule on the one hand, and those that are ruled on the other. . . .

[THE TRUE ATTRIBUTES OF SOVEREIGNTY]

Because there are none on earth, after God, greater than sovereign princes, whom God establishes as His lieutenants to command the rest of mankind, we must enquire carefully into their estate, that we may respect and revere their majesty in all due obedience, speak and think of them with all due honor. He who contemns his sovereign prince, contemns God whose image he is. . . .

Before going any further, one must consider what is meant by *law*. The word law signifies the right command of that person, or those persons, who have absolute authority over all the rest without exception, saving only the law-giver himself, whether the command touches all subjects in general or only some in particular. To put it another way, the law is the rightful command of the sovereign touching all his subjects in general, or matters of general application. . . .

The first attribute of the sovereign prince therefore is the power to make law binding on all his subjects in general and on each in particular. But to avoid any ambiguity one must add that he does so without the consent of any superior, equal, or inferior being necessary. If the prince can only make law with the consent of a superior he is a subject; if of an equal he shares his sovereignty; if of an inferior, whether it be a council of magnates or the people, it is not he who is sovereign. . . .

It may be objected however that not only have magistrates the power of issuing edicts and ordinances, each according to his competence and within his own sphere of jurisdiction, but private citizens can make law in the form of general or local custom. It is agreed that customary law is as binding as statute law. But if the sovereign prince is author of the law, his subjects are the authors of custom. But there is a difference between law and custom. Custom establishes itself gradually over a long period of years, and by common consent, or at any rate the consent of the greater part. Law is made on the instant and draws its force from him who has the right to bind all the rest. Custom is established imperceptibly and without any exercise of compulsion. Law is promulgated and imposed by authority, and often against the wishes of the subject. For this reason Dion Chrysostom compared custom to the king and law to the tyrant. Moreover law can break custom, but custom cannot derogate from the law, nor can the magistrate, or any other responsible for the administration of law, use his discretion about the enforcement of law as he can about custom. Law, unless it is permissive and relaxes the severity of another law, always carries penalties for its breach. Custom only has binding force by the sufferance and during the good pleasure of the sovereign prince, and so far as he is willing to authorize it. Thus the force of both statutes and customary law derives from the authorization of the prince. . . . Included in the power of making and unmaking law is that of promulgating it and amending it when it is obscure, or when the magistrates find contradictions and absurdities. . . .

All the other attributes and rights of sovereignty are included in this power of making and unmaking law, so that strictly speaking this is the unique attribute of sovereign power. It includes all other rights of sovereignty, that is to say of making peace and war, of hearing appeals from the sentences of all courts whatsoever, of appointing and dismissing the great officers of state; of taxing, or granting privileges of exemption to all subjects, of appreciating or depreciating the value and weight of the coinage, of receiving oaths of fidelity from subjects and liege-vassals alike, without exception of any other to whom faith is due. . . .

38
Thomas Hobbes

Thomas Hobbes (1588–1679) was a vigorous defender of the royal prerogatives in England. He is distinguished from his contemporaries in that he justifies his support of absolute sovereignty with a complete theory of human nature and the state. The monarch, he argues, is that person into whose hands all power has been placed for the purpose of maintaining peace and order. Royal authority is the only means of avoiding what, in his view, is infinitely worse, the "war of each against all," which must constantly be waged in a state of nature. As a thoroughgoing individualist, Hobbes was surely no fascist; yet he did play a significant part in the development of the theory of absolute rule.

[THE ORIGIN AND NATURE OF THE STATE]*

OF THE CAUSES, GENERATION, AND DEFINITION OF A COMMONWEALTH. The final cause, end, or design of men, who naturally love liberty, and dominion over others, in the introduction of that restraint upon themselves, in which we see them live in commonwealths, is the foresight of their own preservation, and of a more contented life thereby; that is to say, of getting themselves out from that miserable condition of war, which is necessarily consequent, as hath been shown in chapter xiii, to the natural passions of men, when there is no visible power to keep them in awe, and tie

---

*From T. Hobbes, *Leviathan,* 1651. These passages are from a modernized edition edited by Michael Oakeshott and published by Basil Blackwell, Oxford, 1946.

them by fear of punishment to the performance of their covenants, and observation of those laws of nature set down in the fourteenth and fifteenth chapters.

For the laws of nature, as "justice," "equity," "modesty," "mercy," and, in sum, "doing to others as we would be done to," of themselves, without the terror of some power to cause them to be observed, are contrary to our natural passions, that carry us to partiality, pride, revenge, and the like. And covenants, without the sword, are but words, and of no strength to secure a man at all. Therefore notwithstanding the laws of nature, which everyone hath then kept, when he has the will to keep them, when he can do it safely, if there be no power erected, or not great enough for our security, every man will and may lawfully rely on his own strength and art, for caution against all other men. And in all places where men have lived by small families, to rob and spoil one another has been a trade, and so far from being reputed against the law of nature, that the greater spoils they gained, the greater was their honor; and men observed no other laws therein, but the laws of honor; that is, to abstain from cruelty, leaving to men their lives, and instruments of husbandry. And as small families did then, so now do cities and kingdoms, which are but greater families, for their own security, enlarge their dominions, upon all pretenses of danger, and fear of invasion, or assistance that may be given to invaders, and endeavor as much as they can to subdue or weaken their neighbors, by open force and secret arts, for want of other caution, justly; and are remembered for it in after ages with honor.

Not is it the joining together of a small number of men that gives them this security; because in small numbers, small additions on the one side or the other make the advantage of strength so great as is sufficient to carry the victory; and therefore gives encouragement to an invasion. The multitude sufficient to confide in for our security is not determined by any certain number, but by comparison with the enemy we fear; and is then sufficient, when the odds of the enemy is not of so visible and conspicuous moment to determine the event of war, as to move him to attempt.

And be there never so great a multitude; yet if their actions be directed according to their particular judgments and particular appetites, they can expect thereby no defense, nor protection, neither against a common enemy, nor against the injuries of one another. For being distracted in opinions concerning the best use and application of their strength, they do not help but hinder one another; and reduce their strength by mutual opposition to nothing: whereby they are easily, not only subdued by a very few that agree together; but also when there is no common enemy, they make war upon each other, for their particular interests. For if we could suppose a great multitude of men to consent in the observation of justice, and other laws of nature, without a common power to keep them all in awe, we might as well suppose all mankind to do the same; and then there neither would be nor need to be any civil government or commonwealth at all; because there would be peace without subjection.

Nor is it enough for the security, which men desire should last all the time of their life, that they be governed and directed by one judgment, for a limited time: as in one battle, or one war. For though they obtain a victory by their unanimous endeavor against a foreign enemy; yet afterwards, when either they have no common enemy, or he that by one part is held for an enemy is by another part held for a friend, they must needs by the difference of their interests dissolve, and fall again into a war among themselves. . . .

The only way to erect such a common power as may be able to defend them from the invasion of foreigners and the injuries of one another, and thereby to secure them in such sort as that by their own industry, and by the fruits of the earth, they may nourish themselves and live contentedly, is to confer all their power and strength upon one man, or upon one assembly of men, that may reduce all their wills, by plurality of voices, unto one will: which is as much as to say, to appoint one man, or assembly of men, to bear their person; and everyone to own and acknowledge himself to be author of whatsoever he that so beareth their person shall act, or cause to be acted, in those things which concern the common peace and safety; and therein to submit their wills, every one to his will, and their judgments to his judgment. This is more than consent, or concord; it is a real unity of them all in one and the same person, made by covenant of every man with every man, in such manner as if every man should say to every man, "I authorize and give up my right of governing myself, to this man or to this assembly of men, on this condition, that thou give up thy right to him and authorize all his actions in like manner." This done, the multitude so united in one person is called a "commonwealth," in Latin *civitas*. This is the generation of that great leviathan, or rather, to speak more reverently, of that mortal god, to which we owe under the immortal God, our peace and defense. For by this authority, given him by every particular man in the commonwealth, he hath the use of so much power and strength conferred on him, that by terror thereof, he is enabled to perform the wills of them all, to peace at home, and mutual aid against their enemies abroad. And in him consisteth the essence of the commonwealth; which, to define it, is "one person, of whose acts a great multitude, by mutual covenants one with another, have made themselves every one the author, to the end he may use the strength and means of them all, as he shall think expedient, for their peace and common defense."

And he that carrieth this person is called sovereign, and said to have sovereign power; and everyone besides, his subject.

The attaining to this sovereign power is by two ways. One, by natural force; as when a man maketh his children to submit themselves, and their children, to his government, as being able to destroy them if they refuse; or by war subdueth his enemies to his will, giving them their lives on that condition. The other is when men agree among themselves to submit to some man, or assembly of men, voluntarily, on confidence to be protected by him against all others. This latter may be called a political commonwealth, or commonwealth by institution; and the former, a commonwealth by acquisition. And first, I shall speak of a commonwealth by institution. . . .

2

ORGANICISM

The organic theory of the state was developed most fully in Germany during the nineteenth century. The essential unity of the state as a real being, and the organic interrelation of the subordinate members of the body politic, were there taken to provide a philosophical foundation for the achievement of political unity among the numerous German principalities. "Germany is no longer a state," Hegel had said in his essay on *The Constitution of Germany* in 1802. The political task then became that of creating a strong state government under which all Germans could live in peace and harmony with one another; the philosophical task was that of providing the theory upon which this national unification could be grounded.

The objective of the first of these tasks was attained at last under the leadership of "the man of blood and iron," Bismarck, who became the first Chancellor of the united German Empire in 1871. The latter, philosophical objective had been a challenge to Hegel, and remained a challenge to his followers; their organic theories came to penetrate German life and spirit.

These nineteenth-century thinkers were thus motivated by patriotic aims and aspirations quite similar to those that had inspired Machiavelli and Bodin so many decades before—and indeed Hegel refers to Machiavelli as "a true political genius." But the organicists differed from the earlier defenders of absolute sovereignty in exalting the state itself more than its ruler, in developing the theory of the state as a real person, of superior standing, through whose will and conduct the dialectic of human history is worked out. As manifestations of the world spirit, states are held to be the only institutions in which true human freedom can be realized. The state is not simply the instrument of its citizens, but (said they) the most purely rational representation of their interests; individual citizens are its cells and organs. Because the state is on a level of reality higher than that of any single human being, and because its will is the real will of every citizen, the organicists believed that no real conflict of interest between individual and state could arise. The will of the state is always supreme; its members, should it become necessary, must "be forced to be free."

39
Georg W. F. Hegel

Elements of the philosophy of Hegel were borrowed by both communists and fascists. The Marxist use of the Hegelian dialectic has been discussed earlier in this volume.* Fascist philosophers absorbed not the dialectical methodology but the Hegelian idealization of the national state and the Hegelian arguments against any individuality opposed to, or outside of, state organization. Thus patriotism, Hegel here contends, "is essentially the sentiment of regarding . . . the weal of the community as the substantial basis and the final end."

IDEA AND AIM OF THE STATE*

The State is the realization of the ethical idea. It is the ethical spirit as revealed, self-conscious, substantial will. It is the will which thinks and knows itself, and carries out what it knows, and in so far as it knows. The unreflected existence of the State rests on custom, and its reflected existence on the self-consciousness of the individual, on his knowledge and activity. The individual, in return, has his substantial freedom in the State, as the essence, purpose, and product of his activity.

The true State is the ethical whole and the realization of freedom. It is the absolute purpose of reason that freedom should be realized. The State is the spirit, which lives in the world and there realizes itself consciously; while in nature it is actual only as its own other or as dormant spirit. Only as present in consciousness, knowing itself as an existing object, is it the State. The State is the march of God through the world, its ground is the power of reason realizing itself as will. The idea of the State should not denote any particular State, or particular institution; one must rather consider the Idea only, this actual God, by itself. Because it is more easy to find defects than to grasp the positive meaning, one readily falls into the mistake of emphasizing so much the particular nature of the State as to overlook its inner organic essence. The State is no work of art. It exists in the world, and thus in the realm of caprice, accident, and error. Evil behavior toward it may disfigure it on many sides. But the ugliest man, the criminal, the invalid, and the cripple, are still living human beings. The affirmative, life, persists in spite of defects, and it is this affirmative which alone is here in question.

In the State, everything depends upon the unity of the universal and the particular. In the ancient States the subjective purpose was absolutely one with the will of the State. In modern times, on the contrary, we demand an individual opinion, an individual will and conscience. The ancients had none of these in the modern sense; the final thing for them was the will of the State. While in Asiatic despotisms the individual had no inner self and no self-justification, in the modern world man demands to be honored for the sake of his subjective individuality.

*Reprinted by permission of Charles Scribner's Sons from *Hegel: Selections,* edited by J. Loewenberg.

The union of duty and right has the twofold aspect that what the State demands as duty should directly be the right of the individual, since the State is nothing but the organization of the concept of freedom. The determinations of the individual will are given by the State objectivity, and it is through the State alone that they attain truth and realization. The State is the sole condition of the attainment of the particular end and good.

Political disposition, called patriotism—the assurance resting in truth and the will which has become a custom—is simply the result of the institutions subsisting in the State, institutions in which reason is actually present.

Under patriotism one frequently understands a mere willingness to perform extraordinary acts and sacrifices. But patriotism is essentially the sentiment of regarding, in the ordinary circumstances and ways of life, the weal of the community as the substantial basis and the final end. It is upon this consciousness, present in the ordinary course of life and under all circumstances, that the disposition to heroic effort is founded. But as people are often rather magnanimous than just, they easily persuade themselves that they possess the heroic kind of patriotism, in order to save themselves the trouble of having the truly patriotic sentiment, or to excuse the lack of it.

Political sentiment, as appearance, must be distinguished from what people truly will. What they at bottom will is the real cause, but they cling to particular interests and delight in the vain contemplation of improvements. The conviction of the necessary stability of the State in which alone the particular interests can be realized, people indeed possess, but custom makes invisible that upon which our whole existence rests; it does not occur to anyone, when he safely passes through the streets at night, that it could be otherwise. The habit of safety has become a second nature, and we do not reflect that it is the result of the activity of special institutions. It is through force—this is frequently the superficial opinion—that the State coheres, but what alone holds it together is the fundamental sense of order, which is possessed by all.

The State is an organism or the development of the idea into its differences. These different sides are the different powers of the State with their functions and activities, by means of which the universal is constantly and necessarily producing itself, and, being presupposed in its own productive function, it is thus always actively present. This organism is the political constitution. It eternally springs from the State, just as the State in turn maintains itself through the constitution. If these two things fall asunder, if both different sides become independent of each other, then the unity which the constitution produces is no longer operative; the fable of the stomach and the other organs may be applied to it. It is the nature of an organism that all its parts must constitute a certain unity; if one part asserts its independence the other parts must go to destruction. No predicates, principles, and the like suffice to express the nature of the State; it must be comprehended as an organism.

The State is real, and its reality consists in the interest of the whole being realized in particular ends. Actuality is always the unity of universality and particularity, and the differentiation of the universal into particular ends. These particular ends seem independent, though they are borne and sustained by the whole only. In so far as this unity is absent, no thing is real, though it may exist. A bad State is one which merely exists. A sick body also exists, but it has no true reality. A hand, which is cut off, still looks like a hand and exists, but it has no reality. True reality is necessity. What is real is eternally necessary.

To the complete State belongs, essentially, consciousness and thought. The State knows thus what it wills, and it knows it under the form of thought.

The essential difference between the State and religion consists in that the commands of the State have the form of legal duty, irrespective of the feelings accompanying their performance; the sphere of religion, on the other hand, is in the inner life. Just as the State, were it to frame its commands as religion does, would endanger the right of the inner life, so the church, if it acts as a State and imposes punishment, degenerates into a tyrannical religion.

In the State one must want nothing which is not an expression of rationality. The State is the world which the spirit has made for itself; it has therefore a determinate and self-conscious course. One often speaks of the wisdom of God in nature, but one must not believe that the physical world of nature is higher than the world of spirit. Just as spirit is superior to nature, so is the State superior to the physical life. We must therefore worship the State as the manifestation of the divine on earth, and consider that, if it is difficult to comprehend nature, it is infinitely harder to grasp the essence of the State. . . .

THE CONSTITUTION

The constitution is rational, in so far as the State defines and differentiates its functions according to the nature of its concept.

Who shall make the constitution? This question seems intelligible, yet on closer examination reveals itself as meaningless, for it presupposes the existence of no constitution, but only a mere mass of atomic individuals. How a mass of individuals is to come by a constitution, whether by its own efforts or by those of others, whether by goodness, thought, or force, it must decide for itself, for with a disorganized mob the concept of the State has nothing to do. But if the question does presuppose an already existing constitution, then to make a constitution means only to change it. The presupposition of a constitution implies, however, at once, that any modification in it must take place constitutionally. It is absolutely essential that the constitution, though having a temporal origin, should not be regarded as made. It (the principle of constitution) is rather to be conceived as absolutely perpetual and rational, and therefore as divine, substantial, and above and beyond the sphere of what is made. . . .

Since spirit is real only in what it knows itself to be, and since the State, as the nation's spirit, is the law permeating all its affairs, its ethical code, and the consciousness of its individuals, the constitution of a people chiefly depends upon the kind and the character of its self-consciousness. In it lies both its subjective freedom and the reality of the constitution.

To think of giving people a constitution *a priori*, though according to its content a more or less rational one—such a whim would precisely overlook that element which renders a constitution more than a mere abstract object. Every nation, therefore, has the constitution which is appropriate to it and belongs to it.

The State must, in its constitution, permeate all situations. A constitution is not a thing just made; it is the work of centuries, the idea and the consciousness of what is rational, in so far as it is developed in a people. No constitution, therefore, is merely created by the subjects of the State. The nation must feel that its constitution embodies its right and its status, otherwise the constitution may exist externally, but has no meaning or value. . . .

THE POWER OF THE PRINCE

Because sovereignty contains in ideal all special privileges, the common misconception is quite natural, which takes it to be mere force, empty caprice, and synonymous with despotism. But despotism means a state of lawlessness, in which the particular will as such, whether that of monarch or people (*ochlocracy*), is the law, or rather instead of the law. Sovereignty, on the contrary, constitutes the element of ideality of particular spheres and functions under lawful and constitutional conditions.

The sovereignty of the people, conceived in opposition to the sovereignty residing in the monarch, stands for the common view of democracy, which has come to prevail in modern times. The idea of the sovereignty of the people, taken in this opposition, belongs to a confused idea of what is commonly and crudely understood by "the people." The people without its monarch and without that whole organization necessarily and directly connected with him is a formless mass, which is no longer a State. In a people, not conceived in a lawless and unorganized condition, but as a self-developed and truly organic totality—in such a people sovereignty is the personality of the whole, and this is represented in reality by the person of the monarch.

The State must be regarded as a great architectonic edifice, a hieroglyph of reason, manifesting itself in reality. Everything referring merely to utility, externality, and the like, must be excluded from its philosophic treatment. That the State is the self-determining and the completely sovereign will, the final decision being necessarily referred to it—that is easy to comprehend. The difficulty lies in grasping this "I will" as a person. By this it is not meant that the monarch can act arbitrarily. He is bound, in truth, by the concrete content of the deliberations of his council, and, when the constitution is stable, he has often nothing more to do than sign his name—but this name is important; it is the point than which there is nothing higher.

It may be said that an organic State has already existed in the beautiful democracy of Athens. The Greeks, however, derived the final decision from entirely external phenomena, from oracles, entrails of sacrificed animals, and from the flight of birds. Nature they considered as a power which in this wise made known and gave expression to what was good for the people. Self-consciousness had at that time not yet attained to the abstraction of subjectivity; it had not yet come to the realization that an "I will" must be pronounced by man himself concerning the decisions of the State. This "I will" constitutes the great difference between the ancient and the modern world, and must therefore have its peculiar place in the great edifice of the State. Unfortunately this modern characteristic is regarded as merely external and arbitrary.

It is often maintained against the monarch that since he may be ill-educated or unworthy to stand at the helm, it is therefore absurd to assume the rationality of the institution of the monarch. The presupposition, however, that the fortunes of the State depend upon the particular character of the monarch is false. In the perfect organization of the State the important thing is only the finality of formal decision and the stability against passion. One must not therefore demand objective qualification of the monarch; he has but to say "yes" and to put the dot upon the "i." The crown shall be of such a nature that the particular character of its bearer is of no significance. Beyond his function of administering the final decision, the monarch is a particular being who is of no concern. Situations may indeed arise in which his particularity alone asserts itself, but in that case the State is not yet fully developed, or else is ill constructed. In a well-ordered monarchy the law alone has objective power to which the monarch has but to affix the subjective "I will."

Monarchs do not excel in bodily strength or intellect, and yet millions permit themselves to be ruled by them. To say that the people permit themselves to be governed contrary to their interests, aims, and intentions is preposterous, for people are not so stupid. It is their need, it is the inner power of the idea, which, in opposition to their apparent consciousness, urges them to this situation and retains them therein. . . .

THE MEANING OF WAR

There is an ethical element in war. It must not be regarded as an absolute ill, or as merely an external calamity which is accidentally based upon the passions of despotic individuals or nations, upon acts of injustice, and, in general, upon what ought not to be. The recognition of the finite, such as property and life, as accidental, is necessary. This necessity is at first wont to appear under the form of a force of nature, for all things finite are mortal and transient. In the ethical order, in the State, however, nature is robbed of its force, and the necessity is exalted to a work of freedom, to an ethical law. The transient and negative nature of all things is transformed in the State into an expression of the ethical will. War, often painted by edifying speech as a state in which the vanity of temporal things is demonstrated, now becomes an element whereby the ideal character of the particular receives its right and reality. War has the deep meaning that by it the ethical health of the nations is preserved and their finite aims uprooted. And as the winds which sweep over the ocean prevent the decay that would result from its perpetual calm, so war protects the people from the corruption which an everlasting peace would bring upon it. History shows phases which illustrate how successful wars have checked internal unrest and have strengthened the entire stability of the State.

In peace, civic life becomes more extended, every sphere is hedged in and grows immobile, and at last all men stagnate, their particular nature becoming more and more hardened and ossified. Only in the unity of a body is health, and, where the organs become still, there is death. Eternal peace is often demanded as an ideal toward which mankind should move. Thus Kant proposed an alliance of princes, which should settle the controversies of States, and the Holy Alliance probably aspired to be an institution of this kind. The State, however, is individual, and in individuality negation is essentially contained. A number of States may constitute themselves into a family, but this confederation, as an individuality, must create an opposition and so beget an enemy. Not only do nations issue forth invigorated from their wars, but those nations torn by internal strife win peace at home as a result of war abroad. War indeed causes insecurity in property, but this real insecurity is only a necessary commotion. From the pulpits much is preached concerning the insecurity, vanity, and instability of temporal things, and yet everyone, though he may be touched by his own words, thinks that he, at least, will manage to hold on to his possessions. Let the insecurity finally come, in the form of Hussars with glistening sabers, and show its earnest activity, and that touching edification which foresaw all this now turns upon the enemy with curses. In spite of this, wars will break out whenever necessity demands them; but the seeds spring up anew, and speech is silenced before the grave repetitions of history.

The military class is the class of universality. The defense of the State is its privilege, and its duty is to realize the ideality contained in it, which consists in self-sacrifice. There are different kinds of bravery. The courage of the animal, or the robber, the bravery which arises from a sense of honor, the chivalrous bravery, are not yet the true forms of bravery. In civilized nations true bravery consists in the readiness to give oneself wholly to the service of the State, so that the individual counts but as one among many. Not personal valor alone is significant; the important aspect of it lies in self-subordination to the universal cause. . . .

INTERNATIONAL RELATIONS

Just as the individual is not a real person unless related to other persons, so the State is no real individuality unless related to other States. The legitimate power of a State, and more especially its princely power, is, from the point of view of its foreign relations, a wholly internal affair. A State shall, therefore, not interfere with the internal affairs of another State. On the other hand, for a complete State, it is essential that it be recognized by others; but this recognition demands as a guarantee that it shall recognize those States which recognize it, and shall respect their independence. Hence its internal affairs cannot be a matter of indifference to them.

When Napoleon, before the peace of Campoformio, said, "The French Republic requires recognition as little as the sun needs to be recognized," his words suggest nothing but the strength of existence, which already carries with it the guarantee of recognition, without needing to be expressed.

When the particular wills of the State can come to no agreement their controversy can be decided only by war. What offense shall be regarded as a breach of treaty, or as a violation of respect and honor, must remain indefinite, since many and various injuries can easily accrue from the wide range of the interests of the States and from the complex relations of their citizens. The State may identify its infinitude and honor with every one of its single aspects. And if a State, as a strong individuality, has experienced an unduly protracted internal rest, it will naturally be more inclined to irritability, in order to find an occasion and field for intense activity.

The nations of Europe form a family according to the universal principle of their legislation, their ethical code, and their civilization. But the relation among States fluctuates, and no judge exists to adjust their differences. The higher judge is the universal and absolute Spirit alone—the World-Spirit.

The relation of one particular State to another presents, on the largest possible scale, the most shifting play of individual passions, interests, aims, talents, virtues, power, injustice, vice, and mere external chance. It is a play in which even the ethical whole, the independence of the State, is exposed to accident. The principles which control the many national spirits are limited. Each nation as an existing individuality is guided by its particular principles, and only as a particular individuality can each national spirit win objectivity and self-consciousness; but the fortunes and deeds of States in their relation to one another reveal the dialectic of the finite nature of these spirits. Out of this dialectic rises the universal Spirit, the unlimited World-Spirit, pronouncing its judgment—and its judgment is the highest—upon the finite nations of the world's history; for the history of the world is the world's court of justice.

40
Johann G. Fichte

Johann G. Fichte (1762–1814), building upon an organic theory of the state, wrote *Addresses to the German Nation* in 1808, combining emotion with philosophic reason to plead for German unity. The German nation, internally coherent and eternally real, cries out (said he) for the German state that did not yet exist. He appealed for patriotism above all—a willingness on the part of individuals to sacrifice for love of fatherland. More than a century later, aggressive German nationalism owed much to his impassioned zeal. "Love of fatherland," he wrote, "must itself govern the State and be the supreme, final, and absolute authority."

[THE UNITY OF THE GERMAN NATION]*

I speak for Germans simply, of Germans simply, not recognizing, but setting aside completely and rejecting, all the dissociating distinctions which for centuries unhappy events have caused in this single nation. . . . my spirit gathers round it

*From J. Fichte, *Addresses to the German Nation*, 1808. These passages are from a translation by R.F. Jones and G.H. Turnbull, 1922, and are reprinted by permission of the Open Court Publishing Company, La Salle, Ill.

the educated part of the whole German nation, from all the lands in which they are scattered. It thinks of and considers our common position and relations; it longs that part of the living force, with which these addresses may chance to grip you, may also remain in and breathe from the dumb printed page which alone will come to the eyes of the absent, and may in all places kindle German hearts to decision and action. Only of Germans and simply for Germans, I said. In due course we shall show that any other mark of unity or any other national bond either never had truth and meaning or, if it had, that owing to our present position these bonds of union have been destroyed and torn from us and can never recur; it is only by means of the common characteristic of being German that we can avert the downfall of our nation which is threatened by its fusion with foreign peoples, and win back again an individuality that is self-supporting and quite incapable of any dependence upon others. . . .

To begin with and before all things: the first, original, and truly natural boundaries of States are beyond doubt their internal boundaries. Those who speak the same language are joined to each other by a multitude of invisible bonds by nature herself, long before any human art begins; they understand each other and have the power of continuing to make themselves understood more and more clearly; they belong together and are by nature one and an inseparable whole. Such a whole, if it wishes to absorb and mingle with itself any other people of different descent and language, cannot do so without itself becoming confused, in the beginning at any rate, and violently disturbing the even progress of its culture. From this internal boundary, which is drawn by the spiritual nature of man himself, the marking of the external boundary by dwelling-place results as a consequence; and in the natural view of things it is not because men dwell between certain mountains and rivers that they are a people, but, on the contrary, men dwell together—and, if their luck has so arranged it, are protected by rivers and mountains—because they were a people already by a law of nature which is much higher.

Thus was the German nation placed. . . .

[THE LOVE OF FATHERLAND]

The noble-minded man's belief in the eternal continuance of his influence even on this earth is thus founded on the hope of the eternal continuance of the people from which he has developed, and on the characteristic of that people as indicated in the hidden law of which we have spoken, without admixture of, or corruption by, any alien element which does not belong to the totality of the functions of that law. This characteristic is the eternal thing to which he entrusts the eternity of himself and of his continuing influence, the eternal order of things in which he places his portion of eternity; he must will its continuance, for it alone is to him the means by which the short span of his life here below is extended into continuous life here below. His belief and his struggle to plant what is permanent, his conception in which he comprehends his own life as an eternal life, is the bond which unites first his own nation, and then, through his nation, the whole human race, in a most intimate fashion with himself, and brings all their needs within his widened sympathy until the end of time. This is his love for his people, respecting, trusting, and rejoicing in it, and feeling honored by descent from it. The divine has appeared in it, and that which is original has deemed this people worthy to be made its vesture and its means of directly influencing the world; for this reason there will be further manifestations of the divine in it. Hence, the noble-minded man will be active and effective, and will sacrifice himself for his people. Life merely as such, the mere continuance of changing existence, has in any case never had any value for him; he has wished for it only as the source of what is permanent. But this permanence is promised to him only by the continuous and independent existence of his nation. In order to save his nation he must be ready even to die that it may live, and that he may live in it the only life for which he has ever wished.

So it is. Love that is truly love, and not a mere transitory lust, never clings to what is transient; only in the eternal does it awaken and become kindled, and there alone does it rest. Man is not able to love even himself unless he conceives himself as eternal; apart from that he cannot even respect, much less approve of, himself. Still less can he love anything outside himself without taking it up into the eternity of his faith and of his soul and binding it thereto. He who does not first regard himself as eternal has in him no love of any kind, and, moreover, cannot love a fatherland, a thing which for him does not exist. He who regards his invisible life as eternal, but not his visible life as similarly eternal, may perhaps have a heaven and therein a fatherland, but here below he has no fatherland, for this, too, is regarded only in the image of eternity—eternity visible and made sensuous—and for this reason also he is unable to love his fatherland. If none has been handed down to such a man, he is to be pitied. But he to whom a fatherland has been handed down, and in whose soul heaven and earth, visible and invisible meet and mingle, and thus, and only thus, create a true and enduring heaven—such a man fights to the last drop of his blood to hand on the precious possession unimpaired to his posterity.

So it always has been, although it has not always been expressed in such general terms and so clearly as we express it here. What inspired the men of noble mind among the Romans, whose frame of mind and way of thinking still live and breathe among us in their works of art, to struggles and sacrifices, to patience and endurance for the fatherland? They themselves express it often and distinctly. It was their firm belief in the eternal continuance of their Roma, and their confident expectation that they themselves would eternally continue to live in this eternity in the stream of time. In so far as this belief was well founded, and they themselves would have comprehended it if they had been entirely clear in their own minds, it did not deceive them. To this very day there still lives in our midst what was truly eternal in their eternal Roma; they themselves live with it, and its consequences will continue to live to the very end of time.

People and fatherland in this sense, as a support and guarantee of eternity on earth and as that which can be eternal here below, far transcend the State in the ordinary sense of the word, viz., the social order as comprehended by mere intellectual conception and as established and maintained under the guidance of this conception. The aim of the State is positive law, internal peace, and a condition of affairs in which everyone may by diligence earn his daily bread and satisfy the needs of his material existence, so long as God permits him to live. All this is only a means, a condition, and a framework for what love of fatherland really wants, viz., that the eternal and the divine may blossom in the world and never cease to become more and more pure, perfect, and excellent. That is why this love of fatherland must itself govern the State and be the supreme, final, and absolute authority. . . .

Then, too, it must be love of fatherland that governs the State by placing before it a higher object than the usual one of maintaining internal peace, property, personal freedom, and the life and well-being of all. For this higher object alone, and with no other intention, does the State assemble an armed force. When the question arises of making use of this, when the call comes to stake everything that the State, in the narrow conception of the word, sets before itself as object, viz., property, personal freedom, life, and well-being, nay, even the continued existence of the State itself; when the call comes to make an original decision with responsibility to God alone, and without a clear and reasonable idea that what is intended will surely be attained—for this is never possible in such matters—then, and then only, does there live at the helm of the State a truly original and primary life, and at this point, and not before, the true sovereign rights of government enter, like God, to hazard the lower life for the sake of the higher. In the maintenance of the traditional constitution, the laws, and civil prosperity there is absolutely no real true life and no original decision. Conditions and circumstances, and legislators perhaps long since dead, have created these things; succeeding ages go on faithfully in the paths marked out, and so in fact they have no public life of their own; they merely repeat a life that once existed. In such times there is no need of any real government. But, when this regular course is endangered, and it is a question of making decisions in new and unprecedented cases, then there is need of a life that lives of itself. What spirit is it that in such cases may place itself at the helm, that can make its own decisions with sureness and certainty, untroubled by any hesitation? What spirit has an undisputed right to summon and to order everyone concerned, whether he himself be willing or not, and to compel anyone who resists, to risk everything including his life? Not the spirit of the peaceful citizen's love for the constitution and the laws, but the devouring flame of higher patriotism, which embraces the nation as the vesture of the eternal, for which the noble-minded man joyfully sacrifices himself. . . . The promise of a life here on earth extending beyond the period of life here on earth—that alone it is which can inspire men even unto death for the fatherland.

. . .

From all this it follows that the State, merely as the government of human life in its progress along the ordinary peaceful path, is not something which is primary and which exists for its own sake, but is merely the means to the higher purpose of the eternal, regular, and continuous development of what is purely human in this nation. It follows, too, that the vision and the love of this eternal development, and nothing else, should have the higher supervision of State administration at all times, not excluding periods of peace, and that this alone is able to save the people's independence when it is endangered. In the case of the Germans, among whom as an original people this love of fatherland was possible and, as we firmly believe, did actually exist up to the present time, it has been able up to now to reckon with great confidence on the security of what was most vital to it. As was the case with the ancient Greeks alone, with the Germans the State and the nation were actually separated from each other, and each was represented for itself, the former in the separate German realms and principalities, the latter represented visibly in the imperial connection and invisibly—by virtue of a law, not written, but living and valid in the minds of all, a law whose results struck the eye everywhere—in a mass of customs and institutions. Wherever the German language was spoken, everyone who had first seen the light of day in its domain could consider himself as in a double sense a citizen, on the one hand, of the State where he was born and to whose care he was in the first instance commended, and, on the other hand, of the whole common fatherland of the German nation. . . .

These addresses lay before you the sole remaining means, now that the others have been tried in vain, of preventing this annihilation of every nobler impulse that may break out among us in the future, and of preventing this degradation of our whole nation. They propose that you establish deeply and indelibly in the hearts of all, by means of education, the true and all-powerful love of fatherland, the conception of our people as an eternal people and as the security for our own eternity. What kind of education can do this, and how it is to be done, we shall see in the following addresses. . . .

41
Heinrich von Treitschke

Heinrich von Treitschke (1834–1896), a Prussian historian and philosopher prominent at the time of German unification in the late nineteenth century, culminated, with his *Politics,* the organic nationalism that Hegel had earlier launched. The organic state is a real person, living through the generations. Like every organism, it must fight for its life, exercising its power in defense of itself and its ideals. The essence of the living state is the accomplishment of its will—and that sometimes justifies the use of brute force. The inward assent of the citizens is ideal, but "submission is what the state primarily requires."

THE STATE IDEA*

The State is the people, legally united as an independent entity. By the word "people" we understand briefly a number of families permanently living side by side. This definition implies that the State is primordial and necessary, that it is as

*H. Treitschke, *Politics,* Vol. I, 1870. These passages are from a translation by B. Dugdale and T. de Bille, 1916, and are reprinted by permission of Michael Dugdale and the publisher, Constable and Company, Ltd., London.

enduring as history, and no less essential to mankind than speech. History, however, begins for us with the art of writing; earlier than this men's conscious recollection of the past cannot be reckoned with. Therefore everything which lies beyond this limit is rightly judged to be prehistoric. We, on the other hand, must deal here with man as a historical being, and we can only say that creative political genius is inherent in him, and that the State, like him, subsists from the beginning. The attempt to present it as something artificial, following upon a natural condition, has fallen completely into discredit. We lack all historical knowledge of a nation without a constitution. Wherever Europeans have penetrated they have found some form of State organization, rude though it may have been. This recognition of the primordial character of the State is very widespread at the present day, but was in fact discovered in the eighteenth century. Eichhorn, Niebuhr, and Savigny were the first to show that the State is the constituted people. It was indeed a familiar fact to the Ancients in their great and simple Age. For them the State was a divinely appointed order, the origins of which were not subject to inquiry. The constitutional doctrines of the Philosophers were in complete accord with the naïveté of the popular beliefs. For them the citizen was in his very nature no more than a fragment of the State; it therefore followed that the whole must have been anterior to the parts. . . .

The human race was once for all created with certain innate qualities among which speech and political genius must undoubtedly be counted. Aristotle says truly that man is φύσει,* that is to say in his very nature and essence a ζῶον πολιτικόν.† A being who feels no need for a constitution, he proceeds, must either be a god, and thus superior to man, or a beast, and his inferior. . . .

If, then, political capacity is innate in man, and is to be further developed, it is quite accurate to call the State a necessary evil. We have to deal with it as a lofty necessity of Nature. Even as the possibility of building up a civilization is dependent upon the limitation of our powers combined with the gift of reason, so also the State depends upon our inability to live alone. This Aristotle has already demonstrated. The State, says he, arose in order to make life possible; it endured to make good life possible.

This natural necessity of a constituted order is further displayed by the fact that the political institutions of a people, broadly speaking, appear to be the external forms which are the inevitable outcome of its inner life. Just as its language is not the product of caprice but the immediate expression of its most deep-rooted attitude towards the world, so also its political institutions regarded as a whole, and the whole spirit of its jurisprudence, are the symbols of its political genius and of the outside destinies which have helped to shape the gifts which Nature bestowed. . . .

We may say with certainty that the evolution of the State is, broadly speaking, nothing but the necessary outward form which the inner life of a people bestows upon itself, and that peoples attain to that form of government which their moral

*Phusei, "by nature."—Ed.
†Zoon Politikon, "political animal."—Ed.

capacity enables them to reach. Nothing can be more inverted than the opinion that constitutional laws were artificially evolved in opposition to the conception of a Natural Law. Ultramontanes and Jacobins both start with the assumption that the legislation of a modern State is the work of sinful man. They thus display their total lack of reverence for the objectively revealed Will of God, as unfolded in the life of the State.

When we assert the evolution of the State to be something inherently necessary, we do not thereby deny the power of genius or of creative Will in history. For it is of the essence of political genius to be national. There has never been an example of the contrary. The summit of historical fame was never attained by Wallenstein because he was never a national hero, but a Czech who played the German for the sake of expediency. He was, like Napoleon, a splendid Adventurer of history. The truly great maker of history always stands upon a national basis. This applies equally to men of letters. He only is a great writer who so writes that all his countrymen respond, "Thus it must be. Thus we all feel"—who is in fact a microcosm of his nation.

If we have grasped that the State is the people legally constituted we thereby imply that it aims at establishing a permanent tradition throughout the Ages. A people does not only comprise the individuals living side by side, but also the successive generations of the same stock. This is one of the truths which Materialists dismiss as a mystical doctrine, and yet it is an obvious truth. Only the continuity of human history makes man a ζῶον πολιτικόν. He alone stands upon the achievements of his forebears, and deliberately continues their work in order to transmit it more perfect to his children and children's children. Only a creature like man, needing aid and endowed with reason, can have a history, and it is one of the ineptitudes of the Materialists to speak of animal States. It is just a play upon words to talk of a bee State. Beasts merely reproduce unconsciously what has been from all time, and none but human beings can possess a form of government which is calculated to endure. . . . No one who does not recognize the continued action of the past upon the present can ever understand the nature and necessity of War. Gibbon calls Patriotism "the living sense of my own interest in society"; but if we simply look upon the State as intended to secure life and property to the individual, how comes it that the individual will also sacrifice life and property to the State? It is a false conclusion that wars are waged for the sake of material advantage. Modern wars are not fought for the sake of booty. Here the high moral ideal of national honor is a factor handed down from one generation to another, enshrining something positively sacred, and compelling the individual to sacrifice himself to it. This ideal is above all price and cannot be reduced to pounds, shillings, and pence. Kant says, "Where a price can be paid, an equivalent can be substituted. It is that which is above price and which consequently admits of no equivalent, that possesses real value." Genuine patriotism is the consciousness of cooperating with the body-politic, of being rooted in ancestral achievements and of transmitting them to descendants. Fichte has finely said, "Individual man sees in his country the realization of his earthly immortality."

[THE STATE AS PERSON]

This involves that the State has a personality, primarily in the juridical, and secondly in the politico-moral sense. Every man who is able to exercise his will in law has a legal personality. Now it is quite clear that the State possesses this deliberate will; nay more, that it has the juridical personality in the most complete sense. In State treaties it is the will of the State which is expressed, not the personal desires of the individuals who conclude them, and the treaty is binding as long as the contracting State exists. When a State is incapable of enforcing its will, or of maintaining law and order at home and prestige abroad, it becomes an anomaly and falls a prey either to anarchy or a foreign enemy. The State therefore must have the most emphatic will that can be imagined. Roman Law was not fortunate in its development of the conception of legal personality, for in spite of their marvelous legal acuteness the Romans lacked the talent for philosophical speculation, and this is most disastrously displayed in their doctrine of legal personality. Roman Law assumes that a person in the legal sense must be merely an individual citizen.

That is crude materialism. Rather should all associations possessed of legal will be considered as legal persons. Now it was laid down by the Romans, who also felt this imperfection, that the State should attribute this juridical personality to monasteries, churches, etc., to enable them to transact legal business, and to stand in legal relationship with individuals. Thus the preposterous assertion is made that a human being has a legal personality because he has two legs, while the State has to acquire it, not having it by nature. But the will of the State is not fictitious. It is the most real of all. Moreover, what is the meaning of attributing to the State a personality which is not inherent in it? The aim of knowledge is truth. Knowledge must not invent facts but must state them. A legal fiction is therefore not scientific. It is not scientific for me to pretend, when the State fixes a prescriptive period for certain offenses, that no offense has been committed, for there has actually been one, and the State acts thus on grounds of expediency only. How is it possible, in treating of the fundamental fact of all constitutional and political life, to assert, and to act upon, this legal fiction, that the great collective person, the State—the most supremely real person, in the literal sense of the word, that exists—is first of all obliged to endow itself with a personality? How can we deny this attribute to the very source of all authority?

As our Germanic public life was always very rich in all manner of corporations, our German jurisprudence was the first to abandon the theory of Roman Law which regarded the conception of personality as bound up with the individual, and it defined legal personality by competence to act in law. In this way the dictum becomes applicable to the State as well, for the State is the people's collective will. This does not imply that it is the mere mechanical total of all individual wills, for the individual is able to belong to several corporate bodies at the same time. Rousseau has aptly said, in one of the few maintainable passages of his *Contrat Social, "La volonté générale n'est pas la volonté de tous."* *

---

*"The general will is not the will of all."—*Ed.*

The State, then, has from all time been a legal person. It appears to be so still more clearly in the historico-moral sense. States must be conceived as the great collective personalities of history, thoroughly capable of bearing responsibility and blame. We may even speak of their legal guilt, and still more accurately of their individuality. Even as certain people have certain traits, which they cannot alter however much they try, so also the State has characteristics which cannot be obliterated. Pindar's warning words apply as much to the State as to the individual: "Pawn all thy goods to one, and debt will overtake thee."

We cannot imagine the Roman State humane, or encouraging Art and Science. It would be an implicit contradiction. Who cannot discern, in the course of German history, that excess of individual strength and violence whose centrifugal tendencies have made it so hard for us to establish a central authority? The State would no longer be what it has been and is, did it not stand visibly girt about with armed might. Sallust said truly that there is nothing more dangerous for a State founded by arms than to discard this essential principle of its strength. . . .

[THE STATE AS POWER]

Treat the State as a person, and the necessary and rational multiplicity of States follows. Just as in individual life the ego implies the existence of the non-ego, so it does in the State. The State is power, precisely in order to assert itself as against other equally independent powers. War and the administration of justice are the chief tasks of even the most barbaric States. But these tasks are only conceivable where a plurality of States are found existing side by side. Thus the idea of one universal empire is odious—the ideal of a State co-extensive with humanity is no ideal at all. In a single State the whole range of culture could never be fully spanned; no single people could unite the virtues of aristocracy and democracy. All nations, like all individuals, have their limitations, but it is exactly in the abundance of these limited qualities that the genius of humanity is exhibited. The rays of the Divine light are manifested, broken by countless facets among the separate peoples, each one exhibiting another picture and another idea of the whole. Every people has a right to believe that certain attributes of the Divine reason are exhibited in it to their fullest perfection. No people ever attains to national consciousness without overrating itself. The Germans are always in danger of enervating their nationality through possessing too little of this rugged pride. The average German has very little political pride; but even our Philistines generally reveal in the intellectual boast of the freedom and universality of the German spirit, and this is well, for such a sentiment is necessary if a people is to maintain and assert itself. . . .

The features of history are virile, unsuited to sentimental or feminine natures. Brave peoples alone have an existence, an evolution or a future; the weak and cowardly perish, and perish justly. The grandeur of history lies in the perpetual conflict of nations, and it is simply foolish to desire the suppression of their rivalry. Mankind has ever found it to be so. . . .

Further, if we examine our definition of the State as "the people legally united as an independent entity," we find that it can be more briefly put thus: "The State is the public force for Offense and Defense." It is, above all, Power which makes its will to prevail, it is not the totality of the people as Hegel assumes in his deification of it. The nation is not entirely comprised in the State, but the State protects and embraces the people's life, regulating its external aspects on every side. It does not ask primarily for opinion, but demands obedience, and its laws must be obeyed, whether willingly or no.

A step forward has been taken when the mute obedience of the citizens is transformed into a rational inward assent, but it cannot be said that this is absolutely necessary. Powerful, highly-developed Empires have stood for centuries without its aid. Submission is what the State primarily requires; it insists upon acquiescence; its very essence is the accomplishment of its will. The terrible words βίᾳ βίᾳ βιάζεται* permeate the history of all governments. A State which can no longer carry out its purpose collapses in anarchy. What a contrast to the life of the Church. We may say that power is the vital principle of the State, as faith is that of the Church, and love that of the family. The Church is an essentially spiritual force, having also an external life, but appealing first of all to conscience, insisting above all upon the willing mind, and standing high in proportion to its ability to give profound and intense expression to this its vital principle. Therefore it is said, "He that eateth and drinketh unworthily eateth and drinketh judgment to himself." But if the State were to hold this view, or, for instance, to require from its soldiers more than the fulfillment of their military duties, it would be unbearable. "It does not matter," says the State, "what you think, so long as you obey." It is for this reason that gentle characters find it so hard to understand its nature. It may be said roughly that the normal woman first obtains an insight into justice and government through men's eyes, just as the normal man has no natural aptitude for petty questions of household management. This is easily understood, for undoubtedly power is a stern idea, and its enforcement is here the highest and only aim. For this reason the ruling nations are not so much the races rich in mental endowment, but rather those whose peculiar gift is force of character. In this the thoughtful student of the world's history perceives the awful nature of justice. The sentimentalist may bewail the overthrow of cultured Athens by Sparta, or of Hellas by Rome, but the serious thinker must recognize its necessity, and understand why Florence for all her refinement could not withstand the rivalry of Venice. All these cases took their inevitable course.

The State is not an Academy of Arts. If it neglects its strength in order to promote the idealistic aspirations of man, it repudiates its own nature and perishes. This is in truth for the State equivalent to the sin against the Holy Ghost, for it is indeed a mortal error in the State to subordinate itself for sentimental reasons to a foreign Power, as we Germans have often done to England.

---

*Bia, Bia, Biazetai, "Force forces force."—Ed.

[THE STATE AS SOVEREIGN]

We have described the State as an independent force. This pregnant theory of independence implies firstly so absolute a moral supremacy that the State cannot legitimately tolerate any power above its own, and secondly a temporal freedom entailing a variety of material resources adequate to its protection against hostile influences. Legal sovereignty, the State's complete independence of any other earthly power, is so rooted in its nature that it may be said to be its very standard and criterion.

The State is born in a community whenever a group or an individual has achieved sovereignty by imposing its will upon the whole body. . . .

Human communities do exist which in their own fashion pursue aims no less lofty than those of the State, but which must be legally subject to it in their outward relations with the world. It is obvious that contradictions must arise, and that two such authorities, morally but not legally equal, must sometimes collide with each other. Nor is it to be wished that the conflicts between Church and State should wholly cease, for if they did one party or the other would be soulless and dead, like the Russian Church for example. Sovereignty, however, which is the peculiar attribute of the State, is of necessity supreme, and it is a ridiculous inconsistency to speak of a superior and inferior authority within it. The truth remains that the essence of the State consists in its incompatibility with any power over it. How proudly and truly statesmanlike is Gustavus Adolphus' exclamation, "I recognize no power over me but God and the conqueror's sword." This is so unconditionally true that we see at once that it cannot be the destiny of mankind to form a single State, but that the ideal towards which we strive is a harmonious comity of nations, who, concluding treaties of their own free will, admit restrictions upon their sovereignty without abrogating it.

For the notion of sovereignty must not be rigid, but flexible and relative, like all political conceptions. Every State, in treaty making, will limit its power in certain directions for its own sake. States which conclude treaties with each other thereby curtail their absolute authority to some extent. But the rule still stands, for every treaty is a voluntary curb upon the power of each, and all international agreements are prefaced by the clause *"Rebus sic stantibus."** No State can pledge its future to another. It knows no arbiter, and draws up all its treaties with this implied reservation. This is supported by the axiom that so long as international law exists all treaties lose their force at the very moment when war is declared between the contracting parties; moreover, every sovereign State has the undoubted right to declare war at its pleasure, and is consequently entitled to repudiate its treaties. Upon this constantly recurring alteration of treaties the progress of history depends; every State must take care that its treaties do not survive their effective value, lest another Power should denounce them by a declaration of war; for antiquated treaties must necessarily be denounced and replaced by others more consonant with circumstances.

---

*"Things standing as they now do."—*Ed.*

It is clear that the international agreements which limit the power of a State are not absolute, but voluntary self-restrictions. Hence, it follows that the establishment of a permanent international Arbitration Court is incompatible with the nature of the State, which could at all events only accept the decision of such a tribunal in cases of second- or third-rate importance. When a nation's existence is at stake there is no outside Power whose impartiality can be trusted. Were we to commit the folly of treating the Alsace-Lorraine problem as an open question, by submitting it to arbitration, who would seriously believe that the award could be impartial? It is, moreover, a point of honor for a State to solve such difficulties for itself. International treaties may indeed become more frequent, but a finally decisive tribunal of the nations is an impossibility. The appeal to arms will be valid until the end of history, and therein lies the sacredness of war.

42
Mario Palmieri

The most complete theoretical account of modern fascism—*The Philosophy of Fascism*—was written by Mario Palmieri and published in Chicago in 1936. The absolutism defended by Treitschke and others in the nineteenth century had by that time already been brought to reality in Italy by the Fascist Party of Benito Mussolini. In this passage from *The Philosophy of Fascism* Palmieri explains the explicit incorporation, into Italian Fascism, of the theory of the all-powerful state.

FASCISM AND LIBERTY*

The Fascist conception of life is so radically revolutionary in all its aspects as to justify an extended individual treatment of each one of these aspects in a detailed analysis.

As we have already seen, the general, all-embracing conception is that life is an expression of the soul, and, as such, flowering at its best only when its spiritual claims are fully recognized and satisfied.

Now the nature of these claims is such that they conflict inevitably with all the individual's egotistic aspirations, ambitions and desires.

The Fascist conception of life advances, therefore, demands upon the inner world of man, that the ordinary human being is wary to satisfy. It is from this contrast between the claims of the individual and the claims of the whole that the problem of Liberty arises. Because Fascism finds necessary, at the outset, to

*From Mario Palmieri, *The Philosophy of Fascism*, Chicago, 1936.

take away from the ordinary human being what he has been taught and has grown to cherish the most: personal liberty. And it can be affirmed, without falling into exaggeration, that a curtailment of personal liberty not only has proved to be, but must necessarily be, a fundamental condition of the triumph of Fascism.

Unfortunately, it is just due to such a curtailment that the greatest misunderstanding of Fascism has arisen in the world where personal liberty is made almost the paramount issue of life.

But Fascism holds that personal liberty is not an end to itself. Personal liberty is simply a means to the realization of a much greater end: namely, the liberty of the Spirit; this last meaning the faculty of the human Soul of rising above the power of outward circumstances and inward needs to devote itself to the cult of those ideals which form the true goal of life.

Two radically different conceptions of Liberty are thus in conflict, and there is no hope that the abyss which separates them can ever be bridged.

In the Fascist conception, to be free, means to be no more a slave to one's own passions, ambitions or desires; means to be free to will what is true, and good and just, at all times, in all cases; means, in other words, to realize here in this world the true mission of man.

In the Individualistic conception, instead, to be free is . . . to follow the call of one's own nature; to worship one's own God; to think, to act, or to speak according to the dictates of one's own mind; to earn, to spend, to save or to hoard at will; to accumulate property and deed it following one's own whims or fancy; to reach all hedonistic goals; wealth, health, happiness or pleasure. In other words, to be unhindered by compulsions, restrictions, prohibitions, rules, codes and laws. . . .

What the Individualistic conception of Liberty implies is thus nothing less than freedom from all those external fetters born of the very fact that man is forced to live in a state of society; a state, that is, which makes fundamental claims over all forms of individual freedoms, a state which places iron-clad restrictions to that form of Liberty which would allow complete expression of his instincts, his desires and his needs. . . .

But it is a fact, a conclusively proved historical fact, that the ordinary human being *does not know* how to use his freedom, or rather he knows simply how to use it for the satisfaction of his instincts and desires.

And it is only because he finds himself compelled to live in a state of society that restrains him from bringing to its logical conclusion his assumption that the individual is the center of the whole universe.

All through the ages his life has been thus a sorry compromise between his desire to self expression and the need of curbing this desire if some kind of social life had to be realized at all.

It is high time, instead, says Fascism, that the individual be brought back to the vision of his true place in the universe; it is high time that he learns how to curb and master his self; it is high time that his freedom be taken away from him if he is to realize the greatest aim of life: the furtherance of the Spirit. . . .

According to Fascism, a true, a great spiritual life cannot take place unless the State has risen to a position of pre-eminence in the world of man. The curtailment of liberty thus becomes justified at once, with this need of raising the State to its rightful position.

As Giovanni Gentile says, in his book—"What is Fascism?"—

Liberty is, to be sure, the supreme end and aim of every human life, but insofar as personal and social education realize it by evoking this common will in the individual, it presents itself as law, and hence as the State. The maximum of liberty coincides with the maximum strength of the State.

. . . Liberty, therefore, cannot be concerned with the individual's claims, but must find its maximum concern in the fullest expression of the nation's life, and of the State which of such a life is the concrete realization. . . .

THE FASCIST STATE

Without State there is no Nation. These words reverse the commonly accepted principle of modern political science that without Nation there is no State. They seem at first to run counter to all evidence, but they represent, instead, for Fascism, the expression of a fundamental truth, one of those truths which are at the very basis of the social life of mankind.

To say, in fact, that in the State and through the State a Nation first rises to the consciousness of itself, means that the State gives to the people that political, social and moral unity without which there is no possibility of a true national life. Furthermore, the State is the only organ through which the anonymous will of the people can find the expression of will of a single personality, conscious of its aims, its purposes and its needs.

The State becomes thus invested with the dignity, the attributes and the power of an ethical personality which exists and lives, and develops and progresses or decays, and, finally dies.

Compared to this personality of the State with its characteristics of transcendent values and its problems of momentous magnitude, the personality of the single individual loses all of that importance which it had assumed in the modern times.

It is possible thus for a Fascist writer, G. Corso, to write:

. . . the liberal idea, the democratic idea and the socialistic idea, start from the common presupposition that the individual must be free because only the individual is real. To such a conception Fascism opposes the other that the individual is to be considered as a highly transitory and apparent thing, when compared to the ethnic reality of the race, the spiritual reality of the Nation, the ethical reality of the State.

Or for Mussolini to state:

. . . Liberalism denied the State in the interest of the particular individual; Fascism, instead reaffirms the State as the true reality of the individual.

In this shifting of emphasis from the individual to the State, the very functions of the one become part of the life of the other. The State must, therefore, concern itself not only with social order, political organization and economic problems, but with morality and religion as well.

The Fascist State is, in other words, not only the social, political and economic organization of the people of one nation, but is also the outward manifestation of their moral and religious life, and, as such, is therefore an Ethical State.

The Fascist State presupposes that man beside being an individual is also a social being, and therefore, willing and compelled to come under some form of disciplinary authority for the good of the whole.

It presupposes also that the highest law for man is the moral law, and that right or wrong, good or evil, have well defined meanings in this moral law and are beyond the pale of individual likes or dislikes or individual judgment.

It presupposes, finally, that the Nation-State is gifted with an organic life of its own, which far transcends in meaning the life of the individual, and whose development, growth and progress, follow laws which man cannot ignore or modify, but only discover and obey.

Henceforth the State is no longer a word denoting the authority underlying a complex system of relationships between individuals, classes, organizations, etc., but something of far greater import, far greater meaning than that: it is a living entity, it is the highest spiritual entity of the political world. . . .

To bring mankind back to the true vision of the relative worth of the individual and of the nation, that organism of which the single individual is an integral, although accidental and infinitesimal part, needs a truly superhuman effort.

Gone is forever the time when it was possible to find a way to the heart of man through his devotion to higher things than his personal affairs; gone is the time when it was possible to appeal to the mystic side of his nature through a religious commandment; gone, finally, is the time when it was possible to illuminate the reasoning powers of his mind with the light of ideals whose existence and whose reason of being cannot be proved through the powers of reason.

All that remains is an appeal to force, to compulsion; intellectual as well as physical, an appeal to what lies outside of man, to what he fears and with what he must of necessity abide.

Such a forceful appeal is made at present by Fascism which, compelling the elder or educating the younger, is slowly but surely bringing the Italian people to the comprehension of the worth, the beauty and the significance of the National Ideal.

But if the Fascist State is an Ethical State, it is also, and above all, a Sovereign State. Its power, therefore, is not conditional to the will of the people, the parliament, the King, or any other of its constituent elements: it is rather immanent in its very essence.

Once more we find Individualism with its offsprings: the liberal, democratic and radical doctrines, in antithetic contrast to Fascism on an issue of paramount importance for the whole world of man.

Passing from the Liberal doctrine, which had conceded the sovereignty of the State to the people as a whole, to the democratic doctrine, which this sovereignty gave away to the numerical majority and to the socialistic, communistic doctrine which invested it in one small particular class, we find an always greater abdication of the sovereign attributes to an always more restricted constituent element of the nation.

To affirm instead, as Fascism does, that "All is in the State and for the State; nothing outside the State, nothing against the State," means to affirm that the Ideal State is the one which is above individuals, organizations, castes or classes; or above all particularized interests, needs or ambitions.

The rise of Fascism destroys forever, thus, that Gordian Knot of apparently insoluble social problems born from the clash of conflicting interests of individuals within the State. It destroys also the subjection of the welfare of the State to the welfare of any individual, or any group of individuals, or even the totality of all the people. And, as the resort to the Will of God as final authority in all matters which may affect the welfare of the State has lost all meaning in our modern, individualistic, materialistic Society, in the same way the demagogic appeal to the will of the people is to lose all significance in the coming Fascist Society.

The triumph of Fascism means, in fact, that the role of the people is finally brought back to that secondary importance which it assumes when considered in its proper relation to the other elements of the Nation-State.

3

IRRATIONALISM

The tradition of irrationalism in political philosophy, by its nature, defies systematic statement or reasoned analysis. The intellect, so long considered the ideal ruling faculty, is to be abandoned; we are urged to replace reason with some expressly nonintellectual function: sentiment, intuition, passion, inspiration, force, will. Differing functions have been advanced by irrationalists of various kinds—but whatever the function it cannot be analytically defended, nor must it be subjected to rational criticism. It may be difficult to give good reasons to abandon reason; but once having abandoned reason it will be equally difficult for any goal, or any method, or any course of conduct to be defended rationally.

In politics the clearest expression of irrationalism is found in the work of Georges Sorel, whose doctrine of *the social myth* has had great influence, not only upon the syndicalist movement of which he was a part, but especially upon fascist philosophy in the twentieth century. A true myth, said Sorel, does not aim to provide a rational conception of a future society but is a vision, a dream, a great emotional force that can inspire violent revolutionary activity. Such myths are not to be subjected to scientific analysis or rational discussion. To the contrary, Sorel held that their nature puts analysis out of the question and that their advocates must refuse to engage in any intellectual discussion of their virtues. The function of a myth, above all, is mass inspiration; "the myths are not descriptions of things," Sorel said, "but determinations to act."

For Sorel himself the ideal myth was that of the general strike, which would topple the existing order. For Richard Wagner ancient Norse and Germanic myths were central in art, and the mission of the German folk must be central in politics. For Houston Chamberlain the myth of Aryan supremacy was the key to history. Neitzsche held that as a moral person one must not accept the myth of any another, but must create one's own. In this heady, nonrational spirit Italian and German fascists especially, but also fascist parties in Spain, Greece, and Japan, have rediscovered old myths or developed new ones—irrational concoctions of national power and racial superiority.

43
Georges Sorel

Georges Sorel (1847–1922) formulated his theory of social myths concisely in a letter to Daniel Halevy (1907), from which the following passages are excerpted. Sorel was a socialist, a syndicalist, and after 1917 an admirer of Lenin. His philosophic irrationalism, however, his scorn for intellectualism, and his passion for revolutionary activity in place of talk were highly influential in shaping the direction of twentieth-century fascism.

[THE SOCIAL MYTH]*

. . . Men who are participating in a great social movement always picture their coming action as a battle in which their cause is certain to triumph. These constructions, knowledge of which is so important for historians, I propose to call myths; the syndicalist "general strike" and Marx's catastrophic revolution are such myths. As remarkable examples of such myths, I have given those which were constructed by primitive Christianity, by the Reformation, by the Revolution and by the followers of Mazzini. I now wish to show that we should not attempt to analyze such groups of images in the way that we analyze a thing into its elements, but that they must be taken as a whole, as historical forces, and that we should be especially careful not to make any comparison between accomplished fact and the picture people had formed for themselves before action.

I could have given one more example which is perhaps still more striking: Catholics have never been discouraged even in the hardest trials, because they have always pictured the history of the Church as a series of battles between Satan and the hierarchy supported by Christ; every new difficulty which arises is only an episode in a war which must finally end in the victory of Catholicism.

. . . If Catholicism is in danger at the present time, it is to a great extent owing to the fact that the myth of the Church militant tends to disappear. . . .

In employing the term myth I believed that I had made a happy choice, because I thus put myself in a position to refuse any discussion whatever with the people who wish to submit the idea of a general strike to a detailed criticism, and who accumulate objections against its practical possibility. It appears, on the contrary, that I had made a most unfortunate choice, for while some told me that myths were only suitable to a primitive state of society, others imagined that I thought the modern world might be moved by illusions analogous in nature to those which Renan thought might usefully replace religion. But there has been a worse misunderstanding than this even, for it has been asserted that my theory of myths was

*Reprinted with permission of The Macmillan Company from G. Sorel, *Letter to Daniel Halevy.* Copyright 1950 by The Free Press. These passages are from *Reflections on Violence,* originally written in 1906, translated by T. E. Hulme and J. Roth.

only a kind of lawyer's plea, a falsification of the real opinions of the revolution-aries, the *sophistry of an intellectualist.*

If this were true, I should not have been exactly fortunate, for I have always tried to escape the influence of that intellectual philosophy, which seems to me a great hindrance to the historian who allows himself to be dominated by it. . . .

The whole of this philosophy can be summed up in the following phrase of Renan's: "Human affairs are always an approximation lacking gravity and preci-sion"; and as a matter of fact, for an intellectualist, what lacks precision must also lack gravity. But in Renan the conscientious historian was never entirely asleep, and he at once adds as a corrective: "To have realized this truth is a great result obtained by philosophy; but it is an abdication of any active rôle. The future lies in the hands of those who are not disillusioned."* From this we may conclude that the intellectualist philosophy is entirely unable to explain the great movements of history.

The intellectualist philosophy would have vainly endeavored to convince the ardent Catholics, who for so long struggled successfully against the revolutionary traditions, that the myth of the Church militant was not in harmony with the sci-entific theories formulated by the most learned authors according to the best rules of criticism; it would never have succeeded in persuading them. It would not have been possible to shake the faith that these men had in the promises made to the Church by any argument; and so long as this faith remained, the myth was, in their eyes, incontestable. Similarly, the objections urged by philosophy against the rev-olutionary myths would have made an impression only on those men who were anxious to find a pretext for abandoning any active rôle, for remaining revolution-ary in words only.

I can understand the fear that this myth of the general strike inspires in many *worthy progressives,*† on account of its character of *infinity*‡ the world of today is very much inclined to return to the opinions of the ancients and to subordinate ethics to the smooth working of public affairs, which results in a definition of virtue as the golden mean; as long as socialism remains a *doctrine expressed only in words,* it is very easy to deflect it towards this doctrine of the golden mean; but this transformation is manifestly impossible when the myth of the "general strike" is introduced, as this implies an absolute revolution. You know as well as I do that all that is best in the modern mind is derived from this "torment of the infinite"; you are not one of those people who look upon the tricks by means of which read-ers can be deceived by words, as happy discoveries. That is why you will not con-demn me for having attached great worth to a myth which gives to socialism such

---

*Renan, *Histoire du peuple d'Israël,* vol. iii. p. 497.

†Translator's Note.—In French, *"braves gens."* Sorel is using the words ironically to indicate those naïve, philanthropically disposed people who believe that they have discovered the solution to the problem of social reform—whose attitude, however, is often complicated by a good deal of hypocrisy, they being fre-quently rapacious when their own personal interests are at stake.

‡Parties, as a rule, *define* the reforms that they wish to bring about; but the general strike has a charac-ter of *infinity,* because it puts on one side all discussion of definite reforms and confronts men with a cata-strophe. People who pride themselves on their practical wisdom are very much upset by such a conception, which puts forward no definite project of future social organization.

high moral value and such great sincerity. It is because the theory of myths tends to produce such fine results that so many seek to dispute it. . . .

As long as there are no myths accepted by the masses, one may go on talking of revolts indefinitely, without ever provoking any revolutionary movement; this is what gives such importance to the general strike and renders it so odious to social-ists who are afraid of a revolution; they do all they can to shake the confidence felt by the workers in the preparations they are making for the revolution; and in order to succeed in this they cast ridicule on the idea of the general strike—the only idea that could have any value as a motive force. One of the chief means employed by them is to represent it as a Utopia; this is easy enough, because there are very few myths which are perfectly free from any Utopian element.

The revolutionary myths which exist at the present time are almost free from any such mixture; by means of them it is possible to understand the activity, the feelings and the ideas of the masses preparing themselves to enter on a decisive struggle: the myths are not descriptions of things, but expressions of a determination to act. A Utopia is, on the contrary, an intellectual product; it is the work of theorists who, after observing and discussing the known facts, seek to establish a model to which they can compare existing society in order to estimate the amount of good and evil it contains. It is a combination of imaginary institutions having sufficient analogies to real institutions for the jurist to be able to reason about them; it is a construction which can be taken to pieces, and certain parts of it have been shaped in such a way that they can (with a few alterations by way of adjustment) be fitted into approach-ing legislation. While contemporary myths lead men to prepare themselves for a combat which will destroy the existing state of things, the effect of Utopias has always been to direct men's minds towards reforms which can be brought about by patching up the existing system; it is not surprising, then, that so many makers of Utopias were able to develop into able statesmen when they had acquired a greater experience of political life. A myth cannot be refuted, since it is, at bottom, identi-cal with the convictions of a group, being the expression of these convictions in the language of movement; and it is, in consequence, unanalyzable into parts which could be placed on the plane of historical descriptions. A Utopia, on the contrary, can be discussed like any other social constitution; the spontaneous movements it presupposes can be compared with the movements actually observed in the course of history, and we can in this way evaluate its verisimilitude; it is possible to refute Utopias by showing that the economic system on which they have been made to rest is incompatible with the necessary conditions of modern production.

Liberal political economy is one of the best examples of a Utopia that could be given. A state of society was imagined which could contain only the types pro-duced by commerce, and which would exist under the law of the fullest competi-tion; it is recognized today that this kind of ideal society would be as difficult to realize as that of Plato; but several great statesmen of modern times have owed their fame to the efforts they made to introduce something of this ideal of com-mercial liberty into industrial legislation.

We have here a Utopia free from any mixture of myth; the history of French democracy, however, presents a very remarkable combination of Utopias and myths. The theories that inspired the authors of our first constitutions are regarded today as extremely chimerical; indeed, people are often loth to concede them the value which they have been so long recognized to possess—that of an ideal on which legislators, magistrates, and administrators should constantly fix their eyes, in order to secure for men a little more justice. With these Utopias were mixed up the myths which represented the struggle against the ancient regime; so long as the myths survived, all the refutations of liberal Utopias could produce no result; the myth safeguarded the Utopia with which it was mixed.

For a long time Socialism was scarcely anything but a Utopia; the Marxists were right in claiming for their master the honor of bringing about a change in this state of things; Socialism has now become the preparation of the masses employed in great industries for the suppression of the State and property; and it is no longer necessary, therefore, to discuss how men must organize themselves in order to enjoy future happiness; everything is reduced to the *revolutionary apprenticeship* of the proletariat. Unfortunately Marx was not acquainted with facts which have now become familiar to us; we know better than he did what strikes are, because we have been able to observe economic conflicts of considerable extent and duration; the myth of the "general strike" has become popular, and is now firmly established in the minds of the workers; we possess ideas about violence that it would have been difficult for him to have formed; we can then complete his doctrine, instead of making commentaries on his text, as his unfortunate disciples have done for so long.

In this way Utopias tend to disappear completely from Socialism; Socialism has no longer any need to concern itself with the organization of industry since capitalism does that. I think, moreover, that I have shown that the general strike corresponds to a kind of feeling which is so closely related to those which are necessary to promote production in any very progressive state of industry, that a revolutionary apprenticeship may at the same time be considered as an apprenticeship which will enable the workman to occupy a high rank among the best workmen of his own trade.

People who are living in this world of "myths," are secure from all refutation; this has led many to assert that Socialism is a kind of religion. For a long time people have been struck by the fact that religious convictions are unaffected by criticism, and from that they have concluded that everything which claims to be beyond science must be a religion. It has been observed also that Christianity tends at the present day to be less a system of dogmas than a Christian life, i.e., a moral reform penetrating to the roots of one's being; consequently, a new analogy has been discovered between religion and the revolutionary Socialism which aims at the apprenticeship, preparation, and even reconstruction of the individual—a gigantic task. But Bergson has taught us that it is not only religion which occupies the profounder region of our mental life; revolutionary myths have their place there equally with religion. The arguments which Yves Guyot urges against Socialism on the ground that it is a religion, seem to me, then, to be founded on an imperfect acquaintance with the new psychology.

Renan was very surprised to discover that Socialists are beyond discouragement. "After each abortive experiment they recommence their work: the solution is not yet found, but it will be. The idea that no solution exists never occurs to them, and in this lies their strength." The explanation given by Renan is superficial; it regards Socialism as a Utopia, that is, as a thing which can be compared to observed realities; if this were true, it would be scarcely possible to understand how confidence can survive so many failures. But by the side of the Utopias there have always been myths capable of urging on the workers to revolt. For a long time these myths were founded on the legends of the Revolution, and they preserved all their value as long as these legends remained unshaken. Today the confidence of the Socialists is greater than ever since the myth of the general strike dominates all the truly working-class movement. No failure proves anything against Socialism since the latter has become a work of preparation (for revolution); if they are checked, it merely proves that the apprenticeship has been insufficient; they must set to work again with more courage, persistence, and confidence than before; their experience of labor has taught workmen that it is by means of patient apprenticeship that a man may become a true comrade, and it is also the only way of becoming a true revolutionary.

44
Richard Wagner

Richard Wilhelm Wagner (1813–1883) was more than a titanic figure in the history of music; he was a major influence upon social attitudes in Germany during and after his lifetime. The Teutonic myths his operas exploited would, he thought, plumb the depths of the German soul, and he himself would come to be recognized as the prophet of national greatness yet to come. The universality of spirit in German literature and music, he believed, cried out to be reborn in the sphere of politics, through the victory of German power.

[REBIRTH OF THE GERMAN SPIRIT]*

It is good, and most encouraging for us, to find that the German spirit, when with the second half of last century it raised itself from its deepest decay, did not require a new birth, but merely a resurrection; across two desert centuries it could stretch its hands to the selfsame spirit, which then strewed wide its lusty seeds through all the Holy Roman Empire of the German nation, and whose effect upon even the plastic shape of Europe's civilization we can never deem of small account if we remember that the beautiful, the manifoldly individual, the imaginative Ger-

---

*From the book *Wagner on Music and Drama* by Richard Wagner. Edited and with an intro. by Albert Goldman and Evert Sprinchorn. Published by E. P. Dutton & Co., Inc. and used with their permission as well as that of Curtis Brown, Ltd., London.

man costume of those days was adopted by every European nation. Look at two portraits: here Dürer, there Leibnitz; what a horror at the unhappy period of our downfall is awakened in us by the contrast!

Hail to the glorious spirits who first felt deep this horror, and cast their gaze across the centuries to recognize themselves once more! Then was found that it had not been drowsiness that plunged the German folk into its misery; it had fought its war of thirty years for its spiritual freedom; that was won, and though the body was faint with wounds and loss of blood, the mind stayed free, even beneath French full-bottomed wigs. Hail Winckelmann and Lessing, ye who, beyond the centuries of native German majesty, found the German's ur-kinsmen in the divine Hellenes, and laid bare the pure ideal of human beauty to the powder-bleared eyes of French-civilized mankind! Hail to thee, Goethe, thou who hadst power to wed Helena to our Faust, the Greek ideal to the German spirit! Hail to thee, Schiller, thou who gavest to the reborn spirit the stature of the "German stripling" (*des deutschen Jünglings*), who stands disdainful of the pride of Britain, the sensuous wiles of Paris! Who was this *deutsche Jüngling?* Has anyone heard of a French, an English *Jüngling?* And *yet* how plain and clear beyond mistake, we understand this "German *Jüngling*"! This stripling, who in Mozart's virginal melodies beshamed the Italian capons; in Beethoven's symphony grew up to courage of the man, for dauntless, world-redeeming deeds! And this stripling it was who threw himself at last upon the battlefield when his princes had lost every-thing—empire, country, honor; to reconquer for the folk its freedom, for the princes e'en their forfeit thrones. And how was this *Jüngling* repaid? In all history there is no blacker ingratitude than the German princes' treachery to the spirit of their people; and many a good, a noble and self-sacrificing deed of theirs will it need to atone for that betrayal. We hope for those deeds, and therefore let the sin be told right loudly!

How was it possible that the princes should have passed in total silence the incomparably glorious resurrection of the German spirit, not even have thence derived the smallest change in their opinion of their people's character? How explain this incredible blindness, which absolutely knew not so much as how to use that infinitely stirring spirit for the furthering of their dynastic policy?

The reason of the German heart's perversity in these highest regions of the German nation, of all places, lies certainly both deep and far away; in part, perchance, in just the universal scope of German nature. The German Reich was no narrow national state. . . . the *deutsche Jüngling* was not the man to need the "smile of princes," in the sense of a Racine or a Lully: he was called to throw aside the "curb of rules," and as there, so here in the people's life, to step forth a liberator from oppression.

This calling was recognized by an intelligent statesman at the time of utmost want; and, when all the red-tape armies of our monarchs had been utterly routed by the holder of French power—invading no longer as a curled and frizzled civi-lizer, but as a ravenous lord of war; when the German princes were no longer ser-vants to mere French civilization, but vassals to French political despotism: then was it the German *Jüngling* whose aid was invoked, to prove with weapons in his hand the mettle of this German spirit reborn within him. He showed the world its patent of nobility. To the sound of lyre and sword* he fought its battles. Amazed, the Gallic caesar asked why he no longer could beat the Cossacks and Croats, the Imperial and Royal Guards? Perhaps his nephew is the only man on all the thrones of Europe who really knows the answer to that question: he knows and *fears* the German *Jüngling*. Learn ye to know him too, for ye should *love* him! . . .

Now, we ask what an unheard, what an incommensurable wealth of quickening organizations might not the German state include within it, if *all* the various leanings toward true culture and civilization, as exhibited in German unionism, were drawn, in due analogy with the example of Prussian military organization, into the only sphere of power to further them, into that sphere in which the governments at present hold themselves close-hedged by their bureaucratism?

As we here proposed to deal with politics merely in so far as, in our opinion, they bear upon the German art spirit, we leave it to other inquiries to yield us more precise conclusions as to the political development of the German spirit, when brought into that leavening union with the spirit of the German princes which we desire. If we reserve to ourselves, however, a further discussion of the German spirit's artistic aptitudes, both social and individual, upon the lines of the root idea last broached—we beg, for all our later researches on that domain, to carry over the result of this preliminary disquisition in something like the following sentence:

Universal as the mission of the German folk is seen to have been, since its entrance into history, equally universal are the German spirit's aptitudes for art; the rebirth of the German spirit, which happened in the second half of the preceding century, has shown us an example of the activation of this universality in the weightiest domains of art; the example of that rebirth's evaluation to the end of ennobling the public spiritual life of the German folk, as also to the end of founding a new and truly German civilization, extending its blessings e'en beyond our frontiers, must be set by those in whose hands repose the political fortunes of the German people: for this it needs nothing but that the German princes should themselves be given that right example from their own midst.

45
Friedrich Nietzsche

Friedrich Nietzsche (1844–1900), in his early years a professor of classical philosophy and a disciple of Wagner, died insane after producing some of the most original and provocative works in modern moral philosophy. He came to believe that the fundamental reality is the will to power. In support of that will he

---

*An allusion to Körner's patriotic songs, as set to music by Weber in September, 1814. These songs were the means of arousing the utmost patriotic enthusiasm among the youths and younger men of Germany.—TR.

presents an aristocratic moral ideal characterized by strength, courage, pride, and, above all, assertion of self. He despised the customary morality based upon pity, humility, and altruism, thinking it a code for slaves, adopted in part as the result of a plot by the Jews to revenge themselves upon their Aryan conquerors by foisting upon them ignoble moral standards. Some men are inferiors, knaves, and fools; others are superiors, wise, and deep; the battle of the latter to affirm themselves and their own standards, Nietzsche thought, although sometimes painful to all, is the ultimate joy and satisfaction in life.

[THE WILL TO POWER]*

To refrain mutually from injury, from violence, from exploitation, and put one's will on a par with that of others: this may result in a certain rough sense in good conduct among individuals when the necessary conditions are given (namely, the actual similarity of the individuals in amount of force and degree of worth, and their co-relation within one organisation). As soon, however, as one wished to take this principle more generally, and if possible even as *the fundamental principle of society,* it would immediately disclose what it really is—namely, a Will to the *denial* of life, a principle of dissolution and decay. Here one must think profoundly to the very basis and resist all sentimental weakness: life itself is *essentially* appropriation, injury, conquest of the strange and weak, suppression, severity, obtrusion of peculiar forms, incorporation, and at the least, putting it mildest, exploitation;—but why should one for ever use precisely these words on which for ages a disparaging purpose has been stamped? Even the organisation within which, as was previously supposed, the individuals treat each other as equal—it takes place in every healthy aristocracy—must itself, if it be a living and not a dying organisation, do all that towards other bodies, which the individuals within it refrain from doing to each other: it will have to be the incarnated Will to Power, it will endeavour to grow, to gain ground, attract to itself and acquire ascendency—not owing to any morality or immorality, but because it *lives,* and because life *is* precisely Will to Power. On no point, however, is the ordinary consciousness of Europeans more unwilling to be corrected than on this matter; people now rave everywhere, even under the guise of science, about coming conditions of society in which "the exploiting character" is to be absent:—that sounds to my ears as if they promised to invent a mode of life which should refrain from all organic functions. "Exploitation" does not belong to a depraved, or imperfect and primitive society: it belongs to the *nature* of the living being as a primary organic function; it is a consequence of the intrinsic Will to Power, which is precisely the Will to Life.—Granting that as a theory this is a novelty—as a reality it is the *fundamental fact* of all history: let us be so far honest towards ourselves!

*These passages are from F. Nietzsche, *Beyond Good and Evil* (1886), Helen Zimmern, tr., by permission of the publishers George Allen & Unwin Ltd., London.

[MASTER-MORALITY AND SLAVE-MORALITY]

In a tour through the many finer and coarser moralities which have hitherto prevailed or still prevail on the earth, I found certain traits recurring regularly together, and connected with one another, until finally two primary types revealed themselves to me, and a radical distinction was brought to light. There is *master-morality* and *slave-morality*;—I would at once add, however, that in all higher and mixed civilisations, there are also attempts at the reconciliation of the two moralities; but one finds still oftener the confusion and mutual misunderstanding of them, indeed, sometimes their close juxtaposition—even in the same man, within one soul. The distinctions of moral values have either originated in a ruling caste, pleasantly conscious of being different from the ruled—or among the ruled class, the slaves and dependents of all sorts. In the first case, when it is the rulers who determine the conception "good," it is the exalted, proud disposition which is regarded as the distinguishing feature, and that which determines the order of rank. The noble type of man separates from himself the beings in whom the opposite of this exalted, proud disposition displays itself: he despises them. . . . The noble type of man regards *himself* as a determiner of values; he does not require to be approved of; he passes the judgment: "What is injurious to me is injurious in itself"; he knows that it is he himself only who confers honour on things; he is a *creator of values*. He honours whatever he recognises in himself: such morality is self-glorification. In the foreground there is the feeling of plenitude, of power, which seeks to overflow, the happiness of high tension, the consciousness of a wealth which would fain give and bestow:—the noble man also helps the unfortunate, but not—or scarcely—out of pity, but rather from an impulse generated by the superabundance of power. The noble man honours in himself the powerful one, him also who has power over himself, who knows how to speak and how to keep silence, who takes pleasure in subjecting himself to severity and hardness, and has reverence for all that is severe and hard. "Wotan placed a hard heart in my breast," says an old Scandinavian Saga: it is thus rightly expressed from the soul of a proud Viking. Such a type of man is even proud of *not* being made for sympathy; the hero of the Saga therefore adds warningly: "He who has not a hard heart when young, will never have one." The noble and brave who think thus are the furthest removed from the morality which sees precisely in sympathy, or in acting for the good of others, or in *désintéressement,* the characteristic of the moral; faith in oneself, pride in oneself, a radical enmity and irony towards "selflessness," belong as definitely to noble morality, as do a careless scorn and precaution in presence of sympathy and the "warm heart."—It is the powerful who *know* how to honour, it is their art, their domain for invention. . . .

. . . A morality of the ruling class, however, is more especially foreign and irritating to present-day taste in the sternness of its principle that one has duties only to one's equals; that one may act towards beings of a lower rank, towards all that is foreign, just as seems good to one, or "as the heart desires," and in any case "beyond good and evil": it is here that sympathy and similar sentiments can have a place. The ability and obligation to exercise prolonged gratitude and prolonged revenge—both only within the circle of equals,—artfulness in retaliation, *raffinement* of the idea in friendship, a certain necessity to have enemies (as outlets for the emotions of envy, quarrelsomeness, arrogance—in fact, in order to be a good *friend*): all these are typical characteristics of the noble morality, which, as has been pointed out, is not the morality of "modern ideas," and is therefore at present difficult to realise, and also to unearth and disclose.—It is otherwise with the second type of morality, *slave-morality*. Supposing that the abused, the oppressed, the suffering, the unemancipated, the weary, and those uncertain of themselves, should moralise, what will be the common element in their moral estimates? Probably a pessimistic suspicion with regard to the entire situation of man will find expression, perhaps a condemnation of man, together with his situation. The slave has an unfavourable eye for the virtues of the powerful; he has a scepticism and distrust, a *refinement* of distrust of everything "good" that is there honoured—he would fain persuade himself that the very happiness there is not genuine. On the other hand, *those* qualities which serve to alleviate the existence of sufferers are brought into prominence and flooded with light; it is here that sympathy, the kind, helping hand, the warm heart, patience, diligence, humility, and friendliness attain to honour; for here these are the most useful qualities, and almost the only means of supporting the burden of existence. Slave-morality is essentially the morality of utility. Here is the seat of the origin of the famous antithesis "good" and "*evil*":—power and dangerousness are assumed to reside in the evil, a certain dreadfulness, subtlety, and strength, which do not admit of being despised. According to slave-morality, therefore, the "evil" man arouses fear; according to master-morality, it is precisely the "good" man who arouses fear and seeks to arouse it, while the bad man is regarded as the despicable being. . . . A last fundamental difference: the desire for *freedom,* the instinct for happiness and the refinements of the feeling of liberty belong as necessarily to slave-morals and morality, as artifice and enthusiasm in reverence and devotion are the regular symptoms of an aristocratic mode of thinking and estimating.

The man of noble character must first bring it home forcibly to his mind, especially with the aid of history, that, from time immemorial, in all social strata in any way dependent, the ordinary man *was* only that which he *passed for:*—not being at all accustomed to fix values, he did not assign even to himself any other value than that which his master assigned to him (it is the peculiar *right of masters* to create values). It may be looked upon as the result of an extraordinary atavism, that the ordinary man, even at present, is still always *waiting* for an opinion about himself, and then instinctively submitting himself to it. . . . In fact, conformably to the slow rise of the democratic social order (and its cause, the blending of the blood of masters and slaves), the originally noble and rare impulse of the masters to assign a value to themselves and to "think well" of themselves, will now be more and more encouraged and extended. . . . It is "the slave" in the vain man's blood, the remains of the slave's craftiness—and how much of the "slave" is still left in woman, for instance!—which seeks to *seduce* to good opinions of itself; it is the slave, too, who immediately afterwards falls prostrate himself before these opinions, as though he had not called them forth. . . .

[THE NEED FOR STRUGGLE]

. . . the species needs itself as species, as something which, precisely by virtue of its hardness, its uniformity, and simplicity of structure, can in general prevail and make itself permanent in constant struggle with its neighbours, or with rebellious or rebellion-threatening vassals. The most varied experience teaches it what are the qualities to which it principally owes the fact that it still exists, in spite of all Gods and men, and has hitherto been victorious: these qualities it calls virtues, and these virtues alone it develops to maturity. It does so with severity, indeed it desires severity; every aristocratic morality is intolerant in the education of youth, in the control of women, in the marriage customs, in the relations of old and young, in the penal laws (which have an eye only for the degenerating): it counts intolerance itself among the virtues, under the name of "justice." A type with few, but very marked features, a species of severe, warlike, wisely silent, reserved and reticent men (as as such, with the most delicate sensibility for the charm and *nuances* of society) is thus established, unaffected by the vicissitudes of generations; the constant struggle with uniform *unfavourable* conditions is, as already remarked, the cause of a type becoming stable and hard.

[INSTINCT FOR RANK]

There is an *instinct for rank,* which more than anything else is already the sign of a *high* rank; there is a *delight* in the *nuances* of reverence which leads one to infer noble origin and habits. The refinement, goodness, and loftiness of a soul are put to a perilous test when something passes by that is of the highest rank, but is not yet protected by the awe of authority from obtrusive touches and incivilities: something that goes its way like a living touchstone, undistinguished, undiscovered, and tentative, perhaps voluntarily veiled and disguised. He whose task and practice it is to investigate souls, will avail himself of many varieties of this very art to determine the ultimate value of a soul, the unalterable, innate order of rank to which it belongs: he will test it by its *instinct for reverence.* . . .

At the risk of displeasing innocent ears, I submit that egoism belongs to the essence of a noble soul, I mean the unalterable belief that to a being such as "we," other beings must naturally be in subjection, and have to sacrifice themselves. The noble soul accepts the fact of his egoism without question, and also without consciousness of harshness, constraint, or arbitrariness therein, but rather as something that may have its basis in the primary law of things:—if he sought a designation for it he would say: "It is justice itself." He acknowledges under certain circumstances, which made him hesitate at first, that there are other equally privileged ones; as soon as he has settled this question of rank, he moves among those equals and equally privileged ones with the same assurance, as regards modesty and delicate respect, which he enjoys in intercourse with himself—in accordance with an innate heavenly mechanism which all the stars understand. It is an *additional* instance of his egoism, this artfulness and self-limitation in intercourse with his equals—every star is a similar egoist; he honours *himself* in them, and in the rights which he concedes to them, he has no doubt that the exchange of honours and rights, as the *essence* of all intercourse, belongs also to the natural condition of things. The noble soul gives as he takes, prompted by the passionate and sensitive instinct of requital, which is at the root of his nature. The notion of "favour" has, *inter pares,* neither significance nor good repute; there may be a sublime way of letting gifts as it were light upon one from above, and of drinking them thirstily like dew-drops; but for those arts and displays the noble soul has no aptitude. His egoism hinders him here: in general, he looks "aloft" unwillingly—he looks either *forward,* horizontally and deliberately, or downwards —*he knows that he is on a height.*

46
Houston S. Chamberlain

Houston S. Chamberlain (1855–1927) was an English writer on music and literature in the Wagnerian tradition. His chief work, *Foundations of the Nineteenth Century,* was a massive treatise designed to justify, with what purports to be historical scholarship, the myth of the superiority of the Germanic peoples. Chamberlain's fanaticism contributed substantially to the German myth of the master race. The Aryans are, he argued, "by right . . . the lords of the world."

THE ENTRANCE OF THE GERMANIC PEOPLE INTO THE HISTORY OF THE WORLD*

The entrance of the Jew into European history had, as Herder said, signified the entrance of an alien element—alien to that which Europe had already achieved, alien to all it was still to accomplish; but it was the very reverse with the Germanic peoples. This barbarian, who would rush naked to battle, this savage, who suddenly sprang out of woods and marshes to inspire into a civilized and cultivated world the terrors of a violent conquest won by the strong hand alone, was nevertheless the lawful heir of the Hellene and the Roman, blood of their blood and spirit of their spirit. It was his own property which he, unwitting, snatched from the alien hand. But for him the sun of the Indo-European must have set. The Asiatic and African slave had by assassination wormed his way to the very throne of the Roman Empire, the Syrian mongrel had made himself master of the law, the Jew was using the library at Alexandria to adapt Hellenic philosophy to the Mosaic law, the Egyptian to embalm and bury for boundless ages the fresh bloom of natural science in the ostentatious pyramids of scientific systematization; soon, too, the beautiful flowers of old Aryan life—Indian thought, Indian

*From H. S. Chamberlain, *Foundations of the Nineteenth Century,* Vol. I, 1899. These passages are reprinted from a translation by John Lees, 1911, by permission of Dodd Mead and Co., New York, and of The Bodley Head, London.

poetry—were to be trodden under foot by the savage bloodthirsty Mongolian, and the Bedouin, with his mad delusions bred of the desert, was to reduce to an everlasting wilderness that garden of Eden, Erania, in which for centuries all the symbolism of the world had grown; art had long since vanished; there were nothing but replicas for the rich, and for the poor the circus: accordingly, to use that expression of Schiller which I quoted at the beginning of the first chapter, there were no longer men but only creatures. It is high time for the Saviour to appear. He certainly did not enter into history in the form in which combining, constructive reason, if consulted, would have chosen for the guardian angel, the harbinger of a new day of humanity; but today, when a glance back over past centuries teaches us wisdom, we have only one thing to regret, that the Teuton did not destroy with more thoroughness, wherever his victorious arm penetrated, and that as a consequence of his moderation the so-called "Latinizing," that is, the fusion with the chaos of peoples, once more gradually robbed wide districts of the one quickening influence of pure blood and unbroken youthful vigor, and at the same time deprived them of the rule of those who possessed the highest talents. At any rate it is only shameful indolence of thought, or disgraceful historical falsehood, that can fail to see in the entrance of the Germanic tribes into the history of the world the rescuing of agonizing humanity from the clutches of the everlastingly bestial.

FREEDOM AND LOYALTY

Let us attempt a glance into the depths of the soul. What are the specific intellectual and moral characteristics of this Germanic race? Certain anthropologists would fain teach us that all races are equally gifted; we point to history and answer: that is a lie! The races of mankind are markedly different in the nature and also in the extent of their gifts, and the Germanic races belong to the most highly gifted group, the group usually termed Aryan. Is this human family united and uniform by bonds of blood? Do these stems really all spring from the same root? I do not know and I do not much care; no affinity binds more closely than elective affinity, and in this sense the Indo-European Aryans certainly form a family. In his *Politics* Aristotle writes (i.5): "If there were men who in physical stature alone were so pre-eminent as the representatives of the Gods, then everyone would admit that other men by right must be subject unto them. If this, however, is true in reference to the body, then there is still greater justification for distinguishing between pre-eminent and commonplace souls." Physically and mentally the Aryans are pre-eminent among all peoples; for that reason they are by right, as the Stagirite expresses it, the lords of the world. Aristotle puts the matter still more concisely when he says, "Some men are by nature free, others slaves"; this perfectly expresses the moral aspect. For freedom is by no means an abstract thing, to which every human being has fundamentally a claim; a right to freedom must evidently depend upon capacity for it, and this again presupposes physical and intellectual power. One may make the assertion, that even the mere conception of freedom is quite unknown to most men. Do we not see the *homo syriacus* develop just as well and as happily in the position of slave as of master? Do the Chinese not show us another example of the same nature? Do not all historians tell us that the Semites and half-Semites, in spite of their great intelligence, never succeeded in founding a State that lasted, and that because everyone always endeavored to grasp all power for himself, thus showing that their capabilities were limited to despotism and anarchy, the two opposites of freedom? And here we see at once what great gifts a man must have in order that one may say of him, he is "by nature free," for the first condition of this is the power of creating. Only a State-building race can be free; the gifts which make the individual an artist and philosopher are essentially the same as those which, spread through the whole mass as instinct, found States and give to the individual that which hitherto had remained unknown to all nature: the idea of freedom. As soon as we understand this, the near affinity of the Germanic peoples to the Greeks and Romans strikes us, and at the same time we recognize what separates them. In the case of the Greeks the individualistic creative character predominates, even in the forming of constitutions; in the case of the Romans it is communistic legislation and military authority that predominate; the Germanic races, on the other hand, have individually and collectively perhaps less creative power, but they possess a harmony of qualities, maintaining the balance between the instinct of individual freedom, which finds its highest expression in creative art, and the instinct of public freedom which creates the State; and in this way they prove themselves to be the equals of their great predecessors. Art more perfect in its creations, so far as form is concerned, there may have been, but no art has ever been more powerful in its creations than that which includes the whole range of things human between the winged pen of Shakespeare and the etching-tool of Albrecht Dürer, and which in its own special language—music—penetrates deeper into the heart than any previous attempt to create immortality out of that which is mortal—to transform matter into spirit. And in the meantime the European States, founded by Germanic peoples, in spite of their, so to speak, improvised, always provisional and changeable character—or rather perhaps thanks to this character—proved themselves to be the most enduring as well as the most powerful in the world. In spite of all storms of war, in spite of the deceptions of that ancestral enemy, the chaos of peoples, which carried its poison into the very heart of our nation, freedom and its correlative, the State, remained, through all the ages the creating and saving ideal, even though the balance between the two often seemed to be upset: we recognize that more clearly today than ever.

In order that this might be so, that fundamental and common "Aryan" capacity of free creative power had to be supplemented by another quality, the incomparable and altogether peculiar Germanic loyalty (*Treue*). If that intellectual and physical development which leads to the idea of freedom and which produces on the one hand art, philosophy, science, on the other constitutions (as well as all the phenomena of culture which this word implies), is common to the Hellenes and Romans as well as to the Germanic peoples, so also is the extravagant conception of loyalty a specific characteristic of the Teuton. . . .

A FORWARD GLANCE

I, a modest historian, who can neither influence the course of events nor possess the power of looking clearly into the future, must be satisfied if in fulfilling the purpose of this book I have succeeded in showing the distinction between the Germanic and the Non-Germanic. That the Teuton is one of the greatest, perhaps the very greatest power in the history of mankind, no one will wish to deny, but in order to arrive at a correct appreciation of the present time, it behooved us to settle once for all who could and who could not be regarded as Teuton. In the nineteenth century, as in all former centuries, but of course with widely different grouping and with constantly changing relative power, there stood side by side in Europe these "Heirs"—the chaos of half-breeds, relics of the former Roman Empire, the Germanizing of which is falling off—the Jews—and the Germans, whose contamination by mixture with the half-breeds and the descendants of other Non-Aryan races is on the increase. No arguing about "humanity" can alter the fact that this means a struggle. Where the struggle is not waged with cannon-balls, it goes on silently in the heart of society by marriages, by the annihilation of distances which furthers intercourse, by the varying powers of resistance in the different types of mankind, by the shifting of wealth, by the birth of new influences and the disappearance of others, and by many other motive powers. But this struggle, silent though it be, is above all others a struggle for life and death.

47
Alfredo Rocco

Alfredo Rocco (1875–1935) was Minister of Justice in Italy during the reign of the Fascist Party there. As one of Benito Mussolini's closest advisers, he was among the most prominent of fascist leaders, and one of the first to highlight the essentially nonrational character of fascist philosophy. "Fascism is, above all, action and sentiment," he insisted, "the unconscious reawakening of our profound racial instinct." The passage below is from *The Political Doctrine of Fascism,* a work whose deliberate irrationality Mussolini heartily endorsed.

Fascism as Action, as Feeling, and as Thought

Much has been said, and is now being said for or against this complex political and social phenomenon which in the brief period of six years has taken complete hold of Italian life and, spreading beyond the borders of the Kingdom, has made itself felt in varying degrees of intensity throughout the world. But people have been much more eager to extol or to deplore than to understand—which is natural enough in a period of tumultuous fervor and of political passion. The time has not yet arrived for a dispassionate judgment. For even I, who noticed the very first manifestations of this great development, saw its significance from the start and participated directly in its first doings, carefully watching all its early uncertain and changing developments, even I do not feel competent to pass definite judgment. Fascism is so large a part of myself that it would be both arbitrary and absurd for me to try to dissociate my personality from it, to submit it to impartial scrutiny in order to evaluate it coldly and accurately. What can be done, however, and it seldom is attempted, is to make inquiry into the phenomenon which shall not merely consider its fragmentary and adventitious aspects, but strive to get at its inner essence. The undertaking may not be easy, but it is necessary, and no occasion for attempting it is more suitable than the present one afforded me by my friends of Perugia. Suitable it is in time because, at the inauguration of a course of lectures and lessons principally intended to illustrate that old and glorious trend of the life and history of Italy which takes its name from the humble saint of Assisi, it seemed natural to connect it with the greatest achievement of modern Italy, different in so many ways from the Franciscan movement, but united with it by the mighty common current of Italian History. It is suitable as well in place because at Perugia, which witnessed the growth of our religious ideas, of our political doctrines and of our legal science in the course of the most glorious centuries of our cultural history, the mind is properly disposed and almost oriented towards an investigation of this nature.

First of all let us ask ourselves if there is a political doctrine of Fascism; if there is any ideal content in the Fascist state. For in order to link Fascism, both as concept and system, with the history of Italian thought and find therein a place for it, we must first show that it is thought; that it is a doctrine. Many persons are not quite convinced that it is either the one or the other; and I am not referring solely to those men, cultured or uncultured, as the case may be and very numerous everywhere, who can discern in this political innovation nothing except its local and personal aspects, and who know Fascism only as the particular manner of behavior of this or that well-known Fascist, of this or that group of a certain town; who therefore like or dislike the movement on the basis of their likes and dislikes for the individuals who represent it. Nor do I refer to those intelligent and cultivated persons, very intelligent indeed and very cultivated, who because of their direct or indirect allegiance to the parties that have been dispossessed by the advent of Fascism, have a natural cause of resentment against it and are therefore unable to see, in the blindness of hatred, anything good in it. I am referring rather to those—and there are many in our ranks too—who know Fascism as action and feeling but not yet as thought, who therefore have an intuition but no comprehension of it.

It is true that Fascism is, above all, action and sentiment and that such it must continue to be. Were it otherwise, it could not keep up that immense driving force, that renovating power which it now possesses and would merely be the solitary meditation of a chosen few. Only because it is feeling and sentiment, only because it is the unconscious reawakening of our profound racial instinct, has it the force to stir the soul of the people, and to set free an irresistible current of national will. Only because it is action, and as such actualizes itself in a vast organization and in a huge movement, has it the conditions for determining the historical course of contemporary Italy.

But Fascism is thought as well and it has a theory, which is an essential part of this historical phenomenon, and which is responsible in a great measure for the successes that have been achieved. To the existence of this ideal content of Fascism, to the truth of this Fascist logic we ascribe the fact that though we commit many errors of detail, we very seldom go astray on fundamentals, whereas all the parties of the opposition, deprived as they are of an informing, animating principle, of a unique directing concept, do very often wage their war faultlessly in minor tactics, better trained as they are in parliamentary and journalistic maneuvers, but they constantly break down on the important issues. Fascism, moreover, considered as action, is a typically Italian phenomenon and acquires a universal validity because of the existence of this coherent and organic doctrine. The originality of Fascism is due in great part to the autonomy of its theoretical principles. For even when, in its external behavior and in its conclusions, it seems identical with other political creeds, in reality it possesses an inner originality due to the new spirit which animates it and to an entirely different theoretical approach.

48
Alfred Rosenberg

Alfred Rosenberg (1893–1946) brought irrationalism to extremes earlier undreamed of. *The Myth of the Twentieth Century,* his chief work, exalted the myth of an Aryan super-race, of which the Germans were the contemporary embodiment. No excess of political terror was too great if, on his theory, it advanced the supremacy of the Nordic peoples. The myth of the twentieth century, he urged, was "the myth of the blood." Rosenberg was convicted of crimes against humanity at Nuremberg in 1946 and executed as a war criminal.

[THE MYTH OF NORDIC BLOOD]*

Racial history is thus at the same time natural history and soul-*mystique.* The history of the religion of blood is, conversely, the great world-narrative of the rise and decline of peoples, their heroes and thinkers, their inventors and artists. . . .

The "meaning of world history" has radiated out from the north over the whole world, borne by a blue-eyed blond race which in several great waves determined the spiritual face of the world. . . . These wander-periods were the legendary migration of the Atlantides across north Africa, the migration of the Aryans into India and

*From A. Rosenberg, *The Myth of the Twentieth Century,* 1930. These passages are reprinted from selections appearing in *National Socialism,* a report prepared by the Division of European Affairs, U.S. Department of State; United States Government Printing Office, Washington, 1943.

Persia; the migration of the Dorians, Macedonians, Latins; the migration of the Germanic tribes; the colonization of the world by the Germanic occident. . . .

We stand today before a definitive decision. Either through a new experience and cultivation of the old blood, coupled with an enhanced fighting will, we will rise to a purificatory action, or the last Germanic-western values of morality and state-culture shall sink away in the filthy human masses of the big cities, become stunted on the sterile burning asphalt of a bestialized inhumanity, or trickle away as a morbific agent in the form of emigrants, bastardizing themselves in South America, China, Dutch East India, Africa. . . .

A *new* faith is arising today: the myth of the blood, the faith, to defend with the blood the divine essence of man. The faith, embodied in clearest knowledge, that the Nordic blood represents that *mysterium* which has replaced and overcome the old sacraments. . . .

The new real struggle today is concerned not so much with external changes in power, along with an internal compromise as hitherto, but, conversely, with the new rebuilding of the soul-cells of the Nordic peoples, for the sake of the re-institution in their sovereign rights [*Herrscherrechte*] of those ideals and values from which originates everything which signifies culture to us, and for the sake of the preservation of the racial substance itself. . . .

4

FASCIST PHILOSOPHY
IN ITALY

The word *fasciare* means, in Italian, to bind or envelop; fascism was intended by its founders to be a movement that would finally bind the Italian nation into revitalized unity, a movement that would bring glory to Italy by reviving the traditions of ancient Rome: discipline, order, imperial authority.

Italy was the birthplace of twentieth-century fascism, but fascism there—tied to the career of Benito Mussolini—had a short and painful history. The Fascist Party was founded by Mussolini in 1919; he assumed autocratic power in Italy after the "March on Rome" in 1922; twenty-three years later Mussolini was assassinated; defeated in World War II, Italian fascism turned to ashes.

Mussolini's career was volatile. Originally a socialist and an atheist, he became a bitter critic of socialism and a strong supporter of the Roman Catholic Church. Early in his life he favored republicanism, but later he became a monarchist; once an advocate of a *laissez faire* economy, he came to demand, as dictator, complete state regulation of all economic affairs. These inconsistencies he did not deny; indeed, he gloried in the deliberate rejection of rationality in political philosophy. "No Dogma! Discipline suffices" was one of the slogans of his regime. "My program is action, not thought," Mussolini would often say; to all intellectual criticism of the fascist movement his followers learned to reply, "We think with our blood."

A more coherent exposition of the philosophy of fascism was eventually undertaken by some leading members of the Mussolini government. The central principles of the fascist philosophy were formulated by Alfredo Rocco: fascism was a theory of totalitarian state power, supreme and unrestricted, led by the intuitive genius of an all-powerful ruler. Upon these themes Mussolini himself would later expand; and Giovanni Gentile, perhaps the deepest of the philosophical fascists, along with others, would later weave into them a glorification of heroism, sacrifice, and war.

The fascist movement in Italy (as in Germany later) owed much of its success to the extraordinary enthusiasm it inspired, and to the fanatical loyalty of its disciples to their country and their leaders. At the peak of his career, Mussolini could say to assembled masses: "We have created our myth; it is a faith, a passion. . . . It is a reality by virtue of being a spur, a source of courage. Our myth is the nation, the greatness of the nation. And to this myth, this grandeur . . . we subordinate all the rest."

49
Alfredo Rocco

Italian fascists explicitly rejected the democratic ideals of modern Europe. Rocco, a leader among them, emphasized the integrated cohesion of the social body as central—hence the use of the symbolic *fasces*. He was bitterly opposed to every form of "social atomism," and especially to the liberal individualism that he thought deeply corruptive. An enthusiastic admirer of Machiavelli, and an advocate of supreme power exercised by the ruler of an organic state, he blended these elements into a philosophy that, he claimed, "was to restore Italian thought in the sphere of political doctrine to its own traditions, which are the traditions of Rome."

THE POLITICAL DOCTRINE OF FASCISM*

Premier Mussolini's Endorsement of Signor Rocco's Speech

The following message was sent by Benito Mussolini, the Premier of Italy, to Signor Rocco after he had delivered his speech at Perugia.

> Dear Rocco,
> I have just read your magnificent address which I endorse throughout. You have presented in a masterful way the doctrine of Fascism. For Fascism has a doctrine, or, if you will, a particular philosophy with regard to all the questions which beset the human mind today. All Italian Fascists should read your discourse and derive from it both the clear formulation of the basic principles of our program as well as the reasons why Fascism must be systematically, firmly, and rationally inflexible in its uncompromising attitude towards other parties. Thus and only thus can the word become flesh and the ideas be turned into deeds.
>
> Cordial greetings,
MUSSOLINI.

Common Origins and Common Background of Modern Political Doctrines: From Liberalism to Socialism*

Modern political thought remained, until recently, both in Italy and outside of Italy under the absolute control of those doctrines which, proceeding from the Protestant Reformation and developed by the adepts of natural law in the seven-

---

*A. Rocco, *The Political Doctrine of Fascism,* 1925. Reprinted from *Readings on Fascism and National Socialism,* selected by members of the philosophy department of the University of Colorado, by permission of the publisher, Alan Swallow, Denver.

teenth and eighteenth centuries, were firmly grounded in the institutions and customs of the English, of the American, and of the French Revolutions. Under different and sometimes clashing forms these doctrines have left a determining imprint upon all theories and actions both social and political, of the nineteenth and twentieth centuries down to the rise of Fascism. The common basis of all these doctrines, which stretch from Longuet, from Buchanan, and from Althusen down to Karl Marx, to Wilson and to Lenin is a social and state concept which I shall call mechanical or atomistic.

Society according to this concept is merely a sum total of individuals, a plurality which breaks up into its single components. Therefore the ends of a society, so considered, are nothing more than the ends of the individuals which compose it and for whose sake it exists. An atomistic view of this kind is also necessarily anti-historical, inasmuch as it considers society in its spatial attibutes and not in its temporal ones; and because it reduces social life to the existence of a single generation. Society becomes thus a sum of determined individuals, viz., the generation living at a given moment. This doctrine which I call atomistic and which appears to be anti-historical, reveals from under a concealing cloak a strongly materialistic nature. For in its endeavors to isolate the present from the past and the future, it rejects the spiritual inheritance of ideas and sentiments which each generation receives from those preceding and hands down to the following generation thus destroying the unity and the spiritual life itself of human society.

This common basis shows the close logical connection existing between all political doctrines; the substantial solidarity, which unites all the political movements, from Liberalism to Socialism, that until recently have dominated Europe. For these political schools differ from one another in their methods, but all agree as to the ends to be achieved. All of them consider the welfare and happiness of individuals to be the goal of society, itself considered as composed of individuals of the present generation. All of them see in society and in its juridical organization, the state, the mere instrument and means whereby individuals can attain their ends. They differ only in that the methods pursued for the attainment of these ends vary considerably one from the other.

Thus the Liberals insist that the best manner to secure the welfare of the citizens as individuals is to interfere as little as possible with the free development of their activities and that therefore the essential task of the state is merely to coordinate these several liberties in such a way as to guarantee their coexistence. Kant, who was without doubt the most powerful and thorough philosopher of liberalism, said, "man, who is the end, cannot be assumed to have the value of an instrument." And again, "justice, of which the state is the specific organ, is the condition whereby the freedom of each is conditioned upon the freedom of others, according to the general law of liberty."

Having thus defined the task of the state, Liberalism confines itself to the demand of certain guarantees which are to keep the state from overstepping its functions as general coordinator of liberties and from sacrificing the freedom of individuals more than is absolutely necessary for the accomplishment of its purpose. All the efforts are therefore directed to see to it that the ruler, mandatory of all and entrusted with the realization, through and by liberty, of the harmonious happiness of everybody, should never be clothed with undue power. Hence the creation of a system of checks and limitations designed to keep the rulers within bounds; and among these, first and foremost, the principle of the division of powers, contrived as a means for weakening the state in its relation to the individual, by making it impossible for the state ever to appear, in its dealings with citizens, in the full plenitude of sovereign powers; also the principle of the participation of citizens in the lawmaking power, as a means for securing, in behalf of the individual, a direct check on this, the strongest branch, and an indirect check on the entire government of the state. This system of checks and limitations, which goes by the name of constitutional government, resulted in a moderate and measured liberalism. The checking power was exercised only by those citizens who were deemed worthy and capable, with the result that a small élite was made to represent legally the entire body politic for whose benefit this régime was instituted.

It was evident, however, that this moderate system, being fundamentally illogical and in contradiction with the very principles from which it proceeded, would soon become the object of serious criticism. For if the object of society and of the state is the welfare of individuals, severally considered, how is it possible to admit that this welfare can be secured by the individuals themselves only through the possibilities of such a liberal régime? The inequalities brought about both by nature and by social organizations are so numerous and so serious, that, for the greater part, individuals abandoned to themselves not only would fail to attain happiness, but would also contribute to the perpetuation of their condition of misery and dejection. The state therefore cannot limit itself to the merely negative function of the defense of liberty. It must become active, in behalf of everybody, for the welfare of the people. It must intervene, when necessary, in order to improve the material, intellectual, and moral conditions of the masses; it must find work for the unemployed, instruct and educate the people, and care for health and hygiene. For if the purpose of society and of the state is the welfare of individuals, and if it is just that these individuals themselves control the attainment of their ends, it becomes difficult to understand why Liberalism should not go the whole distance, why it should see fit to distinguish certain individuals from the rest of the mass, and why the functions of the people should be restricted to the exercise of a mere check. Therefore the state, if it exists for all, must be governed by all, and not by a small minority: if the state is for the people, sovereignty must reside in the people: if all individuals have the right to govern the state, liberty is no longer sufficient; equality must be added: and if sovereignty is vested in the people, the people must wield all sovereignty and not merely a part of it. The power to check and curb the government is not sufficient. The people must be the government. Thus, logically developed, Liberalism leads to Democracy, for Democracy contains the promises of Liberalism but oversteps its limitations in that it makes the action of the state positive, proclaims the equality of all citizens through the dogma of popular sovereignty. Democracy therefore necessarily implies a republican form of government even though at times, for reasons of expediency, it temporarily adjusts itself to a monarchical régime.

Once started on this downward grade of logical deductions it was inevitable that this atomistic theory of state and society should pass on to a more advanced position. Great industrial developments and the existence of a huge mass of working men, as yet badly treated and in a condition of semi-servitude, possibly endurable in a régime of domestic industry, became intolerable after the industrial revolution. Hence a state of affairs which towards the middle of the last century appeared to be both cruel and threatening. It was therefore natural that the following question be raised: "If the state is created for the welfare of its citizens, severally considered, how can it tolerate an economic system which divides the population into a small minority of exploiters, the capitalists, on one side, and an immense multitude of exploited, the working people, on the other?" No! The state must again intervene and give rise to a different and less iniquitous economic organization, by abolishing private property, by assuming direct control of all production, and by organizing it in such a way that the products of labor be distributed solely among those who create them, viz., the working classes. Hence we find Socialism, with its new economic organization of society, abolishing private ownership of capital and of the instruments and means of production, socializing the product, suppressing the extra profit of capital, and turning over to the working class the entire output of the productive processes. It is evident that Socialism contains and surpasses Democracy in the same way that Democracy comprises and surpasses Liberalism, being a more advanced development of the same fundamental concept. Socialism in its turn generates the still more extreme doctrine of Bolshevism which demands the violent suppression of the holders of capital, the dictatorship of the proletariat, as means for a fairer economic organization of society and for the rescue of the laboring classes from capitalistic exploitation.

Thus Liberalism, Democracy, and Socialism, appear to be, as they are in reality, not only the offspring of one and the same theory of government, but also logical derivations one of the other. Logically developed Liberalism leads to Democracy; the logical development of Democracy issues into Socialism. It is true that for many years, and with some justification, Socialism was looked upon as antithetical to Liberalism. But the antithesis is purely relative and breaks down as we approach the common origin and foundation of the two doctrines, for we find that the opposition is one of method, not of purpose. The end is the same for both, viz., the welfare of the individual members of society. The difference lies in the fact that Liberalism would be guided to its goal by liberty, whereas Socialism strives to attain it by the collective organization of production. There is therefore no antithesis nor even a divergence as to the nature and scope of the state and the relation of individuals to society. There is only a difference of evaluation of the means for bringing about these ends and establishing these relations, which difference depends entirely on the different economic conditions which prevailed at the time when the various doctrines were formulated. Liberalism arose and began to thrive in the period of small industry; Socialism grew with the rise of industrialism and of world-wide capitalism. The dissension therefore between these two points of view, or the antithesis, if we wish so to call it, is limited to the economic field. Socialism is at odds with Liberalism only on the question of the organization of production and of the division of wealth. In religious, intellectual, and moral matters it is liberal, as it is liberal and democratic in its politics. Even the anti-liberalism and anti-democracy of Bolshevism are in themselves purely contingent.

For Bolshevism is opposed to Liberalism only in so far as the former is revolutionary, not in its socialistic aspect. For if the opposition of the Bolsheviki to liberal and democratic doctrines were to continue, as now seems more and more probable, the result might be a complete break between Bolshevism and Socialism notwithstanding the fact that the ultimate aims of both are identical.

Fascism as an Integral Doctrine of Sociality Antithetical to the Atomism of Liberal, Democratic, and Socialistic Theories

The true antithesis, not to this or that manifestation of the liberal-democratic-socialistic conception of the state but to the concept itself, is to be found in the doctrine of Fascism. For while the disagreement between Liberalism and Democracy, and between Liberalism and Socialism lies in a difference of method, as we have said, the rift between Socialism, Democracy, and Liberalism on one side and Fascism on the other is caused by a difference in concept. As a matter of fact, Fascism never raises the question of methods, using in its political praxis now liberal ways, now democratic means and at times even socialistic devices. This indifference to method often exposes Fascism to the charge of incoherence on the part of superficial observers, who do not see that what counts with us is the end and that therefore even when we employ the same means we act with a radically different spiritual and strive for entirely different results. The Fascist concept then of the nation, of the scope of the state, and of the relations obtaining between society and its individual components, rejects entirely the doctrine which I said proceeded from the theories of natural law developed in the course of the sixteenth, seventeenth, and eighteenth centuries and which form the basis of the liberal, democratic, and socialistic ideology.

I shall not try here to expound this doctrine but shall limit myself to a brief résumé of its fundamental concepts.

Man—the political animal—according to the definition of Aristotle, lives and must live in society. A human being outside the pale of society is an inconceivable thing—a non-man. Humankind in its entirety lives in social groups that are still, today, very numerous and diverse, varying in importance and organization from the tribes of Central Africa to the great Western Empires. These various societies are fractions of the human species each one of them endowed with a unified organization. And as there is no unique organization of the human species, there is not "one" but there are "several" human societies. Humanity therefore exists solely as a biological concept not as a social one.

Each society on the other hand exists in the unity of both its biological and its social contents. Socially considered it is a fraction of the human species endowed with unity of organization for the attainment of the peculiar ends of the species.

This definition brings out all the elements of the social phenomenon and not merely those relating to the preservation and perpetuation of the species. For man is not solely matter; and the ends of the human species, far from being the materialistic ones we have in common with other animals, are, rather, and predominantly, the spiritual finalities which are peculiar to man and which every form of society strives to attain as well as its stage of social development allows. Thus the organization of every social group is more or less pervaded by the spiritual influxes of: unity of language, of culture, of religion, of tradition, of customs, and in general of feeling and of volition, which are as essential as the material elements: unity of economic interests, of living conditions, and of territory. The definition given above demonstrates another truth, which has been ignored by the political doctrines that for the last four centuries have been the foundations of political systems, viz., that the social concept has a biological aspect, because social groups are fractions of the human species, each one possessing a peculiar organization, a particular rank in the development of civilization with certain needs and appropriate ends, in short, a life which is really its own. If social groups are then fractions of the human species, they must possess the same fundamental traits of the human species, which means that they must be considered as a succession of generations and not as a collection of individuals.

It is evident therefore that as the human species is not the total of the living human beings of the world, so the various social groups which compose it are not the sum of the several individuals which at a given moment belong to it, but rather the infinite series of the past, present, and future generations constituting it. And as the ends of the human species are not those of the several individuals living at a certain moment, being occasionally in direct opposition to them, so the ends of the various social groups are not necessarily those of the individuals that belong to the groups but may even possibly be in conflict with such ends, as one sees clearly whenever the preservation and the development of the species demand the sacrifice of the individual, to wit, in times of war.

Fascism replaces therefore the old atomistic and mechanical state theory which was at the basis of the liberal and democratic doctrines with an organic and historic concept. When I say organic I do not wish to convey the impression that I consider society as an organism after the manner of the so-called "organic theories of the state"; but rather to indicate that the social groups as fractions of the species receive thereby a life and scope which transcend the scope and life of the individuals identifying themselves with the history and finalities of the uninterrupted series of generations. It is irrelevant in this connection to determine whether social groups, considered as fractions of the species, constitute organisms. The important thing is to ascertain that this organic concept of the state gives to society a continuous life over and beyond the existence of the several individuals.

The relations therefore between state and citizens are completely reversed by the Fascist doctrine. Instead of the liberal-democratic formula, "society for the individual," we have, "individuals for society" with this difference however: that while the liberal doctrines eliminated society, Fascism does not submerge the individual in the social group. It subordinates him, but does not eliminate him; the individual as a part of his generation even remaining an element of society however transient and insignificant he may be. Moreover the development of individuals in each generation, when coordinated and harmonized, conditions the development and prosperity of the entire social unit.

At this juncture the antithesis between the two theories must appear complete and absolute. Liberalism, Democracy, and Socialism look upon social groups as aggregates of living individuals; for Fascism they are the recapitulating unity of the indefinite series of generations. For Liberalism, society has no purposes other than those of the members living at a given moment. For Fascism, society has historical and immanent ends of preservation, expansion, improvement, quite distinct from those of the individuals which at a given moment compose it; so distinct in fact that they may even be in opposition. Hence the necessity, for which the older doctrines make little allowance, of sacrifice, even up to the total immolation of individuals, in behalf of society; hence the true explanation of war, eternal law of mankind, interpreted by the liberal-democratic doctrines as a degenerate absurdity or as a maddened monstrosity.

For Liberalism, society has no life distinct from the life of the individuals, or as the phrase goes: *solvitur in singularitates.* For Fascism, the life of society overlaps the existence of individuals and projects itself into the succeeding generations through centuries and millennia. Individuals come into being, grow, and die, followed by others, unceasingly; social unity remains always identical to itself. For Liberalism, the individual is the end and society the means; nor is it conceivable that the individual, considered in the dignity of an ultimate finality, be lowered to mere instrumentality. For Fascism, society is the end, individuals the means, and its whole life consists in using individuals as instruments for its social ends. The state therefore guards and protects the welfare and development of individuals not for their exclusive interest, but because of the identity of the needs of individuals with those of society as a whole. We can thus accept and explain institutions and practices, which like the death penalty, are condemned by Liberalism in the name of the preeminence of individualism.

The fundamental problem of society in the old doctrines is the question of the rights of individuals. It may be the right to freedom as the Liberals would have it; or the right to the government of the commonwealth as the Democrats claim it, or the right to economic justice as the Socialists contend; but in every case it is the right of individuals, or groups of individuals (classes). Fascism on the other hand faces squarely the problem of the right of the state and of the duty of individuals. Individual rights are only recognized in so far as they are implied in the rights of the state. In this preeminence of duty we find the highest ethical value of Fascism.

The Problems of Liberty, of Government, and of Social Justice in the Political Doctrine of Fascism

This, however, does not mean that the problems raised by the other schools are ignored by Fascism. It means simply that it faces them and solves them differently, as, for example, the problem of liberty.

There is a Liberal theory of freedom, and there is a Fascist concept of liberty. For we, too, maintain the necessity of safeguarding the conditions that make for the free development of the individual; we, too, believe that the oppression of individual personality can find no place in the modern state. We do not, however, accept a bill of rights which tends to make the individual superior to the state and to empower him to act in opposition to society. Our concept of liberty is that the individual must be allowed to develop his personality in behalf of the state, for these ephemeral and infinitesimal elements of the complex and permanent life of society determine by their normal growth the development of the state. But this individual growth must be normal. A huge and disproportionate development of the individual of classes, would prove as fatal to society as abnormal growths are to living organisms. Freedom therefore is due to the citizen and to classes on condition that they exercise it in the interest of society as a whole and within the limits set by social exigencies, liberty being, like any other individual right, a concession of the state. What I say concerning civil liberties applies to economic freedom as well. Fascism does not look upon the doctrine of economic liberty as an absolute dogma. It does not refer economic problems to individual needs, to individual interest, to individual solutions. On the contrary it considers the economic development, and especially the production of wealth, as an eminently social concern, wealth being for society an essential element of power and prosperity. But Fascism maintains that in the ordinary run of events economic liberty serves the social purposes best; that it is profitable to entrust to individual initiative the task of economic development both as to production and as to distribution; that in the economic world individual ambition is the most effective means for obtaining the best social results with the least effort. Therefore, on the question also of economic liberty the Fascists differ fundamentally from the Liberals; the latter see in liberty a principle, the Fascists accept it as a method. By the Liberals, freedom is recognized in the interest of the citizens; the Fascists grant it in the interest of society. In other terms, Fascists make of the individual an economic instrument for the advancement of society, an instrument which they use so long as it functions and which they subordinate when no longer serviceable. In this guise Fascism solves the eternal problem of economic freedom and of state interference, considering both as mere methods which may or may not be employed in accordance with the social needs of the moment.

What I have said concerning political and economic Liberalism applies also to Democracy. The latter envisages fundamentally the problem of sovereignty; Fascism does also, but in an entirely different manner. Democracy vests sovereignty in the people, that is to say, in the mass of human beings. Fascism discovers sovereignty to be inherent in society when it is juridically organized as a state. Democracy therefore turns over the government of the state to the multitude of living men that they may use it to further their own interests; Fascism insists that the government be entrusted to men capable of rising above their own private interests and of realizing the aspirations of the social collectivity, considered in its unity and in its relation to the past and future. Fascism therefore not only rejects the dogma of popular sovereignty and substitutes for it that of state sovereignty, but it also proclaims that the great mass of citizens is not a suitable advocate of social interests for the reason that the capacity to ignore individual private interests in favor of the higher demands of society and of history is a very rare gift and the privilege of the chosen few. Natural intelligence and cultural preparation are of great service in such tasks. Still more valuable perhaps is the intuitiveness of rare great minds, their traditionalism and their inherited qualities. This must not however be construed to mean that the masses are not to be allowed to exercise any influence on the life of the state. On the contrary, among peoples with a great history and with noble traditions, even the lowest elements of society possess an instinctive discernment of what is necessary for the welfare of the race, which in moments of great historical crises reveals itself to be almost infallible. It is therefore as wise to afford to this instinct the means of declaring itself as it is judicious to entrust the normal control of the commonwealth to a selected élite. . . .

Historical Value of the Doctrine of Fascism

. . . At this point it will not be very difficult to assign a fitting place in history to this great trend of thought which is called Fascism and which, in spite of the initial difficulties, already gives clear indication of the magnitude of its developments.

The liberal-democratic speculation both in its origin and in the manner of its development appears to be essentially a non-Italian formation. Its connection with the Middle Ages already shows it to be foreign to the Latin mind, the medieval disintegration being the result of the triumph of Germanic individualism over the political mentality of the Romans. The barbarians, boring from within and hacking from without, pulled down the great political structure raised by Latin genius and put nothing in its place. Anarchy lasted eight centuries during which time only one institution survived and that a Roman one—the Catholic Church. But, as soon as the laborious process of reconstruction was started with the constitution of the great national states backed by the Roman Church the Protestant Reformation set in followed by the individualistic currents of the seventeenth and eighteenth centuries, and the process of disintegration was started anew. This anti-state tendency was the expression of the Germanic spirit and it therefore became predominant among the Germanic peoples and wherever Germanism had left a deep imprint even if afterward superficially covered by a veneer of Latin culture. . . .

While therefore in other countries such as France, England, Germany, and Holland, the general tradition in the social and political sciences worked in behalf of anti-state individualism, and therefore of liberal and democratic doctrines, Italy, on the other hand, clung to the powerful legacy of its past in virtue of which she proclaims the rights of the state, the preeminence of its authority, and the superiority of its ends. The very fact that the Italian political doctrine in the Middle Ages linked itself with the great political writers of antiquity, Plato and Aristotle, who in a different manner but with an equal firmness advocated a strong state and the subordination of individuals to it, is a sufficient index of the orientation of political philosophy in Italy. We all know how thorough and crushing the authority of Aristotle was in the Middle Ages. But for Aristotle the spiritual cement of the state is "virtue" not absolute virtue but political virtue, which is social devotion. His state is made up solely of its citizens, the citizens being either those who defend it with their arms or who govern it as magistrates. All others who provide it with the materials and services it needs are not citizens. They become such only in the corrupt forms of certain democracies. Society is therefore divided into two classes, the free men or citizens who give their time to noble and virtuous occupations and who profess their subjection to the state, and the laborers and slaves who work for the maintenance of the former. No man in this scheme is his own master. The slaves belong to the freemen, and the freemen belong to the state.

It was therefore natural that St. Thomas Aquinas, the greatest political writer of the Middle Ages, should emphasize the necessity of unity in the political field, the harm of plurality of rulers, the dangers and damaging effects of demagogy. The good of the state, says St. Thomas Aquinas, is unity. And who can procure unity more fittingly than he who is himself one? Moreover the government must follow, as far as possible, the course of nature and in nature power is always one. In the physical body only one organ is dominant—the heart; in the spirit only one faculty has sway—reason. Bees have one sole ruler; and the entire universe one sole sovereign—God. Experience shows that the countries, which are ruled by many, perish because of discord while those that are ruled over by one enjoy peace, justice, and plenty. The States which are not ruled by one are troubled by dissensions, and toil unceasingly. On the contrary the states which are ruled over by one king enjoy peace, thrive in justice and are gladdened by affluence.* The rule of the multitudes cannot be sanctioned, for where the crowd rules it oppresses the rich as would a tyrant.† . . .

The Roman tradition, which was one of practice but not of theories—for Rome constructed the most solid state known to history with extraordinary statesmanship but with hardly any political writings—influenced considerably the founder of modern political science, Niccolo Machiavelli, who was himself in truth not a creator of doctrines but a keen observer of human nature who derived from the study of history practical maxims of political import. He freed the science of politics from the formalism of the scholastic and brought it close to concrete reality. His writings, an inexhaustible mine of practical remarks and precious observations, reveal dominant in him the state idea, no longer abstract but in the full historical concreteness of the national unity of Italy. Machiavelli therefore is not only the greatest of modern political writers, he is also the greatest of our countrymen in full possession of a national Italian consciousness. To liberate Italy, which was in his day "enslaved, torn and pillaged," and to make her more powerful, he would use any means, for to his mind the holiness of the end justified them completely. In this he was sharply rebuked by foreigners who were not as hostile to his means as they were fearful of the end which he propounded. He advocated therefore the constitution of a strong Italian state, supported by the sacrifices and by the blood of the citizens, not defended by mercenary troops; well-ordered internally, aggressive and bent on expansion. . . .

*De reg. princ. I. c. 2.
†Comm. In Polit. L. III. lectio VIII.

A powerful innovating movement, issuing from the war and of which Fascism is the purest expression, was to restore Italian thought in the sphere of political doctrine to its own traditions which are the traditions of Rome.

This task of intellectual liberation, now slowly being accomplished, is no less important than the political deliverance brought about by the Fascist Revolution. It is a great task which continues and integrates the Risorgimento; it is now bringing to an end, after the cessation of our political servitude, the intellectual dependence of Italy.

Thanks to it, Italy again speaks to the world and the world listens to Italy. It is a great task and a great deed and it demands great efforts. To carry it through, we must, each one of us, free ourselves of the dross of ideas and mental habits which two centuries of foreign intellectualistic tradition have heaped upon us; we must not only take on a new culture but create for ourselves a new soul. We must methodically and patiently contribute something towards the organic and complete elaboration of our doctrine, at the same time supporting it both at home and abroad with untiring devotion. We ask this effort of renovation and collaboration of all Fascists, as well as of all who feel themselves to be Italians. After the hour of sacrifice comes the hour of unyielding efforts. To our work, then, fellow countrymen, for the glory of Italy!

50
Benito Mussolini

Benito Mussolini (1883–1945) was the founder of the Fascist party in Italy and dictator from 1922 until his death in 1945. The following article, which first appeared as a contribution to *Enciclopedia Italiana* in 1932, is the most famous statement of that composite known as the philosophy of fascism.

THE DOCTRINE OF FASCISM*

(i) Fundamental Ideas

1 Like every sound political conception, Fascism is both practice and thought; action in which a doctrine is immanent, and a doctrine which, arising out of a given system of historical forces, remains embedded in them and works there from within. Hence it has a form correlative to the contingencies of place and time, but it has also a content of thought which raises it to a formula of truth in the higher level of the history of thought. In the world one does not act spiritually as a human

*Benito Mussolini, *The Doctrine of Fascism,* 1932. This translation is reprinted from *The Social and Political Doctrines of Contemporary Europe,* 1939, edited by Michael Oakeshott, by permission of the Cambridge University Press.

will dominating other wills without a conception of the transient and particular reality under which it is necessary to act, and of the permanent and universal reality in which the first has its being and its life. In order to know men it is necessary to know man; and in order to know man it is necessary to know reality and its laws. There is no concept of the State which is not fundamentally a concept of life: philosophy or intuition, a system of ideas which develops logically or is gathered up into a vision or into a faith, but which is always, at least virtually, an organic conception of the world.

2 Thus Fascism could not be understood in many of its practical manifestations as a party organization, as a system of education, as a discipline, if it were not always looked at in the light of its whole way of conceiving life, a spiritualized way. The world seen through Fascism is not this material world which appears on the surface, in which man is an individual separated from all others and standing by himself, and in which he is governed by a natural law that makes him instinctively live a life of selfish and momentary pleasure. The man of Fascism is an individual who is nation and fatherland, which is a moral law, binding together individuals and the generations into a tradition and a mission, suppressing the instinct for a life enclosed within the brief round of pleasure in order to restore within duty a higher life free from the limits of time and space: a life in which the individual, through the denial of himself, through the sacrifice of his own private interests, through death itself, realizes that completely spiritual existence in which his value as a man lies.

3 Therefore it is a spiritualized conception, itself the result of the general reaction of modern times against the flabby materialistic positivism of the nineteenth century. Anti-positivistic, but positive: not sceptical, nor agnostic, nor pessimistic, nor passively optimistic, as are, in general, the doctrines (all negative) that put the center of life outside man, who with his free will can and must create his own world. Fascism desires an active man, one engaged in activity with all his energies: it desires a man virilely conscious of the difficulties that exist in action and ready to face them. It conceives of life as a struggle, considering that it behooves man to conquer for himself that life truly worthy of him, creating first of all in himself the instrument (physical, moral, intellectual) in order to construct it. Thus for the single individual, thus for the nation, thus for humanity. Hence the high value of culture in all its forms (art, religion, science), and the enormous importance of education. Hence also the essential value of work, with which man conquers nature and creates the human world (economic, political, moral, intellectual).

4 This positive conception of life is clearly an ethical conception. It covers the whole of reality, not merely the human activity which controls it. No action can be divorced from moral judgment; there is nothing in the world which can be deprived of the value which belongs to everything in its relation to moral ends. Life, therefore, as conceived by the Fascist, is serious, austere, religious: the whole of it is poised in a world supported by the moral and responsible forces of the spirit. The Fascist disdains the "comfortable" life.

5 Fascism is a religious conception in which man is seen in his immanent relationship with a superior law and with an objective Will that transcends the particular individual and raises him to conscious membership in a spiritual society.

Whoever has seen in the religious politics of the Fascist regime nothing but mere opportunism has not understood that Fascism besides being a system of government is also, and above all, a system of thought.

6 Fascism is a historical conception, in which man is what he is only in so far as he works with the spiritual process in which he finds himself, in the family or social group, in the nation and in the history in which all nations collaborate. From this follows the great value of tradition, in memories, in language, in customs, in the standards of social life. Outside history man is nothing. Consequently Fascism is opposed to all the individualistic abstractions of a materialistic nature like those of the eighteenth century; and it is opposed to all Jacobin utopias and innovations. It does not consider that "happiness" is possible upon earth, as it appeared to be in the desire of the economic literature of the eighteenth century, and hence it rejects all theological theories according to which mankind would reach a definitive stabilized condition at a certain period in history. This implies putting oneself outside history and life, which is a continual change and coming to be. Politically, Fascism wishes to be a realistic doctrine; practically, it aspires to solve only the problems which arise historically of themselves and that of themselves find or suggest their own solution. To act among men, as to act in the natural world, it is necessary to enter into the process of reality and to master the already operating forces.

7 Against individualism, the Fascist conception is for the State; and it is for the individual in so far as he coincides with the State, which is the conscience and universal will of man in his historical existence. It is opposed to classical Liberalism, which arose from the necessity of reacting against absolutism, and which brought its historical purpose to an end when the State was transformed into the conscience and will of the people. Liberalism denied the State in the interests of the particular individual; Fascism reaffirms the State as the true reality of the individual. And if liberty is to be the attribute of the real man, and not of that abstract puppet envisaged by individualistic Liberalism, Fascism is for liberty. And for the only liberty which can be a real thing, the liberty of the State and of the individual within the State. Therefore, for the Fascist, everything is in the State, and nothing human or spiritual exists, much less has value, outside the State. In this sense Fascism is totalitarian, and the Fascist State, the synthesis and unity of all values, interprets, develops and gives strength to the whole life of the people.

8 Outside the State there can be neither individuals nor groups (political parties, associations, syndicates, classes). Therefore Fascism is opposed to Socialism, which confines the movement of history within the class struggle and ignores the unity of classes established in one economic and moral reality in the State; and analogously it is opposed to class syndicalism. Fascism recognizes the real exigencies for which the socialist and syndicalist movement arose, but while recognizing them wishes to bring them under the control of the State and give them a purpose within the corporative system of interests reconciled within the unity of the State.

9 Individuals form classes according to the similarity of their interests, they form syndicates according to differentiated economic activities within these interests; but they form first, and above all, the State, which is not to be thought of numerically as the sum-total of individuals forming the majority of a nation. And consequently Fascism is opposed to Democracy, which equates the nation to the majority, lowering it to the level of that majority; nevertheless it is the purest form of democracy if the nation is conceived, as it should be, qualitatively and not quantitatively, as the most powerful idea (most powerful because most moral, most coherent, most true) which acts within the nation as the conscience and the will of a few, even of One, which ideal tends to become active within the conscience and the will of all—that is to say, of all those who rightly constitute a nation by reason of nature, history or race, and have set out upon the same line of development and spiritual formation as one conscience and one sole will. Not a race, nor a geographically determined region, but as a community historically perpetuating itself, a multitude unified by a single idea, which is the will to existence and to power: consciousness of itself, personality.

10 This higher personality is truly the nation in so far as it is the State. It is not the nation that generates the State, as according to the old naturalistic concept which served as the basis of the political theories of the national States of the nineteenth century. Rather the nation is created by the State, which gives to the people, conscious of its own moral unity, a will and therefore an effective existence. The right of a nation to independence derives not from a literary and ideal consciousness of its own being, still less from a more or less unconscious and inert acceptance of a *de facto* situation, but from an active consciousness, from a political will in action and ready to demonstrate its own rights: that is to say, from a state already coming into being. The State, in fact, as the universal ethical will, is the creator of right.

11 The nation as the State is an ethical reality which exists and lives in so far as it develops. To arrest its development is to kill it. Therefore the State is not only the authority which governs and gives the form of laws and the value of spiritual life to the wills of individuals, but it is also a power that makes its will felt abroad, making it known and respected, in other words, demonstrating the fact of its universality in all the necessary directions of its development. It is consequently organization and expansion, at least virtually. Thus it can be likened to the human will which knows no limits to its development and realizes itself in testing its own limitlessness.

12 The Fascist State, the highest and most powerful form of personality, is a force, but a spiritual force, which takes over all the forms of the moral and intellectual life of man. It cannot therefore confine itself simply to the functions of order and supervision as Liberalism desired. It is not simply a mechanism which limits the sphere of the supposed liberties of the individual. It is the form, the inner standard and the discipline of the whole person; it saturates the will as well as the intelligence. Its principle, the central inspiration of the human personality living in the civil community, pierces into the depths and makes its home in the heart of the man of action as well as of the thinker, of the artist as well as of the scientist: it is the soul of the soul.

13 Fascism, in short, is not only the giver of laws and the founder of institutions, but the educator and promoter of spiritual life. It wants to remake, not the forms of human life, but its content, man, character, faith. And to this end it requires discipline and authority that can enter into the spirits of men and there govern unopposed. Its sign, therefore, is the Lictors' rods, the symbol of unity, of strength and justice.

(ii) Political and Social Doctrine

1 When in the now distant March of 1919 I summoned to Milan, through the columns of the *Popolo d' Italia,* my surviving supporters who had followed me since the constitution of the Fasces of Revolutionary Action, founded in January 1915, there was no specific doctrinal plan in my mind. I had known and lived through only one doctrine, that of the Socialism of 1903-4 up to the winter of 1914, almost ten years. My experience in this had been that of a follower and of a leader, but not that of a theoretician. My doctrine, even in that period, had been a doctrine of action. . . .

. . . Fascism was not given out to the wet nurse of a doctrine elaborated beforehand round a table: it was born of the need for action; it was not a party, but in its first two years it was a movement against all parties. The name which I gave to the organization defined its characteristics. Nevertheless, whoever rereads, in the now crumpled pages of the time, the account of the constituent assembly of the *Fasci Italiani di Combattimento* will not find a doctrine, but a series of suggestions, of anticipations, of admonitions, which when freed from the inevitable vein of contingency, were destined later, after a few years, to develop into a series of doctrinal attitudes which made of Fascism a self-sufficient political doctrine able to face all others, both past and present. . . . I said at that time: 'We must go forward in opposition to Labor. . . . We want to accustom the working classes to being under a leader, to convince them also that it is not easy to direct an industry or a commercial undertaking successfully. . . . The successors of the present regime still being undecided, we must not be unwilling to fight for it. We must hasten; when the present regime is superseded, we must be the ones to take its place. The right of succession belongs to us because we pushed the country into the War and we lead it to victory. The present method of political representation cannot be sufficient for us, we wish for a direct representation of individual interests.'

·   ·   ·

2 The years preceding the March on Rome were years during which the necessity of action did not tolerate enquiries or complete elaborations of doctrine. Battles were being fought in the cities and villages. There were discussions, but— and this is more sacred and important—there were deaths. People knew how to die. The doctrine—beautiful, well-formed, divided into chapters and paragraphs and surrounded by a commentary—might be missing; but there was present something more decisive to supplant it—Faith. Nevertheless, he who recalls the past with the aid of books, articles, votes in Parliament, the major and the minor speeches, he who knows how to investigate and weigh evidence, will find that the foundations of the doctrine were laid while the battle was raging. It was precisely in these years that Fascist thought armed itself, refined itself, moving towards one organization of its own. The problems of the individual and the State; the problems of authority and liberty; political and social problems and those more specifically national; the struggle against liberal, democratic, socialist, Masonic, demagogic doctrines was carried on at the same time as the "punitive expeditions." But since the "system" was lacking, adversaries ingenuously denied that Fascism had any power to make a doctrine of its own, while the doctrine rose up, even though tumultuously, at first under the aspect of a violent and dogmatic negation, as happens to all ideas that break new ground, then under the positive aspect of a constructive policy which, during the years 1926, 1927, 1928, was realized in the laws and institutions of the regime.

Fascism is today clearly defined not only as a regime but as a doctrine. And I mean by this that Fascism today, self-critical as well as critical of other movements, has an unequivocal point of view of its own, a criterion, and hence an aim, in face of all the material and intellectual problems which oppress the people of the world.

3 Above all, Fascism, in so far as it considers and observes the future and the development of humanity quite apart from the political considerations of the moment, believes neither in the possibility nor in the utility of perpetual peace. It thus repudiates the doctrine of Pacifism—born of a renunciation of the struggle and an act of cowardice in the face of sacrifice. War alone brings up to their highest tension all human energies and puts the stamp of nobility upon the peoples who have the courage to meet it. All other trials are substitutes, which never really put a man in front of himself in the alternative of life and death. A doctrine, therefore, which begins with a prejudice in favor of peace is foreign to Fascism; as are foreign to the spirit of Fascism, even though acceptable by reason of the utility which they might have in given political situations, all internationalistic and socialistic systems which, as history proves, can be blown to the winds when emotional, idealistic and practical movements storm the hearts of peoples. Fascism carries over this anti-pacifist spirit even into the lives of individuals. The proud motto of the *Squadrista, "Me ne frego,"** written on the bandages of a wound is an act of philosophy which is not only stoical, it is the epitome of a doctrine that is not only political: it is education for combat, the acceptance of the risks which it brings; it is a new way of life for Italy. Thus the Fascist accepts and loves life, he knows nothing of suicide and despises it; he looks on life as duty, ascent, conquest: life which must be noble and full: lived for oneself, but above all for those others near and far away, present and future.

4 The "demographic" policy of the regime follows from these premises. Even the Fascist does in fact love his neighbor, but this "neighbor" is not for him a vague and ill-defined concept; love for one's neighbor does not exclude necessary educational severities, and still less differentiations and distances. Fascism rejects universal concord, and, since it lives in the community of civilized peoples, it keeps them vigilantly and suspiciously before its eyes, it follows their states of

---

*Loosely translated: "I don't give a damn."—*Ed.*

mind and the changes in their interests and it does not let itself be deceived by temporary and fallacious appearances.

5 Such a conception of life makes Fascism the precise negation of that doctrine which formed the basis of the so-called Scientific or Marxian Socialism: the doctrine of historical Materialism, according to which the history of human civilizations can be explained only as the struggle of interest between the different social groups and as arising out of change in the means and instruments of production. That economic improvements—discoveries of raw materials, new methods of work, scientific inventions—should have an importance of their own, no one denies, but that they should suffice to explain human history to the exclusion of all other factors is absurd: Fascism believes, now and always, in holiness and in heroism, that is in acts in which no economic motive—remote or immediate—plays a part. With this negation of historical materialism, according to which men would be only by-products of history, who appear and disappear on the surface of the waves while in the depths the real directive forces are at work, there is also denied the immutable and irreparable "class struggle" which is the natural product of this economic conception of history, and above all it is denied that the class struggle can be the primary agent of social changes. Socialism, being thus wounded in these two primary tenets of its doctrine, nothing of it is left save the sentimental aspiration—old as humanity—towards a social order in which the sufferings and the pains of the humblest folk could be alleviated. But here Fascism rejects the concept of an economic "happiness" which would be realized socialistically and almost automatically at a given moment of economic evolution by assuring to all a maximum prosperity. Fascism denies the possibility of the materialistic conception of "happiness" and leaves it to the economists of the first half of the eighteenth century; it denies, that is, the equation of prosperity with happiness, which would transform men into animals with one sole preoccupation: that of being well-fed and fat, degraded in consequence to a merely physical existence.

6 After Socialism, Fascism attacks the whole complex of democratic ideologies and rejects them both in their theoretical premises and in their applications or practical manifestations. Fascism denies that the majority, through the mere fact of being a majority, can rule human societies; it denies that this majority can govern by means of a periodical consultation; it affirms the irremediable, fruitful and beneficent inequality of men, who cannot be leveled by such a mechanical and extrinsic fact as universal suffrage. By democratic regimes we mean those in which from time to time the people is given the illusion of being sovereign, while true effective sovereignty lies in other, perhaps irresponsible and secret, forces. Democracy is a regime without a king, but with very many kings, perhaps more exclusive, tyrannical and violent than one king even though a tyrant. This explains why Fascism, although before 1922 for reasons of expediency it made a gesture of republicanism, renounced it before the March on Rome, convinced that the question of the political forms of a State is not preeminent to-day, and that studying past and present monarchies, past and present Republics it becomes clear that monarchy and republic are not to be judged *sub specie aeternitatis,* but represent forms in which the political evolution, the history, the tradition, the psychology of

a given country are manifested. Now Fascism overcomes the antithesis between monarchy and republic which retarded the movements of democracy, burdening the former with every defect and defending the latter as the regime of perfection. Now it has been seen that there are inherently reactionary and absolutistic republics, and monarchies that welcome the most daring political and social innovations.

7 "Reason, Science," said Renan (who was inspired before Fascism existed) in one of his philosophical Meditations, "are products of humanity, but to expect reason directly from the people and through the people is a chimera. It is not necessary for the existence of reason that everybody should know it. In any case, if such an initiation should be made, it would not be made by means of base democracy, which apparently must lead to the extinction of every difficult culture, and every higher discipline. The principle that society exists only for the prosperity and the liberty of the individuals who compose it does not seem to conform with the plans of nature, plans in which the species alone is taken into consideration and the individual seems to be sacrificed. It is strongly to be feared lest the last word of democracy thus understood (I hasten to say that it can also be understood in other ways) would be a social state in which a degenerate mass would have no other care than to enjoy the ignoble pleasures of vulgar men."

Thus far Renan. Fascism rejects in democracy the absurd conventional lie of political equalitarianism clothed in the dress of collective irresponsibility and the myth of happiness and indefinite progress. But if democracy can be understood in other ways, that is, if democracy means not to relegate the people to the periphery of the State, then Fascism could be defined as an "organized, centralized, authoritarian democracy."

8 In face of Liberal doctrines, Fascism takes up an attitude of absolute opposition both in the field of politics and in that of economics. . . . From 1870–1915 there occurs the period in which the very priests of the new creed had to confess the twilight of their religion: defeated as it was by decadence in literature, by activism in practice. Activism: that is to say, Nationalism, Futurism, Fascism. The "Liberal" century, after having accumulated an infinity of Gordian knots, tried to untie them by the hecatomb of the World War. Never before has any religion imposed such a cruel sacrifice. Were the gods of Liberalism thirsty for blood? Now Liberalism is about to close the doors of its deserted temples because the peoples feel that its agnosticism in economics, its indifferentism in politics and in morals, would lead, as they have led, the States to certain ruin. In this way one can understand why all the political experiences of the contemporary world are anti-Liberal, and it is supremely ridiculous to wish on that account to class them outside of history; as if history were a hunting ground reserved to Liberalism and its professors, as if Liberalism were the definitive and no longer surpassable message of civilization.

9 But the Fascist repudiations of Socialism, Democracy, Liberalism must not make one think that Fascism wishes to make the world return to what it was before 1789, the year which has been indicated as the year of the beginning of the liberal-democratic age. One does not go backwards. The Fascist doctrine has not chosen

De Maistre as its prophet. Monarchical absolutism is a thing of the past and so also is every theocracy. So also feudal privileges and division into impenetrable and isolated castes have had their day. The theory of Fascist authority has nothing to do with the police State. A party that governs a nation in a totalitarian way is a new fact in history. References and comparisons are not possible. Fascism takes over from the ruins of Liberal Socialistic democratic doctrines those elements which still have a living value. It preserves those that can be called the established facts of history, it rejects all the rest, that is to say the idea of a doctrine which holds good for all times and all peoples. If it is admitted that the nineteenth century has been the century of Socialism, Liberalism, and Democracy, it does not follow that the twentieth must also be the century of Liberalism, Socialism and Democracy. Political doctrines pass; peoples remain. It is to be expected that this century may be that of authority, a century of the "Right," a Fascist century. If the nineteenth was the century of the individual (Liberalism means individualism) it may be expected that this one may be the century of "collectivism" and therefore the century of the State. That a new doctrine should use the still vital elements of other doctrines is perfectly logical. No doctrine is born quite new, shining, never before seen. No doctrine can boast of an absolute "originality." It is bound, even if only historically, to other doctrines that have been, and to develop into other doctrines that will be. Thus the scientific socialism of Marx is bound to the Utopian Socialism of the Fouriers, the Owens and the Saint-Simons; thus the Liberalism of the nineteenth century is connected with the whole "Enlightenment" of the eighteenth century. Thus the doctrines of democracy are bound to the *Encyclopédie*. Every doctrine tends to direct the activity of men towards a determined objective; but the activity of man reacts upon the doctrine, transforms it, adapts it to new necessities or transcends it. The doctrine itself, therefore, must be, not words, but an act of life. Hence, the pragmatic veins in Fascism, its will to power, its will to be, its attitude in the face of the fact of "violence" and of its own courage.

10 The keystone of Fascist doctrine is the conception of the State, of its essence, of its tasks, of its ends. For Fascism the State is an absolute before which individuals and groups are relative. Individuals and groups are "thinkable" in so far as they are within the State. The Liberal State does not direct the interplay and the material and spiritual development of the groups, but limits itself to registering the results; the Fascist State has a consciousness of its own, a will of its own, on this account it is called an "ethical" State. In 1929, at the first quinquennial assembly of the regime, I said: "For Fascism, the State is not the night-watchman who is concerned only with the personal security of the citizens; nor is it an organization for purely material ends, such as that of guaranteeing a certain degree of prosperity and a relatively peaceful social order, to achieve which a council of administration would be sufficient, nor is it a creation of mere politics with no contact with the material and complex reality of the lives of individuals and the life of peoples. The State, as conceived by Fascism and as it acts, is a spiritual and moral fact because it makes concrete the political, juridical, economic organization of the nation and such an organization is, in its origin and in its development, a manifestation of the spirit. The State is the guarantor of internal and external security, but it is also the guardian and the transmitter of the spirit of the people as it has been elaborated through the centuries in language, custom, faith. The State is not only present, it is also past, and above all future. It is the State which, transcending the brief limit of individual lives, represents the immanent conscience of the nation. The forms in which States express themselves change, but the necessity of the State remains. It is the State which educates citizens for civic virtue, makes them conscious of their mission, calls them to unity; harmonizes their interests in justice; hands on the achievements of thought in the sciences, the arts, in law, in human solidarity; it carries men from the elementary life of the tribe to the highest human expression of power which is Empire; it entrusts to the ages the names of those who died for its integrity or in obedience to its laws; it puts forward as an example and recommends to the generations that are to come the leaders who increased its territory and the men of genius who gave it glory. When the sense of the State declines and the disintegrating and centrifugal tendencies of individuals and groups prevail, national societies move to their decline."

11 From 1929 up to the present day these doctrinal positions have been strengthened by the whole economico-political evolution of the world. It is the State alone that grows in size, in power. It is the State alone that can solve the dramatic contradictions of capitalism. What is called the crisis cannot be overcome except by the State, within the State. . . . When one says liberalism, one says the individual; when one says Fascism, one says the State. But the Fascist State is unique; it is an original creation. It is not reactionary, but revolutionary in that it anticipates the solutions of certain universal problems. These problems are no longer seen in the same light: in the sphere of politics they are removed from party rivalries, from the supreme power of parliament, from the irresponsibility of assemblies; in the sphere of economics they are removed from the sphere of the syndicates' activities—activities that were ever widening their scope and increasing their power both on the workers' side and on the employers'—removed from their struggles and their designs; in the moral sphere they are divorced from ideas of the need for order, discipline and obedience, and lifted into the plane of the moral commandments of the fatherland. Fascism desires the State to be strong, organic and at the same time founded on a wide popular basis. The Fascist State has also claimed for itself the field of economics and, through the corporative, social and educational institutions which it has created, the meaning of the State reaches out to and includes the farthest off-shoots; and within the State, framed in their respective organizations, there revolve all the political, economic and spiritual forces of the nation. A State founded on millions of individuals who recognize it, feel it, are ready to serve it, is not the tyrannical State of the medieval lord. It has nothing in common with the absolutist States that existed either before or after 1789. In the Fascist State the individual is not suppressed, but rather multiplied, just as in a regiment a soldier is not weakened but multiplied by the number of his comrades. The Fascist State organizes the nation, but it leaves sufficient scope to individuals; it has limited useless or harmful liberties and has preserved those that are essential. It cannot be the individual who decides in this matter, but only the State.

12 The Fascist State does not remain indifferent to the fact of religion in general and to that particular positive religion which is Italian Catholicism. The State has no theology, but it has an ethic. In the Fascist State religion is looked upon as one of the deepest manifestations of the spirit; it is, therefore, not only respected, but defended and protected. The Fascist State does not create a "God" of its own, as Robespierre once, at the height of the Convention's foolishness, wished to do; nor does it vainly seek, like Bolshevism, to expel religion from the minds of men; Fascism respects the God of the ascetics, of the saints, of the heroes, and also God as seen and prayed to by the simple and primitive heart of the people.

13 The Fascist State is a will to power and to government. In it the tradition of Rome is an idea that has force. In the doctrine of Fascism Empire is not only a territorial, military or mercantile expression, but spiritual or moral. One can think of an empire, that is to say a nation that directly or indirectly leads other nations, without needing to conquer a single square kilometer of territory. For Fascism the tendency to Empire, that is to say, to the expansion of nations, is a manifestation of vitality; its opposite, staying at home, is a sign of decadence: peoples who rise or rerise are imperialist, peoples who die are renunciatory. Fascism is the doctrine that is most fitted to represent the aims, the states of mind, of a people, like the Italian people, rising again after many centuries of abandonment or slavery to foreigners. But Empire calls for discipline, coordination of forces, duty and sacrifice; this explains many aspects of the practical working of the regime and the direction of many of the forces of the State and the necessary severity shown to those who would wish to oppose this spontaneous and destined impulse of the Italy of the twentieth century, to oppose it in the name of the superseded ideologies of the nineteenth, repudiated wherever great experiments of political and social transformation have been courageously attempted: especially where, as now, peoples thirst for authority, for leadership, for order. If every age has its own doctrine, it is apparent from a thousand signs that the doctrine of the present age is Fascism. That it is a doctrine of life is shown by the fact that it has resuscitated a faith. That this faith has conquered minds is proved by the fact that Fascism has had its dead and its martyrs.

Fascism henceforward has in the world the universality of all of those doctrines which, by fulfilling themselves, have significance in the history of the human spirit.

51
Giovanni Gentile

Giovanni Gentile (1875–1944) was a Neo-Hegelian philosopher and an intellectual figure of high repute in pre-fascist Italy. His organic spirit and his intense nationalism led him to join the Fascist Party, of which he became the chief theoretician. In *The Philosophic Basis of Fascism* he defends the totalitarian character of the fascist state; the authority of the State over the individual, Gentile insists, is *absolute.* "It does not compromise, it does not bargain, it does not surrender any portion of its field to other moral or religious principles." In the following passage from that work the expressly *anti-intellectual* character of fascist philosophy is also underscored.

THE PHILOSOPHIC BASIS OF FASCISM*

. . . In the definition of Fascism the first point to grasp is the comprehensive, or as Fascists say, the "totalitarian" scope of its doctrine, which concerns itself not only with political organization and political tendency, but with the whole will and thought and feeling of the nation.

There is a second and equally important point. Fascism is not a philosophy. Much less is it a religion. It is not even a political theory which may be stated in a series of formulae. The significance of Fascism is not to be grasped in the special theses which it from time to time assumes. When on occasion it has announced a program, a goal, a concept to be realized in action, Fascism has not hesitated to abandon them when in practice these were found to be inadequate or inconsistent with the principle of Fascism. Fascism has never been willing to compromise its future. Mussolini has boasted that he is a *tempista,* that his real pride is in "good timing." He makes decisions and acts on them at the precise moment when all the conditions and considerations which make them feasible and opportune are properly matured. This is a way of saying that Fascism returns to the most rigorous meaning of Mazzini's "Thought and Action," whereby the two terms are so perfectly coincident that no thought has value which is not already expressed in action. The real "views" of the *Duce* are those which he formulates and executes at one and the same time.

Is Fascism therefore "anti-intellectual," as has been so often charged? It is eminently anti-intellectual, eminently Mazzinian, that is, if by intellectualism we mean the divorce of thought from action, of knowledge from life, of brain from heart, of theory from practice. Fascism is hostile to all Utopian systems which are destined never to face the test of reality. It is hostile to all science and all philosophy which remain matters of mere fancy or intelligence. It is not that Fascism denies value to culture, to the higher intellectual pursuits by which thought is invigorated as a source of action. Fascist anti-intellectualism holds in scorn a product peculiarly typical of the educated classes in Italy: the *leterato*—the man who plays with knowledge and with thought without any sense of responsibility for the practical world. It is hostile not so much to culture as to bad culture, the culture which does not educate, which does not make men, but rather creates pedants and aesthetes, egotists in a word, men morally and politically indifferent. It has no use, for instance, for the man who is "above the conflict" when his country or its important interests are at stake.

By virtue of its repugnance for "intellectualism," Fascism prefers not to waste time constructing abstract theories about itself. But when we say that it is not a

---

*From G. Gentile, *The Philosophic Basis of Fascism,* 1928. Reprinted from *Readings on Fascism and National Socialism,* selected by members of the philosophy department of the University of Colorado, by permission of the publisher. Alan Swallow, Denver.

system or a doctrine we must not conclude that it is a blind praxis or a purely instinctive method. If by system or philosophy we mean a living thought, a principle of universal character daily revealing its inner fertility and significance, then Fascism is a perfect system, with a solidly established foundation and with a rigorous logic in its development; and all who feel the truth and the vitality of the principle work day by day for its development, now doing, now undoing, now going forward, now retracing their steps, according as the things they do prove to be in harmony with the principle or to deviate from it.

And we come finally to a third point.

The Fascist system is not a political system, but it has its center of gravity in politics. Fascism came into being to meet serious problems of politics in post-war Italy. And it presents itself as a political method. But in confronting and solving political problems it is carried by its very nature, that is to say by its method, to consider moral, religious, and philosophical questions and to unfold and demonstrate the comprehensive totalitarian character peculiar to it. It is only after we have grasped the political character of the Fascist principle that we are able adequately to appreciate the deeper concept of life which underlies that principle and from which the principle springs. The political doctrine of Fascism is not the whole of Fascism. It is rather its more prominent aspect and in general its most interesting one.

The politic of Fascism revolves wholly about the concept of the national State; and accordingly it has points of contact with nationalist doctrines, along with distinctions from the latter which it is important to bear in mind.

Both Fascism and nationalism regard the State as the foundation of all rights and the source of all values in the individuals composing it. For the one as for the other the State is not a consequence—it is a principle. But in the case of nationalism, the relation which individualistic liberalism, and for that matter socialism also, assumed between individual and State is inverted. Since the State is a principle, the individual becomes a consequence—he is something which finds an antecedent in the State: the State limits him and determines his manner of existence, restricting his freedom, binding him to a piece of ground whereon he was born, whereon he must live and will die. In the case of Fascism, State and individual are one and the same things, or rather, they are inseparable terms of a necessary synthesis.

Nationalism, in fact, founds the State on the concept of nation, the nation being an entity which transcends the will and the life of the individual because it is conceived as objectively existing apart from the consciousness of individuals, existing even if the individual does nothing to bring it into being. For the nationalist, the nation exists not by virtue of the citizen's will, but as datum, a fact, of nature.

For Fascism, on the contrary, the State is a wholly spiritual creation. It is a national State, because, from the Fascist point of view, the nation itself is a creation of the mind and is not a material presupposition, is not a datum of nature. The nation, says the Fascist, is never really made; neither, therefore, can the State attain an absolute form, since it is merely the nation in the latter's concrete, political manifestation. For the Fascist, the State is always *in fieri*. It is in our hands, wholly; whence our very serious responsibility towards it.

But this State of the Fascists which is created by the consciousness and the will of the citizen, and is not a force descending on the citizen from above or from without, cannot have toward the mass of the population the relationship which was presumed by nationalism.

Nationalism identified State with Nation, and made of the nation an entity preëxisting, which needed not to be created but merely to be recognized or known. The nationalists, therefore, required a ruling class of an intellectual character, which was conscious of the nation and could understand, appreciate and exalt it. The authority of the State, furthermore, was not a product but a presupposition. It could not depend on the people—rather the people depended on the State and on the State's authority as the source of the life which they lived and apart from which they could not live. The nationalistic State was, therefore, an aristocratic State, enforcing itself upon the masses through the power conferred upon it by its origins.

The Fascist State, on the contrary, is a people's state, and, as such, the democratic State *par excellence.* The relationship between State and citizen (not this or that citizen, but all citizens) is accordingly so intimate that the State exists only as, and in so far as, the citizen causes it to exist. Its formation therefore is the formation of a consciousness of it in individuals, in the masses. Hence the need of the Party, and of all the instruments of propaganda and education which Fascism uses to make the thought and will of the *Duce* the thought and will of the masses. Hence the enormous task which Fascism sets itself in trying to bring the whole mass of the people, beginning with the little children, inside the fold of the Party.

On the popular character of the Fascist State likewise depends its greatest social and constitutional reform—the foundation of the Corporations of Syndicates. In this reform Fascism took over from syndicalism the notion of the moral and educational function of the syndicate. But the Corporations of Syndicates were necessary in order to reduce the syndicates to State discipline and make them an expression of the State's organism from within. The Corporations of Syndicates are a device through which the Fascist State goes looking for the individual in order to create itself through the individual's will. But the individual it seeks is not the abstract political individual whom the old liberalism took for granted. He is the only individual who can ever be found, the individual who exists as a specialized productive force, and who, by the fact of his specialization, is brought to unite with other individuals of his same category and comes to belong with them to the one great economic unit which is none other than the nation.

This great reform is already well under way. Toward it nationalism, syndicalism, and even liberalism itself, were already tending in the past. For even liberalism was beginning to criticize the older forms of political representation, seeking some system of organic representation which would correspond to the structural reality of the State.

The Fascist conception of liberty merits passing notice. The *Duce* of Fascism once chose to discuss the theme of "Force or consent?"; and he concluded that the two terms are inseparable, that the one implies the other and cannot exist apart from the other; that, in other words, the authority of the State and the freedom of the citizen constitute a continuous circle wherein authority presupposes liberty and liberty authority. For freedom can exist only within the State, and the State means authority. But the State is not an entity hovering in the air over the heads of its citizens. It is one with the personality of the citizen. Fascism, indeed, envisages the contrast not as between liberty and authority, but as between a true, a concrete liberty which exists, and an abstract, illusory liberty which cannot exist.

Liberalism broke the circle above referred to, setting the individual against the State and liberty against authority. What the liberal desired was liberty as against the State, a liberty which was a limitation of the State; though the liberal had to resign himself, as the lesser of the evils, to a State which was a limitation on liberty. The absurdities inherent in the liberal concept of freedom were apparent to liberals themselves early in the Nineteenth Century. It is no merit of Fascism to have again indicated them. Fascism has its own solution of the paradox of liberty and authority. The authority of the State is absolute. It does not compromise, it does not bargain, it does not surrender any portion of its field to other moral or religious principles which may interfere with the individual conscience. But on the other hand, the State becomes a reality only in the consciousness of its individuals. And the Fascist corporative State supplies a representative system more sincere and more in touch with realities than any other previously devised and is therefore freer than the old liberal State.

52
Mario Palmieri

The "corporative state" was one element of fascist philosophy that was not simply borrowed from earlier thinkers. Its practicality was never fully tested, but the fascists envisaged an economy controlled and managed by the state, one in which all class conflict would be eliminated and all private exploitation forbidden. Palmieri, in *The Philosophy of Fascism,* argues that fascism explicitly rejects both communism and capitalism in favor of this "corporative idea." He expands also on other aspects of fascism not thoroughly dealt with in the speeches and essays of Fascist Party leaders—notably the revival of values and principles absorbed by fascism from the traditions of imperial Rome.

FASCISM AND THE MEANING OF LIFE*

We must never forget that other civilizations of far greater significance than ours from the standpoint of spiritual achievements—the only true standard of comparison possible—have appeared on this earth, flowered forth in magnificent products of spiritual expression and disappeared again, engulfed in the shadows of oblivion and covered by few layers of sand or by the triumphant vegetation of the earth.

*From M. Palmieri, *The Philosophy of Fascism,* 1936.

A new dark age is still possible, and it will dawn upon us soon enough unless we find again a meaning for life, a different purpose than the satisfaction of the senses, and, finally, a new goal for our efforts, nowadays so implacably frustrated by the emptiness, the vacuity, and the futility of the goal which we try so desperately and still so vainly to reach.

It is the possibility of such a Dark Age which Fascism is trying strenuously and successfully to stave off by teaching us anew the truth that we need to visualize and to worship a deeper reality lying behind and beyond the immediate and closely bound world of the self, if we want to find peace, achieve salvation and restore dignity and purpose to our life.

At this extremely critical time of our history, when the fate of a whole civilization is at stake, Fascism takes up once again the challenging and to the perplexing, ages-old query, it answers emphatically that life *has* a meaning, that it has a purpose and a goal, and that it has worth and dignity and beauty.

When we shall become aware that our individuality is truly and fully realized in those institutions and through those institutions called the Family, the Church, the Nation, and the State, then and only then, we shall realize the great significance and the deep import of the Fascist philosophy of life.

Fascism maintains in effect that the meaning of life is found only in the realization of a full life of the Spirit; that this realization in turn is achieved only when the individual's spiritual needs, aspirations and longings are rooted, integrated and nurtured in the Family, the Church, the Nation and the State; that these institutions, forming the framework of all life of the Spirit, enjoy in turn an existence of their own: timeless and absolute, whose essence partakes of the Spirit itself and is not contingent upon the Will and the actions of man.

In the Fascist philosophy of life Man first rises to the capacity of a true spiritual being when in the Family he finds something in which and through which he can express and realize his first spiritual needs—then in the Church, an institution which offers him a new outlet for those spiritual needs not satisfied by the Family. Next, in the Nation, he finds something which expresses the fundamental continuity of his human experience within determinate limits of space, and the fundamental unity which is at the very root of life. Finally, in the State he finds an organism which gives ample scope to the expression of his spiritual life, an organism born of the conscious act of restricting, of his own free will, the full play of his activity and the full extent of his freedom; to allow his own rights, his own liberties, his own opportunities, to those fellow beings bound by the same laws, the same duties, the same authority.

The Family, the Church, the Nation, the State, these are the four cardinal points of the life of man; through them this life can flower forth in an expression of great spiritual achievement; denying them it can only revert to a state of satisfied animal wants unworthy of the name of human. . . .

In conclusion, if man, to achieve salvation, must be led anew to visualize and worship a deeper reality than the immediate and closely bound world of the self, there is one way, and one way only to lead him to the goal, says Fascism, and that way is through the renewed cult of the Family, the Church, the Nation and the State.

This cult will give anew a meaning to life; with this cult life will again find a purpose; through this cult life will finally reach its far off, magnificent goal which is nothing less than the spiritualization of man.

FASCISM AND THE CONDUCT OF LIFE

The conduct of life must rest upon three great, unalterable principles—Fascism maintains—namely: the principle of Unity, the principle of Authority and the principle of Duty.

> One invisible tie binds together the destinies of all the people of one nation. There cannot be any joy or any pain experienced by one single individual, any good or any evil befallen to him which shall not ultimately affect the welfare of the whole nation.

This is the first principle of the Fascist conduct of life, and one whose consequences prove to be the most far-reaching in the life of a nation.

If we have found always, says Fascism, such shifting grounds for the foundations of a durable and satisfactory social life, it is simply because we have forgotten that the good of the whole cannot be dependent upon the material welfare of the individual, that the very life of the individual is dependent upon and is part of the life of an entity much greater and of far deeper meaning than his small ego, namely, the nation of which he is an integral part and which constitutes for him the supreme essence of the race.

Never before, to be sure, had a social and political system advanced such claims upon the inner world of man as this claim of Fascism to determine for him the forms of conduct; never before has that regeneration of social and political life, always dreamed, never effectuated, been so close to realization.

The first principle of the Fascist conduct of life rests upon a mystic belief of the oneness of all living beings; the second principle, the principle of Authority, rests upon another mystic belief: that of the divine essence of the hero. Not the military hero, but hero in the sense meant by Carlyle: hero of the soul.

> Find in any country the ablest man that exists there, raise him to the supreme place and loyalty, reverence him, you have a perfect government for that country; no ballot box, parliamentary eloquence, voting, constitution building or other machinery whatsoever can improve it a whit. It is the perfect State, the ideal Country.

Thus spoke Carlyle in his lecture on the hero as king, delivered the twenty-second of May, 1840. And his words are no less true today than they were a hundred years ago. Nay, still closer to the truth, if that could be possible, and true in a still deeper sense than Carlyle ever thought. Because the ultimate reality of the Universe which lies behind and beyond the deceiving realm of appearances, does not reveal itself indiscriminately and equally to all men.

There is Man in the abstract as a thinking and spiritual being; there are men in the concrete gifted in various degrees with the gifts of these divine elements of thought and soul.

We are all partakers of the divine, but the hero among us is partaker of it in a fuller measure than all. He is in a more direct, more immediate relationship with the fountain-head of all knowledge, all wisdom, all love. What he sees in life we do not see, and it is even useless for us to strive toward a better comprehension of life, a better understanding of nature, because we shall never be able to render asunder the veil of mystery shrouding the ultimate aspect of reality.

Vainly we strive through observation, experimentation, analysis, logic, to reach the core of being. The highest truths are hidden from us. Only that magic flash of a moment of supreme intuition, that flash which renders for an instant man akin to God, can reveal the Truth. And we shall never know the ecstasy of that moment. The supreme gifts of synthesis, intuition, revelation, are denied to us; they belong rightly to the hero and to none other.

And if there is no hero in a country, darkness is upon the land; the darkness originating from the confusion of conflicting ideas, conflicting beliefs, conflicting wills.

It can be realized then at once how utterly impossible it is to conciliate such an article of faith with a naive belief in the wisdom of the mass, the leadership of the many, the supreme worth of Democracy.

The day may come, perhaps, and we all sincerely hope and pray for it, when all men will be heroes, but at the present stage of human evolution, let only the greatest among the great rule and govern, because he sees deeper and further than we shall ever be able to see, because he knows what we shall never be able to know, because he is a gift from God.

But if the principle of Authority recognizes that ultimately there must be a supreme power, it is, nevertheless, not completely exhausted by this recognition. Fascism holds, in fact, that the State must be a social, political, economic, moral and religious organism built as a pyramid at whose vertex is the national hero, the greatest man of his time and his nation, and leading to this national hero by an uninterrupted series of continuously widening powers arranged in hierarchies.

The hierarchy becomes thus the very essence of Authority and the hierarchical arrangement of Society its truest expression in the world of man.

All the recognition of a man's worth is expressed in the place he occupies in the hierarchy; all the functions of a man's social and political life are contained in the functions he must fulfill as a member of the hierarchy.

No man is an outcast in the social system of Fascism, no man is worthless; no man, that is, who belongs to the Fascist nation and to its life.

It is, therefore, not the smallest title of glory of Fascism to have brought about this new realization of the fellowship of man at a time held, by common consent, to be a time of supreme and inevitable moral decadence.

But these two great principles of the unity of all human beings and of devotion to authority as expressed through a scale of human values, cannot be separated— Fascism holds—from the third and greatest principle of all: the principle of Duty.

And it is, perhaps, in this conception of duty as supreme motive power of the actions of man, and in the belief that such a conception can be transformed into living reality, that Fascism reveals most clearly the profound idealism underlying its philosophy.

. . .

Life thus, as conceived by Fascism is "serious, austere, religious, and its development takes place in a world sustained by the moral and responsible forces of the spirit."

This means, in turn, that to be a Fascist is, of all things, the most difficult in the world. He who subscribes to the doctrine of Fascism subscribes also to rules of conduct which make exacting claims upon his will to live a satisfactory sensual life. The life of the Fascist is a life of ascetic self-denial, heroic self-sacrifice, moral abnegation and religious enthusiasm.

The true Fascist works not for himself alone, but for his nation as well; believes not in a godless Universe, but in a universe which exists by the will of God; worships this God not as a remote, abstract entity having no intimate connection with his individual life, but as something from which he parted at birth, to which he can confidently appeal in life and which he shall rejoin at death; the true Fascist forsakes the realization of his rights for the fulfillment of his duties; strives to make of love an expression of the soul rather than an enjoyment of the senses; holds the unity of the family to be a sacred thing and monogamic marriage to be the supreme test and the true end of love; respects that hierarchical arrangement of society which, through successive stages, confers the primary Authority of divine origin to men invested with power to rule over their fellow beings; is willing to sacrifice his personal pleasure for the welfare of his brethren, willing to suffer for the welfare of his family, willing to die for the welfare of his country and, finally, the true Fascist is willing to forego all claims to personal freedom if these claims conflict with the realization of the true goal of life: the spiritualization of man.

THE CORPORATIVE IDEA

Fascism, which is the very antithesis of Individualism, stands as the nemesis of all economic doctrines and all economic practice of both the capitalistic and the communistic systems. Fascism holds that:

1 The economic life of man cannot be abstracted and separated from the whole of his spiritual life. In the words of Mussolini: "The economic man does not exist. Man is integral; he is political, economic, religious, saint and warrior at the same time."

2 The economic life of man is influenced, if not actually determined, by idealistic factors.

3 True economic progress can derive only from the concerted effort of individuals who know how to sacrifice their personal egoism and ambitions for the good of the whole.

4 Economic initiatives cannot be left to the arbitrary decisions of private, individual interests.

5 Open competition, if not wisely directed and restricted, actually destroys wealth instead of creating it.

6 The wealth of a community is something intangible which cannot be identified with the sum of riches of single individuals.

7 The proper function of the State in the Fascist system is that of supervising, regulating and arbitrating the relationships of capital and labor, employers and employees, individuals and associations, private interests and national interests.

8 Class war is avoidable and must be avoided. Class war is deleterious to the orderly and fruitful life of the nation, therefore it has no place in the Fascist State.

9 More important than the production of wealth is its right distribution, distribution which must benefit in the best possible way all the classes of the nation, hence, the nation itself.

10 Private wealth belongs not only to the individual, but, in a symbolic sense, to the State as well.

These fundamental tenets of Fascist economy derive in turn from those basic conceptions of the Fascist doctrine of the State which we have expounded in the chapter of the "Fascist State." We have said there, in fact, that the Fascist State is a Sovereign State. This means that there cannot be any single economic interests which are above the general economic interests of the State, no individual, economic initiatives which do not fall under the supervision and regulation of the State, no relationships of the various classes of the nation which are not the concern of the State.

Furthermore, the Fascist State is an Ethical State. This means that all the factors influencing the life of a nation: the economic, the social, the political, etc., are brought into the Fascist State under the dominion of the moral law, which becomes not only the supreme law of the individual, but the supreme law of the State as well.

"One invisible tie binds together all the people of a nation. There cannot be any joy or any pain experienced by one single individual which shall not ultimately affect the welfare of the whole nation."

This is the principle of Fascist Ethics which, translated and applied to the realm of Economics, has transformed the economic organization of the State.

If it is true that one invisible tie binds together the destinies of all the people of one nation, then it is also true that the terms wealthy and pauper, capitalist and worker, landowner and farmer, employer and employee, lose their antagonistic meaning altogether and remain to signify brethren in spirit if not in flesh, engaged from different angles, on different planes, in the arduous task of building up a nation's life.

We see thus the Fascist State resolutely enter the economic field to dictate what shall be from now on the relationship between capital and labor, employer and employee, landowner and farmhand, industrialist and worker. . . .

By delimiting thus the field of action of capital and labor, by harmonizing production and distribution to the actual needs of the nation, the legislation of Fascism has accomplished in the realm of Economics what no legislation of any other political system has ever been able to accomplish; namely, a co-ordination of all the economic forces of the nation so that the material life of the people may be free of struggles, strikes, unemployment, class war, concentrated wealth and widespread misery.

To bring about such a magic transformation of the economic life of the nation, Fascism has made use of the most characteristic phenomenon of the modern era: the syndicalist phenomenon. Originated as an instrument of the war of classes, syndicalism attempted to organize the various categories of workers in syndical organizations having no other goal than the protection of the material welfare of their own members. These organizations were devoted thus to the furthering of supremely particularized interests, ready to set themselves against each other and against the State itself, whenever those interests were menaced or conflicted with others.

The problem which presented itself as an ominous menace upon the horizon of Fascism at the outset of its very life in Italy was, therefore, to bring at once the phenomenon of syndicalism under the authority of the State, and, successively, to transform its original aim of protecting the interests of the proletariat into protecting the interests of the whole nation.

This could be accomplished only by enlarging the narrow form of the original syndicalist organizations into larger forms which would include all the citizens of the nation into an all-comprehensive national manifestation. This manifestation of the Italians of all classes, all professions, all trades and all creeds into the framework of one enormous and far-reaching organization, which has for its end the material welfare of the whole, is called National Syndicalism.

This National Syndicalism represents the first attempt made to bring the egotistic claims of the individual under the discipline of the Sovereign State; for the realization of an aim which transcends the welfare of the individual and identifies itself with the prosperity of the whole nation.

To make this discipline possible, and the sovereignty effective in practice as well as in theory, Fascism has devised the "Corporazione," an instrument of social life destined to exercise the most far-reaching influence upon the economic development of Fascist States. (The Italian word "Corporazione" which is currently translated into English by the apparently analogous word "Corporation," means, more exactly in the Italian language, what the word "Guild" means in English; that is: associations of persons engaged in kindred pursuits. We shall nevertheless follow the general usage to obviate the danger of misunderstandings.)

Within the Corporations the interests of producers and consumers, employers and employees, individuals and associations are interlocked and integrated in a unique and univocal way, while all types of interests are brought under the aegis of the State.

Finally, through these corporations the State may at any time that it deems fit, or that the need requires, intervene within the economic life of the individual to let the supreme interests of the nation have precedence over his private, particular interests, even to the point where his work, his savings, his whole fortune may need to be pledged, and if absolutely necessary, sacrificed. . . .

The corporative principle which is essentially an anti-individualistic principle, becomes thus the true foundation of the anti-individualistic Fascist State.

That organization to which it gives origin in the field of economics, finds its counterpart in the political field where it gives birth to a new and entirely original social formation.

This is possible because the corporative principle is, in the words of Bottai:

> . . . a principal of political-juridical organization, and at the same time, a principle of social life. To give value and to organize the economic categories, to set them in a certain form of hierarchy at whose vertex is the national interest, means, at the same time, to devise not only the special organs which must realize them, but to devise a whole series or principles of subordination of two kinds: political, that is of interests and facts; juridical, that is of rights and laws. And, inasmuch as the parties of the social relationship are always two: the individual and the commonwealth; and, inasmuch as every political or juridical organization is at bottom only a system of relationships among the various individuals and between the single individual and society, it follows that the corporative principle is a principle of complex and progressive subordination of the individual's economic interests to the greater interests of the various economic categories and the general all-comprehensive national economy.

Whoever thinks of Fascist Economy must think of it, therefore, as of something more than a new form of Economics, because it is first of all, and above all, a translation of Ethics into Economics, an application of Ethical principles to economic facts.

THE LEGACY OF ROME

The historical continuity of political forms, social organization, religious expression and spiritual aspirations, in the life of the Italian people, which had lasted two thousand years and had been broken only in the last few centuries of servitude to foreigners and their foreign ways of living, has been at last restored by Fascism, which is the direct heir of Roman traditions and of Roman ideals.

Fascism means, in fact, the return to Order, to Authority, to Law; the return to the Roman conception of human Society, conception which those centuries of oblivion could obscure but never efface.

Fascism is, in other words, intimately connected to Rome; its mission is the continuation of the mission of Rome; its heritage is the legacy of Rome.

There are some things Rome symbolized in the golden age of its glory which were and still are of supreme significance to mankind; things of the spirit of an eternal and absolute value which Fascism wants restored to their rightful supremacy. . . .

Empire, in the generally accepted meaning, is a political organization whose foundation is always a territorial extension. Empire, in the Fascist meaning of the word denotes, instead, that unification of peoples and nations brought about by the triumph of a universal idea. Hence, the seat of Empire is necessarily there where the realization of this universal idea takes place.

It is not incomprehensible, thus, that Rome has been twice the seat of Empire, and that she has been chosen again by destiny to fill such a role for the third successive time in the twenty-eighth century of her fateful history.

Twice in the past, from Rome, a Universal Idea has sent a message of harmony and unity to divided, warring and ailing mankind. Twice have the seven hills of Rome seen the triumph of this Idea bring about in their midst the realization of Empire.

The triumph of the Idea of Order, of Authority, of equal Justice under Law, saw the Empire of Augustus and of Trajanus give to mankind for the first and only time in human history the life-enhancing blessing of political unity.

The triumph of the Catholic Idea of salvation in Christ and through Christ and His Church, saw the Empire of the Church give to mankind the life-inspiring blessing of spiritual unity.

The triumph of the Fascist Idea of subjection of all individual life to the life of the Whole will see a new Empire rise on the seven hills of Rome, an empire founded not necessarily upon territorial possessions and political conquests, but primarily upon the generalized belief that Fascism may finally furnish man with the long sought solution of the riddle of life.

A spiritual power generated from those great Italian spirits who have been in the past the assertors of Rome's immortal and eternal right to Empire, and the prophets of Rome's third form of Empire, is the leaven which has brought about that fermentation of spiritual forces called Fascism. . . .

"Del Primato morale e civile degli Italiani" ("On the Moral and Civil Primacy of the Italian People")* is one of those books which leave an indelible mark upon the soul of a nation.

But to call the Primato a book is not quite correct, because it is something more than a mere book; it is a message; it is a call and a prophecy. Nowhere else have the claims of Italy and of the Italians to supreme primacy in the moral and social realms—apart from the "De Monarchia" of Dante, which establishes and supports these claims in the political field—found such forceful and thorough expression as in the two large volumes of the Primato.

The main thesis of the Primato is that modern Civilization is built and must rest upon the foundations laid by Christianity and that the true expression of Christianity is found only in Catholicism.

European Civilization must be re-established a second time by recalling it to its Christian and Catholic origins and extinguishing the heterodoxy which for two centuries reigned in all its parts. . . .

When a civilization is to be rebuilt, a moral center of action must be established where the source of motion may reside and whence the movement may be spread to all its parts as from the center to the circumference.

History teaches that every civilization has its special seat in one country or city as its base, which becomes morally the capital of the civilized world.

The center of the civilizing process is where the center of Catholicism is. . . . Now, since Italy is center of the latter, it follows that Italy is the true head of civilization and Rome the ideal metropolis of the world.

*By Vincenzo Gioberti, 1845.—*Ed.*

Providence chose the Italian land for this high destiny, nourishing a spark of divine truth in it "ab antico" and molding there a race wonderfully adapted in genius and intelligence for subjecting the whole world in Christian obedience. . . . Italy is the priestly nation among the great body of redeemed peoples. . . . Nor did the inhabitants of this peninsula give to other peoples merely divine gifts, but also every other civil and human good, and all the great intellects of Europe, who enhanced in any measure the glory of their countries, lit their lamps at the living flame of Italian genius.

Words like these are words of fire, and very little wonder is left, after reading them, at the vision of Italy dreaming once more dreams of glory, dreams of greatness, dreams of empire. . . .

THE HERO AS LEADER

The age of hero-worship appears to us most strange and remote, indeed; the very possibility of a hero appearing in our midst is denied with a vehemence and a finality which reveal our incapacity to understand the true essence of heroism; everything points, in other words, to the low state to which has fallen the cult and the practice of the heroic in man.

But if the age of hero-worship is past forever, it is not true that heroes may not appear in our midst.

What is a hero, the Carlylean hero?

A hero is he who can pierce with the mystic light of an inner vision to the very heart of things; he who can re-discover the greatest and most profound of all truths: viz., that beyond his realm of fugitive appearances there lies, immutable and eternal, what Fichte called the "Divine Idea of the World"; finally, he who, living already in spirit in this realm of timeless and absolute Reality, is able to translate his vision into deeds and to act according to the dictates of an inner voice telling him that ". . . they wrong man greatly who say he is to be seduced by ease. Difficulty, abnegation, martyrdom, death are the allurements that act on the heart of man."

As a god or a prophet, as a saint or a warrior, as a poet or a king; under whatever aspect they might have appeared on this earth, all heroes have always delivered and, for that matter, will ever deliver, the same message to mankind: viz., that man lives a true human life only when his life is devoted to and, if necessary, sacrificed for the triumph of an ideal and that only by living such a life can he ever find happiness on this earth.

And because every age brings forth its own type of hero, the hero as Leader; the new type of hero born of the need of the times, answering the call of history, in delivering anew such a message—a message of hope and trust, of faith and revolt, of abnegation and assertion at the same time—must deliver it not in the form of revealed religion, not in the form of a God-inspired book, of a prophecy, or of a poem encompassing earth and heaven, but in the form of a new way of life: a way of life capable of leading man out of his present unhappy, miserable state.

The hero as Leader!

To acknowledge that a man in our midst, a man of flesh and bone, with our vices and our virtues, with our strength and our weaknesses, with our aspirations and our dreams, is truly a hero: the hero as Leader, we must ask of him first of all, and above all, that through his speech, his actions, his influence, his example, his whole life, in short, he live the very message he is delivering to us.

But this is not sufficient; we want to be certain that he is not a quack, a charlatan or an impostor, but a true and sincere man. Sincerity of purpose, that magic touchstone which serves so well to distinguish the gold from the dross in the actions of men—is what we expect to find in the man to be recognized as hero.

And yet, sincerity, however admirable it may be, by itself achieves nothing everlasting if it is not accompanied by courage. Nothing great, nothing of any value, of any meaning whatsoever can ever be accomplished in this world of ours, if all fear of the known and unknown hostile, belittling or derisive forces is not banished from the heart and the mind of man.

Finally, sincerity and courage must be accompanied by belief, belief in one's own destiny, belief in the role which one is destined to play on the stage of life, belief in one's own powers if the world is to be actually and effectively changed through one's own efforts.

Underlying this magic trinity of sincerity, courage and faith, there must always exist within the soul's deepest recesses a mystic power of immediate knowledge of the truth through the supreme gift of intuition, if the action of a man must share the finality of an act of God.

Once we find all these qualities within the soul of one man, once we discover that they not only exist there, but have taken complete possession of his inner life, blotting out—so to speak—any other virtue, any other vice, then we may rest assured that we have found a man entitled to our admiration, a true hero worthy of inclusion within the sacred cohort of the Carlylean heroes.

But our skeptical brethren—little men without vision, without faith, without belief—ask for pragmatic proof of his right to our admiration, if not to our worship. Such proof is evidently not needed by those who can recognize the hero when they see him, but is sorely needed by those unaware of the bread they eat but blind to the reality of the unseen.

To this category of people, condemned by a mean fate to the worst form of necessity of all, it will be necessary to furnish explanations, it will be necessary to ask them whether an imposter, a quack, a false man could ever bring about the unification of a nation, the resurrection of an empire, the redemption of a land, the regeneration of the moral conscience of a people. What impostor, what quack, what false man has ever accomplished that before? By what miracle of ingenuity, cunning or malice, has he ever been able to fool all the people all of the time? And is that ever possible?

If what was accomplished once is guaranty of what can be accomplished now, if the past is forerunner of the present, if it is true that *"Historia magistra vitae,"* we are forced to acknowledge then that there is here among us on this earth a man marked by Destiny to say a new word to mankind. His words, his deeds, his thoughts, the whole life of this man is a living lesson of heroism for all those timid souls who believe that there is no greater thing on earth than to be satisfied with a routine, commonplace existence.

How deeply, movingly pathetic beyond words it is to see this man, burning with the great flame that he has carried and still carries, deep within; seek here and there and everywhere a refuge, and with the refuge a piece of bread, and with the piece of bread the means to bring forth that inner flame burning deep, deep within. How inspiring to see him follow the call of destiny without being aware of exactly what destiny expected from him; only dimly perceiving in a blurred vision the image of some great thing shaping itself in the mist, and calling to him, leading him, drawing him toward an unknown and perhaps dangerous goal. . . .

But the hour of destiny is calling. Is there no hope left for Italy? Must Italy renounce forever her glorious past? Must she resign herself to a minor role in world history? Is there no significance in all that which forms the substance of the Idea of a nation, the Italian nation? . . .

Questions like these must have agitated the mind and the heart of that man when the hour of destiny struck its call.

But the mist enveloping the vision haunting his dreams since the early days of his youth is finally lifting, the contours of this vision become finally sharp, clear and distinct. . . . What do they reveal to the inner eye of the seer? They reveal the image of the great mother Italy sunk in the mire, seeking light, pleading for help.

It was then that a true, complete revolution of all thoughts, all feelings, all sensations, took the soul of that man by storm and forced him to examine critically his whole past, revise all his beliefs, fashion for himself a new creed, find within himself the capacity to utter a new word, the *word* that a whole people, a whole continent, the whole western civilization was in need to hear and was waiting to hear.

He had then the intuition that something of tremendous import for mankind was at stake, hung precariously on the decision of his life course; he had the revelation that an issue of far-reaching consequence for the future of mankind had to be settled then. It was a question whether, faced by the decay of the liberal-democratic-capitalistic-materialistic organization of society, man had to embrace communism and abjection or choose another way of life in tune with his soul's aspirations, if not with his animal nature's wants.

It was thus that the dumb, inchoate historical forces which shape the destinies of man found suddenly a voice; it was thus that centuries of thought and action were brought suddenly to a climax by such a voice; it was thus that the people themselves acquired suddenly the voice they so earnestly and yet so vainly had sought; because if Fascism is a creature of the man Benito Mussolini, yet, in truth, it belongs to western civilization itself.

The man was simply the mouthpiece chosen by destiny to utter what needed to be uttered at a crucial time of human history; what he said all people were longing to say; what he did many people, perhaps, were trying to do.

He actually expressed in words what remained unexpressed in the inmost heart of the people; he only translated into action what lay dormant in a potential state within the very nature of the people.

Alone, he could achieve nothing. As a leader he could change, and is changing the aspect of the world. . . .

53
The National Fascist Party
and
The Charter of Labor

The philosophy of fascism was embodied in the laws and principles of the Italian government under Benito Mussolini. The preamble to a 1929 statute of that government made very clear the place of the National Fascist Party in Italian society; that preamble is the first of the two short selections below. The second selection is from what was called *The Charter of Labor;* this was not a legislative act but was established and promulgated by the Fascist Grand Council in 1927, and it came to be regarded as the organic law of the Italian nation.

[THE NATIONAL FASCIST PARTY]*

The National Fascist Party is a civil militia for the service of the nation. Its objective: to realize the greatness of the Italian people. From its beginnings, which are indistinguishable from the renaissance of the Italian conscience and the will to victory, until now, the party has always thought of itself as in a state of war, at first in order to combat those who were stifling the will of the nation, today and from henceforth to defend and increase the power of the Italian people. Fascism is not merely an Italian organization connected with a program partly realized and partly still to be realized; it is above all a faith which has had its confessors, and under the impulse of which the new Italians work as soldiers, pledged to achieve victory in the struggle between the nation and its enemies. The Party is an essential part of this new organization, and its function is fundamental and indispensable to the vitality of the regime. In the hour of vigil, its organization was fixed according to the necessities of battle, and the people recognized the Duce by the marks of his will, his strength and his achievements. In that heat of the struggle, action took precedence of law. Every stage was marked by a conquest, and the assemblies were only gatherings of officers and men dominated by the memory of the dead. Without dogmatic formulas or rigid projects, Fascism knows that victory lies in the possibility of its own continuous renewal. Fascism lives today in terms of the future, and regards the new generations as forces destined to achieve the ends appointed by our will. Without order and hierarchy, there can be neither discipline nor effort nor education of the people, which must receive light and guidance from that high place where is to be found the complete vision of rewards, tasks, functions and merits, and where the only guidance is in the general interest.

*The Preamble to the Statute of 20 December 1929. Reprinted from The Political and Social Doctrines of Contemporary Europe, 1939, edited by Michael Oakeshott, by permission of the Cambridge University Press.

THE CHARTER OF LABOR*

I The Italian nation is an organic whole having life, purposes and means of action superior in power and duration to those of the individuals, single or associated, of which it is composed. It is a moral, political and economic unity, which is realized integrally in the Fascist State.

II Work in all its forms—intellectual, technical or manual—whether organization or execution—is a social duty. And for this reason only it is regulated by the State. The process of production, from the national point of view, is a single whole, its aims are united and identified with the well-being of the producers and the promotion of national power.

III Occupational or syndical organization is free; but only the juridically recognized syndicate which submits to the control of State has the right to represent legally the entire category of employers or workers for which it is constituted, in safeguarding its interests vis-à-vis the State and other occupational associations, in making collective contracts of work binding on all the members of the category, in levying contributions and exercising over its members functions delegated to it in the public interest.

IV In the collective contract of work the solidarity of the various factors of production finds its concrete expression in the reconciliation of the conflicting interests of employers and employees and in their subordination to the superior interests of production. . . .

54
The Fascist Decalogue

"The Ten Commandments" of the Italian soldier under Mussolini exhibit the essence of the philosophy of fascism in short compass. There were two versions of these ten commandments; together they illustrate how a political philosophy may be used to direct and control the conduct of individual citizens.

THE FASCIST DECALOGUE†

(i)

1 Know that the Fascist and in particular the soldier, must not believe in perpetual peace.

2 Days of imprisonment are always deserved.

---

*From *The Charter of Labor,* 1927. Reprinted from *The Political and Social Doctrines of Contemporary Europe,* 1939, edited by Michael Oakeshott, by permission of the Cambridge University Press.

†Reprinted from *The Political and Social Doctrines of Contemporary Europe,* 1939, edited by Michael Oakeshott, by permission of the Cambridge University Press.

3 The nation serves as a sentinel even over a can of petrol.

4 A companion must be a brother, first, because he lives with you, and secondly because he thinks like you.

5 The rifle and cartridge belt, and the rest, are confided to you not to rust in leisure, but to be preserved in war.

6 Do not ever say "The Government will pay . . ." because it is *you* who pay; and the Government is that which you willed to have, and for which you put on a uniform.

7 Discipline is the soul of armies; without it there are no soldiers, only confusion and defeat.

8 Mussolini is always right.

9 For a volunteer there are no extenuating circumstances when he is disobedient.

10 One thing must be dear to you above all: the life of the Duce.

1934

(ii)

1 Remember that those who fell for the revolution and for the empire march at the head of your columns.

2 Your comrade is your brother. He lives with you, thinks with you, and is at your side in the battle.

3 Service to Italy can be rendered at all times, in all places, and by every means. It can be paid with toil and also with blood.

4 The enemy of Fascism is your enemy. Give him no quarter.

5 Discipline is the sunshine of armies. It prepares and illuminates the victory.

6 He who advances to the attack with decision has victory already in his grasp.

7 Conscious and complete obedience is the virtue of the Legionary.

8 There do not exist things important and things unimportant. There is only duty.

9 The Fascist revolution has depended in the past and still depends on the bayonets of its Legionaries.

10 Mussolini is always right.*

1938

---

*This slogan appeared ubiquitously in the classrooms of Italian schools, during the days of the Fascist regime, under a portrait of the *Duce*, Benito Mussolini.—*Ed.*

5

FASCIST PHILOSOPHY IN GERMANY

The roots of fascism lay in German philosophy and, in Germany, fascism was culminated. The rule of the National Socialist (Nazi) Party from 1921 to 1945, with Adolph Hitler as absolute dictator, *Führer,* was the fruit of this political movement—a period of ruthless cruelty and genocidal slaughter.

The philosophical principles of fascism that had been laid down in Italy were not much enhanced by the Nazis, but German fascists did exercise totalitarian authority more rigorously, and they developed more effectively than their Italian allies a national spirit that was deliberately and thoroughly irrational. This fanatical irrationality helps to account for the pervasive racism of Nazi leaders, their inhuman persecution of minorities of every kind, and their glorification of armies and of brute force. Aggressive and irrational nationalism under the Nazis led directly to catastrophic world war, and eventually to the total defeat of fascism in Europe.

German and Italian fascists differed in some respects. To justify Italian imperialism in Africa, Mussolini had argued that the state is fundamental and creates the nation. But Hitler, to justify his absorption of Austria and his aggressive claims on German-speaking regions of France and (what was then) Czechoslovakia, insisted that the nation, or people (*volk*), was more fundamental than the state which was its instrument. The myth of Roman grandeur obviously could not suit the German fascists, but they were adept at the propagation of Teutonic myths of their own—above all, the myth of the Aryan super-race, from which all that was valuable in

Europe was claimed to derive. This myth, treated by Nazis in the academic world as scientifically confirmed, paints Jews and Negroes as unwholesome and inferior, corrupters of an Aryan civilization of which the Germans were the last pure representatives. Despite its transparent absurdity, the myth of Aryan superiority proved an inspiring and effective motivator in Germany, where it won widespread acceptance and was given enthusiastic support.

55
Hermann Göring

Hermann Göring (1893–1946) was one of Hitler's closest associates, Prime
Minister of Prussia and commander of the German air forces during the Second
World War. The following short passage from *Germany Reborn* is representative
of fascist hero worship and also of the Nazi claim that they were the last bulwark
of Europe against Soviet Communism.

[SWASTIKA VERSUS STAR]*

May the other peoples realize that the Leader in Germany is the first guarantor of
European peace. For the task which Hitler has taken over, and the fight which he
is waging at home, does not only concern Germany. Hitler's mission is of importance for the history of the whole world, because he took up a war to the death
against Communism and therewith raised a bulwark for the other European
nations. Many times before in world history have mighty spiritual struggles been
decided on German territory. It is our solemn belief that if, in the mighty struggle
between Communism and National Socialism, the former had won, then the
deadly bacillus would have spread from Communist Germany to the other European countries. The day will come when the other countries will begin to realize
this, and on that day France, England and other peoples will be thankful that at the
critical moment there was an Adolf Hitler in Germany.

The great struggle on the outcome of which the future not only of Germany, but
of Europe and the whole world, depended was the struggle between the Swastika
and Soviet Star. If the Soviet Star had been victorious, Germany would have perished in a bloody Communist reign of terror, and the whole of the western world
would have followed Germany into the abyss. The victory of the Swastika has at
any rate averted this terrible danger, and for that we must give thanks to God.
Once more it has become possible for Germany to rise again and for us to create
a healthy Germany. But Germany is, and will remain, the heart of Europe, and
Europe can only be healthy and live in peace when its heart is healthy and intact.
The German people has arisen and Germany will again be healthy. For that we
have the guarantor who is Adolf Hitler, the Chancellor of the German people and
the protector of their honor and freedom.

*From H. Göring, *Germany Reborn,* 1934. Reprinted by permission of George Allen & Unwin Ltd.,
London.

56
Alfred Rosenberg

The myth of the Aryan super-race was blended with passionate nationalism to justify aggressive war in defense of the "honor" of the German people. In Rosenberg's *The Myth of the Twentieth Century,* fascism reached its apogee.

[GERMAN NATIONAL HONOR]*

A German religious movement, which would like to develop into a folk-church, will have to declare that the ideal of neighborly love is unconditionally to be subordinated to the idea of national honor, that no act of a German church may be approved which does not primarily serve the safeguarding of the *Volkstum.* . . .

The idea of honor, national honor, is for us the beginning and end of our entire thinking and doing. It does not admit of any equal-valued center of force alongside of it, no matter of what kind, neither Christian love, nor the Masonic humanity, nor the Roman philosophy. . . .

The essence of the contemporary world revolution lies in the awakening of the racial types. Not in Europe alone but on the whole planet. This awakening is the organic counter movement against the last chaotic remnants of the liberal economic imperialism, whose object of exploitation out of desperation has fallen into the snare of Bolshevik Marxism, in order to complete what democracy had begun, the extirpation of the racial and national consciousness. . . .

[STATE AND FOLK]

The state is nowadays no longer an independent idol, before which everything must bow down; the state is not even an end but is only a means for the preservation of the folk. . . . Forms of the state change, and the laws of the state pass away; the folk remains. From this alone follows that the nation is the first and *last,* that to which everything else has to be subordinated. . . .

The new thought puts folk and race higher than the state and its forms. It declares protection of the folk more important than protection of a religious denomination, a class, the monarchy, or the republic; it sees in treason against the folk a greater crime than high treason against the state. . . .

No folk of Europe is racially unified, including Germany. In accordance with the newest researches, we recognize five races, which exhibit noticeably different types. Now it is beyond question true that the Nordic race primarily has borne the genuine cultural fruits of Europe. The great heroes, artists, founders of states have come from this race. . . . Nordic blood created *German* life above all others. Even

*From A. Rosenberg, *The Myth of the Twentieth Century,* 1930. These passages are reprinted from selections appearing in *National Socialism,* a report prepared by the Division of European Affairs, U.S. Department of State; United States Government Printing Office, Washington, 1943.

those sections, in which only a small part today is pure Nordic, have their basic stock from the Nordic race. Nordic is German and has functioned so as to shape the culture and human types of the *westisch, dinarisch,* and *ostisch-Baltisch* races. Also a type which is predominantly *dinarisch* has often been innerly formed in a Nordic mode. This emphasis on the Nordic race does not mean a sowing of "race-hatred" in Germany but, on the contrary, the conscious acknowledgment of a kind of racial cement within our nationality. . . . On the day when Nordic blood should completely dry up, Germany would fall to ruin, would decline into a characterless chaos. That many forces are consciously working toward this, has been discussed in detail. For this they rely primarily on the Alpine lower stratum, which, without any value of its own, has remained essentially superstitious and slavish despite all Germanization. Now that the external bond of the old idea of the Reich has fallen away, this blood is active, together with other bastard phenomena, in order to put itself in the service of a magic faith or in the service of the democratic chaos, which finds its herald in the parasitic but energetic Judaism. . . .

The foundation for the arising of a *new aristocracy* lies in those men who have stood—in a spiritual, political, and military sense—in the foremost positions in the struggle for the coming Reich. It will appear thereby with inner necessity that up to 80 percent of these men will also externally approach the Nordic type, since the fulfillment of the demanded values lies on a line with the highest values of this blood. With the others the inheritance, which exhibits itself in actions, outweighs personal appearance. . . .

[NORDIC EUROPE]

Europe's states have all been founded and preserved by the Nordic man. This Nordic man through alcohol, the World War, and Marxism has partially degenerated, partially been uprooted. . . . In order to preserve Europe, the Nordic energies of Europe must first be revitalized, strengthened. That means then Germany, Scandinavia with Finland, and England. . . .

Nordic Europe is the fated future, with a *German* central Europe. Germany as racial and national state, as central power of the continent, safeguarding the south and southeast; the Scandinavian states with Finland as a second group, safeguarding the northeast; and Great Britain, safeguarding the west and overseas at those places where required in the interest of the Nordic man. . . .

57
Ernst R. Huber

Ernst R. Huber (1904–1990) was one of the foremost theoreticians of the Third German Reich. In the following passages he develops the three central concepts of German fascism: the *Volk,* or people, the *Führer,* or leader, and the Nazi party, which represents the State.

[THE PEOPLE]*

There is no people without an objective unity, but there is also none without a common consciousness of unity. A people is determined by a number of different factors: by racial derivation and by the character of its land, by language and other forms of life, by religion and history, but also by the common consciousness of its solidarity and by its common will to unity. For the concrete concept of a people, as represented by the various peoples of the earth, it is of decisive significance which of these various factors they regard as determinants for the nature of the people. The new German Reich proceeds from the concept of the political people, determined by the natural characteristics and by the historical idea of a closed community. The political people is formed through the uniformity of its natural characteristics. Race is the natural basis of the people. . . . As a political people the natural community becomes conscious of its solidarity and strives to form itself, to develop itself, to defend itself, to realize itself. "Nationalism" is essentially this striving of a people which has become conscious of itself toward self-direction and self-realization, toward a deepening and renewing of its natural qualities.

This consciousness of self, springing from the consciousness of a historical idea, awakens in a people its will to historical formation: the will to action. The political people is no passive, sluggish mass, no mere object for the efforts of the state at government or protective welfare work. . . . The great misconception of the democracies is that they can see the active participation of the people only in the form of plebiscites according to the principle of majority. In a democracy the people does not act as a unit but as a complex of unrelated individuals who form themselves into parties. . . . The new Reich is based on the principle that real action of a self-determining people is only possible according to the principle of leadership and following. . . .

In the theory of the nationalistic [*völkisch*] Reich, people and state are conceived as an inseparable unity. The people is the prerequisite for the entire political order; the state does not form the people but the people molds the state out of itself as the form in which it achieves historical permanence. . . . The state is a

---

*From E. Huber, *Constitutional Law of the Greater German Reich,* 1939. These passages are reprinted from selections appearing in *National Socialism,* a report prepared by the Division of European Affairs, U.S. Department of State, U.S. Government Printing Office, Washington, 1943.

function of the people, but it is not therefore a subordinate secondary machine which can be used or laid aside at will. It is the form in which the people attains to historical reality. It is the bearer of the historical continuity of the people which remains the same in the center of its being in spite of all changes, revolutions, and transformations. . . .

[THE FÜHRER]

The Führer Reich of the [German] people is founded on the recognition that the true will of the people cannot be disclosed through parliamentary votes and plebiscites but that the will of the people in its pure and uncorrupted form can only be expressed through the Führer. Thus a distinction must be drawn between the supposed will of the people in a parliamentary democracy, which merely reflects the conflict of the various social interests, and the true will of the people in the Führer-state, in which the collective will of the real political unit is manifested. . . .

The Führer is the bearer of the people's will; he is independent of all groups, associations, and interests, but he is bound by laws which are inherent in the nature of his people. In this twofold condition: independence of all factional interests but unconditional dependence of the people, is reflected the true nature of the Führer principle. Thus the Führer has nothing in common with the functionary, the agent, or the exponent who exercises a mandate delegated to him and who is bound to the will of those who appoint him. The Führer is no "representative" of a particular group whose wishes he must carry out. He is no "organ" of the state in the sense of a mere executive agent. He is rather himself the bearer of the collective will of the people. In his will the will of the people is realized. He transforms the mere feelings of the people into a conscious will. . . . Thus it is possible for him, in the name of the true will of the people which he serves, to go against the subjective opinions and convictions of single individuals within the people if these are not in accord with the objective destiny of the people. . . . He shapes the collective will of the people within himself and he embodies the political unity and entirety of the people in opposition to individual interests. . . .

But the Führer, even as the bearer of the people's will, is not arbitrary and free of all responsibility. His will is not the subjective, individual will of a single man, but the collective national will is embodied within him in all its objective, historical greatness. . . . Such a collective will is not a fiction, as is the collective will of the democracies, but it is a political reality which finds its expression in the Führer. The people's collective will has its foundation in the political idea which is given to a people. It is present in the people, but the Führer raises it to consciousness and discloses it. . . .

In the Führer are manifested also the natural laws inherent in the people: It is he who makes them into a code governing all national activity. In disclosing these natural laws he sets up the great ends which are to be attained and draws up the plans for the utilization of all national powers in the achievement of the common goals. Through his planning and directing he gives the national life its true purpose and value. This directing and planning activity is especially manifested in the law-giving power which lies in the Führer's hand. The great change in significance which the law has undergone is characterized therein that it no longer sets up the limits of social life, as in liberalistic times, but that it drafts the plans and the aims of the nation's actions. . . .

The Führer principle rests upon unlimited authority but not upon mere outward force. It has often been said, but it must constantly be repeated, that the Führer principle has nothing in common with arbitrary bureaucracy and represents no system of brutal force, but that it can only be maintained by mutual loyalty which must find its expression in a free relation. The Führer-order depends upon the responsibility of the following, just as it counts on the responsibility and loyalty of the Führer to his mission and to his following. . . . There is no greater responsibility than that upon which the Führer principle is grounded. . . .

The office of the Führer developed out of the National Socialist movement. It was originally not a state office; this fact can never be disregarded if one is to understand the present legal and political position of the Führer. The office of the Führer first took root in the structure of the Reich when the Führer took over the powers of the Chancellor, and then when he assumed the position of the Chief of State. But his primary significance is always as leader of the movement; he has absorbed within himself the two highest offices of the political leadership of the Reich and has created thereby the new office of "Führer of the people and the Reich." That is not a superficial grouping together of various offices, functions, and powers. . . . It is not a union of offices but a unity of office. The Führer does not unite the old offices of Chancellor and President side by side within himself, but he fills a new, unified office. . . .

The Führer unites in himself all the sovereign authority of the Reich; all public authority in the state as well as in the movement is derived from the authority of the Führer. We must speak not of the state's authority but of the Führer's authority if we wish to designate the character of the political authority within the Reich correctly. The state does not hold political authority as an impersonal unit but receives it from the Führer as the executor of the national will. The authority of the Führer is complete and all-embracing; it unites in itself all the means of political direction; it extends into all fields of national life; it embraces the entire people, which is bound to the Führer in loyalty and obedience. The authority of the Führer is not limited by checks and controls, by special autonomous bodies or individual rights, but it is free and independent, all-inclusive and unlimited. It is not, however, self-seeking or arbitrary and its ties are within itself. It is derived from the people; that is, it is entrusted to the Führer by the people. It exists for the people and has its justification in the people; it is free of all outward ties because it is in its innermost nature firmly bound up with the fate, the welfare, the mission, and the honor of the people. . . .

[THE NATIONAL SOCIALIST PARTY]

On July 14, 1933 was issued the law against the formation of new parties which raised the NSDAP* to the only political party in Germany. . . . The overthrow of the old party-state was accompanied by the construction of the new movement-

*National Socialist German Workers' (Nazi) party—*Ed.*

state [*Bewegungsstaat*]. Out of a political fighting organization the NSDAP grew to a community capable of carrying the state and the nation. This process was accomplished step by step in the first months after the National Socialist seizure of power. The assumption of the office of Chancelor by the Führer of the movement formed the basis for this development. Various party leaders were appointed as *Reichsminister;* the governors of the provinces were national leaders or *Gauleiter* of the party, such as General von Epp; the Prussian government officials are as a rule *Gauleiter* of the party; the Prussian police chiefs are mostly high-ranking SA leaders. By this system of a union of the personnel of the party and state offices the unity of party and state was achieved. . . .

The aim of the National Socialist movement is the nationalistic Reich: that is, a state of which the nature and development is determined by the idea of the people, for which the people is the substance of political unity, of which the inward and outward strength is drawn from the whole people, and which is supported by the whole people. . . . The people and the party in the National Socialist Reich are a unit, not in the sense that every citizen must be a member of the party, but in the sense that the movement is only possible as the visible embodiment and realization of the all-embracing unity of the people. The totality of National Socialism is not to be explained therein that all fields of life are penetrated by the political will of the movement but that all members of the people are expected to take part in the common political life and to share in the determination of the common political fate. . . .

[THE INDIVIDUAL AND THE REICH]

Not until the nationalistic political philosophy had become dominant could the liberalistic idea of basic rights be really overcome. The concept of personal liberties of the individual as opposed to the authority of the state had to disappear; it is not to be reconciled with the principle of the nationalistic Reich. There are no personal liberties of the individual which fall outside of the realm of the state and which must be respected by the state. The member of the people, organically connected with the whole community, has replaced the isolated individual; he is included in the totality of the political people and is drawn into the collective action. There can no longer be any question of a private sphere, free of state influence, which is sacred and untouchable before the political unity. The constitution of the nationalistic Reich is therefore not based upon a system of inborn and inalienable rights of the individual. . . .

The legal position of the individual member of the people forms an entirely new concept which is indispensable for the construction of a nationalistic order. The legal position of the individual is always related to the community and conditioned by duty. It is developed not for the sake of the individual but for the community, which can only be filled with life, power, and purpose when a suitable field of action is insured for the individual member. Without a concrete determination of the individual's legal position there can be no real community.

This legal position represents the organic fixation of the individual in the living order. Rights and obligations arise from the application of this legal position to specific individual relationships. . . . But all rights must be regarded as duty-bound rights. Their exercise is always dependent upon the fulfillment by the individual of those duties to which all rights are subordinate. . . .

It is a mistake to claim that the citizen of the Reich has no rights but only duties; that there is no right of choice but only a duty of acclamation. There are, of course, no inborn, inalienable political rights which are inherent in the individual himself and which would tend to limit and hamper the leadership of the Reich. But in every true political community the individual has his legal position which he receives from the Führer and which makes him a true follower. . . .

58
Adolph Hitler

Adolph Hitler (1889–1945) was absolute dictator in Germany from 1933 until his death by suicide in 1945. His early years as a draftsman and enlisted soldier could not have foretold the heights of popularity and power he was later to attain. The National Socialist (Nazi) Party which he founded was outlawed in 1923; while in prison he wrote his massive autobiography, *Mein Kampf (My Battle)*. This extraordinary work—political tract, personal apologia, historical analysis, patriotic ode, and anti-semitic diatribe all in one—became the gospel of the Third German Reich. No written work better exhibits Hitler's mind and spirit, or the character of fascism in Germany. As a tyrant exerting authoritarian control over his state, exploiting terror and launching aggressive war, he has had no equal in all history. But it is the spoken word more than any writings to which, as Hitler himself insisted, his movement owed its phenomenal success. He was a superb orator with the power to inspire almost hysterical enthusiasm in his audiences. The passages from *Mein Kampf* immediately below are followed by some short segments from Hitler's speeches—of which no written rendition can give a full account.

[THE IMPORTANCE OF RACIAL PURITY]*

Any crossing between two beings of not quite the same high standard produces a medium between the standards of the parents. That means: the young one will probably be on a higher level than the racially lower parent, but not as high as the higher one. Consequently, it will succumb later on in the fight against the higher level. But such a mating contradicts Nature's will to breed life as a whole towards

*From Adolf Hitler's *Mein Kampf,* translated by Manheim. Copyright © renewed 1971 by Houghton Mifflin Company. Reprinted by permission of the publisher, Houghton Mifflin Company and Hutchinson Publishing Group Ltd.

a higher level. The presumption for this does not lie in blending the superior with the inferior, but rather in a complete victory of the former. The stronger has to rule and he is not to amalgamate with the weaker one, that he may not sacrifice his own greatness. Only the born weakling can consider this as cruel, but at that he is only a weak and limited human being; for, if this law were not dominating, all conceivable development towards a higher level, on the part of all organically living beings, would be unthinkable for man. . . .

If it were different, every further development towards higher levels would stop, and rather the contrary would happen. For, since according to numbers, the inferior element always outweighs the superior element, under the same preservation of life and under the same propagating possibilities, the inferior element would increase so much more rapidly that finally the best element would be forced to step into the background, if no correction of this condition were carried out. But just this is done by Nature, by subjecting the weaker part to such difficult living conditions that even by this the number is restricted, and finally by preventing the remainder, without choice, from increasing, but by making here a new and ruthless choice, according to strength and health.

Just as little as Nature desires a mating between weaker individuals and stronger ones, far less she desires the mixing of a higher race with a lower one, as in this case her entire work of higher breeding, which has perhaps taken hundreds of thousands of years, would tumble at one blow.

Historical experience offers countless proofs of this. It shows with terrible clarity that with any mixing of the blood of the Aryan with lower races the result was the end of the culture-bearer. North America, the population of which consists for the greatest part of Germanic elements—which mix only very little with the lower, colored races—displays a humanity and a culture different from those of Central and South America, where chiefly the Romanic immigrants have sometimes mixed with the aborigines on a large scale. By this example alone one may clearly and distinctly recognize the influence of the race mixture. The Germanic of the North American continent, who has remained pure and less intermixed, has become the master of that continent, he will remain so until he, too, falls victim to the shame of blood-mixing.

The result of any crossing, in brief, is always the following:

a Lowering of the standard of the higher race.
b Physical and mental regression, and, with it, the beginning of a slowly but steadily progressive lingering illness.

To bring about such a development means nothing less than sinning against the will of the Eternal Creator.

[THE ARYAN RACE]

. . . What we see before us of human culture today, the results of art, science, and techniques, is almost exclusively the creative product of the Aryan. But just this fact admits of the not unfounded conclusion that he alone was the founder of higher humanity as a whole, thus the prototype of what we understand by the word 'man.' He is the Prometheus of mankind, out of whose bright forehead springs the divine spark of genius at all times, forever rekindling that fire which in the form of knowledge lightened up the night of silent secrets and thus made man climb the path towards the position of master of the other beings on this earth. Exclude him—and deep darkness will again fall upon the earth, perhaps even, after a few thousand years, human culture would perish and the world would turn into a desert.

If one were to divide mankind into three groups: culture-founders, culture-bearers, and culture-destroyers, then, as representative of the first kind, only the Aryan would come in question. It is from him that the foundation and the walls of all human creations originate, and only the external form and color depend on the characteristics of the various peoples involved. He furnishes the gigantic building-stones and also the plans for all human progress. . . .

. . . The more primitive the technical presumptions for a cultural activity are, the more necessary is the presence of human auxiliary forces which then, collected and applied with the object of organization, have to replace the force of the machine. Without this possibility of utilizing inferior men, the Aryan would never have been able to take the first steps towards his later culture; exactly as, without the help of various suitable animals which he knew how to tame, he would never have arrived at a technology which now allows him to do without these very animals. The words *'Der Mohr hat seine Schuldigkeit getan, er kann gehen'* [The Moor has done his duty, he may go] has unfortunately too deep a meaning. . . .

Therefore, for the formation of higher cultures, the existence of inferior men was one of the most essential presumptions, because they alone were able to replace the lack of technical means without which a higher development is unthinkable. The first culture of mankind certainly depended less on the tamed animal, but rather on the use of inferior people.

Therefore, it is no accident that the first cultures originated in those places where the Aryan, by meeting lower peoples, subdued them and made them subject to his will. They, then, were the first technical instrument in the service of a growing culture.

With this the way that the Aryan had to go was clearly lined out. As a conqueror he subjected the lower peoples and then he regulated their practical ability according to his command and his will and for his aims. But while he thus led them towards a useful, though hard activity, he not only spared the lives of the subjected, but perhaps he even gave them a fate which was better than that of their former so-called 'freedom.' As long as he kept up ruthlessly the master's standpoint, he not only really remained 'master' but also the preserver and propagator of the culture. For the latter was based exclusively on his abilities, and, with it, on his preservation in purity. But as soon as the subjected peoples themselves began to rise (probably) and approached the conqueror linguistically, the sharp separating wall between master and slave fell. The Aryan gave up the purity of his blood and therefore he also lost his place in the Paradise which he had created for himself. He became submerged in the race-mixture, he gradually lost his cultural ability more and more, till at last not only mentally but also physically he began to resemble more the subjected and aborigines than his ancestors. For some time he may still live on the existing cultural goods, but then petrifaction sets in, and finally oblivion.

In this way cultures and realms collapse in order to make room for new formations.

The blood-mixing, however, with the lowering of the racial level caused by it, is the sole cause of the dying-off of old cultures; for the people do not perish by lost wars, but by the loss of that force of resistance which is contained only in the pure blood.

All that is not race in this world is trash.

All world historical events, however, are only the expression of the races' instinct of self-preservation in its good or in its evil meaning.*

. . .

[STATE AND RACE]

. . .

The highest purpose of the folkish State is the care for the preservation of those racial primal elements which, supplying culture, create the beauty and dignity of a higher humanity. We, as Aryans, are therefore able to imagine a State only to be the living organism of a nationality which not only safeguards the preservation of that nationality, but which, by a further training of its spiritual and ideal abilities, leads it to the highest freedom.

. . .

. . . there is only one most sacred human right, and this right is at the same time the most sacred obligation, namely: to see to it that the blood is preserved pure, so that by the preservation of the best human material a possibility is given for a more noble development of these human beings.

---

*After Hitler's elevation to the supreme leadership, history and science were taught in German schools in strict accord with the doctrines of *Mein Kampf.* As an illustration, the following poem, by Will Vesper, was used as instructional material in classes in German history:

Nun steht um dich, mein Führer, fest dein Volk,
Und wenn du sprichst, in Gute wie im Grimme,
so bist du seine gottgewollte Stimme.
Gestalt und Wille ward in dir das Volk,
du sein Gesetz. In deinen grossen Planen
vollendet sich der reinste Traum der Ahnen.
Die Enkel werden noch in tausend Jahren
auf deinen Strassen, deinen Strömen fahren.

About thee stand thy people, oh my *Führer.*
And when, in kindness or in wrath, thou speakest,
Thou art, by God's decree, the voice this people finds.
In thee do they both form and will assume—
Thou art the law in them. In thy vast planning
The fathers' purest dreams are made come true.
Still in a thousand years our grandchildren
Down roads of thine will travel, down thy streams.

—*Ed.*

Thus a folkish State primarily will have to lift marriage out of the level of a permanent race degradation in order to give it the consecration of that institution which is called upon to beget images of the Lord and not deformities half man and half ape.

. . .

The folkish State has to make up for what is today neglected in this field in all directions. *It has to put the race into the center of life in general. It has to care for its preservation in purity. It has to make the child the most precious possession of a people. It has to take care that only the healthy beget children; that there is only one disgrace: to be sick and to bring children into the world despite one's own deficiencies; but one highest honor: to renounce this. Further, on the other hand this has to be looked upon as objectionable: to keep healthy children from the nation. Thereby the State has to appear as the guardian of a thousand years' future, in the face of which the wish and the egoism of the individual appears as nothing and has to submit. . . .*

[CLOTHES AND BODIES SERVE THE NATION]

The clothes of the young people also have to be adapted to this purpose. It is truly miserable to be compelled to see that our youth also is subject to a lunacy of fashion which helped in converting the meaning of the old proverb *'Kleider machen Leute'* [clothes make people] into a detrimental one.

Particularly with youth, clothes have to be put into the service of education. The young man who during summer walks about in long pipe-like trousers, covered up to the neck, loses, merely through his clothes, a stimulant for his physical fitness. For ambition, too, and we may as well say it, vanity also, have to be applied. Not the vanity in beautiful clothes which not everyone is able to buy, but the vanity in a beautiful, well-shaped body which everyone can help in building up.

This is of use also for the future. The girl should become acquainted with her knight. If today physical beauty were not pushed completely into the background by our dandified fashionableness, the seduction of hundreds of thousands of girls by bow-legged, disgusting Jewish bastards would never be possible. Also this is in the interest of the nation, that the most beautiful bodies find one another and thus help in giving the nation new beauty.

[CITIZENS AND SUBJECTS]

The *folkish State* divides its inhabitants into three classes: State citizens, State subjects, and aliens.

In principle, only birth confers the status of subject. Being a State subject as such does not entitle one to hold public offices, to exercise political activity in the sense of participation in elections, be it actively or passively. In principle, every State subject's race and nationality have to be ascertained. Every State subject is free at any time to abandon his status and to become a State citizen in that country the nationality of which corresponds to his own. The *alien* is distinguished from the State subject only by the fact that he is a State subject of an alien State.

The young State subject of German nationality is obliged to undergo the school training prescribed to every German. By this he subjects himself to be educated to become a fellow citizen, conscious of his race and nation. Later he has to undergo the physical exercises further prescribed by the State, and finally he joins the army. The training in the army is a general one; it has to comprise every German and to educate him for the range of military activities for which he can be used according to his physical and mental abilities. Thereupon the irreproachably healthy young man, after discharging his military duty, is in the most solemn manner given the *State citizenship*. It is the most valuable document for his entire earthly life. With this he enters upon all the rights of the State citizen and takes part in all its advantages. For the State has to draw a sharp distinction between those who as national members are cause and bearers of its existence and its greatness, and those who only as 'earning' elements make their domicile within the State.

The bestowal of the *State citizen certificate* should be combined with the solemn oath to the national community and the State. This certificate must signify a bond that bridges all cleavages and unites all. *It must be a greater honor to be a citizen of this Reich as a street cleaner, than to be a king in a foreign State.*

The State citizen, as compared with the alien, is privileged. He is the master of the Reich. But this higher dignity also involves obligations. One without honor or character, the common criminal, the traitor to the country, etc., can at any time be deprived of this honor. By this he becomes a State subject again.

The German girl is State subject and only becomes a State citizen when she marries. But citizenship can be conferred on those female German State subjects who are active in economic life.

[ORGANIZATION AND HIERARCHY]

A view of life which, by rejecting the democratic mass idea, endeavors to give this world to the best people, that means to the most superior men, has logically to obey the same aristocratic principle also within this people and has to guarantee leadership and highest influence within the respective people to the best heads. With this it does not build up on the idea of the majority, but on that of the personality.

.   .   .

.   .   . To employ [the individual person] profitably for the community is the first and the highest task of the organization of the national community. Indeed, the organization itself has to be only an execution of this principle. Only with this is it freed from the curse of mechanism and becomes something living. *Organization in itself has to be the incorporation of the endeavor of putting the heads above the masses and of subjecting the masses to the heads.*

.   .   .

The folkish State, therefore, has to free the entire leadership—especially the highest, that means the political leadership—from the parliamentary principle of the decision by majority, that means decision by the masses, in order to establish firmly in its place the right of the person.

From this results the following conclusion:

The best State constitution and State form is that which, with the most natural certainty, brings the best heads of the national community to leading importance and to leading influence.

. . .

There must be no decisions by majority, but only responsible persons, and the word 'council' is once more reduced to its original meaning. At every man's side there stand councillors, indeed, but *one man decides.*

The principle which once made the Prussian army the most marvelous instrument of the German people has to be some day in a transformed meaning the principle of the construction of our whole State constitution: *authority of every leader towards below and responsibility towards above.*

[THE ARMY AS THE SCHOOL OF THE GERMAN NATION]

. . . the army was the mightiest school of the German nation. . . . What the German people owes to the army may be simply summed up in one single word, namely: everything.

The army trained for absolute responsibility at a time when this quality had become very rare and the shunning of responsibility had more and more become the order of the day, starting from the model example of all unscrupulousness, the parliament; the army further taught personal courage in a time when cowardice threatened to become a spreading disease, and when the willingness to sacrifice, to stand up for the general welfare, was almost looked upon as stupidity, and when only he seemed to be clever who understood best how to spare himself and to advance his own 'ego'; it was the school which still taught the individual German to seek the salvation of the nation, not in the mendacious phrases of international fraternity between negroes, Germans, Chinese, French, British, etc., but rather in the strength and the unity of his own nationality.

. . .

. . . In the face of the Jewish democratic idea of a blind worship of numbers, the army upheld the faith in personality. . . .

This was the high school of the German nation.

. . .

[THE JEW]

The Jew forms the strongest contrast to the Aryan.

. . .

In the Jewish people, the will to sacrifice oneself does not go beyond the bare instinct of self-preservation of the individual.

. . .

If the Jews were alone in this world, they would suffocate as much in dirt and filth, as they would carry on a detestable struggle to cheat and to ruin each other, although the complete lack of the will to sacrifice, expressed in their cowardice, would also in this instance make the fight a comedy.

Thus it is fundamentally wrong to conclude, merely from the fact of their standing together in a fight, or, more rightly expressed, in their exploiting their fellow human beings, that the Jews have a certain idealistic will to sacrifice themselves.

Here, too, the Jew is led by nothing but pure egoism on the part of the individual.

. . .

The Jewish people, with all its apparent intellectual qualities, is nevertheless without any true culture, especially without a culture of its own. For the sham culture which the Jew possesses today is the property of other peoples, and is mostly spoiled in his hands.

When judging Jewry in its attitude towards the question of human culture, one has to keep before one's eye as an essential characteristic that there never has been and consequently that today also there is no Jewish art; that above all the two queens of all arts, architecture and music, owe nothing original to Jewry. What he achieves in the field of art is either bowdlerization or intellectual theft. With this, the Jew lacks those qualities which distinguish creatively and, with it, culturally blessed races.

. . .

No, the Jew possesses no culture-creating energy whatsoever, as the idealism, without which there can never exist a genuine development of man towards a higher level, does not and never did exist in him. His intellect, therefore, will never have a constructive effect, but only a destructive one, and in very rare cases it is perhaps stimulating, at the utmost, but then in the form of the original prototype of that *'Kraft, die stets das Böse will und doch das Gute schafft'* [that force which always wants evil and nevertheless creates good]. Any progress of mankind takes place not through him but in spite of him.

. . .

In the Jew's life as a parasite in the body of other nations and States, his characteristic is established which once caused Schopenhauer to pronounce the sentence, already mentioned, that the Jew is the 'great master of lying.' Life urges the Jew towards the lie, that is, to a perpetual lie, just as it forces the inhabitants of northern countries to wear warm clothes.

. . .

The Jews were always a people with definite racial qualities and never a religion, only their progress made them probably look very early for a means which could divert disagreeable attention from their person. But what would have been more useful and at the same time more harmless than the 'purloining' of the appearance of being a religious community? For here, too, everything is purloined, or rather, stolen. But resulting from his own original nature the Jew cannot possess a religious institution for the very reason that he lacks all idealism in any form and that he also does not recognize any belief in the hereafter. But in the Aryan conception one cannot conceive of a religion which lacks the conviction of the continuation of life after death in some form. Indeed, the Talmud is then not a book for the preparation for the life to come, but rather for a practical and bearable life in this world.

. . .

Upon this first and greatest lie, that the Jew is not a race but simply a religion, further lies are then built up in necessary consequence. To them also belongs the language spoken at the time by the Jew. For him it is never a means of expressing his thoughts, but for hiding them. When he speaks French, he thinks Jewish, and when he turns out German poetry, he only gives an outlet to the nature of his people.

As long as the Jew has not become the master of the other peoples, he must, whether he likes it or not, speak their languages, and only if they would be his slaves then they might all speak a universal language so that their domination will be made easier (Esperanto!).

How far the entire existence of this people is based on a continuous lie is shown in an incomparable manner and certainty in the 'Protocols of the Wise Men of Zion,' so infinitely hated by the Jews. They are supposed to be a 'forgery' the *Frankfurter Zeitung* moans and cries out to the world once a week; the best proof that they are genuine after all. What many Jews may do unconsciously is here exposed consciously. But this is what matters. It makes no difference from the head of which Jew these disclosures come, but decisive it is that they demonstrate, with a truly horrifying certainty, the nature and the activity of the Jewish people and expose them in their inner connection as well as in their ultimate final aims.* But the best criticism applied to them is reality. He who examines the historical development of the past hundred years, from the points of view of this book, will also immediately understand the clamor of the Jewish press. For once this book has become the common property of a people, the Jewish danger is bound to be considered as broken.

[THE JEWISH THREAT]

. . .

How far they keep the approaching victory before their eyes is seen from the terrible manner which their intercourse with the members of other peoples assumes.

For hours the black-haired Jew boy, diabolic joy in his face, waits in ambush for the unsuspecting girl whom he defiles with his blood and thus robs her from her people. With the aid of all means he tries to ruin the racial foundations of the people to be enslaved. Exactly as he himself systematically demoralizes women and girls, he is not scared from pulling down the barriers of blood and race for others on a large scale. It was and is the Jews who bring the negro to the Rhine, always with the same concealed thought and the clear goal of destroying, by the bastardization which would necessarily set in, the white race which they hate, to throw it down from its cultural and political height and in turn to rise personally to the position of master.

---

*The 'Protocols of the Wise Men of Zion' were first circulated in Russia (where anti-Semitism had long been popular) by certain secret organizations in the early years of the twentieth century. The tract purports to be an exact account of a meeting of Jewish leaders in 1897, in which a horrible plot to undermine society, overthrow governments, and destroy Christianity is revealed. In fact, the "minutes" in the 'Protocols' are copied verbatim from "A Dialogue in Hades Between Machiavelli and Montesquieu," an attack on the Masons and Bonapartists, written in French by Maurice Joly in 1868; in the 'Protocols' the word "Jew" is simply substituted for Joly's devils. Another contributing source is probably the novel *Biarritz* by John Retcliff (1868), in which the author describes an imaginary annual meeting of "the princes of the Twelve Tribes of Israel," in the Jewish cemetery of Prague, at which meeting measures calculated to destroy all Christians are discussed. Editions of the 'Protocols' edited by Alfred Rosenberg and others were widely distributed in Germany and other countries during Hitler's regime. The Reverend Charles Coughlin, an American fascist of the period, defended these 'Protocols' in his periodical *Social Justice* in a way closely paralleling the defense given here by Hitler. The 'Protocols of the Wise men of Zion' continue still to be presented as genuine in the hate literature of anti-semitic organizations around the world.—*Ed.*

For a racially pure people, conscious of its blood, can never be enslaved by the Jew. It will forever only be the master of bastards in this world.

Thus he systematically tries to lower the racial level by a permanent poisoning of the individual.

In the political sphere, however, he begins to replace the idea of democracy by that of the dictatorship of the proletariat.

In the organized mass of Marxism he has found the weapon which makes him now dispense with democracy and which allows him, instead, to enslave and to 'rule' the people dictatorially with the brutal fist.

He now works methodically towards the revolution in a twofold direction: economically and politically.

Thanks to his international influence, he ensnares with a net of enemies those peoples which put up a too violent resistance against the enemy from within, he drives them into war, and finally, if necessary, he plants the flag of revolution on the battlefield.

In the field of economics he undermines the States until the social organizations which have become unprofitable are taken from the State and submitted to his financial control.

Politically he denies to the State all means of self-preservation, he destroys the bases of any national self-dependence and defense, he destroys the confidence in the leaders, he derides history and the past, and he pulls down into the gutter everything which is truly great.

In the domain of culture he infects art, literature, theater, smites natural feeling, overthrows all conceptions of beauty and sublimity, of nobility and quality, and in turn he pulls the people down into the confines of his own swinish nature.

. . .

[The following passages are from speeches by Adolph Hitler. Going beyond their specific content, one must try to imagine the dynamism and the spirit of patriotic fervor with which the speeches were delivered and the mass enthusiasm with which they were received. *Ed.*]

[MIGHT MAKES RIGHT]*

The Strong over the Weak

. . . It is evident that the stronger has the right before God and the world to enforce his will. History shows that the right as such does not mean a thing, unless it is backed up by great power. If one does not have the power to enforce his right, that right alone will profit him absolutely nothing. The stronger have always been victorious. The whole of nature is a continuous struggle between strength and weakness, an eternal victory of the strong over the weak. All nature would be full

---

*This and the following selections are from *Hitler's Words, the Speeches of Adolph Hitler from 1923–1943,* edited by G. Prange and reprinted by permission of the Public Affairs Press, Washington.

of decay if it were otherwise. And the states which do not wish to recognize this law will decay. If you need an example of this kind of decay, look at the present German Reich. (Munich, April 13, 1923; *Völkischer Boebachter,* April 15/16, 1923.)

Only Force Rules

The fundamental motif through all the centuries has been the principle that force and power are the determining factors. All development is struggle. Only force rules. Force is the first law. A struggle has already taken place between original man and his primeval world. Only through struggle have states and the world become great. If one should ask whether this struggle is gruesome, then the only answer could be: For the weak, yes, for humanity as a whole, no.

World history proves that in the struggle between nations, that race has always won out whose drive for self-preservation was the more pronounced, the stronger. . . . Unfortunately, the contemporary world stresses internationalism instead of the innate values of race, democracy and the majority instead of the worth of the great leader. Instead of everlasting struggle the world preaches cowardly pacifism, and everlasting peace. These three things, considered in the light of their ultimate consequences, are the causes of the downfall of all humanity. The practical result of conciliation among nations is the renunciation of a people's own strength and their voluntary enslavement. (Essen, Nov. 22, 1926; *Völkischer Beobachter,* Nov. 26, 1926.)

The Nonsense of Humanitarianism

The inventions of mankind are the result of eternal struggle. Never would aviation have progressed so remarkably had it not been for the war, had not countless thousands sacrificed their lives in this cruel struggle against nature. The struggle against the great beasts is ended, but it is being inexorably carried on against the tiny creatures—against bacteria and bacilli. There is no Marxian reconciliation on this score; it is either you or I, life or death, either extermination or servitude.

From [various] examples we arrive at the fundamental conclusion that there is no humanitarianism but only an eternal struggle, a struggle which is the prerequisite for the development of all humanity.

The borderline between man and the animal is established by man himself. The position which man enjoys today is his own accomplishment. We see before us the Aryan race which is manifestly the bearer of all culture, the true representative of all humanity. All inventions in the field of transportation must be credited to the members of a particular race. Our entire industrial science is without exception the work of the Nordics. All great composers from Beethoven to Richard Wagner are Aryans, even though they were born in Italy or France. Do not say that art is international. The tango, the shimmy, and the jazzband are international but they are not art. Man owes everything that is of any importance to the principle of struggle and to one race which has carried itself forward successfully. Take away the

Nordic Germans and nothing remains but the dance of apes. . . . Because we recognize the fact that our people can endure only through struggle, we National Socialists are fighters. (Munich, April 2, 1927; *Völkischer Beobachter,* April 5, 1927.)

Struggle—The Source of Strength

Politics is nothing else than the struggle of a people for its existence in this world; it is the eternal battle of a people, for better or for worse, for its existence on this planet. How does this struggle take place? Great men of world history have described it. Frederick the Great said that politics is the art of serving one's people with all the means at one's disposal; according to Bismarck, politics is the art of the possible. . . . Clemenceau declared that the politics of peace was nothing else than the continuation of war with other means. Clausewitz asserted that war was nothing else than the continuation of politics with other weapons. In reality, then, politics is the struggle of a people with all weapons to the limit of its power for its existence on this earth.

With what question is struggle primarily related? It is the drive for self-preservation which leads to struggle—that is, the question of love and hunger. These are the two fundamental primitive forces around which everything on this earth centers. The total space on which life is carried on is circumscribed. This leads to a struggle of one against the other for this limited area. In addition, this area is more restricted for certain groups than for others so that their existence is dependent upon the preservation of the particular region which they inhabit.

Thus, the struggle for daily bread becomes in reality a struggle for the soil which produces this daily bread; that is, for space itself. It is an iron principle: the weak fall in order that the strong may live. . . . From all the innumerable creatures a complete species rises and becomes the master of the rest. Such a one is man—the most brutal, the most resolute creature on earth. He knows nothing but the extermination of his enemies in the world. . . . This struggle, this battle has not been carried on by all men in the same way. Certain species stand out, and at the top of the list is the Aryan. The Aryan has forged the weapons with which mankind has made itself master of the animal world. There is scarcely anything in existence which when traced back to its origin cannot claim an Aryan as its creator. . . . Never have votes and majorities added one iota to the culture of mankind. Every accomplishment is solely the result of the work and energy of great men, and as such, a flaming protest against the inertia of the masses.

How does this process then take place? It is an eternal struggle. Every achievement is nothing else than the result of a struggle of give-and-take. Every new invention is a triumph over an old one. Every record is a struggle against that which exists. Every championship performance is a conquest of that which prevailed previously.

Hence the following principles result: The value of man is determined in the first place by his inner racial virtues; second, by the ability of the race to bring forth men who in turn become leaders in the struggle for advancement, third, this entire process takes place in the form of eternal struggle. As a consequence struggle is the father of all things in this world. (Munich, Nov. 21, 1927; *Völkischer Beobachter,* Nov. 23, 1927.)

Originality Plus Brutality

The will to live leads beyond the limitations of the present to the struggle for the prerequisites of life. Struggle is the impulse of self-preservation in nature. Man has become great through struggle.

The first fundamental of any rational *Weltanschauung* is the fact that on earth and in the universe force alone is decisive. Whatever goal man has reached is due to his originality plus his brutality. Whatever man possesses today in the field of culture is the culture of the Aryan race. The Aryan has stamped his character on the whole world. The basis for all development is the creative urge of the individual, not the vote of majorities. The genius of the individual is decisive, not the spirit of the masses. All life is bound up in three theses: Struggle is the father of all things, virtue lies in blood, leadership is primary and decisive. (Chemnitz, April 2, 1928; *Völkischer Beobachter,* April 7, 1928).

Man Must Kill

If men wish to live, then they are forced to kill others. The entire struggle for survival is a conquest of the means of existence which in turn results in the elimination of others from these same sources of subsistence. As long as there are peoples on this earth, there will be nations against nations and they will be forced to protect their vital rights in the same way as the individual is forced to protect his rights.

There is in reality no distinction between peace and war. Life, no matter in what form, is a process which always leads to the same result. Self-preservation will always be the goal of every individual. Struggle is ever-present and will remain. This signifies a constant willingness on the part of man to sacrifice to the utmost. Weapons, methods, instruments, formations, these may change, but in the end the struggle for survival remains. . . .

One is either the hammer or the anvil. We confess that it is our purpose to prepare the German people again for the role of the hammer. . . . We confess further that we will dash anyone to pieces who should dare to hinder us in this undertaking. . . . Our rights will never be represented by others. Our rights will be protected only when the German Reich is again supported by the point of the German dagger. (Munich, March 15, 1929; *Völkischer Beobachter,* March 17, 1929.)

[NATIONALISM VS. INTERNATIONALISM]

Long Live Fanatical Nationalism

Our entire work consists of enlightening our people, of reshaping its mentality. It consists in the creation of a new Movement which will reform our people from top to bottom even reaching into the soul of the common German man, a new Movement which establishes three great postulates without which foreign policy cannot be carried out in the future.

In the first place, our people must be delivered from the hopeless confusion of international convictions, and educated consciously and systematically to fanatical nationalism. We will not declare that our goal is to have the German people sing German songs again in the future. No, our goal is that the German people should again acquire honor and conviction, that it should again bow in adoration before its own history, that it should respect those things which formerly gave it significance, and that it should curse that which damaged its honor. We recognize only two Gods: A God in Heaven and a God on earth and that is our Fatherland.

Second, insofar as we educate the people to fight against the delirium of democracy and bring it again to the recognition of the necessity of authority and of leadership, we tear it away from the nonsense of parliamentarianism; thereby we deliver it from the atmosphere of irresponsibility and lead it to responsibility and to a recognition of duty on the part of the individual person.

Third, insofar as we deliver the people from the atmosphere of pitiable belief in possibilities which lie outside the bounds of one's own strength—such as the belief in reconciliation, understanding, world peace, the League of Nations, and international solidarity—we destroy these ideas. There is only one right in this world and this right is one's own strength.

The people must recognize that its future will not be molded through cowardly belief in the help of others but through faithful devotion to one's own task. Out of this devotion deliverance must one day come—freedom and happiness and life. (Munich, Sept. 22, 1928; *Völkischer Beobachter,* Sept. 23, 1928.)

Racial and National Regeneration

Racial degeneration continues apace. The bastardization of great states has begun. The Negroization of culture, of customs—not only of blood—strides forward. The world becomes democratized. The value of the individual declines. The masses apparently are gaining the victory over the idea of the great leader. Numbers are chosen as the new God.

The poison of pacifism is again scattered about. The world forgets that struggle is the father of all things. State upon state is becoming intoxicated with ideas that must lead to the obliteration of a people. When the bastard, however, stands against the thoroughbred, and the Negro stands against the white man, the one who from the racial standpoint is the strongest, will be victorious. The individual is creative and has given culture to the world. When cowardice is pitted against courage and pacifism against daring, courage and daring gain the victory. That state will be victorious which does not fall prey to the vice of cowardice and pacifism. The people who opposed pacifism with the idea of struggle will with mathematical certainty become the master of its fate.

A people who opposes the bastardization of its spirit and its blood can be saved. The German people has its specific value and cannot be placed on the same level as 70,000,000 Negroes. If the German people will recognize its value it can mold the forces which will lead to victory.

Negro music is now the rage. But if we put the shimmy alongside a Beethoven symphony, then the triumph is clear. Let us think about the German soul, and then faith, creative power, and tenacity will not fail. Our people has always found men who conquered distress. Now it is believed, however, that leaders can be dispensed with; and at present world history is not being made, but, rather, the history of submission. Out of our strong faith will come the strength to help ourselves against this bastardization.

[TO THE GERMAN YOUTH]

"Obedience Über Alles"

The things we want from our youth are different from what was wanted in the past. In our eyes the German youth of the future should be slim and lithe, fast as greyhounds, tough as leather, and hard as Krupp steel. We must bring up a new type of man, so that our people will not succumb to the symptoms of degeneracy of the times.

We do not talk, we act. We undertook to give this people a new type of education, an education that is to begin with our youth and will never end. In the future our young men will pass from one school into the other. It starts with the child and ends with the old fighter of the Movement. No one shall say that there is any time when he can be left entirely to his own devices. It is the duty of everyone to serve his people. Everyone has the duty to prepare himself for this service, to harden himself physically and to prepare and strengthen himself spiritually. The earlier this preparation begins, the better.

.   .   .

We will harden ourselves to such an extent that any storm will find us strong. We will never forget that the sum total of all virtues and all strength can be effective only when it is subservient to one will and to one command. We are standing here now not by mere chance, not because each one of you did as he pleased, but because you were called here by the order of your youth leader, and because that order became a thousand separate orders. And as each of these orders was obeyed, millions of German boys in Germany became one organization; and out of tens of thousands of comrades living in Germany came this demonstration, this present roll call. Nothing is possible unless one will commands, a will which has to be obeyed by others, beginning at the top and ending only at the very bottom. Beside physical training and education, this is our second great task.

We are a following (*Gefolgschaft*) but as the word itself indicates, following means to follow, it means to be a loyal member of a following. We must train our people so that whenever someone has been appointed to command, the others will recognize it as their duty to obey him, for it can happen that an hour later they will be called upon to command, and they can do it then only if others in turn obey. This is the expression of an authoritarian state—not of a weak, babbling democracy—of an authoritarian state where everyone is proud to obey, because he knows: I will likewise be obeyed when I must take command. Germany is no chicken house where everyone runs about at random, cackling and crowing, but we are a people that from its infancy on learns how to be disciplined. If others do not understand us, that is all the same to us. . . . You are the proof that this idea has come to life in the German Reich. You are the proof of how this idea has become reality. Believe me, the day will come when German youth will once again have a wonderful healthy and glowing appearance, healthy, frank, sincere, brave, and peace loving. We are no ruffians. If the rest of the world misunderstands us in our discipline, that is not our fault. From this discipline fewer quarrels will develop for the world than from the parliamentary-democratic confusion of the present day.

   . . . But we must never forget that only the strong deserve friendship and only the strong grant friendship. We want, therefore, to make ourselves strong—that is our motto. You are responsible to me for making this come true. You are the future of the nation, the future of the German Reich. (Nürnberg, Sept. 14, 1935; *Völkischer Beobachter,* Sept. 15, 1935.)

PART **THREE**

DEMOCRACY

Democracy is many things. It is a form of government in which participating citizens take pride. It is an ideal pursued by most of the world's peoples. It is a way of seeking to reach community objectives harmoniously, through a process to which all have given consent. Sometimes democracy is identified with a set of political institutions: a representative parliament, the secret ballot, majority rule; and sometimes democracy is said to lie most fundamentally in the spirit and dispositions of the individual members of a community. Democracy, it is said, is a way of life.

The word "democracy" has enormous appeal, of course, and great propaganda value—so we may expect that many will claim the name for what they defend, whether it be truly democratic or not. And there is no easy resolution of the unavoidable disputes over what democracy really means, since there is neither any person whom we can consult, nor any document to which we can refer, that has ultimate authority in such controversies. Dogmatic democrats there may be, but there can be no democratic dogma.

One may therefore expect democratic philosophers to be inconsistent with one another at times, as they surely have been. Yet there are cords of principle, sometimes tangled, that loosely bind democrats together. They share the core conviction that human beings can, and in most circumstances should, govern themselves. Democracy seems to be at least this much: self-government, government by the people, the rule of a community by its own members. Saying this, however, does little more than set the stage for the discussion of the philosophical issues

343

inescapably confronted by any community that would seriously undertake to govern itself.

The four Sections of this Part present a great variety of arguments all of which aim to contribute to a systematic understanding of the philosophy of democracy.

In the first Section appear assorted answers to the question: *What is democracy?* Leading theories of democracy are introduced, and attempts to state its essence are explored.

In the second Section appear assorted answers to the question: *Why have a democracy?* Two ways of defending the rightness of democracy are examined: justifying it by reference to some higher laws, laws of nature or principles of justice; and justifying it by reference to its consequences, the goodness of the results it promises, or is said to promise.

In the third Section appear assorted answers to the question: *What are the principal instruments upon which democracy must rely?* Here we explore the relations between democracy and majority rule, and the role of representation (as well as different systems of representation) in making democracy work.

In the fourth Section appear a range of answers to the question: *What are the ideals and conditions of democracy?* What are the kinds of liberty that democracy requires, and that it tends to foster? What is the meaning of the equality that democracy seems to suppose and that it therefore must protect?

So much has been written about all these questions that we can reasonably expect one volume to do no more than put before us an array of answers at once provocative, and penetrating, and useful. That is the aim of the selections in this Part, all of which examine reflectively the philosophical foundations of democracy.

WHAT IS DEMOCRACY?

The word "democracy" comes to us from the Greek—"demo" is derived from the Greek word for the people, *demos;* and "cracy" from the Greek word for the power to rule, *kratein.* "We are called a democracy," said Pericles of Athens, because "the administration is in the hands of the many and not of the few." Aristotle, one of the greatest of the classical Greek philosophers, gave the first systematic account of the different forms of government; his discussion of the several kinds of democracy, of which he considers best that in which power is held by the middle class, remains very pertinent and will be found below.

In all the centuries since, from the time of Aristotle to that of the French Revolution, democracy has been much discussed but rarely practiced. The serious enlargement of democratic practice came gradually during the nineteenth and twentieth centuries; but only during the last half of the twentieth century have democratic aspirations become truly worldwide. As a political ideal, roughly understood and loosely described, democracy is now almost universally pursued.

But to pursue it most effectively we must know more precisely what it is. Is it, at the core, a bargaining process among competing interests? A way of reaching decisions? A marketplace for ideas? A process of deliberation? A frame of mind? Or the system of participation in government itself? Philosophers have continued to analyze democracy and it forms, seeking to identify its *essential* features, and to formulate what are believed to be its most fundamental principles. In the selections that follow appear the accounts presented by a number of recent philosophers of democracy, of whom perhaps the greatest is John Dewey, who says of democracy that it is a way of life "controlled by a working faith in the capacity of human beings for intelligent judgment and action if proper conditions are furnished."

59
Pericles

Pericles (498 B.C.–429 B.C.) was the foremost leader of the classical Athenian democracy. He delivered a eulogy after the battle at Megaris during the war with Sparta, honoring those who died for Athens by describing and praising the city-state for which they had fought. This most famous of all funeral orations gives the finest short statement of what democracy meant to the citizens of Athens.

OUR CITY IS THROWN OPEN TO THE WORLD*

. . . But before I praise the dead, I should like to point out by what principles of action we rose to power, and under what institutions and through what manner of life our empire became great. For I conceive that such thoughts are not unsuited to the occasion, and that this numerous assembly of citizens and strangers may profitably listen to them.

"Our form of government does not enter into rivalry with the institutions of others. We do not copy our neighbours, but are an example to them. It is true that we are called a democracy, for the administration is in the hands of the many and not of the few. But while the law secures equal justice to all alike in their private disputes, the claim of excellence is also recognized; and when a citizen is in any way distinguished, he is preferred to the public service, not as a matter of privilege, but as the reward of merit. Neither is poverty a bar, but a man may benefit his country whatever be the obscurity of his condition. There is no exclusiveness in our public life, and in our private intercourse we are not suspicious of one another, nor angry with our neighbor if he does what he likes; we do not put on sour looks at him which, though harmless, are not pleasant. While we are thus unconstrained in our private intercourse, a spirit of reverence pervades our public acts; we are prevented from doing wrong by respect for authority and for the laws, having an especial regard to those which are ordained for the protection of the injured as well as to those unwritten laws which bring upon the transgressor of them the reprobation of the general sentiment.

And we have not forgotten to provide for our weary spirits many relaxations from toil; we have regular games and sacrifices throughout the year; at home the style of our life is refined; and the delight which we daily feel in all these things helps to banish melancholy. Because of the greatness of our city the fruits of the whole earth flow in upon us; so that we enjoy the goods of other countries as freely as of our own.

Then, again, our military training is in many respects superior to that of our adversaries. Our city is thrown open to the world, and we never expel a foreigner

*This eulogy, delivered in 430 B.C., was reported by Thucydides in his history of the Peloponnesian War. The translation used here is by Benjamin Jowett, originally published in 1881, at the Clarendon Press, Oxford.

or prevent him from seeing or learning anything of which the secret if revealed to an enemy might profit him. We rely not upon management or trickery, but upon our own hearts and hands. And in the matter of education, whereas they from early youth are always undergoing laborious exercises which are to make them brave, we live at ease, and yet are equally ready to face the perils which they face. And here is the proof. The Lacedaemonians come into Attica not by themselves, but with their whole confederacy following; we go alone into a neighbor's country; and although our opponents are fighting for their homes and we on a foreign soil, we have seldom any difficulty in overcoming them. Our enemies have never yet felt our united strength; the care of a navy divides our attention, and on land we are obliged to send our own citizens everywhere. But they, if they meet and defeat a part of our army, are as proud as if they had routed us all, and when defeated they pretend to have been vanquished by us all.

If then we prefer to meet danger with a light heart but without laborious training, and with a courage which is gained by habit and not enforced by law, are we not greatly the gainers? Since we do not anticipate the pain, although, when the hour comes, we can be as brave as those who never allow themselves to rest; and thus too our city is equally admirable in peace and in war. For we are lovers of the beautiful, yet simple in our tastes, and we cultivate the mind without loss of manliness. Wealth we employ, not for talk and ostentation, but when there is a real use for it. To avow poverty with us is no disgrace; the true disgrace is in doing nothing to avoid it. An Athenian citizen does not neglect the state because he takes care of his own household; and even those of us who are engaged in business have a very fair idea of politics. We alone regard a man who takes no interest in public affairs, not as a harmless, but as a useless character; and if few of us are originators, we are all sound judges of a policy. The great impediment to action is, in our opinion, not discussion, but the want of that knowledge which is gained by discussion preparatory to action. For we have a peculiar power of thinking before we act and of acting too, whereas other men are courageous from ignorance but hesitate upon reflection. And they are surely to be esteemed the bravest spirits who, having the clearest sense both of the pains and pleasures of life, do not on that account shrink from danger.

In doing good, again, we are unlike others; we make our friends by conferring, not by receiving favors. Now he who confers a favor is the firmer friend, because he would fain by kindness keep alive the memory of an obligation; but the recipient is colder in his feelings, because he knows that in requiting another's generosity he will not be winning gratitude but only paying a debt. We alone do good to our neighbors not upon a calculation of interest, but in the confidence of freedom and in a frank and fearless spirit.

To sum up: I say that Athens is the school of Hellas, and that the individual Athenian in his own person seems to have the power of adapting himself to the most varied forms of action with the utmost versatility and grace. This is no passing and idle word, but truth and fact; and the assertion is verified by the position to which these qualities have raised the state. For in the hour of trial Athens alone among her contemporaries is superior to the report of her. No enemy who comes against her is indignant at the reverses which he sustains at the hands of such a city; no subject complains that his masters are unworthy of him. And we shall assuredly not be without witnesses; there are mighty monuments of our power which will make us the wonder of this and of succeeding ages; we shall not need the praises of Homer or of any other panegyrist whose poetry may please for the moment, although his representation of the facts will not bear the light of day. For we have compelled every land and every sea to open a path for our valor, and have everywhere planted eternal memorials of our friendship and of our enmity. Such is the city for whose sake these men nobly fought and died; they could not bear the thought that she might be taken from them; and every one of us who survive should gladly toil on her behalf.

I have dwelt upon the greatness of Athens because I want to show you that we are contending for a higher prize than those who enjoy none of these privileges, and to establish by manifest proof the merit of these men whom I am now commemorating. Their loftiest praise has been already spoken. For in magnifying the city I have magnified them, and men like them whose virtues made her glorious.

60
Aristotle

Aristotle (384 B.C.–322 B.C.) was a superb political scientist as well as a deep philosopher; having studied the actual constitutions of Greek states, he passed judgment astutely upon the merits and demerits of governments of many different kinds. His *Politics* is one of the greatest treatises in political philosophy ever written. Democracy was not Aristotle's ideal governmental form, but he understood it well: it is a government of the many based upon personal liberty, he reports, and upon the principle (which Aristotle himself finds problematic) that all citizens count equally.

[THE VARIETIES OF DEMOCRACY]*

The first variety of democracy is the variety which is said to follow the principle of equality closest. In this variety the law declares equality to mean that the poor are to count no more than the rich: neither is to be sovereign, and both are to be on a level. § 23. [We may approve this law]; for if we hold, as some thinkers do, that liberty and equality are chiefly to be found in democracy, it will be along these lines—with all sharing alike, as far as possible, in constitutional rights—that they will most likely be found. A constitution of this order is bound to be a democracy; for [while all share alike] the people are the majority, and the will of the majority is sovereign. § 24. A second variety of democracy is that in which offices are assigned on the basis of a property qualification, but the qualification is low: those who attain it have to be admitted to a share in office, and those who lose it are excluded. A third variety is one in which every citizen of unimpeachable descent can share in office, but the law is the final sov-

---

*From Aristotle, *Politics,* Book IV, Chapter 4.

ereign. § 25. A fourth variety is one in which every person [irrespective of descent, and] provided only that he is a citizen, can share in office, but the law is still the final sovereign. A fifth variety of democracy is like the fourth in admitting to office every person who has the status of citizen; but here the people, and not the law, is the final sovereign. This is what happens when popular decrees are sovereign instead of the law; and that is a result which is brought about by leaders of the demagogue type. § 26. In democracies which obey the law there are no demagogues; it is the better class of citizens who preside over affairs. Demagogues arise in states where the laws are not sovereign. The people then becomes an autocrat—a single composite autocrat made up of many members, with the many playing the sovereign, not as individuals, but collectively. § 27. It is not clear what Homer means when he says that 'it is not good to have the rule of many masters': whether he has in mind the collective rule of the many, or the rule of a number of magistrates acting as individuals. However that may be, a democracy of this order, being in the nature of an autocrat and not being governed by law, begins to attempt an autocracy. It grows despotic; flatterers come to be held in honour; it becomes analogous to the tyrannical form of single-person government. § 28. Both show a similar temper; both behave like despots to the better class of citizens; the decrees of the one are like the edicts of the other; the popular leader in the one is the same as, or at any rate like, the flatterer in the other; and in either case the influence of favourites predominates—that of the flatterer in tyrannies, and that of the popular leader in democracies of this variety. § 29. It is popular leaders who, by referring all issues to the decision of the people, are responsible for substituting the sovereignty of decrees for that of the laws. Once the people are sovereign in all matters, *they* are sovereign themselves over its decisions; the multitude follows their guidance; and this is the source of their great position. § 30. But the critics of the magistrates are also responsible. Their argument is, 'The *people* ought to decide': the people accept that invitation readily; and thus the authority of all the magistrates is undermined. There would appear to be solid substance in the view that a democracy of this type is not a true constitution. Where the laws are not sovereign, there is no constitution. § 31. Law should be sovereign on every issue, and the magistrates and the citizen body should only decide about details. The conclusion which emerges is clear. Democracy may be a form of constitution; but this particular system, under which everything is managed merely by decrees, is not even a democracy, in any real sense of the word. Decrees can never be general rules [and any real constitution must be based on general rules].   . . . So far, then, as concerns the different forms of democracy, and the definition of those forms.

[THE VITAL ROLE OF THE MIDDLE CLASS]*

§ 1. We have now to consider what is the best constitution and the best way of life for the *majority* of states and men.* In doing so we shall not employ, [for the purpose of measuring 'the best'], a standard of excellence above the reach of ordinary men, or a standard of education requiring exceptional endowments and equipment, or the standard of a constitution which attains an ideal height. We shall only be

*From Aristotle, *Politics,* Book IV, Chapter 11

concerned with the sort of life which most men are able to share and the sort of constitution which it is possible for most states to enjoy. § 2. The 'aristocracies', so called, of which we have just been treating, [will not serve us for this purpose: they] either lie, at one extreme, beyond the reach of most states, or they approach, at the other, so closely to the constitution called 'polity' that they need not be considered separately and must be treated as identical with it. The issues we have just raised can all be decided in the light of one body of fundamental principles. § 3. If we adopt as true the statements made in the *Ethics*—(1) that a truly happy life is a life of goodness lived in freedom from impediments, and (2) that goodness consists in a mean—it follows that the best way of life [for the *majority* of men] is one which consists in a mean, and a mean of the kind attainable by every individual. Further, the same criteria which determine whether the citizen-body [i.e. all its members, considered as *individuals*] have a good or bad way of life must also apply to the constitution; for a constitution is the way of life of a citizen-body. § 4. In all states there may be distinguished three parts, or classes, of the citizen-body—the very rich; the very poor; and the middle class which forms the mean. Now it is admitted, as a general principle, that moderation and the mean are always best. We may therefore conclude that in the ownership of all gifts of fortune a middle condition will be the best. § 5. Men who are in this condition are the most ready to listen to reason. Those who belong to either extreme—the over-handsome, the over-strong, the over-noble, the over-wealthy; or at the opposite end the over-poor, the over-weak, the utterly ignoble—find it hard to follow the lead of reason. Men in the first class tend more to violence and serious crime: men in the second tend too much to roguery and petty offences; and most wrongdoing arises either from violence or roguery. It is a further merit of the middle class that its members suffer least from ambition, which both in the military and the civil sphere is dangerous to states. § 6. It must also be added that those who enjoy too many advantages—strength, wealth, connexions, and so forth—are both unwilling to obey and ignorant how to obey. This is a defect which appears in them from the first, during childhood and in home-life: nurtured in luxury, they never acquire a habit of discipline, even in the matter of lessons. But there are also defects in those who suffer from the opposite extreme of a lack of advantages: they are far too mean and poor-spirited. § 7. We have thus, on the one hand, people who are ignorant how to rule and only know how to obey, as if they were so many slaves, and, on the other hand, people who are ignorant how to obey any sort of authority and only know how to rule as if they were masters of slaves. The result is a state, not of freemen, but only of slaves and masters: a state of envy on the one side and on the other contempt. Nothing could be further removed from the spirit of friendship or the temper of a political community. Community depends on friendship; and when there is enmity instead of friendship, men will not even share the same path. § 8. A state aims at being, as far as it can be, a society composed of equals and peers [who, as such, can be friends and associates]; and the middle class, more than any other, has this sort of composition. It follows that a state which is based on the middle class is bound to be the best constituted in respect of the elements [i.e. equals and peers] of which, on our view, a state is naturally composed. The middle classes [besides contributing, in this way, to the security of the state] enjoy a greater security themselves than any other class. § 9. They do not, like the poor, covet the goods of others; nor do others covet their possessions, as the poor covet those of the rich. Neither plotting against others, not plotted against themselves, they live in freedom from danger; and we may well approve the prayer of Phocylides

> Many things are best for the middling:
> Fain would I be of the state's middle class.

§ 10. It is clear from our argument, first, that the best form of political society is one where power is vested in the middle class, and, secondly, that good government is attainable in those states where there is a large middle class—large enough, if possible, to be stronger than both of the other classes, but at any rate large enough to be stronger than either of them singly; for in that case its addition to either will suffice to turn the scale, and will prevent either of the opposing extremes from becoming dominant. § 11. It is therefore the greatest of blessings for a state that its members should possess a moderate and adequate property. Where some have great possessions, and others have nothing at all, the result is either an extreme democracy or an unmixed oligarchy; or it may even be—indirectly, and as a reaction against both of these extremes—a tyranny. Tyranny is a form of government which may grow out of the headiest type of democracy, or out of oligarchy; but it is much less likely to grow out of constitutions of the middle order, or those which approximate to them [e.g. moderate oligarchies]. § 12. We shall explain the reason later, when we come to treat of revolutions and constitutional change.

Meanwhile, it is clear that the middle type of constitution is best [for the *majority* of states]. It is the one type free from faction; where the middle class is large, there is least likelihood of faction and dissension among the citizens. § 13. Large states are generally more free from faction just because they have a large middle class. In small states, on the other hand, it is easy for the whole population to be divided into only two classes; nothing is left in the middle, and all—or almost all—are either poor or rich. § 14. The reason why democracies are generally more secure and more permanent than oligarchies is the character of their middle class, which is more numerous, and is allowed a larger share in the government, than it is in oligarchies. Where democracies have no middle class, and the poor are greatly superior in number, trouble ensues, and they are speedily ruined. . . .

[THE ATTRIBUTES OF DEMOCRACY]*

Chapter 2

§ 1. The underlying idea of the democratic type of constitution is liberty. (This, it is commonly said, can only be enjoyed in democracy; and this, it is also said, is the aim of every democracy.) Liberty has more than one form. One of its forms [is

---

*From Aristotle, *Politics,* Book VI, Chapters 2–3.

the political, which] consists in the interchange of ruling and being ruled. § 2. The democratic conception of justice is the enjoyment of arithmetical equality, and not the enjoyment of proportionate equality on the basis of desert. On this arithmetical conception of justice the masses must necessarily be sovereign; the will of the majority must be ultimate and must be the expression of justice. The argument is that each citizen should be on an equality with the rest; and the result which follows in democracies is that the poor—they being in a majority, and the will of the majority being sovereign—are more sovereign than the rich. § 3. Such is the first form of liberty, which all democrats agree in making the aim of their sort of constitution. The other form [is the civil, which] consists in 'living as you like'. Such a life, the democrats argue, is the function of the free man, just as the function of slaves is *not* to live as they like. § 4. This is the second aim of democracy. Its issue is, ideally, freedom from any interference of government, and, failing that, such freedom as comes from the interchange of ruling and being ruled. It contributes, in this way, to a general system of liberty based on equality.

§ 5. Such being the idea of democracy, and the root from which it develops, we can now proceed to study its attributes or institutions. [Under the head of the executive], there is the election of officers *by* all, and *from* all; there is the system of all ruling over each, and each, in his turn, over all; there is the method of appointing by lot to all offices—or, at any rate, to all which do not require some practical experience and professional skill; there is the rule that there should be no property-qualification for office—or, at any rate, the lowest possible; there is the rule that, apart from the military offices, no office should ever be held twice by the same person—or, at any rate, only on few occasions, and those relating only to a few offices; there is, finally, the rule that the tenure of every office—or, at any rate, of as many as possible—should be brief. [Under the head of the judicature], there is the system of popular courts, composed of all the citizens or of persons selected from all, and competent to decide all cases—or, at any rate, most of them, and those the greatest and most important, such as the audit of official accounts, constitutional issues, and matters of contract. [Under the head of the deliberative] there is the rule that the popular assembly should be sovereign in all matters—or, at any rate, in the most important; and conversely that the executive magistracies should be sovereign in none—or, at any rate, in as few as possible.

§ 6. Among the executive magistracies the one most popular in democracies is the Council, wherever there are not adequate means for paying all the citizens to attend the popular assembly. If there *are* adequate means, the Council itself is deprived of its power; and the people, once it is furnished with pay, begins to take everything into its hands, as has already been noticed in the previous section of our inquiry. § 7. This system of payment is a further attribute of democracy. The ideal is payment in every sphere—popular assembly, courts, and executive magistracies; but if that cannot be had, there will at any rate be payment for attending the courts, the council, and the stated meetings of the popular assembly, and also for serving on any board of magistrates—or, at the least, any board whose members are required to have a common table. (It may be remarked that while oligarchy is characterized by good birth, wealth, and culture, the attributes of democracy would appear to be the very opposite—low birth, poverty, and vulgarity.) § 8. Another attribute of democracy is to dispense with all life offices—or at least to curtail the powers of any such offices, if they have been left surviving from some earlier epoch of change, and to make appointments to any life-office depend on the use of the lot and not on election.

§ 9. These are the attributes common to democracies generally. But if we look at the form of democracy and the sort of populace which is generally held to be specially typical, we have to connect it [not so much with these attributes, as] with the conception of justice which is the recognized democratic conception—that of equality of rights for all on an arithmetical basis. Equality here *might* be taken to mean that the poorer class should exercise no greater authority than the rich, or, in other words, that sovereignty should not be exercised only by it, but equally vested in all the citizens on a numerical basis. If that were the interpretation followed, the upholders of democracy could afford to believe that equality—and liberty—was really achieved by their constitution.

Chapter 3

§ 1. This raises the question, 'How is such equality actually to be secured?' Should the assessed *properties* of the citizens be divided into two equal blocks, but with one block containing 500 large and the other 1,000 small owners, and should the 1,000 and the 500 have equal voting power? Or, alternatively, should equality of this order [i.e. equality based on property, and not on personality] be calculated on some other system—a system, for example, by which properties are divided into two equal blocks, as before, but equal numbers of representatives are then selected from the 500 owners in the one block and the 1,000 in the other, and the representatives so selected are given control of the elections [of magistrates] and the law courts? § 2. [Either system means, in effect, the basing of the constitution on property.] Now is a constitution so based the one most in accordance with justice, as justice is conceived in democracies? Or is a constitution based on numbers [i.e. on *persons,* rather than property] more truly in accordance with justice? Democrats reply by saying that justice consists in the will of a majority of persons. Oligarchs reply by saying that it consists in the will of a majority of property-owners, and that decisions should be taken on the basis of weight of property. § 3. Both of these answers involve inequality and injustice. If justice is made to consist in the will of the few [i.e. the few who own the greatest amount of property], tyranny is the logical result; for if we carry the oligarchical conception of justice to its logical consequence, a single person who owns more than all the other owners of property put together will have a just claim to be the sole ruler. If, on the other hand, justice is made to consist in the will of a majority of persons, that majority will be sure to act unjustly, as we have already noted, and to confiscate the property of the rich minority.

§ 4. In this position we have to ask, in the light of the definitions of justice propounded by both sides, 'What is the sort of equality to which both sides can agree?' . . .

To find theoretically where truth resides, in these matters of equality and justice, is a very difficult task. Difficult as it may be, it is an easier task than that of persuading men to act justly, if they have power enough to secure their own selfish interests. The weaker are always anxious for equality and justice. The strong pay no heed to either.

61
Carl Cohen

Carl Cohen (1931–   ) is a professor of philosophy at The University of Michigan. His book, *Democracy,* presents a general theory of democracy, dealing in turn with its nature, presuppositions, instruments, conditions, prospects, and defense. The core of the democratic process, he argues, is the *participation* of the members of a community in making the decisions that govern the community as a whole. The degree to which democracy is genuinely realized in any community, therefore, is determined by the quality and quantity of that citizen participation, direct or indirect.

WHAT DEMOCRACY IS*

Some Short Definitions of Democracy

Democracy is government by the people. This is a definition most dictionaries report and one likely to meet with general approval. It also fits the etymology of the term: *demos,* the people, and *kratein,* to rule, are its Greek roots. Ancient philosophers and statesmen used this concept in a reasonably straightforward way. "We are called a democracy," said Pericles, "because the administration is in the hands of the many and not of the few." Aristotle, after distinguishing several kinds of democracy, says at last, "We may lay it down generally that a system which does not allow every citizen to share is oligarchical (*oligos,* few) and that one which does so is democratic" (*Politics,* IV, 6). In more recent times, Abraham Lincoln's often quoted phrase, "government of the people, by the people, and for the people," suggests the same general idea. Democracy is a system in which the people govern themselves.

Short expressions that purport to define democracy do not explain much, however, even when they meet with general accord, because they seek to put too simply a matter that is not at all simple. Some further examples are: "Government by consent," "Rule by the majority," "Government with equal rights for all," "Sovereignty of the people," and so on. Such epigrammatic definitions are usually not mistaken, but they cannot reach the heart of the matter. When we examine any

*From Carl Cohen, *Democracy* (NY: The Free Press, 1972). Copyright C. Cohen.

such expression critically its inadequacy becomes apparent. Government by consent of whom? Consent to what? Equal rights to what? What constitutes consent or equality of right? What is sovereignty, and when do the people possess it? Rule by the majority of whom? Is majority rule always democratic, and do democratic decisions always require majority approval? Surely there is a difference between government *for* the people and government *by* the people; what shall we say of a government that is one and not the other? Where does government *of* the people fit in? Puzzles of this sort abound. It is necessary to begin afresh if we are to understand clearly and thoroughly what is meant by the correct assertion that democracy is government by the people.

The Paradox of Self-Rule

We say that in a democracy the people rule themselves, that the people are sovereign. This is a figurative mode of speech from at least one point of view. The concepts 'rule' and 'sovereign' are relational: there is no ruler without ruled, no sovereign without subject. Part of what is involved in ruling is the power of over-ruling, of compelling the ruled or of acting against their will. In this important sense the people cannot rule themselves, although one part of the people may rule another part. "It was now perceived," John Stuart Mill wrote in 1859, "that such phrases as 'self-government,' and 'the power of the people over themselves,' do not express the true state of the case. The 'people' who exercise the power are not always the same people with those over whom it is exercised . . .." (*On Liberty,* Chap. 1). Almost a century later this concern had hardened into these assertions by Walter Lippmann: "The people . . . cannot administer the government. They cannot themselves perform. They cannot normally initiate and propose the necessary legislation. A mass cannot govern" (*The Public Philosophy,* 1955, p. 19). No one has put the point more elegantly than Gladstone: "No people of a magnitude to be called a nation has ever, in strictness, governed itself; the utmost which appears to be attainable, under the conditions of human life, is that it should choose its governors, and that it should on select occasions bear directly on their action" (*The Nineteenth Century,* July 1878).

In the world of practical politics it is evident that the people cannot, in the sense indicated, rule themselves. The government obeyed may be of the people's own selection, but the people do not enact or execute the laws. This distinction between rulers and ruled, at least in large communities, is not difficult to draw. Most men are governed but not governors.

Still the notion of self-government is not foolish, and when we use the expression to describe certain states of affairs we seem to make sense. Democratic government *is* self-government, government of the people by themselves. In some contexts such government is a reality. Yet if the earlier objection be taken seriously the people cannot govern themselves. How is this paradox to be resolved?

Consider the use of the expression "self-government" in a nonpolitical context. We speak of an individual as potentially self-governed, governed by himself alone. The usage may be figurative here also, for no single person can over-rule himself, although conceivably his higher faculties may over-rule his lower faculties, if that distinction among faculties can be drawn. Nevertheless, the distinction between governing one's self and being governed by others is of the first importance to every human being. An understanding of self-government on this personal level may serve as the key to the resolution of the paradox of community self-rule.

As an individual I enjoy self-rule when I am not directed, controlled by anyone else. I govern myself when I decide for myself the goals I shall seek, and choose my own means for attaining them. Every person experiences such individual control in at least some of the affairs of life. Where then is the difficulty? The paradox arises from the fact that the verb "to govern" has a double meaning. In one sense the power to govern includes the power to over-rule, to compel, and therefore implies a bifurcation of governors and governed. This may be called the *administrative* sense of government. In another, deeper sense, to govern is to establish goals or policy, to give direction to the body governed. The latter is the original meaning of the verb "to govern," coming from the Latin *gubernare,* and in turn from the Greek *kybernan,* to steer, or pilot a ship. This may be called the *directive* sense of government.

In any community the government may command, forbid, overrule; these are its administrative functions experienced directly in daily life, and the ones focused upon by those who argue that a community cannot govern itself. More fundamentally, however, who governs the community guides it, steers it. When this directive function is understood as primary in governing, the paradox of self-rule melts away. Insofar as government is conceived administratively, it involves the conflict of wills and the subordination of some to others, and it must be a portion of the community that governs, not the whole. But insofar as government is conceived directively, involving the determination of policy and the objectives which guide communal life, it may be a few or it may be the many who govern. In principle it is possible for all the members of a community to participate in the establishment of the ends sought in common. If all, or most, do participate in this task, we may fairly describe that community as self-governed.

The Essence of Democracy

Democracy is a kind of community government. To specify the nature of democracy, therefore, it is necessary to differentiate this kind of community government from all other kinds. This, in turn, requires an appreciation of the great scope of the concept of community. There is no practical limit to the number or variety of human communities. The purposes that bind men into community may range from the trivial to the world-shaking; the size of communities may range from very small to very large. The boundaries of a community need by no means be geographical; the principle of its unity may lie in fraternal, charitable, ethnic, religious, or economic concerns. What is held in common by the members of a community may be of passing or secondary concern to them, or it may call forth their most permanent and profound loyalties. In reflecting upon the communities in which democracy can subsist, it is most important that one not focus exclusively upon national states. These are very important communities, and we are understandably very much interested in the way democracy functions in them. But a satisfactory theory of democracy must be applicable to a range of community types and sizes far exceeding that of national states. Communities of greatly different kinds and sizes may be governed democratically.

What does the democratic government of a community entail? The analogy between the life of a community and the life of an individual is again helpful. An individual can be self-governing in choosing his own ends; he can be self-directing, autonomous. Such self-direction or autonomy on an interpersonal scale is democracy.

Democracy is government by the people in that it is the system within which the people, the members of the community, participate in the determination of policy for the community as a whole. The directive function of government is central to any account of self-government; it is the fact that this directive function can be widely shared that renders democracy possible.

What is involved in the notion of determining policy for the community as a whole? Clearly that is not a function that the members of a community can perform once and be done with. Policy is constantly being formed and re-formed; the direction of a community requires continual attention. Self-government, therefore, requires a continuing series of decisions, of greater or lesser importance, and it is in the making of these decisions, choices, that participation in policy-making becomes concrete. When the most important decisions of the community are reached through the general participation of its members, we may call that community self-governed.

Which decisions are the most important ones, those upon which the entire membership of the community should have some voice? The natural reply is that the membership should have a voice in making decisions that affect them all, or that seriously affect them all. But which decisions are these? This question has no general answer. In many specific contexts it is answered clearly enough by the nature of the community. In other contexts there just may be no agreement upon which issues are rightly dealt with by the membership at large. Conflict on this matter may stem from disagreement over the basic purposes of the community; or (if these be agreed upon) conflict may lie in disagreement over what spheres of activity must be under collective control if those larger purposes are to be realized. Which issues are the proper business of the community is inevitably a controversial question.

Happily this question, however difficult in particular cases, does not have to be answered in order to grasp the essential nature of democracy itself. A statement of that essence, a definition of democracy, I now present with the understanding that it is to receive a good deal of further refinement. *Democracy is that system of community government in which, by and large, the members of a community participate, or may participate, directly or indirectly, in the making of decisions which affect them all.*

Upon this foundation we can build a coherent theory of democracy. A necessary first step is the more careful analysis of *participation* and its dimensions. . . .

62
A. D. Lindsay

Alexander D. Lindsay (1892–1952) was a professor of moral philosophy at Glasgow University and long-time Master of Balliol College, Oxford. Confident in the ability of ordinary people to judge wisely in matters of community concern, he emphasized the critical role of *discussion* in a democracy. Not the equality of citizen-participants in itself, but the special deliberative process in which they engage, he argued, is what makes democracy unique.

[DEMOCRATIC PROBLEMS AND PARADOXES]*

It is a commonplace of political theory that direct democracy became impossible when the size of the community outgrew the limits of a single public meeting. But long before that limit is reached most members of the community have ceased to take any part in the discussion or to contribute anything to the meeting. No one can really do business at a big meeting. Men can say Yes or No to cut-and-dried proposals, or compelling and spellbinding speeches may turn votes, but the real discussion and largely the real government is in the hands of the committee who prepare the business.

The real point is that when a society has grown beyond the limits of a public meeting, then even the pretence of direct government has to be given up, and something has to be done about it. And that the limit of direct democracy was felt to be determined by the limit in the size of the public meeting, and not by the much earlier limit of the effective discussion, has been of sinister importance in the theory of democracy. It has suggested that what matters is not that the people should rule, but that they should think they rule; and it has given undue emphasis to the element of consent over the element of discussion.

But the practical man will be listening to all this with growing impatience. How far away all such discussions seem from the actual necessities of government even in the seventeenth century! The population of the nation state even then ran into millions. What relation could there possibly be between the government of millions, scattered

---

*These passages are from A. D. Lindsay (Lord Lindsay of Birker), *The Essentials of Democracy,* 2nd ed., (Oxford: The Clarendon Press, 1929) by permission of the publisher. This small book consists of the William J. Cooper Foundation Lectures, delivered at Swarthmore College, Pennsylvania, in January 1929.

over a wide area, with little knowledge of one another, and the government of a congregation? Ought we not to say frankly that in these circumstances government by the people is an obvious impossibility? Government, even if it be government by means of discussion, can only be carried on by a few, and that is surely the end of it.

We are accustomed to say that this problem was solved by representative government. That representative government was adopted because of this difficulty of size is true enough. . . . It was the great invention of representative government (so the accepted theory of government runs) which enabled modern democracy to pass the narrow limits within which Greek democracy was confined—limits defined by Aristotle as the range of an orator's voice.

[But] democratic theory . . . has never been entirely happy about the representative. He is a necessary evil, to be done without if possible. Think of the disputes which have raged round the difference between representative and delegate—round the proper relation of a representative to his constituents—of Walt Whitman's protest against 'the never-ending audacity of elected persons'—of the very different answers given to the puzzling question, 'What does a representative represent?' . . . Rousseau confirmed this attitude in his statement that the people of England are free only at a general election, and that then they enslave themselves. From Rousseau till the present day there is a continuous tradition in democratic theory which had denounced representative government as essentially undemocratic—or at least as a makeshift to be controlled and limited as much as possible, and democratic practice in Switzerland and America, if not in England, has made experiment after experiment to embody this tradition in practice.

Let us accept the position of the Levellers that the consent to government and to acts of government by each and every member of the community is the one thing needful to democracy—that therefore government by the public meeting, where such is possible, is its ideal form—and with that in mind let us think again of Aristotle's limit of democracy—the range of an orator's voice; and remember that there are now other ways than representative government of setting back these limits. Thanks to broadcasting, the whole world might become in some sense a public meeting. . . .

The logical conclusion of the whole process is that if we can make the whole country one public meeting, we can make it govern and say Yes or No at the end of the discussion, and so we are to regard the referendum as the logical outcome of democracy. We may even go further and let there be demands from the body of the hall that something else should be discussed—instead of letting the preparation of the agenda be confined entirely to the platform, and then we shall add to the referendum the initiative. . . .

In spite however of the help which democracy now gets from modern science, this process of widening the area of democratic government is disillusioning. Modern democracy does not feel like the simple town meeting or the congregation. What has gone wrong? . . .

Let us ask ourselves whether we really want to make government like an immense public meeting. Does any sane man think that a desirable end to bring about? What did anyone ever *do* at a public meeting except produce enthusiasm? Look at the practice of largish democratic societies, and observe that when they hold their congresses they may have public meetings for propaganda purposes, but they never attempt more than the most formal business at them. Government by public meeting is an impossibility, as anyone must recognize who will think what a public meeting can actually do, or has seen a public meeting unexpectedly asked to do something. When we think of modern democracy as Greek democracy enlarged by modern inventions, we should remember that the Greeks did not think that a state which was, as we say, governed by a public meeting was necessarily a democracy. For them the test question was—what was the constitution of the body which arranged the agenda for and managed the public meeting? Only if that were elected by lot (were what President Lowell calls a sample democracy) did they call the state a democracy. Otherwise it was an oligarchy, governed by the few who arranged the business, settled what questions were to be asked, and arranged the discussion. It is not merely that a public meeting can only say Yes or No to questions put to it, or that public meetings whether of visible or invisible audiences are notoriously susceptible to mass suggestion, but that whether they say Yes or No depends enormously on how the questions are put, and on what sort of discussion there is.

Further it is worth noting that most of (though not all) the effective criticisms of democracy are criticisms of what happens at the public meeting, visible and invisible. The anti-democrat calls democracy government by a mob. But a collection of people is not in itself a mob, and it is not made a mob because its members are common or ordinary or stupid people, but because and in so far as they are under the influence of mass suggestion. The individual members of the most howling mob would be found to be sensible decent people in their own circle when dealing with familiar problems which they have to face as a matter of business. The anti-democrat who contemplates certain aspects of the public meeting may well say of democracy, if it is government by public meeting, that it is government by mass suggestion; that its implication is that people govern best by getting themselves into a state of mind in which they would never dream of getting to solve their own comparatively simple problems. No one supposes that in ordinary life the responses of people under mass suggestion are of any serious value whatever. No one in his senses, if he had to solve an ordinary scientific or practical problem, would put himself under mass suggestion. The anti-democrat contemplating much that goes on at a general election may well ask—what are we to think of a form of government in which people deliberately make themselves drunk, or allow themselves to be made drunk, before they decide the most important questions of government? For there is no very essential difference in the effects on the judgement of mass suggestion and of alcohol. And the cynically-minded might say that it was not an accident that in the early days of democracy election days were great days of drunkenness: that if the liquor has now largely disappeared, that is partly because the required result can be produced without it; the effectiveness of mass suggestion has so much increased. . . .

The theory which forces men to acquiesce in these evils is the theory of the Levellers that the essence of democracy is government by the consent of all the governed—that that result is more important than are the means by which it is attained. . . .

[DISCUSSION AS THE ESSENTIAL ELEMENT IN DEMOCRATIC PARTICIPATION]

Now surely, if we reflect upon it, what matters most in the tiny democratic societies which we feel to be thoroughly satisfactory forms of government is what comes out of the free give and take of discussion. When men who are serving a common purpose meet to pool their experience, to air their difficulties and even their discontents, there comes about a real process of collective thinking. The narrowness and onesidedness of each person's point of view are corrected, and something emerges which each can recognize as embodying the truth of what he stood for, and yet (or rather therefore) is seen to serve the purpose of the society better than what anyone conceived for himself. That is of course an ideal. Such perfect agreement is not often reached. But it is an ideal which is always to some extent realized when there is open and frank discussion. And any one with experience of the effectiveness of discussion in a small democratic society must recognize how valuable is the contribution of those who are not easily convinced but can stand up resolutely for their own point of view. Where discussion of that kind prevails, we recognize that democracy is not a makeshift or a compromise or a means of keeping people quiet by the production of a sham unanimity, or a process of counting heads to save the trouble of breaking them, but the ideal form of government.

Observe further that the moment we take discussion seriously, we are committed to the view that we are concerned not primarily to obtain or register consent, but to find something out. What it is that democratic discussion is trying to find out we shall discuss later. The root of the matter is that if the discussion is at all successful, we discover something from it which could have been discovered in no other way. I am only concerned now to note and insist on this fact, and to note its likeness to the discovery of truth in other spheres. Modern science is a great realm of co-operative thinking where discoveries are made originally by the work of isolated individuals, but where they are tested and enlarged by criticism and discussion. Every scientific discoverer knows that what he most wants to know is not what can be said for, but what can be said against his theory. What he most wants is an opposition. The example of scientific co-operative thinking may remind us that democratic discussion is entirely compatible with leadership and with any amount of difference in the weight of the contributions made by different members. Democracy assumes that each member of the community has something to contribute if it can be got out of him. It does not for a moment assume that what each member contributes is of equal value.

Now if, with all this in mind, we approach the problem created by the large scale of political democracy, we shall say that what matters is not that the final decision of government should be assented to by every one, but that every one should have somehow made his contribution to that decision. There cannot possibly be one enormous discussion, but there may be smaller areas of discussion, and the results of these may be conveyed by the representative to a further discussion, and so on. If we examine the means by which non-political democratic societies which have grown beyond the area of a discussion group try to keep the society democratic, we find the process of representation at its best. . . .

[VOTING]

. . . It is of paramount importance to the health of a representative assembly that public opinion should be focussed on its doings. We must have real discussion, and we must insist therefore that our representative assemblies shall be so constituted, and have such a procedure, that real discussion is possible in them. But that discussion is to take place, if possible, with the invisible public listening; and the function of a general election is not simply to choose representatives but to express the approval or disapproval of the general public on the doings of the representative assembly. Of course, in a healthy and educated democracy, discussion, as we have already said, will not be confined to the discussions of the representative assembly. The discussion of the assembly will define issues. Profitable discussion in even the smallest group, as we all know, needs a chairman to define issues and focus attention on the points where discussion will be profitable. In a healthy democracy the discussions of the representative assembly will as it were act as chairman for the multifarious informal discussion of the nation as a whole, and the measure of the successful working of democracy is the extent to which the voting of the ordinary man and woman has been informed by this widely diffused public discussion.

But when all this is said, the importance of voting, of taking part in the decision, saying Yes or No on the broad issues formulated by the representative assembly, remains. However strongly we may hold that discussion rather than consent is the thing most worth having in democracy, we know this to be the case. It was no answer to the advocates of female suffrage that women could take part in political discussion as well as men, and therefore could without the vote already make their contribution. It was demanded that their discussion and influence should have behind it the power of the vote, and that that was a real demand was universally recognized.

.   .   .

Now all this process of discussion is, however complicated and arranged for, a natural process—grounded in the facts of human nature. In comparison, is there not something curiously artificial about voting? The purpose of discussion is to achieve a real unity of purpose out of differences. The principle of voting says that all are to count alike. Democratic instinct has always rejected, and surely rightly, schemes to differentiate voters—to give men more votes because they are richer or better educated than other people. There have of course been many attempts in modern democratic governments to weight votes; but such proposals or enactments have ordinarily, and I think justly, been held to be undemocratic. The democratic opponents of such devices would say that they do not deny the difference between men's political capacities, but would maintain that wealth or wisdom or leadership will have their natural effect in the discussion that precedes the voting, and no doubt therefore on the voting. But in the voting itself, they would maintain, each is to count for one and no one for more than one. Votes are not really all of equal value, but they are all to be counted as equal. That is the real paradox of democratic government which continually provokes the scorn of nondemocratic critics, and yet it is, I think, a paradox which the democrat must somehow defend at all costs.

In the second place, the principle of voting rests on the convention that what commands the assent of the majority of voters (either a bare majority or some specified majority of voters) shall be deemed to be the decision of the whole. That again is something conventional which needs justification.

We shall best approach this question, I believe, by going back to our simple small democracy. There what strikes us is that in a sufficiently small democratic group which is working well there is often very little voting. The part elsewhere played by voting is there played by what is called the sense of the meeting. Let us ask ourselves what that part is. . . . The sense of the meeting, when it is effective, ensures that the discussion shall serve and be controlled by the common purpose. To that end every one contributes, and the contribution of all is necessary.

In such a meeting voting is usually unnecessary, but it is wanted when anything goes wrong. . . .

Of course voting is also used much more often for purposes of convenience. When there is not time or possibility of resolving differences, when the one creative proposal which would unite all differences has not been discovered, and we have to choose between more or less satisfactory proposals, the necessity for acting in this world will not wait on our finding the entirely satisfactory solution which would resolve all our differences. We have to act, and to act promptly with what light we have, and action is decisive. Therefore we have to have a rough-and-ready way of deciding between such alternatives as have presented themselves. Equal counting of heads and agreement to abide by the majority vote are rough-and-ready means of getting a second best decision.

There is a special kind of majority rule, very important in politics, which is worth noting and helps to elucidate the point I am making, and that is the rule of a majority party. There may be differences within a community which cannot be resolved by discussion but only by action. The necessary maintaining and organizing of opposition may and often does set up differences too sharply held to be reconciled. 'It is the business of an opposition to oppose,' as the maxim says. But these differences may be and often are reconciled by giving each party a turn to carry out its policy. Then it is found that for all the fire with which the opposition opposed each and every clause of a government's bill, they do not reverse it all when they get the chance. Good representative government, as we all recognize, needs not only a strong opposition. It needs also that the opposition should be an alternative government. In the alternation in power of political parties there is often worked out in practical dialectic what discussion could not discover.

The theory behind the whole procedure is that we are trying by expression and discussion of different standpoints to find out what the purpose of the community requires, and that of *that* the ordinary member of the community is as good a judge as anyone else, provided (and the proviso is, as we shall see, of enormous importance)—provided that he understands what the proposals between which he is judging really amount to. Rousseau is often supposed to have said that the general will is always right. He did not. He said it was always honest. What he was insisting on was the power of the ordinary man to judge of fair play, of honesty, of conformance with the spirit of the community. It is this sense which the ordinary man can contribute and to which the expert, absorbed as he naturally is in his own solution and in his special contribution, often fails to contribute.

63
Joseph A. Schumpeter

Joseph A. Schumpeter (1883–1950) was an internationally renowned political economist (and Austrian Minister of Finance) whose account of democracy departed from the classical view; for him the democratic process is genuine if and only if the leaders of a community acquire their power to make decisions for that community by competing for the support of the citizenry. His influential book, *Capitalism, Socialism, and Democracy,* elaborates upon this theory: that the essence of democratic government is *competition for leadership.*

[DEMOCRACY AS COMPETITION FOR POLITICAL LEADERSHIP]*

I think that most students of politics have by now come to accept the criticisms leveled at the classical doctrine of democracy in the preceding chapter. I also think that most of them agree, or will agree before long, in accepting another theory which is much truer to life and at the same time salvages much of what sponsors of the democratic method really mean by this term. Like the classical theory, it may be put into the nutshell of a definition.

It will be remembered that our chief troubles about the classical theory centered in the proposition that "the people" hold a definite and rational opinion about every individual question and that they give effect to this opinion—in a democracy—by choosing "representatives" who will see to it that that opinion is carried out. Thus the selection of the representatives is made secondary to the primary purpose of the democratic arrangement which is to vest the power of deciding

---

*Reprinted from *Capitalism, Socialism, and Democracy,* 3rd. edition 1950, pp. 269–273. By permission of Harper & Row Publishers, Inc. and Allen & Unwin Ltd. London.

political issues in the electorate. Suppose we reverse the roles of these two elements and make the deciding of issues by the electorate secondary to the election
of the men who are to do the deciding. To put it differently, we now take the view
that the role of the people is to produce a government, or else an intermediate body
which in turn will produce a national executive* or government. And we define:
the democratic method is that institutional arrangement for arriving at political
decisions in which individuals acquire the power to decide by means of a competitive struggle for the people's vote.

Defense and explanation of this idea will speedily show that, as to both plausibility of assumptions and tenability of propositions, it greatly improves the theory
of the democratic process.

First of all, we are provided with a reasonably efficient criterion by which to
distinguish democratic governments from others. We have seen that the classical
theory meets with difficulties on that score because both the will and the good of
the people may be, and in many historical instances have been, served just as well
or better by governments that cannot be described as democratic according to any
accepted usage of the term. Now we are in a somewhat better position partly
because we are resolved to stress a *modus procedendi* the presence or absence of
which it is in most cases easy to verify.[†]

For instance, a parliamentary monarchy like the English one fulfills the requirements of the democratic method because the monarch is practically constrained to
appoint to cabinet office the same people as parliament would elect. A "constitutional" monarchy does not qualify to be called democratic because electorates and
parliaments, while having all the other rights that electorates and parliaments have
in parliamentary monarchies, lack the power to impose their choice as to the governing committee: the cabinet ministers are in this case servants of the monarch,
in substance as well as in name, and can in principle be dismissed as well as
appointed by him. Such an arrangement may satisfy the people. The electorate
may reaffirm this fact by voting against any proposal for change. The monarch
may be so popular as to be able to defeat any competition for the supreme office.
But since no machinery is provided for making this competition effective the case
does not come within our definition.

Second, the theory embodied in this definition leaves all the room we may wish
to have for a proper recognition of the vital fact of leadership. The classical theory
did not do this but, as we have seen, attributed to the electorate an altogether unrealistic degree of initiative which practically amounted to ignoring leadership. But
collectives act almost exclusively by accepting leadership—this is the dominant
mechanism of practically any collective action which is more than a reflex. Propositions about the working and the results of the democratic method that take
account of this are bound to be infinitely more realistic than propositions which do

---

*The insincere word "executive" really points in the wrong direction. It ceases however to do so if we
use it in the sense in which we speak of the "executives" of a business corporation who also do a great deal
more than "execute" the will of stockholders.

†See however the fourth point below.

not. They will not stop at the execution of a *volonté générale* but will go some way toward showing how it emerges or how it is substituted or faked. What we have termed Manufactured Will is no longer outside the theory, an aberration for the absence of which we piously pray; it enters on the ground floor as it should.

Third, however, so far as there are genuine group-wise volitions at all—for instance the will of the unemployed to receive unemployment benefit or the will of other groups to help—our theory does not neglect them. On the contrary we are now able to insert them in exactly the role they actually play. Such volitions do not as a rule assert themselves directly. Even if strong and definite they remain latent, often for decades, until they are called to life by some political leader who turns them into political factors. This he does, or else his agents do it for him, by organizing these volitions, by working them up and by including eventually appropriate items in his competitive offering. The interaction between sectional interests and public opinion and the way in which they produce the pattern we call the political situation appear from this angle in a new and much clearer light.

Fourth, our theory is of course no more definite than is the concept of competition for leadership. This concept presents similar difficulties as the concept of competition in the economic sphere, with which it may be usefully compared. In economic life competition is never completely lacking, but hardly ever is it perfect. Similarly, in political life there is always some competition, though perhaps only a potential one, for the allegiance of the people. To simplify matters we have restricted the kind of competition for leadership which is to define democracy, to free competition for a free vote. The justification for this is that democracy seems to imply a recognized method by which to conduct the competitive struggle, and that the electoral method is practically the only one available for communities of any size. But though this excludes many ways of securing leadership which should be excluded,* such as competition by military insurrection, it does not exclude the cases that are strikingly analogous to the economic phenomena we label "unfair" or "fraudulent" competition or restraint of competition. And we cannot exclude them because if we did we should be left with a completely unrealistic ideal.† Between this ideal case which does not exist and the cases in which all competition with the established leader is prevented by force, there is a continuous range of variation within which the democratic method of government shades off into the autocratic one by imperceptible steps. But if we wish to understand and not to philosophize, this is as it should be. The value of our criterion is not seriously impaired thereby.

Fifth, our theory seems to clarify the relation that subsists between democracy and individual freedom. If by the latter we mean the existence of a sphere of indi-

---

*It also excludes methods which should not be excluded, for instance, the acquisition of political leadership by the people's tacit acceptance of it or by election *quasi per inspirationem*. The latter differs from election by voting only by a technicality. But the former is not quite without importance even in modern politics; the sway held by a party boss *within his party* is often based on nothing but tacit acceptance of his leadership. Comparatively speaking however these are details which may, I think, be neglected in a sketch like this.

†As in the economic field, *some* restrictions are implicit in the legal and moral principles of the community.

vidual self-government the boundaries of which are historically variable—*no* society tolerates absolute freedom even of conscience and of speech, *no* society reduces that sphere to zero—the question clearly becomes a matter of degree. We have seen that the democratic method does not necessarily guarantee a greater amount of individual freedom than another political method would permit in similar circumstances. It may well be the other way round. But there is still a relation between the two. If, on principle at least, everyone is free to compete for political leadership* by presenting himself to the electorate, this will in most cases though not in all mean a considerable amount of freedom of discussion *for all*. In particular it will normally mean a considerable amount of freedom of the press. This relation between democracy and freedom is not absolutely stringent and can be tampered with. But, from the standpoint of the intellectual, it is nevertheless very important. At the same time, it is all there is to that relation.

Sixth, it should be observed that in making it the primary function of the electorate to produce a government (directly or through an intermediate body) I intended to include in this phrase also the function of evicting it. The one means simply the acceptance of a leader or a group of leaders, the other means simply the withdrawal of this acceptance. This takes care of an element the reader may have missed. He may have thought that the electorate controls as well as installs. But since electorates normally do not control their political leaders in any way except by refusing to reelect them or the parliamentary majorities that support them, it seems well to reduce our ideas about this control in the way indicated by our definition. Occasionally, spontaneous revulsions occur which upset a government or an individual minister directly or else enforce a certain course of action. But they are not only exceptional, they are, as we shall see, contrary to the spirit of the democratic method.

Seventh, our theory sheds much-needed light on an old controversy. Whoever accepts the classical doctrine of democracy and in consequence believes that the democratic method is to guarantee that issues be decided and policies framed according to the will of the people must be struck by the fact that, even if that will were undeniably real and definite, decision by simple majorities would in many cases distort it rather than give effect to it. Evidently the will of the majority is the will of the majority and not the will of "the people." The latter is a mosaic that the former completely fails to "represent." To equate both by definition is not to solve the problem. Attempts at real solutions have however been made by the authors of the various plans for proportional representation.

These plans have met with adverse criticism on practical grounds. It is in fact obvious not only that proportional representation will offer opportunities for all sorts of idiosyncrasies to assert themselves but also that it may prevent democracy from producing efficient governments and thus prove a danger in times of stress. But before concluding that democracy becomes unworkable if its principle is carried out consistently, it is just as well to ask ourselves whether this principle really implies proportional representation. As a matter of fact it does not. If acceptance

---

*Free, that is, in the same sense in which everyone is free to start another textile mill.

of leadership is the true function of the electorate's vote, the case for proportional representation collapses because its premises are no longer binding. The principle of democracy then merely means that the reins of government should be handed to those who command more support than do any of the competing individuals or teams. And this in turn seems to assure the standing of the majority system within the logic of the democratic method, although we might still condemn it on grounds that lie outside of that logic.

64
Henry B. Mayo

Henry B. Mayo (1911–   ) is an American philosopher who believes that democratic governments are distinguished from all others by their reliance upon four central principles: (1) popular control of policy makers; (2) political equality; (3) political freedoms; and (4) rule of the majority. Building upon these principles Mayo constructs a theory of democracy that is coherent and widely applicable.

THE THEORY OF DEMOCRACY OUTLINED*

The approach taken in this study is to regard democracy as a political system with a theory to explain and justify it. The first problem is, then, to identify the working principles of the political system generally called democratic.

In order to arrive at these distinguishing principles, several starting points are possible. We could, for example, begin with some of the older classic statements of democracy, or with a contemporary definition, or with the institutions of one of the existing democratic systems. Although all these sources will be tapped from time to time, I shall take as the starting point the Athenian example. . . . This need not be misleading if we do take it as no more than a starting point, and do not regard Athens and its unique institutional features as a small scale model of contemporary democracies.

The original democratic system of Athens could be described in one phrase as "rule by the people," if "people" was construed narrowly to mean adult male citizens, comprising a small proportion of the total persons in a small state. This definitive operating principle, traced out into secondary principles and institutions, made it easy for Athenians—and for us—to distinguish the democracy from other ancient political systems. Such a principle was both accurately descriptive and

*From *An Introduction to Democratic Theory* by Henry B. Mayo. Copyright © 1960 by Oxford University Press, Inc. Reprinted by permission.

quite workable, given the scale of operations. But the principle is neither descriptive of nor feasible in any modern state. It makes sense to say that one person rules, or that a few persons do, no matter how large the state; but it makes almost no sense to say that the people rule in any modern state, in any ordinary sense of the word "rule." . . . Or as MacIver was always concerned to put it:

> Democracy is not a way of governing, whether by majority or otherwise, but primarily a way of determining who shall govern and, broadly, to what ends . . . The people, let us repeat, do not and cannot govern; they control the government.*

The only exception to this is the occasional use of "direct democratic devices" such as the referendum.

Democracy, then, as a political system must have identifiable features other than the people's actually "governing," to distinguish it from other methods of making public policies. The problem is to separate the accidental features from the characteristic. Some political features, such as whether the government is federal or unitary, presidential or parliamentary, unicameral or bicameral, republican or monarchical, are by general agreement accidental variations from a common type. So, too, is the kind of economic system with which the political system is associated—although this is more debatable. These and other features are not necessarily related, either in logic or practice, with features of the political system ordinarily listed as democratic. Since one cannot analyze all of a system, except perhaps in a treatise on comparative democratic systems, we seek here only the differentiating features or principles of organization typical of all democracies and not typical of any other systems.

What, then, in any contemporary state corresponds to the "rule by the people" in the Athenian system? We are inevitably driven to conclude, I think, that such a corresponding factor lies in the effectiveness of the popular control over the rulers or decision-makers. In short, a political system is democratic to the extent that the decision-makers are under effective popular control. (One should perhaps add: to the extent to which decisions are *influenced* by the people, but this is a more amorphous concept, for which allowance will be made later.)

Plainly however, this, although in the spirit of the Athenian democracy, is a much vaguer test to apply than the Athenian. To distinguish ancient democracy from other types of the Greek *polis* was easy, and there could scarcely be dispute about it. But when the test is the extent of effective popular control, then the existence of democracy in any system is obviously a matter of degree. At one extreme will be the absolute ruler—a Hitler, a Stalin, a Peron—who, however despotic, must sometimes take popular sentiment into account (but who will endeavor, through education, censorship, propaganda, and other means, to engineer the popular sentiment which he wishes), and whose elections and plebiscites, if they are held at all, are carefully "rigged." At the other will be an elected government anxious to be re-elected, and an opposition anxious to become the government, both

*R. M. MacIver, *The Web of Government,* New York, 1947, p. 198. *The Ramparts We Guard,* New York, 1950, p. 51.

of them therefore sensitive to public opinion, with a wide range of political free-doms through which continuing influence as well as periodic control can be exercised.

Popular control of policy-makers is then the basic feature or principle, and political systems can be classified as more or less democratic according to a number of criteria associated with popular control and designed to make it effective; only if a particular system meets the tests of a substantial number of these criteria do we, by common consent, agree to call it democratic. But although the existence of democracy then becomes a matter of degree, the distinction is valid enough as we shall see, and the criteria will enable us to say in what respects and to what extent a system is democratic.

It must now be our purpose to try to make this somewhat vague language more precise. Accordingly I shall first sketch what I take to be a consistent and coherent theory of democracy in the form of the minimum number of distinguishing principles. At the same time, the outline will be reasonably close to contemporary usage, and is recognizably approximated by a number of existing democracies. The analysis and justification of these principles and of the system as a whole, together with the chief questions or problems which arise, will be given in later chapters.

DISTINGUISHING PRINCIPLES OF A DEMOCRATIC SYSTEM

Influence over decision-makers and hence over public policies may be exercised in many ways, even in a non-democratic system. The policies of an absolute ruler or of an oligarchy, for instance, may be affected by palace intrigue and court favorites, or by careful calculation of what the subjects will stand in the way of taxes and the like; it is possible to conceive of a benevolent autocrat who will in fact keep his ear to the ground and often graciously accede to public demands. But popular influence, although necessary, is not enough even if institutionalized to make a political system democratic.

1 *Popular control of policy-makers,* however, is a democratic stigmatum, and this is our first and most general principle. The one institutional embodiment of the principle universally regarded as indispensable in modern democracies is that of choosing the policy-makers (representatives) at elections held at more or less regular intervals. This is as close as we usually get—which is not very close—to imitating the making and control of decisions in the Athenian *ecclesia.*

Other methods of choosing and authorizing representatives—e.g. by lot or heredity—have died out, except for remnants of the lot such as are left in the choice of a jury. Even the Soviet type of "democracy" pays tribute to the method of electing representatives, although their practice of it is quite different from that in other kinds of democracies. In this as in other respects, the Soviet Union has borrowed some of the forms and language of democracy and stripped them of their spirit and meaning.

Three riders must be added to our general principle at the outset in order to avoid misunderstanding:

a On the whole, no democratic system operates on the principle that voters directly decide public policies at elections. The control over policy is much more indirect—through the representatives. This will be made clear later . . . but if we accept provisionally that voters choose representatives at elections and do not normally decide policies, then the usual criticism aimed at modern democracies on grounds of the incompetence of voters to judge policies is wide of the mark, however true it may have been of Athens where the citizens did decide directly.

b The popular influence upon policies, as distinct from control over policy-makers, goes on all the time and may take many institutionalized and legitimate forms. The extent of such influence, however, cannot be reduced to any public test which can be incorporated at the present time into a general theory. The reason is that popular influence and consultation take such an infinity of forms—of which interest or pressure groups are perhaps the best known—that hardly any general principle can as yet be enunciated. What gives popular influence its sanction is that it can affect the chances of a representative at election time, or, more accurately, the representative's estimate of his chances.

c Popular control by means of modern elections has only a faint resemblance to the old principle that, in some sense, authority stems from the people, and to old practices such as an elective monarchy. The assumption or belief that authority *should* derive from the people—sometimes called the doctrine of popular sovereignty—does of course underlie the practice of popular elections, but our immediate concern is with the translation of the assumption into an operating principle or institutional practice.

2 The second principle of democracy is that of *political equality,* which in turn is institutionalized as the equality of all adult citizens in voting.

It makes little difference whether we think of this principle as coordinate with the first, or derivative—a widening of the meaning of "popular." Political equality is a principle common to Athenian and modern democracies. There is, of course, more to citizenship than voting, and hence other ways in which political equality or inequality can prevail, but it is not debatable today that in any democracy the principle of equality of voting is taken for granted.

Although the general principle may be cast in the Athenian form, the modern expression of it is quite different. For one thing, equality of voting is not, as in Athens, an equal share directly over the decisions; the share in the decisions is indirect—only the share in the control of the decision-makers is direct. For another, political equality today covers a wider range of citizens and voters than the Athenian, and in this respect we should call modern democracies more democratic than Athens.

Political equality is complex, like all general principles, and may be broken down into several elements, consisting at least of the following:

a Every adult should have the vote—the familiar device of the universal adult suffrage. Popular control defines the "people" as all adult citizens, although there are of course minor differences in the definitions of an "adult."

b One person should have one vote—that is, there should be no plural voting.

c Each vote should count equally—that is, votes are not weighted in any way.

In terms of representation, the belief in equal voting is expressed in the old slogan of "Representation by population" or in Bentham's formula regarding happiness, that "everybody is to count for one, nobody for more than one." In terms of control over policy-makers, it is expressed by saying that every vote should have an equal share in that control.

d If every vote is to count equally, the corollary follows that the number of representatives elected should be directly proportional to the number of votes cast for them. If we assume, for simplicity of argument, a two-party system, then the number of representatives elected from each party will be proportional to the number of votes cast for that party. Thus, in a two-party system, if party A gets 60 per cent of the popular vote it will get 60 per cent of the seats, and party B will get 40 per cent. Any other result would not be counting each vote equally.* It is just at this point, however, as we shall see, that the practice of many democracies diverges from this aspect of political equality, and often does so for very good reasons.

A little reflection will show that equality of voting, even if followed to the letter, is not enough of itself to distinguish a democratic system from an elected dictatorship. The belief and indeed the practice of equal voting are both official in the Soviet Union. Equality of voting, with its corollary, may thus be regarded as a necessary, but not a sufficient, principle of democracy. Is there, then, anything else about political equality and the franchise to distinguish a democratic political system? The answer must lie in the fact that voting alone does not ensure the reality of popular control; the mechanism may be manipulated to prevent such control.

3 The third principle may be stated either in terms of the *effectiveness of the popular control* or in terms of *political freedoms.*

Again, it makes little difference whether we regard "effectiveness" as part of the first principle (popular control) or as specifying the conditions of effective control. Can one set of decision-makers be turned out of office at elections and another set installed? Is there a free choice among alternatives, whether independent candidates or parties? That is, is the voting merely ritual, or does it effectively (freely) control the decision makers?

This again is a very general statement of what prevails in a democracy. To make the general standard specific enough to test in practice, we must once more break it into components.

a To say that the voting must be effective is to say that there must be free choice, without coercion or intimidation of the voters. This in turn drives us back upon the secrecy of the ballot, whether we draw the conclusion from reflecting on human nature—that we live in an imperfect world of imperfect people—or from reflecting upon the historical experience of many countries with open voting. Yet the condition of the secret ballot alone is not enough to ensure free choice, since even a Soviet election may provide the voter with privacy in the voting booth.

b In order that voting may be effective, it must, then, be free in another sense, i.e. at least two candidates for each position must be able to come forward if they

---

*Note that the reference is in terms of actual votes, not in terms of eligible adults—a point to which fuller reference is made later.

wish. This minimum in itself is also not enough, because it could be cleverly imitated even in the Soviet Union by the simple device of putting forward more official candidates than seats to be filled.

An effective choice for the voter entails freedom for candidates to stand for election outside of the single party, not deterred by legal obstacles. (The question of *de facto* obstacles such as poverty is explored later.) At this point we come close to the most characteristic feature of a modern democracy: the meaningful choice or control when candidates are free to run for office, when they and their supporters are free to press their claims publicly, to put forward alternative policies, to criticize the present decision-makers and other candidates; in short, when there is what Schumpeter has called a competitive biding for votes.

The effectiveness of popular control thus entails a range of political freedoms. Among them are certainly the freedoms of speech, assembly, and organization, as well as the freedom to run for office. These widespread political liberties were characteristic of the Athenian form of democracy, and are likewise typical of all other historical versions, though lacking in the Soviet system.

These formal rules or conditions or devices of effective choice—secret ballot, freedom to run for office, and freedom to speak, assemble, and organize for political purposes—are procedural political freedoms, necessary if there is to be any meaningful choice at the polls, if the voters are to control the decision-makers at election times and through them indirectly to sanction the decisions. Or they may be looked upon as the rules which insure free competition for office, men being what they are and the world being what it is.

Among those political freedoms, that of organization leads almost inevitably (as we shall see later) to the formation of political parties, with different sets of candidates and sometimes with different outlooks and policy alternatives. The pure theory, of itself, will hardly tell us whether or not political parties will make their appearance in a democracy. They are not, so to speak, logically entailed as part of popular control, of effective choice in free and equal voting, and they do not always appear at local levels of government. Experience and history, however, give an enormous weight of evidence to show that political parties invariably do appear, despite the early, and mostly non-democratic, objection to "factions."

The existence and extent of these political liberties, as manifested above all in political opposition, is perhaps the most crucial test of the extent of democracy within a country. They are often summed up in the single concept "freedom to oppose." The touchstone of a democratic system is political freedoms, opposition, and parties. . . .

The result of political activity taking place within these rules—equality of voting and political liberties—is to enable the effective choice of representatives to take place, i.e. to ensure the popular control of decision-makers at election time, and to keep the channels open to legitimate influence at all times. From the viewpoint of the individual voter, the vote is the formal means by which he takes his share in political power. It scarcely needs pointing out that other implications also follow, for instance that the outvoted citizens accept the verdict of the polls with fortitude if not with gladness.

Although equality of voting within the context of political freedoms is a basic part of a democratic system, it is not all. Another essential part, already implicit, is that the policy decisions are made by the elected representatives, since only these are susceptible to popular control. The policies are not made, for instance, by others behind the scenes—as Marxists allege—nor by any non-elected body, such as a hereditary upper house. Insofar as they are made elsewhere, to that extent we say democracy is lacking. (To say this, however, is not to ignore the political reality of executive or Cabinet leadership.)

It is plain that we cannot expect the representatives to be unanimous, any more than we can expect the electorate to be so. Political systems are devised *because* there is conflict and disagreement. There must, then, be a principle or rule according to which decisions are made among the representatives themselves.

4 The fourth principle is that *when the representatives are divided, the decision of the majority prevails.*

This is, in fact, the nearly universal rule for decision-making in all legislatures. Let us be clear how it links with the previous principles. Equality of voting, in a context of political freedoms, turns up representatives who are authorized to make the policies for the time being. This may be loosely called "consent of the governed" in the sense that there is a choice and one set of representatives rather than another is chosen. But "consent" is a slippery term, and it is better to think of election results as authorizing the successful candidates to make decisions, or in other words, as investing the government and its policies with legitimacy.

The common assumption is that with an electoral system based on equality of voting a majority of the representatives have been chosen by a majority of the voters, and hence the majority rule in the legislature yields decisions as legitimate "as if" they had been made directly by a majority of the voters, and indeed by a majority of all the adult citizens. That is why this fourth principle is sometimes called "majority rule." In fact, however, if governments depended for their legitimacy on this strict relation of votes to representatives, half the democratic governments of the world could at times claim no rightful authority from the "people."

The principle of decision-making by a majority of representatives is much disputed, and is examined *in extenso* later, particularly the justification for the majority principle. The case *against* may be put in a nutshell: that it is both necessary and feasible to maintain legal limits upon a majority of the decision-makers (and hence by implication upon a majority of the citizens), and by so doing we may achieve the best of all possible systems: a "wise" minority veto of "unwise" majority decisions. Democracy would then be identical with ideal government, and the historic search for a government with power to rule wisely, but powerless to do wrong, would be over. To state the case is almost enough to refute it.

From this method of policy-making there follow certain implications, which may be called the rules of the game for representatives.

First, the majority of the representatives makes the policy decisions within the framework of the political freedoms mentioned earlier. These freedoms are taken as given, as part of the formal principles or essential conditions of democracy. Whatever else the majority may do—and it may mete very ill treatment through some of its decisions—it does not shut up the opposition, the critics, the dissenters, whether these are within or without the legislature. Opponents may be coerced into obedience to law, but not abolished or silenced or shorn of their political liberties: this is the one inhibition upon the majority decisions so long as a democracy exists. When the political liberties and the legitimate opposition are gone, so, too, is democracy.

Second, the minority of representatives and their supporters among the public obey even though under protest, while working either to alter the policy to which they object or to dislodge the government and if possible to become a majority—by all peaceful political means, but only by these. . . .

Third, when the opposition in its turn has grown into a majority and attains office, the play begins all over again with different actors in the roles of government and opposition. The minority also agrees beforehand that they, too, will extend the same political freedoms and follow the same rules of the game should they arrive in the seats of office. The problem which arises here is that created by the existence of a minority party which uses the political freedoms in order to abolish democracy.

Many social conditions are, of course, necessary if the majority principle is to work well, but those formal conditions just stated are the minimum rules of the game for majorities and minorities in the legislature if democracy is to work *at all*. Moreover, in any functioning democracy, regardless of the niceties of the electoral system, the rules apply in those common cases where the majority of representatives happen to be elected by the minority of voters. No identity of voters and representatives need be assumed as long as the unwritten constitution does not require it, although there is, I think, an obligation to reduce the likelihood of wide discrepancies by eliminating abuses from the electoral system and thus closely approximating the principle of political equality.

The foregoing is a simplified, formal, abstract sketch of a democratic political system—its essential principles of operation for political policy-making. It concentrates upon how the binding decisions, related to government and arising from conflict and dispute, are made in the context of political freedoms. In other terms, the outline concentrates upon the ways in which policy-makers get their power and authorization—their legitimacy, always a prime concern to any political theory. The principles are close enough to common usage, and to some political systems in existence, to warrant the description democratic.

Each of the principles can be cast in operational terms. This has the great advantage of giving us practical tests which, taken together, enable us to distinguish democratic from non-democratic systems, and also to identify democracies empirically as more or less democratic, in this or that respect. One need not attempt, however, to solve the impossible problem of exact summation—of trying to construct a single index number which will register all the tests for democracy. Some criteria are more important than others, and all are a matter of degree.*

Each of the principles can also be cast in normative (moral) terms—for example, that political equality *should* prevail—and in this form they constitute the moral justification of a theory of democracy. They are moral beliefs for which a case can be made, and which may be traced further back until we lay bare the "ultimates" or postulates to which the principles commit us.

Considered in both operational and normative terms, the principles may thus fairly be described as making up a democratic political theory which both explains and justifies a democratic political system.

A working definition may be constructed from the above: a democratic political system is one in which public policies are made, on a majority basis, by representatives subject to effective popular control at periodic elections which are conducted on the principle of political equality and under conditions of political freedom. The definition is hardly remarkable; others of a similar kind have frequently been constructed.[†]

I am aware that the bare outline bristles with questions, as any model does when it is made up of an abstraction of formal principles. Moreover, even when the skeleton has been given flesh and blood, there are a number of other far-reaching queries which at once suggest themselves, among them: what values (if any) inhere in a political system operating on such principles? What case can be made for the system as a whole other than that involved in the justification of the separate principles?

65
John Dewey

John Dewey is rightly known as the philosopher of democracy. In every sphere—in the school, in local and national American politics, and in international relations—he sought tirelessly to apply the principles of democracy. At the core of those principles, he believed, lay "a faith in the capacities of human nature; faith in human intelligence and in the power of pooled and cooperative experience." More than a form of government, democracy was for him a way of life.

---

*See Russell H. Fitzgibbon, "A Statistical Evaluation of Latin-American Democracy," *Western Political Quarterly,* IX, September 1956, pp. 607 ff., for an attempt to measure (in "a crude and groping way," as the author says) which countries of Latin America are more democratic. At that time, Uruguay, Costa Rica, and Chile were at the top of the list.

[†]For instance, John Morley's: Democracy is "the name for a form of government by which the ultimate control of the machinery of government is committed to a numerical majority of the community." *Oracles on Man and Government,* London, 1923, p. 29. Or again: Democracy is "government of the whole, by the majority, generally through representatives elected by secret ballot of adults." E. F. Carritt, *Ethical and Political Thinking,* Oxford, 1957, p. 150.

[THE FOUNDATION OF DEMOCRACY]*

Democracy is much broader than a special political form, a method of conducting government, of making laws and carrying on governmental administration by means of popular suffrage and elected officers. It is that, of course. But it is something broader and deeper than that. The political and governmental phase of democracy is a means, the best means so far found, for realizing ends that lie in the wide domain of human relationships and the development of human personality. It is, as we often say, though perhaps without appreciating all that is involved in the saying, a way of life, social and individual. The keynote of democracy as a way of life may be expressed, it seems to me, as the necessity for the participation of every mature human being in formation of the values that regulate the living of men together: which is necessary from the standpoint of both the general social welfare and the full development of human beings as individuals.

Universal suffrage, recurring elections, responsibility of those who are in political power to the voters, and the other factors of democratic government are means that have been found expedient for realizing democracy as the truly human way of living. They are not a final end and a final value. They are to be judged on the basis of their contribution to end. It is a form of idolatry to erect means into the end which they serve. Democratic political forms are simply the best means that human wit has devised up to a special time in history. But they rest back upon the idea that no man or limited set of men is wise enough or good enough to rule others without their consent; the positive meaning of this statement is that all those who are affected by social institutions must have a share in producing and managing them. The two facts that each one is influenced in what he does and enjoys and in what he becomes by the institutions under which he lives, and that therefore he shall have, in a democracy, a voice in shaping them, are the passive and active sides of the same fact.

The development of political democracy came about through substitution of the method of mutual consultation and voluntary agreement for the method of subordination of the many to the few enforced from above. Social arrangements which involve fixed subordination are maintained by coercion. The coercion need not be physical. There have existed, for short periods, benevolent despotisms. But coercion of some sort there has been; perhaps economic, certainly psychological and moral. The very fact of exclusion from participation is a subtle form of suppression. It gives individuals no opportunity to reflect and decide upon what is good for them. Others who are supposed to be wiser and who in any case have more power decide the question for them and also decide the methods and means by which subjects may arrive at the enjoyment of what is good for them. This form of coercion and suppression is more subtle and more effective than are overt intimidation and restraint. When it is habitual and embodied in social institutions, it seems the normal and natural state of affairs. The mass usually become unaware

---

*From J. Dewey, "Democracy and Educational Administration," an address before the National Education Association, Feb. 22, 1937. Reprinted from *Intelligence in the Modern World,* edited by Joseph Ratner, and published by The Modern Library, Random House, New York, 1939.

that they have a claim to a development of their own powers. Their experience is so restricted that they are not conscious of restriction. It is part of the democratic conception that they as individuals are not the only sufferers, but that the whole social body is deprived of the potential resources that should be at its service. The individuals of the submerged mass may not be very wise. But there is one thing they are wiser about than anybody else can be, and that is where the shoe pinches, the troubles they suffer from.

The foundation of democracy is faith in the capacities of human nature; faith in human intelligence and in the power of pooled and coöperative experience. It is not belief that these things are complete but that if given a show they will grow and be able to generate progressively the knowledge and wisdom needed to guide collective action. Every autocratic and authoritarian scheme of social action rests on a belief that the needed intelligence is confined to a superior few, who because of inherent natural gifts are endowed with the ability and the right to control the conduct of others; laying down principles and rules and directing the ways in which they are carried out. It would be foolish to deny that much can be said for this point of view. It is that which controlled human relations in social groups for much the greater part of human history. The democratic faith has emerged very, very recently in the history of mankind. Even where democracies now exist, men's minds and feelings are still permeated with ideas about leadership imposed from above, ideas that developed in the long early history of mankind. After democratic political institutions were nominally established, beliefs and ways of looking at life and of acting that originated when men and women were externally controlled and subjected to arbitrary power, persisted in the family, the church, business and the school, and experience shows that as long as they persist there, political democracy is not secure.

Belief in equality is an element of the democratic credo. It is not, however, belief in equality of natural endowments. Those who proclaimed the idea of equality did not suppose they were enunciating a psychological doctrine, but a legal and political one. All individuals are entitled to equality of treatment by law and in its administration. Each one is affected equally in quality if not in quantity by the institutions under which he lives and has an equal right to express his judgment, although the weight of his judgment may not be equal in amount when it enters into the pooled result to that of others. In short, each one is equally an individual and entitled to equal opportunity of development of his own capacities, be they large or small in range. Moreover, each has needs of his own, as significant to him as those of others are to them. The very fact of natural and psychological inequality is all the more reason for establishment by law of equality of opportunity, since otherwise the former becomes a means of oppression of the less gifted.

While what we call intelligence may be distributed in unequal amounts, it is the democratic faith that it is sufficiently general so that each individual has something to contribute, and the value of each contribution can be assessed only as it enters into the final pooled intelligence constituted by the contributions of all. Every authoritarian scheme, on the contrary, assumes that its value may be assessed by some *prior* principle, if not of family and birth or race and color or possession of material wealth, then by the position and rank a person occupies in the existing social scheme. The democratic faith in equality is the faith that each individual shall have the chance and opportunity to contribute whatever he is capable of contributing and that the value of his contribution be decided by its place and function in the organized total of similar contributions, not on the basis of prior status of any kind whatever.

I have emphasized in what precedes the importance of the effective release of intelligence in connection with personal experience in the democratic way of living. I have done so purposely because democracy is so often and so naturally associated in our minds with freedom of *action,* forgetting the importance of freed intelligence which is necessary to direct and to warrant freedom of action. Unless freedom of individual action has intelligence and informed conviction back of it, its manifestation is almost sure to result in confusion and disorder. The democratic idea of freedom is not the right of each individual to *do* as he pleases, even if it be qualified by adding "provided he does not interfere with the same freedom on the part of others." While the idea is not always, not often enough, expressed in words, the basic freedom is that of freedom of *mind* and of whatever degree of freedom of action and experience is necessary to produce freedom of intelligence. The modes of freedom guaranteed in the Bill of Rights are all of this nature: Freedom of belief and conscience, of expression of opinion, of assembly for discussion and conference, of the press as an organ of communication. They are guaranteed because without them individuals are not free to develop and society is deprived of what they might contribute.

CREATIVE DEMOCRACY*

At the present time, the frontier is moral, not physical. The period of free lands that seemed boundless in extent has vanished. Unused resources are now human rather than material. They are found in the waste of grown men and women who are without the chance to work, and in the young men and young women who find doors closed where there was once opportunity. The crisis that one hundred and fifty years ago called out social and political inventiveness is with us in a form which puts a heavier demand on human creativeness.

At all events this is what I mean when I say that we now have to recreate by deliberate and determined endeavor the kind of democracy which in its origin one hundred and fifty years ago was largely the product of a fortunate combination of men and circumstances. We have lived for a long time upon the heritage that came to us from the happy conjunction of men and events in an earlier day. The present state of the world is more than a reminder that we have now to put forth every energy of our own to prove worthy of our heritage. It is a challenge to do for the critical and complex conditions of today what the men of an earlier day did for simpler conditions.

*Reprinted by permission of G. P. Putnam's Sons from *The Philosopher of the Common Man* by Horace M. Kallen.

. . .

Democracy as a personal, an individual, way of life involves nothing fundamentally new. But when applied it puts a new practical meaning in old ideas. Put into effect it signifies that powerful present enemies of democracy can be successfully met only by the creation of personal attitudes in individual human beings; that we must get over our tendency to think that its defense can be found in any external means whatever, whether military or civil, if they are separated from individual attitudes so deep-seated as to constitute personal character.

Democracy is a way of life controlled by a working faith in the possibilities of human nature. Belief in the Common Man is a familiar article in the democratic creed. That belief is without basis and significance save as it means faith in the potentialities of human nature as that nature is exhibited in every human being irrespective of race, color, sex, birth, and family, of material or cultural wealth. This faith may be enacted in statutes, but it is only on paper unless it is put in force in the attitudes which human beings display to one another in all the incidents and relations of daily life. To denounce Naziism for intolerance, cruelty and stimulation of hatred amounts to fostering insincerity if, in our personal relations to other persons, if, in our daily walk and conversation, we are moved by racial, color, or other class prejudice; indeed, by anything save a generous belief in their possibilities as human beings, a belief which brings with it the need for providing conditions which will enable these capacities to reach fulfillment. The democratic faith in human equality is belief that every human being, independent of the quantity or range of his personal endowment, has the right to equal opportunity with every other person for development of whatever gifts he has. The democratic belief in the principle of leadership is a generous one. It is universal. It is belief in the capacity of every person to lead his own life free from coercion and imposition by others provided right conditions are supplied.

Democracy is a way of personal life controlled not merely by faith in human nature in general but by faith in the capacity of human beings for intelligent judgment and action if proper conditions are furnished. I have been accused more than once and from opposed quarters of an undue, a utopian, faith in the possibilities of intelligence and in education as a correlate of intelligence. At all events I did not invent this faith. I acquired it from my surroundings as far as those surroundings were animated by the democratic spirit. For what is the faith of democracy in the rôle of consultation, of conference, of persuasion, of discussion, in formation of public opinion, which in the long run is self-corrective, except faith in the capacity of the intelligence of the common man to respond with common sense to the free play of facts and ideas which are secured by effective guarantees of free inquiry, free assembly, and free communication? I am willing to leave to upholders of totalitarian states of the right and the left the view that faith in the capacities of intelligence is utopian. For the faith is so deeply embedded in the methods which are intrinsic to democracy that when a professed democrat denies the faith he convicts himself of treachery to his profession.

. . . The heart and final guarantee of democracy is in free gatherings of neighbors on the street corner to discuss back and forth what is read in uncensored news of the day, and in gatherings of friends in the living rooms of houses and apartments to converse freely with one another. Intolerance, abuse, calling of names because of differences of opinion about religion or politics or business, as well as because of differences of race, color, wealth, or degree of culture, are treason to the democratic way of life. For everything which bars freedom and fullness of communication sets up barriers that divide human beings into sets and cliques, into antagonistic sects and factions, and thereby undermines the democratic way of life. Merely legal guarantees of the civil liberties of free belief, free expression, free assembly are of little avail if in daily life freedom of communication, the give and take of ideas, facts, experiences, is choked by mutual suspicion, by abuse, by fear and hatred. These things destroy the essential condition of the democratic way of living even more effectually than open coercion, which—as the example of totalitarian states proves—is effective only when it succeeds in breeding hate, suspicion, intolerance in the minds of individual human beings.

Finally, given the two conditions just mentioned, democracy as a way of life is controlled by personal faith in personal day-by-day working together with others. Democracy is the belief that even when needs and ends or consequences are different for each individual, the habit of amicable co-operation—which may include, as in sport, rivalry and competition—is itself a priceless addition to life. To take as far as possible every conflict which arises—and they are bound to arise—out of the atmosphere and medium of force, of violence as a means of settlement, into that of discussion and of intelligence, is to treat those who disagree—even profoundly—with us as those from whom we may learn, and in so far, as friends. A genuinely democratic faith in peace is faith in the possibility of conducting disputes, controversies, and conflicts as co-operative undertakings in which both parties learn by giving the other a chance to express itself, instead of having one party conquer by forceful suppression of the other—a suppression which is none the less one of violence when it takes place by psychological means of ridicule, abuse, intimidation, instead of by overt imprisonment or in concentration camps. To co-operate by giving differences a chance to show themselves because of the belief that the expression of difference is not only a right of the other persons but is a means of enriching one's own life-experience, is inherent in the democratic personal way of life.

If what has been said is charged with being a set of moral commonplaces, my only reply is that that is just the point in saying them. For to get rid of the habit of thinking of democracy as something institutional and external and to acquire the habit of treating it as a way of personal life is to realize that democracy is a moral ideal and so far as it becomes a fact is a moral fact. It is to realize that democracy is a reality only as it is indeed a commonplace of living.

Since my adult years have been given to the pursuit of philosophy, I shall ask your indulgence if in concluding I state briefly the democratic faith in the formal terms of a philosophic position. So stated, democracy is belief in the ability of human experience to generate the aims and methods by which further experience will grow in ordered richness. Every other form of moral and social faith rests upon the idea that experience must be subjected at some point or other to some form of external control; to some "authority" alleged to exist outside the processes of experience. Democracy is the faith that the process of experience is more important than any special result attained, so that special results achieved are of ultimate value only as they are used to enrich and order the ongoing process. Since the process of experience is capable of being educative, faith in democracy is all one with faith in experience and education. All ends and values that are cut off from the ongoing process become arrests, fixations. They strive to fixate what has been gained instead of using it to open the road and point the way to new and better experiences.

If one asks what is meant by experience in this connection, my reply is that it is that free interaction of individual human beings with surrounding conditions, especially the human surroundings, which develops and satisfies need and desire by increasing knowledge of things as they are. Knowledge of conditions as they are is the only solid ground for communication and sharing; all other communication means the subjection of some persons to the personal opinion of other persons. Need and desire—out of which grow purpose and direction of energy—go beyond what exists, and hence beyond knowledge, beyond science. They continually open the way into the unexplored and unattained future.

Democracy as compared with other ways of life is the sole way of living which believes wholeheartedly in the process of experience as end and as means; as that which is capable of generating the science which is the sole dependable authority for the direction of further experience and which releases emotions, needs, and desires so as to call into being the things that have not existed in the past. For every way of life that fails in its democracy limits the contacts, the exchanges, the communications, the interactions by which experience is steadied while it is also enlarged and enriched. The task of this release and enrichment is one that has to be carried on day by day. Since it is one that can have no end till experience itself comes to an end, the task of democracy is forever that of creation of a freer and more humane experience in which all share and to which all contribute.

2

THE JUSTIFICATION
OF DEMOCRACY

Whatever the essential nature of democratic government is believed to be, its advocates have the burden of showing that it is *justifiable,* that of all the alternative forms it is most preferable and worthy of defense. For this task rhetoric will not suffice; good arguments are needed.

Arguments presented to justify democracy, whether classical or modern, are essentially of two kinds. One family of justificatory arguments aims to establish the essential *rightness* of democracy, to show that it is the logical product of fundamental principles of justice universally accepted. From these moral principles—chief among them being the intrinsic equality of all persons—it is claimed that government of the community by its own members may be rationally derived. Arguments of this general kind—justification under the laws of nature—are found below in Sub-Section A.

A second family of justificatory arguments aims to show that some very desirable states of affairs, some goods universally sought, are the likely *consequences* of democracy. From this perspective democratic governments are more likely to do for the members of the community what they want done than are any of its alternatives. Arguments of this general kind—justification by consequences—are found below in Sub-Section B.

An argument of the first sort seeks to embed democracy in some theoretical structure, and looks to *principles* above all; an argument of the second sort focuses upon the outcomes of democratic practice, and looks to *results* above all. The one is essentially rationalistic in spirit, and relies upon the strength of underlying moral convictions and inferences drawn from them; the other is essentially empirical in spirit and relies upon the strength of factual evidence that may be brought to bear.

Attacks upon these kinds of argument will differ substantially also, of course. Those who reject the justification of democracy under the laws of nature may question the principles upon which they rest, or may accept those principles but question the reasoning with which democracy is claimed to be derived from them. Those who reject the consequentialist justification of democracy may dispute claims regarding what democracy really does produce; or they may accept those claims but deny that those outcomes really are good, or good enough.

These two families of justificatory arguments are logically independent of one another; therefore, the strength of neither is affected by alleged weaknesses in the other. Without inconsistency it is possible to accept arguments of one kind while rejecting the other; depending upon one's philosophical outlook, such preference could go either way. One may also accept and uphold justificatory defenses of democracy of both kinds without contradiction.

JUSTIFICATION
OF DEMOCRACY UNDER
THE LAWS OF NATURE

That humans have the *right* to self-government and may not be deprived of that right by any worldly authority is the conviction that underlies the defense of democracy by its most famous classical advocates. The formulations of such defenses vary, of course, but the spirit does not. Democracy is defended as *just,* as morally required.

The natural law foundation of this defense has been explicitly theological for some. That all human beings are "created equal" and "endowed by their Creator with certain unalienable rights" were premises absolutely central to the moral position of the founders of the American republic. Their views owed much to John Locke's *Second Treatise of Government* published a century before. Locke had said, and his successors believed and believe still, that humans possess, by nature and because they are the children of God, certain *natural rights.* Those rights are recognized, and made secure, in a civil government to which citizens have given their consent, explicit or implicit. Absent that consent, no authority may be exercised justly over them. Therefore some variety of *contract*—a binding agreement under principles that precede government and make possible its creation—has played a central role in this tradition.

Whatever the religious or metaphysical foundations of such defenses, they invariably incorporate a principle of human equality. The evident differences among human beings are not denied, but beneath superficial variations there lies (it is held) an equal moral worth, or dignity, in all citizens. This principle of human equality lies at the core of the justification of democracy under the laws of nature. Democracy alone is just, these arguments suggest, because the equality of all persons can be given adequate recognition only where all may participate in their common government.

66
John Locke

John Locke (1632–1704) is the most important single philosopher in the tradition of natural rights democracy. The central ideas of classical democratic theory—individual rights and natural law—were certainly not originated by him, but his *Second Treatise of Government* weaves these ideas together as no other work before him did. It is one of the most influential philosophical treatises of all time. Locke develops a coherent theory of government as the product of a social contract into which persons who possess rights by nature may enter by giving their consent. When any government violates that contract by failing to do what it was created to do, its citizens are entitled to replace it with a new and better instrument for the protection of their lives, liberties, and estates.

OF THE STATE OF NATURE*

To understand political power right, and derive it from its original, we must consider what state all men are naturally in, and that is, a state of perfect freedom to order their actions and dispose of their possessions and persons as they think fit, within the bounds of the law of nature, without asking leave or depending upon the will of any other man.

A state also of equality, wherein all the power and jurisdiction is reciprocal, no one having more than another; there being nothing more evident than that creatures of the same species and rank, promiscuously born to all the same advantages of nature and the use of the same faculties, should also be equal one among another without subordination or subjection; unless the Lord and Master of them all should, by any manifest declaration of his will, set one above another, and confer on him, by an evident and clear appointment, an undoubted right to dominion and sovereignty. . . .

But though this be a state of liberty, yet it is not a state of license; though man in that state have an uncontrollable liberty to dispose of his person or possessions, yet he has not liberty to destroy himself, or so much as any creature in his possession, but where some nobler use than its bare preservation calls for it. The state of nature has a law of nature to govern it, which obliges everyone; and reason, which is that law, teaches all mankind who will but consult it that being all equal and independent, no one ought to harm another in his life, health, liberty, or possessions; for men being all the workmanship of one omnipotent and infinitely wise Maker—all the servants of one sovereign Master, sent into the world by his order, and about his business—they are his property, whose workmanship they are, made to last during his, not one another's pleasure; and being furnished with like facul-

---

*From J. Locke, *Second Treatise of Government,* 1690. These passages are from an edition of Locke's works published in London, by Thomas Tegg and others, in 1823.

ties, sharing all in one community of nature, there cannot be supposed any such subordination among us that may authorize us to destroy another, as if we were made for one another's uses, as the inferior ranks of creatures are for ours. Everyone, as he is bound to preserve himself, and not to quit his station willfully, so by the like reason, when his own preservation comes not in competition, ought he, as much as he can, to preserve the rest of mankind, and may not, unless it be to do justice to an offender, take away or impair the life (or what tends to the preservation of life) the liberty, health, limb, or goods of another.

And that all men may be restrained from invading others' rights, and from doing hurt to one another, and the law of nature be observed, which wills the peace and preservation of all mankind, the execution of the law of nature is, in that state, put into every man's hands, whereby everyone has a right to punish the transgressors of that law to such a degree as may hinder its violation; for the law of nature would, as all other laws that concern men in this world, be in vain, if there were nobody that in that state of nature had a power to execute that law and thereby preserve the innocent and restrain offenders. And if anyone in the state of nature may punish another for any evil he has done, everyone may do so; for in that state of perfect equality, where naturally there is no superiority or jurisdiction of one over another, what any may do in prosecution of that law everyone must needs have a right to do. . . .

It is often asked as a mighty objection, "Where are or ever were there any men in such a state of nature?" To which it may suffice as an answer at present, that since all princes and rulers of independent governments all through the world are in a state of nature, it is plain the world never was, nor ever will be, without numbers of men in that state. I have named all governors of independent communities, whether they are, or are not, in league with others; for it is not every compact that puts an end to the state of nature between men, but only this one of agreeing together mutually to enter into one community, and make one body politic; other promises and compacts men may make one with another, and yet still be in the state of nature; . . . for truth and keeping of faith belongs to men as men, and not as members of society.

To those that say there were never any men in the state of nature . . . I moreover affirm that all men are naturally in that state and remain so till by their own consents they make themselves members of some politic society; and I doubt not in the sequel of this discourse to make it very clear.

OF THE STATE OF WAR

The state of war is a state of enmity and destruction; and therefore declaring by word or action, not a passionate and hasty, but a sedate, settled design upon another man's life, puts him in a state of war with him against whom he has declared such an intention, and so has exposed his life to the other's power to be taken away by him, or anyone that joins with him in his defense and espouses his quarrel; it being reasonable and just I should have a right to destroy that which threatens me with destruction; for, by the fundamental law of nature, man being to be preserved as much as possible, when all cannot be preserved, the safety of the innocent is to be preferred; and one may destroy a man who makes war upon him, or has discovered an enmity to his being, for the same reason that he may kill a wolf or a lion; because such men are not under the ties of the common law of reason, have no other rule but that of force and violence, and so may be treated as beasts of prey, those dangerous and noxious creatures that will be sure to destroy him whenever he falls into their power.

And hence it is that he who attempts to get another man into his absolute power, does thereby put himself into a state of war with him; it being to be understood as a declaration of a design upon his life; for I have reason to conclude that he who would get me into his power without my consent would use me as he pleased when he got me there, and destroy me too when he had a fancy to it; for nobody can desire to have me in his absolute power, unless it be to compel me by force to that which is against the right of my freedom, i.e., make me a slave. To be free from such force is the only security of my preservation; and reason bids me look on him as an enemy to my preservation, who would take away that freedom which is the fence to it; so that he who makes an attempt to enslave me thereby puts himself into a state of war with me. He that, in the state of nature, would take away the freedom that belongs to anyone in that state, must necessarily be supposed to have a design to take away everything else, that freedom being the foundation of all the rest; as he that, in the state of society, would take away the freedom belonging to those of that society or commonwealth, must be supposed to design to take away from them everything else, and so be looked on as in a state of war. . . .

And here we have the plain "difference between the state of nature and the state of war," which, however some men* have confounded [them], are as far distant as a state of peace, good-will, mutual assistance and preservation, and state of enmity, malice, violence, and mutual destruction, are one from another. Men living together according to reason, without a common superior on earth with authority to judge between them, is properly the state of nature. But force, or a declared design of force, upon the person of another, where there is no common superior on earth to appeal to for relief, is the state of war; and it is the want of such an appeal [that] gives a man the right of war even against an aggressor, though he be in society, and a fellow subject. Thus a thief, whom I cannot harm but by appeal to the law, for having stolen all that I am worth, I may kill when he sets on me to rob me but of my horse or coat; because the law, which was made for my preservation, where it cannot interpose to secure my life from present force, which, if lost, is capable of no reparation, permits me my own defense, and the right of war, a liberty to kill the aggressor, because the aggressor allows not time to appeal to our common judge, nor the decision of the law, for remedy in a case where the mischief may be irreparable. Want of a common judge with authority puts all men in a state of nature; force without right upon a man's person makes a state of war both where there is and is not a common judge. . . .

To avoid this state of war (wherein there is no appeal but to Heaven, and wherein every least difference is apt to end, where there is no authority to decide

---

*The reference is almost certainly to Thomas Hobbes.—*Ed.*

between the contenders) is one great reason of men's putting themselves into society and quitting the state of nature; for where there is an authority, a power on earth from which relief can be had by appeal, there the continuance of the state of war is excluded, and the controversy is decided by that power. . . .

OF POLITICAL OR CIVIL SOCIETY

Man being born, as has been proved, with a title to perfect freedom and uncontrolled enjoyment of all the rights and privileges of the law of nature equally with any other man or number of men in the world, has by nature a power not only to preserve his property—that is, his life, liberty, and estate—against the injuries and attempts of other men, but to judge of and punish the breaches of that law in others as he is persuaded the offense deserves, even with death itself in crimes where the heinousness of the fact in his opinion requires it. But because no political society can be, nor subsist, without having in itself the power to preserve the property and, in order thereunto, punish the offenses of all those of that society, there and there only is political society where every one of the members has quitted his natural power, resigned it up into the hands of the community in all cases that exclude him not from appealing for protection to the law established by it. And thus all private judgment of every particular member being excluded, the community comes to be umpire by settled standing rules, indifferent and the same to all parties; and by men having authority from the community for the execution of those rules decides all the differences that may happen between any members of that society concerning any matter of right; and punishes those offenses which any member has committed against the society, with such penalties as the law has established; whereby it is easy to discern who are, and who are not, in political society together. Those who are united into one body, and have a common established law and judicature to appeal to, with authority to decide controversies between them, and punish offenders, are in civil society one with another; but those who have no such common appeal, I mean on earth, are still in the state of nature, each being, where there is no other, judge for himself, and executioner, which is, as I have before shown it, the perfect state of nature.

And thus the commonwealth comes by a power to set down what punishment shall belong to the several transgressions which they think worthy of it, committed among the members of that society (which is the power of making laws) as well as it has the power to punish any injury done unto any of its members, by anyone that is not of it (which is the power of war and peace): and all this for the preservation of the property of all the members of that society as far as is possible. But though every man who has entered into civil society, and is become a member of any commonwealth, has thereby quitted his power to punish offenses against the law of nature, in prosecution of his own private judgment; yet, with the judgment of offenses, which he has given up to the legislative in all cases, where he can appeal to the magistrate, he has given a right to the commonwealth to employ his force for the execution of the judgments of the commonwealth, whenever he shall be called to it; which, indeed, are his own judgments, they being made by himself or his representative. And herein we have the original of the leg-islative and executive power of civil society, which is to judge by standing laws how far offenses are to be punished when committed within the commonwealth, and also to determine, by occasional judgments founded on the present circum-stances of the fact, how far injuries from without are to be vindicated; and in both these to employ all the force of all the members, when there shall be need.

Whenever, therefore, any number of men are so united into one society, as to quit every one his executive power of the law of nature, and to resign it to the pub-lic, there and there only is a political or civil society. And this is done wherever any number of men, in the state of nature, enter into society to make one people, one body politic, under one supreme government; or else when any one joins him-self to, and incorporates with, any government already made; for hereby he autho-rizes the society or, which is all one, the legislative thereof, to make laws for him, as the public good of the society shall require, to the execution whereof his own assistance (as to his own decrees) is due. And this puts men out of a state of nature into that of a commonwealth by setting up a judge on earth, with authority to determine all the controversies, and redress the injuries that may happen to any member of the commonwealth; which judge is the legislative, or magistrate appointed by it. And wherever there are any number of men, however associated, that have no such decisive power to appeal to, there they are still in the state of nature.

Hence it is evident that absolute monarchy, which by some men is counted the only government in the world, is indeed inconsistent with civil society, and so can be no form of civil government at all; for the end of civil society being to avoid and remedy those inconveniences of the state of nature which necessarily follow from every man being judge in his own case, by setting up a known authority, to which everyone of that society may appeal upon any injury received or contro-versy that may arise, and which everyone of the society ought to obey. Wherever any persons are who have not such an authority to appeal to for the decision of any difference between them, there those persons are still in the state of nature; and so is every absolute prince, in respect of those who are under his dominion.

For he being supposed to have all, both legislative and executive power in him-self alone, there is no judge to be found, no appeal lies open to anyone who may fairly and indifferently and with authority decide, and from whose decision relief and redress may be expected of any injury or inconvenience that may be suffered from the prince, or by his order; so that such a man, however entitled, "czar," or "grand seignoir," or how you please, is as much in the state of nature with all under his dominion, as he is with the rest of mankind; for wherever any two men are who have no standing rule, and common judge to appeal to on earth, for the determination of controversies of right betwixt them, there they are still in the state of nature, and under all the inconveniences of it, with only this woeful dif-ference to the subject, or rather slave, of an absolute prince: that whereas in the ordinary state of nature he has a liberty to judge of his right and, according to the best of his power to maintain it; now, whenever his property is invaded by the will and order of his monarch, he has not only no appeal as those in society ought to have but, as if he were degraded from the common state of rational creatures, is denied a liberty to judge of, or to defend his right; and so is exposed to all the misery and inconveniences that a man can fear from one who, being in the unrestrained state of nature, is yet corrupted with flattery and armed with power. . . .

OF THE BEGINNING OF POLITICAL SOCIETIES

Men, being, as has been said, by nature all free, equal, and independent, no one can be put out of this estate and subjected to the political power of another without his own consent. The only way whereby anyone divests himself of his natural liberty and puts on the bonds of civil society is by agreeing with other men to join and unite into a community for their comfortable, safe, and peaceable living one among another, in a secure enjoyment of their properties and a greater security against any that are not of it. This any number of men may do, because it injures not the freedom of the rest; they are left as they were in the liberty of the state of nature. When any number of men have so consented to make one community or government, they are thereby presently incorporated and make one body politic wherein the majority have a right to act and conclude the rest.

For when any number of men have, by the consent of every individual, made a community, they have thereby made that community one body, with a power to act as one body, which is only by the will and determination of the majority; for that which acts any community being only the consent of the individuals of it, and it being necessary to that which is one body to move one way, it is necessary the body should move that way whither the greater force carries it, which is the consent of the majority; or else it is impossible it should act or continue one body, one community, which the consent of every individual that united into it agreed that it should; and so everyone is bound by that consent to be concluded by the majority. And therefore we see that in assemblies impowered to act by positive laws, where no number is set by that positive law which impowers them, the act of the majority passes for the act of the whole, and of course determines, as having by the law of nature and reason the power of the whole.

And thus every man, by consenting with others to make one body politic under one government, puts himself under an obligation to everyone of that society to submit to the determination of the majority, and to be concluded by it; or else this original compact, whereby he with others incorporates into one society, would signify nothing, and be no compact, if he be left free, and under no other ties than he was in before in the state of nature. For what appearance would there be of any compact? What new engagement if he were no further tied by any decrees of the society than he himself thought fit and did actually consent to? This would be still as great a liberty as he himself had before his compact, or anyone else in the state of nature has, who may submit himself and consent to any acts of it if he thinks fit.

For if the consent of the majority shall not, in reason, be received as the act of the whole, and conclude every individual, nothing but the consent of every individual can make anything to be the act of the whole; but such a consent is next to impossible ever to be had if we consider the infirmities of health and avocations of business, which in a number, though much less than that of a commonwealth, will necessarily keep many away from the public assembly. To which, if we add the variety of opinions and contrariety of interests which unavoidably happen in all collections of men, the coming into society upon such terms would be only like Cato's coming into the theater only to go out again. Such a constitution as this would make the mighty leviathan of a shorter duration than the feeblest creatures, and not let it outlast the day it was born in; which cannot be supposed till we can think that rational creatures should desire and constitute societies only to be dissolved; for where the majority cannot conclude the rest, there they cannot act as one body, and consequently will be immediately dissolved again.

Whosoever, therefore, out of a state of nature unite into a community must be understood to give up all the power necessary to the ends for which they unite into society to the majority of the community, unless they expressly agreed in any number greater than the majority. And this is done by barely agreeing to unite into one political society, which is all the compact that is, or needs be, between the individuals that enter into or make up a commonwealth. And thus that which begins and actually constitutes any political society is nothing but the consent of any number of freemen capable of a majority to unite and incorporate into such a society. And this is that, and that only, which did or could give beginning to any lawful government in the world.

To this I find two objections made:

First, "That there are no instances to be found in story of a company of men independent and equal one among another, that met together, and in this way began and set up a government."

Secondly, "It is impossible of right, that men should do so, because all men being born under government, they are to submit to that, and are not at liberty to begin a new one."

To the first there is this to answer: that it is not at all to be wondered that history gives us but a very little account of men that lived together in the state of nature. The inconveniences of that condition, and the love and want of society, no sooner brought any number of them together, but they presently united and incorporated if they designed to continue together. And if we may not suppose men ever to have been in the state of nature, because we hear not much of them in such a state, we may as well suppose the armies of Salmanasser or Xerxes were never children, because we hear little of them till they were men and embodied in armies. Government is everywhere antecedent to records, and letters seldom come in among a people till a long continuation of civil society has, by other more necessary arts, provided for their safety, ease, and plenty; and then they begin to look after the history of their founders and search into their original, when they have outlived the memory of it; for it is with commonwealths as with particular persons—they are commonly ignorant of their own births and infancies; and if they know anything of their original, they are beholden for it to the accidental records that others have kept of it. And those that we have of the beginning of any politics in the world, excepting that of the Jews, where God himself immediately interposed, and which favors not at all paternal dominion, are all either plain instances of such a beginning as I have mentioned, or at least have manifest footsteps of it. . . .

But to conclude, reason being plain on our side, that men are naturally free, and the examples of history showing that the governments of the world, that were begun in peace, had their beginning laid on that foundation, and were made by the consent of the people, there can be little room for doubt, either where the right is, or what has been the opinion or practice of mankind about the first erecting of governments. . . .

The other objection I find urged against the beginning of politics in the way I have mentioned is this:

"That all men being born under government, some or other, it is impossible any of them should ever be free and at liberty to unite together and begin a new one, or ever be able to erect a lawful government."

If this argument be good, I ask, how came so many lawful monarchies into the world? For if anybody, upon this supposition, can show me any one man in any age of the world free to begin a lawful monarchy, I will be bound to show him ten other free men at liberty at the same time to unite and begin a new government under a regal or any other form, it being demonstration that if anyone, born under the dominion of another, may be so free as to have a right to command others in a new and distinct empire, everyone that is born under the dominion of another may be so free, too, and may become a ruler, or subject of a distinct separate government. And so, by this their own principle, either all men, however born, are free, or else there is but one lawful prince, one lawful government in the world. And then they have nothing to do, but barely to show us which that is; which, when they have done, I doubt not but all mankind will easily agree to pay obedience to him.

Though it be a sufficient answer to their objection, to show that it involves them in the same difficulties that it does those they use it against, yet I shall endeavor to discover the weakness of this argument a little further. "All men," say they, "are born under government, and therefore they cannot be at liberty to begin a new one. Everyone is born a subject to his father, or his prince, and is therefore under the perpetual tie of subjection and allegiance." It is plain mankind never owned nor considered any such natural subjection that they were born in, to one or to the other, that tied them without their own consents, to a subjection to them and their heirs.

For there are no examples so frequent in history, both sacred and profane, as those of men withdrawing themselves, and their obedience, from the jurisdiction they were born under, and the family or community they were bred up in, and setting up new governments in other places; from whence sprang all that number of petty commonwealths in the beginning of ages, and which always multiplied as long as there was room enough, till the stronger or more fortunate swallowed the weaker, and those great ones, again breaking to pieces, dissolved into lesser dominions. All which are so many testimonies against paternal sovereignty, and plainly prove that it was not the natural right of the father descending to his heirs that made governments in the beginning, since it was impossible, upon that ground, there should have been so many little kingdoms; all must have been but only one universal monarchy, if men had not been at liberty to separate themselves from their families and the government, be it what it will, that was set up in it, and go and make distinct commonwealths and other governments, as they thought fit. . . .

Every man being, as has been shown, naturally free, and nothing being able to put him into subjection to any earthly power but only his own consent, it is to be considered what shall be understood to be a sufficient declaration of a man's consent to make him subject to the laws of any government. There is a common distinction of an express and a tacit consent, which will concern our present case. Nobody doubts but an express consent of any man entering into any society makes him a perfect member of that society, a subject of that government. The difficulty is, what ought to be looked upon as a tacit consent, and how far it binds—i.e., how far anyone shall be looked upon to have consented and thereby submitted to any government, where he has made no expressions of it at all. And to this I say that every man that has any possessions or enjoyment of any part of the dominions of any government does thereby give his tacit consent, and is as far forth obliged to obedience to the laws of that government, during such enjoyment, as anyone under it; whether this his possession be of land to him and his heirs forever, or a lodging only for a week, or whether it be barely traveling freely on the highway; and, in effect, it reaches as far as the very being of anyone within the territories of that government.

To understand this the better, it is fit to consider that every man, when he at first incorporates himself into any commonwealth, he, by his uniting himself thereunto, annexes also, and submits to the community those possessions which he has, or shall acquire, that do not already belong to any other government; for it would be a direct contradiction for anyone to enter into society with others for the securing and regulating of property, and yet to suppose his land, whose property is to be regulated by the laws of the society, should be exempt from the jurisdiction of that government to which he himself, the proprietor of the land, is a subject. By the same act therefore, whereby anyone unites his person, which was before free, to any commonwealth, by the same he unites his possessions, which were before free, to it also; and they become, both of them, person and possession, subject to the government and dominion of that commonwealth as long as it has a being. Whoever, therefore, from thenceforth by inheritance, purchase, permission, or otherwise, enjoys any part of the land so annexed to, and under the government of that commonwealth, must take it with the condition it is under—that is, of submitting to the government of the commonwealth, under whose jurisdiction it is, as far forth as any subject of it.

But since the government has a direct jurisdiction only over the land, and reaches the possessor of it (before he has actually incorporated himself in the society) only as he dwells upon and enjoys that, the obligation anyone is under by virtue of such enjoyment, to submit to the government, begins and ends with the enjoyment; so that whenever the owner, who has given nothing but such a tacit consent to the government, will, by donation, sale, or otherwise, quit the said possession, he is at liberty to go and incorporate himself into any other commonwealth, or to agree with others to begin a new one, *in vacuis locis,* in any part of the world they can find free and unpossessed. Whereas he that has once, by actual agreement, and any express declaration, given his consent to be of any commonwealth, is perpetually and indispensably obliged to be and remain unalterably a subject to it, and can never be again in the liberty of the state of nature, unless, by any calamity, the government he was under comes to be dissolved, or else by some public act, cuts him off from being any longer a member of it.

But submitting to the laws of any country, living quietly, and enjoying privileges and protection under them, makes not a man a member of that society; this is only a local protection and homage due to and from all those who, not being in a state of war, come within the territories belonging to any government, to all parts whereof the force of its laws extends. But this no more makes a man a member of that society, a perpetual subject of that commonwealth, than it would make a man a subject to another, in whose family he found it convenient to abide for some time, though, while he continued in it, he were obliged to comply with the laws, and submit to the government he found there. And thus we see that foreigners, by living all their lives under another government, and enjoying the privileges and protection of it, though they are bound, even in conscience, to submit to its administration, as far forth as any denizen, yet do not thereby come to be subjects or members of that commonwealth. Nothing can make any man so but his actually entering into it by positive engagement, and express promise and compact. That is that which I think concerning the beginning of political societies, and that consent which makes anyone a member of any commonwealth.

OF THE ENDS OF POLITICAL SOCIETY AND GOVERNMENT

If man in the state of nature be so free as has been said; if he be absolute lord of his own person and possessions, equal to the greatest, and subject to nobody, why will he part with his freedom, why will he give up his empire, and subject himself to the dominion and control of any other power? To which it is obvious to answer that though in the state of nature he has such a right, yet the enjoyment of it is very uncertain, and constantly exposed to the invasion of others; for all being kings as much as he, every man his equal, and the greater part no strict observers of equity and justice, the enjoyment of the property he has in this state is very unsafe, very unsecure. This makes him willing to quit a condition which, however free, is full of fears and continual dangers; and it is not without reason that he seeks out and is willing to join in society with others who are already united, or have a mind to unite, for the mutual preservation of their lives, liberties, and estates, which I call by the general name "property."

The great and chief end, therefore, of men's uniting into commonwealths and putting themselves under government is the preservation of their property. To which in the state of nature there are many things wanting:

First, there wants an established, settled, known law, received and allowed by common consent to be the standard of right and wrong, and the common measure to decide all controversies between them; for though the law of nature be plain and intelligible to all rational creatures, yet men being biased by their interest, as well as ignorant for want of studying it, are not apt to allow of it as a law binding to them in the application of it to their particular cases.

Secondly, in the state of nature there wants a known and indifferent judge, with authority to determine all differences according to the established law; for everyone in that state being both judge and executioner of the law of nature, men being partial to themselves, passion and revenge is very apt to carry them too far and with too much heat in their own cases, as well as negligence and unconcernedness to make them too remiss in other men's.

Thirdly, in the state of nature there often wants power to back and support the sentence when right, and to give it due execution. They who by any injustice offend, will seldom fail, where they are able, by force to make good their injustice; such resistance many times makes the punishment dangerous, and frequently destructive to those who attempt it.

Thus mankind, notwithstanding all the privileges of the state of nature, being but in an ill condition while they remain in it, are quickly driven into society. Hence it comes to pass that we seldom find any number of men live any time together in this state. The inconveniences that they are therein exposed to, by the irregular and uncertain exercise of the power every man has of punishing the transgressions of others, make them take sanctuary under the established laws of government and therein seek the preservation of their property. It is this makes them so willingly give up every one his single power of punishing, to be exercised by such alone as shall be appointed to it among them; and by such rules as the community, or those authorized by them to that purpose, shall agree on. And in this we have the original right of both the legislative and executive power, as well as of the governments and societies themselves.

For in the state of nature, to omit the liberty he has of innocent delights, a man has two powers:

The first is to do whatsoever he thinks fit for the preservation of himself and others within the permission of the law of nature, by which law, common to them all, he and all the rest of mankind are one community, make up one society, distinct from all other creatures. And, were it not for the corruption and viciousness of degenerate men, there would be no need of any other, no necessity that men should separate from this great and natural community, and by positive agreements combine into smaller and divided associations.

The other power a man has in the state of nature is the power to punish the crimes committed against that law. Both these he gives up when he joins in a private, if I may so call it, or particular politic society and incorporates into any commonwealth separate from the rest of mankind.

The first power, viz., of doing whatsoever he thought fit for the preservation of himself and the rest of mankind, he gives up to be regulated by laws made by the society, so far forth as the preservation of himself and the rest of that society shall require; which laws of the society in many things confine the liberty he had by the law of nature.

Secondly, the power of punishing he wholly gives up, and engages his natural force (which he might before employ in the execution of the law of nature, by his own single authority, as he thought fit) to assist the executive power of the society, as the law thereof shall require; for being now in a new state, wherein he is to enjoy many conveniences from the labor, assistance, and society of others in the same community as well as protection from its whole strength, he is to part also with as much of his natural liberty, in providing for himself, as the good, prosperity, and safety of the society shall require, which is not only necessary, but just, since the other members of the society do the like.

But though men when they enter into society, give up the equality, liberty, and executive power they had in the state of nature, into the hands of the society, to be so far disposed of by the legislative as the good of the society shall require; yet it being only with an intention in everyone the better to preserve himself, his liberty and property (for no rational creature can be supposed to change his condition with an intention to be worse), the power of the society, or legislative constituted by them, can never be supposed to extend farther than the common good, but is obliged to secure everyone's property by providing against those three defects above-mentioned that made the state of nature so unsafe and uneasy. And so whoever has the legislative or supreme power of any commonwealth is bound to govern by established standing laws, promulgated and known to the people, and not by extemporary decrees; by indifferent and upright judges who are to decide controversies by those laws; and to employ the force of the community at home only in the execution of such laws, or abroad to prevent or redress foreign injuries, and secure the community from inroads and invasion. And all this to be directed to no other end but the peace, safety, and public good of the people. . . .

OF THE EXTENT OF THE LEGISLATIVE POWER

The great end of men's entering into society being the enjoyment of their properties in peace and safety, and the great instrument and means of that being the laws established in that society, the first and fundamental positive law of all commonwealths is the establishing of the legislative power; as the first and fundamental natural law, which is to govern even the legislative itself, is the preservation of the society, and (as far as will consist with the public good) of every person in it. This legislative is not only the supreme power of the commonwealth, but sacred and unalterable in the hands where the community have once placed it; nor can any edict of anybody else, in what form soever conceived or by what power soever backed, have the force and obligation of a law, which has not its sanction from that legislative which the public has chosen and appointed; for without this the law could not have that which is absolutely necessary to its being a law: the consent of the society over whom nobody can have a power to make laws, but by their own consent, and by authority received from them.* And therefore all the obedience,

---

*"The lawful power of making laws to command whole politic societies of men, belonging so properly unto the same entire societies, that for any prince or potentate of what kind soever upon earth, to exercise the same of himself, and not by express commission immediately and personally received from God, or else by authority derived at the first from their consent, upon whose persons they impose laws, it is no better than mere tyranny. Laws they are not, therefore, which public approbation hath not made so" (Hooker's *Eccl. Pol.* lib. i. sect. 10).

"Of this point, therefore, we are to note, that such men naturally have no full and perfect power to command whole politic multitudes of men, therefore utterly without our consent, we could in such sort be at no man's commandment living. And to be commanded we do consent, when that society, whereof we be a part, hath at any time before consented, without revoking the same by the like universal agreement. Laws therefore human, of what kind soever, are available by consent" (*Ibid.*).

which by the most solemn ties anyone can be obliged to pay, ultimately terminates in this supreme power, and is directed by those laws which it enacts; nor can any oaths to any foreign power whatsoever, or any domestic subordinate power, discharge any member of the society from his obedience to the legislative acting pursuant to their trust, nor oblige him to any obedience contrary to the laws so enacted, or farther than they do allow; it being ridiculous to imagine one can be tied ultimately to obey any power in the society which is not supreme.

Though the legislative, whether placed in one or more, whether it be always in being, or only by intervals, though it be the supreme power in every commonwealth; yet:

First, it is not, nor can possibly be absolutely arbitrary over the lives and fortunes of the people; for it being but the joint power of every member of the society given up to that person or assembly which is legislator, it can be no more than those persons had in a state of nature before they entered into society and gave up to the community; for nobody can transfer to another more power than he has in himself, and nobody has an absolute arbitrary power over himself, or over any other, to destroy his own life, or take away the life or property of another. A man, as has been proved, cannot subject himself to the arbitrary power of another; and having in the state of nature no arbitrary power over the life, liberty, or possession of another, but only so much as the law of nature gave him for the preservation of himself and the rest of mankind, this is all he does or can give up to the commonwealth, and by it to the legislative power, so that the legislative can have no more than this. Their power, in the utmost bounds of it, is limited to the public good of the society. It is a power that has no other end but preservation, and therefore can never have a right to destroy, enslave, or designedly to impoverish the subjects. The obligations of the law of nature cease not in society but only in many cases are drawn closer and have by human laws known penalties annexed to them to enforce their observation. Thus the law of nature stands as an eternal rule to all men, legislators as well as others. The rules that they make for other men's actions must, as well as their own and other men's actions be conformable to the law of nature, i.e., to the will of God, of which that is a declaration, and the fundamental law of nature being the preservation of mankind, no human sanction can be good or valid against it.

Secondly, the legislative or supreme authority cannot assume to itself a power to rule by extemporary, arbitrary decrees, but is bound to dispense justice, and to decide the rights of the subject by promulgated, standing laws, and known authorized judges. For the law of nature being unwritten, and so nowhere to be found but in the minds of men, they who through passion or interest shall miscite or misapply it, cannot so easily be convinced of their mistake where there is no established judge; and so it serves not, as it ought, to determine the rights and fence the properties of those that live under it, especially where everyone is judge, interpreter, and executioner of it too, and that in his own case; and he that has right on his side, having ordinarily but his own single strength, has not force enough to defend himself from injuries or to punish delinquents. To avoid these inconveniences which disorder men's properties in the state of nature, men unite into societies that they may have the united strength of the whole society to secure and defend their properties, and may have standing rules to bound it by which every-one may know what is his. To this end it is that men give up all their natural power to the society which they enter into, and the community put the legislative power into such hands as they think fit with this trust, that they shall be governed by declared laws, or else their peace, quiet, and property will still be at the same uncertainty as it was in the state of nature.

Absolute arbitrary power or governing without settled standing laws can neither of them consist with the ends of society and government which men would not quit the freedom of the state of nature for, and tie themselves up under, were it not to preserve their lives, liberties, and fortunes, and by stated rules of right and prop-erty to secure their peace and quiet. It cannot be supposed that they should intend, had they a power so to do, to give to any one, or more, an absolute arbitrary power over their persons and estates, and put a force into the magistrate's hand to exe-cute his unlimited will arbitrarily upon them. This were to put themselves into a worse condition than the state of nature, wherein they had a liberty to defend their right against the injuries of others, and were upon equal terms of force to maintain it, whether invaded by a single man or many in combination. Whereas, by sup-posing they have given up themselves to the absolute arbitrary power and will of a legislator, they have disarmed themselves, and armed him, to make a prey of them when he pleases; he being in a much worse condition who is exposed to the arbitrary power of one man, who has the command of 100,000, than he that is exposed to the arbitrary power of 100,000 single men, nobody being secure that his will, who has such a command, is better than that of other men, though his force be 100,000 times stronger. And therefore, whatever form the commonwealth is under, the ruling power ought to govern by declared and received laws and not by extemporary dictates and undetermined resolutions; for then mankind will be in a far worse condition than in the state of nature if they shall have armed one or a few men with the joint power of a multitude, to force them to obey at pleasure the exorbitant and unlimited decrees of their sudden thoughts, or unrestrained, and till that moment unknown wills, without having any measures set down which may guide and justify their actions. For all the power the government has being only for the good of the society, as it ought not to be arbitrary and at pleasure, so it ought to be exercised by established and promulgated laws; that both the people may know their duty and be safe and secure within the limits of the law; and the rulers, too, kept within their bounds, and not be tempted by the power they have in their hands to employ it to such purposes and by such measures as they would not have known, and own not willingly.

Thirdly, the supreme power cannot take from any man part of his property with-out his own consent; for the preservation of property being the end of government, and that for which men enter into society, it necessarily supposes and requires, that the people should have property; without which they must be supposed to lose that, by entering into society, which was the end for which they entered into it—too gross an absurdity for any man to own. Men, therefore, in society having prop-erty, they have such right to the goods, which by the law of the community are theirs, that nobody has a right to take their substance or any part of it from them, without their own consent; without this they have no property at all; for I have truly no property in that which another can by right take from me when he pleases, against my consent. Hence it is a mistake to think that the supreme or legislative power of any commonwealth can do what it will and dispose of the estates of the subject arbitrarily, or take any part of them at pleasure. This is not much to be feared in governments where the legislative consists, wholly or in part, in assemblies which are variable, whose members, upon the dissolution of the assembly, are subjects under the common laws of their country, equally with the rest. But in governments where the legislative is in one lasting assembly always in being, or in one man, as in absolute monarchies, there is danger still that they will think themselves to have a distinct interest from the rest of the community, and so will be apt to increase their own riches and power by taking what they think fit from the people; for a man's property is not at all secure, though there be good and equitable laws to set the bounds of it between him and his fellow subjects, if he who commands those subjects have power to take from any private man what part he pleases of his property and use and dispose of it as he thinks good.

But government, into whatsoever hands it is put, being, as I have before shown, entrusted with this condition, and for this end, that men might have and secure their properties; the prince, or senate, however it may have power to make laws for the regulating of property between the subjects one among another, yet can never have a power to take to themselves the whole or any part of the subject's property without their own consent; for this would be in effect to leave them no property at all. All to let us see that even absolute power, where it is necessary, is not arbitrary by being absolute, but is still limited by that reason and confined to those ends, which required it in some cases to be absolute, we need look no farther than the common practice of martial discipline; for the preservation of the army, and in it of the whole commonwealth, requires an absolute obedience to the command of every superior officer, and it is justly death to disobey or dispute the most dangerous or unreasonable of them; but yet we see, that neither the sergeant, that could command a soldier to march up to the mouth of a cannon, or stand in a breach where he is almost sure to perish, can command that soldier to give him one penny of his money; nor the general, that can condemn him to death for deserting his post, or for not obeying the most desperate orders, can yet, with all his absolute power of life and death, dispose of one farthing of that soldier's estate or seize one jot of his goods, whom yet he can command anything, and hang for the least disobedience. Because such a blind obedience is necessary to that end for which the commander has his power, viz., the preservation of the rest; but the disposing of his goods has nothing to do with it.

It is true, governments cannot be supported without great charge, and it is fit everyone who enjoys his share of the protection should pay out of his estate his proportion for the maintenance of it. But still it must be with his own consent, i.e., the consent of the majority, giving it either by themselves or their representatives chosen by them. For if anyone shall claim a power to lay and levy taxes on the people, by his own authority and without such consent of the people, he thereby invades the fundamental law of property and subverts the end of government; for what property have I in that which another may by right take, when he pleases, to himself?

Fourthly, the legislative cannot transfer the power of making laws to any other hands; for it being but a delegated power from the people, they who have it cannot pass it over to others. The people alone can appoint the form of the commonwealth, which is by constituting the legislative and appointing in whose hands that shall be. And when the people have said, we will submit to rules and be governed by laws made by such men, and in such forms, nobody else can say other men shall make laws for them; nor can the people be bound by any laws but such as are enacted by those whom they have chosen and authorized to make laws for them. The power of the legislative being derived from the people by a positive voluntary grant and institution, can be no other than what that positive grant conveyed, which being only to make laws, and not to make legislators, the legislative can have no power to transfer their authority of making laws and place it in other hands.

These are the bounds which the trust that is put in them by the society, and the law of God and nature, have set to the legislative power of every commonwealth, in all forms of government:

First, they are to govern by promulgated established laws, not to be varied in particular cases, but to have one rule for rich and poor, for the favorite at court and the countryman at plow.

Secondly, these laws also ought to be designed for no other end ultimately, but the good of the people.

Thirdly, they must not raise taxes on the property of the people without the consent of the people, given by themselves or their deputies. And this properly concerns only such governments where the legislative is always in being, or at least where the people have not reserved any part of the legislative to deputies to be from time to time chosen by themselves.

Fourthly, the legislative neither must nor can transfer the power of making laws to anybody else, or place it anywhere but where the people have.

OF THE LEGISLATIVE, EXECUTIVE, AND FEDERATIVE POWER OF THE COMMONWEALTH

The legislative power is that which has a right to direct how the force of the commonwealth shall be employed for preserving the community and the members of it. But because those laws which are constantly to be executed, and whose force is always to continue, may be made in a little time, therefore there is no need that the legislative should be always in being, not having always business to do. And because it may be too great a temptation to human frailty, apt to grasp at power, for the same persons who have the power of making laws to have also in their hands the power to execute them, whereby they may exempt themselves from obedience to the laws they make, and suit the law, both in its making and execution, to their own private advantage, and thereby come to have a distinct interest from the rest of the community, contrary to the end of society and government; therefore, in well ordered commonwealths, where the good of the whole is so considered, as it ought, the legislative power is put into the hands of diverse persons, who, duly assembled, have by themselves, or jointly with others, a power to make laws; which when they have done, being separated again, they are themselves subject to the laws they have made, which is a new and near tie upon them to take care that they make them for the public good.

But because the laws that are at once and in a short time made have a constant and lasting force and need a perpetual execution, or an attendance thereunto; therefore, it is necessary there should be a power always in being which should see to the execution of the laws that are made and remain in force. And thus the legislative and executive power come often to be separated.

There is another power in every commonwealth which one may call natural, because it is that which answers to the power every man naturally had before he entered into society; for though in a commonwealth, the members of it are distinct persons still in reference to one another, and as such are governed by the laws of the society, yet, in reference to the rest of mankind, they make one body which is, as every member of it before was, still in the state of nature with the rest of mankind. Hence it is, that the controversies that happen between any man of the society with those that are out of it are managed by the public, and an injury done to a member of their body engages the whole in the reparation of it. So that, under this consideration, the whole community is one body in the state of nature, in respect of all other states or persons out of its community.

This therefore contains the power of war and peace, leagues and alliances, and all the transactions with all persons and communities without the commonwealth, and may be called "federative," if anyone pleases. So the thing be understood, I am indifferent as to the name. . . .

Though, as I said, the executive and federative power of every community be really distinct in themselves, yet they are hardly to be separated and placed at the same time in the hands of distinct persons; for both of them requiring the force of the society for their exercise, it is almost impracticable to place the force of the commonwealth in distinct and not subordinate hands, or that the executive and federative power should be placed in persons that might act separately, whereby the force of the public would be under different commands, which would be apt some time or other to cause disorder and ruin.

OF THE SUBORDINATION OF THE POWERS OF THE COMMONWEALTH

Though in a constituted commonwealth, standing upon its own basis, and acting according to its own nature, that is, acting for the preservation of the community, there can be but one supreme power, which is the legislative, to which all the rest are and must be subordinate; yet, the legislative being only a fiduciary power to act for certain ends, there remains still in the people a supreme power to remove or alter the legislative, when they find the legislative act contrary to the trust reposed in them; for all power given with trust for the attaining an end, being limited by that end; whenever that end is manifestly neglected or opposed, the trust must necessarily be forfeited and the power devolve into the hands of those that gave it, who may place it anew where they shall think best for their safety and security. And thus the community perpetually retains a supreme power of saving themselves from the attempts and designs of anybody, even of their legislators, whenever they shall be so foolish or so wicked as to lay and carry on designs against the liberties and properties of the subject; for no man, or society of men, having a power to deliver up their preservation, or consequently the means of it, to the absolute will and arbitrary dominion of another, whenever anyone shall go about to bring them into such a slavish condition, they will always have a right to preserve what they have not a power to part with, and to rid themselves of those who invade this fundamental, sacred, and unalterable law of self-preservation, for which they entered into society. And thus the community may be said in this respect to be always the supreme power, but not as considered under any form of government, because this power of the people can never take place till the government be dissolved.

In all cases, while the government subsists, the legislative is the supreme power; for what can give laws to another must needs be superior to him; and since the legislative is not otherwise legislative of the society, but by the right it has to make laws for all the parts and for every member of the society, prescribing rules to their actions, and giving power of execution where they are transgressed, the legislative must needs be the supreme, and all other powers in any members or parts of the society, derived from and subordinate to it.

In some commonwealths, where the legislative is not always in being, and the executive is vested in a single person who has also a share in the legislative, there that single person in a very tolerable sense may also be called supreme; not that he has in himself all the supreme power, which is that of lawmaking, but because he has in him the supreme execution, from whom all inferior magistrates derive all their several subordinate powers, or at least the greatest part of them. Having also no legislative superior to him, there being no law to be made without his consent which cannot be expected should ever subject him to the other part of the legislative, he is properly enough in this sense supreme. But yet it is to be observed that though oaths of allegiance and fealty are taken to him, it is not to him as supreme legislator, but as supreme executor of the law made by a joint power of him with others; allegiance being nothing but an obedience according to law, which when he violates, he has no right to obedience, nor can claim it otherwise than as the public person invested with the power of the law, and so is to be considered as the image, phantom, or representative of the commonwealth, acted by the will of the society, declared in its laws; and thus he has no will, no power, but that of the law. But when he quits this representation, this public will, and acts by his own private will, he degrades himself and is but a single private person without power and without will that has no right to obedience—the members owing no obedience but to the public will of the society.

The executive power, placed anywhere but in a person that has also a share in the legislative, is visibly subordinate and accountable to it and may be at pleasure changed and displaced, so that it is not the supreme executive power that is exempt from subordination, but the supreme executive power vested in one, who

having a share in the legislative, has no distinct superior legislative to be subordinate and accountable to, farther than he himself shall join and consent; so that he
is no more subordinate than he himself shall think fit, which one may certainly
conclude will be but very little. Of other ministerial and subordinate powers in a
commonwealth we need not speak, they being so multiplied with infinite variety,
in the different customs and constitutions of distinct commonwealths, that it is
impossible to give a particular account of them all. Only thus much, which is necessary to our present purpose, we may take notice of concerning them, that they
have no manner of authority, any of them, beyond what is by positive grant and
commission delegated to them, and are all of them accountable to some other
power in the commonwealth.

It is not necessary, no, nor so much as convenient, that the legislative should be
always in being; but absolutely necessary that the executive power should,
because there is not always need of new laws to be made, but always need of execution of the laws that are made. When the legislative has put the execution of the
laws they make into other hands, they have a power still to resume it out of those
hands, when they find cause, and to punish for any maladministration against the
laws. The same holds also in regard of the federative power, that and the executive being both ministerial and subordinate to the legislative which, as has been
shown, in a constituted commonwealth is the supreme. . . .

The power of assembling and dismissing the legislative, placed in the executive, gives not the executive a superiority over it, but is a fiduciary trust placed in
him for the safety of the people, in a case where the uncertainty and variableness
of human affairs could not bear a steady fixed rule; for it not being possible that
the first framers of the government should, by any foresight, be so much masters
of future events as to be able to prefix so just periods of return and duration to the
assemblies of the legislative, in all times to come, that might exactly answer all the
exigencies of the commonwealth, the best remedy could be found for this defect
was to trust this to the prudence of one who was always to be present and whose
business it was to watch over the public good. Constant, frequent meetings of the
legislative, and long continuations of their assemblies without necessary occasion,
could not but be burdensome to the people and must necessarily in time produce
more dangerous inconveniences, and yet the quick turn of affairs might be sometimes such as to need their present help. Any delay of their convening might
endanger the public; and sometimes, too, their business might be so great that the
limited time of their sitting might be too short for their work, and rob the public
of that benefit which could be had only from their mature deliberation. What then
could be done in this case to prevent the community from being exposed, some
time or other, to eminent hazard, on one side or the other, by fixed intervals and
periods, set to the meeting and acting of the legislative, but to entrust it to the prudence of some who, being present and acquainted with the state of public affairs,
might make use of this prerogative for the public good? And where else could this
be so well placed as in his hands who was entrusted with the execution of the laws
for the same end? Thus supposing the regulation of times for the assembling and
sitting of the legislative not settled by the original constitution, it naturally fell into

the hands of the executive, not as an arbitrary power depending on his good pleasure, but with this trust always to have it exercised only for the public weal, as the
occurrences of times and change of affairs might require. Whether settled periods
of their convening, or a liberty left to the prince for convoking the legislative, or
perhaps a mixture of both, has the least inconvenience attending it, it is not my
business here to inquire; but only to show, that though the executive power may
have the prerogative of convoking and dissolving such conventions of the legislative, yet it is not thereby superior to it. . . .

OF THE DISSOLUTION OF GOVERNMENT

He that will with any clearness speak of the dissolution of government, ought in
the first place to distinguish between the dissolution of the society and the dissolution of the government. That which makes the community and brings men out of
the loose state of nature into one politic society is the agreement which everyone
has with the rest to incorporate and act as one body, and so be one distinct commonwealth. The usual, and almost only, way whereby this union is dissolved is the
inroad of foreign force making a conquest upon them; for in that case (not being
able to maintain and support themselves as one entire and independent body) the
union belonging to that body which consisted therein must necessarily cease, and
so everyone return to the state he was in before, with a liberty to shift for himself
and provide for his own safety, as he thinks fit, in some other society. Whenever
the society is dissolved, it is certain the government of that society cannot remain.
Thus conquerors' swords often cut up governments by the roots and mangle societies to pieces, separating the subdued or scattered multitude from the protection
of, and dependence on, that society which ought to have preserved them from violence. The world is too well instructed in, and too forward to allow of, this way of
dissolving of governments to need any more to be said of it; and there wants not
much argument to prove, that where the society is dissolved, the government cannot remain—that being as impossible as for the frame of a house to subsist when
the materials of it are scattered and dissipated by a whirlwind, or jumbled into a
confused heap by an earthquake.

Besides this overturning from without, governments are dissolved from within.

First, when the legislative is altered. Civil society being a state of peace among
those who are of it, from whom the state of war is excluded by the umpirage
which they have provided in their legislative for the ending all differences that
may arise among any of them; it is in their legislative that the members of a commonwealth are united and combined together into one coherent living body. This
is the soul that gives form, life, and unity to the commonwealth; from hence the
several members have their mutual influence, sympathy, and connection; and,
therefore, when the legislative is broken or dissolved, dissolution and death follows; for the essence and union of the society consisting in having one will, the
legislative, when once established by the majority, has the declaring and, as it
were, keeping of that will. The constitution of the legislative is the first and fundamental act of society, whereby provision is made for the continuation of their

union under the direction of persons and bonds of laws made by persons authorized thereunto by the consent and appointment of the people, without which no
one man, or number of men, among them can have authority of making laws that
shall be binding to the rest. When any one, or more, shall take upon them to make
laws, whom the people have not appointed so to do, they make laws without
authority, which the people are not therefore bound to obey; by which means they
come again to be out of subjection and may constitute to themselves a new legislative as they think best, being in full liberty to resist the force of those who
without authority would impose anything upon them. Everyone is at the disposure
of his own will when those who had, by the delegation of the society, the declaring of the public will are excluded from it, and others usurp the place, who have
no such authority or delegation. . . .

There is therefore, secondly, another way whereby governments are dissolved,
and that is when the legislative or the prince, either of them, act contrary to their
trust.

First, the legislative acts against the trust reposed in them, when they endeavor
to invade the property of the subject, and to make themselves, or any part of the
community, masters or arbitrary disposers of the lives, liberties, or fortunes of the
people.

The reason why men enter into society is the preservation of their property; and
the end why they choose and authorize a legislative is that there may be laws
made, and rules set, as guards and fences to the properties of all the members of
the society, to limit the power, and moderate the dominion of every part and member of the society; for since it can never be supposed to be the will of the society
that the legislative should have a power to destroy that which everyone designs to
secure by entering into society, and for which the people submitted themselves to
legislators of their own making. Whenever the legislators endeavor to take away
and destroy the property of the people, or to reduce them to slavery under arbitrary
power, they put themselves into a state of war with the people, who are thereupon
absolved from any further obedience, and are left to the common refuge which
God has provided for all men against force and violence. Whensoever therefore
the legislative shall transgress this fundamental rule of society, and either by ambition, fear, folly, or corruption, endeavor to grasp themselves, or put into the hands
of any other, an absolute power over the lives, liberties, and estates of the people,
by this breach of trust they forfeit the power the people had put into their hands
for quite contrary ends, and it devolves to the people, who have a right to resume
their original liberty, and, by the establishment of a new legislative, such as they
shall think fit, provide for their own safety and security, which is the end for which
they are in society. What I have said here concerning the legislative in general
holds true also concerning the supreme executor, who having a double trust put in
him, both to have a part in the legislative and the supreme execution of the law,
acts against both when he goes about to set up his own arbitrary will as the law of
the society. He acts also contrary to his trust when he either employs the force,
treasure, and offices of the society to corrupt the representatives and gain them to
his purposes, or openly pre-engages the electors and prescribes to their choice

such whom he has by solicitations, threats, promises, or otherwise won to his designs, and employs them to bring in such who have promised beforehand what to vote and what to enact. Thus to regulate candidates and electors, and new-model the ways of election, what is it but to cut up the government by the roots, and poison the very fountain of public security? For the people having reserved to themselves the choice of their representatives, as the fence to their properties, could do it for no other end but that they might always be freely chosen, and, so chosen, freely act and advise as the necessity of the commonwealth and the public good should, upon examination and mature debate, be judged to require. This, those who give their votes before they hear the debate and have weighed the reasons on all sides are not capable of doing. To prepare such an assembly as this, and endeavor to set up the declared abettors of his own will for the true representatives of the people and the lawmakers of the society, is certainly as great a breach of trust and as perfect a declaration of a design to subvert the government as is possible to be met with. To which if one shall add rewards and punishments visibly employed to the same end, and all the arts of perverted law made use of to take off and destroy all that stand in the way of such a design, and will not comply and consent to betray the liberties of their country, it will be past doubt what is doing. What power they ought to have in the society, who thus employ it contrary to the trust that went along with it in its first institution, is easy to determine; and one cannot but see that he who has once attempted any such thing as this cannot any longer be trusted.

To this perhaps it will be said, that the people being ignorant, and always discontented, to lay the foundation of government in the unsteady opinion and uncertain humor of the people, is to expose it to certain ruin; and no government will be able long to subsist if the people may set up a new legislative, whenever they take offense at the old one. To this I answer: Quite the contrary. People are not so easily got out of their old forms as some are apt to suggest. They are hardly to be prevailed with to amend the acknowledged faults in the frame they have been accustomed to. And if there be any original defects, or adventitious ones introduced by time or corruption, it is not an easy thing to get them changed, even when all the world sees there is an opportunity for it. This slowness and aversion in the people to quit their old constitutions has, in the many revolutions which have been seen in this kingdom, in this and former ages, still kept us to, or after some interval of fruitless attempts still brought us back again to, our old legislative of king, lords, and commons; and whatever provocations have made the crown be taken from some of our princes' heads, they never carried the people so far as to place it in another line.

But it will be said this hypothesis lays a ferment for frequent rebellion. To which I answer.

First, no more than any other hypothesis; for when the people are made miserable, and find themselves exposed to the ill-usage of arbitrary power, cry up their governors as much as you will for sons of Jupiter, let them be sacred or divine, descended or authorized from heaven, give them out for whom or what you please, the same will happen. The people generally ill-treated, and contrary to right, will be ready upon any occasion to ease themselves of a burden that sits heavy upon them. They will wish and seek for the opportunity, which in the change, weakness, and accidents of human affairs seldom delays long to offer itself. He must have lived but a little while in the world who has not seen examples of this in his time, and he must have read very little who cannot produce examples of it in all sorts of governments in the world.

Secondly, I answer, such revolutions happen not upon every little mismanagement in public affairs. Great mistakes in the ruling part, many wrong and inconvenient laws, and all the slips of human frailty will be borne by the people without mutiny or murmur. But if a long train of abuses, prevarications, and artifices, all tending the same way, make the design visible to the people, and they cannot but feel what they lie under, and see whither they are going, it is not to be wondered that they should then rouse themselves and endeavor to put the rule into such hands which may secure to them the ends for which government was at first erected, and without which ancient names and specious forms are so far from being better that they are much worse than the state of nature or pure anarchy—the inconveniences being all as great and as near, but the remedy farther off and more difficult.

Thirdly, I answer that this doctrine of a power in the people of providing for their safety anew by a new legislative, when their legislators have acted contrary to their trust by invading their property, is the best fence against rebellion, and the probablest means to hinder it; for rebellion being an opposition, not to persons, but authority which is founded only in the constitutions and laws of the government, those, whoever they be, who by force break through, and by force justify their violation of them, are truly and properly rebels; for when men, by entering into society and civil government, have excluded force and introduced laws for the preservation of property, peace, and unity among themselves, those who set up force again in opposition to the laws do *rebellare,* that is, bring back again the state of war, and are properly rebels; which they who are in power (by the pretense they have to authority, the temptation of force they have in their hands, and the flattery of those about them), being likeliest to do, the properest way to prevent the evil is to show them the danger and injustice of it who are under the greatest temptation to run into it.

In both the forementioned cases, when either the legislative is changed, or the legislators act contrary to the end for which they were constituted, those who are guilty are guilty of rebellion; for if anyone by force takes away the established legislative of any society, and the laws of them made pursuant to their trust, he thereby takes away the umpirage which everyone had consented to for a peaceable decision of all their controversies, and a bar to the state of war among them. They who remove or change the legislative take away this decisive power which nobody can have but by the appointment and consent of the people, and so destroying the authority which the people did, and nobody else can, set up, and introducing a power which the people has not authorized, they actually introduce a state of war which is that of force without authority; and thus, by removing the legislative established by the society (in whose decisions the people acquiesced and united as to that of their own will), they untie the knot and expose the people anew to the state of war. And if those, who by force take away the legislative, are rebels, the legislators themselves, as has been shown, can be no less esteemed so, when they who were set up for the protection and preservation of the people, their liberties and properties, shall by force invade and endeavor to take them away; and so they putting themselves into a state of war with those who made them the protectors and guardians of their peace, are properly, and with the greatest aggravation, *rebellantes,* rebels.

But if they who say "it lays a foundation for rebellion" mean that it may occasion civil wars or intestine broils, to tell the people they are absolved from obedience when illegal attempts are made upon their liberties or properties, and may oppose the unlawful violence of those who were their magistrates when they invade their properties contrary to the trust put in them, and that therefore this doctrine is not to be allowed, being so destructive to the peace of the world; they may as well say, upon the same ground, that honest men may not oppose robbers or pirates because this may occasion disorder or bloodshed. If any mischief come in such cases, it is not to be charged upon him who defends his own right, but on him that invades his neighbor's. If the innocent honest man must quietly quit all he has, for peace's sake, to him who will lay violent hands upon it, I desire it may be considered, what a kind of peace there will be in the world, which consists only in violence and rapine, and which is to be maintained only for the benefit of robbers and oppressors. Who would not think it an admirable peace betwixt the mighty and the mean when the lamb without resistance yielded his throat to be torn by the imperious wolf? Polyphemus' den gives us a perfect pattern of such a peace and such a government, wherein Ulysses and his companions had nothing to do but quietly to suffer themselves to be devoured. And no doubt Ulysses, who was a prudent man, preached up passive obedience, and exhorted them to a quiet submission by representing to them of what concernment peace was to mankind, and by showing the inconveniences which might happen if they should offer to resist Polyphemus, who had now the power over them.

The end of government is the good of mankind. And which is best for mankind: that the people should be always exposed to the boundless will of tyranny, or that the rulers should be sometimes liable to be opposed when they grow exorbitant in the use of their power and employ it for the destruction and not the preservation of the properties of their people?

Nor let anyone say that mischief can arise from hence as often as it shall please a busy head, or turbulent spirit, to desire the alteration of the government. It is true such men may stir whenever they please, but it will be only to their own just ruin and perdition; for till the mischief be grown general, and the ill designs of the rulers become visible, or their attempts sensible to the greater part, the people, who are more disposed to suffer than right themselves by resistance, are not apt to stir. The examples of particular injustice or oppression of here and there an unfortunate man moves them not. But if they universally have a persuasion, grounded upon manifest evidence, that designs are carrying on against their liberties, and the general course and tendency of things cannot but give them strong suspicions of the evil intention of their governors, who is to be blamed for it? Who can help it if they who might avoid it bring themselves into this suspicion? Are the people to be blamed if they have the sense of rational creatures and can think of things no otherwise than as they find and feel them? And is it not rather their fault who put things into such a posture that they would not have them thought to be as they are? I grant that the pride, ambition, and turbulence of private men have sometimes caused great disorders in commonwealths, and factions have been fatal to states and kingdoms. But whether the mischief has oftener begun in the people's wantonness and a desire to cast off the lawful authority of their rulers, or in the rulers' insolence and endeavors to get and exercise an arbitrary power over their people— whether oppression or disobedience gave the first rise to the disorder, I leave it to impartial history to determine. This I am sure: whoever, either ruler or subject, by force goes about to invade the rights of either prince or people and lays the foundation for overturning the constitution and frame of any just government is highly guilty of the greatest crime I think a man is capable of—being to answer for all those mischiefs of blood, rapine, and desolation, which the breaking to pieces of governments bring on a country. And he who does it is justly to be esteemed the common enemy and pest of mankind, and is to be treated accordingly.

That subjects or foreigners, attempting by force on the properties of any people, may be resisted with force, is agreed on all hands. But that magistrates doing the same thing may be resisted, has of late been denied; as if those who had the greatest privileges and advantages by the law, had thereby a power to break those laws by which alone they were set in a better place than their brethren; whereas their offense is thereby the greater, both as being ungrateful for the greater share they have by the law, and breaking also that trust which is put into their hands by their brethren.

Whosoever uses force without right, as everyone does in society who does it without law, puts himself into a state of war with those against whom he so uses it; and in that state all former ties are canceled, all other rights cease, and everyone has a right to defend himself and to resist the aggressor. . . .

Here, it is like, the common question will be made: Who shall be judge whether the prince or legislative act contrary to their trust? This, perhaps, ill-affected and factious men may spread among the people, when the prince only makes use of his due prerogative. To this I reply: The people shall be judge; for who shall be judge whether his trustee or deputy acts well and according to the trust reposed in him, but he who deputes him, and must, by having deputed him, have still a power to discard him when he fails in his trust? If this be reasonable in particular cases of private men, why should it be otherwise in that of the greatest moment, where the welfare of millions is concerned, and also where the evil, if not prevented, is greater, and the redress very difficult, dear, and dangerous?

But further, this question, "Who shall be judge?" cannot mean that there is no judge at all; for where there is no judicature on earth, to decide controversies among men, God in heaven is Judge. He alone, it is true, is Judge of the right. But every man is judge for himself, as in all other cases, so in this, whether another has put himself into a state of war with him, and whether he should appeal to the Supreme Judge, as Jephthah did.

If a controversy arise betwixt a prince and some of the people in a matter where the law is silent or doubtful, and the thing be of great consequence, I should think the proper umpire, in such a case, should be the body of the people; for in cases where the prince has a trust reposed in him and is dispensed from the common ordinary rules of the law, there, if any men find themselves aggrieved, and think the prince acts contrary to or beyond that trust, who so proper to judge as the body of the people (who, at first, lodged that trust in him) how far they meant it should extend? But if the prince, or whoever they be in the administration, decline that way of determination, the appeal then lies nowhere but to Heaven; force between either persons who have no known superior on earth, or which permits no appeal to a judge on earth, being properly a state of war, wherein the appeal lies only to Heaven; and in that state the injured party must judge for himself, when he will think fit to make use of that appeal, and put himself upon it.

To conclude, the power that every individual gave the society when he entered into it can never revert to the individuals again as long as the society lasts, but will always remain in the community, because without this there can be no community, no commonwealth, which is contrary to the original agreement; so also when the society has placed the legislative in an assembly of men, to continue in them and their successors, with direction and authority for providing such successors, the legislative can never revert to the people while that government lasts; because having provided a legislative with power to continue forever, they have given up their political power to the legislative and cannot resume it. But if they have set limits to the duration of their legislative, and made this supreme power in any person or assembly, only temporary, or else, when by the miscarriages of those in authority it is forfeited, upon the forfeiture, or at the determination of the time set, it reverts to the society, and the people have a right to act as supreme and continue the legislative in themselves, or erect a new form, or under the old form place it in new hands, as they think good.

67
Jean Jacques Rousseau

Jean Jacques Rousseau (1712–1778) built his theory of government on the notion of a social contract also—but for him that contract was not so much an agreement on the legal model, between ruler and ruled, as it was a fundamental compact through which the original social unity is achieved, the instrument that forms the community in which government can arise. The larger body of humanity, whose well-being Rousseau thought paramount, always pursues the ideals of democracy, later inscribed on the banners of the great revolution in France: *liberty,* through the sovereignty of the people; *equality* of all citizens united by the original compact, and *fraternity* resulting from each giving himself to all. Rousseau is cryptic at times; adherents of conflicting political theories have claimed to find support in his work. But however he may be classified, the vision of a human family whose members are genuinely free and equal was fundamental for him, and for the democracies he inspired.

THE SOCIAL CONTRACT*

Man is born free, and everywhere he is in chains. Many a man believes himself to be the master of others who is, no less than they, a slave. How did this change take place? I do not know. What can make it legitimate? To this question I hope to be able to furnish an answer. . . . The social order is a sacred right which serves as a foundation for all other rights. This right, however, since it comes not by nature, must have been built upon conventions. To discover what these conventions are is the matter of our inquiry.

OF THE RIGHT OF THE STRONGEST

However strong a man, he is never strong enough to remain master always, unless he transform his Might into Right, and Obedience into Duty. Hence we have come to speak of the Right of the Strongest, a right which, seemingly assumed in irony, has, in fact, become established in principle. But the meaning of the phrase has never been adequately explained. Strength is a physical attribute, and I fail to see how any moral sanction can attach to its effects. To yield to the strong is an act of necessity, not of will. At most it is the result of a dictate of prudence. How, then, can it become a duty?

Let us assume for a moment that some such Right does really exist. The only deduction from this premise is inexplicable gibberish. For to admit that Might makes Right is to reverse the process of effect and cause. The mighty man who defeats his rival becomes heir to his Right. So soon as we can disobey with impunity, disobedience becomes legitimate. And, since the Mightiest is always right, it merely remains for us to become possessed of Might. But what validity can there be in a Right which ceases to exist when Might changes hands? If a man be constrained by Might to obey, what need has he to obey by Duty? And if he is not constrained to obey, there is no further obligation on him to do so. It follows, therefore, that the word Right adds nothing to the idea of Might. It becomes, in this connection, completely meaningless.

Obey the Powers that be. If that means Yield to Force, the precept is admirable but redundant. My reply to those who advance it is that no case will ever be found of its violation. All power comes from God. Certainly, but so do all ailments. Are we to conclude from such an argument that we are never to call in the doctor? If I am waylaid by a footpad at the corner of a wood, I am constrained by force to give him my purse. But if I manage to keep it from him, is it my duty to hand it over? His pistol is also a symbol of Power. It must, then, be admitted that Might does not create Right, and that no man is under an obligation to obey any but the legitimate powers of the State. And so I continually come back to the question I first asked.

---

*From *Social Contract: Essays by Locke, Hume, and Rousseau,* edited by Sir Ernest Barker. Oxford University Press. 1947. Reprinted by permission.

OF SLAVERY

Since no man has natural authority over his fellows, and since Might can produce no Right, the only foundation left for legitimate authority in human societies is Agreement.

If a private citizen, says Grotius, can alienate his liberty and make himself another man's slave, why should not a whole people do the same, and subject themselves to the will of a King? The argument contains a number of ambiguous words which stand in need of explanation. But let us confine our attention to one only—*alienate*. To alienate means to give or to sell. Now a man who becomes the slave of another does not give himself. He sells himself in return for bare subsistence, if for nothing more. But why should a whole people sell themselves? So far from furnishing subsistence to his subjects, a King draws his own from them, and from them alone. According to Rabelais, it takes a lot to keep a King. Do we, then, maintain that a subject surrenders his person on condition that his property be taken too? It is difficult to see what he will have left.

It will be said that the despot guarantees civil peace to his subjects. So be it. But how are they the gainers if the wars to which his ambition may expose them, his insatiable greed, and the vexatious demands of his Ministers cause them more loss than would any outbreak of internal dissension? How do they benefit if that very condition of civil peace be one of the causes of their wretchedness? One can live peacefully enough in a dungeon, but such peace will hardly, of itself, ensures one's happiness. The Greeks imprisoned in the cave of Cyclops lived peacefully while awaiting their turn to be devoured.

To say that a man gives himself for nothing is to commit oneself to an absurd and inconceivable statement. Such an act of surrender is illegitimate, null, and void by the mere fact that he who makes it is not in his right mind. To say the same thing of a whole People is tantamount to admitting that the People in question are a nation of imbeciles. Imbecility does not produce Right.

Even if a man can alienate himself, he cannot alienate his children. They are born free, their liberty belongs to them, and no one but themselves has a right to dispose of it. Before they have attained the age of reason their father may make, on their behalf, certain rules with a view to ensuring their preservation and well-being. But any such limitation of their freedom of choice must be regarded as neither irrevocable nor unconditional, for to alienate another's liberty is contrary to the natural order, and is an abuse of the father's rights. It follows that an arbitrary government can be legitimate only on condition that each successive generation of subjects is free either to accept or to reject it, and if this is so, then the government will no longer be arbitrary.

When a man renounces his liberty he renounces his essential manhood, his rights, and even his duty as a human being. There is no compensation possible for such complete renunciation. It is incompatible with man's nature, and to deprive him of his free will is to deprive his actions of all moral sanction. The convention, in short, which sets up on one side an absolute authority, and on the other an obligation to obey without question, is vain and meaningless. Is it not obvious that

where we can demand everything we owe nothing? Where there is no mutual obligation, no interchange of duties, it must, surely, be clear that the actions of the commanded cease to have any moral value? For how can it be maintained that my slave
has any "right" against me when everything that he has is my property? His right
being *my* right, it is absurd to speak of it as ever operating to my disadvantage. . . .

THAT WE MUST ALWAYS GO BACK TO AN ORIGINAL COMPACT

Even were I to grant all that I have so far refuted, the champions of despotism
would not be one whit the better off. There will always be a vast difference
between subduing a mob and governing a social group. No matter how many isolated individuals may submit to the enforced control of a single conqueror, the
resulting relationship will ever be that of Master and Slave, never of People and
Ruler. The body of men so controlled may be an agglomeration; it is not an association. It implies neither public welfare nor a body politic. An individual may
conquer half the world, but he is still only an individual. His interests, wholly different from those of his subjects, are private to himself. When he dies his empire
is left scattered and disintegrated. He is like an oak which crumbles and collapses
in ashes so soon as the fire consumes it.

"A People," says Grotius, "may give themselves to a king." His argument implies
that the said People were already a People before this act of surrender. The very act
of gift was that of a political group and presupposed public deliberation. Before,
therefore, we consider the act by which a People chooses their king, it were well if
we considered the act by which a People is constituted as such. For it necessarily
precedes the other, and is the true foundation on which all Societies rest.

Had there been no original compact, why, unless the choice were unanimous,
should the minority ever have agreed to accept the decision of the majority? What
right have the hundred who desire a master to vote for the ten who do not? The
institution of the franchise is, in itself, a form of compact, and assumes that, at
least once in its operation, complete unanimity existed.

OF THE SOCIAL PACT

I assume, for the sake of argument, that a point was reached in the history of
mankind when the obstacles to continuing in a state of Nature were stronger than
the forces which each individual could employ to the end of continuing in it. The
original state of Nature, therefore, could no longer endure, and the human race
would have perished had it not changed its manner of existence.

Now, since men can by no means engender new powers, but can only unite and
control those of which they are already possessed, there is no way in which they can
maintain themselves save by coming together and pooling their strength in a way
that will enable them to withstand any resistance exerted upon them from without.
They must develop some sort of central direction and learn to act in concert.

Such a concentration of powers can be brought about only as the consequence of an agreement reached between individuals. But the self-preservation of each single man derives primarily from his own strength and from his own freedom. How, then, can he limit these without, at the same time, doing himself an injury and neglecting that care which it is his duty to devote to his own concerns? This difficulty, in so far as it is relevant to my subject, can be expressed as follows:

"Some form of association must be found as a result of which the whole strength of the community will be enlisted for the protection of the person and property of each constituent member, in such a way that each, when united to his fellows, renders obedience to his own will, and remains as free as he was before." That is the basic problem of which the Social Contract provides the solution.

The clauses of this Contract are determined by the Act of Association in such a way that the least modification must render them null and void. Even though they may never have been formally enunciated, they must be everywhere the same, and everywhere tacitly admitted and recognized. So completely must this be the case that, should the social compact be violated, each associated individual would at once resume all the rights which once were his, and regain his natural liberty, by the mere fact of losing the agreed liberty for which he renounced it.

It must be clearly understood that the clauses in question can be reduced, in the last analysis, to one only, to wit, the complete alienation by each associate member to the community of *all his rights*. For, in the first place, since each has made surrender of himself without reservation, the resultant conditions are the same for all: and, because they are the same for all, it is in the interest of none to make them onerous to his fellows.

Furthermore, this alienation having been made unreservedly, the union of individuals is as perfect as it well can be, none of the associated members having any claim against the community. For should there be any rights left to individuals, and no common authority be empowered to pronounce as between them and the public, then each, being in some things his own judge, would soon claim to be so in all. Were that so, a state of Nature would still remain in being, the conditions of association becoming either despotic or ineffective.

In short, whose gives himself to all gives himself to none. And, since there is no member of the social group over whom we do not acquire precisely the same rights as those over ourselves which we have surrendered to him, it follows that we gain the exact equivalent of what we lose, as well as an added power to conserve what we already have.

If, then, we take from the social pact everything which is not essential to it, we shall find it to be reduced to the following terms: "each of us contributes to the group his person and the powers which he wields as a person, and we receive into the body politic each individual as forming an indivisible part of the whole."

As soon as the act of association becomes a reality, it substitutes for a person of each of the contracting parties a moral and collective body made up of as many members as the constituting assembly has votes, which body receives from this very act of constitution its unity, its dispersed *self,* and its will. The public person thus formed by the union of individuals was known in the old days as a *City,* but now as the *Republic* or *Body Politic.* . . .

OF THE CIVIL STATE

The passage from the state of nature to the civil state produces a truly remarkable change in the individual. It substitutes justice for instinct in his behavior, and gives to his actions a moral basis which formerly was lacking. Only when the voice of duty replaces physical impulse and the cravings of appetite does the man who, till then, was concerned solely with himself, realize that he is under compulsion to obey quite different principles, and that he must now consult his reason and not merely respond to the promptings of desire. Although he may find himself deprived of many advantages which were his in a state of nature, he will recognize that he has gained others which are of far greater value. By dint of being exercised, his faculties will develop, his ideas take on a wider scope, his sentiments become ennobled, and his whole soul be so elevated, that, but for the fact that misuse of the new conditions still, at times, degrades him to a point below that from which he has emerged, he would unceasingly bless the day which freed him for ever from his ancient state, and turned him from a limited and stupid animal into an intelligent being and a Man.

Let us reduce all this to terms which can be easily comprehended. What a man loses as a result of the Social Contract is his natural liberty and his unqualified right to lay hands on all that tempts him, provided only that he can compass its possession. What he gains is civil liberty and the ownership of what belongs to him. That we may labor under no illusion concerning these compensations, it is well that we distinguish between natural liberty which the individual enjoys so long as he is strong enough to maintain it, and civil liberty which is curtailed by the general will. Between possessions which derive from physical strength and the right of the first-comer, and ownership which can be based only on a positive title.

To the benefits conferred by the status of citizenship might be added that of Moral Freedom, which alone makes a man his own master. For to be subject to appetite is to be a slave, while to obey the laws laid down by society is to be free. . . .

OF THE LIMITS OF THE SOVEREIGN POWER

If the State or the City is nothing but a moral person the life of which consists in the union of its members, and if the most important of its concerns is the maintenance of its own being, then it follows that it must have at its disposition a power of compulsion covering the whole field of its operations in order that it may be in a position to shift and adjust each single part in a way that shall be most beneficial to the whole. As nature gives to each man complete power over his limbs, so, too, the social compact gives to the body politic complete power over its members: and it is this power, directed by the general will, which, as I have already pointed out, bears the name of sovereignty.

But we have to consider not only the State as a public person, but those individual persons, too, who compose it, and whose lives and liberties are, in nature, independent of it. It is important, therefore, that we carefully distinguish between the rights of the citizens and the rights of the sovereign, between the duties which the former owe as subjects, and the natural rights which, as men, they are entitled to enjoy.

It is agreed that what, as a result of the social compact, each man alienates of power, property, and liberty is only so much as concerns the well-being of the community. But, further, it must be admitted that the sovereign alone can determine how much, precisely, this is.

Such services as the citizen owes to the State must be rendered by him whenever the sovereign demands. But the sovereign cannot lay upon its subjects any burden not necessitated by the well-being of the community. It cannot even wish to do so, for in the realm of reason, as of nature, nothing is ever done without cause.

The undertakings which bind us to the Commonwealth are obligatory only because they are mutual: their nature being such that we cannot labor for others without, at the same time, laboring for ourselves. For how can the general will be always right, and how can all constantly will the happiness of each, if every single individual does not include himself in that word *each,* so that in voting for the general interest he may feel that he is voting for his own? Which goes to show that the equality of rights and the idea of justice which it produces derive from the preference which each man has for his own concerns—in other words, from human nature: that the general will, if it be deserving of its name, must be general, not in its origins only, but in its objects, applicable to all as well as operated *by* all, and that it loses its natural validity as soon as it is concerned to achieve a merely individual and limited end, since, in that case, we, pronouncing judgment on something outside ourselves, cease to be possessed of that true principle of equity which is our guide.

In fact, as soon as issue is joined on some *particular* point, on some *specific* right arising out of a situation which has not previously been regulated by some form of general agreement, we are in the realm of debate. The matter becomes a trial in which certain interested individuals are ranged against the public, but where there is no certainty about what law is applicable nor about who can rightly act as judge. It would be absurd in such a case to demand an *ad hoc* decision of the general will, since the general will would then be the decision of one of the parties only. To the other it would appear in the guise of a pronouncement made by some outside power, sectarian in its nature, tending to injustice in the particular instance, and subject to error. Thus, just as the will of the individual cannot represent the general will, so, too, the general will changes its nature when called upon to pronounce upon a particular object. In so far as it is general, it cannot judge of an individual person or an isolated fact. When, for instance, the people of Athens appointed or removed their leaders, according honors to one and penalties to another: when, in other words, using the machinery supplied by a multiplicity of specific decrees, they exercised, in a muddled sort of way, all the functions of government, they ceased, strictly speaking, to have any general will at all, and behaved not as sovereign so much as magistrate. This statement may seem to be at variance with generally accepted ideas. I ask only that I may be granted time in which to develop my own. What makes the will general is not the number of citizens concerned but the common interest by which they are united. For in the sort of community with which I am dealing, each citizen necessarily submits to the conditions which he imposes on his neighbors. When comes that admirable identity of interest and justice which gives to the common deliberations of the People a complexion of equity. When, however, discussion turns on specific issues, this complexion vanishes, because there is no longer any common interest uniting and identifying the pronouncement of the judge with that of the interested party.

No matter by what way we return to our general principle, the conclusion must always be the same, to wit, that the social compact establishes between all the citizens of a State a degree of equality such that all undertake to observe the same obligations and to claim the same rights. Consequently, by the very nature of the pact, every act of Sovereignty—that is to say, every authentic act of the general will—lays the same obligations and confers the same benefits on all. The sovereign knows only the nation as a whole and does not distinguish between the individuals who compose it.

What, then, is a true act of sovereignty? It is not a convention established between a superior and an inferior, but between the body politic and each of its members: a convention having the force of law because it is based upon the social contract: equitable, because it affects all alike: useful, because its sole object is the general good: firm, because it is backed by public force and the supreme power. So long as the subjects of a State observe only conventions of this kind, they are obeying not a single person, but the decision of their own wills. To ask what are the limits of the respective rights of sovereign and citizens is merely to ask to what extent the latter can enter into an undertaking with themselves, each in relation to all, and all in relation to each. . . .

68
Thomas Jefferson

Thomas Jefferson (1743–1826) was the most eloquent, and perhaps also the most politically effective advocate of natural rights democracy. The *Second Treatise of Government* was published by Locke in 1690 in part to justify the Glorious Revolution of 1688 in England, a revolution that had already taken place. Jefferson, a profound student of Locke and of Rousseau, applied Locke's principles to the circumstances of the British colonies in America a century later, in part to justify the revolution he himself had helped to inspire. The *Declaration of Independence of the United States of America* was the product of Jefferson's pen. In his many famous letters Jefferson exhibits not only his conviction that democracy is a moral consequence of the *rights* of citizens, but also his confidence in its workability, in the *capacity* of educated citizens to govern themselves wisely.

THE DECLARATION OF INDEPENDENCE

When in the Course of human events it becomes necessary for one people to dissolve the political bands which have connected them with another, and to assume among the powers of the earth, the separate and equal station to which the Laws of Nature and of Nature's God entitle them, a decent respect to the opinions of mankind requires that they should declare the causes which impel them to the separation.

We hold these truths to be self-evident, that all men are created equal, that they are endowed by their Creator with certain unalienable Rights, that among these are Life, Liberty and the pursuit of Happiness.—That to secure these rights, Governments are instituted among Men, deriving their just powers from the consent of the governed.—That whenever any Form of Government becomes destructive of these ends, it is the Right of the People to alter or to abolish it, and to institute new Government, laying its foundation on such principles, and organizing its powers in such form, as to them shall seem most likely to effect their Safety and Happiness. Prudence, indeed, will dictate that Governments long established should not be changed for light and transient causes; and accordingly all experience hath shewn, that mankind are more disposed to suffer, while evils are sufferable, than to right themselves by abolishing the forms to which they are accustomed. But when a long train of abuses and usurpations, pursuing invariably the same Object, evinces a design to reduce them under absolute Despotism, it is their right, it is their duty, to throw off such Government, and to provide new Guards for their future security.—Such has been the patient sufferance of these Colonies; and such is now the necessity which constrains them to alter their former Systems of Government. The history of the present King of Great Britain is a history of repeated injuries and usurpations, all having in direct object the establishment of an absolute Tyranny over these States. To prove this, let Facts be submitted to a candid world. . . .

In every stage of these Oppressions We have Petitioned for Redress in the most humble terms: Our repeated Petitions have been answered only by repeated injury. A Prince, whose character is thus marked by every act which may define a Tyrant, is unfit to be the ruler of a free people.

Nor have We been wanting in attentions to our British brethren. We have warned them from time to time of attempts by their legislature to extend an unwarrantable jurisdiction over us. We have reminded them of the circumstances of our emigration and settlement here. We have appealed to their native justice and magnanimity, and we have conjured them by the ties of our common kindred to disavow these usurpations, which would inevitably interrupt our connections and correspondence. They too have been deaf to the voice of justice and of consanguinity. We must, therefore, acquiesce in the necessity, which denounces our Separation, and hold them, as we hold the rest of mankind, Enemies in War, in Peace Friends.

We, therefore, the Representatives of the united States of America, in General Congress, Assembled, appealing to the Supreme Judge of the world for the rectitude of our intentions, do, in the Name, and by Authority of the good People of these Colonies solemnly publish and declare, That these United Colonies are, and of Right ought to be Free and Independent States; that they are Absolved from all

Allegiance to the British Crown, and that all political connection between them and the State of Great Britain, is and ought to be totally dissolved; and that as Free and Independent States, they have full Power to levy War, conclude Peace, contract Alliances, establish Commerce, and to do all other Acts and Things which Independent States may of right do.

And for the support of this Declaration, with a firm reliance on the protection of divine Providence, we mutually pledge to each other our Lives, our Fortunes and our sacred Honor.

[ON REBELLION]*

God forbid we should ever be twenty years without such a rebellion [Shays's Rebellion]. The people cannot be all, and always, well-informed. The part which is wrong will be discontented in proportion to the importance of the facts they misconceive. If they remain quiet under such misconceptions, it is a lethargy, the forerunner of death to the public liberty. We have had thirteen States independent for eleven years. There has been one rebellion. That comes to one rebellion in a century and a half for each State. What country before ever existed a century and a half without a rebellion? And what country can preserve its liberties if its rulers are not warned from time to time that this people preserve the spirit of resistance? Let them take arms. The remedy is to set them right as to facts, pardon and pacify them. What signify a few lives lost in a century or two? The tree of liberty must be refreshed from time to time with the blood of patriots and tyrants. It is its natural manure.

To William S. Smith, Paris, November 13, 1787.

[ON MONARCHY AND AMERICA]

I was much an enemy to monarchies before I came to Europe. I am ten thousand times more so since I have seen what they are. There is scarcely an evil known in these countries which may not be traced to their king as its source, nor a good which is not derived from the small fibers of republicanism existing among them. I can further say, with safety, there is not a crowned head in Europe whose talents or merits would entitle him to be elected a vestryman by the people of any parish in America.

To George Washington, Paris, May 2, 1788.

I am sensible that there are defects in our federal government, yet they are so much lighter than those of monarchies that I view them with much indulgence. I rely, too, on the good sense of the people for remedy, whereas the evils of monarchical government are beyond remedy. If any of our countrymen wish for a king, give them Aesop's fable of the frogs who asked for a king; if this does not cure them, send them to Europe. They will go back good republicans.

To David Ramsay, Paris, August 4, 1787.

*This and the following selections from the letters of Jefferson are from *The Political Writings of Thomas Jefferson,* edited by Edward Dumbauld, New York, 1955. Reprinted by permission of the publishers, The Liberal Arts Press, Inc.

I sincerely wish you may find it convenient to come here; the pleasure of the trip will be less than you expect, but the utility greater. It will make you adore your own country—its soil, its climate, its equality, liberty, laws, people, and manners. My God! how little do my countrymen know what precious blessings they are in possession of and which no other people on earth enjoy. I confess I had no idea of it myself. While we shall see multiplied instances of Europeans going to live in America, I will venture to say no man now living will ever see an instance of an American removing to settle in Europe and continuing there. Come, then, and see the proofs of this, and on your return add your testimony to that of every thinking American in order to satisfy our countrymen how much it is their interest to preserve, uninfected by contagion, those peculiarities in their government and manners to which they are indebted for those blessings.

To James Monroe, Paris, June 17, 1785.

[ON GOVERNMENT BY THE PEOPLE]

I have no fear but that the result of our experiment will be that men may be trusted to govern themselves without a master. Could the contrary of this be proved, I should conclude either that there is no God or that he is a malevolent being.

To David Hartley, Paris, July 2, 1787.

I consider the people who constitute a society or nation as the source of all authority in that nation; as free to transact their common concerns by any agents they think proper; to change these agents individually or the organization of them in form or function whenever they please; that all the acts done by these agents under the authority of the nation are the acts of the nation, are obligatory on them and enure to their use, and can in no wise be annulled or affected by any change in the form of the government, or of the persons administering it.

Cabinet Opinion, April 28, 1793.

In every country where man is free to think and to speak, differences of opinion will arise from difference of perception and the imperfection of reason; but these differences, when permitted, as in this happy country, to purify themselves by free discussion, are but as passing clouds overspreading our land transiently and leaving our horizon more bright and serene. That love of order and obedience to the laws, which so remarkably characterize the citizens of the United States, are sure pledges of internal tranquility; and the elective franchise, if guarded as the ark of our safety, will peaceably dissipate all combinations to subvert a Constitution dictated by the wisdom and resting on the will of the people. That will is the only legitimate foundation of any government, and to protect its free expression should be our first object.

To Benjamin Waring, Washington, March 23, 1801.

The first principle of republicanism is that the *lex majoris partis* is the fundamental law of every society of individuals of equal rights; to consider the will of the society enounced by the majority of a single vote as sacred as if unanimous is the first of all lessons in importance, yet the last which is thoroughly learnt. This law once disregarded, no other remains but that of force, which ends necessarily in military despotism.

To Alexander Humboldt, Monticello, June 13, 1817.

[ON EDUCATION]

And say, finally, whether peace is best preserved by giving energy to the government or information to the people. This last is the most certain and the most legitimate engine of government. Educate and inform the whole mass of the people. Enable them to see that it is their interest to preserve peace and order, and they will preserve them. And it requires no very high degree of education to convince them of this. They are the only sure reliance for the preservation of our liberty.

To James Madison, Paris, December 20, 1787.

I know of no safe depository of the ultimate powers of the society but the people themselves, and if we think them not enlightened enough to exercise their control with a wholesome discretion, the remedy is not to take it from them but to inform their discretion by education.

To William C. Jarvis, Monticello, September 28, 1820.

It is an axiom in my mind that our liberty can never be safe but in the hands of the people themselves, and that, too, of the people with a certain degree of instruction. This it is the business of the state to effect and on a general plan.

To George Washington, Paris, January 4, 1786.

If a nation expects to be ignorant and free in a state of civilization, it expects what never was and never will be. The functionaries of every government have propensities to command at will the liberty and property of their constituents. There is no safe deposit for these but with the people themselves, nor can they be safe with them without information. Where the press is free and every man able to read all is safe.

To Charles Yancey, Monticello, January 6, 1816.

69
Carl Cohen

The justification of democracy under natural law, its moral rightness, is rooted in
the principle of human equality. The argument in which that principle of equality
is applied, and its consequences defended, is carefully laid out in Carl Cohen's
Democracy. Principles implicit in classical defenses of democracy are here made
explicit. Equals must be treated equally. In any community of which the members
are genuinely equal, therefore, all are entitled equally to participate in their
common government. The state, or political community, is indeed a community
of persons intrinsically equal. Therefore, democracy is morally justified in it.

[THE ARGUMENT OUTLINED]*

By "democracy" I mean that form of community government in which the members of a community may participate equally in making directive decisions that
concern the community as a whole. Supposing general agreement on this—that
democratic government is government by the people, government of a community
by the body of its members—I now open the question: Why have it?

The defense of democracy that follows proceeds in two phases. In the first I
shall try to show what would be required to justify democratic government in *any*
given community context. This I call the justifiability of democracy in general. In
the second phase I shall try to show how democratic government can be justified
in the context of the *political* community. This I call the justification of democracy
in the body politic. The expression "the justification of political democracy," I
avoid because the phrase "political democracy" suggests, incorrectly, that there are
kinds of democracy of which the political is one. In fact there are different *spheres*
in which democracy may be operative, of which the political is one.

The justifiability of democracy in general rests essentially upon one moral principle likely to meet with universal acceptance: that equals should be treated
equally. This is a formal principle purely; it says nothing about who are or are not
equals. Therefore, any effort using this principle to justify democracy in a particular community or kind of community needs to be supplemented by argument
showing that the members of that community (or kind of community) are indeed
equal in the necessary relevant sense.

The justification of democracy in the body politic requires that this supplemen-
tary argument be provided specifically with reference to the political community.
To do this it will be necessary to maintain that there is one fundamental respect in
which all persons are equal—all persons because, in principle, any person may be
a member of the body politic. And it will be necessary to maintain further that that
respect in which all persons are equal is so related to the political community that
it serves to justify democracy in that community.

*From Carl Cohen, *Democracy,* (NY: The Free Press, 1972). Copyright C. Cohen.

Three key principles, then, will be discussed in the following two sections; each is crucial to justificatory arguments used in defense of democracy. They are:

1 That equals should be treated equally.
2 That all persons are equal in one fundamental respect.
3 That the respect in which all persons are equal is precisely that necessary to justify democracy in the body politic.

THE JUSTIFICATION OF DEMOCRACY IN GENERAL

That equals should be treated equally is a basic principle of distributive justice. So fundamental is this principle and so universally accepted that it is likely to be thought of as at least part of what is normally meant by justice, part of what is meant by "giving to every one his due." It is not my present purpose to defend this principle. Rather I aim to show that, supposing its truth, democracy is generally justifiable for those communities in which certain equalities are realized.

From the time of Aristotle, at least, there has been wide agreement that "persons who are equal should have assigned to them equal things." But a principle so general in formulation cannot be applied until supplemented by specific claims about actual equalities, and about what equalities are relevant in a particular context. No sooner do we assert the general principle than, as Aristotle continues, "there arises a question which must not be overlooked. Equals and unequals—yes; but equals and unequals *in what?*"

It is largely the result of fundamental disagreement on these questions—*who* are equal, and equal in *what*—that attitudes toward democracy and social policy in general have varied so over the ages. In the assignment of any given set of goods, tangible or intangible, justice requires that equals be assigned equal portions. But for the just assignment of a particular set of goods some equalities and inequalities will be important, and some will be irrelevant. Aristotle makes this point crisply:

> It is possible to argue that offices and honors ought to be distributed unequally [i.e., that superior amounts should be assigned to superior persons] on the basis of superiority *in any respect whatsoever*—even though there were similarity, and no shadow of any difference, in every other respect. . . . If this argument were accepted, the mere fact of a better complexion, or greater height, or any other such advantage, would establish a claim for a greater share of political rights to be given to its possessor. But is not the argument obviously wrong? To be clear that it is, we have only to study the other arts and sciences. If you were dealing with a number of flute-players who were equal in their art, you would not assign them flutes on the principle that the better born should have a greater amount. Nobody will play the better for being better born; . . . If our point is not yet plain, it can be made so if we push it still further. Let us suppose a man who is superior to others in flute-playing, but far inferior in birth and beauty. Birth and beauty may be greater goods than ability to play the flute, and those who possess them may, upon balance, surpass the flute-player more in these qualities than he surpasses them in his flute-playing; but the fact remains that *he* is the man who ought to get the better supply of flutes. (*Politics,* III, 12)

The point is that where an equality (or inequality) among persons is not properly relevant to the use of the goods to be distributed (as noble birth is irrelevant to flute-playing ability) that equality (or inequality) ought not affect the allocation.

Furthermore, Aristotle argues, it must be the case that some equalities (or inequalities) are relevant to a given allocation while others are not. For if we could not distinguish the relevant from the irrelevant we should have to weigh *all* equalities and inequalities in making the allocation. But to suppose that we can weigh them all is to suppose that every quality of a person is commensurable with every other—and that is plainly false. One man exceeds another in height but is exceeded by him in wealth. Now if it were possible to say in the particular case that A excels B in height to a greater degree than B excels A in wealth, we seem committed to the position that, in general, it is possible to measure the relative merits of height and wealth. But this is absurd. There is no degree of height equal or even properly comparable to a degree of wealth. So, depending on the goods to be assigned, it may be the one, or the other, or neither of these respects in which the equality or inequality of A and B is to be measured. (*Politics,* III, 12)

These arguments are compelling and their conclusions correct. To achieve a just distribution of a given set of goods in a given community, we must distinguish relevant from irrelevant equalities and inequalities, and weigh only the former in making the allocation.

Now, selecting the most just form of government for a given community may be viewed as a problem of distributive justice within that community. The task is one of deciding to whom, and in what degree, the right to participate in making decisions which affect the whole should be given. Alternative governmental forms may be conceived as alternative patterns of distribution of a special good—that good being the right to a voice in community decision-making.

A democratically governed community is one in which that right is distributed to all members equally. What would justify this pattern of distribution for any given community? Two claims would have to be made good: first, that equals should be treated equally; and second, that all members of that community are equal in the respect(s) properly relevant to the allocation of the right to participate in government.

To show that these are the claims the justification of democracy requires (and to make clearer what is involved in them) we may suppose a genuine community—Xcom—of which nothing is at first known save that it has a specified membership. If now we must choose a form of government for Xcom, nothing further being known about the members of Xcom, there is a strong presumption in favor of democracy. By hypothesis we have no information that could justify the unequal distribution of rights of participation. So far as we know, the members of Xcom are equals; at least they are equals in being members of Xcom. Regarding the right to a voice in the affairs of Xcom we have no rational way to justify any preference among them. The choice of any alternative to democracy entails that preference be given to some over others; upon one who would give such preference lies the obligation to justify such preference.

How might one seek to meet that obligation? Were one to deny that all the members of Xcom have an equal right to a voice in its affairs, he would be forced to claim either that the members of Xcom are unequal in some fundamental and relevant respect, or that, although equal, they should not be treated equally. The latter claim no one is likely to make or to accept. The denial that democracy in a given community is just will be defended by trying to show the important and relevant inequalities among its members. Where such claims of inequality cannot be made good we reject the denial, and view the preference of some to others as ungrounded and unjust. All of which is to say that we invariably do believe that equals ought to be treated equally. And we are likely to act on the presumption that where important and relevant inequalities cannot be shown, the members of a community are entitled to equal treatment with regard to the right to participate in common affairs.

There are two kinds of inequality which might be used to justify the denial of the equal right of members of a community to participate in their government. These are: inequalities of *concern,* and inequalities of *standing*. I discuss these in turn.

Inequalities of Concern   Every member of a community, by virtue of being a member of it, has a stake in the outcome of the decisions of that community. He is concerned in the result; if it affects the community it affects him as one of its constituents. But, of course, the outcome need not concern all members equally. Each member (inequalities of standing aside) is entitled to some voice in the outcome in which he has a *stake*; each would be entitled to an equal voice only if the stake of each were equal, or nearly so. Where it is clear that some members have a much larger stake in the outcome of the decision-making process than do others, we are faced with inequalities of concern. In such cases the basic principle, that equals should be treated equally, calls for a stronger voice to be given to those more greatly concerned in the result. The classic illustration is that of shareholders in a private corporation, to whom votes are assigned on the basis of the number of shares owned. If equals are to be treated equally, one's voice in the government of any community of which he is a member should be proportionate to his relative stake in the outcome of its decisions.

A vital qualification must accompany this conclusion, however. There are many cases in which inequalities of concern must, as a practical matter, be disregarded. Sometimes it may seem clear that some in the community have a greater interest (material or spiritual) in the outcome of certain decisions than do others. Yet it may be impossible or wholly infeasible to identify those having a greater interest, or to measure the differences of interest, and hence it may be impossible to assign differing rights of participation justly. The only practical course in dealing with such cases is to treat as a class the many decisions facing the community, then to attend to those equalities and inequalities that can be pretty clearly determined and which are relevant to that whole class of decisions. Therefore we normally and properly weigh such factors as registered membership in the community, or the number of shares owned, while ignoring equalities and inequalities we cannot reasonably decide upon.

Inequalities of Standing   The claim of a community member to an equal voice in the government of that community supposes not only that his concern in the results of its decisions is roughly equal to that of all other members, but supposes also that *the nature of his membership* in that community is fundamentally the same as that of every other membership. The large shareholder in a corporation may claim a voice proportionate to the number of his shares just when all shareholders are shareholders in precisely the same sense. If that is in doubt we must look to the nature of the claimant's shares, to their "class," and should they differ in kind from the rest his claim to a voice proportionate to the number of his shares may not prove valid. The claim to equal treatment supposes equality of kind as well as equality of interest. But many communities have members in different categories, memberships of different kinds. Where these different categories of membership can be specified, and the differences are relevant to the right to participate, the principle that equals should be treated equally will not serve to justify participation proportionate to interest only. In such communities, even supposing equality of concern, democracy may not be justifiable because of inequalities in standing.

Some illustrations from everyday experience will serve to confirm this analysis. There are communities in which we recognize an essential inequality with respect to the nature of the membership of their members; in these we are likely to think democracy inappropriate, or applicable only in limited degree or special cases. The family community is an excellent case in point. Minor children are likely to have a stake at least equal to that of the parent in the outcome of many decisions that the family must make. But while parent and child are both members of that community, their memberships are of different category, and it is rarely believed that important family decisions should be reached by majority vote. Where the obligations which arise out of such decisions fall chiefly on the parents, children may be listened to with respect, and may be properly overruled. On the other hand, there may be circumstances in which all the members of the family have not only an essentially equal stake, but have as well an essentially like membership with regard to the issue to be decided. What shall be the destination of a day's outing? What kind of dog shall the family acquire? On such questions we may deem it appropriate to count the vote of parent and child equally.

Classroom situations exhibit similar disparities of standing in a community. We do not normally permit full democracy in the classroom, even though the stake of the pupil in some of the decisions made may be as great or greater than that of the teacher. The clear inequality of status in that community justifies unequal voice in its government. Where this difference between instructor and student is enormous—as in primary school classes—we think democracy largely absurd as a way of making classroom decisions. Where the gap between instructor and student has greatly narrowed—as in a graduate seminar in philosophy—we are likely to think that a good measure of democracy can be justified.

Turning the matter about, whenever we begin with the assumption that a community, whatever its size or function, is essentially a community of equals, all having an essentially equal stake in its affairs, we are likely to insist upon an equal voice for each in the making of its directive decisions. The members of a chess club have, as members, precisely equal standing within that community and a concern roughly equal in its joint affairs; each may therefore claim, as a matter of justice, an equal voice in deciding whether the club shall hold a tournament or not. Fraternal orders tend to be highly democratic internally (however discriminatory they may be in choosing members) just because the significance of membership is confraternity—equal status in a social group. In any group so organized the equality enjoyed by members *as* members is a paramount feature of that community. This is often the reason membership in some "exclusive" club is prized; believing the members of that club superior to the mass, the member (or potential member) regards membership in it as a badge of equality with its other members. And in treating membership as a symbol of equality within that community he is correct. Therefore democracy is readily justified within fraternal communities, and is almost universally practiced—internally—by them.

To this point the argument has been concerned only with democracy in general—with what would have to be established regarding any community to justify democracy in it. In general we may conclude that:

First. In any community, if the members have an equal concern in the outcome of community decisions, and have an equal standing as community members, they are equal in the respects relevant to the assignment of the right to participate in the government of that community.

Second. If the principle be accepted, that equals should be treated equally, and the members of any community are equal in the respects relevant to the assignment of the right to participate in government, democracy in that community is justified.

The principles employed here are principles of justice. Their application to particular communities requires knowledge or beliefs about where the relevant equalities or inequalities lie. The argument so far has involved no claim (save for those implied in the illustrations given) about actual equalities or inequalities, and hence no claims about the justifiability of democracy in specific contexts. Of course, what constitutes equality of concern or equality of standing cannot be settled for all communities in the same way. Each community or kind of community must be examined separately. But with regard to any particular community, or kind of community, these principles indicate how we might justify, or show unjustifiable, democracy in it.

THE JUSTIFICATION OF DEMOCRACY IN THE BODY POLITIC

There is one kind of community in which the rightness or wrongness of democracy is of special interest and importance, and that is the political community. So closely do we associate democracy with the body politic that, for many, democracy means only a form of government in that body. This is an unreasonably narrow conception of democracy, but the concern for democracy in this sphere is understandable enough; and in just this sphere the most fundamental disputes concerning its justifiability arise.

The justificatory defense of democracy now enters its second phase. In the preceding section I indicated what kinds of claims regarding equality would have to be defended to justify democracy in any given community; here I shall argue that claims of just these kinds can be defended with respect to the political community, and that therefore democracy can be justified in it.

The political community encompasses all persons (or virtually all) who reside in a given geographical area. This does not define such communities but does indicate their essentially universal scope. With certain possible but minor exceptions, every sort of person could be a citizen of a given body politic. Therefore, to justify democracy in this body one must be prepared to maintain: (a) that all persons are equal in some fundamental respect; and (b) that the respect in which all persons are equal does justify the equal assignment of the right to participate in the government of the polity. That the claim should be made for "all persons" may appear unnecessarily strong, since *all* persons would be citizens only of a world-state; but if, in principle, *any* person could be a member of a democratic state, it is the equality of all that the democrat is obliged to maintain.

A *That all persons are equal.* I disclaim at the outset any effort to prove that all persons are equal; it is unlikely that it can be proved. I begin here with the assumption that is in some important sense true. My aim is chiefly to explicate the sense in which this claim is commonly believed true, and to show that its truth is, if not certain, at least plausible.

I begin with two denials, both important. First, it is commonly and correctly pointed out that one may believe all persons are fundamentally equal and consistently deny that they are equal in every or even in many respects. The principle of human equality is not concerned with the empirically determinable characteristics of humans—their size or strength or color or intelligence or temperament, or with any other of those innumerable features which the most ordinary experience tells us vary so greatly from person to person. If such equality were being claimed for all persons the principle would be patently false, and of no use whatever in justifying democracy. In many important respects persons are obviously not equal, nor would one wish them to be, nor does any sensible person claim them to be. Democracy in the body politic does not suppose persons to be equal in empirical respects; it is entirely consistent with the facts of human variety and uniqueness.

Second, it is not necessary, for the defense of democracy, to provide some more ultimate ground upon which human equality must be founded. The attempt to do so is likely to lead to an infinite regress in the quest for ultimacy. But even those proposals which claim to avoid this regress by specifying some absolutely ultimate foundations are not likely to enhance the justification of democracy. For such solutions inevitably take the form of some theological or metaphysical claims about the nature of the world (and/or God) which are sure to meet with less universal acceptance than the principle of human equality itself. For example, this principle has often been defended as a logical consequence of the common fatherhood of a divine being. But that this filial relationship does certify human equality appears very doubtful when we recall that, historically, the same belief in divine fatherhood has most frequently been used (and often is still) to justify sharply stratified social systems and to defend the fundamental *in*equality of persons, classes, castes, and races. Quite apart from the difficulty of establishing the truth of religious doctrines, the resort to them adds nothing to the argument for equality. Nothing I shall say, however, is logically inconsistent with the possible further claim that human equality somehow stems from the fatherhood of God. Similarly, one may resort to some set of metaphysical principles of a nontheological character to provide an ultimate foundation for human equality. But any such set is at least as disputable as the principle of human equality itself. In the present context, therefore, nothing is to be gained by such a metaphysical quest. It will not enhance the defense of democracy, and is likely to detract from it in suggesting that this defense presupposes the adoption of some single metaphysical viewpoint. Still, there is nothing in this argument for democracy that is logically inconsistent with the claim that the principle of human equality it employs has some more ultimate metaphysical ground.

I turn now to the core of the matter. What is the sense of the principle of human equality upon which the justification of democracy in the body politic depends? It is, simply, that beneath all the undeniable differences among persons there is in every human being an element, or aspect, or essential quality which justifies our treating him as the equal of every other in the largest sphere of human life.

In the *Fundamental Principles of the Metaphysics of Morals* Immanuel Kant distinguishes the possession of *value* from the possession of *dignity*. "Whatever has a value can be replaced by something else which is *equivalent* in value; whatever, on the other hand, is above all value, and therefore admits of no equivalent, has a dignity." So commodities which satisfy human wants and needs have a market value; what appeals to human tastes (even in the absence of need) may be said to have emotional or imaginative value. But some things in the world cannot be measured on any scale of values; they are invaluable, priceless. That is the case with every human being. One person may be a better cook than another, or a better student or legislator, and in restricted spheres of conduct we may and often must appraise their relative merit. But *as persons* they do not have relative merit; for what has relative merit may, insofar as it has that merit, be replaced by another like entity with equal or greater merit. A good cook may be replaced by a better cook; a good legislator by one at least his equal in legislation. But *as a person* no human being can possibly be replaced by another. What entitles him to a place in this sphere is simply his having human dignity; it is a quality intrinsic to his being. Just this thought is expressed in the now commonplace remark that the dignity of every human being must be respected. Dignity here connotes not pride or manner, but the intrinsic worthiness of every human being, without regard to his intelligence, skills, talents, rank, property, or beliefs. Who affirms the principle of human equality normally asserts the universal possession of dignity in this sense.

A paradox arises here. It seems to be a feature of things equal to one another that they are mutually substitutable, interchangeable. But if all persons are equal in possessing dignity just that interchangeability is being denied with respect to them. The paradox is resolved simply by distinguishing the sense of equality here employed from the sense in which equal things are verified as equal by measurement. In this latter sense replaceable elements in a machine or system are equal to their replacements. And if human equality were of a kind to be so verifiable we should be rightly astounded if some, at least, did not measure out different from others. But it is an irrelevant objection to the principle of human equality that there is no empirical respect in which all persons measure out the same. If true it would only show that this equality must lie beyond or beneath any qualities empirically measurable. If all persons are equal they are so in possessing an intrinsic dignity which does not admit of any relative evaluation.

John Dewey wrote:

> In social and moral matters, equality does not mean mathematical equivalence. It means rather the inapplicability of considerations of greater and less, superior and inferior. It means that no matter how great the quantitative differences of ability, strength, position, wealth, such differences are negligible in comparison with something else—the fact of individuality, the manifestation of something irreplaceable. It means, in short, a world in which an existence must be reckoned with on its own account, not as something capable of equation with and transformation into something else. It implies, so to speak, a metaphysical mathematics of the incommensurable in which each speaks for itself and demands consideration on its own behalf. (*Characters and Events,* 1929, Vol. II, p. 854)

And Walter Lippmann has put the matter more colloquially:

> There is no worldly sense in this feeling [of ultimate equality and fellowship with all others], for it is reasoned from the heart: 'there you are, sir, and there is your neighbor. You are better born than he, you are richer, you are stronger, you are handsomer, nay, you are better, wiser, kinder, and more likeable; you have given more to your fellow men and taken less than he. By any and every test of intelligence, of virtue, of usefulness, you are demonstrably a better man than he, and yet—absurd as it sounds—these differences do not matter, for the last part of him is untouchable and incomparable, and unique and universal.' Either you feel this or you do not; when you do not feel it, the superiorities that the world acknowledges seem like mountainous waves at sea; when you do feel it they are slight and impermanent ripples upon a vast ocean. Men were possessed by this feeling long before they had imagined the possibility of democratic government. They spoke of it in many ways, but the essential quality of feeling is the same from Buddha to St. Francis to Whitman. . . .
>
> There is felt to be a spiritual reality behind and independent of the visible character and behavior of a man. We have no scientific evidence that this reality exists, and in the nature of things we can have none. But we know, each of us, in a way too certain for doubting, that, after all the weighing and comparing and judging of us is done, there is something left over which is the heart of the matter. (*Men of Destiny,* 1927, pp. 49–50)

. . .

B *That the equality all men enjoy justifies their equal possession of the right to participate in their own government.*

We come now to the second hurdle in justifying democracy for the body politic. Supposing that the possession of dignity is the fundamental respect in which all persons are equal, does equality in that respect justify the equal right of persons to participate in their government? Allowing that equals should be treated equally, does *this* kind of equality justify *that* kind of equal treatment? Showing that it does requires again two stages. First, I shall argue that human equality as described above gives to every person an equal *concern* in the political community. Second, I shall argue that human equality as described above gives to every person an equal *standing* in the political community.

Stage One   Every community has some reason for being. The common pursuit of some objectives held in common is the unifying principle of every community, and hence of every political community. But the political community is importantly different from all other communities in being, within its domain, universally inclusive. Within it all other communities of interest are organized and all other human ends are pursued. Because of this inclusive nature, the objectives every political community can be said to have are of the most general sort. It aims to achieve what is in the interest of all its members; particular ends arise only out of this general service function. When, therefore, it appears necessary to formulate the purposes of the body politic, the most general concepts are employed—the public interest, the common weal, the general good. So the *Constitution of the United States* was ordained to ". . . establish Justice, insure domestic Tranquility, provide for the common defense, promote the general Welfare, and secure the Blessings of Liberty. . . ." In short, the purpose of the political community is to help meet the universal needs of human beings living together.

Precisely because these needs are universal every person has an equal concern in the effort to meet them. Every person has an equal concern in the establishment of justice, the protection of liberty, and the promotion of general welfare, because these goals are crucial to the pursuit of all his other ends, and hence crucial to the conduct of his own life. Every human being has a life to lead; it is a life unique, irreplaceable, having dignity but no price. In living such a life all persons are equal, and that is why they have, every single one, an equal stake in the decisions of the community whose general purpose is the protection and improvement of the lives of its members. In summary: the special and inclusive nature of the political community gives to every person an equal concern in the outcome of its decisions.

On precisely this ground we deny (in a democracy) that some have a right to a stronger voice in government than others. We may admit that in some respects the interests of one segment of the community may be more seriously affected than those of other segments by certain decisions. So it was long believed, even in countries now professing democracy, that the right to participate should be the prerogative only of those with property, or other significant economic stake in the community. Similarly, a university education was long believed to entitle one to a louder voice in government than those not so educated. But now it is generally agreed that differences in economic interests and education do not justify such discrimination. However great these differences may be they are relatively unimportant when compared with the interests shared equally by all. Whatever his rank or wealth, every human being has not only a stake in the political community, but equally with all others the highest stake; for it is his life which is under that government, and that is a matter which concerns no citizen less than any other. Insofar as his having a stake entitles him to a voice in the outcome, his having an equal stake entitles him to an equal voice.

· · ·

Stage Two   Not only an equal *stake*, but as well an equal *standing* in the political community must be shown if democracy is to be justified within it. It is precisely upon this issue that much of the traditional debate over the rightness of democracy has centered.

As the most inclusive of organized human communities, the political must comprise all, or virtually all, of the human inhabitants of a given geographical area; occasional exceptions to this (the cases of aliens, minors, convicts, etc.) will be given special justification. Within its physical domain the political community is essentially universal. Every person, by virtue of being a person, is entitled to membership in some polity; the man without a country is a puzzling anomaly. Furthermore, one's membership in his polity has no ground other than that he is a human being. The origin and foundation of his membership is—equally with all others—the simple fact that he was born or lives there, just as the others do. Our common practice is silent testimony to this principle of universal membership. Barring deliberate changes, we say everyone is a citizen of a state who is born on its territory, or (where patrimony takes precedence over domicile) we may say that he is a citizen who is born the son of a citizen. We do not require that he be born rich, or healthy, or clever, but only that he be born there or in that family, and that when he comes to maturity he be not lacking in essential human characteristics. These established, his citizenship, his equal membership in the political community, is unquestioned.

This is why the respect in which all persons are equal does justify their equal standing in the political community. That standing is their standing as members, and as a member of the polity each person is exactly the equal of the rest. The dignity and irreplaceability of his human life entitles him to a membership in the body politic essentially no different from the membership enjoyed by any other citizen.

Earlier illustrations may be recalled to advantage. Communities in which membership arises from different sources—the family consisting of parents and children, or the classroom in which sit students and teacher—exhibit a fundamental dissimilarity in the nature of membership enjoyed by their members. Student and teacher are both members of the classroom community, but they are not members on the same ground; they acquire their membership in very different ways requiring very different qualifications; even the authority which certifies their membership is likely to be different. Members of chess clubs or fraternal orders, on the other hand, however different in some respects, are exactly equal with respect to the nature of their membership in that club or society. Whatever their playing skill or social graces, they are, as members of these communities, of equal standing. The political community—although of incomparably greater importance—is essentially of the latter sort. It is essentially one whose members are members equally, and whose membership rests upon a common foundation. In the case of the political community the chief element of that foundation is their common humanity.

OBJECTIONS AND REPLIES

Two objections to the foregoing justification of democracy in the body politic must now be discussed.

The First Objection   That humans are not all equal in the sense described, but are in fact fundamentally unequal. This position, if substantiated, cuts the ground from under every justificatory argument for democracy. If the essence of some persons is gold, and that of others iron, then equality of standing in the polity cannot be defended and membership in it must be of fundamentally different kinds. The principle that equals should be treated equally cannot then justify universally equal rights of participation. If, as Aristotle claims, "It is clear that, just as some men are by nature free, so others are by nature slaves, and for these latter the condition of slavery is both beneficial and just," (*Politics,* I, 5) then the relation of the slave to the political community must be essentially different from that of the free man to the same community. To treat them as equals if basically they are not equals is clearly not justifiable. On this view, therefore, democracy might prove a reasonably satisfactory expedient in some circumstances, but it cannot be defended as a just ideal.

This objection is not likely to be persuasive in these times, but I do not know how it can be refuted absolutely. I think that human beings are equal in the fundamental sense described above, and I certainly believe that all ought to be treated as though they are; but I do not know how to demonstrate that equality, nor do I think it can be demonstrated to the satisfaction of one who begins with a hierarchical view of the world and a metaphysical commitment to basic inequality among persons. I do not see how those who assert and those why deny the fundamental equality of humans can (while such disagreement prevails) reach any accord regarding the justifiability of democracy. They start from opposed foundations. As Plato remarks of another fundamental conflict, "those who are agreed and those who are not agreed upon this point have no common ground, and can only despise one another when they see how widely they differ." (*Crito,* 49.) He who denies this ultimate equality may yet be persuaded to accept democracy on pragmatic grounds, but for him no argument for democracy that is justificatory in the strong sense can succeed.

This is understandable. Traditionally the differences between democrats and antidemocrats have been traceable to differences of view regarding the nature and capacities of persons. Insofar as a commitment to the fundamental equality of humans is now more widespread than ever before, and more than ever an inspiration for social reform, we may expect that the foregoing justification of democracy, and democracy itself, will be now more widely and more intelligently defended.

The Second Objection   That although humans may be equal in some fundamental sense, they are nevertheless unequal in respects crucial to their right to participate in government. This objection is more serious than the first because more moderate and more plausible. In one form or another it is presented by almost every defender of government by an elite. The classic statement, again, is to be found in Aristotle.

> Claims to political rights must be based on the ground of contribution to the elements which constitute the being of the state. There is thus good ground for the claims to honor and office which are made by persons of good descent, free birth, or wealth. (*Politics,* III, 12.)

This objection need not rely upon the claim that some persons are, *by nature,* better than others. Aristotle and many others have believed that. But differences of wealth and intelligence, whether natural or not, are certainly real. The question raised here is whether such real differences can justify preference in the government of the political community. Are the rich, the wellborn, and/or the intelligent, entitled to a stronger voice in the community? Note that the preference here at issue is not merely preference arising out of public esteem or community choice, but preference by right.

Aristotle and his followers could argue straightforwardly that inequalities of birth, wealth, or intellectual capacity do justify political preference by right. For them the being of a state and its goodness are constituted by such elements as culture, economic power, and nobility. Hence those who excel in the possession of these can contribute most to the well-being of the state, and are therefore by right entitled to a stronger claim on the honors and offices which make that contribution possible.

The mistake in this view is fundamental and, unfortunately, pervasive. It is the underlying premise (explicit in Aristotle) that what is chiefly to be considered in assigning political rights is the individual's *capacity to contribute to the welfare of the community*. This premise is essential to most elitist argument—Aristotelian or modern—because if it were not true there would be no rational ground for choosing the chosen few.

The adoption of this premise has two serious consequences. First, viewing political rights as ultimately justified by contribution to the state seems to suppose the prior and independent existence of the state to whose welfare contribution may be made. The logical priority of the community to the individual may be implicit, or again as in Aristotle explicit, but it appears in any case to underlie this not uncommon approach to political right. But the notion that the state has an independent welfare, a reality and purpose separable from the reality and purposes of its human citizens, can be dangerous. While there are important insights provided by this organic view of the political community, it tends to suggest that the state is somehow "out there," a body of higher order than its citizens and one whom they must serve. As a practical matter this belief can lead, where democracy is practiced, to much groundless fear of community action. Where democracy is not practiced, the conception of the state as a higher body, assigning political rights on the basis of contribution to its welfare, has often led to outrageous oppression and abuse.

The second consequence of the view that contribution to the state's welfare should be the ground of political rights is that some persons, at least, must be supposed to know what the state's welfare is, to know what the state is for and what is good for it. The premise supposes, that is, knowledge of what the state ought to be and how it can become so—*antecedent to the operation of political processes*. Supposing all that, it might indeed be reasonable to give much stronger voice to those in the community who have this knowledge and can thereby best further the state's objectives.

I submit, however, that the knowledge thus supposed is impossible to obtain. For in order to know which members of the community have the greatest capacities to contribute to the common good we must know with some concreteness the forms that the common good will take. But what those forms will be cannot be known prior to the expression of the interests, needs, and desires of the members generally, and therefore knowledge of the common good cannot be used in *allocating* the right to express those interests, needs, and desires, and have them fairly weighed. It is only after the general exercise of these rights of participation that knowledge of the community's particular aims can be acquired. Before their exercise we may, perhaps, formulate the purposes of the political community in very vague and general terms; but so unspecific must these notions be that they can give no ground for discrimination among its members. Prior to the participation of the membership, therefore, it cannot be adequately known what the ends are to which contribution may prove valuable. The selection and re-formation of particular community objectives is the outcome of the political process, not its ground. In sum, the well-being of a body politic cannot be ascertained in advance of the directive decisions made by its members, and therefore contributions to such well-being, or the capacity so to contribute, cannot be used to determine who shall have a right to participate in those fundamental decisions.

After the specific objectives of a political community have been selected, its members may indeed choose to give office and honor to those believed best able to forward those objectives. Perhaps the wealthy or the intelligent will be elected to serve as legislators or administrators, as in a democracy they often are. That election itself is the chief means available to the community membership to express its directive choices. But the very general and inclusive nature of the political community requires that these choices be made by the membership of the community at large. These choices inevitably result in preference to some over others, *but no preference can rightly be given to any elite in the process of making the choices themselves.* In that fundamental process the standing of every constituent is equal to that of every other.

The critic whose objection to the defense of democracy rests upon the conviction that the greater capacity of some to contribute to the good of the state entitles them to antecedent political preference may hold that conviction without realizing that a judgment concerning what the state's good is has been presupposed. He may, on the other hand, acknowledge that presupposition explicitly and claim direct and certain knowledge of where the good of the community lies and who the best contributors to it will be. In the latter case, again, antidemocrat and democrat reach a fundamental parting of ways, the one claiming knowledge and knowledge channels that the other does not recognize or accept. I do not see how it could be proved beyond doubt that such antecedent knowledge is impossible. But beside the argument registered above, there are two considerations which weigh heavily in favor of the democrat on this issue. The first is that where the antidemocrat claims (or presupposes) such knowledge, the burden of establishing the validity of this knowledge claim rests upon him. If he fails to sustain this burden, the objection to democracy which presupposes the possession of such knowledge must be discounted. The second consideration centers about a misconception. The claim that the greater knowledge or intelligence of some entitles them to a stronger voice in the direction of the community seems to suppose that the real interests of a community's members are subject to discovery in just the way any set of public facts is discovered. Hence the more intelligent or more well educated are thought likely to choose community objectives more wisely. But this misapprehends how community interests take shape. In some degree they may be simply knowable. But in large measure the interests of the members congeal and become known, even by the members themselves, only in the very process of their choosing. Many community interests, therefore, are impossible to know prior to such choosing. To this degree antecedent knowledge of the community's good would have to be supernatural, or is impossible.

Objections of this second sort generally aim to show that real inequalities among men justify unequal allocation of rights in the political process. They do not succeed in showing that. What they do show in fact every democrat may readily allow—that there are human inequalities which may properly be considered when, as participants, we make political decisions. But what may reasonably affect our judgments as participants need have no bearing whatever on our equal right to participate. Differences among persons are indeed relevant to political judgments, but cannot be shown relevant in determining who shall have the primary right to engage in the process of community direction. Such a right is enjoyed by every citizen by virtue of his being a member of the polity, having a life to lead within that community. And in living such lives all citizens—without regard to attainments or intellect—are fundamentally equal.

EQUALITY AS AN HYPOTHESIS

A The Intermediate View of Justification   The argument justifying democracy in the body politic depends upon universal human equality of a fundamental kind. I have specifically disclaimed the attempt to prove this equality; even if real it is probably not confirmable by empirical evidence. Therefore one who doubts the ultimate equality of human beings, and will act on it only if empirically established, is likely to find this (and every) effort to justify democracy incomplete and ineffective in achieving its stated aim. But it does not follow, even for the doubter, that the argument accomplishes nothing. For if valid it shows that democracy in the political sphere is justified *if* human equality be granted.

Then we may employ the justificatory argument hypothetically. Are all human beings *known* to be equal in embodying a priceless dignity? Perhaps not. We may be receptive to empirical support for ultimate human equality while remaining, in the absence of such support, genuinely in doubt. Nevertheless we may treat universal human equality as an hypothesis. *If* this hypothesis is acted upon, *then* we will be inclined to defend democracy in political communities. This surely might be a reasonable procedure. Not knowing that human beings are ultimately equal, or that they are not so equal, I may decide to proceed by treating them as equals for the purposes of dealing with pressing problems in some sphere, while recognizing that I am acting on that assumption.

B The Burden of Proof Regarding Equality   Is there an obligation to assume the equality of persons in the absence of knowledge to the contrary? This is a difficult question; essentially it asks where the burden of proof on this matter should lie. Must the equalitarian first refute the claims for inequality among persons, and then provide additional positive evidence for their equality? Or does the burden lie chiefly upon the inequalitarian to support his case, failing which equality is reasonably assumed? Traditional defenses of the equality of persons have generally supposed the latter approach correct, although the frequent adoption of a "natural rights" terminology has given the appearance that some were willing to accept a heavier burden. Their normal procedure—Rousseau and Locke are good examples—was reasonable enough. They argued, in effect, that if the reasons usually given to legitimize moral and political inequality can be discredited, equality is properly supposed.

Whatever Rousseau and Locke might have said or believed concerning this burden of proof, it does appear that there are but two alternative procedures in this area, and that there are good reasons for choosing a specific member of the pair. When we face the question of who shall have (and have to what degree) the right to participate in the political process, we cannot suspend judgment on the question of equality. Either we will treat all members of the polity as equal or we will not. Concerning the burden of proof, then, we must proceed using one of two principles:

1 In the absence of good grounds for discriminating among persons it is reasonable to treat them as equal.

2 In the absence of good grounds for treating persons as equal, it is reasonable to treat them as unequal.

While it is doubtful that the burden of proof can be conclusively shown to lie on one side or the other, I suggest that the former of these operating principles is the more plausible and the more natural, for two reasons.

First. In any real political community political rights have got to be allocated in some fashion. Inevitably this allocation will take place in the light of such knowledge and beliefs as are common or in authority at the time the basic decisions are made. Now if, to the best knowledge and belief of those who must act on this matter, there is no good ground for discriminating among persons in a given context, those persons are *in that context of action and belief,* equal to one another. This is not equality positively shown, but it is a real equality from the point of view of those who must decide either to discriminate or not to discriminate.

Second. With no good grounds to discriminate among persons, it is simpler to assume their equality than their inequality. For the assumption of equality provides some usable guides in deciding subsequently how persons shall be treated. To assume inequality, on the other hand, leaves one in a very awkward position; it is an embarrassingly incomplete assumption in a way the assumption of equality is not. The former principle directs that the humans concerned are not to be treated as equals, but gives no clues about how to make the discriminations it implies must be made. Perhaps this is one reason human equality has often been viewed as "natural," inequality as unnatural.

C Human Equality as a Regulative Principle If these considerations do not suffice to justify the placement of the burden of proof on the inequalitarian, we may at least conclude that there is no good reason to place it upon the equalitarian. In the absence of good reasons to discriminate, it is at least as reasonable to proceed on the assumption of human equality as any other, and the selection of one among equally reasonable alternatives in this sphere becomes a matter of choice. What will govern such a choice may depend upon the temperament and philosophical inclinations of the chooser. If one chooses to proceed upon the assumption of human equality he may accept the justificatory argument presented above, realizing that it is based not upon a certain truth but upon his resolve under the circumstances to treat human beings in that way until there is good reason to do otherwise. When the argument rests upon such conscious resolution it becomes explicitly hypothetical—the supposition of human equality is its *hypo*-thesis, its underlying proposition. So construed the force of the foregoing argument for democracy in the body politic is reduced; how much reduced it will be depends upon the strength given to the equalitarian resolution to which it is anchored.

Now one may insist that the force of the argument is reduced very little (if at all) so long as the resolution to treat persons as equals (in the sense described earlier) is maintained universally. On this view the principle of human equality will be a rule governing all interpersonal conduct, but which provides no information regarding the actual conditions or relations of human beings. In Immanuel Kant's discussion of the transcendental ideas—the ideas of self, world, and of God—he repeatedly insists upon a fundamental distinction of this kind, a distinction between their *regulative* and *constitutive* use. Construed constitutively, as though supplying actual concepts of certain objects, these ideas (he argues) are pseudorational and lead to intellectual disaster. Employed as regulators of reason the transcendental ideas have an excellent and valuable function; self, world, and God are ideas which focus the efforts of reason, leading thereby to the systematic unity of empirical knowledge in general. Properly employed these ideas regulate the operations of reason, he argues, but cannot supply the intellect with objective knowledge. Kant speaks similarly of that rational principle which bids us to treat every phenomenon in space and time as conditioned by some other, and forbids us to treat any such object as absolutely unconditioned. This principle, also, is regulative but not constitutive. It cannot tell us what is or is not conditioned; it serves only as a rule, "postulating what we ought to do" but never saying what is the case beyond or behind experience.

So, analogically, the idea of human equality may be viewed as having, if not constitutive, then regulative employment. The principle that, having no good grounds to discriminate one should treat all men as equals, may be construed as a regulative principle in the moral and political sphere. If one cannot honestly assert that he knows men to be equal, he may still insist that their being treated as equals (there being no good grounds to do otherwise) be a general rule of political conduct.

What would justify the adoption of such a rule? When Kant faced the need to justify the regulative employment of the transcendental ideas he could point only to the effects of the adoption of these regulators upon the growth of the knowledge thus regulated. When these ideas are so employed, heuristically, he said, ". . . empirical knowledge is more adequately secured within its own limits and more effectively improved than would be possible in the absence of such ideas." ("Appendix, Transcendental Dialectic," *Critique of Pure Reason.*) So, likewise, the regulative use of the principle of human equality can only be justified by the effects of this use upon the people and societies among whom it is in force. Evaluating these effects obliges one to look, again prospectively, at the consequences of the democracy to which the assumption of equalitarianism leads. With this we are thrown back into the frame of vindicatory arguments in defense of democracy. This outcome should prove no surprise; it is the inescapable consequence of treating the base of the argument as hypothesis. For any defense of democracy to be wholly free of the need to evaluate its consequences, that defense must rest upon principles quite beyond doubt. In the case of the present justification of democracy such principles would be those asserting the equality of human beings and their consequent possession of equal rights in the polity. The complete success of this justificatory argument supposes not only the adoption of these principles as regulative, but the knowledge of their truth as constitutive. Whether they be true in that full sense is a question whose definitive answer appears forever elusive.

JUSTIFICATION
OF DEMOCRACY
BY ITS CONSEQUENCES

Many modern defenders of democracy rest their case not upon antecedent principles (whose truth they may think forever in doubt) but upon the *consequences* of democracy, results that are evident to all, empirically verifiable. The underlying spirit of these defenses is utilitarian, pragmatic in the best sense of that term. Certainty is not claimed; perfection is not thought attainable. The claims of these advocates are more modest. Democracy, they say, is the best of the alternatives open to us; in practice it is the best of all forms of government if the measure of goodness is the achievement of the objectives of citizens.

Those objectives are various, of course. Just laws, a wise administration of foreign policy, the protection of minorities, reliable respect for the civil liberties of citizens, the development of a tolerant spirit and the disposition to compromise, the encouragement of loyalty and good order, the reasonably harmonious resolution of disputes—all these and more are consequences that have been claimed for democratic government. Occasional serious failures will be admitted. Yet no other form of government is as *likely* to achieve these goals, or to achieve them as often and as dependably, as is a government in which the people rule themselves. This is true, say these advocates, because government in which the members participate is naturally *self-correcting*. No form of government is likely to eliminate every injustice, but for that very reason a good government must provide reliable channels through which remedies for abuse can be pursued. Democracy does that as no other form of government can.

Moreover, democracy encourages (these arguments contend) the very qualities and attitudes its practice requires: flexibility, fallibilism, an optimism tempered by the recognition of great and continuing differences among the factions of the community. Bitter disagreements can be at least mitigated by compromise—and that, in any event, is the best we can hope for. Democracy rarely functions smoothly; inefficiencies are common, dissatisfactions linger. But in judging democratic government we must be careful always to compare the realities of its practice with the realities (and not the ideals) of the practice of its alternatives.

70
John Stuart Mill

John Stuart Mill (1806–1873) was one of the great philosophers in the utilitarian tradition. His arguments for parliamentary reform in England, and in defense of intellectual freedom, and in defense of representative self-government, were eloquent and compelling. The best arguments, he believed, are those showing the good consequences of the position defended. "I forgo any advantage," he wrote in *On Liberty,* "which could be derived to my argument from the idea of abstract right as a thing independent of utility. I regard utility as the ultimate appeal on all ethical questions; but it must be utility in the largest sense, grounded on the permanent interests of man as a progressive being." In that spirit Mill labored for a fairer system of representation, for broadened suffrage, for equal rights for women—and for every reform that would result in more effective control over the government by the citizenry. In *Considerations on Representative Government,* Mill argues that the business of the public is conducted best when citizens participate vigorously, and furthermore that such participation improves the character and abilities of the citizens themselves. Representative democracy, *because of its results,* is "the ideally best polity."

THE IDEALLY BEST POLITY*

There is no difficulty in showing that the ideally best form of government is that in which the sovereignty, or supreme controlling power in the last resort, is vested in the entire aggregate of the community, every citizen not only having a voice in the exercise of the ultimate sovereignty, but being, at least occasionally, called on to take an actual part in the government by the personal discharge of some public function, local or general.

To test this proposition, it has to be examined in reference to the two branches into which, as pointed out in the last chapter, the inquiry into the goodness of a government conveniently divides itself, namely, how far it promotes the good management of the affairs of society by means of the existing faculties, moral, intellectual, and active, of its various members, and what is its effect in improving or deteriorating those faculties.

The ideally best form of government, it is scarcely necessary to say, does not mean one which is practicable or eligible in all states of civilization, but the one which, in the circumstances in which it is practicable and eligible, is attended with the greatest amount of beneficial consequences, immediate and prospective. A completely popular government is the only polity which can make out any claim to this character. It is pre-eminent in both the departments between which the excellence of a political Constitution is divided. It is both more favorable to pre-

---

*From J. S. Mill, *Considerations on Representative Government,* 1861. These passages are reprinted from an edition published by Harper and Brothers, New York, 1862.

sent good government, and promotes a better and higher form of national character than any other polity whatsoever.

Its superiority in reference to present well-being rests upon two principles, of as universal truth and applicability as any general propositions which can be laid down respecting human affairs. The first is that the rights and interests of every or any person are only secure from being disregarded when the person interested is himself able, and habitually disposed, to stand up for them. The second is, that the general prosperity attains a greater height, and is more widely diffused, in proportion to the amount and variety of the personal energies enlisted in promoting it.

Putting these two propositions into a shape more special to their present application—human beings are only secure from evil at the hands of others in proportion as they have the power of being, and are, self-*protecting;* and they only achieve a high degree of success in their struggle with Nature in proportion as they are self-*dependent,* relying on what they themselves can do, either separately or in concert, rather than on what others do for them.

. . .

It is an inherent condition of human affairs that no intention, however sincere, of protecting the interests of others can make it safe or salutary to tie up their own hands. Still more obviously true is it that by their own hands only can any positive and durable improvement of their circumstances in life be worked out. Through the joint influence of these two principles, all free communities have both been more exempt from social injustice and crime, and have attained more brilliant prosperity than any others, or than they themselves after they lost their freedom. Contrast the free states of the world, while their freedom lasted, with the contemporary subjects of monarchical or oligarchical despotism: the Greek cities with the Persian satrapies, the Italian republics, and the free towns of Flanders and Germany, with the feudal monarchies of Europe; Switzerland, Holland, and England with Austria or ante-revolutionary France. Their superior prosperity was too obvious ever to have been gainsaid; while their superiority in good government and social relations is proved by the prosperity, and is manifest besides in every page of history. If we compare, not one age with another, but the different governments which coexisted in the same age, no amount of disorder which exaggeration itself can pretend to have existed amidst the publicity of the free states can be compared for a moment with the contemptuous trampling upon the mass of the people which pervaded the whole life of the monarchical countries, or the disgusting individual tyranny which was of more than daily occurrence under the systems of plunder which they called fiscal arrangements, and in the secrecy of their frightful courts of justice.

It must be acknowledged that the benefits of freedom, so far as they have hitherto been enjoyed, were obtained by the extension of its privileges to a part only of the community, and that a government in which they are extended impartially to all is a desideratum still unrealized. But, though every approach to this has an independent value, and in many cases more than an approach could not, in the existing state of general improvement, be made, the participation of all in these benefits is the ideally perfect conception of free government. In proportion as any, no matter who, are excluded from it, the interests of the excluded are left without the guaranty accorded to the rest, and they themselves have less scope and encouragement than they might otherwise have to that exertion of their energies for the good of themselves and of the community, to which the general prosperity is always proportioned.

Thus stands the case as regards present well-being—the good management of the affairs of the existing generation. If we now pass to the influence of the form of government upon character, we shall find the superiority of popular government over every other to be, if possible, still more decided and indisputable.

This question really depends upon a still more fundamental one, viz., which of two common types of character, for the general good of humanity, it is most desirable should predominate—the active or the passive type; that which struggles against evils or that which endures them; that which bends to circumstances, or that which endeavors to make circumstances bend to itself.

The commonplaces of moralists and the general sympathies of mankind, are in favor of the passive type. Energetic characters may be admired, but the acquiescent and submissive are those which most men personally prefer. The passiveness of our neighbors increases our own sense of security, and plays into the hands of our willfulness. Passive characters, if we do not happen to need their activity, seem an obstruction the less in our own path. A contented character is not a dangerous rival. Yet nothing is more certain than that improvement in human affairs is wholly the work of the uncontented characters; and, moreover, that it is much easier for an active mind to acquire the virtues of patience, than for a passive one to assume those of energy. . . .

The people who think it a shame when anything goes wrong—who rush to the conclusion that the evil could and ought to have been prevented, are those who, in the long run, do most to make the world better. If the desires are low placed, if they extend to little beyond physical comfort, and the show of riches, the immediate results of the energy will not be much more than the continual extension of man's power over material objects; but even this makes room, and prepares the mechanical appliances for the greatest intellectual and social achievements; and while the energy is there, some persons will apply it, and it will be applied more and more, to the perfecting not of outward circumstances alone, but of man's inward nature. Inactivity, unaspiringness, absence of desire, is a more fatal hindrance to improvement than any misdirection of energy, and is that through which alone, when existing in the mass, any very formidable misdirection by an energetic few becomes possible. It is this, mainly, which retains in a savage or semi-savage state the great majority of the human race.

Now there can be no kind of doubt that the passive type of character is favored by the government of one or a few, and the active self-helping type by that of the many. Irresponsible rulers need the quiescence of the ruled more than they need any activity but that which they can compel. Submissiveness to the prescriptions of men as necessities of nature is the lesson inculcated by all governments upon those who are wholly without participation in them. The will of superiors, and the law as the will of superiors, must be passively yielded to. But no men are mere instruments or materials in the hands of their rulers who have will, or spirit, or a spring of internal activity in the rest of their proceedings, and any manifestation of these qualities, instead of receiving encouragement from despots, has to get itself forgiven by them. Even when irresponsible rulers are not sufficiently conscious of danger from the mental activity of their subjects to be desirous of repressing it, the position itself is a repression. Endeavor is even more effectually restrained by the certainty of its impotence than by any positive discouragement. Between subjection to the will of others and the virtues of self-help and self-government, there is a natural incompatibility. This is more or less complete, according as the bondage is strained or relaxed. Rulers differ very much in the length to which they carry the control of the free agency of their subjects, or the suppression of it by managing their business for them. But the difference is in degree, not in principle; and the best despots often go the greatest lengths in chaining up the free agency of their subjects. A bad despot, when his own personal indulgences have been provided for, may sometimes be willing to let the people alone; but a good despot insists on doing them good by making them do their own business in a better way than they themselves know of. . . .

Very different is the state of the human faculties where a human being feels himself under no other external restraint than the necessities of nature, or mandates of society which he has his share in imposing, and which it is open to him, if he thinks them wrong, publicly to dissent from, and exert himself actively to get altered. No doubt, under a government partially popular, this freedom may be exercised even by those who are not partakers in the full privileges of citizenship; but it is a great additional stimulus to anyone's self-help and self-reliance when he starts from even ground, and has not to feel that his success depends on the impression he can make upon the sentiments and dispositions of a body of whom he is not one. It is a great discouragement to an individual, and a still greater one to a class, to be left out of the constitution; to be reduced to plead from outside the door to the arbiters of their destiny, not taken into consultation within. The maximum of the invigorating effect of freedom upon the character is only obtained when the person acted on either is, or is looking forward to become a citizen as fully privileged as any other. What is still more important than even this matter of feeling is the practical discipline which the character obtains from the occasional demand made upon the citizens to exercise, for a time and in their turn, some social function. It is not sufficiently considered how little there is in most men's ordinary life to give any largeness either to their conceptions or to their sentiments. Their work is a routine; not a labor of love, but of self-interest in the most elementary form, the satisfaction of daily wants; neither the thing done, nor the process of doing it, introduces the mind to thoughts or feelings extending beyond individuals; if instructive books are within their reach, there is no stimulus to read them; and, in most cases, the individual has no access to any person of cultivation much superior to his own. Giving him something to do for the public supplies, in a measure, all these deficiencies. If circumstances allow the amount of public duty assigned him to be considerable, it makes him an educated man.

Notwithstanding the defects of the social system and moral ideas of antiquity, the practice of the dicastery and the ecclesia raised the intellectual standard of an average Athenian citizen far beyond anything of which there is yet an example in any other mass of men, ancient or modern. The proofs of this are apparent in every page of our great historian of Greece; but we need scarcely look further than to the high quality of the addresses which their great orators deemed best calculated to act with effect on their understanding and will. A benefit of the same kind, though far less in degree, is produced on Englishmen of the lower middle class by their liability to be placed on juries and to serve parish offices, which, though it does not occur to so many, nor is so continuous, nor introduces them to so great a variety of elevated considerations as to admit of comparison with the public education which every citizen of Athens obtained from her democratic institutions, makes them nevertheless very different beings, in range of ideas and development of faculties, from those who have done nothing in their lives but drive a quill, or sell goods over a counter.

Still more salutary is the moral part of the instruction afforded by the participation of the private citizen, if even rarely, in public functions. He is called upon, while so engaged, to weigh interests not his own; to be guided, in case of conflicting claims, by another rule than his private partialities; to apply, at every turn, principles and maxims which have for their reason of existence the general good; and he usually finds associated with him in the same work minds more familiarized than his own with these ideas and operations, whose study it will be to supply reason to his understanding, and stimulation to his feeling for the general good. He is made to feel himself one of the public, and whatever is their interest to be his interest. Where this school of public spirit does not exist, scarcely any sense is entertained that private persons, in no eminent social situation, owe any duties to society except to obey the laws and submit to the government. There is no unselfish sentiment of identification with the public. Every thought or feeling, either of interest or of duty, is absorbed in the individual and in the family. The man never thinks of any collective interest, of any objects to be pursued jointly with others, but only in competition with them, and in some measure at their expense. A neighbor, not being an ally or an associate, since he is never engaged in any common undertaking for joint benefit, is therefore only a rival. Thus even private morality suffers, while public is actually extinct. Were this the universal and only possible state of things, the utmost aspirations of the lawgiver or the moralist could only stretch to make the bulk of the community a flock of sheep innocently nibbling the grass side by side.

From these accumulated considerations, it is evident that the only government which can fully satisfy all the exigencies of the social state is one in which the whole people participate; that any participation, even in the smallest public function, is useful; that the participation should everywhere be as great as the general degree of improvement of the community will allow; and that nothing less can be ultimately desirable than the admission of all to a share in the sovereign power of the state. But since all cannot, in a community exceeding a single small town, participate personally in any but some very minor portions of the public business, it follows that the ideal type of a perfect government must be representative.

71
Alexis de Tocqueville

Alexis de Tocqueville (1805–1859) was a French statesman who wrote *Democracy in America* after traveling widely in this country in 1831/32. His candid and penetrating account of American democracy retains freshness and relevance to this day. Aristocratic by temperament and training, troubled by widespread mediocrity, de Tocqueville was sharply critical of much that he saw in America. But he was also very favorably impressed by the vigor of American public life, and by the great good sense exhibited by popularly elected legislatures. The involvement of people in their common government, he observed, promotes their deeper public spirit, and leads to greater respect by the people for laws of their own making. Most fundamentally, he concluded, the purposes of a democracy, however clumsily pursued, are inevitably "more useful to humanity" than those of an aristocracy, however wise. The point is that the "majority of the citizens, who are subject to error . . . cannot have an interest opposed to their own advantage." When democracies blunder, they do so in the right direction; that is the deep merit of government by the people.

THE REAL ADVANTAGES OF A DEMOCRACY*

Before entering upon the present chapter, I must remind the reader of what I have more than once observed in this book. The political Constitution of the United States appears to me to be one of the forms of government that a democracy may adopt; but I do not regard the American Constitution as the best, or as the only one, that a democratic people may establish. In showing the advantages which the Americans derive from the government of democracy, I am therefore very far from affirming, or believing, that similar advantages can be obtained only from the same laws.

1 General Tendency of the Laws

The defects and weaknesses of a democratic government may readily be discovered; they can be proved by obvious facts, whereas their healthy influence becomes evident in ways which are not obvious and are, so to speak, hidden. A glance suffices to detect its faults, but its good qualities can be discerned only by long observation. The laws of the American democracy are frequently defective or incomplete; they sometimes attack vested rights, or sanction others which are dangerous to the community; and even if they were good, their frequency would still be a great evil. How comes it, then, that the American republics prosper and continue?

---

*From A. de Tocqueville, *Democracy in America,* 1835. These passages are reprinted from a translation by Henry Reeve, revised by Francis Bowen, and further corrected and edited by Phillips Bradley, by permission of the publisher, Alfred A. Knopf, Inc., New York, and Vintage Books, Inc. Copyright 1945 by Alfred A. Knopf, Inc.

In the consideration of laws, a distinction must be carefully observed between the end at which they aim, and the means by which they pursue that end; between their absolute and their relative excellence. If it be the intention of the legislator to favor the interests of the minority at the expense of the majority, and if the measures he takes are so combined as to accomplish the object he has in view with the least possible expense of time and exertion, the law may be well drawn up, although its purpose is bad; and the more efficacious it is, the more dangerous it will be.

Democratic laws generally tend to promote the welfare of the greatest possible number; for they emanate from the majority of the citizens, who are subject to error, but who cannot have an interest opposed to their own advantage. The laws of an aristocracy tend, on the contrary, to concentrate wealth and power in the hands of the minority; because an aristocracy, by its very nature, constitutes a minority. It may therefore be asserted, as a general proposition, that the purpose of a democracy in its legislation is more useful to humanity than that of an aristocracy. This, however, is the sum total of its advantages.

Aristocracies are infinitely more expert in the science of legislation than democracies ever can be. They are possessed of a self-control that protects them from the errors of temporary excitement; and they form far-reaching designs, which they know how to mature till a favorable opportunity arrives. Aristocratic government proceeds with the dexterity of art; it understands how to make the collective force of all its laws converge at the same time to a given point. Such is not the case with democracies, whose laws are almost always ineffective or inopportune. The means of democracy are therefore more imperfect than those of aristocracy, and the measures that it unwittingly adopts are frequently opposed to its own cause; but the object it has in view is more useful.

Let us now imagine a community so organized by nature or by its constitution that it can support the transitory action of bad laws, and that it can await, without destruction, the general tendency of its legislation: we shall then conceive how a democratic government, notwithstanding its faults, may be best fitted to produce the prosperity of this community. This is precisely what has occurred in the United States; and I repeat what I have before remarked, that the great advantage of the Americans consists in their being able to commit faults which they may afterwards repair.

An analogous observation may be made respecting public officers. It is easy to perceive that American democracy frequently errs in the choice of the individuals to whom it entrusts the power of the administration; but it is more difficult to say why the state prospers under their rule. In the first place, it is to be remarked that if, in a democratic state, the governors have less honesty and less capacity than elsewhere, the governed are more enlightened and more attentive to their interests. As the people in democracies are more constantly vigilant in their affairs and more jealous of their rights, they prevent their representatives from abandoning that general line of conduct which their own interest prescribes. In the second place, it must be remembered that if the democratic magistrate is more apt to misuse his power, he possesses it for a shorter time. But there is yet another reason which is still more general and conclusive. It is no doubt of importance to the welfare of nations that they should be governed by men of talents and virtue; but it is perhaps still more important for them that the interests of those men should not differ from the interests of the community at large; for if such were the case, their virtues might become almost useless and their talents might be turned to a bad account. I have said that it is important that the interests of the persons in authority should not differ from or oppose the interests of the community at large; but I do not insist upon their having the same interests as the *whole* population, because I am not aware that such a state of things ever existed in any country.

No political form has hitherto been discovered that is equally favorable to the prosperity and the development of all the classes into which society is divided. These classes continue to form, as it were, so many distinct communities in the same nation; and experience has shown that it is no less dangerous to place the fate of these classes exclusively in the hands of any one of them than it is to make one people the arbiter of the destiny of another. When the rich alone govern, the interest of the poor is always endangered; and when the poor make the laws, that of the rich incurs very serious risks. The advantage of democracy does not consist, therefore, as has sometimes been asserted, in favoring the prosperity of all, but simply in contributing to the well-being of the greatest number.

The men who are entrusted with the direction of public affairs in the United States are frequently inferior, in both capacity and morality, to those whom an aristocracy would raise to power. But their interest is identified and mingled with that of the majority of their fellow citizens. They may frequently be faithless and frequently mistaken but they will never systematically adopt a line of conduct hostile to the majority; and they cannot give a dangerous or exclusive tendency to the government.

The maladministration of a democratic magistrate, moreover, is an isolated fact, which has influence only during the short period for which he is elected. Corruption and incapacity do not act as common interests which may connect men permanently with one another. A corrupt or incapable magistrate will not combine his measures with another magistrate simply because the latter is as corrupt and incapable as himself; and these two men will never unite their endeavors to promote the corruption and inaptitude of their remote posterity. The ambition and the maneuvers of the one will serve, on the contrary, to unmask the other. The vices of a magistrate in democratic states are usually wholly personal.

. . .

In the United States, where public officers have no class interests to promote, the general and constant influence of the government is beneficial, although the individuals who conduct it are frequently unskillful and sometimes contemptible. There is, indeed, a secret tendency in democratic institutions that makes the exertions of the citizens subservient to the prosperity of the community in spite of their vices and mistakes; while in aristocratic institutions there is a secret bias which, notwithstanding the talents and virtues of those who conduct the government, leads them to contribute to the evils that oppress their fellow creatures. In aristocratic governments public men may frequently do harm without intending it; and in democratic states they bring about good results of which they have never thought.

2 Public Spirit

There is one sort of patriotic attachment which principally arises from that instinctive, disinterested, and undefinable feeling which connects the affections of man with his birthplace. This natural fondness is united with a taste for ancient customs and a reverence for traditions of the past; those who cherish it love their country as they love the mansion of their fathers. They love the tranquility that it affords them; they cling to the peaceful habits that they have contracted within its bosom; they are attached to the reminiscences that it awakens; and they are even pleased by living there in a state of obedience. This patriotism is sometimes stimulated by religious enthusiasm, and then it is capable of making prodigious efforts. It is in itself a kind of religion: it does not reason, but it acts from the impulse of faith and sentiment. In some nations the monarch is regarded as a personification of the country; and, the fervor of patriotism being converted into the fervor of loyalty, they take a sympathetic pride in his conquests, and glory in his power. There was a time under the ancient monarchy when the French felt a sort of satisfaction in the sense of their dependence upon the arbitrary will of their king; and they were wont to say with pride: "We live under the most powerful king in the world."

But, like all instinctive passions, this kind of patriotism incites great transient exertions, but no continuity of effort. It may save the state in critical circumstances, but often allows it to decline in times of peace. While the manners of a people are simple and its faith unshaken, while society is steadily based upon traditional institutions whose legitimacy has never been contested, this instinctive patriotism is wont to endure.

But there is another species of attachment to country which is more rational than the one I have been describing. It is perhaps less generous and less ardent, but it is more fruitful and more lasting: it springs from knowledge; it is nurtured by the laws; it grows by the exercise of civil rights; and, in the end, it is confounded with the personal interests of the citizen. A man comprehends the influence which the well-being of his country has upon his own; he is aware that the laws permit him to contribute to that prosperity, and he labors to promote it, first because it benefits him, and secondly because it is in part his own work.

. . . I maintain that the most powerful and perhaps the only means that we still possess of interesting men in the welfare of their country is to make them partakers in the government. At the present time civic zeal seems to me to be inseparable from the exercise of political rights; and I think that the number of citizens will be found to augment or decrease in Europe in proportion as those rights are extended.

How does it happen that in the United States, where the inhabitants have only recently immigrated to the land which they now occupy, and brought neither customs nor traditions with them there; where they met one another for the first time with no previous acquaintance; where, in short, the instinctive love of country can scarcely exist; how does it happen that everyone takes as zealous an interest in the affairs of his township, his county, and the whole state as if they were his own? It is because everyone, in his sphere, takes an active part in the government of society.

The lower orders in the United States understand the influence exercised by the general prosperity upon their own welfare; simple as this observation is, it is too rarely made by the people. Besides, they are accustomed to regard this prosperity as the fruit of their own exertions. The citizen looks upon the fortune of the public as his own, and he labors for the good of the state, not merely from a sense of pride or duty, but from what I venture to term cupidity.

It is unnecessary to study the institutions and the history of the Americans in order to know the truth of this remark, for their manners render it sufficiently evident. As the American participates in all that is done in his country, he thinks himself obliged to defend whatever may be censured in it; for it is not only his country that is then attacked, it is himself. The consequence is that his national pride resorts to a thousand artifices and descends to all the petty tricks of personal vanity.

Nothing is more embarrassing in the ordinary intercourse of life than this irritable patriotism of the Americans. A stranger may be well inclined to praise many of the institutions of their country, but he begs permission to blame some things in it, a permission that is inexorably refused. America is therefore a free country in which, lest anybody should be hurt by your remarks, you are not allowed to speak freely of private individuals or of the state, of the citizens or of the authorities, of public or of private undertakings, or, in short, of anything at all except, perhaps, the climate and the soil; and even then Americans will be found ready to defend both as if they had co-operated in producing them.

In our times we must choose between the patriotism of all and the government of a few; for the social force and activity which the first confers are irreconcilable with the pledges of tranquillity which are given by the second.

3 Respect for Right

I am persuaded that the only means which we possess, at the present time of inculcating the idea of right and of rendering it, as it were, palpable to the senses is to endow all with the peaceful exercise of certain rights; this is very clearly seen in children, who are men without the strength and the experience of manhood. When a child begins to move in the midst of the objects that surround him, he is instinctively led to appropriate to himself everything that he can lay his hands upon; he has no notion of the property of others; but as he gradually learns the value of things, and begins to perceive that he may in his turn be despoiled, he becomes more circumspect, and he ends by respecting those rights in others which he wishes to have respected in himself. The principle which the child derives from the possession of his toys is taught to the man by the objects which he may call his own. . . .

The same thing occurs in the political world. In America, the lowest classes have conceived a very high notion of political rights, because they exercise those rights; and they refrain from attacking the rights of others in order that their own may not be violated. While in Europe the same classes sometimes resist even the supreme power, the American submits without a murmur to the authority of the pettiest magistrate.

. . .

But I do not wish to exaggerate the example that America furnishes. There the people were invested with political rights at a time when they could not be abused, for the inhabitants were few in number and simple in their manners. As they have increased, the Americans have not augmented the power of the democracy; they have rather extended its domain.

It cannot be doubted that the moment at which political rights are granted to a people that had before been without them is a very critical one, that the measure, though often necessary, is always dangerous. A child may kill before he is aware of the value of life; and he may deprive another person of his property before he is aware that his own may be taken from him. The lower orders, when they are first invested with political rights, stand in reason to those rights in the same position as the child does to the whole of nature; and the celebrated adage may then be applied to them: *Homo puer robustus*. This truth may be perceived even in America. The states in which the citizens have enjoyed their rights longest are those in which they make the best use of them.

It cannot be repeated too often that nothing is more fertile in prodigies than the art of being free; but there is nothing more arduous than the apprenticeship of liberty. It is not so with despotism: despotism often promises to make amends for a thousand previous ills; it supports the right, it protects the oppressed, and it maintains public order. The nation is lulled by the temporary prosperity that it produces, until it is roused to a sense of its misery. Liberty, on the contrary, is generally established with difficulty in the midst of storms; it is perfected by civil discord; and its benefits cannot be appreciated until it is already old.

4 Respect for Law

It is not always feasible to consult the whole people, either directly or indirectly, in the formation of law; but it cannot be denied that, when this is possible, the authority of law is much augmented. This popular origin, which impairs the excellence and the wisdom of legislation, contributes much to increase its power. There is an amazing strength in the expression of the will of a whole people; and when it declares itself, even the imagination of those who would wish to contest it is overawed. The truth of this fact is well known by parties, and they consequently strive to make out a majority whenever they can. If they have not the greater number of voters on their side, they assert that the true majority abstained from voting; and if they are foiled even there, they have recourse to those persons who had no right to vote.

In the United States, except slaves, servants, and paupers supported by the townships, there is no class of persons who do not exercise the elective franchise and who do not indirectly contribute to make the laws. Those who wish to attack the laws must consequently either change the opinion of the nation or trample upon its decision.

A second reason, which is still more direct and weighty, may be adduced: in the United States everyone is personally interested in enforcing the obedience of the whole community to the law; for as the minority may shortly rally the majority to its principles, it is interested in professing that respect for the decrees of the legislator which it may soon have occasion to claim for its own. However irksome an enactment may be, the citizen of the United States complies with it, not only because it is the work of the majority, but because it is his own, and he regards it as a contract to which he is himself a party.

In the United States, then, that numerous and turbulent multitude does not exist who, regarding the law as their natural enemy, look upon it with fear and distrust. It is impossible, on the contrary, not to perceive that all classes display the utmost reliance upon the legislation of their country and are attached to it by a kind of parental affection.

I am wrong, however, in saying all classes; for as in America the European scale of authority is inverted, there the wealthy are placed in a position analogous to that of the poor in the Old World, and it is the opulent classes who frequently look upon law with suspicion. I have already observed that the advantage of democracy is not, as has been sometimes asserted, that it protects the interests of all, but simply that it protects those of the majority. In the United States, where the poor rule, the rich have always something to fear from the abuse of their power. This natural anxiety of the rich may produce a secret dissatisfaction; but society is not disturbed by it, for the same reason that withholds the confidence of the rich from the legislative authority makes them obey its mandates: their wealth, which prevents them from making the law, prevents them from withstanding it. Among civilized nations, only those who have nothing to lose ever revolt; and if the laws of a democracy are not always worthy of respect, they are always respected; for those who usually infringe the laws cannot fail to obey those which they have themselves made and by which they are benefited; while the citizens who might be interested in their infraction are induced, by their character and station, to submit to the decisions of the legislature, whatever they may be. Besides, the people in America obey the law, not only because it is their own work, but because it may be changed if it is harmful; a law is observed because, first, it is a self-imposed evil, and, secondly, it is an evil of transient duration.

5 All-Pervading Political Activity

On passing from a free country into one which is not free the traveler is struck by the change; in the former all is bustle and activity; in the latter everything seems calm and motionless. In the one, amelioration and progress are the topics of inquiry; in the other, it seems as if the community wished only to repose in the enjoyment of advantages already acquired. Nevertheless, the country which exerts itself so strenuously to become happy is generally more wealthy and prosperous than that which appears so contented with its lot; and when we compare them, we can scarcely conceive how so many new wants are daily felt in the former, while so few seem to exist in the latter.

If this remark is applicable to those free countries which have preserved monarchical forms and aristocratic institutions, it is still more so to democratic republics.

In these states it is not a portion only of the people who endeavor to improve the state of society, but the whole community is engaged in the task; and it is not the exigencies and convenience of a single class for which provision is to be made, but the exigencies and convenience of all classes at once.

It is not impossible to conceive the surprising liberty that the Americans enjoy; some idea may likewise be formed of their extreme equality; but the political activity that pervades the United States must be seen in order to be understood. No sooner do you set foot upon American ground than you are stunned by a kind of tumult; a confused clamor is heard on every side, and a thousand simultaneous voices demand the satisfaction of their social wants. Everything is in motion around you; here the people of one quarter of a town are met to decide upon the building of a church; there the election of a representative is going on; a little farther, the delegates of a district are hastening to the town in order to consult upon some local improvements; in another place, the laborers of a village quit their plows to deliberate upon the project of a road or a public school. Meetings are called for the sole purpose of declaring their disapprobation of the conduct of the government; while in other assemblies citizens salute the authorities of the day as the fathers of their country. Societies are formed which regard drunkenness as the principal cause of the evils of the state, and solemnly bind themselves to give an example of temperance.

The great political agitation of American legislative bodies, which is the only one that attracts the attention of foreigners, is a mere episode, or a sort of continuation, of that universal movement which originates in the lowest classes of the people and extends successively to all the ranks of society. It is impossible to spend more effort in the pursuit of happiness.

It is difficult to say what place is taken up in the life of an inhabitant of the United States by his concern for politics. To take a hand in the regulation of society and to discuss it is his biggest concern and, so to speak, the only pleasure an American knows. This feeling pervades the most trifling habits of life; even the women frequently attend public meetings and listen to political harangues as a recreation from their household labors. Debating clubs are, to a certain extent, a substitute for theatrical entertainments: an American cannot converse, but he can discuss, and his talk falls into a dissertation. He speaks to you as if he was addressing a meeting; and if he should chance to become warm in the discussion, he will say "Gentlemen" to the person with whom he is conversing.

In some countries the inhabitants seem unwilling to avail themselves of the political privileges which the law gives them; it would seem that they set too high a value upon their time to spend it on the interests of the community; and they shut themselves up in a narrow selfishness, marked out by four sunk fences and a quickset hedge. But if an American were condemned to confine his activity to his own affairs, he would be robbed of one half of his existence; he would feel an immense void in the life which he is accustomed to lead, and his wretchedness would be unbearable. I am persuaded that if ever a despotism should be established in America, it will be more difficult to overcome the habits that freedom has formed than to conquer the love of freedom itself.

This ceaseless agitation which democratic government has introduced into the political world influences all social intercourse. I am not sure that, on the whole, this is not the greatest advantage of democracy; and I am less inclined to applaud it for what it does than for what it causes to be done.

It is incontestable that the people frequently conduct public business very badly; but it is impossible that the lower orders should take a part in public business without extending the circle of their ideas and quitting the ordinary routine of their thoughts. The humblest individual who cooperates in the government of society acquires a certain degree of self-respect; and as he possesses authority, he can command the services of minds more enlightened than his own. He is canvassed by a multitude of applicants, and in seeking to deceive him in a thousand ways, they really enlighten him. He takes a part in political undertakings which he did not originate, but which give him a taste for undertakings of the kind. New improvements are daily pointed out to him in the common property, and this gives him the desire of improving that property which is his own. He is perhaps neither happier nor better than those who came before him, but he is better informed and more active. I have no doubt that the democratic institutions of the United States, joined to the physical constitution of the country, are the cause (not the direct, as is so often asserted, but the indirect cause) of the prodigious commercial activity of the inhabitants. It is not created by the laws, but the people learn how to promote it by the experience derived from legislation.

When the opponents of democracy assert that a single man performs what he undertakes better than the government of all, it appears to me that they are right. The government of an individual, supposing an equality of knowledge on either side, is more consistent, more persevering, more uniform, and more accurate in details than that of a multitude, and it selects with more discrimination the men whom it employs. If any deny this, they have never seen a democratic government, or have judged upon partial evidence. It is true that, even when local circumstances and the dispositions of the people allow democratic institutions to exist, they do not display a regular and methodical system of government. Democratic liberty is far from accomplishing all its projects with the skill of an adroit despotism. It frequently abandons them before they have borne their fruits, or risks them when the consequences may be dangerous; but in the end it produces more than any absolute government; if it does fewer things well, it does a greater number of things. Under its sway the grandeur is not in what the public administration does, but in what is done without it or outside of it. Democracy does not give the people the most skillful government, but it produces what the ablest governments are frequently unable to create: namely, an all-pervading and restless activity, a superabundant force, and an energy which is inseparable from it and which may, however unfavorable circumstances may be, produce wonders. These are the true advantages of democracy.

In the present age, when the destinies of Christendom seem to be in suspense, some hasten to assail democracy as a hostile power while it is yet growing; and others already adore this new deity which is springing forth from chaos. But both parties are imperfectly acquainted with the object of their hatred or their worship; they strike in the dark and distribute their blows at random.

We must first understand what is wanted of society and its government. Do you wish to give a certain elevation to the human mind and teach it to regard the things of this world with generous feelings, to inspire men with a scorn of mere temporal advantages, to form and nourish strong convictions and keep alive the spirit of honorable devotedness? Is it your object to refine the habits, embellish the manners, and cultivate the arts, to promote the love of poetry, beauty, and glory? Would you constitute a people fitted to act powerfully upon all other nations, and prepared for those high enterprises which, whatever be their results, will leave a name forever famous in history? If you believe such to be the principal object of society, avoid the government of the democracy, for it would not lead you with certainty to the goal.

But if you hold it expedient to divert the moral and intellectual activity of man to the production of comfort and the promotion of general well-being; if a clear understanding be more profitable to man than genius; if your object is not to stimulate the virtues of heroism, but the habits of peace; if you had rather witness vices than crimes, and are content to meet with fewer noble deeds, provided offenses be diminished in the same proportion; if, instead of living in the midst of a brilliant society, you are contented to have prosperity around you; if, in short, you are of the opinion that the principal object of a government is not to confer the greatest possible power and glory upon the body of the nation, but to ensure the greatest enjoyment and to avoid the most misery to each of the individuals who compose it—if such be your desire, then equalize the conditions of men and establish democratic institutions.

But if the time is past at which such a choice was possible, and if some power superior to that of man already hurries us, without consulting our wishes, towards one or the other of these two governments, let us endeavor to make the best of that which is allotted to us and, by finding out both its good and its evil tendencies, be able to foster the former and repress the latter to the utmost.

GENERAL SURVEY OF THE SUBJECT

Although the revolution that is taking place in the social condition, the laws, the opinions, and the feelings of men is still very far from being terminated, yet its results already admit of no comparison with anything that the world has ever before witnessed. I go back from age to age up to the remotest antiquity, but I find no parallel to what is occurring before my eyes; as the past has ceased to throw its light upon the future, the mind of man wanders in obscurity.

Nevertheless, in the midst of a prospect so wide, so novel, and so confused, some of the more prominent characteristics may already be discerned and pointed out. The good things and the evils of life are more equally distributed in the world: great wealth tends to disappear, the number of small fortunes to increase; desires and gratifications are multiplied, but extraordinary prosperity and irremediable penury are alike unknown. The sentiment of ambition is universal, but the scope of ambition is seldom vast. Each individual stands apart in solitary weakness, but society at large is active, provident, and powerful; the performances of private persons are insignificant, those of the state immense.

There is little energy of character, but customs are mild and laws humane. If there are few instances of exalted heroism or of virtues of the highest, brightest, and purest temper, men's habits are regular, violence is rare, and cruelty almost unknown. Human existence becomes longer and property more secure; life is not adorned with brilliant trophies, but it is extremely easy and tranquil. Few pleasures are either very refined or very coarse, and highly polished manners are as uncommon as great brutality of tastes. Neither men of great learning nor extremely ignorant communities are to be met with; genius becomes more rare, information more diffused. The human mind is impelled by the small effort of all mankind combined together, not by the strenuous activity of a few men. There is less perfection, but more abundance, in all the productions of the arts. The ties of race, of rank, and of country are relaxed; the great bond of humanity is strengthened.

If I endeavor to find out the most general and most prominent of all these different characteristics, I perceive that what is taking place in men's fortunes manifests itself under a thousand other forms. Almost all extremes are softened or blunted: all that was most prominent is superseded by some middle term, at once less lofty and less low, less brilliant and less obscure, than what before existed in the world.

When I survey this countless multitude of beings, shaped in each other's likeness, amid whom nothing rises and nothing falls, the sight of such universal uniformity saddens and chills me and I am tempted to regret that state of society which has ceased to be. When the world was full of men of great importance and extreme insignificance, of great wealth and extreme poverty, of great learning and extreme ignorance, I turned aside from the latter to fix my observation on the former alone, who gratified my sympathies. But I admit that this gratification arose from my own weakness; it is because I am unable to see at once all that is around me that I am allowed thus to select and separate the objects of my predilection from among so many others. Such is not the case with that Almighty and Eternal Being whose gaze necessarily includes the whole of created things and who surveys distinctly, though all at once, mankind and man.

We may naturally believe that it is not the singular prosperity of the few, but the greater well-being of all that is most pleasing in the sight of the Creator and Preserver of men. What appears to me to be man's decline is, to His eye, advancement; what afflicts me is acceptable to Him. A state of equality is perhaps less elevated, but it is more just: and its justice constitutes its greatness and its beauty. I would strive, then, to raise myself to this point of the divine contemplation and thence to view and to judge the concerns of men.

．　．　．

For myself, who now look back from this extreme limit of my task and discover from afar, but at once, the various objects which have attracted my more attentive investigation upon my way, I am full of apprehensions and of hopes. I perceive mighty dangers which it is possible to ward off, mighty evils which may be avoided or alleviated; and I cling with a firmer hold to the belief that for democratic nations to be virtuous and prosperous, they require but to will it.

. . . The nations of our time cannot prevent the conditions of men from becoming equal, but it depends upon themselves whether the principle of equality is to lead them to servitude or freedom, to knowledge or barbarism, to prosperity or wretchedness.

72
Ernest Barker

Ernest Barker (1874–1960), a profound British student of Plato and Aristotle, sought to embody the political ideals of ancient Greece in a theory of contemporary democracy. Only a democratic state, he contends, can do full justice to the variety and complexity of the ideas and interests of its citizens, because only in a democracy can those ideas and interests fully and richly interact. In resolving conflicts among them, he argues, best results in the long run are likely to be achieved through the debate and discussion of the many "when they meet together." Taken individually, the citizens may exhibit no remarkable abilities; through conference and deliberation they can achieve a wisdom greater than that possible for any autocracy.

[DEMOCRACY AND THE PLURALITY OF IDEAS]*

If the State can be regarded as mediating social thought about justice to its members, and as expressing in its law the product of such thought, we may draw from that premiss the conclusion that the State should itself correspond, in its own nature and operation, to the process of social thought which it mediates, and should thus be a broad open channel for the flow of the product which it expresses. The process of social thought is a process in which all the members of Society can freely share, and to which they can all contribute freely. It follows that, if there is to be correspondence and a broad open flow, the process of the activity of the State should also be a process in which all its members can freely share and to which they can all freely contribute. We may argue that this demand is satisfied, and satisfied only, by the democratic State; first in the form of its constitution and the way of its coming into being, and next in its method of government and the way of its operation.

In their actual coming into being, as has already been noted, States are historical products of very various patterns, due to a variety of historical causes. But the question before us here is not a question of the far-off origins, back in the mists of time, of the States we know today in their changed and developed form as the modern States of our Western world. It is a question of the basis and *raison d'être* of the modern State *as we know it now*, in the form which it has now assumed in the world in which we now live. What set of ideas, and what motions of the mind, have formed and brought into being the State we now know in the form it now has? Some answer to that question has already been given; and it is only necessary to summarize briefly the heads of the answer. A national Society, in the course of a process of social thought, creates and sustains an idea and ideal of a right of

*From E. Barker, *Principles of Social and Political Theory*, 1951. Reprinted by permission of the Clarendon Press, Oxford.

order relations between its members: an idea and ideal of justice. But it cannot attain its ends, or turn the idea into fact and the ideal into reality, without an organized system for the declaration and enforcement of the dictates of justice. We must therefore conceive the society as making itself, or "constituting" itself, an organized system *for this purpose,* or, in other words, as forming itself into a *legal* association or State, while still continuing to exist and act as a Society, and still continuing, as such, to maintain and develop that process of social thought which is continually fertilizing the idea and ideal of justice. This act of the "constitution" of a State by the members of a national Society results, and expresses itself, in a "constitution" in another and further sense of the word: the Constitution with a capital C; the articles of association (both written and unwritten) which warrant, authorize, and control the actions and the organs of the legal association. We may say that this Constitution, or set of articles of association, is of the nature of a contract, which we may call the political contract; and in that sense, as has already been noted, we may say that the State has a contractual basis. We may also say that the constitution of a State by a national Society and by all the members of that Society, or in other words by the people, is the first stage and the foundation of the democratic method of government. In it, and by it, the people have given themselves the basis of political action by a first democratic act of creation. Will they not then go on, still following the same path, and give themselves a method of government and a way of permanent operation in which they are equally active?*

To find a firm basis for a theory of the democratic method of government in the modern State, we must go back to the process of social thought from which the State issues and to which it always remains attached. The process of social thought is naturally and necessarily a process of discussion. Ideas emerge here and there: each emergent idea becomes a magnet which attracts a clustering group of adherents: the various ideas, and the various groups they attract, must either engage in a war of competition with one another to achieve a victory, or attempt a method of composition which fuses and blends them together in peace. The military idea of a war of competition between ideas is prominent in the philosophy of Hegel. His dialectical idealism (which Marx turned upside down, or as he preferred to say "right side up again," in his dialectical materialism) assumes a war of ideas, in which "one shrewd thought devours another": a battle of thesis and antithesis, in which each side fights for itself. But even Hegel's military conception of the war of ideas ends in a sort of composition between thesis and antithesis; or, more

---

*To avoid misunderstanding, and to make the argument clear, it should be noted that the argument here advanced is simply, and only, an argument that the modern State is the product of a shift of ideas, which may be traced in England from the beginning of the Civil War to the Revolution of 1688 and the Hanoverian settlement; which showed itself in North America and France in the last quarter of the eighteenth century; and which spread over Western Europe, South America, and the countries of the British Commonwealth, during the nineteenth century. Whatever the State may hitherto have been, it became, with this shifting of ideas, a specifically legal association, created by the sentiment and action of the national Society, and based on a constitution which is of the nature of a contract. It would be a folly to argue that the State (in the sense of all States, at all times) is based upon contract. It is not a folly to argue that the modern State, in all the parts of the world which have been stirred by this shift of ideas, is so based.

exactly, it ends by producing the synthesis of a higher truth in which the partial truths of the thesis and the antithesis are abolished and transcended. It has thus, after all, some approach to the principle of discussion; but Hegel's theory of discussion is rather that of a logical process inside a solitary mind (even if that mind be conceived as the "objective" mind of a whole Society) than that of a social process among and between a number of minds. The theory which is implied in Aristotle's *Politics* is much nearer to the idea of such a social process. Instead of assuming a war of two conflicting ideas, to be ended by a transcendent and triumphant synthesis, he assumes a plurality of social ideas, to be fused and blended together in a "scheme of composition." Just as it takes all sorts of men to make a world, so it takes all sorts of ideas to produce a "catholic" and all-round view. Aristotle applies this conception to the field of culture and the province of artistic judgment: here, he says, "some appreciate one aspect, and some another, but all together appreciate all." But he also applies it generally to the whole field of social thought; and he applies it, in particular, to matters of political judgment. The Many, he holds, "when they meet together," and put their minds fairly to one another, can achieve a composition of ideas which gives their judgment a general validity.

If we follow the guidance of Aristotle, we shall say that social thought proceeds by the way of a plurality of ideas, by the way of debate and discussion between the different ideas, "when they meet together" and come into contact with one another and by the way of a composition of ideas attained through such debate and discussion. We shall also say that this social way must also be, and also is, the political way: in other words it must also be, and also is, the method of the State's government and the way of the State's operation. This is not only because the State should be true to the Society from which it comes and on which it continues to rest: it is also because the way of Society (the way of plurality of ideas, debate among them, and composition of them) is right in itself and universally right— right for Society, right for the State, and right wherever men are gathered together and have to act together. The one way to get at practical truth, the right thing to do, the straight line of action, is, in any form of group, the way of thinking things over together and talking them over together, with a view to finding some composition of the different threads of thought. It is the way of the Friends, when they seek what they call "the sense of the meeting." It is the way of democracy, which is not a solution, but a way of seeking solutions—not a form of State devoted to this or that particular end (whether private enterprise or public management), but a form of State devoted, whatever its end may be, to a single means and method of determining that end. The core of democracy is choice, and not something chosen; choice among a number of ideas, and choice, too, of the scheme on which those ideas are eventually composed. Democracy is incompatible with any form of one-idea State, because its essence is hospitality to a plurality of ideas, and because its method (which is also its essence) consists in holding together a number of different ideas with a view to comparison and composition of their difference. The democratic criticism of the one-idea State is not a criticism of its object (which may also be the object of the democratic State, or at any rate part of its object): it is a criticism of its whole process of life.

This last phrase, "process of life," suggests a further consideration which is of vital importance in the theory of democracy. One of the archbishops of Canterbury, Frederic Temple, once said that there were two schools of political thought: one which held that politics existed for the production of a result, or the *ergon* school; and another which held that politics was valuable in itself as a process of activity, or the *energeia* school. The school of production judged politics by the results which it produced: the school of process preferred to judge on a different basis, and it was content, and more than content, if the process of the political life of a community elicited and enlisted for its operation the minds and wills of its members, thus aiding, and indeed in its measure constituting, the development of their capacities as persons. The distinction here suggested, which goes back to Aristotle,* is a just and pregnant distinction. We are naturally apt to think of politics in terms of making, rather than of doing, as if our political activity were directed wholly to achieving an object outside itself (and not immanent in itself), such as a scheme of legal order, or an adjustment of economic relations, or some other similar structure. But this is not the whole of the matter, or even the greater part. It is certainly true, and indeed it has already been urged in the course of our argument, that the State as a legal association must necessarily produce a result: it must produce a scheme of declared and enforced law which gives expression to the idea of justice. But there are two other things which must also be borne in mind. First, the ultimate purpose behind justice, and therefore behind law, is the development of the capacities of human personality in as many persons as possible to the greatest possible extent. That is the final result which the State must produce—or rather help to produce; for the result produces itself in each person through his own internal activity, even if it needs help, in the way of removal of hindrances and the offering of opportunities, in order to produce itself fully. This first reflection naturally leads to the second. If we hold that behind and beyond the *production* of law by the State there is a *process* of personal activity and personal development in its members, we may go on to say that the production should itself be drawn into the process. In other words we may argue that the productive effort of the State, the effort of declaring and enforcing a system of law, should also be a process in which and through which, each member of the State is spurred into personal development, because he is drawn into free participation in one of the greatest of all our secular human activities.

These reflections suggest a second main justification of the democratic system. Not only is it justified, as we saw at the beginning of this section, by the fact that it makes the State true to the method of general discussion and composition of ideas which is the method of Society; it is also justified, as we now see, by the fact

---

*The distinction between production *(poiesis)* and action *(praxis)* is discussed in the *Ethics,* Book VI, cc. iii–v. The gist of the argument is that "Production has an end other than itself: action cannot have; for good action is itself its own end."

that it makes the State, in the very process of its own operation, true to the fundamental purpose which lies behind its operation, the purpose of the development in action of the capacities of personality.

73
Charles Frankel

Charles Frankel (1917–1979) was a professor of philosophy at Columbia University whose active public life enriched his theoretical account of the merits of democracy. It is a risky system, he thought, and an exhausting one—but it promotes certain public virtues as no other system of government can. Success within a democracy requires that conflicts be controlled and violence avoided. Democracy obliges restraint and promotes compromise, and encourages the moral education of its leaders. It teaches all citizens that a life of public "sportsmanship"—accepting one's losses gracefully, not with resignation but with the understanding that the issue may be reopened and that there will be an opportunity to wage the battle yet again—is both satisfying and profitable. We ought to choose a democracy, Frankel argued, because it, more than any other form of government, encourages its members to treat one another with respect and decency.

WHY CHOOSE DEMOCRACY?*

Choosing a political ideal is not like demonstrating the truth of a theorem in some geometry, and those who think that democracy needs that kind of justification are indirectly responsible for the uncertainty about it. Despite the semantic inflation from which the current discussion of political ideals suffers, the reasons for choosing democracy are neither mysterious nor difficult. But they are unsettling reasons, and they ask those who accept them to bet a great deal on their capacity to live with what they have chosen.

THE SIGNIFICANCE OF THE DEMOCRATIC POLITICAL METHOD

In an area so full of grandiose claims, it is safest to begin by using the word "democracy" in its narrowest sense. So conceived, democracy is the method of choosing a government through competitive elections in which people who are not members of the governing groups participate. Whatever may be said for or against democracy so conceived, it is surely not a supreme ideal of life. It is doubtful that anyone has ever treated the right to cast a ballot once every year or so as an end

---

*Reprinted from *The Democratic Prospect* by Charles Frankel. Copyright © 1962 by Charles Frankel. Reprinted by permission of Harper & Row Publishers, Inc.

in itself. A society in which the democratic political method has been consolidated, to be sure, has a tremendous source of reassurance. It possesses a peaceful method for determining who shall hold power and for effecting changes in the structure of power. Yet even peace is only one value among others. It is worth something to have security and order, but how much it is worth depends on the kind of security and order it is. The importance of the democratic political method lies mainly in its nonpolitical by-products. It is important because a society in which it is well established will probably be different in at least four respects—in the conditions that protect its liberties, in the kind of consensus that prevails, in the character of the conflicts that go on within it, and in the manner in which it educates its rulers and citizens.

First, liberties. Construed strictly as a method for choosing governments, democracy does not guarantee the citizen's personal liberties. Democratic governments have attacked personal liberties, as in colonial New England, and undemocratic governments have often protected them, as in Vienna before World War I. Yet competitive elections have their points, and it is only one of their points that they allow a society to choose its government. For in order to maintain competitive elections, it is necessary to have an opposition, the opposition must have some independent rights and powers of its own, the good opinion of some people outside government must be sought, and at least some members of the society must have protections against the vengefulness of the powers that be. And this carries a whole train of institutions behind it—courts, a press not wholly devoted to promoting the interests of those in power, and independent agencies for social inquiry and criticism.

It is these necessitating conditions for elections that give elections their long-range significance. So far as political democracy is concerned, these conditions are only means to ends: they make competitive elections possible. But it is because a system of competitive elections requires and fosters such conditions that it justifies itself. The conditions required for maintaining an honest electoral system are the best reasons for wishing to maintain it. Indeed, a man might value such a system even though he thought all elections frivolous and foolish. He would have as good a reason to do so, and perhaps a better reason, than the man who always finds himself voting happily for the winning side. The outsider and the loser are the peculiar beneficiaries of a political system that creates institutions with a vested interest in liberty.

The democratic political method, furthermore, helps to foster a different kind of social consensus. There have been many kinds of political arrangement that have allowed men to feel that the government under which they live is *their* government. There is no clear evidence that democracy is necessarily superior to other systems in promoting a sense of oneness between rulers and ruled. But the special virtue of a democratic political system is that it permits men to feel at home within it who do not regard their political leaders as their own kind, and who would lose their self-respect, indeed, if they gave their unprovisional loyalty to any human institution. Despite all that is said about democratic pressures towards conformity—and a little of what is said is true—the democratic political system ceremonializes the fact of disagreement and the virtue of independent judgment. If it is to work, it requires an extraordinarily sophisticated human attitude—loyal opposition. The mark of a civilized man, in Justice Holmes' famous maxim, is that he can act with conviction while questioning his first principles. The ultimate claim of a democratic government to authority is that it permits dissent and survives it. In this respect, it dwells on the same moral landscape as the civilized man.

The democratic political method also changes the character of the conflicts that take place in a society. The perennial problem of politics is to manage conflict. And what happens in a conflict depends in part on who the onlookers are, how they react, and what powers they have. A significant fact about political democracy is that it immensely expands the audience that looks on and that feels itself affected and involved. This is why democratic citizens so often find democracy tiring and feel that their societies are peculiarly fragile. Hobbes, who said that he and fear were born as twins, recommended despotism in the interests of psychological security as well as physical safety.

But to say that democracy expands the scope of a conflict is also to say that democracy is a technique for the socialization of conflict. It brings a wider variety of pressures to bear on those who are quarreling and extends public control over private fights and private arrangements. And it does so whether these private fights are inside the government or outside. The association of democracy with the conception of private enterprise has something paradoxical about it. In one sense, there is more important enterprise that is private—free from outside discussion and surveillance—in totalitarian systems than in democratic systems. The persistent problem in a democratic system, indeed, is to know where to draw the line, where to say that outside surveillance is out of place. That line is drawn very firmly by those who make the important decisions in totalitarian societies.

But the final contribution that the democratic political method makes to the character of the society in which it is practiced is its contribution to education. Begin with the impact of political democracy on its leaders. The democratic method, like any other political method, is a system of rules for governing political competition. And such rules have both a selective and an educational force. They favor certain kinds of men, and make certain kinds of virtue more profitable and certain kinds of vice more possible. From this point of view, the significant characteristic of democratic rules of competition is that the loser is allowed to lose with honor, and permitted to live and try again if he wants. The stakes are heavy but limited. Such a system of competition gives men with sporting moral instincts a somewhat better chance to succeed. Even its typical kind of corruption has something to be said in its favor. The greased palm is bad but it is preferable to the mailed fist.

The democratic political method, furthermore, rests on methods of mutual consultation between leaders and followers. There are various ways in which support for the policies of political leaders is obtained in a democracy, but one of the most important is that of giving men the sense that they have been asked for their opinions and that their views have been taken into account. This makes leadership in a democracy a nerve-racking affair. One of the great dangers in a democratic political system, in fact, is simply that leaders will not have the privacy and quiet necessary for serene long-range decisions. But this is the defect of a virtue. In general, power insulates. The democratic system is a calculated effort to break in on such insulation. The conditions under which democratic leaders hold power are conditions for educating them in the complexity and subtlety of the problems for which they are responsible.

And the coin has its other side. "We Athenians," said Pericles, "are able to judge policy even if we cannot originate it, and instead of looking on discussion as a stumbling-block in the way of action, we think it an indispensable preliminary to any wise action at all." But the fruits of free discussion do not show themselves only in public policy. They show themselves in the attitudes and capacities of the discussants. Democratic political arrangements are among the factors that have produced one of the painful and more promising characteristics of modern existence—men's sense that their education is inadequate, men's assertion that they have a right to be educated. And democratic politics help to promote a classic conception of education—it must be social as well as technical, general as well as special, free and not doctrinaire. We can reverse the classic conception of the relation of education to democracy and not be any further from the truth: education is not simply a prerequisite for democracy; democracy is a contribution to education.

USES OF DEMOCRACY

But enough of political systems. In any liberal view of men's business, politics is a subordinate enterprise. It has its soul-testing challenges and pleasures, and its great work to do. But like the work of commerce and industry, the work of politics is essentially servile labor. The State is not the place to turn if you want a free commentary on human experience, and governments do not produce science, philosophy, music, literature, or children—or at any rate they do not produce very convincing specimens of any of these things. Politics may achieve its own forms of excellence, but the more important human excellences are achieved elsewhere. And it is from this point of view, I think, that democracy should in the end be considered.

For the democratic idea is based on the assumption that the important ends of life are defined by private individuals in their own voluntary pursuits. Politics, for liberal democracy, is only one aspect of a civilization, a condition for civilization but not its total environment. That is probably why the air seems lighter as one travels from controlled societies to free ones. One receives an impression of vitality, the vitality of people who are going about their own business and generating their own momentum. They may be going off in more different directions than the members of a centrally organized society, but the directions are their own. The best reasons for choosing democracy lie in the qualities it is capable of bringing to our daily lives, in the ways in which it can furnish our minds, imaginations, and consciences. These qualities, I would say, are freedom, variety, self-consciousness, and the democratic attitude itself.

That democracy is hostile to distinction and prefers mediocrity is not a recent view. And there is an obvious sense in which it is true that democracy makes for homogeneity. Democracy erodes the clear distinctions between classes. It destroys ready-made status-symbols so rapidly that the manufacture of new ones becomes the occupation of a major industry. Most obvious of all, democracy increases the demand for a great many good things, from shoes to education. By increasing the demand, it also puts itself under pressure to cheapen the supply.

Yet certain pertinent facts must be set against these tendencies. First, more good things *are* more generally available in democracies. Second, egalitarianism's twin is the morality of achievement. There is a tension between the democratic suspicion of the man who sets himself apart and the democratic admiration for the man who stands out, but the egalitarian hostility towards ostentatious social distinctions is normally rooted in the belief that each man should be given a chance on his own to show what he can do. And finally, pressures towards uniformity are great in all societies. Is suspicion of the eccentric in egalitarian metropolitan America greater than in an eighteenth-century village? It is difficult to think so. "The fallacy of the aristocrat," Bertrand Russell has remarked, "consists in judging a society by the kind of life it affords a privileged few." Standing alone takes courage anywhere. Usually it also takes money; almost invariably it requires the guarantee that the individual will still retain his basic rights. In these respects modern liberal democracy, despite all the complaints about conformity, has made it easier for the ordinary unprivileged man to stand alone, if he has the will to do so, than any other kind of society known in history.

For however ambiguous some of the facts may be, the official commitment of liberal democracy is to the view that each man has his idiosyncrasies, that these idiosyncrasies deserve respect, and that if the individual does not know what is good for him, it is highly unlikely that a self-perpetuating elite will know better. And this is not just an official commitment. The institutions of liberal democracy go very far in giving it concrete embodiment. Assuming that the members of a democratic society have minimal economic securities, there is a flexibility in their situation which not many ordinary men have enjoyed in the past. If they fall out of favor with one set of authorities, they have a chance to turn around and look elsewhere.

It is unquestionable that there are great constellations of concentrated power in contemporary democratic societies; it is equally unquestionable that there is some freedom in any society. For in dealing with power, bright men learn how to work the angles. But in a democratic society there are more angles to work. Individual freedom of choice is not an absolute value. Any society must limit it; indeed, one man's freedom often rests on restricting the next man's. But while freedom of choice is not an absolute value, the democratic doctrine that each man has certain fundamental rights assigns an intrinsic value to his freedom of choice. If it has to be limited, it is recognized that something of value has been sacrificed. Social planning in a democracy is for this reason fundamentally different from social planning in undemocratic environments. The vague phrase "social utility," in a democratic setting, implicitly includes as one of its elements the value of freedom of choice.

What difference does this make? One difference is that variety is promoted; a second is that individuals are educated in self-consciousness. Needless to say, variety, too, has its limits. We do not have to protect dope peddlers in its name. But the full import of variety, of the mere existence of differences and alternatives, is frequently overlooked. It does not merely give us more choices, or offer us a break in the routine. It affects the immediate quality of our experience; it changes our relation to whatever it is that we choose to have to do or be. This is what is forgotten when freedom is defined simply as the absence of felt frustrations, or when it is said that if a man has just what he wants, it makes little difference whether he has any choice or not. A good that is voluntarily chosen, a good which a man is always free to reconsider, belongs to him in a way that a passively accepted good does not. It is his responsibility.

And this means that democratic variety has another use as well. No one can say with assurance that democracy makes people wiser or more virtuous. But political democracy invites men to think that there may be alternatives to the way they are governed. And social democracy, in reducing the barriers of class, caste, and inherited privilege that stand between men, adds to the variety of people and occasions the individual meets and puts greater pressure on his capacity to adapt to the new and different. Political democracy and a socially mobile society thus invite the individual to a greater degree of consciousness about the relativity of his own ways and a greater degree of self-consciousness in the choice of the standards by which he lives. These are conditions for intensified personal experience. The role of democracy in the extension of these attitudes represents one of its principal contributions to the progress of liberal civilization.

The extension of such attitudes, to be sure, has its risks, which explains much of our uneasiness about what the democratic revolution means. Fads and fashions engage and distract larger groups in modern democratic societies. And social mobility, though it gives breadth and variety to men's experience, may well foreshorten their sense of time. Cut loose from fixed ranks and stations, each with its legends, rationale, and sense of historic vocation, the citizens of a modern democracy face a peculiar temptation to live experimentally, with the help of the latest book, as though no one had ever lived before. But these are the risks not simply of democracy but of modernity, and they can be controlled. The courts, the organized professions, the churches, and the universities are storehouses of funded experience. In a society in which they are given independence from the political urgencies of the moment, they can serve as protections against the dictatorship of the specious present. Modernity implies a revolution in human consciousness. Democratic social arrangements reflect that revolution and accept it; but they also provide instruments for guiding and controlling it. None of democracy's contemporary rivals possess these two qualities to the same extent.

In the end, indeed, the risks of democracy are simply the risks implicit in suggesting to men that the answers are not all in. Democracy gives political form to the principle that also regulates the scientific community—the principle that inquiry must be kept open, that there are no sacred books, that no conclusion that men have ever reached can be taken to be the necessary final word. Cant, obscurantism, and lies are of course a good part of the diet of most democracies. Man is a truth-fearing animal, and it would be a miracle if any social system could quickly change this fact. But the institutions of liberal democracy are unique in that they require men to hold no irreversible beliefs in anything except in the method of free criticism and peaceful change itself, and in the ethic on which this method rests. Such a social system permits men to give their highest loyalty, not to temporary human beliefs or institutions, but to the continuing pursuit after the truth, whatever it may be. The intellectual rationale of democracy is precisely that it does not need to make the foolish and arrogant claim that it rests on infallible truths. Men can believe in it and still believe that the truth is larger than anything they may think they know.

Yet the question that probably gnaws at us most deeply still remains. Freedom, variety, self-consciousness, a sane awareness of human fallibility, and loyalty to the principle that inquiry must be kept open—obviously, these have much in their favor. But they are refined values. Has liberal democracy priced itself out of the competition? Does it have anything to say, not to those who already know and enjoy it, but to the many more who must come to want it if human liberties are to be a little more secure in the world than they now are?

One of the debilitating illusions of many Western liberals is that the values of liberal culture are only our own values, that they have little point for those who look at the world differently, and no point at all for those whose lives are poor, mean, brutish, and short. Although colonialists used this view for different purposes, they shared it, and it betrays an inexact understanding of the nature of liberal values. Freedom, variety, self-consciousness, and the chance to seek the truth are all taxing experiences. Their virtues may be hard to conceive by those who have never enjoyed them. Yet in spite of the discomforts these values bring, the evidence indicates, I think, that most men would be happy to have them, and would think their lives enhanced. The difficulty with the most characteristic liberal values is not that they are parochial values. The difficulty is that men have other more imperious wants, like the need for medicines, schooling, bread, release from usurers, or a chance to get out from under corrupt and exploitative regimes. Illiberal programs promise these substantial material improvements and frequently deliver. And liberal programs, if they speak of freedom and leave out the usury and corruption, do not generally bring freedom either.

But let us assume, as there is every reason to assume, that liberal programs, if they are willing to recognize that they, too, must make a revolution, can also improve men's material condition. What can be said to the young man or the young—or old—nation in a hurry? What good reasons can we give, reasons that take account of their present condition and justified impatience, when we try to explain to them—and to ourselves—why the liberal path, despite its meanderings, is preferable to the authoritarian path?

One thing that can be said, quite simply, is that the authoritarian path closes up behind the traveler as he moves. The virtue of liberal democracy is that it permits second thoughts. To choose an authoritarian regime is to bet everything on a single throw of the dice; if the bet is bad, there is no way out save through violence, and not much hope in that direction. To choose a liberal approach, while it does not guarantee against errors, guarantees against the error so fatal that there is no peaceful way out or back. But there is another reason as well. The reason for choosing democracy is that it makes democrats.

Imagine a regime wholly committed to the welfare of those it rules. Imagine, against all the practical difficulties, that it is intelligent, honest, courageous, and that it does not have to enter into any deals with any of the international blocs that dominate the modern scene. And imagine, too, that this regime aims, in the end, to bring democracy and liberal values to the country it rules. But assume only that it claims, for the present, to be the one true spokesman for the public interest, the only group in the society that knows what truth and justice mean. What is the consequence? The consequence is that a democratic attitude is impossible. That attitude has been described in various ways—as a love for liberty, equality, and fraternity, as respect for the dignity of the individual, as a consistent regard for individual rights. The descriptions are not wrong, but they overintellectualize the attitude. At bottom, the democratic attitude is simply an attitude of good faith plus a working belief in the probable rationality of others. And that is what political authoritarianism destroys. Once a society is governed by the doctrine that some one group monopolizes all wisdom, it is divided into the Enlightened and the Unenlightened, and the Enlightened determine who shall be accorded membership in the club. In a modern State this makes almost impossible the growth of that mutual trust between opposing groups which is a fundamental condition for the growth of a strong political community that is also free.

The competition that takes place in a democracy is an instance of cooperative competition. It is a struggle in which both sides work to maintain the conditions necessary for a decent struggle. Accordingly, it rests on the assumption that there are no irreconcilable conflicts, that differences can be negotiated or compromised, if men have good will. Such a system requires men to deal with one another honestly, to make a serious effort to reach agreements, and to keep them after they have been made. It requires them to recognize, therefore, that the other side has its interests and to be prepared to make concessions to these interests when such concessions are not inconsistent with fundamental principles. A democratic ethic does not ask men to be fools. They do not have to assume that their opponents have put all their cards on the table. But democratic competition is impossible if the parties to the competition cannot assume that their opponents will recognize their victory if they win and will cooperate with them afterwards. The intention to annihilate the opposition or to win at all costs destroys the possibility of a regulated struggle. In this sense democracy is an exercise in the ethic of good faith. It is a system that makes it possible for men, not to love their enemies, but at least to live without fearing them. That kind of mutual trust between enemies is what authoritarianism destroys.

No doubt, such an argument may seem pathetically beside the point to men who live in societies that have been torn by distrust for centuries and that have known government only as a name for cruelty and dishonesty. If such men succeed in installing democratic regimes in their countries, they will do so by recognizing their enemies and distrusting them. But the harshness that goes with any deep social revolution is one thing if it is recognized as a bitter and dangerous necessity and is kept within limits. It is another if the violence is doctrinal, and the assumption is made that men can never cooperate unless they have the same interests and ideas. Such an assumption, as all the evidence suggests, encourages the adoption of terror as an official policy and condemns a society to an indefinite period in which power will be monopolistically controlled. In a diversified modern society, indeed in any society that has even begun the movement towards modernity, the doctrine of governmental infallibility trains men in suspiciousness and conspiracy. Perhaps other objectives will be achieved, but under such circumstances their taste will be sour.

Nor does the doctrine of infallibility destroy only good faith. It is also incompatible with a belief in the probable rationality of others. To hold a democratic attitude is to proceed on the assumption that other men may have their own persuasive reasons for thinking as they do. If they disagree with you, this does not necessarily make them candidates for correction and cure. This is the homely meaning of the oft-repeated assertion that democracy has faith in the reasonableness and equality of human beings. The faith does not assert that all men are in fact reasonable, or that they are equal in the capacity to think well or live sensibly. The faith is pragmatic: it expresses a policy. And the policy is simply to credit others with minds of their own, and to hold them responsible for their actions, until there are strong and quite specific reasons for thinking otherwise. Such a policy allows room for the idiosyncrasies of men and permits the varieties of human intelligence to be recognized and used.

In the end, the man who asks himself why he should choose democracy is asking himself to decide with which of two policies he would rather live. One is the policy of normally thinking that his fellows are dangerous to him and to themselves. The other is the policy of thinking that they are reasonable until they show themselves dangerous. To act on either policy has its risks. Why should a man choose one rather than the other? One reason can be found if he asks himself about the consequences the policy he adopts will have for the elementary feelings he will entertain towards his fellows, not in some transfigured world to come, but here and now. The point of the democratic policy is that it makes for democratic feelings. Those who do not wish to see human society divided into exploiters and exploited, those who wish to see each man come into his own free estate, believe that in that ultimate condition men will treat each other with the respect and fellow-feeling that equals show to equals. It is in the name of such moral attitudes that they seek democracy. The final reason for choosing the democratic method is that it provides a training ground, here and now, in just these attitudes.

3

DEMOCRACY, REPRESENTATION, AND MAJORITY RULE

Any system in which the members of a community govern themselves must devise institutions and practices, *instruments* with which the will of the people is made effective, transformed concretely into policy and law. Of all such instruments there are two employed by virtually every democracy, and these two have therefore become so closely associated with it as to be sometimes confused with democracy itself. These are, first, a *system of representation* through which the voice of the people may be heard, and second, a *decision-making rule*—most often the rule of the majority—to determine the winners when laws and other matters are contested.

Representation is a perennial problem in democratic government. For some it is an evil, accepted only because it is believed unavoidable in any democracy of substantial size; for others it is desirable in itself, a wholesome device through which the voice of the people may be refined and their excesses on occasion restrained. The spirit of healthy representation is another matter upon which democrats disagree. Are elected representatives rightly viewed as *spokespersons* for their constituents, obliged to act as they believe the electors would act in their place? Or are representatives rightly viewed as *delegates,* chosen by their constituents for their wisdom and character, and expected to use their judgment in the work of the parliament, even when that judgment leads to unpopular outcomes?

But the most critical questions regarding the uses of representation in a democracy concern the ideal nature of the *constituency* itself: how ought the electors to be divided for the purposes of selecting representatives? Representation by geo-

graphical district has been most common, of course, and it is in many circumstances taken for granted; but many philosophers have sought systems of representation that more fully reflect, in the legislature, the variety of views in the electorate at large, representatives chosen not by the voters living in some region, but
by voters supporting some specific position, or who are of some specific inclination. A system consisting of electoral districts made more homogenous in this way
has important merits that heterogeneous systems (like geographical representation)
lack, but also has important demerits that they avoid. The theoretical issues here at
stake are made more sensitive by conflicts among racial and ethnic groups within
the community. Where a given system of representation appears to frustrate the
efforts of some ethnic minority to achieve effective representation, dispute over
the justice of competing principles of representation is likely to become bitter.
Probably there is no single best system of representation; the virtues and vices of
competing systems, proportional and geographical, homogenous and heterogeneous, will be a continuing concern in every healthy democracy.

In the selection of representatives, and in the formal acts of representative legislatures, there must also be some *rule* for determining who wins. Usually, in a
democracy, we agree to abide by the rule of the majority, and some even think
that rule to be part of the essence of self-government. But not every democratic
decision need be determined by majority rule. For the amendment of their most
fundamental charter a community may employ a rule much more protective than
that of the simple majority ("qualified majority" rules, or "super-majority"
rules)—as Americans do with respect to the amendment of the Constitution of
the United States. On the other hand, in the election of representatives when candidates are many, a democratic community may choose to apply the rule of plurality, resulting often in the election of persons who do not have the support of
any majority but have received more votes than any of their competitors. Some
decision-making rules (like that of the plurality) are *more efficient but less protective;* some rules (like the rule of unanimity in a jury deciding a criminal case,
or the two-thirds rule for ending debate in a public meeting) are *more protective
but less efficient.* As in the case of representative systems, there is probably not
one best rule, but many rules that the people may use in their self-government,
the wisdom of that choice depending upon the context and the kinds of issues to
be confronted.

The philosophical selections that follow explore many arguments arising in
debates over the instruments of democracy. These arguments should be
approached by democrats with an open mind, never supposing that the one system
of representation to which we happen to be accustomed, or the one set of rules that
we happen to have long employed, is necessarily wisest or best. The overriding
question should be this: if democracy is government by the people, what institutions and practices best help the people to govern themselves? What systems of
representation, and what decision-making rules, serve to make citizen participation
wise and effective?

74
James Madison

James Madison (1751–1836), Alexander Hamilton (1757–1804), and John Jay (1745–1829) were the authors of *The Federalist*—a series of 85 essays published in 1887–88 in defense of the proposed Constitution of the United States which they had helped to design at the Constitutional Convention in Philadelphia only months before. Jefferson called these essays—appearing anonymously over the signature "Publius" in a New York newspaper, the *Independent Journal*—"the best commentaries on the principles of government . . . ever written." Their objective was to encourage the ratification of the new Constitution, and to do that they needed to show that the system of representation devised in that Constitution was fair, wise, and well-calculated to protect and advance the interests of the people of the several American states.

Excerpts from two of the greatest *Federalist* essays, both authored by Madison, appear below. From the most famous of them all, #10, appears the passage in which Madison gives a forthright defense of *representation* as an essential instrument with which the excesses of popular rule may be restrained, and the "violence of faction" counteracted. Even a great number of citizens over a great extent of territory can (he argues) with a just electoral system select representatives "whose wisdom may best discern the true interest of their country." His own wisdom led to Madison's election as fourth President of the United States. In #51 Madison argues that institutions, such as those devised in the Constitution, are needed which "divide and arrange the several offices [of government] in such a manner as that each may be a check on the other"—a system of checks and balances that has kept the American republic reasonably steady for more than two centuries.

[HOW RETAIN A POPULAR GOVERNMENT WHILE GUARDING AGAINST THE DANGERS OF FACTION?]*

Among the numerous advantages promised by a well-constructed Union, none deserves to be more accurately developed than its tendency to break and control the violence of faction. . . .

By a faction, I understand a number of citizens, whether amounting to a majority or minority of the whole, who are united and actuated by some common impulse of passion, or of interest, adverse to the rights of other citizens, or to the permanent and aggregate interests of the community.

There are two methods of curing the mischiefs of faction: the one, by removing its cause; the other, by controlling its effects.

There are again two methods of removing the causes of faction: the one, by destroying the liberty which is essential to its existence; the other, by giving to every citizen the same opinions, the same passions, and the same interests.

*From *The Federalist #10*, by James Madison.

It could never be more truly said than of the first remedy, that it was worse than the disease. Liberty is to faction what air is to fire, an aliment without which it instantly expires. But it could not be less folly to abolish liberty, which is essential to political life, because it nourishes faction, than it would be to wish the annihilation of air, which is essential to animal life, because it imparts to fire its destructive agency.

The second expedient is as impracticable as the first would be unwise. As long as the reason of man continues fallible, and he is at liberty to exercise it, different opinions will be formed. As long as the connection subsists between his reason and his self-love, his opinions and his passions will have a reciprocal influence on each other; and the former will be objects to which the latter will attach themselves. The diversity in the faculties of men, from which the rights of property originate, is not less an insuperable obstacle to a uniformity of interests. The protection of these faculties is the first object of government. From the protection of different and unequal faculties of acquiring property, the possession of different degrees and kinds of property immediately results; and from the influence of these on the sentiments and views of the respective proprietors, ensues a division of the society into different interests and parties.

The latent causes of faction are thus sown in the nature of man and we see them everywhere brought into different degrees of activity, according to the different circumstances of civil society. . . .

The inference to which we are brought is, that the *causes* of faction cannot be removed, and that relief is only to be sought in the means of controlling its *effects*.

If a faction consists of less than a majority, relief is supplied by the republican principle, which enables the majority to defeat its sinister views by regular vote. It may clog the administration, it may convulse the society; but it will be unable to execute and mask its violence under the forms of the Constitution. When a majority is included in a faction, the form of popular government, on the other hand, enables it to sacrifice to its ruling passion or interest both the public good and the rights of other citizens. To secure the public good and private rights against the danger of such a faction, and at the same time to preserve the spirit and the form of popular government, is then the great object to which our inquiries are directed. . . .

By what means is this object obtainable? . . . A pure democracy, by which I mean a society consisting of a small number of citizens, who assemble and administer the government in person, can admit of no cure for the mischiefs of faction. A common passion or interest will, in almost every case, be felt by a majority of the whole; a communication and concert result from the form of government itself; and there is nothing to check the inducements to sacrifice the weaker party or an obnoxious individual. . . .

A republic, by which I mean a government in which the scheme of representation takes place, opens a different prospect, and promises the cure for which we are seeking. Let us examine the points in which it varies from pure democracy, and we shall comprehend both the nature of the cure and the efficacy which it must derive from the Union.

The two great points of difference between a democracy and a republic are: first, the delegation of the government, in the latter, to a small number of citizens elected by the rest; secondly, the greater number of citizens, and greater sphere of country, over which the latter may be extended.

The effect of the first difference is, on the one hand, to refine and enlarge the public views, by passing them through the medium of a chosen body of citizens, whose wisdom may best discern the true interest of their country, and whose patriotism and love of justice will be least likely to sacrifice it to temporary or partial considerations. . . .

The other point of difference is, the greater number of citizens and extent of territory which may be brought within the compass of republican than of democratic government; and it is this circumstance principally which renders factious combinations less to be dreaded in the former than in the latter. The smaller the society, the fewer probably will be the distinct parties and interests composing it; the fewer the distinct parties and interests, the more frequently will a majority be found of the same party; and the smaller the number of individuals composing a majority, and the smaller the compass within which they are placed, the more easily will they concert and execute their plans of oppression. Extend the sphere and you take in a greater variety of parties and interests; you make it less probable that a majority of the whole will have a common motive to invade the rights of other citizens; or if such a common motive exists, it will be more difficult for all who feel it to discover their own strength, and to act in unison with each other. . . .

Hence, it clearly appears, that the same advantage which a republic has over a democracy, in controlling the effects of faction, is enjoyed by a large over a small republic—is enjoyed by the Union over the States composing it. . . .

The influence of factious leaders may kindle a flame within their particular States, but will be unable to spread a general conflagration through the other States. A religious sect may degenerate into a political faction in a part of the Confederacy; but the variety of sects dispersed over the entire face of it must secure the national councils against any danger from that source. A rage for paper money, for an abolition of debts, for an equal division of property, or for any other improper or wicked project, will be less apt to pervade the whole body of the Union than a particular member of it; in the same proportion as such a malady is more likely to taint a particular county or district, than an entire State.

In the extent and proper structure of the Union, therefore, we behold a republican remedy for the diseases most incident to republican government. And according to the degree of pleasure and pride we feel in being republicans, ought to be our zeal in cherishing the spirit and supporting the character of Federalists.

[HOW BALANCE THE POWERS OF GOVERNMENT?]*

To what expedient, then, shall we finally resort, for maintaining in practice the necessary partition of power among the several departments, as laid down in the Constitution? The only answer that can be given is, that as all these exterior provisions are found to be inadequate, the defect must be supplied, by so contriving the interior structure of the government as that its several constituent parts may,

*From *The Federalist #51,* by James Madison.

by their mutual relations, be the means of keeping each other in their proper places. . . .

The great security against a gradual concentration of the several powers in the same department, consists in giving to those who administer each department the necessary constitutional means and personal motives to resist encroachments of the others. The provision for defence must in this, as in all other cases, be made commensurate to the danger of attack. Ambition must be made to counteract ambition. The interest of the man must be connected with the constitutional rights of the place. It may be a reflection on human nature, that such devices should be necessary to control the abuses of government. But what is government itself, but the greatest of all reflections on human nature? If men were angels, no government would be necessary. If angels were to govern men, neither external nor internal controls on government would be necessary. In framing a government which is to be administered by men over men, the great difficulty lies in this: you must first enable the government to control the governed; and in the next place oblige it to control itself. A dependence on the people is, no doubt, the primary control on the government; but experience has taught mankind the necessity of auxiliary precautions.

This policy of supplying, by opposite and rival interests, the defect of better motives, might be traced through the whole system of human affairs, private as well as public. We see it particularly displayed in all the subordinate distributions of power, where the constant aim is to divide and arrange the several offices in such a manner as that each may be a check on the other—that the private interest of every individual may be a sentinel over the public rights. These inventions of prudence cannot be less requisite in the distribution of the supreme powers of the State.

75
Edmund Burke

Edmund Burke (1730–1797), Irish-English philosopher and statesman, is revered by many as the greatest spokesman for the conservative ideals of parliamentary democracy. While Rousseau had in part inspired the revolution in France, Burke was horrified by its excesses; while Rousseau had questioned the genuineness of a democracy in which participation was not direct, Burke defended a parliamentary system in which representatives, well qualified and prepared for their roles, would use their own judgment in behalf of their constituents. Like most of his contemporaries, Burke did look to an ideal order superior to that of the present—but for him that order was the ongoing system created by untold generations as they worked out the forms of representative government and the traditions and usages of those venerable forms. Like Rousseau he was profoundly concerned with the rights of human beings and of citizens; but he thought those rights best protected by looking beyond immediate desires to the distant past and future, always restraining government in such ways as to render it impossible for the passions of a passing majority to cause it to invade private liberties.

A PARLIAMENTARY REPRESENTATIVE IS NOT A MERE DELEGATE*

It ought to be the happiness and glory of a representative to live in the strictest union, the closest correspondence, and the most unreserved communication with his constituents. Their wishes ought to have great weight with him; their opinion, high respect; their business, unremitted attention. It is his duty to sacrifice his repose, his pleasures, his satisfactions, to theirs; and, above all, ever and in all cases to prefer their interest to his own. But his unbiassed opinion, his mature judgment, his enlightened conscience, he ought not to sacrifice to you, to any man, or to any set of men living. These he does not derive from your pleasure, no, nor from the law and the Constitution. They are a trust from Providence, for the abuse of which he is deeply answerable. Your representative owes you, not his industry only, but his judgment; and he betrays, instead of serving you, if he sacrifices it to your opinion.

My worthy colleague says his will ought to be subservient to yours. If that be all, the thing is innocent. If government were a matter of will upon any side, yours, without question, ought to be superior. But government and legislation are matters of reason and judgment, and not of inclination; and what sort of reason is that in which the determination precedes the discussion; in which one set of men deliberate and another decide; and where those who form the conclusion are perhaps three hundred miles distant from those who hear the arguments?

To deliver an opinion is the right of all men; that of constituents is a weighty and respectable opinion, which a representative ought always to rejoice to hear, and which he ought always most seriously to consider. But *authoritative* instructions, *mandates* issued, which the member is bound blindly and implicitly to obey, to vote, and to argue for, though contrary to the clearest conviction of his judgment and conscience; these are things utterly unknown to the laws of this land, and which arise from a fundamental mistake of the whole order and tenour of our constitution.

Parliament is not a *congress* of ambassadors from different and hostile interests; which interests each must maintain, as an agent and advocate against other agents and advocates; but Parliament is a *deliberative* assembly of *one* nation, with *one* interest, that of the whole. You choose a member indeed; but when you have chosen him, he is not member of Bristol, but he is a member of *Parliament.* If the local constituent should have an interest, or should form a hasty opinion, evidently opposite to the real good of the rest of the community, the members for that place ought to be as far as any other from any endeavour to give it effect. . . . Your faithful friend, your devoted servant, I shall be to the end of my life; a flatterer you do not wish for.

---

*From a speech delivered (in 1774) to the citizens of Bristol, while campaigning for election to Parliament from that constituency. [Burke was elected.—*Ed.*]

76
J. Ramsay MacDonald

James Ramsay MacDonald (1866–1937) was long-time leader of the British
Labour Party and three times Prime Minister of Great Britain in the early years of
the twentieth century. A brilliant socialist theoretician and advocate of
revolutionary change, he never abandoned his commitment to parliamentary
procedures in the quest for progress. In *Parliament and Democracy,* from which
the passage below is taken, he asks: Can a parliament succeed in making the will
of those who elected it truly effective? How? It can succeed, he answers, but only
if the larger democratic community is constituted by a host of smaller
communities themselves fully democratic; the active role of the citizen, the
involvement of individual persons, must be cultivated first of all at the *local* level.
A genuine democracy must be participatory through and through.

[THE PARLIAMENTARY IDEA]*

It is true that a body representing the citizenship of the whole nation must be concerned with so many things that it can respond but slowly to the affairs, even when
pressing, of the industrial community, and it must in ordinary times be somewhat
remote from the day to day interests of the man in the street. It is charged with so
much that it can do nothing swiftly and well. Its business must therefore tend to
lose interest; it must ever be liable to be controlled by manipulators fighting sham
battles and to develop rules of discussion which mean that contests in it are conducted not upon affairs of real importance but of partisanship and of party management; its elections must tend to deteriorate until they become appeals to a
crowd that is but little interested or instructed in the real issues; it must always be
watched and threatened by outside movements arising out of its neglect or its
faults. The complexity of Parliamentary work is a menace to democracy as a system, and to Parliament as an institution. Hence arises the attack upon democracy
and Parliament which has become prevalent to-day. I have indicated how industrial administration can be carried on in accordance with the principles of an
organic Socialism, and how industrial self-administration can be secured without
a dissolution of the organic unity of political society through its institutions. I
retain the Parliamentary idea and the Parliamentary institution, and I have now to
consider how it can be protected against the deterioration to which I have referred
and which I have admitted. The question we have to answer to-day is no less than
this: Is democracy played out?

The satisfactory working of Parliament undoubtedly presupposes a keen political intelligence on the part of such a large number of electors as to influence the
conduct of elections and the work of the Parliamentary sections. At bottom, the
view of those who would supplant civic institutions by industrial ones is that the

*From *Parliament and Democracy,* National Labour Press, Ltd., Manchester, 1920.

civic unity is so many-sided that it cannot be represented and that intelligence cannot become good enough to make political democracy in its fullest meaning successful.

But how are we to meet the admitted fact that the complexity of Parliamentary representation makes not only Parliament itself ineffective but democracy a mere tool of a capitalist dictatorship or a mere plaything in the hands of demagogues and party managers? What we hear is that the ordinary elector cannot protect himself against his political enemies, and that, strive as we may, he is taken in in the end. Up to now that is true, but the argument amounts to no more than this: that democrats are not yet intelligent enough to run a democracy. Let us note the force of this. If the lack of intelligence will not allow the existence of self-government, but turns it into a capitalist dictatorship, what hope is there for any form of free government? All our ideals are wrong; all our aims are false. Obedience and authority become the inevitable condition of government. Socialists must reject such a conclusion *sans phrase.* They must proceed to deal with intelligence. They can have no art or part with those who, whether inspired by reaction or revolution, regard democracy with the Olympian airs of the superior being or the *blasé* yawn of the disillusioned one. This anti-democratic pose, whatever its motive, belongs to reaction, not to progress. The "Dictatorship of the Proletariat" as used in Russia, though not as used by Marx, is far more akin to the spirit of old-fashioned English Toryism with the House of Lords as its citadel than it is to popular government.

The Socialist State can have no foundation but intelligence, which is the only reliable power in society. The biologist may explain how and why the crowd is moved by instinct: our problem is to strengthen intelligence in that crowd and weaken the conditions and diminish the opportunities which make instinctive feelings arbitrary motives. The analytical critic may expose the self-regarding motives of groups and functions and compel us to face the fact that group and class interests war against each other and the community: our problem is to create by strenuous propaganda the higher and truer conception of a social unity which in a well-ordered society would embrace in harmonious working all those rivalries, and to devise our programmes with that unity in view. The society we would create is not a patchwork of the existing one, but one which corresponds to ideal conceptions.

We must extend the activities of discussion; we must raise discussion from being the engagement of armies to being the exploration of truth seekers. . . . The key-word is self-teaching—self-teaching by contact, not by textbooks—the development of the adult mind, not in relation to some world outside itself, but in relation to its own world. A robust mental independence, a capacity to reflect from the standpoint of one's own fireside and experience, a power to respect one's people, one's self, and one's own life—that is education. Intelligence is the only dictator who can justify himself—a robust intelligence. . . . This cannot be emphasised too much, for to create intelligence is the necessary preparation for Socialist success.

Given, then, the intelligent citizen, how is his political State to be organised so as to keep him in touch with it and draw from him intelligent judgments upon it?

Can we remedy it, so that Parliament ceases to be vague, ceases to be the sport of demagogues, ceases to be the creation of a non-political crowd? It is largely a problem in contact. At what points does the individual life come into contact with the organisations of his complex communal life? I have dealt with the industrial side. What of the political side? Through the workshop, through the district, through the shop committee, the trade branch, the guild, the workman gets his contact with the national economic bodies. Through what has he to reestablish his broken contact with Parliament?

The individual's first and most intimate contact is with his family. Hence, I believe that everything which takes from the family its essential responsibilities has an evil effect both upon the individual and the community. Let us establish families on an independent economic and moral foundation, let the father and mother be the heads of the little State of the home, with an income equal to its needs, with a life in accordance with its nature, with an experience which roots for ever the minds of its people in reality and companionship and the co-operation of duty, and we shall have laid the foundations of a great State, because we have enabled the individual to find himself. . . .

The next system of contact which an individual makes is his town or village, and the problem of the Socialist is to make this again a real civic unity, to make its government something important, something in which the individual feels concern. This means, on the mechanical side, that the powers of local self-government must be greatly enhanced. Far greater freedom must be given to local authorities; the red tape which binds them to a Whitehall bureaucracy must be cut. Local governing bodies should be given liberty to develop themselves, and powers now granted them by legislation, or which they can exercise only with Whitehall sanction, must be given to them absolutely. The provision of education, within certain national limits prescribed by Parliament, should be their responsibility, and no uniform system should be imposed; control of such interests as land and housing should be in their hands, and they should have power to supply collectively what they desire. A judiciary power should also be restored to these unities, so that their completeness may be easily felt and their responsibilities may commend them to the regard of their people. In a sentence, they should organise their local life in accordance with the intelligence of the local unity, and no obstacle should be put in their way.

Thus the sense and the responsibility of citizenship on a scale which the citizen can comprehend will be developed. He will understand what it is to belong to a community, and if education enables him to grasp that community in its historical sense, if his neighbourhood appeals to him as being rich in tradition and in men, he will understand the secret of living in community and of devoting himself to his community. The local government unit must be a real and a big thing, something in which the citizen can take an interest and a pride. The first organised unit of government with which the citizen comes in contact should fulfil two conditions: it should be so important as to be held in esteem, and it should be so close up to him that he can grasp its work with his mind.

The community idea must be the dominant note; the thought must be the co-operation of citizens, not of workmen nor of consumers. And I would put in a plea that in local government areas historical tradition may not be wholly sacrificed to economic convenience. Tradition is the only inheritance which men need care about. It alone links up the generations so that no good thing ceases to live.

The merely bureaucratic and materialist Socialist of the Fabian and Economic schools accepts the hard, grey, mechanical world, impoverished by capitalism, and would organise it. He would take the industrial unit of the workshop as the primary unit of his State. But . . . [the] world we desire is not achieved by the removal of differences and the creation of featureless things, either as men or communities. Families with individuality, villages and towns with individuality, counties with individuality, nations with individuality—from these comes the grand humanity. We detest Capitalism because it has brought all life and all communities down to machine levels, to standard sizes, to featureless averages. Its conception of union is sameness; its conception of efficiency is averages. It cannot afford to nurture traditions; when it preserves tradition, it vulgarises it for its own personal adornment. The Socialist must move on totally different lines. By enlivening democracy and enriching it right through in widening group after widening group, he invigorates the life of the widest of all the groups—the nation and humanity. Upon this plan we can give Parliament a definiteness and a meaning; we can make it a democratic reality; we can invigorate democratic intelligence and interest until the national representative body is chosen by reflecting citizens, is composed of men with a genius and a character fitting to their work, and is really a mirror of the national will.

The Socialist political State, sub-divided into a gradation of organisations determined by the various historical contacts which the individual makes in expanding his self from his fireside over the whole world until he finds himself at rest in the all-comprehending unity of humanity, is a State of vigilant and intelligent democracy, a State every grade of which will be guided by the opinion, the criticism and the ideals of citizens conscious of their responsibility to play a part in the life of the whole.

Such is the idea which the Socialist should place in rivalry to the pluralists in sovereignty and materialists in administration who would construct the organisation of society from industrial functions. The region is a unity of life, the workshop is only a unity of economic function. Representation must overcome the difficulties of complex interests, but the way to do that is not to simplify the complexities until they cease to be real, but to simplify them into their containing unities, taking care all the time that the simplified unity is still social and not merely a functional part of the social unity. The citizen finds it difficult to express himself in terms of his full citizenship, but the problem must not be given up: it can be solved by allowing him to function effectively in natural groups of ever-widening complexity. We must cling to citizenship in these days of revolutionary turmoil and of materialist aims as an outcast on a stormy sea clings to the spar upon which his chances of life depend. The subdivisions of the State must, each in itself, contain in embryo the State in full, and the mind that is working in it must be the same mind throughout. Voluntary association and industrial combination ought to fructify in the life of the community, but can claim no authority in the State except through the organisation of citizens.

77
John C. Calhoun

John C. Calhoun (1782–1850) resigned as Vice President of the United States to become Senator from the State of South Carolina. As a defender of slavery and advocate of the beleaguered Southern cause in the years before the Civil War, he concluded that for a democracy to maintain its equilibrium, it must deliberately incorporate devices that give minorities reliable protection against the inevitable tendency of the numerical majority to oppress. Members of every minority—ethnic or ideological or economic—are likely to share his concern. The structural safeguard he thought required to give this protection was what he called (in *A Disquisition on Government*) the rule of the "concurrent majority"—the power of a minority to veto adverse legislation, to block action and by so doing to force compromise. Governments that are genuinely *constitutional,* Calhoun argued, rest fundamentally upon compromise; absolute governments (whether ruled by one person or by a numerical majority) rely ultimately upon the threat or the use of force. No national democracy can last, Calhoun believed, unless its structure encouraged and rewarded all parties when they exhibit the "disposition to harmonize." If there are issues—like slavery—upon which no compromise is acceptable, the community will shatter, perhaps in war. Calhoun's theory of the concurrent majority, some contend, is realized indirectly through devices by which powers are distributed within the legislature to the advocates of minority interests.

[MAN AND GOVERNMENT]*

. . . What is that constitution or law of our nature, without which government would not exist, and with which its existence is necessary?

In considering this, I assume, as an incontestable fact, that man is so constituted as to be a social being. His inclinations and wants, physical and moral, irresistibly impel him to associate with his kind; and he has, accordingly, never been found, in any age or country, in any state other than the social. In no other, indeed, could he exist; and in no other—were it possible for him to exist—could he attain to a full development of his moral and intellectual faculties, or raise himself, in the scale of being, much above the level of the brute creation.

I next assume also, as a fact not less incontestable, that, while man is so constituted as to make the social state necessary to his existence and the full development of his faculties, this state itself cannot exist without government. The assumption rests on universal experience. In no age or country has any society or community ever been found, whether enlightened or savage, without government of some description.

*From J. C. Calhoun, *A Disquisition on Government.* These passages are from the text of the first edition of the *Disquisition,* published under the direction of the General Assembly of the State of South Carolina, Columbia, SC, 1851.

Having assumed these as unquestionable phenomena of our nature, I shall, without further remark, proceed to the investigation of the primary and important question, What is that constitution of our nature which, while it impels man to associate with his kind, renders it impossible for society to exist without government?

The answer will be found in the fact (not less incontestable than either of the others) that, while man is created for the social state, and is accordingly so formed as to feel what affects others as well as what affects himself, he is, at the same time, so constituted as to feel more intensely what affects him directly, than what affects him indirectly through others; or, to express it differently, he is so constituted that his direct or individual affections are stronger than his sympathetic or social feelings.

.   .   .

But that constitution of our nature which makes us feel more intensely what affects us directly than what affects us indirectly through others necessarily leads to conflict between individuals. Each, in consequence, has a greater regard for his own safety or happiness, than for the safety or happiness of others; and, where these come in opposition, is ready to sacrifice the interests of others to his own. And hence the tendency to a universal state of conflict between individual and individual, accompanied by the connected passions of suspicion, jealousy, anger, and revenge—followed by insolence, fraud, and cruelty—and, if not prevented by some controlling power, ending in a state of universal discord and confusion, destructive of the social state and the ends for which it is ordained. This controlling power, wherever vested or by whomsoever exercised, is *Government.*

It follows, then, that man is so constituted that government is necessary to the existence of society, and society to his existence and the perfection of his faculties. It follows, also, that government has its origin in this twofold constitution of his nature; the sympathetic or social feelings constituting the remote, and the individual or direct the proximate, cause.

If man had been differently constituted in either particular—if, instead of being social in his nature, he had been created without sympathy for his kind, and independent of others for his safety and existence; or if, on the other hand, he had been so created as to feel more intensely what affected others than what affected himself (if that were possible), or even had this supposed interest been equal—it is manifest that, in either case, there would have been no necessity for government, and that none would ever have existed. But although society and government are thus intimately connected with and dependent on each other—of the two, society is the greater. It is the first in the order of things, and in the dignity of its object; that of society being primary—to preserve and perfect our race—and that of government secondary and subordinate—to preserve and perfect society. Both are, however, necessary to the existence and well-being of our race, and equally of divine ordination. . . .

[GOVERNMENT AND CONSTITUTION]

But government, although intended to protect and preserve society, has itself a strong tendency to disorder and abuse of its powers, as all experience and almost every page of history testify. The cause is to be found in the same constitution of our nature which makes government indispensable. The powers which it is necessary for government to possess, in order to repress violence and preserve order, cannot execute themselves. They must be administered by men in whom, like others, the individual are stronger than the social feelings. And hence the powers vested in them to prevent injustice and oppression on the part of others will, if left unguarded, be by them converted into instruments to oppress the rest of the community. That by which this is prevented, by whatever name called, is what is meant by *constitution,* in its most comprehensive sense, when applied to *government.*

Having its origin in the same principle of our nature, *constitution* stands to *government,* as *government* stands to *society;* and, as the end for which society is ordained, would be defeated without government, so that for which government is ordained would, in a great measure, be defeated without constitution. But they differ in this striking particular. There is no difficulty in forming government. It is not even a matter of choice, whether there shall be one or not. Like breathing, it is not permitted to depend on our volition. Necessity will force it on all communities in some one form or another. Very different is the case as to constitution. Instead of a matter of necessity, it is one of the most difficult tasks imposed on man to form a constitution worthy of the name; while, to form a perfect one—one that would completely counteract the tendency of government to oppression and abuse, and hold it strictly to the great ends for which it is ordained—has thus far exceeded human wisdom, and possibly ever will. From this, another striking difference results. Constitution is the contrivance of man, while government is of divine ordination. Man is left to perfect what the wisdom of the Infinite ordained as necessary to preserve the race.

With these remarks I proceed to the consideration of the important and difficult question: How is this tendency of government to be counteracted? Or, to express it more fully, How can those who are invested with the powers of government be prevented from employing them as the means of aggrandizing themselves instead of using them to protect and preserve society? It cannot be done by instituting a higher power to control the government and those who administer it. This would be but to change the seat of authority, and to make this higher power, in reality, the government, with the same tendency, on the part of those who might control its powers, to pervert them into instruments of aggrandizement. Nor can it be done by limiting the powers of government, so as to make it too feeble to be made an instrument of abuse; for, passing by the difficulty of so limiting its powers without creating a power higher than the government itself to enforce the observance of the limitations, it is a sufficient objection that it would, if practicable, defeat the end for which government is ordained, by making it too feeble to protect and preserve society. The powers necessary for this purpose will ever prove sufficient to aggrandize those who control it, at the expense of the rest of the community. . . . .

In answering the important question under consideration, it is not necessary to enter into an examination of the various contrivances adopted by these celebrated governments to counteract this tendency to disorder and abuse, nor to undertake to treat of constitution in its most comprehensive sense. What I propose is far more limited: to explain on what principles government must be formed, in order to resist, by its own interior structure—or, to use a single term, *organism*—the tendency to abuse of power. This structure, or organism, is what is meant by constitution, in its strict and more usual sense; and it is this which distinguishes what are called "constitutional" governments from "absolute." It is in this strict and more usual sense that I propose to use the term hereafter.

How government, then, must be constructed, in order to counteract, through its organism, this tendency on the part of those who make and execute the laws to oppress those subject to their operation, is the next question which claims attention.

There is but one way in which this can possibly be done; and that is, by such an organism as will furnish the ruled with the means of resisting successfully this tendency on the part of the rulers to oppression and abuse. Power can only be resisted by power—and tendency by tendency. Those who exercise power and those subject to its exercise—the rulers and the ruled—stand in antagonistic relations to each other. The same constitution of our nature which leads rulers to oppress the ruled—regardless of the object for which government is ordained—will, with equal strength, lead the ruled to resist, when possessed of the means of making peaceable and effective resistance. Such an organism, then, as will furnish the means by which resistance may be systematically and peaceably made on the part of the ruled, to oppression and abuse of power on the part of the rulers, is the first and indispensable step toward *forming* a constitutional government. And as this can only be effected by or through the right of suffrage—the right on the part of the ruled to choose their rulers at proper intervals, and to hold them thereby responsible for their conduct—the responsibility of the rulers to the ruled, through the right of suffrage, is the indispensable and primary principle in the *foundation* of a constitutional government. When this right is properly guarded, and the people sufficiently enlightened to understand their own rights and the interests of the community, and duly to appreciate the motives and conduct of those appointed to make and execute the laws, it is all-sufficient to give to those who elect effective control over those they have elected.

I call the right of suffrage the indispensable and primary principle; for it would be a great and dangerous mistake to suppose, as many do, that it is, of itself, sufficient to form constitutional governments. To this erroneous opinion may be traced one of the causes why so few attempts to form constitutional governments have succeeded, and why, of the few which have, so small a number have had durable existence. It has led, not only to mistakes in the attempts to form such governments, but to their overthrow when they have, by some good fortune, been correctly formed. So far from being, of itself, sufficient—however well guarded it might be, and however enlightened the people—it would, unaided by other provisions, leave the government as absolute as it would be in the hands of irresponsible rulers; and with a tendency, at least as strong, toward oppression and abuse of its powers, as I shall next proceed to explain.

The right of suffrage, of itself, can do no more than give complete control to those who elect, over the conduct of those they have elected. In doing this, it accomplishes all it possibly can accomplish. This is its aim—and when this is attained, its end is fulfilled. It can do no more, however enlightened the people, or however extended or well guarded the right may be. The sum total, then, of its effects, when most successful, is to make those elected the true and faithful representatives of those who elected them—instead of irresponsible rulers, as they would be without it; and thus, by converting it into an agency, and the rulers into agents, to divest government of all claims to sovereignty, and to retain it unimpaired to the community. But it is manifest that the right of suffrage, in making these changes transfers, in reality, the actual control over the government, from those who make and execute the laws, to the body of the community, and thereby places the powers of the government as fully in the mass of the community as they would be if they, in fact, had assembled, made, and executed the laws themselves, without the intervention of representatives or agents. The more perfectly it does this, the more perfectly it accomplishes its ends; but in doing so, it only changes the seat of authority, without counteracting, in the least, the tendency of the government to oppression and abuse of its powers.

If the whole community had the same interests, so that the interests of each and every portion would be so affected by the action of the government that the laws which oppressed or impoverished one portion would necessarily oppress and impoverish all others—or the reverse—then the right of suffrage, of itself, would be all-sufficient to counteract the tendency of the government to oppression and abuse of its powers, and, of course, would form, of itself, a perfect constitutional government. The interest of all being the same, by supposition, as far as the action of the government was concerned, all would have like interests as to what laws should be made, and how they should be executed. All strife and struggle would cease as to who should be elected to make and execute them. The only question would be, who was most fit, who the wisest and most capable of understanding the common interest of the whole. This decided, the election would pass off quietly, and without party discord, as no one portion could advance its own peculiar interest without regard to the rest by electing a favorite candidate.

But such is not the case. On the contrary, nothing is more difficult than to equalize the action of the government, in reference to the various and diversified interests of the community; and nothing more easy than to pervert its powers into instruments to aggrandize and enrich one or more interests by oppressing and impoverishing the others; and this too, under the operation of laws couched in general terms—and which, on their face, appear fair and equal. Nor is this the case in some particular communities only. It is so in all—the small and the great, the poor and the rich—irrespective of pursuits, productions, or degrees of civilization; with, however, this difference, that the more extensive and populous the country, the more diversified the condition and pursuits of its population, and the richer, more luxurious, and dissimilar the people, the more difficult is it to equalize the action of the government, and the more easy for one portion of the community to pervert its powers to oppress and plunder the other.

Such being the case, it necessarily results that the right of suffrage, by placing the control of the government in the community, must, from the same constitution of our nature which makes government necessary to preserve society, lead to conflict among its different interests—each striving to obtain possession of its powers, as the means of protecting itself against the others, or of advancing its respective interests regardless of the interests of others. For this purpose, a struggle will take place between the various interests to obtain a majority in order to control the government. If no one interest be strong enough, of itself, to obtain it, a combination will be formed between those whose interests are most alike—each conceding something to the others until a sufficient number is obtained to make a majority. The process may be slow, and much time may be required before a compact, organized majority can be thus formed, but formed it will be in time, even without pre-concert or design, by the sure workings of that principle or constitution of our nature in which government itself originates. When once formed, the community will be divided into two great parties—a major and minor—between which there will be incessant struggles on the one side to retain, and on the other to obtain the majority, and, thereby, the control of the government and the advantages it confers.

So deeply seated, indeed, is this tendency to conflict between the different interests or portions of the community, that it would result from the action of the government itself, even though it were possible to find a community where the people were all of the same pursuits, placed in the same condition of life, and in every respect so situated, as to be without inequality of condition or diversity of interests. The advantages of possessing the control of the powers of the government, and, thereby, of its honors and emoluments, are, of themselves, exclusive of all other considerations, ample to divide even such a community into two great hostile parties.

In order to form a just estimate of the full force of these advantages, without reference to any other consideration, it must be remembered that government—to fulfill the ends for which it is ordained, and more especially that of protection against external dangers—must, in the present condition of the world, be clothed with powers sufficient to call forth the resources of the community, and be prepared, at all times, to command them promptly in every emergency which may possibly arise. For this purpose large establishments are necessary, both civil and military (including naval, where, from situation, that description of force may be required), with all the means necessary for prompt and effective action, such as fortifications, fleets, armories, arsenals, magazines, arms of all descriptions, with well-trained forces, in sufficient numbers to wield them with skill and energy, whenever the occasion requires it. The administration and management of a government with such vast establishments must necessarily require a host of employees, agents, and officers—of whom many must be vested with high and responsible trusts, and occupy exalted stations accompanied with much influence and patronage. To meet the necessary expenses, large sums must be collected and disbursed; and, for this purpose, heavy taxes must be imposed, requiring a multitude of officers for their collection and disbursement. The whole united must necessarily place under the control of government an amount of honors and emoluments sufficient to excite profoundly the ambition of the aspiring and the cupidity of the avaricious, and to lead to the formation of hostile parties, and violent party conflicts and struggles to obtain the control of the government. And what makes this evil remediless through the right of suffrage of itself, however modified or carefully guarded or however enlightened the people, is the fact that, as far as the honors and emoluments of the government and its fiscal action are concerned, it is impossible to equalize it. The reason is obvious. Its honors and emoluments, however great, can fall to the lot of but a few, compared to the entire number of the community and the multitude who will seek to participate in them. . . .

That it [the power of government] *will* be so used, unless prevented, is, from the constitution of man, just as certain as that it *can* be so used; and that, if not prevented, it must give rise to two parties, and to violent conflicts and struggles between them, to obtain the control of the government, is, for the same reason, not less certain.

Nor is it less certain, from the operation of all these causes, that the dominant majority, for the time, would have the same tendency to oppression and abuse of power which, without the right of suffrage, irresponsible rulers would have. No reason, indeed, can be assigned, why the latter would abuse their power, which would not apply, with equal force, to the former. The dominant majority, for the time, would, in reality, through the right of suffrage, be the rulers—the controlling, governing, and irresponsible power; and those who make and execute the laws would, for the time, be, in reality but *their* representatives and agents.

Nor would the fact that the former would constitute a majority of the community, counteract a tendency originating in the constitution of man, and which, as such, cannot depend on the number by whom the powers of the government may be wielded. Be it greater or smaller, a majority or minority, it must equally partake of an attribute inherent in each individual composing it; and, as in each the individual is stronger than the social feelings, the one would have the same tendency as the other to oppression and abuse of power. The reason applies to government in all its forms—whether it be that of the one, the few, or the many. In each there must, of necessity, be a governing and a governed—a ruling and a subject portion. The one implies the other; and in all, the two bear the same relation to each other—and have, on the part of the governing portion, the same tendency to oppression and abuse of power. Where the majority is that portion, it matters not how its powers may be exercised—whether directly by themselves, or indirectly, through representatives or agents. Be it which it may, the minority, for the time, will be as much the governed or subject portion, as are the people in an aristocracy, or the subjects in a monarchy. The only difference in this respect is, that in the government of a majority the minority may become the majority, and the majority the minority, through the right of suffrage, and thereby change their relative positions without the intervention of force and revolution. But the duration, or uncertainty of the tenure, by which power is held, cannot, of itself, counteract the tendency inherent in government to oppression and abuse of power. On the contrary, the very uncertainty of the tenure, combined with the violent party warfare which must ever precede a change of parties under such governments, would rather tend to increase than diminish the tendency to oppression.

[THE CONCURRENT MAJORITY]

As, then, the right of suffrage, without some other provision, cannot counteract this tendency of government, the next question for consideration is, What is that other provision? This demands the most serious consideration; for of all the questions embraced in the science of government, it involves a principle, the most important, and the least understood, and when understood, the most difficult of application in practice. It is, indeed, emphatically, that principle which *makes* the constitution, in its strict and limited sense.

From what has been said, it is manifest, that this provision must be of a character calculated to prevent any one interest, or combination of interests, from using the powers of government to aggrandize itself at the expense of the others. Here lies the evil: and just in proportion as it shall prevent, or fail to prevent it, in the same degree it will effect, or fail to effect, the end intended to be accomplished. There is but one certain mode in which this result can be secured; and that is, by the adoption of some restriction or limitation which shall so effectually prevent any one interest, or combination of interests, from obtaining the exclusive control of the government, as to render hopeless all attempts directed to that end. There is, again, but one mode in which this can be effected; and that is, by taking the sense of each interest or portion of the community, which may be unequally and injuriously affected by the action of the government, separately, through its own majority, or in some other way by which its voice may be fairly expressed, and to require the consent of each interest, either to put or to keep the government in action. This, too, can be accomplished only in one way, and that is, by such an organism of the government—and, if necessary for the purpose, of the community also—as will, by dividing and distributing the powers of government, give to each division or interest, through its appropriate organ, either a concurrent voice in making and executing the laws, or a veto on their execution. It is only by such an organism that the assent of each can be made necessary to put the government in motion, or the power made effectual to arrest its action when put in motion; and it is only by the one or the other that the different interests, orders, classes, or portions into which the community may be divided can be protected, and all conflict and struggle between them prevented—by rendering it impossible to put or to keep it in action, without the concurrent consent of all.

Such an organism as this, combined with the right of suffrage, constitutes, in fact, the elements of constitutional government. The one, by rendering those who make and execute the laws responsible to those on whom they operate, prevents the rulers from oppressing the ruled; and the other, by making it impossible for any one interest or combination of interests, or class, or order, or portion of the community, to obtain exclusive control, prevents any one of them from oppressing the other. It is clear, that oppression and abuse of power must come, if at all, from the one or the other quarter. From no other can they come. It follows, that the two, suffrage and proper organism combined, are sufficient to counteract the tendency of government to oppression and abuse of power, and to restrict it to the fulfillment of the great ends for which it is ordained.

In coming to this conclusion, I have assumed the organism to be perfect, and the different interests, portions, or classes of the community, to be sufficiently enlightened to understand its character and object, and to exercise, with due intelligence, the right of suffrage. To the extent that either may be defective, to the same extent the government would fall short of fulfilling its end. But this does not impeach the truth of the principles on which it rests. In reducing them to proper form, in applying them to practical uses, all elementary principles are liable to difficulties; but they are not, on this account, the less true or valuable. Where the organism is perfect, every interest will be truly and fully represented, and of course the whole community must be so. It may be difficult, or even impossible, to make a perfect organism—but, although this be true, yet even when, instead of the sense of each and of all, it takes that of a few great and prominent interests only, it would still, in a great measure, if not altogether, fulfill the end intended by a constitution. For, in such case, it would require so large a portion of the community, compared with the whole, to concur, or acquiesce in the action of the government, that the number to be plundered would be too few, and the number to be aggrandized too many, to afford adequate motives to oppression and the abuse of its powers. Indeed, however imperfect the organism, it must have more or less effect in diminishing such tendency.

It may be readily inferred, from what has been stated, that the effect of organism is neither to supersede nor diminish the importance of the right of suffrage, but to aid and perfect it. The object of the latter is, to collect the sense of the community. The more fully and perfectly it accomplishes this, the more fully and perfectly it fulfills its end. But the most it can do, of itself, is to collect the sense of the greater number; that is, of the stronger interests or combination of interests, and to assume this to be the sense of the community. It is only when aided by a proper organism that it can collect the sense of the entire community, of each and all its interests: of each, through its appropriate organ, and of the whole, through all of them united. This would truly be the sense of the entire community; for whatever diversity each interest might have within itself—as all would have the same interest in reference to the action of the government—the individuals composing each would be fully and truly represented by its own majority or appropriate organ, regarded in reference to the other interests. In brief, every individual of every interest might trust, with confidence, its majority or appropriate organ, against that of every other interest.

[NUMERICAL AND CONCURRENT MAJORITIES DISTINGUISHED]

It results, from what has been said, that there are two different modes in which the sense of the community may be taken: one, simply by the right of suffrage, unaided; the other, by the right through a proper organism. Each collects the sense of the majority. But one regards numbers only, and considers the whole community as a unit, having but one common interest throughout, and collects the sense of the greater number of the whole, as that of the community. The other, on the contrary, regards interests as well as numbers—considering the community as made up of different and conflicting interests, as far as the action of the government is concerned—and takes the sense of each, through its majority or appropriate organ, and the united sense of all, as the sense of the entire community. The former of these I shall call the numerical, or absolute majority; and the latter, the concurrent, or constitutional majority. I call it the constitutional majority because it is an essential element in every constitutional government, be its form what it may. So great is the difference, politically speaking, between the two majorities, that they cannot be confounded without leading to great and fatal errors; and yet the distinction between them has been so entirely overlooked, that when the term "majority" is used in political discussions, it is applied exclusively to designate the numerical—as if there were no other. Until this distinction is recognized, and better understood, there will continue to be great liability to error in properly constructing constitutional governments, especially of the popular form, and of preserving them when properly constructed. . . .

The first and leading error which naturally arises from overlooking the distinction referred to is to confound the numerical majority with the people, and this so completely as to regard them as identical. . . .

This radical error . . . has contributed more than any other cause to prevent the formation of popular constitutional governments, and to destroy them even when they have been formed. It leads to the conclusion that, in their formation and establishment, nothing more is necessary than the right of suffrage, and the allotment to each division of the community a representation in the government in proportion to numbers. If the numerical majority were really the people, and if to take its sense truly were to take the sense of the people truly, a government so constituted would be a true and perfect model of a popular constitutional government; and every departure from it would detract from its excellence. But, as such is not the case, as the numerical majority, instead of being the people, is only a portion of them, such a government, instead of being a true and perfect model of the people's government, that is, a people self-governed, is but the government of a part over a part—the major over the minor portion.

But this misconception of the true elements of constitutional government does not stop here. It leads to others equally false and fatal, in reference to the best means of preserving and perpetuating them, when, from some fortunate combination of circumstances, they are correctly formed. For they who fall into these errors regard the restrictions which organism imposes on the will of the numerical majority as restrictions on the will of the people, and, therefore, as not only useless, but wrongful and mischievous. And hence they endeavor to destroy organism, under the delusive hope of making government more democratic.

Such are some of the consequences of confounding the two, and of regarding the numerical as the only majority. And in this may be found the reason why so few popular governments have been properly constructed, and why, of these few, so small a number have proved durable. Such must continue to be the result, as long as these errors continue to be prevalent. . . .

[THE CONCURRENT MAJORITY AND CONSTITUTIONAL GOVERNMENT]

I shall next proceed to explain, more fully, why the concurrent majority is an indispensable element in forming constitutional governments, and why the numerical majority, of itself, must, in all cases, make governments absolute.

The necessary consequence of taking the sense of the community by the concurrent majority is, as has been explained, to give to each interest or the portion of the community a negative on the others. It is this mutual negative among its various conflicting interests, which invests each with the power of protecting itself, and places the rights and safety of each where only they can be securely placed, under its own guardianship. Without this there can be no systematic, peaceful, or effective resistance to the natural tendency of each to come into conflict with the others; and without this there can be no constitution. It is this negative power—the power of preventing or arresting the action of the government, be it called by what term it may, veto, interposition, nullification, check, or balance of power—which, in fact, forms the constitution. They are all but different names for the negative power. In all its forms, and under all its names, it results from the concurrent majority. Without this there can be no negative; and without a negative, no constitution. The assertion is true in reference to all constitutional governments, be their forms what they may. It is, indeed, the negative power which makes the constitution, and the positive which makes the government. The one is the power of acting; and the other the power of preventing or arresting action. The two, combined, make constitutional governments.

But as there can be no constitution without the negative power, and no negative power without the concurrent majority, it follows, necessarily, that where the numerical majority has the sole control of the government, there can be no constitution, as constitution implies limitation or restriction—and, of course, is inconsistent with the idea of sole or exclusive power. And hence, the numerical, unmixed with the concurrent, majority necessarily forms, in all cases, absolute government.

It is, indeed, the single or *one power* which excludes the negative, and constitutes absolute government, and not the *number* in whom the power is vested. The numerical majority is as truly a *single power*—and excludes the negative as completely as the absolute government of one, or of the few. The former is as much the absolute government of the democratic, or popular form, as the latter of the monarchical or aristocratical. It has, accordingly, in common with them, the same tendency to oppression and abuse of power.

Constitutional governments, of whatever form, are, indeed, much more similar to each other, in their structure and character, than they are, respectively, to the absolute governments, even of their own class. All constitutional governments, of whatever class they may be, take the sense of the community by its parts—each through its appropriate organ—and regard the sense of all its parts as the sense of the whole. They all rest on the right of suffrage and the responsibility of rulers, directly or indirectly. On the contrary, all absolute governments, of whatever form, concentrate power in one uncontrolled and irresponsible individual or body, whose will is regarded as the sense of the community. And hence the great and broad distinction between governments is not that of the one, the few, or the many, but of the constitutional and the absolute.

From this there results another distinction which, although secondary in its character, very strongly marks the difference between these forms of government. I refer to their respective conservative principle—that is, the principle by which they are upheld and preserved. This principle in constitutional governments is *compromise;* and in absolute governments is *force,* as will be next explained.

It has been already shown, that the same constitution of man which leads those who govern to oppress the governed, if not prevented, will, with equal force and certainty, lead the latter to resist oppression when possessed of the means of doing so peaceably and successfully. But absolute governments, of all forms, exclude all other means of resistance to their authority, than that of force, and, of course, leave no other alternative to the governed but to acquiesce in oppression, however great it may be, or to resort to force to put down the government. But the dread of such a resort must necessarily lead the government to prepare to meet force in order to protect itself, and hence, of necessity, force becomes the conservative principle of all such governments.

On the contrary, the government of the concurrent majority, where the organism is perfect, excludes the possibility of oppression, by giving to each interest, or portion, or order—where there are established classes—the means of protecting itself, by its negative, against all measures calculated to advance the peculiar interests of others at its expense. Its effect, then, is to cause the different interests, portions, or orders, as the case may be, to desist from attempting to adopt any measure calculated to promote the prosperity of one, or more, by sacrificing that of others; and thus to force them to unite in such measures only as would promote the prosperity of all, as the only means to prevent the suspension of the action of the government, and, thereby, to avoid anarchy, the greatest of all evils. It is by means of such authorized and effectual resistance that oppression is prevented, and the necessity of resorting to force superseded, in governments of the concurrent majority; and hence compromise, instead of force, becomes their conservative principle.

It would, perhaps, be more strictly correct to trace the conservative principle of constitutional governments to the necessity which compels the different interests, or portions, or orders to compromise—as the only way to promote their respective prosperity and to avoid anarchy—rather than to the compromise itself. No necessity can be more urgent and imperious, than that of avoiding anarchy. It is the same as that which makes government indispensable to preserve society, and is not less imperative than that which compels obedience to superior force. Traced to this source, the voice of a people—uttered under the necessity of avoiding the greatest of calamities, through the organs of a government so constructed as to suppress the expression of all partial and selfish interests, and to give a full and faithful utterance to the sense of the whole community, in reference to its common welfare—may, without impiety, be called *the voice of God.* To call any other so would be impious. . . .

[OBJECTIONS AND REPLIES]

Such are the many and striking advantages of the concurrent over the numerical majority. Against the former but two objections can be made. The one is that it is difficult of construction, which has already been sufficiently noticed; and the other that it would be impracticable to obtain the concurrence of conflicting interests, where they were numerous and diversified; or, if not, that the process for this purpose would be too tardy to meet, with sufficient promptness, the many and dangerous emergencies to which all communities are exposed. This objection is plausible, and deserves a fuller notice than it has yet received.

The diversity of opinion is usually so great, on almost all questions of policy, that it is not surprising, on a slight view of the subject, it should be thought impracticable to bring the various conflicting interests of a community to unite on any one line of policy, or that a government founded on such a principle would be too slow in its movements and too weak in its foundation to succeed in practice. But plausible as it may seem at the first glance, a more deliberate view will show that this opinion is erroneous. It is true that, when there is no urgent necessity, it is difficult to bring those who differ to agree on any one line of action. Each will naturally insist on taking the course he may think best, and, from pride of opinion, will be unwilling to yield to others. But the case is different when there is an urgent necessity to unite on some common course of action, as reason and experience both prove. When something *must* be done—and when it can be done only by the united consent of all—the necessity of the case will force to a compromise, be the case of that necessity what it may. On all questions of acting, necessity, where it exists, is the overruling motive; and where, in such cases, compromise among the parties is an indispensable condition to acting, it exerts an overruling influence in predisposing them to acquiesce in some one opinion or course of action. Experience furnishes many examples in confirmation of this important truth. Among these, the trial by jury is the most familiar, and on that account, will be selected for illustration.

In these, twelve individuals, selected without discrimination, must unanimously concur in opinion—under the obligations of an oath to find a true verdict according to law and evidence, and this, too, not unfrequently under such great difficulty and doubt that the ablest and most experienced judges and advocates differ in opinion, after careful examination. And yet, as impracticable as this mode of trial would seem to a superficial observer, it is found, in practice, not only to succeed, but to be the safest, the wisest, and the best that human ingenuity has ever devised. When closely investigated, the cause will be found in the necessity, under which the jury is placed, to agree unanimously in order to find a verdict. This necessity acts as the predisposing cause of concurrence in some common opinion, and with such efficacy, that a jury rarely fails to find a verdict.

Under its potent influence, the jurors take their seats with the disposition to give a fair and impartial hearing to the arguments on both sides—meet together in the jury-room, not as disputants, but calmly to hear the opinions of each other, and to compare and weigh the arguments on which they are founded, and finally to adopt that which, on the whole, is thought to be true. Under the influence of this *dispo-*

sition to harmonize, one after another falls into the same opinion until unanimity is obtained. Hence its practicability—and hence also its peculiar excellence. Nothing, indeed, can be more favorable to the success of truth and justice, than this predisposing influence caused by the necessity of being unanimous. It is so much so as to compensate for the defect of legal knowledge and a high degree of intelligence on the part of those who usually compose juries. If the necessity of unanimity were dispensed with, and the finding of a jury made to depend on a bare majority, jury trial, instead of being one of the greatest improvements in the judicial department of government, would be one of the greatest evils that could be inflicted on the community. It would be, in such case, the conduit through which all the factious feelings of the day would enter and contaminate justice at its source.

But the same cause would act with still greater force in predisposing the various interests of the community to agree in a well-organized government, founded on the concurrent majority. The necessity for unanimity, in order to keep the government in motion, would be far more urgent, and would act under circumstances still more favorable to secure it. It would be superfluous, after what has been stated, to add other reasons in order to show that no necessity, physical or moral, can be more imperious than that of government. It is so much so that, to suspend its action altogether, even for an inconsiderable period, would subject the community to convulsions and anarchy. But in governments of the concurrent majority such fatal consequences can only be avoided by the unanimous concurrence or acquiescence of the various portions of the community. Such is the imperious character of the necessity which impels to compromise under governments of this description.

But to have a just conception of the overpowering influence it would exert, the circumstances under which it would act must be taken into consideration. These will be found, on comparison, much more favorable than those under which juries act. In the latter case there is nothing besides the necessity of unanimity in finding a verdict, and the inconvenience to which they might be subjected in the event of division, to induce juries to agree, except the love of truth and justice, which, when not counteracted by some improper motive or bias, more or less influences all, not excepting the most depraved. In the case of governments of the concurrent majority, there is, besides these, the love of country, than which, if not counteracted by the unequal and oppressive action of government, or other causes, few motives exert a greater sway. It comprehends, indeed, within itself, a large portion both of our individual and social feelings; and hence its almost boundless control when left free to act. But the government of the concurrent majority leaves it free, by preventing abuse and oppression, and, with them, the whole train of feelings and passions which lead to discord and conflict between different portions of the community. Impelled by the imperious necessity of preventing the suspension of the action of government, with the fatal consequences to which it would lead, and by the strong additional impulse derived from an ardent love of country, each portion would regard the sacrifice it might have to make by yielding its peculiar interest to secure the common interest and safety of all, including its own, as nothing compared to the evils that would be inflicted on all, including its own, by pertinaciously adhering to a different line of action. So powerful, indeed, would be the motives for concurring, and, under such circumstances, so weak would be those opposed to it, the wonder would be, not that there should, but that there should not be a compromise.

But to form a juster estimate of the full force of this impulse to compromise, there must be added that, in governments of the concurrent majority, each portion, in order to advance its own peculiar interests, would have to conciliate all others by showing a disposition to advance theirs; and, for this purpose, each would select those to represent it whose wisdom, patriotism, and weight of character would command the confidence of the others. Under its influence—and with representatives so well qualified to accomplish the object for which they were selected—the prevailing desire would be to promote the common interests of the whole; and hence the competition would be, not which should yield the least to promote the common good, but which should yield the most. It is thus that concession would cease to be considered a sacrifice—would become a free-will offering on the altar of the country and lose the name of compromise. And herein is to be found the feature which distinguishes governments of the concurrent majority so strikingly from those of the numerical. In the latter, each faction, in the struggle to obtain the control of the government, elevates to power the designing, the artful, and unscrupulous, who in their devotion to party—instead of aiming at the good of the whole—aim exclusively at securing the ascendency of party.

When traced to its source, this difference will be found to originate in the fact that in governments of the concurrent majority individual feelings are, from its organism, necessarily enlisted on the side of the social, and made to unite with them in promoting the interests of the whole, as the best way of promoting the separate interests of each; while, in those of the numerical majority, the social are necessarily enlisted on the side of the individual and made to contribute to the interest of parties, regardless of that of the whole. To effect the former—to enlist the individual on the side of the social feelings to promote the good of the whole—is the greatest possible achievement of the science of government; while to enlist the social on the side of the individual to promote the interest of parties at the expense of the good of the whole is the greatest blunder which ignorance can possibly commit.

To this, also, may be referred the greater solidity of foundation on which governments of the concurrent majority repose. Both, ultimately, rest on necessity; for force, by which those of the numerical majority are upheld, is only acquiesced in from necessity—in a necessity not more imperious, however, than that which compels the different portions, in governments of the concurrent majority, to acquiesce in compromise. There is, however, a great difference in the motive, the feeling, the aim which characterize the act in the two cases. In the one, it is done with that reluctance and hostility ever incident to enforced submission to what is regarded as injustice and oppression, accompanied by the desire and purpose to seize on the first favorable opportunity for resistance; but in the other, willingly and cheerfully, under the impulse of an exalted patriotism, impelling all to acquiesce in whatever the common good requires. . . .

78
The Supreme Court of the United States:
Baker v. Carr

The oppression of minorities by a numerical majority became manifest a century after the Civil War in the electoral system in the State of Tennessee (and other American states) in which population shifts over the years had resulted in rural districts electing the same number of representatives to the General Assembly as did urban districts having ten times as many citizens. Representatives elected under this unequal system repeatedly refused, for a period of 60 years, to reapportion seats in the Assembly—obliging underrepresented citizens to appeal to the Federal courts and ultimately to the Supreme Court of the United States. In *Baker v. Carr* (which Chief Justice Warren thought the most important case decided during his tenure on the Court) such departures from equal representation were viewed as violations of the constitutional guarantee of the equal protection of the laws.

The procedural and numerical analyses of the Court need not be detailed here; the principle that a just representative system requires the roughly equal representation of all citizens was expressed most forcefully by Justice Clark in his concurring opinion, from which the following passages (footnotes omitted) are taken.

[JUST REPRESENTATION MUST PROTECT THE EQUALITY OF CITIZENS]*

The controlling facts cannot be disputed. It appears from the record that 37% of the voters of Tennessee elect 20 of the 33 Senators while 40% of the voters elect 63 of the 99 members of the House. But this might not on its face be an "invidious discrimination," for a "statutory discrimination will not be set aside if any state of facts reasonably may be conceived to justify it."

It is true that the apportionment policy incorporated in Tennessee's Constitution, i.e., state-wide numerical equality of representation with certain minor qualifications, is a rational one. . . .

However, the root of the trouble is not in Tennessee's Constitution, for admittedly its policy has not been followed. The discrimination lies in the action of Tennessee's Assembly in allocating legislative seats to counties or districts created by it. Try as one may, Tennessee's apportionment just cannot be made to fit the pattern cut by its Constitution. This was the finding of the District Court. The policy of the Constitution referred to by the dissenters, therefore, is of no relevance here. We must examine what the Assembly has done. The frequency and magnitude of the inequalities in the present districting admit of no policy whatever. . . .

The apportionment picture in Tennessee is a topsy-turvical of gigantic proportions. This is not to say that some of the disparity cannot be explained, but when

*From *Baker v. Carr,* (Justice Clark, concurring) 369 U.S. 186 (1962).

the entire table is examined—comparing the voting strength of counties of like population as well as contrasting that of the smaller with the larger counties—it leaves but one conclusion, namely that Tennessee's apportionment is a crazy quilt without rational basis. At the risk of being accused of picking out a few of the horribles I shall allude to a series of examples. . . .

As is admitted, there is a wide disparity of voting strength between the large and small counties. Some samples are: Moore County has a total representation of two with a population (2,340) of only one-eleventh of Rutherford County (25,316) with the same representation; Decatur County (5,563) has the same representation as Carter (23,303) though the latter has four times the population; likewise, Loudon County (13,264), Houston (3,084), and Anderson County (33,990) have the same representation, i.e., 1.25 each. . . .

Likewise, counties with no municipality of over 10,000 suffer a similar discrimination:

County	Population	Representation
Grundy	6,540	0.95
Chester	6,391	2.00
Cumberland	9,593	0.63
Crockett	9,676	2.00
Loudon	13,264	1.25
Fayette	13,577	2.50

This could not be an effort to attain political balance between rural and urban populations. Since discrimination is present among counties of like population, the plan is neither consistent nor rational. It discriminates horizontally creating gross disparities between rural areas themselves as well as between urban areas themselves, still maintaining the wide vertical disparity already pointed out between rural and urban.

The truth is that—although this case has been here for two years and has had over six hours' argument (three times the ordinary case) and has been most carefully considered over and over again by us in Conference and individually—no one, not even the State nor the dissenters, has come up with any rational basis for Tennessee's apportionment statute.

No one—except the dissenters advocating the HARLAN "adjusted 'total representation'" formula—contends that mathematical equality among voters is required by the Equal Protection Clause. But certainly there must be some rational design to a State's districting. The discrimination here does not fit any pattern—as I have said, it is but a crazy quilt. . . . If present representation has a policy at all, it is to maintain the *status quo* of invidious discrimination at any cost. Like the District Court, I conclude that appellants have met the burden of showing "Tennessee is guilty of a clear violation of the state constitution and of the [federal] rights of the plaintiffs. . . ."

Although I find the Tennessee apportionment statute offends the Equal Protection Clause, I would not consider intervention by this Court into so delicate
a field if there were any other relief available to the people of Tennessee. But
the majority of the people of Tennessee have no "practical opportunities for
exerting their political weight at the polls" to correct the existing "invidious
discrimination." Tennessee has no initiative and referendum. I have searched
diligently for other "practical opportunities" present under the law. I find none
other than through the federal courts. The majority of the voters have been
caught up in a legislative strait jacket. Tennessee has an "informed, civically
militant electorate" and "an aroused popular conscience," but it does not sear
"the conscience of the people's representatives." This is because the legislative
policy has riveted the present seats in the Assembly to their respective constituencies, and by the votes of their incumbents a reapportionment of any kind
is prevented. The people have been rebuffed at the hands of the Assembly; they
have tried the constitutional convention route, but since the call must originate
in the Assembly it, too, has been fruitless. They have tried Tennessee courts
with the same result, and Governors have fought the tide only to flounder. It is
said that there is recourse in Congress and perhaps that may be, but from a
practical standpoint this is without substance. To date Congress has never
undertaken such a task in any State. We therefore must conclude that the people of Tennessee are stymied and without judicial intervention will be saddled
with the present discrimination in the affairs of their state government. . . .

As John Rutledge (later Chief Justice) said 175 years ago in the course of the
Constitutional Convention, a chief function of the Court is to secure the national
rights. Its decision today supports the proposition for which our forebears fought
and many died, namely, that to be fully conformable to the principle of right, the
form of government must be representative. That is the keystone upon which our
government was founded and lacking which no republic can survive. It is well for
this Court to practice self-restraint and discipline in constitutional adjudication,
but never in its history have those principles received sanction where the national
rights of so many have been so clearly infringed for so long a time. National
respect for the courts is more enhanced through the forthright enforcement of
those rights rather than by rendering them nugatory through the interposition of
subterfuges. In my view the ultimate decision today is in the greatest tradition
of this Court.

79
Lani Guinier

Lani Guinier (1950–) is a politically active professor of law who holds that the representative system in the American democracy must be revised, in the interest of justice, to empower the large black minority. She argues that this should be done not by giving preference to black voters, or by gerrymandering voting districts to insure black majorities, but by redesigning the system of voting in such a way that the black minority, or any other minority, may enhance its opportunity to elect representatives, and thus have its interests safeguarded within the legislature. To achieve this enhancement, she proposes a system of *proportionate interest representation* in which all voters cast multiple votes and may either spread or concentrate the support they give. A voting system of this kind, she contends, will enable minority voters to clump or cumulate their support, and that will result in minority representation that, while remaining fair to all, will yield a more just outcome than the existing single-vote system.

[THE ELUSIVE QUEST FOR EQUALITY OF PARTICIPATION]*

For African-Americans, the struggle for political empowerment has been an elusive quest for equality of political participation through more representative and more responsive government. After first fighting for the basic right to vote, the traditional voting rights advocates have turned their attention to obtaining a "meaningful" vote, defined as a vote capable of electing candidates of the black community's choice. On the assumption that racial bloc voting by a white electoral majority will invariably result in the defeat of black representatives, second-generation voting rights litigants seek to integrate the legislature primarily through the subdivision of predominantly white electorates into single-member districts. The second-generation remedial agenda is premised on the notion that black representatives, elected from majority-black subdistricts and electorally accountable only to black voters, will represent those voters' concerns from their newly established legislative seats. Once integrated, legislative bodies will deliberate more effectively and will be "legitimated" as a result of their more inclusive character.

Under this model, representation protects the right to be "present," whereas the right to control government policy is reserved to those who can organize a majority. The result is a "descriptively" integrated legislature in which white majority rule in its self-interest is legitimate so long as some black representatives are there when the majority acts.

The strategic, remedial, and jurisprudential assumptions underlying this second-generation litigation agenda fail to account for the interactive effect of prejudice

*From Lani Guinier, "No Two Seats: The Elusive Quest for Political Equality," *Virginia Law Review,* Vol. 77, No. 8, November 1991. Reprinted by permission. Footnotes, exceedingly numerous in law review articles, have been omitted.

and white majority rule on black political opportunity. Indeed, the history of minority political empowerment has been one in which each litigation victory is ultimately emptied of importance. This theme of pyrrhic victories has been termed . . . the "Law of Racial Thermodynamics." Litigation to ensure descriptive representation predictably transfers the problem of disenfranchisement from the electorate to the legislature. A discrete and insular electoral minority often remains an outvoted legislative minority. Consequently, legislative seats alone do not enfranchise.

I argue that a new conceptual approach is necessary to structure majoritarian collective decisionmaking bodies to ensure meaningful minority interest representation and participation at both the electoral and legislative stages of the political process. . . .

[WHEN IS A REPRESENTATIVE SYSTEM FAIR?]

For the sake of argument, I am prepared for the moment to assume that, under certain conditions, majority rule may be possible. I am also prepared to concede that, as normally understood, the preferences of a bare political majority often are perceived as having greater legitimacy than those of a plurality. But I would argue that majority approval is legitimate *only* if we can assume that neither the majority nor the minority has disproportionate power. To put the point differently: majority rule legitimates a voting procedure, if at all, only to the extent the procedure is fair. To be fair, a procedure must be more than just efficient. It also must comport with the stability, accountability, and reciprocity assumptions.

The claim I press here, but develop later, is that, even in the absence of direct proof of legislative racism, a system in which a permanent and homogeneous majority consistently exercises disproportionate power is neither stable, accountable, nor reciprocal. Proponents of winner-take-all majority rule claim proportionality exists, meaning that the majority is not likely to exercise 100% of the power solely in its self-interest. In my view, however, under the political equality and political empowerment norms of the Voting Rights Act, majority rule is a fair voting procedure to the extent it provides each voter an equal opportunity to influence legislative decisionmaking, or a proportional stake in the legislative outcome. If this is true, then the Voting Rights Act's political equality and empowerment norms are not achieved through the traditional second-generation remedy of creating equipopulous, winner-take-all subdistricts, no matter how much the district lines or district demographics are adjusted, because single-member districts retain majority rule principles but fail to ensure proportional legislative power.

As a remedy, subdistricting primarily attempts to equalize gross population (and therefore votes), without measuring the intensity of voter preferences. In doing so, it equalizes voting weights but not voting power. Even majority-black subdistricts, drawn to compensate for unequally weighted votes at the electoral level, still do nothing to ensure equally powerful, as opposed to equally weighted, legislative votes, for two related reasons. First, it is possible that majoritarian decisionmaking minimizes the legislative power of minorities as a result of their numerical weakness. Second, the operation of prejudice in a winner-take-all system denies blacks elected from single-member districts the ability to exercise even minimal legislative power. The winner-take-all approach may simply increase the majority's representation at the expense of the representational power of electoral minorities. Even though blacks may win a proportionate share of representation through a single-member districting strategy, the ruling coalition is still one elected by white voters. Indeed, a minority of white voters may elect a bare numerical legislative minority, yet exercise 100% of the power. For example, in a 1000 voter/10 seat jurisdiction, with 750 white and 250 black voters, blacks would be proportionately represented with two majority-black districts. Majority rule tells us, however, that the ruling coalition only needs 6 votes on the legislature to control all decisions. Six white representatives might each actually be elected by bare majorities. In such a case, 306 people (6 districts with 51% majorities) have the potential to decide all issues. Such a ruling coalition would represent neither a majority of the total voters nor even a majority of the 750 white voters.

Yet, just as it would be illegitimate for an advantaged minority to exercise majority power, it is illegitimate for an advantaged majority to exercise disproportionate power. From the excluded minority's perspective, such a system exaggerates its difficulty in winning any power and is unlikely to be stable, accountable, or reciprocal. In sum, to the extent majority rule is associated with winner-take-all voting procedures, it does not ensure minority confidence in the system's fairness.

The majoritarian paradigm, of course, already includes constraints on the tyranny of the majority through checks and balances, federalism, and judicial review to unblock the political processes and to protect fundamental rights. I argue, however, that . . . where it consistently produces disproportionate majority control, an efficient or technically fair voting process simply is illegitimate. . . .

[BLACK POLITICAL EMPOWERMENT]*

I propose to shift the analysis of black political empowerment in two ways. First, as a matter of broader democratic theory, voting rights activists and litigators should begin to worry more about the fundamental fairness of permanent majority hegemony in a political system whose legitimacy is based solely on the consent of a simple, racially homogenous majority. Consistent with fairness, equality, and legitimacy, the original civil rights vision suggests fundamentally different trade-offs between majority rule and minority rights.

Second, I propose to refocus on the problems affecting marginalized groups within the legislative decisionmaking process. This renewed focus builds on the civil rights movement's view that the values for which our society stands are defined by what we do for the dispossessed. Thus, a theory of representation that derives its authority from the original civil rights' vision must address concerns of qualitative fairness involving equal recognition and just results. For those at

---

*From Lani Guinier, "The Triumph of Tokenism," *Michigan Law Review,* Vol. 89, No. 5, March, 1991. Reprinted by permission. Footnotes omitted.

the bottom, a system that gives everyone an equal chance of having their political preferences *physically represented* is inadequate. A fair system of political representation would provide mechanisms to ensure that disadvantaged and stigmatized minority groups also have a fair chance to have their policy preferences *satisfied.* . . .

To achieve this limited but important objective, I propose the concept of "proportionate interest" representation. Proportionate interest representation is a general term subsuming a number of implementation strategies. Proportionate interest representation addresses the black electoral success model's failure to develop a realistic enforcement mechanism for achieving legislative responsiveness.

PROPORTIONATE INTEREST REPRESENTATION

Proportionate interest representation disavows the pluralist conception of fairness, which falsely assumes equal bargaining power simply based on access, or numerically proportionate electoral success for all groups. Fairness and responsiveness should be related objectives. Yet, in a racially polarized environment, some systems may be procedurally fair but fundamentally unresponsive. For example, while improving the prospects of black electoral success, black single-member districts may undermine the possibility of effecting true policy change. In a system shaped by irrational, majority prejudice, remedial mechanisms that eliminate pure majority rule and enforce principles of interest proportionality may provide better proxies for political fairness.

At this stage, I am simply assuming, without definitive explication, that qualitative fairness is incompatible with majority bias, where such bias systematically tends to produce inequalities in preference satisfaction because of prejudice. This assumption makes sense in light of our ostensible national commitment to ensuring that blacks achieve meaningful legislative representation, or "a fair chance to influence the political process." The implications of qualitative fairness as a principle of remediation, and its complementary premises and enforcement mechanisms, can best be understood by referring to a concrete example.

Suppose a jurisdiction contained two kinds of people: the yellow and the blue. The yellow people constituted 75% of the population, were geographically dispersed around the jurisdiction's perimeter, and were politically cohesive to the extent that a substantial majority would only vote for yellow candidates. A small group of yellow people were more tolerant. Their interests were subsidiary, however, because they represented only 17% of the jurisdiction's total population. The blue people, who were concentrated in the jurisdiction's inner center, were also politically cohesive. As a numerical minority of 25%, however, they never elected any blue people to the jurisdiction's four governing positions.

Black electoral success theory would criticize the exclusionary at large election format in this jurisdiction because essentially it would allow a bloc voting racial majority to control all four of the elected positions. Because exclusionary at large elections require a 50% plus one majority to win *any* representation, 58% of the population (the yellow people minus the more "liberal" contingent) would decide

100% of the elections. The blue minority would be permanently excluded from meaningful participation. In this situation, black electoral success theory would focus on electing more blue officials by creating one majority-blue single-member district. With one blue legislator out of four, however, the blues would only be technically represented if the other three districts contain only the politically cohesive yellows.

A remedy based on qualitative fairness would retain the at large format but modify the threshold of exclusion. Instead of requiring the 50% plus one vote for election jurisdiction-wide, the votes needed for election would be reduced, for example, to 20% plus one of all votes cast. Any candidate receiving more than 20% of the votes would be elected. All voters would be given four votes. They could, however, use their votes to express the intensity of their preferences through cumulative voting. In other words, voters could "plump," or cumulate, all four of their votes on any one candidate. As a result, a politically cohesive numerical minority of at least 20% could elect one legislator.

In addition, because 17% of the population in our hypothetical jurisdiction are "liberal" yellows, the proportionality principle permits a cross-racial electoral coalition. Assuming the blues could be organized to take maximum advantage of their political cohesion, only 84% of the blues (21% of the total jurisdiction electorate and just over the threshold of exclusion) would be needed to elect a blue candidate. Thus, the blues could use their otherwise wasted votes (16% of the blues, 4% of the total electorate) to join the 17% "liberal" yellows. Given the 20% plus one threshold of exclusion, the blue/yellow coalition of 21% would also have enough votes to elect a representative. The legislature would then contain one blue member, one "green" member, and two yellows. The two yellows would no longer enjoy complete majority hegemony and the blue member would finally have a green "ally" to second her motions and to join with her in demanding access to the governing coalition. In this way, proportionate interest representation would disaggregate the majority.

If modifying the exclusion threshold alone did not yield proportionate interest representation, winner-take-all majority rule by a permanent, hostile legislative majority could be modified. Where majority representatives refuse to bargain with representatives of the minority, simple majority vote rules would be replaced. "A minority veto" for legislation of vital importance to minority interests would respond to evidence of gross "deliberative gerrymanders." Alternatively, depending on the proof of disproportionate majority power, plaintiffs might seek minority assent through other supermajority arrangements, concurrent legislative majorities, consociational arrangements, or rotation in office.

Coalition building has always raised two issues: one, how to encourage alliances between members of the dominant white majority and economically depressed minorities; and two, how to keep those alliances reciprocal and empowering. Interest proportionality, complemented by a minority veto, addresses both problems.

Proportionate interest representation would urge courts, lawyers, and voting rights activists to consider black voters' claims in the context of remedies that "soften the harshness of majority rule." Although remedies that deviate from pure majority rule may not always be feasible in litigation, such proposals may be experimentally implemented through settlement negotiations or political initiatives.

By making black representatives necessary participants in the governing process, by giving minority groups additional bargaining power, and by granting blacks a minority veto on issues affecting vital minority interests, proportionate interest representation helps protect substantive minority interests. Proportionate interest representation may split fixed, racially homogeneous majority constituencies into subgroups who would enjoy greater political leverage through preelection coalition building with other politically cohesive electoral minorities.

In addition to its strategic value, proportionate interest representation serves the collegial function of encouraging more open deliberation. To the extent that legislators would be accountable to a larger, more heterogeneous electorate, threshold lowering arrangements might influence legislators to be more "public regarding" because technically, each legislator would be elected from the entire constituency. By giving dignity to strongly held sentiments of minorities, interest proportionality principles may also produce more reasoned, just decisions.

Finally, proportionate interest representation structures political competition so as to formalize coalitions and intergroup interaction. For example, formalizing intergroup coalitions might ultimately promote minority political parties by causing changes in election structures. Formal coalitions, negotiated by a political party representing minority political interests, might be preferable to diffused minority presence within an umbrella political organization.

The proportionate interest representation principle proposed here is therefore based on a view of politics that is both interest-based and deliberative.

CRITICISM OF PROPORTIONATE INTEREST REPRESENTATION

As an interest-based approach, proportionate interest representation nevertheless may be criticized on the ground that it contains all of the flaws of the pluralist bargain without its stabilizing thrust of majority rule. According to some critics, the potential for promoting special interest representation is a fatal defect. These critics argue that despite institutional structures or incentives for fair minded bargaining special interest representation may not yield transformative politics. Proportionate interest representation is actually construed by some as an argument for legislative set-asides, electoral quotas, or equality of representation based simply on the election of descriptively black representatives.

Proportionate interest representation arguably weakens the two-party system by facilitating the formation of minor parties. By proliferating the number of parties, and by highlighting the importance of interests, proportionate interest representation may facilitate the representation of extremist viewpoints, make compromise more difficult, and simply lead to political paralysis or ungovernability because of the absence of a governing majority. In particular, disadvantaged minorities with an interest in changing the status quo may not find salvation by deviating from majority rule. Rules that protect minorities against unfriendly legislation may also make it more difficult to pass friendly legislation.

Some scholars contend that district representation strikes a better balance between group representation and stalemate. Although district representation assumes geography is an adequate proxy for interests, it does not emphasize unyielding interest representation. District-based representation simply facilitates community organization because it focuses on a smaller geographic area and promotes knowledgeable voters whose representative is more socially and geographically accessible.

Finally, many commentators object to proportionate interest representation on separation of powers and judicial management grounds. Given the demand for justiciability that irresistibly shaped the black electoral success litigation strategy, judicial monitoring to remedy inequality of consideration within the legislative process is arguably neither feasible nor desirable. Legal intervention to change legislative procedural rules may seem unlikely when those rules ensure that each person can put issues on the agenda, propose solutions, and offer support or criticisms of proposals.

I am undeterred by these criticisms for five reasons. First, I emphasize the importance of disaggregating majority interests in a system dominated by irrational prejudice. By disaggregating the majority, proportionate interest representation promotes democratic decision-making by a more diverse and engaged electorate. This result is consistent with the original civil rights vision.

Thus, proportionate interest representation emphasizes the illegitimacy of majority rule where the majority is permanent and constituted on the basis of prejudice. Proportionate interest representation weighs the illegitimacy of a permanent majority more heavily than concerns about efficiency and stability, which are used to justify majoritarian regimes. The argument for proportionate interest representation therefore starts with a legitimacy critique. Mirroring the theory of black electoral success, proportionate interest representation relies heavily on legitimacy considerations: people who have a meaningful voice in governmental decisions are more willing to lend their consent to decisions with which they disagree.

Second, although proportionate interest representation rests on legitimacy derived from minority representation, the concept is not essentialist. Proportionate interest representation is an attempt to construct a deliberative decisionmaking body that represents, in proportion to their presence in the population, minority group interests not minority group voters. The concept is, however, also consistent with the one person/one vote principle because each voter gets the same number of votes.

Third, the promotion of self-identified, rather than geographically predetermined, interest preferences arguably sharpens issue conflict while it helps alleviate social conflict and political alienation. Black representatives elected under the proportionate interest model would be potentially more effective within legislative deliberations because they would not be elected from isolated districts. If the minority also had a mutual veto, blacks would enjoy a valuable, strategic, bargaining position, which assures that the majority would be able to get anything done without their assent.

Fourth, the concept specifically addresses the mobilization and responsiveness aspects of representation. Once elected, minority representatives would be more responsive to their constituents because individual incumbents would not be assured of reelection. Effective representatives would be continuously engaged in issue identification and articulation. Indeed, proportionate interest representation hypothesizes increased black turnout as elected officials respond to core black interests.

In addition, the concept of proportionate representation would not deplete the electoral energy generated by black electoral success theory. That proportionate interest arrangements depend on political cohesion and organization is a potential advantage for the black community. Despite their disproportionately depressed socioeconomic status, political activity is salient for blacks.

Fifth, by modifying the threshold of exclusion in at large election systems, proportionate interest representation also avoids the gerrymandering problem common to district-based systems. By avoiding the need to draw subdistrict boundaries, proportionate interest representation obviates contemporary preoccupation with redistricting decisions. Any system that relies on district representation, no matter how subtly gerrymandered, cannot equalize prospects of electoral success as effectively as a proportionate interest system. Given geographical constituencies, some voters will always vote for losers. In addition, even where blacks are extremely geographically insular, they may not all be captured in a single relatively compact district. Some blacks will thus reside outside the district, and will be unrepresented or only *virtually* represented. Other blacks, for reasons of political expediency, may be "packed" into a majority-black district, where their votes will be wasted.

Even if doctrinally acceptable as a remedial strategy, proportionate interest representation may be politically unsuccessful in a time of retrenchment and regression. The political status quo factors that defeat the traditional electoral success model will predictably dilute any concerted litigation effort to improve legislative performance on behalf of black interests. It may be that no electoral strategy, unaccompanied by a protest-based model of insurgent politics, can mobilize sustained commitment either to incremental reform or to more substantive conceptions of political justice. Moreover, the transformative effect of political power at the local political level is questionable.

While formidable, these concerns do not alter the proposal's political and doctrinal plausibility at the electoral level and its aspirational value for legislative deliberation. Proportionate interest representation disaggregates the majority to benefit some whites as well as blacks. At the electoral level, lowering the threshold of exclusion potentially empowers all numerically significant groups, including minority political parties, organized groups of women, the elderly, as well as any group of working class or poor people presently politically disadvantaged under a majoritarian model. Retaining at large elections eliminates the decennial contestation over political power, including the inevitable fight between incumbent politicians and minority groups seeking representation. . . .

[PROPORTIONATE INTEREST REPRESENTATION AS A DEMOCRATIC IDEAL]

The concept of proportionate interest representation represents an initial foray into a previously neglected field of research critically exploring pluralist theories of black political participation. . . . I offer this set of suggestions as a political and remedial position most advantageous to civil rights advocates. Proportionate interest representation contains strategies for reform at both the electoral and legislative level to address some of the process defects in black electoral success theory that have failed to yield substantive justice. Proportionate interest representation is tied both to the congressional and the civil rights vision underlying the Voting Rights Act. The proposals discussed here apply whether civil rights advocates adopt an exclusively pluralist conception of political bargaining or a civically virtuous notion of deliberation.

By extending my speculative reconstruction of political equality to legislative deliberations, however, I am not articulating a grand moral theory of politics. Nor do I argue that these proposals are statutorily or constitutionally required. My purpose has been to attempt to conceive of a deliberative process in which racism does not control all outcomes. I do not articulate a general principle of judicial review, but have limited my suggestions to the specific context of racial discrimination as a remedial approach to statutory violations.

Without regard to the fact that these proposals may not be immediately implemented, at least political and civil rights activists can measure the failures of the current model assisted by an understanding of political equality that begins to define a future vision. Even if unrealistic, proportionate interest representation serves as an ideal to guide further efforts. Proportionate interest representation is an empowering concept to the extent it enables black voters to "name [their] political reality" or to develop their political imagination.

80
Carl Cohen

Both the *decision-making rules* and the *system of representation* through which the members of the community express their will are analyzed in Carl Cohen's *Democracy*. Majority rule is not, he concludes, a necessary instrument in every democratic context, although it is a natural and fitting rule in most contexts. Other rules seek a different balance between the need for efficiency and the need to protect minority interests. Representative systems also vary. Some (in which constituencies are more homogenous) aim chiefly at accord between the representatives and those responsible for their election. Others (in which constituencies are more heterogeneous) aim chiefly at representation likely to advance the interests of the community as a whole. Alternative instruments compete with one another; democrats, weighing their merits and demerits, must choose among them.

A. DECISION-MAKING RULES AS THE INSTRUMENT OF DEMOCRACY*

The Need for Decision-Making Rules

Community life requires that some decisions be reached, some specific courses of action chosen. Centrally important, therefore, are the rules according to which particular decisions are made; if the community is or wants to be democratic, it is through these decision-making rules that the will of the membership is given concrete effect.

There are many decision-making rules consistent with democratic government. Their kinds need to be distinguished, their respective merits and limitations understood. In reviewing them, I shall argue that democracy is not logically tied to any single decision-making rule. Depending upon the nature of the community and its problems, different rules may serve as the valuable instruments of democracy.

A given democratic community need not employ the same rule in reaching all decisions; different kinds of issues render different kinds of decision-making rules appropriate. The rule for establishing everyday regulations, statutes or bylaws, may greatly differ from the rule for amending the fundamental law, the constitution, of the community. Successful democracy requires intelligence in the choice of its operating rules.

EFFICIENT RULES AND PROTECTIVE RULES

Democratic rules almost invariably will specify what percentage of those who do participate are needed to decide the matter at hand. But it is not the case that an increase in the percentage of participants required for decision necessarily yields a correlative increase in democraticity. Democracy may be frustrated if either too few, or too many, of those participating are required to agree to make decisions binding. Choosing the best decision-making rule for a given context is a complex matter.

Appraisal of any decision-making rule in a democracy must be made in view of the total consequences of its employment. Of these consequences there are two major kinds. The first is the tendency of a rule to provide protection to each member of the community, protection against decisions that somehow injure him, or affect him adversely. The second is the tendency of a rule to make the will of the community effective, by making it possible to reach decisions and to reach them efficiently. In appraising a democratic decision-making rule, therefore, one must weigh both its *protectiveness* and its *efficiency*. Unfortunately, between these two large objectives there is considerable tension.

Greater protection will flow from decision-making rules as they become more *inclusive,* that is, as they require the explicit agreement of a greater percentage of the deciding body for positive action. The more inclusive the rule, the less likely any individual (of unspecified interest) will be to find himself in the minority, and the easier it will be for an adversely affected minority to gather the votes needed to block action.

---

*From Carl Cohen, *Democracy,* New York: The Free Press, 1972. Copyright C. Cohen.

Inclusiveness may be absolute or relative. A rule is inclusive in the absolute sense (to whatever degree) when the agreeing percentage required is a percentage of the entire membership—e.g., when a majority of all the members of some committee, or two-thirds of all the members of some senate, are required for action. Inclusiveness is relative when the percentage required is a percentage of some fluctuating body, those actually voting, or those actually present. Absolute inclusiveness is more cumbersome than relative inclusiveness, and is employed only in special cases; it has the merit, however, of encouraging democraticity by requiring for action a breadth of participation that might not have been otherwise attained. Less inclusive, or only relatively inclusive rules do not entail that the number of actual participants will be fewer, but they permit decisions with fewer participants. That is a danger as well as a convenience. To limit this danger quorum rules are effective in some contexts, insuring that no formal action may be taken without a fixed minimum of participation, or at least presence, by the membership.

Greater efficiency, on the other hand, will tend to flow from rules that are less inclusive, a smaller percentage of the deciding body being required for action. This is true whether the requirements be imposed absolutely or relatively, but the former category may be put aside as exceptional. Among normal rules, framed in terms of those voting (or occasionally those present) the less demanding the requirement for agreement, the more readily will agreement be achieved. Of two rules, one requiring agreement of three-fourths of those voting, the other a bare majority, the latter will obviously permit positive action to be taken more quickly, and supported more stably than will the former. The less inclusive rule permits more immediate response to needs felt in the community. It is likely to prove more effective, too, in making possible some action (say, with majority support) where no proposal whatever could be enacted if the support of three-fourths were required. The cost of this efficiency and effectiveness is risk. Any citizen not knowing at a given time what issues will be decided by a rule about to be chosen should certainly expect to be more frequently in the losing minority under the rule of the majority than under the rule of three-fourths.

Because the objectives of protection and efficiency necessarily conflict, no rule can fully maximize both. At one extreme, the rule giving power of directive decision to one person, the autocrat, may avoid haggling and delay, but gives everyone else no protection whatever against the autocrat's use or abuse of his power. At the other extreme, the rule permitting action only when the community is in unanimous agreement gives complete protection to every member against positive decisions adverse to his interests, but is likely to impose intolerable burdens on all by rendering it virtually impossible to take any community action whatever. Every other decision-making rule occupies some point between these extremes. Ideally, we seek that intermediate point which effects the best available compromise, assuring democraticity and reasonable protection, while imposing the lightest practical burdens upon the community in the actual process of reaching agreement.

What rule proves to be the happiest compromise depends upon many factual circumstances of the community—its size, the character and homogeneity of its members, the kinds of issues it must face. Successful democracy needs different rules for different communities, different situations, and different kinds of issues. No single rule is optimal for all.

Even the most complete information about the character of a rule tells us nothing about the variety of questions on which it is applied and respected. Appraising the democracy of a community, therefore, one must ask not only *what* rules are in effect, but *where* they are in effect, and how consistently they are used. Maximizing the democracy of the whole demands not only maximal range of participation, but within that range the use of differing rules of appropriate inclusiveness. Decision-making rules are the instruments of democracy; the entire pattern of their use is only one index of the health of any democracy, but it is a most important one.

Majority Rule and Its Varieties

Of all decision-making rules, the rule of the majority is the most familiar and the most important. So closely is it associated with democracy that the two are often mistakenly identified. Majority rule, in fact, is only one of many consistent with democracy, and is sometimes less appropriate than others. Because of the combination of efficiency and protectiveness it provides, however, majority rule is commonly chosen as the happiest available compromise.

The concept of "majority rule" is itself ambiguous, on two levels. There is, first, uncertainty as to the meaning of "majority"—i.e., as to what proportion of a given body it refers to; and there is, second, uncertainty regarding the nature of the body within which the majority is required. I treat these two levels in turn.

(1) The "majority" normally means "more than half" of the group in question, but is sometimes loosely used as synonymous with "plurality," the largest single part of the group, whether or not more than half. Obviously majority rule and plurality rule are importantly different, since they can lead to very different outcomes. Plurality rule permits (but does not entail) decision-making by a distinct minority of the whole. Clearly, rule by majority (sometimes specified as "the simple majority") is more inclusive than plurality rule; it therefore provides more protection for the interests of the members, but is less efficient.

On some kinds of issues rule by the simple majority may be thought not protective enough. Rules are then devised requiring the active agreement of two-thirds, or even three-fourths, before certain kinds of action can be taken. These are often called "qualified majority" rules, each named after the fraction it requires—"two-thirds majority," "three-fourths majority," and so on. Qualified majority rules are entirely appropriate for matters of great consequence to the community. So, for example, the Constitution of the United States may be altered only when both (a) an amendment has been properly proposed by either two-thirds of both houses of Congress, or by a convention called by the legislatures of two-thirds of the states; *and* (b) an amendment so proposed has been ratified by the legislatures, or by conventions, in three-fourths of the several states. This double use of the qualified majority is highly protective; citizens may rest assured that the fundamental law of the land cannot be amended easily, or carelessly, or without the overwhelming endorsement of the people's representatives. Such protectiveness can be afforded, however, only when the need for change is very rare, and where speed and efficiency in making change is not essential, perhaps even not desirable. On matters like constitutional change, highly inclusive qualified majority rules, offering much protection and little convenience, may be a democracy's most suitable instrument.

(2) With the meaning of "majority" specified, it remains to determine the precise body within which it must be garnered. The majority of whom? There are three major alternatives. Rule by the majority may signify: (a) rule by the majority of those who actually vote; (b) rule by the majority of those who may vote; (c) rule by the majority of all members.

These alternatives may be viewed as points on a continuum extending from relative inclusiveness to absolute inclusiveness. Another point on that continuum is the rule requiring a majority of those members qualified to vote who are actually present. This would be intermediate in absoluteness between (a) and (b) above; but its restricted applicability only to communities small enough to permit all members to meet together renders it of lesser interest. Still another possibility is rule by the majority of those members known to be affected by the outcome, assuming an issue affects some but not all. Restricting decision to those so affected is an appealing notion, but is seldom feasible because it supposes that criteria marking out the affected sub-group can be precisely specified and fairly applied. In effect, this variant of the rule seeks to circumscribe a new, smaller community within the original, larger one. Within that smaller community the three alternatives above arise once again.

Consider a hypothetical community of 100 members, all of whom will be affected by the democratic resolution of a given issue. Suppose that only 80 are permitted by law to vote (the "qualified voters"), and that only 60 cast a ballot (the "actual voters"). Seriously respecting the principle that the will of the majority should govern, of which body shall we specify that a majority should be required?

(a) Most workable (especially when the community is very large) is the rule requiring only a majority of the votes cast. In our hypothetical case that would mean a majority of the 60 actual voters, resulting in control by as few as 31 of the community's members. This is the rule most commonly employed, but it has the unhappy consequence that, if the number of actual voters should be small, the number needed for control may be very small. If, in our hypothetical community, only 25 had voted, 13 members may decide the matter for 100. (Quorum rules designed to minimize this risk can guard only against the extreme case, and are impractical in elections of large scale.) Usually we do not boggle at the consequences of this system. We know that the controlling minority is likely to be genuinely concerned, and also likely to represent, in fact, a large proportion of the non-voters. Moreover, no other rule may be feasible. Yet this interpretation of majority rule could result in outcomes in conflict with the general wishes of the community.

(b) For greater protection a majority of the qualified voters may be required. This sets a floor below which breadth of participation cannot fall—41 voters in the hypothetical case proposed. The worth of that floor depends, of course, upon the assumption that suffrage in the community is universal, or nearly so. In communities of which a significant percentage of the members are not permitted to vote, even this stronger variant of majority rule may be delusive, resulting in decisions by a small minority of the whole.

(c) In special contexts rule by the majority is interpreted in the strongest sense, as rule by more than half of the total membership of a specific community. Positive action then must have relatively wide support. To apply this rule a community must consist of a determinate number of voting members whose identities are precisely known. In the nominating conventions of political parties, for example, voting delegates are carefully identified and nominations usually require support of at least one-half the total of all delegates plus one. Such a rule may delay positive action (requiring repeated balloting) or block it entirely. It is usually feasible only where the community is relatively small, and where the common need for some action will keep large minorities from remaining stubbornly immovable. Where suffrage is substantially universal (i.e., virtually all members are qualified voters) this and the preceding interpretation are substantially identical.

Concerning each of these interpretations we want to know the degree of efficiency and the degree of protectiveness it provides. Efficiency is an inverse function of inclusiveness (though perhaps not of inclusiveness only); since the three interpretations of majority rule are progressively more inclusive, they are progressively less efficient. Even the most efficient of the three is often clumsy; therefore the majority most commonly required in democratic communities is the majority of those who do actually vote. Anything beyond that is almost certain to retard decision-making, perhaps unduly.

Protectiveness too is largely determined by inclusiveness, hence the risk of minority control is heightened under the first, most common interpretation. However, when actual participants approach in number those qualified to participate, and those qualified approach the number of the whole, the differences in protectiveness may not be very great.

Conclusions both theoretically and practically important for democracy may be drawn. After satisfactory breadth of participation has been attained, majority rule of some variety is usually a reasonable instrument to make the popular will effective. But the rule of the majority cannot by itself guarantee satisfactory breadth. Perhaps the common identification of democracy with majority rule flows from the uncritical assumption that with such a rule breadth of participation is assured. The assumption is not always warranted; majority rule, although a valuable instrument, may prove deceptive as an index of democraticity.

What varieties of what rules a democratic community should employ must depend upon the degrees of efficiency and protectiveness it demands, the degrees of inefficiency and risk it can tolerate. Possible combinations are unlimited, ranging from highly protective and clumsy qualified majority rules, to relatively efficient but risky plurality rules. In view of its own circumstances, and the needs and wants of its own members, a democracy must choose its instruments.

Majority Rule as the Special Instrument of Democracy

Majority rule, the *lex majoris partis,* is no more, or less, than one principle through which the will of the participating membership of a community is made effective. Reasonably interpreted, its use promises that, whatever the breadth of participation already achieved, a fair weighing will be given to the voices of the several participants. No procedural principle can be invoked to judge the wisdom of individual contributions, since that judgment is precisely the one that cannot be antecedently made. Nor can the depth of members' contributions be controlling, since that cannot be accurately or fairly determined. What remains to measure the popular will is, in most cases, the numerical majority, the greater part.

That majority rule is an instrument of democracy and not its substance is further evidenced by the following considerations. *First:* the fact that it is a principle appropriately subject to various interpretations and that one of these must be deliberately selected, is indicative of its instrumental character. No particular decision-making rule is forced upon a community because it is a democracy—although some rules, it is true, will be precluded for that reason.

Second: the importance of plurality rule, and the frequency of its use, is instructive. Rule by plurality may be operative in fact, even where it has not been explicitly agreed upon. Beneath the surface of two-party conflict many points of view are likely to be contending. By receiving the support of the largest minority in the majority party (or even the largest minority within the largest minority within the majority party) one position finally wins the day. It is arguable that in this way minorities almost always, and majorities rarely, rule in a large democracy. The power of minorities is often hidden by the need for compromise within political parties, and by the technical requirement that legislative enactments receive a majority vote in the parliament.

Third: it is noteworthy that some democracies employ devices specifically designed to prevent the majority from being absolutely decisive. In the United States, such institutions as the judicial review of legislative action, the Electoral College, and the representation of each state by two senators regardless of its population, are invoked deliberately to protect minorities from exploitation by a majority. A democracy may respect and use majority rule, and at the same time rationally seek to mitigate the absolute control of the majority.

Fourth: some democratic communities do not count votes at all, when the participation of the members can be made effective through the grasp of the "sense of the meeting," its *con-sensus,* by its presiding officer. This power of leadership can be seriously misused, deliberately or inadvertently, but when employed sensitively and in the spirit of democracy it can result in decisions superior to those of a vote count.

All varieties of decision-making rules are attended by considerable risk; all, including the rule of the majority, have merits as well as limitations. Of all the possibilities, however, only the rule of the simple majority has this special advantage: it is the single rule that both prevents any minority, by itself, from taking positive action for the whole, and prevents any minority, by itself, from blocking the positive action of the whole. Any less inclusive role—rule of the plurality, for example—does not accomplish the former goal; any more inclusive rule—a qualified majority rule, for example—does not accomplish the latter goal. The power to block action is in some ways as important as the power to take action; any minority possessing that power can force the community to keep things as they are, a positive decision often of great consequence. The rule of the simple majority, therefore, exhibits a unique merit, and in most democratic contexts is likely to prove simplest, fairest, and most workable. This is why it has come to be viewed as the natural instrument of democracy. In just this instrumental spirit John Locke wrote of it in his *Second Treatise of Government* (1690).

> For when any number of men have, by the consent of every individual, made a community, they have thereby made that community one body, with a power to act as one body, which is only by the will and determination of the majority; for that which acts any community being only the consent of the individuals of it, and it being necessary to that which is one body to move one way, it is necessary the body should move that way whither the greater force carries it, which is the consent of the majority; or else it is impossible it should act or continue one body, one community, which the consent of every individual that united into it agreed that it should; and so everyone is bound by that consent to be concluded by the majority. And therefore we see that in assemblies impowered to act by positive laws, where no number is set by that positive law which impowers them, the act of the majority passes for the act of the whole and, of course, determines, as having by the law of nature and reason the power of the whole.
>
> And thus every man, by consenting with others to make one body politic under one government, puts himself under an obligation to everyone of that society to submit to the determination of the majority, and to be concluded by it. . . .

Rule by Fluctuating Majorities

What keeps the power of majorities from being abused in healthy democracies? The threat of a tyrannical majority is real, and has been much feared and emphasized by critics of democracy. There are democracies, however, in which majority power is used tyrannically and exploitatively rarely, if at all. How is the danger met?

Many factors may contribute to majority restraint, of course, among them constitutional prohibitions and guarantees. But if the majority is large enough, and determined enough to have its way, no external restrictions will long bind it; laws and institutions can be altered, customs can be ignored, even formal constitutions can be amended or suspended. Yet majority restraint is reasonably common (though far from universal) even where the members of the community are neither unusually altruistic nor unusually sophisticated. What keeps the natural drive for power and self-interest from wrecking a democracy?

Two elements above all encourage successful restraint. First, the habits and temperament of the individual members must be such as to permit general participation in government to continue. Certain attitudes and dispositions are psychological conditions for the success of democracy. Second, an institutional balance must be developed where majority rule is applied by a democracy over a considerable range of issues, and over a considerable stretch of time. The majority that rules on any given issue is not likely to be the same majority as that which rules on many other issues facing the same membership. So, while an equal (or nearly equal) percentage of the community may continue to control, as "the majority," the constituents of that percentage will be constantly varying, from issue to issue, and from time to time. What really rules, in a moderately healthy democracy, is not the majority, but majori*ties* (and often, only pluralities) constantly changing in membership. I call this "rule by fluctuating majorities." The rule of fluctuating majorities is operative when membership in a decisive majority is experienced by all (or almost all) of the community's members at one time or another, and when, on a range of different questions being decided during a given period, any member is likely to find himself a constituent of the ruling majority on some issues, and of a ruled minority on others.

The rule of fluctuating majorities is a key factor in the health of any large democracy. It keeps each citizen conscious of his several roles within the community: ruler, when he sides with the many; ruled, in that he is committed to obey the laws, whether he sides with the many or with the few. That he frequently finds himself one of a minority—indeed, that he is always a member of some minority—is likely to cause him, as it causes his fellow citizens also, to restrain those oppressive tendencies which the possession of power can excite. What the majority of which I am a member does to others today, a majority of which I am not a member may do to me tomorrow. Here enters into the political realm one of the noblest of ethical maxims, the Golden Rule. It enters not because of its nobility, but because of its cold practicality; and it enters in negative form, in which it is more easily understood and more readily applied. Within democracies which realize the principle of rule by fluctuating majorities, this is the Golden Rule of politics: Refrain from doing to others what you would have them refrain from doing to you.

Some have argued that the fluctuating character of rule in a democracy has the reverse effect—that rather than tending to restrain oppressive tendencies it reinforces them. John C. Calhoun, for example, in his *Disquisition on Government* (1851), wrote: "But the duration or uncertainty of the tenure by which power is held cannot, of itself, counteract the tendency inherent in government to oppression and abuse of power. On the contrary, the very uncertainty of the tenure, combined with the violent party warfare which must ever precede a change of parties under such [i.e., pure majoritarian] governments, would rather tend to increase than diminish the tendency to oppression." Similarly, Robert Michels (*Political Parties,* 1911), contended that where the turnover of power is frequent, "everyone who attains to power thinks chiefly of making a profitable use of that power while it lasts," and he concludes that the genuine advantages for democracy provided by rotation in office are outweighed by "the exploitative methods of ephemeral leaders, with all their disastrous consequences."

Such arguments would be more persuasive if they were more generally supported by the facts. Dreading the tyranny of the majority, these critics are convinced that the natural lust for power must make that tyranny unavoidable. Their fears cause them to view "the majority" as a monolith, hungry and irresistible. They ignore the actual condition of democratic communities and one of the most notable features of rule by majority. The search for private profit is tempered by the insecurity of elected office, and the possibility of future catastrophe. Even one who would be rapacious if he could must weigh the fact that the issues in which he has an interest are many, and that he (like all others) enjoys concurrent membership in various majority and minority groups. Intelligent self-interest must cause every citizen of a democracy to remain conscious of the uncertainty of power under majority rule and the possible consequences, to *him*,—on another issue or at another time—of his abuse of power.

This is the core of the argument in Madison's justly famous *Federalist #10:* The continuing contest of a multiplicity of parties and interests can effectively restrain the abusive tendencies of any single party or interest. This argument he marshals in support of the proposed American union.

> Extend the sphere, and you take in a greater variety of parties and interests; you make it less probable that a majority of the whole will have a common motive to invade the rights of other citizens; or if such a common motive exists, it will be more difficult for all who feel it to discover their own strength, and to act in unison with each other. . . .

> Does it [the advantage of a healthy republic] consist in the greater security afforded by a greater variety of parties, against the event of any one party being able to outnumber and oppress the rest? In an equal degree does the increased variety of parties comprised within the Union, increase this security. Does it, in fine, consist in the greater obstacles opposed to the concert and accomplishment of the secret wishes of an unjust and interested majority? Here, again, the extent of the Union gives it the most palpable advantage.

Madison himself distrusted direct democracy, and therefore carefully avoided the term "democracy" in referring to the system he defended, which he called a "republic." But Madison's republic is nothing different from the indirect, representative democracy (of considerable size) here being discussed. Since "the *causes* of faction cannot be removed . . . relief is only to be sought in the means of controlling its *effects*." Thus, in a healthy polity, a reasonably restrained and stable balance can be achieved among a multiplicity and variety of factions. The continuing and widespread use of majority rule can greatly mitigate its own dangers.

The Misuse of Majority Power

Decisive majorities do not always fluctuate. Where they do not, or do not fluctuate with sufficient frequency (all questions in this sphere being questions of degree) the rule of the majority may undermine the practice of general participation, and thereby subvert the very democracy whose instrument it is. Hence there is real danger, for a democracy, in the development of a *fixed majority* in the community. A fixed or permanent majority is released from the healthy check of fluctuation; it can maintain absolute control in the areas of its interest; those who oppose it have no leverage to use against it; its use of power may become abusive, even repressive. At its worst a fixed majority can utterly destroy the delicate equilibrium of many contending interests upon which the practice of democracy so fundamentally depends.

This danger, ironically, tends to be greater where the differences of interest within the community tend to be most marked, and the need for tolerance and restraint most acute. The relatively homogeneous community need not so greatly fear the abuse of power by some of its members. Needing less in the way of protection for the individual in the decision-making rule, it can afford to provide that protection more readily, since even more inclusive rules for decision are not likely to stymie needed activities. In very heterogeneous communities, on the other hand (or at least those having sharply distinguished, stable, and intensely committed sub-groups), individual citizens have much to fear from the power of opponents, and therefore need inclusive, protective, decision-making rules. But in just these communities the operation of such protective rules is likely to prove a cause of serious inefficiency, and even to block needed community action entirely. In these more divided communities, therefore, democracy must be more fragile, its instrument of fluctuating majorities being less effective.

In such heterogeneous contexts democracy may be made safer for its own members, and hence more viable, if the range of issues subjected to community action be restricted to those upon which there is some measure of community consensus. But the degree of such consensus varies enormously among national communities. So, for example, what can be done effectively by collective action in a small, relatively homogeneous nation—say, Holland—may be more wisely left in private hands in a large, relatively heterogeneous nation—say, India—if the operation of the democracy is not to result in the fragmentation of the entire community. Unfortunately, the severe community problems—economic and social—of thickly populated and industrially underdeveloped lands may make essential community control over matters which (given the nature of those communities) do not lend themselves to democratic resolution. The consequent tension may be so severe as to render democracy unworkable in some communities of this kind.

Even where majorities do fluctuate, it can happen that the will of a particular majority, on particular procedural questions, may unwisely restrict the participation of some significant portion of the community on other substantive issues. It is thus entirely possible that decisions reached democratically may cripple the continuation of that very democratic procedure.

There can be no absolute guarantees against such misuse of power. The rule of fluctuating majorities, and a widespread sensitivity to the requirements of democracy, can build restraint in the use of power but cannot insure it. James Thurber put it well: "There is no safety in numbers—or in anything else, for that matter."

B. REPRESENTATION AS THE INSTRUMENT OF DEMOCRACY

Direct and Indirect Democracy

The distinction between *direct* and *indirect* democracy is both common and reasonable. We may participate in the governing process ourselves, or we may participate in the selection of others who will govern for us. The members of a democratic community, in choosing some among themselves to represent all, do not give up ultimate control of community policy. They do give to those so elected the power to act, in certain ways and for a specified period, in the place of their constituents. These representatives then perform what I have earlier called the "administrative" functions of government. Collectively they may properly be called a chamber of deputies, or a representative assembly, or simply the parliament.

The principle of representation, concisely formulated, is this: the administration of government may be conducted by relatively few persons, responsible to the constituent members of the community who elect them, and deriving all their authority from their constituents. All elected office holders, regardless of the branch of government in which they serve, and with them the conduct of virtually all government business, rely ultimately on this principle. It is crucial, therefore, that the citizens of any large democracy understand the proper relations between themselves and their representatives.

When the mass of citizens are believed incapable of governing themselves, a representative system will be deemed not merely a necessity but a positive good, allowing administration to remain in the hands of those thought to be more judicious and more enlightened. Having that consequence was believed, by its authors, to be one great merit of the proposed Constitution of the United States. Madison wrote: "The effect [of the delegation of the government] is . . . to refine and enlarge the public views, by passing them through the medium of a chosen body of citizens, whose wisdom may best discern the true interest of their country, and whose patriotism and love of justice will be least likely to sacrifice it to temporary or partial considerations. Under such a regulation, it may well happen that the public voice, pronounced by the representatives of the people, will be more consonant to the public good than if pronounced by the people themselves, convened for the purpose" (*The Federalist #10*, 1787).*

Whether viewed as a positive advantage or a necessary evil, representation is (like majority rule), an instrument of democracy; it is not identical with democracy. As majoritarianism is a way of making the participation of the membership of a community decisive, representation is a way of channeling that participation so as to enable individual voices to be heard fairly, while increasing the likelihood that difficult decisions will be made wisely. Both instruments are extremely valuable, yet there are circumstances in which either or both may properly be rejected. In some very small democracies no system of representation may be needed or wanted, in large ones representation becomes a practical necessity. Democracy is government through general participation; representation helps make that participation effective. To suppose the identity of the two is to confuse the essence of democracy with one of the instruments through which it is realized.

The proper functioning of any instrument depends both on its quality and the wisdom with which it is used. A large democracy, therefore, needs first a system

*See above, Selection #74.

of representation that is just, designed to reflect the will of the people fully and accurately. Inferior representative machinery may stymie and frustrate even an intelligent and concerned citizenry. The most excellent representative schemes can be abused, however; if the citizenry is corrupt, uninterested, or uninformed, no machinery by itself will provide wise governors. In the last analysis, representatives will represent, as well as lead, their constituents.

A democrat should recognize the necessary consequences of any representative system, and its limitations. In it, each citizen's voice will be diminished, sometimes drowned, by the voices of the many others whom his representative also represents, and by the representatives of other constituencies within the community. But representation itself is not to blame for a reduction in the influence of each citizen; that reduction is a direct result of increasing community size. In a democracy of 500 one must expect to play a smaller role in decision-making than in a democracy of 50. With or without a representative system that will be so. When the community is one of fifty thousand or fifty million, the dimunition in the relative importance of each is proportionate. Beyond a certain size a democracy is compelled by practical considerations to use representative machinery if the individual is to be heard at all. We ought not blame the machinery for the consequence of the size that made it essential.

There are two great spheres in which a representative system must function, and be appraised. The first of these is the choosing of the representatives themselves, the elections. The second comprises all other occasions, between elections, for the people to be heard. If the system for selection is not intelligent and fair, the democracy may be undone; but after selection, too, the system must promote responsiveness by the deputies to their constituents.

Many of the issues relating to representative systems are highly technical, and are properly in the province of the political scientist. Still we can lay out a philosophical framework within which concrete systems may be understood and judged. We must identify the central aspects of all representative systems, and indicate the kinds of advantages and disadvantages offered by the several basic alternatives. And we must grapple with certain fundamental questions arising in every representative system.

The Elements of Every Representative System

Electoral systems are extremely complicated. Ignorance and misunderstanding of them is common, and may be exploited by those whose real intent is to frustrate democracy while professing it. It is unfortunate but true that just here, in this technical arena, the forces for and against democracy often fight their battles.

The basic elements of every representative system are these: *(1)* the degrees of representation; *(2)* the decision-making rule for selecting representatives; *(3)* the decision-making rule(s) used within the representative body; *(4)* the bases of representation; *(5)* the levels of representation. Each of these elements has an important role; in practice, however, it is their combined effect in one system that determines the effectiveness and justice of that system.*

Degrees of Representation

The degree of representation is the degree to which the system approximates direct democracy; the upper limit upon the degree of representation is a system in which everyone speaks for himself. A high degree of representation is realized where the number of persons who must be heard through each representative is small, that is, where the ratio of representatives to total membership is high. As the number of constituents represented by each deputy goes down, the degree of representation goes up. The degree of representation can therefore be expressed as a percentage figure: the percentage of the total membership that will represent the whole. In large democracies it will be an extremely small percentage. So, in general, the degree of representation in a community will *in*crease as the number of representatives increases (supposing the total population constant); that degree will *de*crease as the total population increases (supposing the size of the representative body constant).

Ideally, a democracy will strive for the highest degree of representation feasible. We depart from direct democracy chiefly because size has made it impractical. Representation seeks to overcome the impracticalities of direct general participation, while keeping participation general. The lower the degree of representation (i.e., the more constituents per representative), the greater the distance between the individual citizen and the final decision-making process. I can participate more effectively in the making of laws and policies if I am one of ten electing a representative than if I am one of ten thousand. Participation may continue, but is reduced in effectiveness by the sheer force of numbers.

At the same time, the number of representatives in the governing body must not become so great as to frustrate the purposes of the representative system. Whatever the decision-making rule within that body, its efficiency in resolving the issues before it will drop as the number in the body increases. It must not be allowed to grow indefinitely. The highest possible degree of representation means, in practice, the highest degree of representation consistent with effective function in representative bodies.

The ratios that will best realize this ideal depend upon the kinds of issues dealt with by the representatives, and upon the total size of the community. Some kinds of issues can be debated in an assembly of hundreds; some can be intelligently resolved only in very small deliberative bodies. Legislatures are often quite large; executive committees of large organizations are likely to be very small.

The total size of the community affects the ratio fundamentally because there is virtually an absolute limit on the size of an effective representative assembly. The

---

*For a more detailed, mathematical account of some of these elements and their interrelations, see J. M. Buchanan and J. Tullock's brilliant study, *The Calculus of Consent* (1962), University of Michigan Press, Ann Arbor, to which the following discussion is much indebted.

United States House of Representatives, with 435 members, surely nears that limit. As national democracies grow larger, therefore, they must suffer lower and lower degrees of representation. There is no escaping it. The larger the community, the smaller is the percentage of it who can sit as deputies, and the greater the distance between citizen and decisions. In general, democracy is adversely affected by great size.

Decision-making Rules and Representative Bodies

There must be a rule according to which representatives are chosen, possibly different rules for different bodies. The rule of the simple majority of actual voters is most common for this selection, and works reasonably well where a two-party system is solidly ensconced. Where there are three or more major candidates for an office to be filled, the requirement of a simple majority may necessitate a second, run-off election. The inefficiency of any run-off system can be avoided only by restricting the number of candidates to two (in which case the inefficiencies may be moved to the primary elections in which the candidates are chosen), or by changing from majority to plurality rule, which would make it possible for the successful candidate to be opposed by a majority of the voters. This choice of decision-making rule for elections is most important since it is in the electing of representatives that citizen participation in government is most concrete. Ideally the rule for selecting representatives will be as inclusive, as protective, as it can be without imposing undue inefficiencies on the conduct of elections.

There must be rules, also, for the making of decisions within a representative body already elected. It will be normal for differing rules (simple majority of actual voters, qualified majorities of various sizes, etc.) to be applied to issues of different kinds. In this context, too, we seek to combine efficiency with safety.

The protectiveness of the decision-making rules within the representative body is commonly increased through the use of a bicameral legislature. The two houses will normally exhibit different degrees of representation, and different bases of representation; therefore the requirement that legislation must be approved by both houses is an effective (but sometimes inefficient) way of protecting minority interests against oppressive or careless action, without imposing a decision-making rule that would require an impossibly high percentage of support for any positive action. As the degrees of representation and the bases for representation in the two houses are more nearly alike, the protectiveness of the bicameral system is reduced. Whether the safety it affords fully compensates for the inefficiencies it imposes is a question that can be answered only with full knowledge of the specific circumstances.

Between the two kinds of context just distinguished (decision in the selection of representatives, and decision within the representative body) there is an interesting complementarity. Decision-making rules may be more protective and less efficient, or less protective and more efficient. Now greater protectiveness on the one level (say, in the selection of representatives) may reasonably encourage the use of more efficient, if less protective rules at the other level (say, within the representative body). This could work the other way as well. Very protective rules within the assembly may tend to justify more efficient if less protective rules in selecting representatives. In the end it is the combined effect of the entire system that must be appraised.

Bases of Representation

Assuming the degree of representation known, and the rules both for the selection of representatives and for decisions within the representative body fixed, a key question remains: What kind of constituency is each representative to have? On what principle(s) are the several constituencies to be formed? These principles determine the *bases* of representation. Selecting them is the most difficult and the most important task in developing a good representative system.

There are many possible bases, all of which can be ordered on one very general continuum. At one extreme the constituency of each representative may be entirely *homogeneous,* comprising only persons with interests importantly similar; at the other, it may be entirely *heterogeneous,* comprising persons with diverse, random interests. Each of the two extremes is much superior in some respects, much inferior in others. Intermediate points on this continuum offer compromises in which advantages of one kind are traded off for advantages of other kinds. No solution is perfectly ideal; each democracy must devise the instruments best suited to its circumstances.

Illustrations will be helpful. Suppose the representative body were to consist of deputies each elected by a fixed number of members of some trade or profession. Constituencies would then be very homogeneous, and representation would be functional, in that each constituency would be delineated by the productive role or function of its members. The interests the deputy would defend would be those of lawyers, or plumbers, or teachers, and so on. Systems of roughly this kind have long been advocated by guild socialists and others. Suppose (at the other extreme) each member of the community had been assigned an identification number on a random basis, and that the representative body were to consist of deputies each elected by a fixed number of persons whose identification numbers lay within arbitrarily chosen ranges. Constituencies would then be very heterogeneous, and representation would be non-functional, because neither the special interests nor the productive role of a citizen would have any bearing upon the constituency of which he was a member. The interests the deputy would then defend would be those he believed to be the interests of the coalition, within his randomly selected constituency, responsible for his election and likely to support his reelection. He might find it difficult to know what these interests were, but would try to learn them indirectly by judging the apparent effectiveness of the several elements of his election platform. Such heterogeneity is quite nearly approached in practice, but never fully realized, in the senatorial constituencies of large and populous American states.

The full realization of neither extreme is feasible. But what are the respective advantages and disadvantages of systems near the two ends of the continuum?

Functional representation has the enormous advantage of providing clear lines of responsibility for the deputy. On the one side, he knows precisely who elected him, and what interests he is therefore obliged to represent; on the other, his constituency, being homogeneous, can judge more readily and accurately how well he does his job of representing their common concerns. In such systems the rule for the selection of a representative (so long as it offers some small degree of protectiveness) is not of great moment, since the failure to represent the group's interests will be quickly noted whatever the rule, and punished by rejection at the first opportunity. The nonrepresentation of minorities within the constituency is not a serious danger, since the deputy is pretty certain to respond to the main functional concerns universally shared by his constituents. In general, such a system, to be fair, need only insure that each functional group is genuinely free to choose its own representative, and that the chamber of deputies include representatives of each of the community's major functional groups in proportionate number. So far, excellent. But within the representative body so composed the importance of protection being built into the rule for decision-making is much magnified. When the several competing interests have been institutionally divided and set in opposition, the losing interests (or losing coalition of interests) may lose everything, their concerns being defended only incidentally, if at all, by those in the majority coalition. Furthermore, as a result of the sharp demarcation of interests, the activities of each representative are likely to focus so sharply upon the concerns of his specialized constituency that his vision of community affairs as a whole may be somewhat myopic, with the result that, each looking out only for his own, the larger concerns of the community may be seriously threatened.

Non-functional representation, on the other hand, is very much more likely to result in a concern, by the individual deputy, for the needs of the community as a whole. His constituency being a random sample of the whole, he is likely to believe, correctly, that the interests of a majority of his constituents and those of a majority of the community are substantially identical, and that in defending the latter he defends the former, and so best enhances the chances of his own re-election. Provincialism is thereby much reduced. Moreover, the random nature of the several constituencies much reduces the probability that any significant minority will be entirely without representation in the ruling majority, since any effective coalition is likely to include some defenders of every major interest. The danger of minorities being oppressed by the majority is thereby reduced. So far, excellent. But the lines of responsibility between representatives and constituents in such a system will be most unclear. It will be hard for the deputy to know which of his randomly chosen constituents voted for him, or to know why they voted for him; and it will be therefore difficult for him to learn how to be of particular service to his supporting constituency. In the confusion it is possible, even likely, that some groups will get inadequate attention and defense. Where constituencies are heterogeneous the rule for the selection of representatives from the constituency becomes (in contrast to the other extreme) of high importance. That very heterogeneity calls for the greater emphasis upon protection of minorities that may lie wholly within that constituency, and must therefore be represented through it, or not at all. But the effectiveness and wisdom of any rule, even one highly protective (and therefore inefficient), will be very difficult to judge, as it will be practically impossible to say how well each deputy is doing the job of representing those who elected him.

Every large democracy is likely to devise some compromise between these two extremes, a compromise that seeks to maximize their respective advantages, while keeping their disadvantages to a minimum. James Madison and his colleagues thought the Constitution of the United States provided such a compromise. Supposing, reasonably, that an increasing number of constituents entailed increasing heterogeneity, he wrote: "It must be confessed that in this, as in most other cases, there is a mean, on both sides of which inconveniences will be found to lie. By enlarging too much the number of electors, you render the representatives too little acquainted with all their local circumstances and lesser interests; as by reducing it too much, you render him unduly attached to these, and too little fit to comprehend and pursue great and national objects. The federal Constitution forms a happy combination in this respect . . ." (*The Federalist #10*, 1787).* Representation in the United States has much changed from Madison's day, but the effort to find the appropriate mean goes on. To this problem there is no final solution, because the needs and circumstances of large communities are forever changing.

Geographical and Proportional Representation

In establishing the bases for representation in a democracy two solutions predominate. Both are compromises; both have serious flaws; both work moderately well. On one system, the geographical, a fixed number of districts (wards, townships, states) are each permitted a fixed number of elected representatives. On the other system, the proportional, various devices are employed to insure that each elected deputy has a known and relatively homogeneous constituency supporting him specifically as the representative of their common concern. Under the latter system, if the supporters of Parties x, y and z comprise 60, 25, and 15 percent of the total population respectively, the mixture of representatives in the parliament will approximate that same proportion, each deputy sitting as a representative of voters all of whom share his views on some key issue.

Proportional representation is clearly intended to increase homogeneity, functionality in the representative system. Under it the members of each constituency will not be completely alike, of course, since voters united on some issues will be at odds on others, but it must lead to far more homogeneity than constituencies geographically determined. Geographical representation is not wholly non-functional, because many interests tend to cluster in certain places. Industrial interests (those of farming or mining, for example) or ethnic interests, often concentrate in specific areas. But a geographical district may encompass great heterogeneity, and is likely to encompass at least a good deal of it. Although neither of the two systems is pure, therefore, their relative merits are essentially the merits of the functional and non-functional ends of

*See above, Selection #74.

the continuum described above. There are, of course, many variants of each, and they can even be in some degree combined.

Geographical representation is subject to a particular flaw that is both very common and very serious. In essence, that flaw is the distortion of the geographical districts in a way that subverts genuine and balanced representation. The "rotten boroughs" of England before 1832 (electoral districts with populations near zero), and the "gerrymandering" sometimes still practiced in America (shaping the district to concentrate the votes of a favored minority), are instances of deliberate distortion. More serious, if less blatant, injustices frequently result from accidental distortion caused by the growth and movement of populations. Where the total number of representatives in a legislative body is fixed, and the number from each geographical district is fixed, significant changes in the relative population of the several districts may result in severe under-representation of citizens in more densely populated districts, and over-representation of voters in sparsely populated areas. In effect, the degrees of representation in the several districts then show great disparities; a rural district having half the population of a metropolitan one, but the same number of representatives in a common assembly, unfairly enjoys a degree of representation twice as high.

The population changes that create these disparities take place gradually, but their cumulative impact is enormous. With great cities grossly under-represented, it is inevitable that their needs will be inadequately met by the representative body as a whole. The metropolitan districts will contribute more than their share to the communal treasury, receive less than their share in tax expenditures. In just this fashion have American cities often been abused.

Remedy for the distortion of representative districts is very difficult to achieve. Changing the number of representatives in the assembly, or the relative number from the several districts, is generally not feasible. The remaining alternative is the redrawing of the electoral districts on the map of the community, the painful process of legislative reapportionment. Even when the need for it is widely appreciated, reapportionment is difficult to effect. Any system of representation, once in operation, becomes habitual and ensconced. Moreover, the task of reapportioning falls naturally to the representatives themselves, and they are not likely to want to alter the system in which they have been elected to leadership and have strong vested interests. If the representatives cannot be persuaded or driven by their own constituents to reapportion, external pressure from the judiciary may be the only recourse. In the United States, the landmark Supreme Court case of *Baker v. Carr* (1962)* opened the path to judicial remedy for inequitable apportionment in the several states, and brought to the surface a host of injustices in our representative systems of which few had realized the full extent. The slogan "one person, one vote," has been shorthand for the expression of the democratic ideal of equal degrees of representation for all—for every vote an equal voice.

Proportional representation has the merit of encouraging the responsiveness of the deputy to his constituency; it also tends to give minority parties large enough

*See above, Selection #78.

to elect one or two representatives under that system a voice they would probably be denied under a geographical system.* But its flaws are serious too. Some versions of it oblige the use of signed "voting papers" on which the voter lists his preferences among the candidates; the need to keep these on file makes impossible a wholly secret ballot. Some versions result in the representation of so many minor parties in the parliament that definitive action requires coalitions difficult to maintain. Governmental efficiency is thus reduced. In some cases, the functional division of interests that proportional representation encourages can result in severe damage to minorities wholly unrepresented in the ruling coalition; then the decision-making rules applied within the parliament become most delicate matters. And systems of proportional representation are invariably complicated to operate. But, whether for good or ill, all versions of proportional representation may have results quite different from those that would have emerged had representatives been chosen from geographical districts by majority rule.

Every representative system—geographical, proportional, or other—is an instrument whose purpose is to make effective the participation of citizens in communities too large to permit each a direct voice in substantive affairs. No such system will be perfect; but the continuing effort to improve old forms and devise new ones so as to make representation more just and more effective is an enterprise no democracy can wisely abandon.

Levels of Representation

Any system of representation moves the sphere of actual decision-making one level away from the members represented. That process of removal is sometimes repeated, creating a second level of representation, and even a third. In each case the representatives at a given level become the represented at the next higher level, and the original body of electors come to be represented by a hierarchy of deputies, on several levels. The number of levels of representation in any given system is the number of steps above the membership at large at which substantive decisions are made. Members of a parliament elected through universal suffrage, for example, are representatives on the first level; ministers elected by the members of that parliament are representatives on a second level; administrative officers appointed by those ministers are representatives on a third level. The greater the number of levels, the less direct is the participation of the people, the less pure the democracy.

Such levels of representation are now taken for granted in most large democracies. Sometimes the indirection is a deliberate effort to insulate decisions from masses thought not competent or trustworthy enough to choose their own leaders—as with the original design of the Electoral College that was to choose the President of the United States. Open distrust of the people is less common now, but it is still widely believed that top executives, or administrators requiring technical skills, will be more wisely chosen by the elected representatives of the peo-

*See above, Selection #79.

ple than by the people themselves. The first level representatives, it is argued, will have a clearer understanding of the administrative tasks to be performed, and the talents those tasks require, than citizens at large. Such devices, in any event, although they may not defeat democracy, do tend to mute it. In some cases the argument for a second level of representation is based not on the incompetence of the masses, but on an alleged need to shelter officeholders of some kinds—judges, for example, or members of regulatory agencies—from the political pressures that would inevitably be applied to them if their selection took place on the first level of representation. There is often good sense in this argument.

Increased levels of representation do not remove ultimate authority from the hands of the members of the democratic community, but they do tend to reduce the power of the members to make their authority concretely effective. Wise or foolish, such levels are refinements of the tool of representation itself. Representation is an instrument to enable the members of a community to do for themselves indirectly what they cannot do, or do as well, directly; second and third levels of representation are modifications of that instrument to make possible the accomplishment for the community of what first level representatives cannot accomplish, or accomplish as well.

Representation Between Elections

When democracy operates through representatives, its depth will depend partly upon the quality of the participation of citizens in the election of representatives, and partly upon the effectiveness of the influence of constituents upon their representatives after election. This influence, between elections, is backed up ultimately by the promise of support or the threat of opposition at the next election. But whatever the sanction, that representative system is a better instrument of democracy which provides more and better channels through which public participation may be continuously operative.

Lenin said that, in Western democracies, the people have only the right to decide, at elections, who is to misrepresent them in parliament. Were he right, those democracies would indeed be fraudulent; if the consequence of the representative system is the frustration of the people's will, democracy has been subverted, not served by it. Some so-called democracies are fraudulent in this way; the mere existence of a chamber of deputies is not proof that democracy has been realized. One must know that the deputies represent their constituents truly and steadily; the representative system is only a tool that may function well or badly.

Recall, initiative, and referendum, are institutions devised to help insure better and more constant representation between elections. Recall permits the removal of a public official, by the vote of his constituency, when such a vote is demanded by a specified number of electors. This threat of removal even before the next regular election tends to maintain pressure on representatives to act as faithful deputies, to be sensitive to the intense desires of their constituents, and thus to make indirect participation by those constituents more continuously effective. Initiative and referendum have the same tendency, but operate quite differently.

Instead of threatening the tenure of representatives, they threaten to take certain questions out of the hands of the representatives, and return them to the direct control of the citizens. Initiative provides that a statute or amendment having a specified degree of support must come to popular vote. Referendum permits measures already before some legislative body to be submitted to the vote of the electorate for approval or rejection. These devices aim to sensitize the representative machinery by giving the voters the power to punish or to bypass their representatives without awaiting the next general election. The mere presence of these powers, not to mention specific threats of their use, can inhibit a representative who might seek to abuse his position, and can help to keep representatives alert to the strongly felt needs of their constituents.

Such institutions may increase the depth of a democracy, but they do not always improve the democracy; their net effects upon it may prove to be adverse. The very considerations of community size and complexity of issues necessitating representation in the first place may render damaging instruments designed to suspend representative government on specific issues and reinstitute direct democracy. At critical moments in the life of a community recall, too, may do harm. Although honestly intended to increase the effectiveness of participation, these devices may have precisely the reverse effect, by interfering with the proper fulfillment of the tasks of legislative or executive bodies. They may be employed in such a way as to subordinate long-range policy to short-run desires, while the participation of the people is made truly effective by the representative system as a whole, and over the long run.

Tension invariably arises between the need to keep the will of the membership continuously effective, and the need to encourage reasonable stability of policy and leadership. That stability it will normally be desirable to insure by protecting the authority and tenure of elected representatives. Yet on some occasions in some communities it may be appropriate to return from representative to direct democracy in order to insure the sovereignty of the people. What set of representative institutions best resolves this tension in a given community can be determined only by it, in view of its own circumstances.

The Dilemma of the Representative

The problem of maintaining equilibrium between the need for stability and the need for continuing citizen control between elections, has thus far been viewed from the perspective of the citizens. Consider the problem now from the perspective of the representative, one who serves his constituency with integrity in a system functioning with reasonable success. When he finds himself in honest and serious disagreement with the majority of his electors he may face an agonizing dilemma.

In such circumstances, is it the obligation of the representative to act as he knows his constituents wish him to act (say, support Policy P), or as he genuinely believes to be in their best interests (say, support Policy Q)? On most issues this conflict does not arise; but when the constituents' wishes and his judgment do conflict, what is the representative's overriding duty?

At first glance it would appear that, his position being that of deputy, he ought to vote for P if he really knows that P is what a majority of his constituents want. He has been selected, after all, to represent them, to participate in decision-making for them. To defy them would seem to betray their trust in him. His job (he may reason) is not to pass judgment on the people's wishes, but to implement those wishes. On the other hand, it is easy enough to see that certain questions arising in the parliament may be of so complex a nature that the mass of citizens do not have the time or opportunity to acquire the information necessary for intelligent decision, or the ability to organize or apply such information. In such cases the honest representative may feel that, in acting contrary to the people's will, voting against P, he is only doing what they would themselves do had they the information and understanding that he has. And he has been chosen, the argument continues, precisely for this task—to gather and apply relevant information with a thoroughness not possible for each single citizen he represents. Therefore (he may reason) it is his duty to follow the course that he honestly believes to be in the best interests of his constituents, even if they do not presently agree with him. Edmund Burke said to the electors of Bristol in 1775: "Your representative owes you not his industry only, but his judgment; and he betrays instead of serving you if he sacrifices it to your opinion."*

The same general tension between continuity of citizen participation and stability of leadership described in the preceding section is here manifested in the smaller and clearer context of this deputy's dilemma. If the representative thinks his proper conduct in this situation is that of acting as he knows his constituents really wish him to, he exhibits prime concern for the continuing effectiveness of general participation in government. If he thinks it proper for him to act as he believes the best interests of his constituents require, in spite of their disagreement, he exhibits concern for the successful completion of certain tasks with which the representative body of which he is a member has been charged. There is no simple answer available to him, and the question will not down.

This tension will prove less worrisome, however, if the important distinction between questions of policy and questions of implementation is kept in mind. Our inclination to swing now to one and now to the other horn of the dilemma is partly caused by the difference in our attitudes toward these different kinds of issues. When the question is one of general policy formation, it is appropriate that its resolution be undertaken by general participation. When the question is one of policy implementation its wise resolution is likely to require technical competence and information far greater than that of the ordinary citizen, and is then appropriately the task of representatives selected for just that purpose.

Every particular question, of course, will encompass some elements of policy formation and some of implementation. There can be no simple rule which permits the definitive classification of every issue the representative confronts. Furthermore, what is an issue of policy implementation in one context may be an issue of policy formation in another, smaller context. As a matter of practical fact, the rep-

*See above, Selection #75.

resentative is likely to have a keen appreciation of the community context within which he functions as deputy; without it he could hardly succeed at his job. Given an understanding of that context, the difference between policy formation and implementation, though never sharp, is clear enough on most matters. In the case of a member of a national parliament, should his constituents have indicated their strong support for the conservation of natural resources, or more social welfare legislation, or the reverse of these, it surely is the representative's duty to work for these general objectives. In the smaller context of city government, a councilman is likely to be conscious of his constituents' express desire for public housing or an improved system of public transit, and he is then under the obligation to work for these ends. If the member of parliament or the councilman cannot support known community objectives in good conscience he is at liberty to resign his representative office—he is likely to lose it at the next election in any event. On the other hand, technical questions concerning the rules governing the use of state-owned resources, or the fares to be charged on a public transit system, are not reasonably put before the general populace. It is to resolve just such questions, as best to implement the general aims of nation or city, that representatives have been chosen.

The problem here is that of determining the proper *range* of direct participation within a democracy that is itself largely indirect. Which questions, or kinds of questions, are properly left to the judgment of the representatives, and which are properly decided by the popular will even when a representative system is functioning smoothly? The problem has no general resolution. But the dilemma facing the representative is not so burdensome as at first it might appear. In the first place, on most questions (in communities where representatives are fairly and frequently chosen) their will and the will of their constituents are likely to be identical or nearly so. This is more likely to be the case, of course, where the constituency is relatively homogeneous—and this approximation of identity is an important consideration weighing in favor of a more functional system of representation. In the second place, where representative and constituents are not known to be in agreement, they will very often not be known to be in disagreement either, for the will of the constituents will not normally have been clearly and unambiguously expressed. In such common circumstances the dilemma does not arise; the conscientious deputy ought to act as he supposes they who elected him would act in the light of such knowledge as he possesses. Finally, in those rare cases in which the representative finds himself in conflict with the known will of the majority of his constituents, he must determine whether the question is chiefly one of policy, upon which the popular will ought to be decisive, or one of technique, upon which his election and professional qualifications entitle him to act in opposition to popular will, on the ground that, were his constituents in a position to know or understand the situation as thoroughly as he, they would judge the merits of the question as he does. He makes this decision knowing that he will have to answer to his constituents no later than the time of the next election.

Who, in practice, is to decide whether a given issue is chiefly one of policy or of technique? Is he, the representative alone, to make that decision? Yes; there is no one who can do it for him. But will he not always be inclined to treat questions of policy as technical questions upon which his special competence entitles him to overrule the popular opinion? No doubt there will be that inclination. The integrity of representatives, however, can never be guaranteed by written rules or prescribed codes of conduct. In being elected by the members of a community to administer the governing process in their stead, each representative occupies a position of the highest and most delicate trust. If the members of a democratic community are not capable of selecting, at least in the great run of cases, representatives whose integrity and conscientious attention to their responsibilities as trustees are sufficient to qualify them even to determine the limits of their own jurisdiction, that community will not long remain a democracy.

THE IDEALS OF DEMOCRACY

The ideals of the French Revolution—Liberty, Equality, Fraternity—are the classical ideals of democracy itself. The history of modern democracy may be viewed as an on-going struggle to realize these ideals in actual human communities. Fraternity is the *presupposition* of democracy; liberty is the condition for the successful *practice* of democracy; equality is central to the *justification* of democracy. Consider these ideals in turn, briefly:

The members of any self-governing community must recognize that they share some common enterprise, and recognize also with whom that enterprise is shared. There must be known boundaries, therefore, within which the citizens have the authority to establish policies and laws. Democracy is not even possible where there is no underlying community; and therefore threats to the continuation of an existing community elicit, in a democracy, the impassioned defense of union. Fraternity underlies all that a democracy may accomplish.

Liberty is the most palpable of the three great ideals, the most readily identified in everyday life. Of the three it is liberty that is for most persons the dearest and whose infringement is most quickly and sensitively felt. For any people actually to govern itself there must be wide freedom to speak and to publish, to propose and to oppose, and (within some broad limits) to act without the hindrance of the state. Nearly every major issue in a democracy will touch upon freedom of one kind or another, and every party will contend, as they honestly believe, that the policies they support will extend freedom while those they attack will restrict it. In the day-to-day life of a healthy political democracy *freedom* is likely to be the nub of the most heated controversies.

Equality, of the three ideals, is closest to the heart of democracy, because the commitment to human equality is the theoretical ground of the right of all to participate. The denial of equality, even if only implicit, therefore threatens the loss of moral foundations. Democracy can be justified in any community only to the degree that a relevant underlying equality among its members has been established or supposed. Without fraternity a democracy will not be instituted, and without liberty it will not succeed, but without equality there is little good reason to believe that democracy ought to succeed, or to defend it as right.

Autonomy is not so much an ideal of democracy as its essence. Just as in the life of the individual person it is the imposition of moral laws *upon one's self* that is the mark of a moral will, so, in the life of a community the imposition of rules that govern the members *by the members themselves* is the mark of a moral social life.

FRATERNITY

81
George Washington

Two American presidents, Washington and Lincoln, among the greatest of
political and intellectual heroes, defended the unity of the nation as the
foundation of its democracy. Of union, George Washington (1732–1799) said that
it was "a main Pillar in the Edifice" of independence, and a "main prop" to
liberty. The short passage below is taken from Washington's Farewell Address to
his countrymen upon retiring from the Presidency.

[UNION AS THE BULWARK OF AMERICAN ASPIRATIONS]*

Union . . . is a main Pillar in the Edifice of your real independence; the support
of your tranquillity at home; your peace abroad; of your safety; of your prosperity
in every shape; of that very Liberty which you so highly prize. . . . [I]t is of infinite moment, that you should properly estimate the immense value of your
national Union to your collective and individual happiness;—that you should cherish a cordial, habitual, and immoveable attachment to it; accustoming yourselves

*From George Washington, Farewell Address, September 17, 1796.

to think and speak of it as the Palladium of your political safety and prosperity; watching for its preservation with jealous anxiety; discountenancing whatever may suggest even a suspicion, that it can in any event be abandoned, and indignantly frowning upon the first dawning of every attempt to alienate any portion of our Country from the rest, or to enfeeble the sacred ties which now link together the various parts. . . . [Y]our union ought to be considered as a main prop to your liberty, and . . . the love of the one ought to endear you to the preservation of the other.

82
Abraham Lincoln

The dissolution of the American Union was gravely threatened by the election of Abraham Lincoln (1809–1865) as 16th president in 1860. By February of 1861 seven Southern states had seceded, the provisional constitution of the Confederacy had been adopted and its provisional president inaugurated. The American Civil War—the War of Secession—began in April of 1961, only six weeks after Lincoln's passionate argument, in his Inaugural Address, for the peaceful preservation of the Union. He spoke directly to those who would dissolve the Union, appealing to "the better angels of our nature." Continuing democracy, the peaceful solution to the troubles of the nation, depend utterly upon "the restoration of fraternal sympathies and affections." No statesman ever had a deeper understanding of the role of *fraternity* in the life of a democracy.

[THE AMERICAN UNION IS PERPETUAL]*

FELLOW-CITIZENS of the United States: In compliance with a custom as old as the government itself, I appear before you to address you briefly, and to take in your presence the oath prescribed by the Constitution of the United States to be taken by the President "before he enters on the execution of his office." . . .

It is seventy-two years since the first inauguration of a President under our National Constitution. During that period fifteen different and greatly distinguished citizens have, in succession, administered the executive branch of the government. They have conducted it through many perils, and generally with great success. Yet, with all this scope of precedent, I now enter upon the same task for the brief constitutional term of four years under great and peculiar difficulty. A disruption of the Federal Union, heretofore only menaced, is now formidably attempted.

I hold that, in contemplation of universal law and of the Constitution, the Union of these States is perpetual. Perpetuity is implied, if not expressed, in the funda-

*From Abraham Lincoln, First Inaugural Address, March 4, 1861.

ɯental law of all national governments. It is safe to assert that no government proper ever had a provision in its organic law for its own termination.

Continue to execute all the express provisions of our National Constitution, and the Union will endure forever—it being impossible to destroy it except by some action not provided for in the instrument itself.

Again, if the United States be not a government proper, but an association of States in the nature of contract merely, can it, as a contract, be peaceably unmade by less than all the parties who made it? One party to a contract may violate it— break it, so to speak; but does it not require all to lawfully rescind it?

Descending from these general principles, we find the proposition that, in legal contemplation the Union is perpetual confirmed by the history of the Union itself. The Union is much older than the Constitution. It was formed, in fact, by the Articles of Association in 1774. It was matured and continued by the Declaration of Independence in 1776. It was further matured, and the faith of all the then thirteen States expressly plighted and engaged that it should be perpetual, by the Articles of Confederation in 1778. And, finally, in 1787 one of the declared objects for ordaining and establishing the Constitution was "to form a more perfect Union."

But if the destruction of the Union by one or by a part only of the States be law fully possible, the Union is less perfect than before the Constitution, having lost the vital element of perpetuity.

It follows from these views that no State upon its own mere motion can law fully get out of the Union; that resolves and ordinances to that effect are legally void; and that acts of violence, within any State or States, against the authority of the United States, are insurrectionary or revolutionary, according to circum stances.

I therefore consider that, in view of the Constitution and the laws, the Union is unbroken; and to the extent of my ability I shall take care, as the Constitution itself expressly enjoins upon me, that the laws of the Union be faithfully executed in all the States. Doing this I deem to be only a simple duty on my part; and I shall per form it so far as practicable, unless my rightful masters, the American people, shall withhold the requisite means, or in some authoritative manner direct the con trary. I trust this will not be regarded as a menace, but only as the declared pur pose of the Union that it will constitutionally defend and maintain itself.

In doing this there needs to be no bloodshed or violence; and there shall be none, unless it be forced upon the national authority. The power confided to me will be used to hold, occupy, and possess the property and places belonging to the government, and to collect the duties and imposts; but beyond what may be nec essary for these objects, there will be no invasion, no using of force against or among the people anywhere. Where hostility to the United States, in any interior locality, shall be so great and universal as to prevent competent resident citizens from holding the Federal offices, there will be no attempt to force obnoxious strangers among the people for that object. While the strict legal right may exist in the government to enforce the exercise of these offices, the attempt to do so would be so irritating, and so nearly impracticable withal, that I deem it better to forego for the time the uses of such offices.

The mails, unless repelled, will continue to be furnished in all parts of the Union. So far as possible, the people everywhere shall have that sense of perfect security which is most favorable to calm thought and reflection. The course here indicated will be followed unless current events and experience shall show a modification or change to be proper, and in every case and exigency my best discretion will be exercised according to circumstances actually existing, and with a view and a hope of a peaceful solution of the national troubles and the restoration of fraternal sympathies and affections.

That there are persons in one section or another who seek to destroy the Union at all events, and are glad of any pretext to do it, I will neither affirm nor deny; but if there be such, I need address no word to them. To those, however, who really love the Union may I not speak? . . .

Plainly, the central idea of secession is the essence of anarchy. A majority held in restraint by constitutional checks and limitations, and always changing easily with deliberate changes of popular opinions and sentiments, is the only true sovereign of a free people. Whoever rejects it does, of necessity, fly to anarchy or to despotism. Unanimity is impossible; the rule of a minority, as a permanent arrangement, is wholly inadmissible; so that, rejecting the majority principle, anarchy or despotism in some form is all that is left. . . .

Physically speaking, we cannot separate. We cannot remove our respective sections from each other, nor build an impassable wall between them. A husband and wife may be divorced, and go out of the presence and beyond the reach of each other; but the different parts of our country cannot do this. They cannot but remain face to face, and intercourse, either amicable or hostile, must continue between them. Is it possible, then, to make that intercourse more advantageous or more satisfactory after separation than before? Can aliens make treaties easier than friends can make laws? Can treaties be more faithfully enforced between aliens than laws can among friends? Suppose you go to war, you cannot fight always; and when, after much loss on both sides, and no gain on either, you cease fighting, the identical old questions as to terms of intercourse are again upon you.

This country, with its institutions, belongs to the people who inhabit it. Whenever they shall grow weary of the existing government, they can exercise their constitutional right of amending it, or their revolutionary right to dismember or overthrow it. . . .

Why should there not be a patient confidence in the ultimate justice of the people? Is there any better or equal hope in the world? In our present differences is either party without faith of being in the right? If the Almighty Ruler of Nations, with his eternal truth and justice, be on your side of the North, or on yours of the South, that truth and that justice will surely prevail by the judgment of this great tribunal of the American people. . . .

In your hands, my dissatisfied fellow-countrymen, and not in mine, is the momentous issue of civil war. The government will not assail you. You can have no conflict without being yourselves the aggressors. You have no oath registered in heaven to destroy the government, while I shall have the most solemn one to "preserve, protect, and defend it."

I am loath to close. We are not enemies, but friends. We must not be enemies. Though passion may have strained, it must not break our bonds of affection. The mystic chords of memory, stretching from every battlefield and patriot grave to every living heart and hearthstone all over this broad land, will yet swell the chorus of the Union when again touched, as surely they will be, by the better angels of our nature.

SUBSECTION B

LIBERTY

Liberties of thought and expression—freedom of speech, and of the press, and of assembly, and the like—are universally acknowledged as critical to self-government, and therefore the limitation of these freedoms, and the justification of any such limits, must remain a perpetual problem in democracies. *Economic liberty*, and the relation of democracy to different economic systems, has given rise to theoretical controversy of a very different kind, partly because of conflicting conclusions reached from the study of history. Both families of liberty are dealt with in the selections below.

83
John Stuart Mill

The most famous and perhaps the most powerfully argued defense of individual freedom in the English language was given by J. S. Mill in *On Liberty* (1859). The widest range of liberty ought to be protected, Mill argued, not out of obedience to some command or constitution, but because of the advantages, moral and intellectual, such liberty will bring to the community as a whole over the long run. Especially with respect to the freedom of thought and speech, repression proves in the end to be self-defeating. These utilitarian arguments, presented a century and a half ago, are commonly cited in contemporary controversies over the freedom of speech. It is as though Mill wrote just yesterday, for today and tomorrow.

[THE TYRANNY OF THE MAJORITY]*

. . . in political and philosophical theories, as well as in persons, success discloses faults and infirmities which failure might have concealed from observation. The notion, that the people have no need to limit their power over themselves, might seem axiomatic, when popular government was a thing only dreamed about, or read of as having existed at some distant period of the past. . . .

In time, however, a democratic republic came to occupy a large portion of the earth's surface, and made itself felt as one of the most powerful members of the community of nations; and elective and responsible government became subject to the observations and criticisms which wait upon a great existing fact. It was now perceived that such phrases as "self-government," and "the power of the people over themselves," do not express the true state of the case. The "people" who exercise the power are not always the same people with those over whom it is exercised; and the "self-government" spoken of is not the government of each by himself, but of each by all the rest. The will of the people, moreover, practically means the will of the most numerous or the most active *part* of the people; the majority, or those who succeed in making themselves accepted as the majority; the people, consequently, *may* desire to oppress a part of their number; and precautions are as much needed against this as against any other abuse of power. The limitation, therefore, of the power of government over individuals loses none of its importance when the holders of power are regularly accountable to the community, that is, to the strongest party therein. This view of things, recommending itself equally to the intelligence of thinkers and to the inclination of those important classes in European society to whose real or supposed interests democracy is adverse, has had no difficulty in establishing itself; and in political speculations "the tyranny of the majority" is now generally included among the evils against which society requires to be on its guard.

*From John Stuart Mill, *On Liberty,* 1859.

Like other tyrannies, the tyranny of the majority was at first, and is still vul-
garly, held in dread, chiefly as operating through the acts of the public authorities.
But reflecting persons perceived that when society is itself the tyrant—society collectively, over the separate individuals who compose it—its means of tyrannizing
are not restricted to the acts which it may do by the hands of its political functionaries. Society can and does execute its own mandates: and if it issues wrong
mandates instead of right, or any mandates at all in things with which it ought not
to meddle, it practices a social tyranny more formidable than many kinds of political oppression, since, though not usually upheld by such extreme penalties, it
leaves fewer means of escape, penetrating much more deeply into the details of
life, and enslaving the soul itself. Protection, therefore, against the tyranny of the
magistrate is not enough: there needs protection also against the tyranny of the
prevailing opinion and feeling; against the tendency of society to impose, by other
means than civil penalties, its own ideas and practices as rules of conduct on those
who dissent from them; to fetter the development, and, if possible, prevent the formation, of any individuality not in harmony with its ways, and compel all characters to fashion themselves upon the model of its own. There is a limit to the legitimate interference of collective opinion with individual independence: and to find
that limit, and maintain it against encroachment, is as indispensable to a good condition of human affairs, as protection against political despotism. . . .

[THE DOMAIN OF HUMAN LIBERTY]

The object of this Essay is to assert one very simple principle, as entitled to govern absolutely the dealings of society with the individual in the way of compulsion
and control, whether the means used be physical force in the form of legal penalties, or the moral coercion of public opinion. That principle is, that the sole end for
which mankind are warranted, individually or collectively, in interfering with the
liberty of action of any of their number, is self-protection. That the only purpose
for which power can be rightfully exercised over any member of a civilized community, against his will, is to prevent harm to others. His own good, either physical or moral, is not a sufficient warrant. He cannot rightfully be compelled to do
or forbear because it will be better for him to do so, because it will make him happier, because, in the opinions of others, to do so would be wise, or even right.
These are good reasons for remonstrating with him, or reasoning with him, or persuading him, or entreating him, but not for compelling him, or visiting him with
any evil in case he do otherwise. To justify that, the conduct from which it is
desired to deter him, must be calculated to produce evil to someone else. The only
part of the conduct of anyone, for which he is amenable to society, is that which
concerns others. In the part which merely concerns himself, his independence is,
of right, absolute. Over himself, over his own body and mind, the individual is
sovereign. . . .

It is proper to state that I forgo any advantage which could be derived to my
argument from the idea of abstract right, as a thing independent of utility. I regard
utility as the ultimate appeal on all ethical questions; but it must be utility in the

largest sense, grounded on the permanent interests of man as a progressive being. Those interests, I contend, authorize the subjection of individual spontaneity to external control, only in respect to those actions of each, which concern the interest of other people. . . .

But there is a sphere of action in which society, as distinguished from the individual, has, if any, only an indirect interest; comprehending all that portion of a person's life and conduct which affects only himself, or if it also affects others, only with their free, voluntary, and undeceived consent and participation. When I say only himself, I mean directly, and in the first instance: for whatever affects himself, may affect others through himself; and the objection which may be grounded on this contingency will receive consideration in the sequel. This, then, is the appropriate region of human liberty. It comprises, first, the inward domain of consciousness; demanding liberty of conscience, in the most comprehensive sense; liberty of thought and feeling; absolute freedom of opinion and sentiment on all subjects, practical or speculative, scientific, moral, or theological. The liberty of expressing and publishing opinions may seem to fall under a different principle, since it belongs to that part of the conduct of an individual which concerns other people; but, being almost of as much importance as the liberty of thought itself, and resting in great part on the same reasons, is practically inseparable from it. Secondly, the principle requires liberty of tastes and pursuits; of framing the plan of our life to suit our own character; of doing as we like, subject to such consequences as may follow: without impediment from our fellow creatures, so long as what we do does not harm them, even though they should think our conduct foolish, perverse, or wrong. Thirdly, from this liberty of each individual, follows the liberty, within the same limits, of combination among individuals; freedom to unite, for any purpose not involving harm to others: the persons combining being supposed to be of full age, and not forced or deceived.

No society in which these liberties are not, on the whole, respected, is free, whatever may be its form of government; and none is completely free in which they do not exist absolute and unqualified. The only freedom which deserves the name, is that of pursuing our own good in our own way, so long as we do not attempt to deprive others of theirs, or impede their efforts to obtain it. Each is the proper guardian of his own health, whether bodily, or mental and spiritual. Mankind are greater gainers by suffering each other to live as seems good to themselves, than by compelling each to live as seems good to the rest. . . .

There is . . . in the world at large an increasing inclination to stretch unduly the powers of society over the individual, both by the force of opinion and even by that of legislation: and as the tendency of all the changes taking place in the world is to strengthen society, and diminish the power of the individual, this encroachment is not one of the evils which tend spontaneously to disappear, but, on the contrary, to grow more and more formidable. The disposition of mankind, whether as rulers or as fellow citizens, to impose their own opinions and inclinations as a rule of conduct on others, is so energetically supported by some of the best and by some of the worst feelings incident to human nature, that it is hardly ever kept under restraint by anything but want of power; and as the power is not declining, but growing, unless a strong barrier of moral conviction can be raised against the mischief, we must expect, in the present circumstances of the world, to see it increase.

. . .

OF THE LIBERTY OF THOUGHT AND DISCUSSION

The time, it is to be hoped, is gone by, when any defense would be necessary of the "liberty of the press" as one of the securities against corrupt or tyrannical government. No argument, we may suppose, can now be needed, against permitting a legislature or an executive, not identified in interest with the people, to prescribe opinions to them, and determine what doctrines or what arguments they shall be allowed to hear. This aspect of the question, besides, has been so often and so triumphantly enforced by preceding writers, that it needs not be specially insisted on in this place. . . . Let us suppose, therefore, that the government is entirely at one with the people, and never thinks of exerting any power of coercion unless in agreement with what it conceives to be their voice. But I deny the right of the people to exercise such coercion, either by themselves or by their government. The power itself is illegitimate. The best government has no more title to it than the worst. It is as noxious, or more noxious, when exerted in accordance with public opinion, than when in opposition to it. If all mankind minus one, were of one opinion, and only one person were of the contrary opinion, mankind would be no more justified in silencing that one person, than he, if he had the power, would be justified in silencing mankind. Were an opinion a personal possession of no value except to the owner; if to be obstructed in the enjoyment of it were simply a private injury, it would make some difference whether the injury was inflicted only on a few persons or on many. But the peculiar evil of silencing the expression of an opinion is, that it is robbing the human race; posterity as well as the existing generation; those who dissent from the opinion, still more than those who hold it. If the opinion is right, they are deprived of the opportunity of exchanging error for truth: if wrong, they lose, what is almost as great a benefit, the clearer perception and livelier impression of truth, produced by its collision with error.

It is necessary to consider separately these two hypotheses, each of which has a distinct branch of the argument corresponding to it. We can never be sure that the opinion we are endeavoring to stifle is a false opinion; and if we were sure, stifling it would be an evil still.

First: the opinion which it is attempted to suppress by authority may possibly be true. Those who desire to suppress it, of course deny its truth; but they are not infallible. They have no authority to decide the question for all mankind, and exclude every other person from the means of judging. To refuse a hearing to an opinion, because they are sure that it is false, is to assume that *their* certainty is the same thing as *absolute* certainty. All silencing of discussion is an assumption of infallibility. Its condemnation may be allowed to rest on this common argument, not the worse for being common.

Unfortunately for the good sense of mankind, the fact of their fallibility is far from carrying the weight in their practical judgment, which is always allowed to it in theory; for while everyone well knows himself to be fallible, few think it necessary to take any precautions against their own fallibility, or admit the supposition that any opinion, of which they feel very certain, may be one of the examples of the error to which they acknowledge themselves to be liable. Absolute princes, or others who are accustomed to unlimited deference, usually feel this complete confidence in their own opinions on nearly all subjects. People more happily situated, who sometimes hear their opinions disputed, and are not wholly unused to be set right when they are wrong, place the same unbounded reliance only on such of their opinions as are shared by all who surround them, or to whom they habitually defer: for in proportion to a man's want of confidence in his own solitary judgment, does he usually repose, with implicit trust, on the infallibility of "the world" in general. And the world, to each individual, means the part of it with which he comes in contact; his party, his sect, his church, his class of society: the man may be called, by comparison, almost liberal and large-minded to whom it means anything so comprehensive as his own country or his own age. Nor is his faith in this collective authority at all shaken by his being aware that other ages, countries, sects, churches, classes, and parties have thought, and even now think, the exact reverse. He devolves upon his own world the responsibility of being in the right against the dissentient worlds of other people; and it never troubles him that mere accident has decided which of these numerous worlds is the object of his reliance, and that the same causes which make him a Churchman in London, would have made him a Buddhist or a Confucian in Pekin. Yet it is as evident in itself, as any amount of argument can make it, that ages are no more infallible than individuals; every age having held many opinions which subsequent ages have deemed not only false but absurd; and it is as certain that many opinions, now general, will be rejected by future ages, as it is that many, once general, are rejected by the present.

The objection likely to be made to this argument would probably take some such form as the following. There is no greater assumption of infallibility in forbidding the propagation of error, than in any other thing which is done by public authority on its own judgment and responsibility. Judgment is given to men that they may use it. Because it may be used erroneously, are men to be told that they ought not to use it at all? To prohibit what they think pernicious, is not claiming exemption from error, but fulfilling the duty incumbent on them, although fallible, of acting on their conscientious conviction. If we were never to act on our opinions, because those opinions may be wrong, we should leave all our interests uncared for, and all our duties unperformed. An objection which applies to all conduct, can be no valid objection to any conduct, in particular. It is the duty of governments, and of individuals, to form the truest opinions they can; to form them carefully, and never impose them upon others unless they are quite sure of being right. But when they are sure (such reasoners may say), it is not conscientiousness but cowardice to shrink from acting on their opinions, and allow doctrines which they honestly think dangerous to the welfare of mankind, either in this life or in another, to be scattered abroad without restraint, because other people, in less enlightened times, have persecuted opinions now believed to be true. Let us take care, it may be said, not to make the same mistake: but governments and nations have made mistakes in other things, which are not denied to be fit subjects for the exercise of authority: they have laid on bad taxes, made unjust wars. Ought we therefore to lay on no taxes, and, under whatever provocation, make no wars? Men, and governments, must act to the best of their ability. There is no such thing as absolute certainty, but there is assurance sufficient for the purposes of human life. We may, and must, assume our opinion to be true for the guidance of our own conduct: and it is assuming no more when we forbid bad men to pervert society by the propagation of opinions which we regard as false and pernicious.

I answer, that it is assuming very much more. There is the greatest difference between presuming an opinion to be true, because, with every opportunity for contesting it, it has not been refuted, and assuming its truth for the purpose of not permitting its refutation. Complete liberty of contradicting and disproving our opinion, is the very condition which justifies us in assuming its truth for purposes of action; and on no other terms can a being with human faculties have any rational assurance of being right.

When we consider either the history of opinion, or the ordinary conduct of human life, to what is it to be ascribed that the one and the other are no worse than they are? Not certainly to the inherent force of the human understanding; for, on any matter not self-evident, there are ninety-nine persons totally incapable of judging of it, for one who is capable; and the capacity of the hundredth person is only comparative; for the majority of the eminent men of every past generation held many opinions now known to be erroneous, and did or approved numerous things which no one will now justify. Why is it, then, that there is on the whole a preponderance among mankind of rational opinions and rational conduct? If there really is this preponderance—which there must be unless human affairs are, and have always been, in an almost desperate state—it is owing to a quality of the human mind, the source of everything respectable in man either as an intellectual or as a moral being, namely, that his errors are corrigible. He is capable of rectifying his mistakes, by discussion and experience. Not by experience alone. There must be discussion, to show how experience is to be interpreted. Wrong opinions and practices gradually yield to fact and argument: but facts and arguments, to produce any effect on the mind, must be brought before it. Very few facts are able to tell their own story, without comments to bring out their meaning. The whole strength and value, then, of human judgment, depending on the one property, that it can be set right when it is wrong, reliance can be placed on it only when the means of setting it right are kept constantly at hand. In the case of any person whose judgment is really deserving of confidence, how has it become so? Because he has kept his mind open to criticism of his opinions and conduct. Because it has been his practice to listen to all that could be said against him; to profit by as much of it as was just, and expound to himself, and upon occasion to others, the fallacy of what was fallacious. Because he has felt, that the only way in which a human being can make some approach to knowing the whole of a subject, is by hearing what can be said about it by persons of every variety of opinion, and studying all modes in which it can be looked at by every character of mind. No wise man ever acquired his wisdom in any mode but this; nor is it in the nature of human intellect to become wise in any other manner. The steady habit of correcting and completing his own opinion by collating it with those of others, so far from causing doubt and hesitation in carrying it into practice, is the only stable foundation for a just reliance on it: for, being cognizant of all that can, at least obviously, be said against him, and having taken up his position against all gain-sayers—knowing that he has sought for objections and difficulties, instead of avoiding them, and has shut out no light which can be thrown upon the subject from any quarter—he has a right to think his judgment better than that of any person, or any multitude, who have not gone through a similar process.

. . . The beliefs which we have most warrant for, have no safeguard to rest on, but a standing invitation to the whole world to prove them unfounded. If the challenge is not accepted, or is accepted and the attempt fails, we are far enough from certainty still; but we have done the best that the existing state of human reason admits of; we have neglected nothing that could give the truth a chance of reaching us: if the lists are kept open, we may hope that if there be a better truth, it will be found when the human mind is capable of receiving it; and in the meantime we may rely on having attained such approach to truth, as is possible in our own day. This is the amount of certainty attainable by a fallible being, and this the sole way of attaining it.

Strange it is, that men should admit the validity of the arguments for free discussion, but object to their being "pushed to an extreme"; not seeing that unless the reasons are good for an extreme case, they are not good for any case. Strange that they should imagine that they are not assuming infallibility, when they acknowledge that there should be free discussion on all subjects which can possibly be *doubtful,* but think that some particular principle or doctrine should be forbidden to be questioned because it is so *certain,* that is, because *they are certain* that it is certain. To call my proposition certain, while there is any one who would deny its certainty if permitted, but who is not permitted, is to assume that we ourselves, and those who agree with us, are the judges of certainty, and judges without hearing the other side.

. . .

For a long time past, the chief mischief of the legal penalties is that they strengthen the social stigma. It is that stigma which is really effective. . . . Our merely social intolerance kills no one, roots out no opinions, but induces men to disguise them, or to abstain from any active effort for their diffusion. With us, heretical opinions do not perceptibly gain, or even lose, ground in each decade or generation; they never blaze out far and wide, but continue to smolder in the narrow circles of thinking and studious persons among whom they originate, without ever lighting up the general affairs of mankind with either a true or a deceptive light. And thus is kept up a state of things very satisfactory to some minds, because, without the unpleasant process of fining or imprisoning anybody, it maintains all prevailing opinions outwardly undisturbed, while it does not absolutely interdict the exercise of reason by dissentients afflicted with the malady of thought. A convenient plan for having peace in the intellectual world, and keeping all things going on therein very much as they do already. But the price paid for this sort of intellectual pacification, is the sacrifice of the entire moral courage of the human mind. A state of things in which a large portion of the most active and inquiring intellects find it advisable to keep the general principles and grounds of their convictions within their own breasts, and attempt, in what they address to the public, to fit as much as they can of their own conclusions to premises which they have internally renounced, cannot send forth the open, fearless characters, and logical, consistent intellects who once adorned the thinking world. The sort of men who can be looked for under it, are either mere conformers to commonplace, or timeservers for truth, whose arguments on all great subjects are meant for their hearers, and are not those which have convinced themselves. Those who avoid this alternative, do so by narrowing their thoughts and interest to things which can be spoken of without venturing within the region of principles, that is, to small practical matters, which would come right of themselves, if but the minds of mankind were strengthened and enlarged, and which will never be made effectually right until then: while that which would strengthen and enlarge men's minds, free and daring speculation on the highest subjects, is abandoned.

Those in whose eyes this reticence on the part of heretics is no evil, should consider in the first place, that in consequence of it there is never any fair and thorough discussion of heretical opinions; and that such of them as could not stand such a discussion, though they may be prevented from spreading, do not disappear. But it is not the minds of heretics that are deteriorated most, by the ban placed on all inquiry which does not end in the orthodox conclusions. The greatest harm done is to those who are not heretics, and whose whole mental development is cramped, and their reason cowed, by the fear of heresy. Who can compute what the world loses in the multitude of promising intellects combined with timid characters, who dare not follow out any bold, vigorous, independent train of thought, lest it should land them in something which would admit of being considered irreligious or immoral? Among them we may occasionally see some man of deep conscientiousness, and subtle and refined understanding, who spends a life in sophisticating with an intellect which he cannot silence, and exhausts the resources of ingenuity in attempting to reconcile the promptings of his conscience and reason with orthodoxy, which yet he does not, perhaps, to the end succeed in doing. No one can be a great thinker who does not recognize, that as a thinker it is his first duty to follow his intellect to whatever conclusions it may lead. Truth gains more even by the errors of one who, with due study and preparation, thinks for himself, than by the true opinions of those who only hold them because they do not suffer themselves to think. Not that it is solely, or chiefly, to form great thinkers, that freedom of thinking is required. On the contrary, it is as much and even more indispensable, to enable average human beings to attain the mental stature which they are capable of. There have been, and may again be, great individual thinkers, in a general atmosphere of mental slavery. But there never has been, nor ever will be, in that atmosphere, an intellectually active people. When any people has made

a temporary approach to such a character, it has been because the dread of hetero-
dox speculation was for a time suspended. Where there is a tacit convention that
principles are not to be disputed; where the discussion of the greatest questions
which can occupy humanity is considered to be closed, we cannot hope to find that
generally high scale of mental activity which has made some periods of history so
remarkable. . . .

Let us now pass to the second division of the argument, and dismissing the supposition that any of the received opinions may be false, let us assume them to be
true, and examine into the worth of the manner in which they are likely to be held,
when their truth is not freely and openly canvassed. However unwillingly a person
who has a strong opinion may admit the possibility that his opinion may be false,
he ought to be moved by the consideration that however true it may be, if it is not
fully, frequently, and fearlessly discussed, it will be held as a dead dogma, not a
living truth.

There is a class of persons (happily not quite so numerous as formerly) who
think it enough if a person assents undoubtingly to what they think true, though he
has no knowledge whatever of the grounds of the opinion, and could not make a
tenable defense of it against the most superficial objections. Such persons, if they
can once get their creed taught from authority, naturally think that no good, and
some harm, comes of its being allowed to be questioned. Where their influence
prevails, they make it nearly impossible for the received opinion to be rejected
wisely and considerately, though it may still be rejected rashly and ignorantly; for
to shut out discussion entirely is seldom possible, and when it once gets in, beliefs
not grounded on conviction are apt to give way before the slightest semblance of
an argument. Waiving, however, this possibility—assuming that the true opinion
abides in the mind, but abides as a prejudice, a belief independent of, and proof
against, argument—this is not the way in which truth ought to be held by a rational being. This is not knowing the truth. Truth, thus held, is but one superstition the
more accidentally clinging to the words which enunciate a truth.

If the intellect and judgment of mankind ought to be cultivated, a thing which
Protestants at least do not deny, on what can these faculties be more appropriately exercised by anyone, than on the things which concern him so much that it
is considered necessary for him to hold opinions on them? If the cultivation of
the understanding consists in one thing more than in another, it is surely in learning the grounds of one's own opinion. Whatever people believe, on subjects on
which it is of the first importance to believe rightly, they ought to be able to
defend against at least the common objections. But, some one may say, "Let
them be *taught* the grounds of their opinions. It does not follow that opinions
must be merely parroted because they are never heard controverted. Persons who
learn geometry do not simply commit the theorems to memory, but understand
and learn likewise the demonstrations; and it would be absurd to say that they
remain ignorant of the grounds of geometrical truths, because they never hear
anyone deny, and attempt to disprove them." Undoubtedly: and such teaching
suffices on a subject like mathematics, where there is nothing at all to be said on
the wrong side of the question. The peculiarity of the evidence of mathematical

truths is, that all the argument is on one side. There are no objections, and no answers to objections. But on every subject on which difference of opinion is possible, the truth depends on a balance to be struck between two sets of conflicting reasons. Even in natural philosophy, there is always some other explanation possible of the same facts; some geocentric theory instead of heliocentric, some phlogiston instead of oxygen; and it has to be shown why that other theory cannot be the true one: and until this is shown, and until we know how it is shown, we do not understand the grounds of our opinion. But when we turn to subjects infinitely more complicated, to morals, religion, politics, social relations, and the business of life, three-fourths of the arguments for every disputed opinion consist in dispelling the appearances which favor some opinion different from it. The greatest orator, save one, of antiquity, has left it on record that he always studied his adversary's case with as great, if not with still greater, intensity than even his own. What Cicero practiced as the means of forensic success, requires to be imitated by all who study any subject in order to arrive at the truth. He who knows only his own side of the case, knows little of that. His reasons may be good, and no one may have been able to refute them. But if he is equally unable to refute the reasons on the opposite side; if he does not so much as know what they are, he has no ground for preferring either opinion. The rational position for him would be suspension of judgment, and unless he contents himself with that, he is either led by authority, or adopts, like the generality of the world, the side to which he feels most inclination. Nor is it enough that he should hear the arguments of adversaries from his own teachers, presented as they state them, and accompanied by what they offer as refutations. That is not the way to do justice to the arguments, or bring them into real contact with his own mind. He must be able to hear them from persons who actually believe them; who defend them in earnest, and do their very utmost for them. He must know them in their most plausible and persuasive form; he must feel the whole force of the difficulty which the true view of the subject has to encounter and dispose of; else he will never really possess himself of the portion of truth which meets and removes that difficulty. Ninety-nine in a hundred of what are called educated men are in this condition; even of those who can argue fluently for their opinions. Their conclusion may be true, but it might be false for anything they know: they have never thrown themselves into the mental position of those who think differently from them, and considered what such persons may have to say; and consequently they do not, in any proper sense of the word, know the doctrine which they themselves profess. They do not know those parts of it which explain and justify the remainder; the considerations which show that a fact which seemingly conflicts with another is reconcilable with it, or that, of two apparently strong reasons, one and not the other ought to be preferred. All that part of the truth which turns the scale, and decides the judgment of a completely informed mind, they are strangers to; nor is it ever really known, but to those who have attended equally and impartially to both sides, and endeavored to see the reasons of both in the strongest light. So essential is this discipline to a real understanding of moral and human subjects, that if opponents of all important truths do not exist, it is indispensable to imagine them, and supply them with the strongest arguments which the most skillful devil's advocate can conjure up.

.   .   .

If, however, the mischievous operation of the absence of free discussion, when the received opinions are true, were confined to leaving men ignorant of the grounds of those opinions, it might be thought that this, if an intellectual, is no moral evil, and does not affect the worth of the opinions, regarded in their influence on the character. The fact, however, is, that not only the grounds of the opinion are forgotten in the absence of discussion, but too often the meaning of the opinion itself. The words which convey it, cease to suggest ideas, or suggest only a small portion of those they were originally employed to communicate. Instead of a vivid conception and a living belief, there remain only a few phrases retained by rote; or, if any part, the shell and husk only of the meaning is retained, the finer essence being lost. The great chapter in human history which this fact occupies and fills, cannot be too earnestly studied and meditated on.

It is illustrated in the experience of almost all ethical doctrines and religious creeds. They are all full of meaning and vitality to those who originate them, and to the direct disciples of the originators. Their meaning continues to be felt in undiminished strength, and is perhaps brought out into even fuller consciousness, so long as the struggle lasts to give the doctrine or creed an ascendancy over other creeds. At last it either prevails, and becomes the general opinion, or its progress stops; it keeps possession of the ground it has gained, but ceases to spread further. When either of these results has become apparent, controversy on the subject flags, and gradually dies away. The doctrine has taken its place, if not as a received opinion, as one of the admitted sects or divisions of opinion: those who hold it have generally inherited, not adopted it; and conversion from one of these doctrines to another, being now an exceptional fact, occupies little place in the thoughts of their professors. Instead of being, as at first, constantly on the alert either to defend themselves against the world, or to bring the world over to them, they have subsided into acquiescence, and neither listen, when they can help it, to arguments against their creed, nor trouble dissentients (if there be such) with arguments in its favor. From this time may usually be dated the decline in the living power of the doctrine. We often hear the teachers of all creeds lamenting the difficulty of keeping up in the minds of believers a lively apprehension of the truth which they nominally recognize, so that it may penetrate the feelings, and acquire a real mastery over the conduct. No such difficulty is complained of while the creed is still fighting for its existence: even the weaker combatants then know and feel what they are fighting for, and the difference between it and other doctrines; and in that period of every creed's existence, not a few persons may be found, who have realized its fundamental principles in all the forms of thought, have weighed and considered them in all their important bearings, and have experienced the full effect on the character, which belief in that creed ought to produce in a mind thoroughly imbued with it. But when it has come to be an hereditary creed, and to be received passively, not actively—when the mind is no longer compelled, in the same degree as at first, to exercise its vital powers on the questions which its belief presents to it, there is a progressive tendency to forget all of the belief except the formularies, or to give it a dull and torpid assent, as if accepting it on trust dispensed with the necessity of realizing it in consciousness, or testing it by personal experience; until it almost ceases to connect itself at all with the inner life of the human being. Then are seen the cases, so frequent in this age of the world as almost to form the majority, in which the creed remains as it were outside the mind, encrusting and petrifying it against all other influences addressed to the higher parts of our nature; manifesting its power by not suffering any fresh and living conviction to get in, but itself doing nothing for the mind or heart, except standing sentinel over them to keep them vacant.

. . .

But what! (it may be asked) Is the absence of unanimity an indispensable condition of true knowledge? Is it necessary that some part of mankind should persist in error, to enable any to realize the truth? Does a belief cease to be real and vital as soon as it is generally received—and is a proposition never thoroughly understood and felt unless some doubt of it remains? As soon as mankind have unanimously accepted a truth, does the truth perish within them? The highest aim and best result of improved intelligence, it has hitherto been thought, is to unite mankind more and more in the acknowledgment of all important truths: and does the intelligence only last as long as it has not achieved its object? Do the fruits of conquest perish by the very completeness of the victory?

I affirm no such thing. As mankind improve, the number of doctrines which are no longer disputed or doubted will be constantly on the increase: and the well-being of mankind may almost be measured by the number and gravity of the truths which have reached the point of being uncontested. The cessation, on one question after another, of serious controversy, is one of the necessary incidents of the consolidation of opinion; a consolidation as salutary in the case of true opinions, as it is dangerous and noxious when the opinions are erroneous. But though this gradual narrowing of the bounds of diversity of opinion is necessary in both senses of the term, being at once inevitable and indispensable, we are not therefore obliged to conclude that all its consequences must be beneficial. The loss of so important an aid to the intelligent and living apprehension of a truth, as is afforded by the necessity of explaining it to, or defending it against, opponents, though not sufficient to outweigh, is no trifling drawback from, the benefit of its universal recognition. Where this advantage can no longer be had, I confess I should like to see the teachers of mankind endeavoring to provide a substitute for it; some contrivance for making the difficulties of the question as present to the learner's consciousness, as if they were pressed upon him by a dissentient champion, eager for his conversion.

. . . A person who derives all his instruction from teachers or books, even if he escape the besetting temptation of contenting himself with cram, is under no compulsion to hear both sides; accordingly it is far from a frequent accomplishment, even among thinkers, to know both sides; and the weakest part of what everybody says in defense of his opinion, is what he intends as a reply to antagonists. It is the fashion of the present time to disparage negative logic—that which points out weaknesses in theory or errors in practice, without establishing positive truths. Such negative criticism would indeed be poor enough as an ultimate result; but as a means to attaining any positive knowledge or conviction worthy the name, it cannot be valued too highly; and until people are again systematically trained to it, there will be few great thinkers, and a low general average of intellect, in any but the mathematical and physical departments of speculation. On any other subject no one's opinions deserve the name of knowledge, except so far as he has either had forced upon him by others, or gone through of himself, the same mental process which would have been required of him in carrying on an active controversy with opponents. That, therefore, which when absent, it is so indispensable, but so difficult, to create, how worse than absurd it is to forego, when spontaneously offering itself! If there are any persons who contest a received opinion, or who will do so if law or opinion will let them, let us thank them for it, open our minds to listen to them, and rejoice that there is someone to do for us what we otherwise ought, if we have any regard for either the certainty or the vitality of our convictions, to do with much greater labor for ourselves.

. . . We have hitherto considered only two possibilities: that the received opinion may be false, and some other opinion, consequently, true; or that, the received opinion being true, a conflict with the opposite error is essential to a clear apprehension and deep feeling of its truth. But there is a commoner case than either of these; when the conflicting doctrines, instead of being one true and the other false, share the truth between them; and the nonconforming opinion is needed to supply the remainder of the truth, of which the received doctrine embodies only a part. Popular opinions, on subjects not palpable to sense, are often true, but seldom or never the whole truth. They are a part of the truth; sometimes a greater, sometimes a smaller part, but exaggerated, distorted, and disjoined from the truths by which they ought to be accompanied and limited. Heretical opinions, on the other hand, are generally some of these suppressed and neglected truths, bursting the bonds which kept them down, and either seeking reconciliation with the truth contained in the common opinion, or fronting it as enemies, and setting themselves up, with similar exclusiveness, as the whole truth. The latter case is hitherto the most frequent, as, in the human mind, one-sidedness has always been the rule, and many-sidedness the exception. Hence, even in revolutions of opinion, one part of the truth usually sets while another rises. Even progress, which ought to superadd, for the most part only substitutes, one partial and incomplete truth for another; improvement consisting chiefly in this, that the new fragment of truth is more wanted, more adapted to the needs of the time, than that which it displaces. Such being the partial character of prevailing opinions, even when resting on a true foundation, every opinion which embodies somewhat of the portion of truth which the common opinion omits, ought to be considered precious, with whatever amount of error and confusion that truth may be blended. No sober judge of human affairs will feel bound to be indignant because those who force on our notice truths which we should otherwise have overlooked, overlooks some of those which we see. Rather, he will think that so long as popular truth is one-sided, it is more desirable than otherwise that unpopular truth should have one-sided asserters too; such being usually the most energetic, and the most likely to compel reluctant attention to the fragment of wisdom which they proclaim as if it were the whole.

. . . Unless opinions favorable to democracy and to aristocracy, to property and to equality, to cooperation and to competition, to luxury and to abstinence, to sociality and individuality, to liberty and discipline, and all the other standing antagonisms of practical life, are expressed with equal freedom, and enforced and defended with equal talent and energy, there is no chance of both elements obtaining their due; one scale is sure to go up, and the other down. Truth, in the great practical concerns of life, is so much a question of the reconciling and combining of opposites, that very few have minds sufficiently capacious and impartial to make the adjustment with an approach to correctness, and it has to be made by the rough process of a struggle between combatants fighting under hostile banners. On any of the great open questions just enumerated, if either of the two opinions has a better claim than the other, not merely to be tolerated, but to be encouraged and countenanced, it is the one which happens at the particular time and place to be in a minority. That is the opinion which, for the time being, represents the neglected interests, the side of human well-being which is in danger of obtaining less than its share. . . . When there are persons to be found, who form an exception to the apparent unanimity of the world on any subject, even if the world is in the right, it is always probable that dissentients have something worth hearing to say for themselves, and that truth would lose something by their silence.

. . . I acknowledge that the tendency of all opinions to become sectarian is not cured by the freest discussion, but is often heightened and exacerbated thereby; the truth which ought to have been, but was not, seen, being rejected all the more violently because proclaimed by persons regarded as opponents. But it is not on the impassioned partisan, it is on the calmer and more disinterested bystander, that this collision of opinions works its salutary effect. Not the violent conflict between parts of the truth, but the quiet suppression of half of it, is the formidable evil; there is always hope when people are forced to listen to both sides; it is when they attend only to one that errors harden into prejudices, and truth itself ceases to have the effect of truth, by being exaggerated into falsehood. And since there are few mental attributes more rare than that judicial faculty which can sit in intelligent judgment between two sides of a question, of which only one is represented by an advocate before it, truth has no chance but in proportion as every side of it, every opinion which embodies any fraction of the truth, not only finds advocates, but is so advocated as to be listened to.

. . .

We have now recognized the necessity to the mental well-being of mankind (on which all their other well-being depends) of freedom of opinion, and freedom of the expression of opinion, on four distinct grounds; which we will now briefly recapitulate.

First, if any opinion is compelled to silence, that opinion may, for aught we can certainly know, be true. To deny this is to assume our own infallibility.

Secondly, though the silenced opinion be an error, it may, and very commonly does, contain a portion of truth; and since the general or prevailing opinion of any subject is rarely or never the whole truth, it is only by the collision of adverse opinions that the remainder of the truth has any chance of being supplied.

Thirdly, even if the received opinion be not only true, but the whole truth; unless it is suffered to be, and actually is, vigorously and earnestly contested, it will, by most of those who receive it, be held in the manner of a prejudice, with little comprehension or feeling of its rational grounds. And not only this, but, fourthly, the meaning of the doctrine itself will be in danger of being lost, or enfeebled, and deprived of its vital effect on the character and conduct: the dogma becoming a mere formal profession, inefficacious for good, but cumbering the ground, and preventing the growth of any real and heartfelt conviction, from reason or personal experience.

Before quitting the subject of freedom of opinion, it is fit to take some notice of those who say, that the free expression of all opinions should be permitted, on condition that the manner be temperate, and do not pass the bounds of fair discussion. Much might be said on the impossibility of fixing where these supposed bounds are to be placed; for if the test be offense to those whose opinion is attacked, I think experience testifies that this offense is given whenever the attack is telling and powerful, and that every opponent who pushes them hard, and whom they find it difficult to answer, appears to them, if he shows any strong feeling on the subject, an intemperate opponent. But this, though an important consideration in a practical point of view, merges in a more fundamental objection. Undoubtedly the manner of asserting an opinion, even though it be a true one, may be very objectionable, and may justly incur severe censure. But the principal offenses of the kind are such as it is mostly impossible, unless by accidental self-betrayal, to bring home to conviction. The gravest of them is, to argue sophistically, to suppress facts or arguments, to misstate the elements of the case, or misrepresent the opposite opinion. But all this, even to the most aggravated degree, is so continually done in perfect good faith, by persons who are not considered, and in many other respects may not deserve to be considered, ignorant or incompetent, that it is rarely possible on adequate grounds conscientiously to stamp the misrepresentation as morally culpable; and still less could law presume to interfere with this kind of controversial misconduct. With regard to what is commonly meant by intemperate discussion, namely invective, sarcasm, personality, and the like, the denunciation of these weapons would deserve more sympathy if it were ever proposed to interdict them equally to both sides; but it is only desired to restrain the employment of them against the prevailing opinion: against the unprevailing they may not only be used without general disapproval, but will be likely to obtain for him who uses them the praise of honest zeal and righteous indignation. Yet whatever mischief arises from their use, is greatest when they are employed against the comparatively defenseless; and whatever unfair advantage can be derived by any opinion from this mode of asserting it, accrues almost exclusively to received opinions. The worst offense of this kind which can be committed by a polemic, is to stigmatize those who hold the contrary opinion as bad and immoral men. To calumny of this sort, those who hold any unpopular opinion are peculiarly exposed, because they are in general few and uninfluential, and nobody but themselves feels much interested in seeing justice done them; but this weapon is, from the nature of the case, denied to those who attack a prevailing opinion: they can neither use it with safety to themselves, nor, if they could, would it do anything but recoil on their own cause. In general, opinions contrary to those commonly received can only obtain a hearing by studied moderation of language, and the most cautious avoidance of unnecessary offense, from which they hardly ever deviate even in a slight degree without losing ground: while unmeasured vituperation employed on the side of the prevailing opinion, really does deter people from professing contrary opinions, and from listening to those who profess them. For the interest, therefore, of truth and justice, it is far more important to restrain this employment of vituperative language than the other; and, for example, if it were necessary to choose, there would be much more need to discourage offensive attacks on infidelity, than on religion. It is, however, obvious that law and authority have no business with restraining either, while opinion ought, in every instance, to determine its verdict by the circumstances of the individual case; condemning everyone, on whichever side of the argument he places himself, in whose mode of advocacy either want of candor, or malignity, bigotry, or intolerance of feeling manifest themselves; but not inferring these vices from the side which a person takes, though it be the contrary side of the question to our own: and giving merited honor to everyone, whatever opinion he may hold, who has calmness to see and honesty to state what his opponents and their opinions really are, exaggerating nothing to their discredit, keeping nothing back which tells, or can be supposed to tell, in their favor. This is the real morality of public discussion: and if often violated, I am happy to think that there are many controversialists who to a great extent observe it, and a still greater number who conscientiously strive towards it.

84
The Supreme Court of the United States: Cases on the Freedom of Speech

How far must the freedom of speech extend? In a self-governing community, what limits may be put on free speech, or on a free press, because of the dangers to the community created by those freedoms? This issue has arisen repeatedly in great cases coming before the U.S. Supreme Court. The Justices of that Court, confronting difficult and sensitive issues, must often decide on philosophical grounds how the U.S. Constitution *ought* to be interpreted. Their reasoning has often been presented with eloquence and depth; some of the Justices' opinions constitute memorable chapters in American Constitutional history.

In each case below the essential question before the Court is very briefly summarized, and the Justice whose opinion is cited is identified. References are to *United States Reports,* abbreviated U.S., preceded by the volume number and followed by the page number in that volume, with the date of the decision in parentheses. Footnotes have been omitted.

SCHENCK v. UNITED STATES   249 U.S. 47 (1919)

Schenk, who was general secretary of the Socialist Party during the first World War, was convicted of violating the Espionage Act for sending leaflets to prospective draftees, urging them to resist military conscription. His conviction was upheld by the Supreme Court, in an opinion by Justice Oliver Wendell Holmes in which first appears the very famous "clear and present danger" standard for determining the limits of free speech in a democracy.

Justice Holmes delivered the opinion of the Court:

. . . The document would not have been sent unless it had been intended to have some effect, and we do not see what effect it could be expected to have upon persons subject to the draft except to influence them to obstruct the carrying of it out. . . . We admit that in many places and in ordinary times the defendants, in saying all that was said in the circular, would have been within their constitutional rights. But the character of every act depends upon the circumstances in which it is done. . . . The most stringent protection of free speech would not protect a man in falsely shouting fire in a theater, and causing a panic. It does not even protect a man from an injunction against uttering words that may have all the effect of force. . . . The question in every case is whether the words used are used in such circumstances and are of such a nature as to create a clear and present danger that they will bring about the substantive evils that Congress has a right to prevent. It is a question of proximity and degree. When a nation is at war many things that might be said in time of peace are such a hindrance to its effort that their utterance will not be endured so long as men fight, and that no Court could regard them as protected by any constitutional right.

ABRAMS v. UNITED STATES   250 U.S. 616 (1919)

Later that same year Justice Holmes, joined by Justice Brandeis, expressed greater confidence in the citizens of a democracy. Abrams had been convicted for distributing a left-wing pamphlet directed against the dispatch of U.S. troops to attack Russia just after the Soviet Revolution. "The best test of truth," Holmes had now come to believe, "is the power of the thought to get itself accepted in the competition of the market, and that truth is the only ground upon which their wishes safely can be carried out." Holmes was called "the great dissenter"; this is one of his greatest dissents.

Justice Clarke delivered the opinion of the Court:

. . . It will not do to say . . . that the only intent of these defendants was to prevent injury to the Russian cause. Men must be held to have intended, and to be accountable for, the effects which their acts were likely to produce. Even if their primary purpose and intent was to aid the cause of the Russian Revolution, the plan of action which they adopted *necessarily* involved, before it could be realized, defeat of the war program of the United States, for the obvious effect of this appeal, if it should become effective, as they hoped it might, would be to persuade persons . . . not to aid government loans and not to work in ammunition factories. . . .

Justice Holmes, dissenting:

This indictment is founded wholly upon the publication of two leaflets. . . .

The first of these leaflets says that the President's cowardly silence about the intervention in Russia reveals the hypocrisy of the plutocratic gang in Washington. . . . It says that there is only one enemy of the workers of the world and that is capitalism; that it is a crime for workers of America, etc., to fight the worker's republic of Russia, and ends "Awake! Awake, you Workers of the World! Revolutionists". . . .

The other leaflet, headed "Workers—Wake Up," with abusive language . . . winds up by saying "Workers, our reply to this barbarous intervention has to be a general strike!" . . . "Woe unto those who will be in the way of progress. Let solidarity live! The Rebels."

. . . to make the conduct criminal . . . [the] statute requires that it should be "with intent by such curtailment to cripple or hinder the United States in the prosecution of the war." It seems to me that no such intent is proved.

. . . it is only the present danger of immediate evil or an intent to bring it about that warrants Congress in setting a limit to the expression of opinion. . . . An intent to prevent interference with the revolution in Russia might have been satisfied without any hindrance to carrying on the war in which we were engaged.

I do not see how anyone can find the intent required by the statute in any of the defendant's words. . . . To say that two phrases taken literally might import a suggestion of conduct that would have interference with the war as an indirect and probably undesired effect seems to me by no means enough to show an attempt to produce that effect.

. . . In this case sentences of twenty years imprisonment have been imposed for the publishing of two leaflets that I believe the defendants had as much right to publish as the Government has to publish the Constitution of the United States now vainly invoked by them. Even if I am technically wrong and enough can be squeezed from these poor and puny anonymities to turn the color of legal litmus paper; I will add, even if what I think the necessary intent were shown; the most nominal punishment seems to me all that possibly could be inflicted, unless the defendants are to be made to suffer not for what the indictment alleges but for the creed that they avow. . . .

Persecution for the expression of opinions seems to me perfectly logical. If you have no doubt of your premises or your power and want a certain result with all your heart you naturally express your wishes in law and sweep away all opposition. To allow opposition by speech seems to indicate that you think the speech impotent, as when a man says that he has squared the circle, or that you do not care whole-heartedly for the result, or that you doubt either your power or your premises. But when men have realized that time has upset many fighting faiths, they may come to believe even more than they believe the very foundations of their own conduct that the ultimate good desired is better reached by free trade in ideas—that the best test of truth is the power of the thought to get itself accepted in the competition of the market, and that truth is the only ground upon which their wishes safely can be carried out. That at any rate is the theory of our Constitution. It is an experiment, as all life is an experiment. Every year if not every day we have to wager out salvation upon some prophecy based upon imperfect knowledge. While that experiment is part of our system I think that we should be eternally vigilant against attempts to check the expression of opinions that we loathe and believe to be fraught with death, unless they so imminently threaten immediate interference with the lawful and pressing purposes of the law that an immediate check is required to save the country. I wholly disagree with the argument of the Government that the First Amendment left the common law as to seditious libel in force. History seems to me against the notion. I had conceived that the United States through many years had shown its repentance for the Sedition Act of 1798, by repaying fines that it imposed. Only the emergency that makes it immediately dangerous to leave the correction of evil counsels to time warrants making any exception to the sweeping command, "Congress shall make no law . . . abridging the freedom of speech." Of course I am speaking only of expressions of opinion and exhortations, which were all that were uttered here, but I regret that I cannot put into more impressive words my belief that in their conviction upon this indictment the defendants were deprived of their rights under the Constitution of the United States.

GITLOW v. NEW YORK   268 U.S. 652 (1925)

Gitlow was an anarchist, convicted for violating the New York criminal anarchy statute by distributing a pamphlet entitled "The Left Wing Manifesto." Justice Sanford, affirming his conviction, held that the danger created by such a pamphlet was immediate even though not entirely clear, and was therefore within the authority of the state to punish.

Justice Sanford delivered the opinion of the Court:

Benjamin Gitlow was indicted in the supreme court of New York, with three others, for the statutory crime of criminal anarchy. . . .

. . . Criminal anarchy is the doctrine that organized government should be overthrown by force or violence. . . . The advocacy of such doctrine either by word of mouth or writing is a felony. . . . The indictment . . . charged that the defendant had advocated, advised, and taught the duty, necessity, and propriety of overthrowing and overturning organized government by force, violence, and unlawful means, by certain writings therein set forth, entitled, "The Left Wing Manifesto." . . . The defendant is a member of the Left Wing section of the Socialist party, a dissenting branch or faction of that party, formed in opposition to its dominant policy of "moderate Socialism". . . . The sole contention here is, essentially, that, as there was no evidence of any concrete result flowing from the publication of the Manifesto, or of circumstances showing the likelihood of such result, the statute as construed and applied by the trial court penalizes the mere utterance, as such, of "doctrine" having no quality of incitement. . . . The argument in support of this contention rests primarily upon the following propositions: 1st, that the "liberty" protected by the 14th Amendment includes the liberty of speech and of the press; and 2nd, that while liberty of expression "is not absolute," it may be restrained "only in circumstances where its exercise bears a causal relation with some substantive evil, consummated, attempted, or likely;" and as the statute "takes no account of circumstances," it unduly restrains this liberty, and is therefore unconstitutional. . . .

The statute does not penalize the utterance or publication of abstract "doctrine" or academic discussion having no quality of incitement to any concrete action. It is not aimed against mere historical or philosophical essays. It does not restrain the advocacy of changes in the form of government by constitutional and lawful means. What it prohibits is language advocating, advising, or teaching the overthrow of organized government by unlawful means. These words imply urging to action. . . .

The Manifesto, plainly, is neither the statement of abstract doctrine nor, as suggested by counsel, mere prediction that industrial disturbances and revolutionary mass strikes will result spontaneously in an inevitable process of evolution in the economic system. It advocates and urges in fervent language mass action which shall progressively foment industrial disturbances, and, through political mass strikes and revolutionary mass action, overthrow and destroy organized parliamentary government. It concludes with a call to action. . . .

For present purposes we may and do assume that freedom of speech and of the press—which are protected by the First Amendment from abridgment by Congress—are among the fundamental personal rights and "liberties" protected by the due process clause of the Fourteenth Amendment from impairment by the States. . . . That utterances inciting to the overthrow of organized government by unlawful means present a sufficient danger of substantive evil to bring their punishment within the range of legislative discretion is clear. Such utterances, by their very nature, involve danger to the public peace and to the security of the state. . . . And the immediate danger is none the less real and substantial because the effect of a given utterance cannot be accurately foreseen. The state cannot reasonably be required to measure the danger from every such utterance in the nice balance of a jeweler's scale. A single revolutionary spark may kindle a fire that, smoldering for a time, may burst into a sweeping and destructive conflagration. It cannot be said that the state is acting arbitrarily or unreasonably when, in the exercise of its judgment as to the measures necessary to protect the public peace and safety, it seeks to extinguish the spark without waiting until it has kindled the flame or blazed into the conflagration. . . . it may, in the exercise of its judgment, suppress the threatened danger in its incipiency. . . .

We cannot hold that the present statute is an arbitrary or unreasonable exercise of the police power of the state, unwarrantably infringing the freedom of speech or press; and we must and do sustain its constitutionality. . . .

Once again Justice Holmes, joined by Justice Brandeis, issued a ringing dissent:

. . . If what I think the correct test is applied, it is manifest that there was no present danger of an attempt to overthrow the government by force on the part of the admittedly small minority who shared the defendant's views. It is said that this Manifesto was more than a theory, that it was an incitement. Every idea is an incitement. It offers itself for belief, and, if believed, it is acted on unless some other belief outweighs it, or some failure of energy stifles the movement at its birth. The only difference between the expression of an opinion and an incitement in the narrower sense is the speaker's enthusiasm for the result. Eloquence may set fire to reason. But whatever may be thought of the redundant discourse before us, it had no chance of starting a present conflagration. If, in the long run, the beliefs expressed in proletarian dictatorship are destined to be accepted by the dominant forces of the community, the only meaning of free speech is that they should be given their chance and have their way.

WHITNEY v. CALIFORNIA   274 U.S. 357 (1927)

Perhaps the most cogent formulation by the judiciary of the justification of maximal free speech in a democracy was authored by Justice Louis Brandeis in 1927. The crime for which Anita Whitney was convicted was attendance at a radical convention, for which she was held to have violated California's criminal syndicalism act. Brandeis is passionate: "To courageous, self-reliant men, with confidence in the power of free and fearless reasoning applied through the processes of popular government, no danger flowing from speech can be deemed clear and present, unless the incidence of the evil apprehended is so imminent that it may befall before there is opportunity for full discussion. If there be time to expose through discussion the falsehood and fallacies . . . the remedy to be applied is more speech, not enforced silence."

Justice Brandeis, concurring:

. . . This court has not yet fixed the standard by which to determine when a danger shall be deemed clear; how remote the danger may be and yet be deemed present; and what degree of evil shall be deemed sufficiently substantial to justify resort to abridgment of free speech and assembly as the means of protection. To reach sound conclusions on these matters, we must bear in mind why a state is, ordinarily, denied the power to prohibit dissemination of social, economic and political doctrine which a vast majority of citizens believes to be false and fraught with evil consequence.

Those who won our independence believed that the final end of the state was to make men free to develop their faculties; and that in its government the deliberative forces should prevail over the arbitrary. They valued liberty both as an end and as a means. They believed liberty to be the secret of happiness and courage to be the secret of liberty. They believed that freedom to think as you will and to speak as you think are means indispensable to the discovery and spread of political truth; that without free speech and assembly discussion would be futile; that with them, discussion affords ordinarily adequate protection against the dissemination of noxious doctrine; that the greatest menace to freedom is an inert people; that public discussion is a political duty; and that this should be a fundamental principle of the American government. They recognized the risks to which all human institutions are subject. But they knew that order cannot be secured merely through fear of punishment for its infraction; that it is hazardous to discourage thought, hope and imagination; that fear breeds repression; that repression breeds hate; that hate menaces stable government; that the path of safety lies in the opportunity to discuss freely supposed grievances and proposed remedies; and that the fitting remedy for evil counsels is good ones. Believing in the power of reason as applied through public discussion, they eschewed silence coerced by law—the argument of force in its worst form. Recognizing the occasional tyrannies of governing majorities, they amended the Constitution so that free speech and assembly should be guaranteed.

Fear of serious injury cannot alone justify suppression of free speech and assembly. Men feared witches and burned women. It is the function of speech to free men from the bondage of irrational fears. To justify suppression of free speech there must be reasonable ground to fear that serious evil will result if free speech is practiced. There must be reasonable ground to believe that the danger apprehended is imminent. There must be reasonable ground to believe that the evil to be prevented is a serious one. Every denunciation of existing law tends in some measure to increase the probability that there will be violation of it. Condonation of a breach enhances the probability. Expressions of approval add to the probability. Propagation of the criminal state of mind by teaching syndicalism increases it. Advocacy of lawbreaking heightens it still further. But even advocacy of violation, however reprehensible morally, is not a justification for denying free speech where the advocacy falls short of incitement and there is nothing to indicate that the advocacy would be immediately acted on. The wide difference between advocacy and incitement, between preparation and attempt, between assembling and conspiracy, must be borne in mind. In order to support a finding of clear and present danger it must be shown either that immediate serious violence was to be expected or was advocated, or that the past conduct furnished reason to believe that such advocacy was then contemplated.

Those who won our independence by revolution were not cowards. They did not fear political change. They did not exalt order at the cost of liberty. To courageous, self-reliant men, with confidence in the power of free and fearless reasoning applied through the processes of popular government, no danger flowing from speech can be deemed clear and present, unless the incidence of the evil apprehended is so imminent that it may befall before there is opportunity for full discussion. If there be time to expose through discussion the falsehood and fallacies, to avert the evil by the processes of education, the remedy to be applied is more speech, not enforced silence. Only an emergency can justify repression. Such must be the rule if authority is to be reconciled with freedom. Such, in my opinion, is the command of the Constitution. It is, therefore, always open to Americans to challenge a law abridging free speech and assembly by showing that there was no emergency justifying it.

Moreover, even imminent danger cannot justify resort to prohibition of these functions essential to effective democracy, unless the evil apprehended is relatively serious. Prohibition of free speech and assembly is a measure so stringent that it would be inappropriate as the means for averting a relatively trivial harm to society. A police measure may be unconstitutional merely because the remedy, although effective as means of protection, is unduly harsh or oppressive. Thus, a state might, in the exercise of its police power, make any trespass upon the land of another a crime, regardless of the results or of the intent or purpose of the trespasser. It might, also, punish an attempt, a conspiracy, or an incitement to commit the trespass. But it is hardly conceivable that this court would hold constitutional a statute which punished as a felony the mere voluntary assembly with a society formed to teach that pedestrians had the moral right to cross unenclosed, unposted, waste lands and to advocate their doing so, even if there was imminent danger that advocacy would lead to a trespass. The fact that speech is likely to result in some violence or in destruction of property is not enough to justify its suppression. There must be the probability of serious injury to the state. Among freemen, the deterrents ordinarily to be applied to prevent crime are education and punishment for violations of the law, not abridgement of the rights of free speech and assembly.

WEST VIRGINIA STATE BOARD OF EDUCATION v. BARNETTE
319 U.S. 624 (1943)

Democracy requires not only the freedom to say and publish what one believes, but the freedom to refuse to say what is ordered by the state if one does not believe it. In West Virginia during the Second World War the recitation of the Pledge of Allegiance to the flag of the United States was obligatory for all students. Barnette, a Jehovah's Witness, viewed this ritual as forced idolatry, and refused to allow his child to participate. The coercion exercised by West Virginia in this matter was found by the Court to be unconstitutional. "If there is any fixed star in our constitutional constellation, it is that no official, high or petty, can prescribe what shall be orthodox in politics, nationalism, religion, or other matters of opinion or force citizens to confess by word or act their faith therein."

Justice Jackson delivered the opinion of the Court:

. . . We are dealing with a compulsion of students to declare a belief. They are not merely made acquainted with the flag salute so that they may be informed as to what it is or even what it means. The issue here is whether this slow and easily neglected route to aroused loyalties constitutionally may be short-cut by substituting a compulsory salute and slogan. . . .

There is no doubt that, in connection with the pledges, the flag salute is a form of utterance. Symbolism is a primitive but effective way of communicating ideas . . . a short cut from mind to mind. . . .

It is now a commonplace that censorship or suppression of expression of opinion is tolerated by our Constitution only when the expression presents a clear and present danger of action of a kind the State is empowered to prevent and punish. It would seem that involuntary affirmation could be commanded only on even more immediate and urgent grounds than silence. But here the power of compulsion is invoked without any allegation that remaining passive during a flag salute ritual creates a clear and present danger that would justify an effort even to muffle expression. To sustain the compulsory flag salute we are required to say that a Bill of Rights which guards the individual's right to speak his own mind, left it open to public authorities to compel him to utter what is not in his mind.

Whether the First Amendment to the Constitution will permit officials to order observance of ritual of this nature does not depend upon whether as a voluntary exercise we would think it to be good, bad or merely innocuous. . . .

Nor does the issue as we see it turn on one's possession of particular religious views or the sincerity with which they are held. While religion supplies appellees' motive for enduring the discomforts of making the issue in this case, many citizens who do not share these religious views hold such a compulsory rite to infringe constitutional liberty of the individual. . . .

Government of limited power need not be anemic government. . . . Without promise of a limiting Bill of Rights it is doubtful if our Constitution could have mustered enough strength to enable its ratification. To enforce those rights today is not to choose weak government over strong government. It is only to adhere as a means of strength to individual freedom of mind in preference to officially disciplined uniformity for which history indicates a disappointing and disastrous end. . . .

The Fourteenth Amendment, as now applied to the States, protects the citizen against the State itself and all of its creatures—Boards of Education not excepted. These have, of course, important, delicate, and highly discretionary functions, but none that they may not perform within the limits of the Bill of Rights. . . . There are village tyrants as well as village Hampdens, but none who acts under color of law is beyond reach of the Constitution. . . .

The very purpose of a Bill of Rights was to withdraw certain subjects from the vicissitudes of political controversy, to place them beyond the reach of majorities and officials and to establish them as legal principles to be applied by the courts. One's right to life, liberty, and property, to free speech, a free press, freedom of worship and assembly, and other fundamental rights may not be submitted to vote; they depend on the outcome of no elections. . . .

National unity as an end which officials may foster by persuasion and example is not in question. The problem is whether under our Constitution compulsion as here employed is a permissible means for its achievement.

Struggles to coerce uniformity of sentiment in support of some end thought essential to their time and country have been waged by many good as well as by evil men. . . . As governmental pressure toward unity becomes greater, so strife becomes more bitter as to whose unity it shall be. . . . Those who begin coercive elimination of dissent soon find themselves exterminating dissenters. Compulsory unification of opinion achieves only the unanimity of the graveyard.

It seems trite but necessary to say that the First Amendment to our Constitution was designed to avoid these ends by avoiding these beginnings. . . . Authority here is to be controlled by public opinion, not public opinion by authority. . . . To believe that patriotism will not flourish if patriotic ceremonies are voluntary and spontaneous instead of a compulsory routine is to make an unflattering estimate of the appeal of our institutions to free minds. . . .

If there is any fixed star in our constitutional constellation, it is that no official, high or petty, can prescribe what shall be orthodox in politics, nationalism, religion, or other matters of opinion or force citizens to confess by word or act their faith therein. If there are any circumstances which permit an exception, they do not now occur to us.

We think the action of the local authorities in compelling the flag salute and pledge transcends constitutional limitations on their power and invades the sphere of intellect and spirit which it is the purpose of the First Amendment to our Constitution to reserve from all official control.

UNITED STATES v. DENNIS   341 U.S. 494 (1951)

Widespread fear of communism, and of the Soviet Union, led to a series of controversial free speech cases in the years following the Second World War. Eugene Dennis was General Secretary of the Communist Party of the United States; along with ten other communist leaders, he was convicted, under the Smith Act, for advocating and conspiring to advocate the forcible overthrow of the United States government. His conviction was upheld by the Supreme Court, applying once again the "clear and present danger" standard.

Chief Justice Vinson delivered the opinion of the Court:

. . . Whatever theoretical merit there may be to the argument that there is a "right" to rebellion against dictatorial governments is without force where the existing structure of government provides for peaceful and orderly change. We reject any principle of governmental helplessness in the face of preparation for revolution, which principle, carried to its logical conclusion, must lead to anarchy. . . the Smith Act . . . is directed at advocacy, not discussion. Thus, the trial judge properly charged the jury that they could not convict if they found that petitioners did "no more than pursue peaceful studies and discussions or teaching and advocacy in the realm of ideas". . . . where an offense is specified by a statute in nonspeech or nonpress terms, a conviction relying upon speech or press as evidence of violation may be sustained only when the speech or publication created a "clear and present danger" of attempting or accomplishing the prohibited crime. . . . To those who would paralyze our Government in the face of impending threat by encasing it in a semantic strait-jacket we must reply that all concepts are relative.

. . . In this case we are squarely presented with the application of the "clear and present danger" test, and must decide what that phrase imports. . . . Obviously, the words cannot mean that before the Government may act, it must wait until the *putsch* is about to be executed, the plans have been laid and the signal is awaited. . . . Certainly an attempt to overthrow the Government by force, even though doomed from the outset because of inadequate numbers or power of the revolutionists, is a sufficient evil for Congress to prevent. The damage which such attempts create both physically and politically to a nation makes it impossible to measure the validity in terms of the probability of success, or the immediacy of a successful attempt. . . . We must therefore reject the contention that success or probability of success is the criterion.

. . . Chief Judge Learned Hand . . . interpreted the phrase as follows: "In each case [courts] must ask whether the gravity of the 'evil,' discounted by its improbability, justifies such invasion of free speech as is necessary to avoid the danger". . . . We adopt this statement of the rule. As articulated by Chief Judge Hand, it is as succinct and inclusive as any other we might devise at this time. It takes into consideration those factors which we deem relevant, and relates their significance. More we cannot expect from words.

. . . Likewise, we are in accord with the court below, which affirmed the trial court's finding that the requisite danger existed. . . . If the ingredients of the reaction are present, we cannot bind the Government to wait until the catalyst is added.

. . . The judgments of conviction are affirmed.

Justice Frankfurter, concurring:

. . . No matter how rapidly we utter the phrase "clear and present danger," or how closely we hyphenate the words, they are not a substitute for the weighing of values.

. . . The defendants have been convicted of conspiring to organize a party of persons who advocate the overthrow of the Government by force and violence. The jury has found that the object of the conspiracy is advocacy as "a rule or principle of action," "by language reasonably and ordinarily calculated to incite persons to such action," and with the intent to cause the overthrow "as speedily as circumstances would permit."

On any scale of values which we have hitherto recognized, speech of this sort ranks low. . . .

It is true that there is no divining rod by which we may locate "advocacy." Exposition of ideas readily merges into advocacy. The same Justice who gave currency to application of the incitement doctrine in this field dissented four times from what he thought was its misapplication. As he said in the *Gitlow* dissent, "Every idea is an incitement." . . .

But there is underlying validity in the distinction between advocacy and the interchange of ideas, and we do not discard a useful tool because it may be misused. That such a distinction could be used unreasonably by those in power against hostile or unorthodox views does not negate the fact that it may be used reasonably against an organization wielding the power of the centrally controlled international Communist movement. The object of the conspiracy before us is clear enough that the chance of error in saying that the defendants conspired to advocate rather than to express ideas is slight. Mr. Justice Douglas quite properly points out that the conspiracy before us is not a conspiracy to overthrow the Government. But it would be equally wrong to treat it as a seminar in political theory.

On the Supreme Court in this period the most stalwart defenders of free speech were Justices Black and Douglas. Both dissented vigorously in this case.

Justice Black, dissenting:

. . . At the outset I want to emphasize what the crime involved in this case is, and what it is not. These petitioners were not charged with an attempt to overthrow the Government. They were not charged with overt acts of any kind designed to overthrow the Government. They were not even charged with saying anything or writing anything designed to overthrow the Government. The charge was that they agreed to assemble and to talk and publish certain ideas at a later date. . . . No matter how it is worded, this is a virulent form of prior censorship of speech and press, which I believe the First Amendment forbids. . . .

So long as this Court exercises the power of judicial review of legislation, I cannot agree that the First Amendment permits us to sustain laws suppressing freedom of speech and press on the basis of Congress' or our own notions of mere "reasonableness." Such a doctrine waters down the First Amendment so that it amounts to little more than an admonition to Congress. The Amendment as so construed is not likely to protect any but those "safe" or orthodox views which rarely need its protection.

Justice Douglas, dissenting:

There is a statute which makes a seditious conspiracy unlawful. Petitioners, however, were not charged with a "conspiracy to overthrow" the Government. They were charged with a conspiracy to form a party and groups and assemblies of people who teach and advocate the overthrow of our Government by force or violence and with a conspiracy to advocate and teach its overthrow by force and violence. . . .

So far as the present record is concerned, what petitioners did was to organize people to teach and themselves teach the Marxist-Leninist doctrine contained chiefly in four books. . . . But if the books themselves are not outlawed, if they can lawfully remain on library shelves, by what reasoning does their use in a classroom become a crime? . . . The Act, as construed, requires the element of intent—that those who teach the creed believe in it. The crime then depends not on what is taught but on who the teacher is. That is to make freedom of speech turn not on *what is said,* but on the *intent* with which it is said. Once we start down that road we enter territory dangerous to the liberties of every citizen.

There was a time in England when the concept of constructive treason flourished. Men were punished not for raising a hand against the king but for thinking murderous thoughts about him. The Framers of the Constitution were alive to that abuse and took steps to see that the practice would not flourish here. Treason was defined to require overt acts. . . . The present case is not one of treason. But the analogy is close when the illegality is made to turn on intent, not on the nature of the act. We then start probing men's minds for motive and purpose; they become entangled in the law not for what they did but *for what they thought;* they get convicted not for what they said but for the purpose with which they said it.

. . . I repeat that we deal here with speech alone, not with speech *plus* acts of sabotage or unlawful conduct. Not a single seditious act is charged in the indictment. . . .

The nature of Communism as a force on the world scene would, of course, be relevant to the issue of clear and present danger of petitioner's advocacy within the United States. But the primary consideration is the strength and tactical position of petitioners and their converts in this country. On that there is no evidence in the record. . . .

How it can be said that there is a clear and present danger that this advocacy will succeed is, therefore, a mystery. Some nations less resilient than the United States, where illiteracy is high and where democratic traditions are only budding, might have to take drastic steps and jail these men for merely speaking their creed. But in America they are miserable merchants of unwanted ideas; their wares remain unsold. The fact that their ideas are abhorrent does not make them powerful.

. . . Free speech—the glory of our system of government—should not be sacrificed on anything less than plain and objective proof of danger that the evil advocated is imminent. . . . This does not mean, however, that the Nation need hold its hand until it is in such weakened condition that there is no time to protect itself from incitement to revolution. Seditious conduct can always be punished. . . . The First Amendment reflects the philosophy of Jefferson "that it is time enough for the rightful purposes of civil government for its officers to interfere when principles break out into overt acts against peace and good order."

YATES v. UNITED STATES   354 U.S. 298 (1957)

The Supreme Court majority in the *Dennis* decision had tried to draw a line between the "discussion" of seditious doctrine (permissible) and the "advocacy" of it (not permissible). But that distinction is very hard to apply in practice. Fourteen more communist leaders were convicted under the Smith Act—but the connection between what they had said or written and any revolution as its consequence was very tenuous. The Court now drew the critical distinction differently, between advocacy of abstract doctrine (permissible) and advocacy of action (not permissible). This distinction not having been applied by the lower court, the convictions in this case were reversed.

Justice Harlan delivered the opinion of the Court:

. . . The distinction between advocacy of abstract doctrine and advocacy directed at promoting unlawful action is one that has been consistently recognized in the opinions of this Court. . . . The legislative history of the Smith Act and related bills shows beyond all question that Congress was aware of the distinction between the advocacy or teaching of abstract doctrine and the advocacy or teaching of action, and that it did not intend to disregard it. The statute was aimed at the advocacy and teaching of concrete action for the forcible overthrow of the Government, and not of principles divorced from action. . . .

In failing to distinguish between advocacy of forcible overthrow as an abstract doctrine and advocacy of action to that end, the District Court appears to have been led astray by the holding in *Dennis* that advocacy of violent action to be taken at some future time was enough. It seems to have considered that, since "inciting" speech is usually thought of as calculated to induce immediate action, and since *Dennis* held advocacy of action for future overthrow sufficient, this meant that advocacy, irrespective of its tendency to generate action, is punishable, provided only that it is uttered with a specific intent to accomplish overthrow. . . .

This misconceives the situation confronting the Court in *Dennis* and what was held there. . . . The essential distinction is that those to whom the advocacy is addressed must be urged to *do* something, now or in the future, rather than merely to *believe* in something. At best the expressions used by the trial court were equivocal. . . .

We recognize that distinctions between advocacy or teaching of abstract doctrines, with evil intent, and that which is directed to stirring people to action, are often subtle and difficult to grasp. . . . But the very subtlety of these distinctions required the most clear and explicit instructions with reference to them, for they concerned an issue which went to the very heart of the charges against these petitioners.

BARENBLATT v. UNITED STATES   360 U.S. 109 (1959)

The Committee on Un-American Activities of the U.S. House of Representatives (HUAC) had been authorized, by the House, to investigate "the extent, character, and objects of un-American propaganda activities in the United States." Prying into the personal and political beliefs of private citizens, HUAC appeared to infringe First Amendment freedoms of speech and association. Many witnesses called before the Committee claimed their Fifth Amendment privilege against self-incrimination. Lloyd Barenblatt, who was reported to have been a communist while a graduate student and teaching fellow at The University of Michigan, took a different tack. He flatly refused to answer the Committee's questions, asserting that HUAC was violating the Constitution by abridging his freedom of speech, thought, press, and association. His conviction for contempt of Congress was affirmed by the Supreme Court. Justices Black, Brennan, Douglas, and Chief Justice Warren vehemently disagreed. The case of Lloyd Barenblatt highlights two critical questions: (1) Does the First Amendment to the Constitution, which reads in part "Congress shall make no law . . . abridging the freedom of speech, or of the press" mean what those words seem to say? (2) How is a democracy to control the excesses of a democratically elected legislature when it acts in ways likely to erode the conditions of self-government in the national community that legislature represents? Justice Black's tightly argued and passionate dissent, emphasizing the *constitutional* foundation of the liberties democracy requires, is perhaps the highest point reached on the Supreme Court in the defense of free speech and association in a democracy.

Justice Black dissenting:

The Court today affirms, and thereby sanctions, the use of the contempt power to enforce questioning by congressional committees in the realm of speech and association. I cannot agree with this disposition of the case for I believe that the resolution establishing the House Un-American Activities Committee and the questions that Committee asked Barenblatt violate the Constitution in several respects. (1) Rule XI creating the Committee authorizes such a sweeping, unlimited, all-inclusive, and undiscriminating compulsory examination of witnesses in the field of speech, press, petition, and assembly that it violates the procedural requirements of the Due Process Clause of the Fifth Amendment. (2) Compelling an answer to the questions asked Barenblatt abridges freedom of speech and association in contravention of the First Amendment. (3) The Committee proceedings were part of a legislative program to stigmatize and punish by public identification and exposure all witnesses considered by the Committee to be guilty of Communist affiliations, as well as all witnesses who refused to answer Committee questions on constitutional grounds; the Committee was thus improperly seeking to try, convict, and punish suspects, a task which the Constitution expressly denies to Congress and grants exclusively to the courts, to be exercised by them only after indictment and in full compliance with all the safeguards provided by the Bill of Rights.

The First Amendment says in no equivocal language that Congress shall pass no law abridging freedom of speech, press, assembly, or petition. The activities of this Committee, authorized by Congress, do precisely that, through exposure, obloquy, and public scorn. The Court does not really deny this fact but relies on a combination of three reasons for permitting the infringement: (A) The notion that despite the First Amendment's command Congress can abridge speech and association if this Court decides that the governmental interest in abridging speech is greater than an individual's interest in exercising that freedom, (B) the Government's right to "preserve itself," (C) the fact that the Committee is only after Communists or suspected Communists in this investigation.

(A) I do not agree that laws directly abridging First Amendment freedoms can be justified by a congressional or judicial balancing process. There are, of course, cases suggesting that a law which primarily regulates conduct but which might also indirectly affect speech can be upheld if the effect on speech is minor in relation to the need for control of the conduct. With these cases I agree. Typical of them are *Cantwell v. Connecticut,* 310 U.S. 296, and *Schneider v. Irvington,* 308 U.S. 147. Both of these involved the right of a city to control its streets. In *Cantwell,* a man had been convicted of breach of the peace for playing a phonograph on the street. He defended on the ground that he was disseminating religious views and could not, therefore, be stopped. We upheld his defense, but in so doing we pointed out that the city did have substantial power over conduct on the streets even where this power might to some extent affect speech. A State, we said, might "by general and non-discriminatory legislation regulate the times, the places, and the manner of soliciting upon its streets and holding meetings thereon." But even such laws governing conduct, we emphasized, must be tested, though only by a balancing process, if they indirectly affect ideas. On one side of the balance, we pointed out, is the interest of the United States in seeing that its fundamental law protecting freedom of communication is not abridged; on the other, the obvious interest of the State to regulate conduct within its boundaries. In *Cantwell* we held that the need to control the streets could not justify the restriction made on speech. We stressed the fact that where a man had a right to be on a street, "he had a right peacefully to impart his views to others." Similar views were expressed in *Schneider,* which concerned ordinances prohibiting the distribution of handbills to prevent littering. We forbade application of such ordinances when they affected literature designed to spread ideas. There were other ways, we said, to protect the city from littering which would not sacrifice the right of the people to be informed. In so holding, we, of course, found it necessary to "weigh the circumstances." But we did not in *Schneider,* any more than in *Cantwell,* even remotely suggest that a law directly aimed at curtailing speech and political persuasion could be saved through a balancing process. Neither these cases, nor any others, can be read as allowing legislative bodies to pass laws abridging freedom of speech, press, and association merely because of hostility to views peacefully expressed in a place where the speaker had a right to be. Rule XI, on its face and as here applied, since it attempts inquiry into beliefs, not action—ideas and associations, not conduct, does just that.

To apply the Court's balancing test under such circumstances is to read the First Amendment to say "Congress shall pass no law abridging freedom of speech, press, assembly and petition, unless Congress and the Supreme Court reach the joint conclusion that on balance the interests of Government in stifling these freedoms is greater than the interest of the people in having them exercised." This is closely akin to the notion that neither the First Amendment nor any other provision of the Bill of Rights should be enforced unless the Court believes it is *reasonable* to do so. Not only does this violate the genius of our *written* Constitution, but it runs expressly counter to the injunction to Court and Congress made by Madison when he introduced the Bill of Rights. "If they [the First Ten Amendments] are incorporated into the Constitution, independent tribunals of justice will consider themselves in a peculiar manner the guardians of those rights; they will be an impenetrable bulwark against *every* assumption of power in the Legislative or Executive; they will be naturally led to resist *every* encroachment upon rights expressly stipulated for in the Constitution by the declaration of rights." Unless we return to this view of our judicial function, unless we once again accept the notion that the Bill of Rights means what it says and that this Court must enforce that meaning, I am of the opinion that our great charter of liberty will be more honored in the breach than in the observance.

But even assuming what I cannot assume, that some balancing is proper in this case, I feel that the Court after stating the test ignores it completely. At most it balances the right of the Government to preserve itself, against Barenblatt's right to refrain from revealing Communist affiliations. Such a balance, however, mistakes the factors to be weighed. In the first place, it completely leaves out the real interest in Barenblatt's silence, the interest of the people as a whole in being able to join organizations, advocate causes, and make political "mistakes" without later being subjected to governmental penalties for having dared to think for themselves. It is this right, the right to err politically, which keeps us strong as a Nation. For no number of laws against Communism can have as much effect as the personal conviction which comes from having heard its arguments and rejected them, or from having once accepted its tenets and later recognized their worthlessness. Instead, the obloquy which results from investigations such as this not only stifles "mistakes" but prevents all but the most courageous from hazarding any views which might at some later time become disfavored. This result, whose importance cannot be overestimated, is doubly crucial when it affects the universities, on which we must largely rely for the experimentation and development of new ideas essential to our country's welfare. It is these interests of society, rather than Barenblatt's own right to silence, which I think the Court should put on the balance against the demands of the Government, if any balancing process is to be tolerated. Instead they are not mentioned, while on the other side the demands of the Government are vastly overstated and called "self preservation." It is admitted that this Committee can only seek information for the purpose of suggesting laws, and that Congress' power to make laws in the realm of speech and association is quite limited, even on the Court's test. Its interest in making such laws in the field of education, primarily a state function, is clearly narrower still. Yet the Court styles this attenuated interest self-preservation and allows it to overcome the need our country has to let us all think, speak, and associate politically as we like and without fear of reprisal. Such a result reduces "balancing" to a mere play on words and is completely inconsistent with the rules this Court has previously given for applying a "balancing test," where it is proper: "[T]he courts should be *astute* to examine the *effect* of the challenged legislation. Mere *legislative preferences or beliefs* . . . may well support regulation directed at other personal activities, but be insufficient to justify such as diminishes the exercise of rights so vital to the maintenance of democratic institutions." *Schneider v. Irvington,* 308 U.S. 147.

(B) Moreover, I cannot agree with the Court's notion that First Amendment freedoms must be abridged in order to "preserve" our country. That notion rests on the unarticulated premise that this Nation's security hangs upon its power to punish people because of what they think, speak, or write about, or because of those with whom they associate for political purposes. The Government, in its brief, virtually admits this position when it speaks of the "communication of unlawful ideas." I challenge this premise, and deny that ideas can be proscribed under our

Constitution. I agree that despotic governments cannot exist without stifling the voice of opposition to their oppressive practices. The First Amendment means to me, however, that the only constitutional way our Government can preserve itself is to leave its people the fullest possible freedom to praise, criticize, or discuss, as they see fit, all governmental policies and to suggest, if they desire, that even its most fundamental postulates are bad and should be changed; "Therein lies the security of the Republic, the very foundation of constitutional government."* On that premise this land was created, and on that premise it has grown to greatness. Our Constitution assumes that the common sense of the people and their attachment to our country will enable them, after free discussion, to withstand ideas that are wrong. To say that our patriotism must be protected against false ideas by means other than these is, I think, to make a baseless charge. Unless we can rely on these qualities—if, in short, we begin to punish speech—we cannot honestly proclaim ourselves to be a free Nation and we have lost what the Founders of this land risked their lives and their sacred honor to defend.

(C) The Court implies, however, that the ordinary rules and requirements of the Constitution do not apply because the Committee is merely after Communists and they do not constitute a political party but only a criminal gang. "[T]he long and widely accepted view," the Court says, is "that the tenets of the Communist Party include the ultimate overthrow of the Government of the United States by force and violence."† This justifies the investigation undertaken. By accepting this charge and allowing it to support treatment of the Communist Party and its members which would violate the Constitution if applied to other groups, the Court, in effect, declares that Party outlawed. It has been only a few years since there was a practically unanimous feeling throughout the country and in our courts that this could not be done in our free land. Of course, it has always been recognized that members of the Party who, either individually or in combination, commit acts in violation of valid laws can be prosecuted. But the Party as a whole and innocent members of it could not be attainted merely because it had some illegal aims and because some of its members were lawbreakers. Thus in *De Jonge v. Oregon,* 299 U.S. 353, on stipulated facts that the Communist Party advocated criminal syndicalism—"crime, physical violence, sabotage or any unlawful acts or methods as a means of accomplishing or effecting industrial or political change or revolution"— a unanimous Court, speaking through Chief Justice Hughes, held that a Communist addressing a Communist rally could be found guilty of no offense so long as no violence or crime was urged at the meeting. The Court absolutely refused to

---

*"The greater the importance of safeguarding the community from incitements to the overthrow of our institutions by force and violence, the more imperative is the need to preserve inviolate the constitutional rights of free speech, free press and free assembly in order to maintain the opportunity for free political discussion, to the end that government may be responsive to the will of the people and that changes, if desired, may be obtained by peaceful means. Therein lies the security of the Republic, the very foundation of constitutional government." *De Jonge v. Oregon,* 299 U.S. 353.

†Cf. statement of Sir Richard Nagle presenting a bill of attainder against between two and three thousand persons for political offenses, "'Many of the persons here attainted,' said he, 'have been proved traitors by such evidence as satisfies us. As to the rest we have followed common fame.'" Cited in *Joint Anti-Fascist Committee v. McGrath,* 341 U.S. 123.

concede that either De Jonge or the Communist Party forfeited the protections of the First and Fourteenth Amendments because one of the Party's purposes was to effect a violent change of government. . . .

. . . No matter how often or how quickly we repeat the claim that the Communist Party is not a political party, we cannot outlaw it, as a group, without endangering the liberty of all of us. The reason is not hard to find, for mixed among those aims of Communism which are illegal are perfectly normal political and social goals. And muddled with its revolutionary tenets is a drive to achieve power through the ballot, if it can be done. These things necessarily make it a political party whatever other, illegal, aims it may have. Significantly, until recently the Communist Party was on the ballot in many states. When that was so, many Communists undoubtedly hoped to accomplish its lawful goals through support of Communist candidates. Even now some such may still remain. To attribute to them, and to those who have left the Party, the taint of the group is to ignore both our traditions that guilt like belief is "personal and not a matter of mere association" and the obvious fact that "men adhering to a political party or other organization notoriously do not subscribe unqualifiedly to all of its platforms or asserted principles." *Schneiderman v. United States,* 320 U.S. 118.

The fact is that once we allow any group which has some political aims or ideas to be driven from the ballot and from the battle for men's minds because some of its members are bad and some of its tenets are illegal, no group is safe. Today we deal with Communists or suspected Communists. In 1920, instead, the New York Assembly suspended duly elected legislators on the ground that, being Socialists, they were disloyal to the country's principles. In the 1830's the Masons were hunted as outlaws and subversives, and abolitionists were considered revolutionaries of the most dangerous kind in both North and South. Earlier still, at the time of the universally unlamented Alien and Sedition laws, Thomas Jefferson's party was attacked and its members were derisively called "Jacobins." Fisher Ames described the party as a "French faction" guilty of "subversion" and "officered, regimented and formed to subordination." Its members, he claimed, intended to "take arms against the laws as soon as they dare." History should teach us then, that in times of high emotional excitement minority parties and groups which advocate extremely unpopular social or governmental innovations will always be typed as criminal gangs and attempts will always be made to drive them out. It was knowledge of this fact, and of its great dangers, that caused the Founders of our land to enact the First Amendment as a guarantee that neither Congress nor the people would do anything to hinder or destroy the capacity of individuals and groups to seek converts and votes for any cause, however radical or unpalatable their principles might seem under the accepted notions of the time. Whatever the States were left free to do, the First Amendment sought to leave Congress devoid of any kind or quality of power to direct any type of national laws against the freedom of individuals to think what they please, advocate whatever policy they choose, and join with others to bring about the social, religious, political, and governmental changes which seem best to them. Today's holding, in my judgment, marks another major step in the progressively increasing retreat from the safeguards of the First Amendment.

It is, sadly, no answer to say that this Court will not allow the trend to over-whelm us; that today's holding will be strictly confined to "Communists," as the Court's language implies. This decision can no more be contained than could the holding in *American Communications Asso. CIO v. Douds,* 339 U.S. 382. In that case the Court sustained as an exercise of the commerce power an Act which required labor union officials to take an oath that they were not members of the Communist Party. The Court rejected the idea that the *Douds* holding meant that the Party and all its members could be attainted because of their Communist beliefs. It went to great lengths to explain that the Act held valid "touches only a relative handful of persons, leaving the great majority of persons of the identified affiliations and beliefs completely free from restraint." "[W]hile this Court sits," the Court proclaimed, no wholesale proscription of Communists or their Party can occur. I dissented and said:

"Under such circumstances, restrictions imposed on proscribed groups are sel-dom static, even though the rate of expansion may not move in geometric pro-gression from discrimination to armband to ghetto and worse. Thus I cannot regard the Court's holding as one which merely bars Communists from holding union office and nothing more. For its reasoning would apply just as forcibly to statutes barring Communists and their respective sympathizers from election to political office, mere membership in unions, and in fact from getting or holding any job whereby they could earn a living."

My prediction was all too accurate. Today, Communists or suspected Com-munists have been denied an opportunity to work as government employees, lawyers, doctors, teachers, pharmacists, veterinarians, subway conductors, indus-trial workers, and in just about any other job. In today's holding they are singled out and, as a class, are subjected to inquisitions which the Court suggests would be unconstitutional but for the fact of "Communism." Nevertheless, this Court still sits!* . . .

Finally, I think Barenblatt's conviction violates the Constitution because the chief aim, purpose, and practice of the House Un-American Activities Committee, as disclosed by its many reports, is to try witnesses and punish them because they are or have been Communists or because they refuse to admit or deny Communist affiliations. The punishment imposed is generally punishment by humiliation and public shame. There is nothing strange or novel about this kind of punishment. It is in fact one of the oldest forms of governmental punishment known to mankind; branding, the pillory, ostracism, and subjection to public hatred being but a few examples of it. . . .

The Un-American Activities Committee was created in 1938. It immediately conceived of its function on a grand scale as one of ferreting out "subversives" and

---

*The record in this very case indicates how easily such restrictions spread. During the testimony of one witness an organization known as the Americans for Democratic Action was mentioned. Despite testimony that this organization did not admit Communists, one member of the Committee insisted that it was a Com-munist front because "it followed a party line, almost identical in many particulars with the Communist Party line." Presumably if this accusation were repeated frequently and loudly enough that organization, or any other, would also be called a "criminal gang."

especially of having them removed from government jobs.* It made many reports to the House urging removal of such employees. Finally, at the instigation of the Committee, the House put a rider on an appropriation bill to bar three government workers from collecting their salary. The House action was based on Committee findings that each of the three employees was a member of, or associated with, organizations deemed undesirable and that the "views and philosophies" of these workers "as expressed in various statements and writings constitute subversive activity within the definition adopted by your committee, and that [they are], therefore, unfit for the present to continue in Government employment." The Senate and the President agreed to the rider, though not without protest. We held that statute void as a bill of attainder in *United States v. Lovett,* 328 U.S. 303, (1946), stating that its "effect was to inflict punishment without the safeguards of a judicial trial" and that this "cannot be done either by a State or by the United States."

Even after our *Lovett* holding, however, the Committee continued to view itself as the "only agency of government that has the power of exposure," and to work unceasingly and sincerely to identify and expose all suspected Communists and "subversives" in order to eliminate them from virtually all fields of employment. How well it has succeeded in its declared program of "pitiless publicity and exposure" is a matter of public record. It is enough to cite the experience of a man who masqueraded as a Communist for the FBI and who reported to this same Committee that since 1952 when his "membership" became known he has been unable to hold any job. To accomplish this kind of result, the Committee has called witnesses who are suspected of Communist affiliation, has subjected them to severe questioning and has insisted that each tell the name of every person he has ever known at any time to have been a Communist, and, if possible, to give the addresses and occupations of the people named. These names are then indexed, published, and reported to Congress, and often to the press. The same technique is employed to cripple the job opportunities of those who strongly criticize the Committee or take other actions it deems undesirable.† Thus, in 1949, the Committee

---

*In its very first report it stated, "The Committee has felt that it is its sworn duty and solemn obligation to the people of this country to focus the spotlight of publicity upon every individual and organization engaged in subversive activities regardless of politics or partisanship." It further claimed that, "While Congress does not have the power to deny to citizens the right to believe in, teach, or advocate, communism, fascism, and nazism, it does have the right to focus the spotlight of publicity upon their activities." See also the statement of the Committee's first Chairman, "I am not in a position to say whether we can legislate effectively in reference to this matter, but I do know that exposure in a democracy of subversive activities is the most effective weapon that we have in our possession." 83 Cong. Rec. 7570 (1938).

†It is impossible even to begin to catalogue people who have been stigmatized by the Committee for criticizing it. In 1942 the Committee reported "Henry Luce's *Time* magazine has been drawn sucker-fashion into this movement to alter our form of government. . . ." In 1946 Harold Laski and Socialists generally were attacked for their "impertinence in suggesting that the United States should trade its system of free economy for some brand of Socialism." The Committee deemed it "imperative" that it ascertain the "methods used to enable Mr. Laski to broadcast to [a] rally." In 1951 a full report was issued on a "Communist lobby"—a committee formed to urge defeat of a Communist control bill before Congress. Among the distinguished sponsors of the group listed by the Committee was the late Prof. Zechariah Chafee. The Committee, nevertheless, advised "the American public that individuals who knowingly and actively support such a propaganda outlet . . . are actually aiding and abetting the Communist program in the United States."

reported that it had indexed and printed some 335,000 names of people who had signed "Communist" petitions of one kind or another. All this the Committee did and does to punish by exposure the many phases of "un-American" activities that it reports cannot be reached by legislation, by administrative action, or by any other agency of Government, which, of course, includes the courts.

The same intent to expose and punish is manifest in the Committee's investigation which led to Barenblatt's conviction. The declared purpose of the investigation was to identify to the people of Michigan the individuals responsible for the, alleged, Communist success there. The Committee claimed that its investigation "uncovered" members of the Communist Party holding positions in the school systems in Michigan; that most of the teachers subpoenaed before the Committee refused to answer questions on the ground that to do so might result in self-incrimination, and that most of these teachers had lost their jobs. It then stated that "the Committee on Un-American Activities approves of this action. . . ." Similarly, as a result of its Michigan investigation, the Committee called upon American labor unions to amend their constitutions, if necessary, in order to deny membership to any Communist Party member.* This would, of course, prevent many workers from getting or holding the only kind of jobs their particular skills qualified them for. The Court, today, barely mentions these statements, which, especially when read in the context of past reports by the Committee, show unmistakably what the Committee was doing. I cannot understand why these reports are deemed relevant to a determination of a congressional intent to investigate Communism in education, but irrelevant to any finding of congressional intent to bring about exposure for its own sake or for the purposes of punishment.

I do not question the Committee's patriotism and sincerity in doing all this.[†] I merely feel that it cannot be done by Congress under our Constitution. For, even assuming that the Federal Government can compel witnesses to testify as to Communist affiliations in order to subject them to ridicule and social and economic retaliation. I cannot agree that this is a legislative function. Such publicity is clearly punishment, and the Constitution allows only one way in which people can be convicted and punished. As we said in *Lovett,* "Those who wrote our Constitution well knew the danger inherent in special legislative acts which take away the life, liberty or property of particular named persons because the legislature thinks them guilty of conduct which deserves punishment. *They intended to safeguard the people of this country from punishment without trial by duly constituted courts.*" 328 U.S., at 317. Thus if Communism is to be made a crime, and Communists are to be subjected to "pains and penalties," I would still hold this conviction bad, for the crime of Communism, like all others, can be punished only by court and jury after a trial with all judicial safeguards.

---

*"[T]he Committee on Un-American Activities calls upon the American labor movement . . . to amend its constitutions where necessary in order to deny membership to a member of the Communist Party or any other group which dedicates itself to the destruction of America's way of life." Ibid.

[†]Sincerity and patriotism do not, unfortunately, insure against unconstitutional acts. Indeed, some of the most lamentable and tragic deaths of history were instigated by able, patriotic, and sincere men. See generally Mill, *On Liberty.*

It is no answer to all this to suggest that legislative committees should be allowed to punish if they grant the accused some rules of courtesy or allow him counsel. For the Constitution proscribes *all* bills of attainder by State or Nation, not merely those which lack counsel or courtesy. It does this because the Founders believed that punishment was too serious a matter to be entrusted to any group other than an independent judiciary and a jury of twelve men acting on previously passed, unambiguous laws, with all the procedural safeguards they put in the Constitution as essential to a fair trial—safeguards which included the right to counsel, compulsory process for witnesses, specific indictments, confrontation of accusers, as well as protection against self-incrimination, double jeopardy, and cruel and unusual punishment—in short, due process of law. They believed this because not long before, worthy men had been deprived of their liberties, and indeed their lives, through parliamentary trials without these safeguards. The memory of one of these, John Lilburne—banished and disgraced by a parliamentary committee on penalty of death if he returned to his country—was particularly vivid when our Constitution was written. His attack on trials by such committees and his warning that "what is done unto any one, may be done unto every one" was part of the history of the times which moved those who wrote our Constitution to determine that no such arbitrary punishments should ever occur here. It is the protection from arbitrary punishments through the right to a judicial trial with all these safeguards which over the years has distinguished America from lands where drumhead courts and other similar "tribunals" deprive the weak and the unorthodox of life, liberty, and property without due process of law. It is this same right which is denied to Barenblatt, because the Court today fails to see what is here for all to see—that exposure and punishment is the aim of this Committee and the reason for its existence. To deny this is to ignore the Committee's own claims and the reports it has issued ever since it was established. I cannot believe that the nature of our judicial office requires us to be so blind, and must conclude that the Un-American Activities Committee's "identification" and "exposure" of Communists and suspected Communists amount to an encroachment on the judiciary which bodes ill for the liberties of the people of this land.

Ultimately all the questions in this case really boil down to one—whether we as a people will try fearfully and futilely to preserve democracy by adopting totalitarian methods, or whether in accordance with our traditions and our Constitution we will have the confidence and courage to be free.

I would reverse this conviction.

85
Alexander Meiklejohn

Alexander Meiklejohn (1872–1964) was a distinguished American political philosopher whose central interest was the freedom of speech, and the role of free speech in a democracy. In the selections below from *Political Freedom,* Meiklejohn first gives a very famous interpretation of the free speech clause of the First Amendment as a principle absolutely essential to self-government. He then goes on to attack the "clear and present danger" test as used to justify limits on free speech, a test that has led our Supreme Court, he argues, to disastrous outcomes. If the citizens who are to decide an issue are denied *any* opinion, or doubt, or criticism, or disbelief relevant to that issue, the impact will be adverse to the general good. "It is that mutilation of the thinking process of the community against which the First Amendment to the Constitution is directed."

[HOW IS THE FIRST AMENDMENT TO BE UNDERSTOOD?]*

And now, after this long introduction, we are, I hope, ready for the task of interpreting the First Amendment to the Constitution, of trying to clear away the confusions by which its meaning has been obscured and even lost.

"Congress shall make no law . . . abridging the freedom of speech . . ." says the First Amendment to the Constitution. As we turn now to the interpreting of those words, three preliminary remarks should be made.

First, let it be noted that, by those words, Congress is not debarred from all action upon freedom of speech. Legislation which abridges that freedom is forbidden, but not legislation to enlarge and enrich it. The freedom of mind which befits the members of a self-governing society is not a given and fixed part of human nature. It can be increased and established by learning, by teaching, by the unhindered flow of accurate information, by giving men health and vigor and security, by bringing them together in activities of communication and mutual understanding. And the federal legislature is not forbidden to engage in that positive enterprise of cultivating the general intelligence upon which the success of self-government so obviously depends. On the contrary, in that positive field the Congress of the United States has a heavy and basic responsibility to promote the freedom of speech.

And second, no one who reads with care the text of the First Amendment can fail to be startled by its absoluteness. The phrase, "Congress shall make no law . . . abridging the freedom of speech," is unqualified. It admits of no exceptions. To say that no laws of a given type shall be made means that no laws of that type

*From Alexander Meiklejohn, *Political Freedom,* New York, Harper and Brothers, 1948.

shall, under any circumstances, be made. That prohibition holds good in war as in peace, in danger as in security. The men who adopted the Bill of Rights were not ignorant of the necessities of war or of national danger. It would, in fact, be nearer to the truth to say that it was exactly those necessities which they had in mind as they planned to defend freedom of discussion against them. Out of their own bitter experience they knew how terror and hatred, how war and strife, can drive men into acts of unreasoning suppression. They planned, therefore, both for the peace which they desired and for the wars which they feared. And in both cases they established an absolute, unqualified prohibition of the abridgment of the freedom of speech. That same requirement, for the same reasons, under the same Constitution, holds good today. . . .

But, third, this dictum which we rightly take to express the most vital wisdom which men have won in their striving for political freedom is yet—it must be admitted—strangely paradoxical. No one can doubt that, in any well-governed society, the legislature has both the right and the duty to prohibit certain forms of speech. Libellous assertions may be, and must be, forbidden and punished. So too must slander. Words which incite men to crime are themselves criminal and must be dealt with as such. Sedition and treason may be expressed by speech or writing. And, in those cases, decisive repressive action by the government is imperative for the sake of the general welfare. All these necessities that speech be limited are recognized and provided for under the Constitution. They were not unknown to the writers of the First Amendment. That amendment, then, we may take it for granted, *does not forbid the abridging of speech.* But, at the same time, *it does forbid the abridging of the freedom of speech.* It is to the solving of that paradox, that apparent self-contradiction, that we are summoned if, as free men, we wish to know what the right of freedom of speech is. . . .

The difficulties of the paradox of freedom as applied to speech may perhaps be lessened if we now examine the procedure of the traditional American town meeting. That institution is commonly, and rightly, regarded as a model by which free political procedures may be measured. It is self-government in its simplest, most obvious form.

In the town meeting the people of a community assemble to discuss and to act upon matters of public interest—roads, schools, poorhouses, health, external defense, and the like. Every man is free to come. They meet as political equals. Each has a right and a duty to think his own thoughts, to express them, and to listen to the arguments of others. The basic principle is that the freedom of speech shall be unabridged. And yet the meeting cannot even be opened unless, by common consent, speech is abridged. A chairman or moderator is, or has been, chosen. He "calls the meeting to order." And the hush which follows that call is a clear indication that restrictions upon speech have been set up. The moderator assumes, or arranges, that in the conduct of the business, certain rules of order will be observed. Except as he is overruled by the meeting as a whole, he will enforce those rules. His business on its negative side is to abridge speech. For example, it is usually agreed that no one shall speak unless "recognized by the chair." Also, debaters must confine their remarks to "the question before the house." If one man "has the floor," no one else may interrupt him except as provided by the rules. The meeting has assembled, not primarily to talk, but primarily by means of talking to get business done. And the talking must be regulated and abridged as the doing of the business under actual conditions may require. If a speaker wanders from the point at issue, if he is abusive or in other ways threatens to defeat the purpose of the meeting, he may be and should be declared "out of order." He must then stop speaking, at least in that way. And if he persists in breaking the rules, he may be "denied the floor" or, in the last resort, "thrown out" of the meeting. The town meeting, as it seeks for freedom of public discussion of public problems, would be wholly ineffectual unless speech were thus abridged. It is not a Hyde Park. It is a parliament or congress. It is a group of free and equal men, cooperating in a common enterprise, and using for that enterprise responsible and regulated discussion. It is not a dialectical free-for-all. It is self-government.

These speech-abridging activities of the town meeting indicate what the First Amendment to the Constitution does not forbid. When self-governing men demand freedom of speech they are not saying that every individual has an unalienable right to speak whenever, wherever, however he chooses. They do not declare that any man may talk as he pleases, when he pleases, about what he pleases, about whom he pleases, to whom he pleases. The common sense of any reasonable society would deny the existence of that unqualified right. No one, for example, may, without consent of nurse or doctor, rise up in a sickroom to argue for his principles or his candidate. In the sickroom, that question is not "before the house." The discussion is, therefore, "out of order." To you who now listen to my words, it is allowable to differ with me, but it is not allowable for you to state that difference in words until I have finished my reading. Anyone who would thus irresponsibly interrupt the activities of a lecture, a hospital, a concert hall, a church, a machine shop, a classroom, a football field, or a home, does not thereby exhibit his freedom. Rather, he shows himself to be a boor, a public nuisance, who must be abated, by force if necessary.

What, then, does the First Amendment forbid? Here again the town meeting suggests an answer. That meeting is called to discuss and, on the basis of such discussion, to decide matters of public policy. For example, shall there be a school? Where shall it be located? Who shall teach? What shall be taught? The community has agreed that such questions as these shall be freely discussed and that, when the discussion is ended, decision upon them will be made by vote of the citizens. Now, in that method of political self-government, the point of ultimate interest is not the words of the speakers, but the minds of the hearers. The final aim of the meeting is the voting of wise decisions. The voters, therefore, must be made as wise as possible. The welfare of the community requires that those who decide issues shall understand them. They must know what they are voting about. And this, in turn, requires that so far as time allows, all facts and interests relevant to the problem shall be fully and fairly presented to the meeting. Both facts and interests must be given in such a way that all the alternative lines of action can be wisely measured in relation to one another. As the self-governing community seeks, by the method of voting, to gain wisdom in action, it can find it only in the minds of its individual citizens. If they fail, it fails. That is why freedom of discussion for those minds may not be abridged.

The First Amendment, then, is not the guardian of unregulated talkativeness. It does not require that, on every occasion, every citizen shall take part in public debate. Nor can it even give assurance that everyone shall have opportunity to do so. If, for example, at a town meeting, twenty like-minded citizens have become a "party," and if one of them has read to the meeting an argument which they have all approved, it would be ludicrously out of order for each of the others to insist on reading it again. No competent moderator would tolerate that wasting of the time available for free discussion. What is essential is not that everyone shall speak, but that everything worth saying shall be said. To this end, for example, it may be arranged that each of the known conflicting points of view shall have, and shall be limited to, an assigned share of the time available. But however it be arranged, the vital point, as stated negatively, is that no suggestion of policy shall be denied a hearing because it is on one side of the issue rather than another. And this means that though citizens may, on other grounds, be barred from speaking, they may not be barred because their views are thought to be false or dangerous. No plan of action shall be outlawed because someone in control thinks it unwise, unfair, un-American. No speaker may be declared "out of order" because we disagree with what he intends to say. And the reason for this equality of status in the field of ideas lies deep in the very foundations of the self-governing process. When men govern themselves, it is they—and no one else—who must pass judgment upon unwisdom and unfairness and danger. And that means that unwise ideas must have a hearing as well as wise ones, unfair as well as fair, dangerous as well as safe, un-American as well as American. Just so far as, at any point, the citizens who are to decide an issue are denied acquaintance with information or opinion or doubt or disbelief or criticism which is relevant to that issue, just so far the result must be ill-considered, ill-balanced planning for the general good. *It is that mutilation of the thinking process of the community against which the First Amendment to the Constitution is directed.* The principle of the freedom of speech springs from the necessities of the program of self-government. It is not a Law of Nature or of Reason in the abstract. It is a deduction from the basic American agreement that public issues shall be decided by universal suffrage.

If, then, on any occasion in the United States it is allowable to say that the Constitution is a good document it is equally allowable, in that situation, to say that the Constitution is a bad document. If a public building may be used in which to say, in time of war, that the war is justified, then the same building may be used in which to say that it is not justified. If it be publicly argued that conscription for armed service is moral and necessary, it may likewise be publicly argued that it is immoral and unnecessary. If it may be said that American political institutions are superior to those of England or Russia or Germany, it may, with equal freedom, be said that those of England or Russia or Germany are superior to ours. These conflicting views may be expressed, must be expressed, not because they are valid, but because they are relevant. If they are responsibly entertained by anyone, we, the voters, need to hear them. When a question of policy is "before the house," free men choose to meet it not with their eyes shut, but with their eyes open. To be afraid of ideas, any idea, is to be unfit for self-government. To be afraid of ideas, any idea, is to be unfit for self-government. Any such suppression of ideas about the common good, the First Amendment condemns with its absolute disapproval. The freedom of ideas shall not be abridged.

[THE "CLEAR AND PRESENT DANGER" TEST REJECTED]

Now the primary purpose of this lecture is to challenge the interpretation of the freedom-of-speech principle which, since 1919, has been adopted by the Supreme Court of the United States. In that year, and in the years which have ensued, the court, following the lead of Justice Oliver Wendell Holmes, has persistently ruled that the freedom of speech of the American community may constitutionally be abridged by legislative action. That ruling annuls the most significant purpose of the First Amendment. It destroys the intellectual basis of our plan of self-government. The court has interpreted the dictum that Congress shall not abridge the freedom of speech by defining the conditions under which such abridging is allowable. Congress, we are now told, is forbidden to destroy our freedom except when it finds it advisable to do so.

The 1919 decision of which I am speaking arose from a review by the Supreme Court of the conviction, during World War I, of a group of persons who were accused of obstructing the drafting of men into the army. In the course of the trial in the lower court it had been shown that the defendants had mailed circulars to men who had been passed by the exemption boards. These circulars contained violent denunciations of the Conscription Act under which the draft was being administered. They impressed upon their readers "the right to assert your opposition to the draft," and urged the draftees to exercise that right. The Supreme Court unanimously sustained the conviction and Mr. Holmes wrote the opinion. In doing so, he formulated a new test of the freedom of speech guarantee. During the twenty-eight years which have passed since that decision was handed down, that test in varying forms has been accepted as expressing the law of the land. It is known as the principle of "clear and present danger."

The words in which Mr. Holmes explained and justified his decision have often been quoted. "We admit," he said, "that in many places and in ordinary times, the defendants in saying all that was said in the circular, would have been within their constitutional rights. But the character of every act depends upon the circumstances in which it is done. The most stringent protection of free speech would not protect a man in falsely shouting fire in a theatre, and causing a panic. It does not even protect a man from an injunction against uttering words which may have all the effect of force. . . . The question in every case is whether the words used are used in such circumstances and are of such a nature as to create a clear and present danger that they will bring about the substantive evils that Congress has a right to prevent. It is a question of proximity and degree. When a nation is at war many things that might be said in time of peace are such a hindrance to its effort that their utterance will not be endured so long as men fight, and that no court could regard them as protected by any constitutional right. It seems to be admitted that, if an actual obstruction of the recruiting service were proved, liability for words that produced that effect might be enforced." . . .

As we gather up the import of a series of opinions and decisions in which, since 1919, the phrase, "clear and present danger," has held a dominating influence, I wish to argue that their effect upon our understanding of self-government has been one of disaster. The philosophizing of Mr. Holmes has, I think, led us astray. As already remarked, it has, in effect, led to the annulment of the First Amendment rather than to its interpretation. . . .

What is the line, the principle, which marks off those speech activities which are liable to legislative abridgment from those which, under the Constitution, the legislature is forbidden to regulate or to suppress? Here is the critical question which must be studied, not only by the Supreme Court, but by every American who wishes to meet the intellectual responsibilities of his citizenship.

In the Constitution as it stood before it was amended by the Bill of Rights, the principle of the freedom of public discussion had been already clearly recognized and adopted. Article I, section 6, of the Constitution, as it defines the duties and privileges of the members of Congress, says, ". . . and for any speech or debate in either House, they shall not be questioned in any other place." Here is a prohibition against abridgment of the freedom of speech which is equally uncompromising, equally absolute, with that of the First Amendment. Unqualifiedly, the freedom of debate of our representatives upon the floor of either house is protected from abridging interference. May that protection, under the Constitution, be limited or withdrawn in time of clear and present danger? And if not, why not?

No one can possibly doubt or deny that congressional debate, on occasion, brings serious and immediate threat to the general welfare. For example, military conscription, both in principle and in procedure, has been bitterly attacked by our federal representatives. On the floors of both houses, in time of peace as well as in war, national policies have been criticized with an effectiveness which the words of private citizens could never achieve. Shall we, then, as we guard against "substantive evils that we have a right to prevent," call our representatives to account in some other place? . . . If congressional immunity were not absolute and unconditional, the whole program of representative self-government would be broken down. And likewise, by common consent, the same kind of immunity is guaranteed to the judges in our courts. Everyone knows that the dissenting opinions of members of the Supreme Court are a clear and present threat to the effectiveness of majority decisions. And yet the freedom of the minorities on the bench to challenge and to dissent has not been legally abridged. Nor will it be.

And that fact throws strong and direct light upon the provision of the First Amendment that the public discussions of "citizens" shall have the same immunity. In the last resort, it is not our representatives who govern us. We govern ourselves, using them. And we do so in such ways as our own free judgment may decide. And, that being true, it is essential that when we speak in the open forum, we "shall not be questioned in any other place." It is not enough for us, as self-governing men, that we be governed wisely and justly, by someone else. We insist on doing our own governing. The freedom which we grant to our representatives is merely a derivative of the prior freedom which belongs to us as voters. In spite of all the dangers which it involves, Article I, section 6, suggests that the First

Amendment means what it says: In the field of common action, of public discussion, the freedom of speech shall not be abridged. . . .

The heart of Mr. Holmes is in the right place. He demands freedom not merely for idle contemplation, but for the vigorous thinking and deciding which determine public action. Human discourse, as the First Amendment sees it, is not "a mere academic and harmless discussion." If it were, the advocates of self-government would be as little concerned about it as they would be concerned about the freedom of men playing solitaire or chess. The First Amendment was not written primarily for the protection of those intellectual aristocrats who pursue knowledge solely for the fun of the game, whose search for truth expresses nothing more than a private intellectual curiosity or an equally private delight and pride in mental achievement. It was written to clear the way for thinking which serves the general welfare. It offers defense to men who plan and advocate and incite toward corporate action for the common good. On behalf of such men it tells us that every plan of action must have a hearing, every relevant idea of fact or value must have full consideration, whatever may be the dangers which that activity involves. It makes no difference whether a man is advocating conscription or opposing it, speaking in favor of a war or against it, defending democracy or attacking it, planning a communist reconstruction of our economy or criticising it. So long as his active words are those of participation in public discussion and public decision of matters of public policy, the freedom of those words may not be abridged. That freedom is the basic postulate of a society which is governed by the votes of its citizens. . . .

The "clear and present danger" argument, which Mr. Holmes here offers, moves quickly from deliberate obstruction of a law to reasonable protest against it. Taken as it stands, his formula tells us that whenever the expression of a minority opinion involves clear and present danger to the public safety it may be denied the protection of the First Amendment. And that means that whenever crucial and dangerous issues have come upon the nation, free and unhindered discussion of them must stop. If, for example, a majority in Congress is taking action against "substantive evils which Congress has a right to prevent," a minority which opposes such action is not entitled to the freedom of speech of Article I, section 6. Under that ruling, dissenting judges might, in "dangerous" situations, be forbidden to record their dissents. Minority citizens might, in like situations, be required to hold their peace. No one, of course, believes that this is what Mr. Holmes or the court intended to say. But it is what, in plain words, they did say. The "clear and present danger" opinion stands on the record of the court as a peculiarly inept and unsuccessful attempt to formulate an exception to the principle of the freedom of speech.

In support of this criticism it is worthy of note that, both by Mr. Holmes and by Mr. Brandeis who, in general, concurred with him, the "clear and present danger" formula was very quickly found to be unsatisfactory. Within the same year, 1919, in which the principle had found its first expression, these two gallant defenders of freedom were confronted by the fact that the great majority of their colleagues were taking very seriously the assertion of Mr. Holmes that whenever any utterance creates clear and present danger to the public safety, that utterance may be forbidden and punished. Against that doctrine, the two dissenters spoke out with insistent passion. It is not enough, they said, that a danger created by speech be clear and present. It must also be very serious. In this vein, Mr. Holmes, with the approval of Mr. Brandeis, wrote, "I think we should be eternally vigilant against attempts to check the expression of opinions that we loathe and think to be fraught with death, unless they so imminently threaten interference with the lawful and pressing purposes of the law that an immediate check is required to save the country."* If the modification here suggested had been made when the principle was first devised it could not possibly have been applied to the case then before the court. But in the ten years which followed, this additional test of the extreme gravity of the danger involved is so strongly urged by both justices that the basic meaning of the test is, for them, radically altered. By implication, at least, it becomes no longer recognizable as the principle of "clear and present danger." The danger must be clear and present, but, also, terrific.

The character of this change begins to appear when Mr. Brandeis, with Mr. Holmes agreeing, says, "The fact that speech is likely to result in some violence or destruction of property is not enough to justify its suppression. There must be probability of serious injury to the State."† And again, we read from the same source, "Moreover, even imminent danger cannot justify resort to prohibition of these functions essential to effective democracy, unless the evil apprehended is relatively serious. Prohibition of free speech and assembly is a measure so stringent that it would be inappropriate as the means for averting a relatively trivial harm to society."‡

But the transformation of the principle does not stop with the addition of seriousness to clarity and immediacy . . . in the expositions of the formula of "clear and present danger," the most difficult and tantalizing factor for a reader has always been the insistence that a danger must be imminent, rather than remote, if it is to justify suppression. What is the basis for that insistence? It is relatively easy to understand why such a danger must be "clear." But why is it necessary that it be "present"? If the justification of suppression is, as Mr. Holmes says, that Congress is required and empowered to guard against dangers to the public safety, why should not that justification apply to clear and remote evils as well as to those which are clear and present? Surely we are not being told that, as Congress guards the common welfare, shortsightedness on its part is a virtue. Why, then, may it not take the same action in providing against the dangers of the future? As one reads the words of the advocates of the doctrine one feels certain that there is a valid reason for this differentiation which they are making. But in the early opinions, at least, that reason is never brought to light.

Eight years after the first formulation of the doctrine, however, Mr. Brandeis, writing with the approval of Mr. Holmes, moved forward toward an explanation of this immediacy. But the logical effect of this change was to lead the way toward

---

*Abrams v. U.S., 250 U.S. 616 (1919).
†Whitney v. California, 274 U.S. 352 (1927).
‡Ibid.

the substitution of a valid principle of freedom for that given in the "clear and present danger" test. "Those who won our independence by revolution," he says, "were not cowards. They did not fear political change. They did not exalt order at the cost of liberty. To courageous, self-reliant men, with confidence in the power of free and fearless reasoning applied through the processes of popular government, no danger flowing from speech can be deemed clear and present, unless the incidence of the evil apprehended is so imminent that it may befall before there is opportunity for free discussion. If there be time to expose through discussion the falsehood and fallacies, to avert the evil by the processes of education, the remedy to be applied is more speech, not enforced silence. Only an emergency can justify suppression. Such must be the rule if authority is to be reconciled with freedom. Such, in my opinion, is the command of the Constitution. It is, therefore, always open to Americans to challenge a law abridging free speech and assembly by showing that there was no emergency justifying it.*

In making that statement, Mr. Brandeis, though he keeps the traditional legal words, has abandoned the idea of "clear and present danger." He has brought us far along the road toward that very different principle of the absolute freedom of public discussion which was advocated in the first lecture of this series. Dangers, he now says, do not, as such, justify suppression. We Americans are not afraid of ideas, of any idea, if only we can have a fair chance to think about it. Under our plan of government, only an "emergency" can justify suppression.

And if we wish to see how far Mr. Brandeis has departed, or is departing, from the position originally taken by Mr. Holmes, we need only examine what are for him the defining characteristics of an "emergency." It is a situation in which there is "no opportunity for full discussion," in which there is no "time to expose through discussion the falsehood and fallacies, to avert the evil by the processes of education." Never when the ordinary civil processes of discussion and education are available, says Mr. Brandeis, will the Constitution tolerate the resort to suppression. The only allowable justification of it is to be found, not in the dangerous character of a specific set of ideas, but in the social situation which, for the time, renders the community incapable of the reasonable consideration of the issues of policy which confront it. In an emergency, as so defined, there can be no assurance that partisan ideas will be given by the citizens a fair and intelligent hearing. There can be no assurance that all ideas will be fairly and adequately presented. In a word, when such a civil or military emergency comes upon us, the processes of public discussion have broken down. In that situation as so defined, no advocate of the freedom of speech, however ardent, could deny the right and the duty of the government to declare that public discussion must be, not by one party alone, but by all parties alike, stopped until the order necessary for fruitful discussion has been restored. When the roof falls in, a moderator may, without violating the First Amendment, declare the meeting adjourned.

But to say these things is to deny at its very roots the principle which had been formulated by Mr. Holmes. That principle was directed toward the suppression of

Ibid.

some one partisan set of ideas. And it did so at the same time and under the same conditions in which opposed and competing partisan ideas were allowed free expression. "Dangerous" ideas were suppressed while "safe" ideas were encouraged. The doctrine, as stated, assumed that the normal processes of free public discussion were going on. But in the very midst of those processes it attacked and punished the advocates of some one point of view on the ground that their beliefs seemed to those in authority dangerous. That procedure Mr. Brandeis, if I understand him, now flatly repudiates. "If there be time to expose through discussion the falsehood and fallacies, to avert the evil by the processes of education, the remedy to be applied is more speech, not enforced silence." The logical integrity, the social passion of Mr. Brandeis, could not tolerate the essential incoherence, the rabid intolerance, of the "clear and present danger" principle, which would give a hearing to one side while denying it to the other. His lucid and painstaking mind fought its way through the self-contradictions of that doctrine as a theory of self-government. And as he did so, he brought nearer the day when we Americans can again hold up our heads and reaffirm our loyalty to the fundamental principles of the Constitution, can say without equivocation, with confidence that the words mean what they say, "Congress shall make no law abridging the freedom of speech."

86
Milton Friedman

Milton Friedman (1912–   ) is a distinguished economist who argues that the ideal of political freedom cherished by democrats is tied essentially to *economic freedom.* Democracy, he therefore holds, requires a *free private enterprise exchange economy.* Only open markets produce that wide dispersion of decision-making power that blocks potential tyrants; this, he contends, accounts for the fact that capitalism appears historically to be a necessary condition for the political freedoms we call democratic.

[POLITICAL AND ECONOMIC FREEDOM]*

To the free man, the country is the collection of individuals who compose it, not something over and above them. He is proud of a common heritage and loyal to common traditions. But he regards government as a means, an instrumentality, neither a grantor of favors and gifts, nor a master or god to be blindly worshipped and served. He recognizes no national goal except as it is the consensus of the goals that the citizens severally serve. He recognizes no national purpose except as it is the consensus of the purposes for which the citizens severally strive.

*From Milton Friedman, *Capitalism and Freedom,* University of Chicago Press, 1962.

The free man will ask neither what his country can do for him nor what he can do for his country. He will ask rather "What can I and my compatriots do through government" to help us discharge our individual responsibilities, to achieve our several goals and purposes, and above all, to protect our freedom? And he will accompany this question with another: How can we keep the government we create from becoming a Frankenstein that will destroy the very freedom we establish it to protect? Freedom is a rare and delicate plant. Our minds tell us, and history confirms, that the great threat to freedom is the concentration of power. Government is necessary to preserve our freedom, it is an instrument through which we can exercise our freedom; yet by concentrating power in political hands, it is also a threat to freedom. Even though the men who wield this power initially be of good will and even though they be not corrupted by the power they exercise, the power will both attract and form men of a different stamp.

How can we benefit from the promise of government while avoiding the threat to freedom? Two broad principles embodied in our Constitution give an answer that has preserved our freedom so far, though they have been violated repeatedly in practice while proclaimed as precept.

First, the scope of government must be limited. Its major function must be to protect our freedom both from the enemies outside our gates and from our fellow-citizens: to preserve law and order, to enforce private contracts, to foster competitive markets. Beyond this major function, government may enable us at times to accomplish jointly what we would find it more difficult or expensive to accomplish severally. However, any such use of government is fraught with danger. We should not and cannot avoid using government in this way. But there should be a clear and large balance of advantages before we do. By relying primarily on voluntary co-operation and private enterprise, in both economic and other activities, we can insure that the private sector is a check on the powers of the governmental sector and an effective protection of freedom of speech, of religion, and of thought.

The second broad principle is that government power must be dispersed. If government is to exercise power, better in the county than in the state, better in the state than in Washington. If I do not like what my local community does, be it in sewage disposal, or zoning, or schools, I can move to another local community, and though few may take this step, the mere possibility acts as a check. If I do not like what my state does, I can move to another. If I do not like what Washington imposes, I have few alternatives in this world of jealous nations.

The very difficulty of avoiding the enactments of the federal government is of course the great attraction of centralization to many of its proponents. It will enable them more effectively, they believe, to legislate programs that—as they see it—are in the interest of the public, whether it be the transfer of income from the rich to the poor or from private to governmental purposes. They are in a sense right. But this coin has two sides. The power to do good is also the power to do harm; those who control the power today may not tomorrow; and, more important, what one man regards as good, another may regard as harm. The great tragedy of the drive to centralization, as of the drive to extend the scope of government in general, is that it is mostly led by men of good will who will be the first to rue its consequences.

The preservation of freedom is the protective reason for limiting and decentralizing governmental power. But there is also a constructive reason. The great advances of civilization, whether in architecture or painting, in science or literature, in industry or agriculture, have never come from centralized government.

. . . Newton and Leibnitz; Einstein and Bohr; Shakespeare, Milton, and Pasternak; Whitney, McCormick, Edison, and Ford; Jane Addams, Florence Nightingale, and Albert Schweitzer; no one of these opened new frontiers in human knowledge and understanding, in literature, in technical possibilities, or in the relief of human misery in response to governmental directives. Their achievements were the product of individual genius, of strongly held minority views, of a social climate permitting variety and diversity.

Government can never duplicate the variety and diversity of individual action. At any moment in time, by imposing uniform standards in housing, or nutrition, or clothing, government could undoubtedly improve the level of living of many individuals; by imposing uniform standards in schooling, road construction, or sanitation, central government could undoubtedly improve the level of performance in many local areas and perhaps even on the average of all communities. But in the process, government would replace progress by stagnation, it would substitute uniform mediocrity for the variety essential for that experimentation which can bring tomorrow's laggards above today's mean.

This book discusses some of these great issues. Its major theme is the role of competitive capitalism—the organization of the bulk of economic activity through private enterprise operating in a free market—as a system of economic freedom and a necessary condition for political freedom. . . .

[ECONOMIC FREEDOM SUPPORTS POLITICAL FREEDOM]

It is widely believed that politics and economics are separate and largely unconnected; that individual freedom is a political problem and material welfare an economic problem; and that any kind of political arrangements can be combined with any kind of economic arrangements. The chief contemporary manifestation of this idea is the advocacy of "democratic socialism" by many who condemn out of hand the restrictions on individual freedom imposed by "totalitarian socialism" in Russia, and who are persuaded that it is possible for a country to adopt the essential features of Russian economic arrangements and yet to ensure individual freedom through political arrangements. The thesis of this chapter is that such a view is a delusion, that there is an intimate connection between economics and politics, that only certain combinations of political and economic arrangements are possible, and that in particular, a society which is socialist cannot also be democratic, in the sense of guaranteeing individual freedom.

Economic arrangements play a dual role in the promotion of a free society. On the one hand, freedom in economic arrangements is itself a component of freedom broadly understood, so economic freedom is an end in itself. In the second place, economic freedom is also an indispensable means toward the achievement of political freedom.

The first of these roles of economic freedom needs special emphasis because intellectuals in particular have a strong bias against regarding this aspect of freedom as important. They tend to express contempt for what they regard as material aspects of life, and to regard their own pursuit of allegedly higher values as on a different plane of significance and as deserving of special attention. For most citizens of the country, however, if not for the intellectual, the direct importance of economic freedom is at least comparable in significance to the indirect importance of economic freedom as a means to political freedom. . . .

Viewed as a means to the end of political freedom, economic arrangements are important because of their effect on the concentration or dispersion of power. The kind of economic organization that provides economic freedom directly, namely, competitive capitalism, also promotes political freedom because it separates economic power from political power and in this way enables the one to offset the other.

Historical evidence speaks with a single voice on the relation between political freedom and a free market. I know of no example in time or place of a society that has been marked by a large measure of political freedom, and that has not also used something comparable to a free market to organize the bulk of economic activity.

Because we live in a largely free society, we tend to forget how limited is the span of time and the part of the globe for which there has ever been anything like political freedom: the typical state of mankind is tyranny, servitude, and misery. The nineteenth century and early twentieth century in the Western world stand out as striking exceptions to the general trend of historical development. Political freedom in this instance clearly came along with the free market and the development of capitalist institutions. So also did political freedom in the golden age of Greece and in the early days of the Roman era.

History suggests only that capitalism is a necessary condition for political freedom. Clearly it is not a sufficient condition. Fascist Italy and Fascist Spain, Germany at various times in the last seventy years, Japan before World Wars I and II, tzarist Russia in the decades before World War I—are all societies that cannot conceivably be described as politically free. Yet, in each, private enterprise was the dominant form of economic organization. It is therefore clearly possible to have economic arrangements that are fundamentally capitalist and political arrangements that are not free.

Even in those societies, the citizenry had a good deal more freedom than citizens of a modern totalitarian state like Russia or Nazi Germany, in which economic totalitarianism is combined with political totalitarianism. Even in Russia under the Tzars, it was possible for some citizens, under some circumstances, to change their jobs without getting permission from political authority because capitalism and the existence of private property provided some check to the centralized power of the state.

The relation between political and economic freedom is complex and by no means unilateral. In the early nineteenth century, Bentham and the Philosophical

Radicals were inclined to regard political freedom as a means to economic freedom. They believed that the masses were being hampered by the restrictions that were being imposed upon them, and that if political reform gave the bulk of the people the vote, they would do what was good for them, which was to vote for laissez faire. In retrospect, one cannot say that they were wrong. There was a large measure of political reform that was accompanied by economic reform in the direction of a great deal of laissez faire. An enormous increase in the well-being of the masses followed this change in economic arrangements.

The triumph of Benthamite liberalism in nineteenth-century England was followed by a reaction toward increasing intervention by government in economic affairs. This tendency to collectivism was greatly accelerated, both in England and elsewhere, by the two World Wars. Welfare rather than freedom became the dominant note in democratic countries. Recognizing the implicit threat to individualism, the intellectual descendants of the Philosophical Radicals—Dicey, Mises, Hayek, and Simons, to mention only a few—feared that a continued movement toward centralized control of economic activity would prove *The Road to Serfdom,* as Hayek entitled his penetrating analysis of the process. Their emphasis was on economic freedom as a means toward political freedom.

Historical evidence by itself can never be convincing. Perhaps it was sheer coincidence that the expansion of freedom occurred at the same time as the development of capitalist and market institutions. Why should there be a connection? What are the logical links between economic and political freedom? In discussing these questions we shall consider first the market as a direct component of freedom, and then the indirect relation between market arrangements and political freedom. A by-product will be an outline of the ideal economic arrangements for a free society. . . .

The basic problem of social organization is how to co-ordinate the economic activities of large numbers of people. Even in relatively backward societies, extensive division of labor and specialization of function is required to make effective use of available resources. In advanced societies, the scale on which coordination is needed, to take full advantage of the opportunities offered by modern science and technology, is enormously greater. Literally millions of people are involved in providing one another with their daily bread, let alone with their yearly automobiles. The challenge to the believer in liberty is to reconcile this widespread interdependence with individual freedom.

Fundamentally, there are only two ways of co-ordinating the economic activities of millions. One is central direction involving the use of coercion—the technique of the army and of the modern totalitarian state. The other is voluntary co-operation of individuals—the technique of the market place.

The possibility of co-ordination through voluntary co-operation rests on the elementary—yet frequently denied—proposition that both parties to an economic transaction benefit from it, *provided the transaction is bi-laterally voluntary and informed.*

Exchange can therefore bring about co-ordination without coercion. A working model of a society organized through voluntary exchange is a *free private enterprise exchange economy*—what we have been calling competitive capitalism. . . .

Despite the important role of enterprises and of money in our actual economy, and despite the numerous and complex problems they raise, the central characteristic of the market technique of achieving co-ordination is fully displayed in the simple exchange economy that contains neither enterprises nor money. As in that simple model, so in the complex enterprise and money-exchange economy, co-operation is strictly individual and voluntary *provided: (a)* that enterprises are private, so that the ultimate contracting parties are individuals and *(b)* that individuals are effectively free to enter or not to enter into any particular exchange, so that every transaction is strictly voluntary.

It is far easier to state these provisos in general terms than to spell them out in detail, or to specify precisely the institutional arrangements most conducive to their maintenance. Indeed, much of technical economic literature is concerned with precisely these questions. The basic requisite is the maintenance of law and order to prevent physical coercion of one individual by another and to enforce contracts voluntarily entered into, thus giving substance to "private." Aside from this, perhaps the most difficult problems arise from monopoly—which inhibits effective freedom by denying individuals alternatives to the particular exchange—and from "neighborhood effects"—effects on third parties for which it is not feasible to charge or recompense them. . . .

[A FREE SOCIETY REQUIRES A MARKET ECONOMY]

So long as effective freedom of exchange is maintained, the central feature of the market organization of economic activity is that it prevents one person from interfering with another in respect of most of his activities. The consumer is protected from coercion by the seller because of the presence of other sellers with whom he can deal. The seller is protected from coercion by the consumer because of other consumers to whom he can sell. The employee is protected from coercion by the employer because of other employers for whom he can work, and so on. And the market does this impersonally and without centralized authority.

Indeed, a major source of objection to a free economy is precisely that it does this task so well. It gives people what they want instead of what a particular group thinks they ought to want. Underlying most arguments against the free market is a lack of belief in freedom itself.

The existence of a free market does not of course eliminate the need for government. On the contrary, government is essential both as a forum for determining the "rules of the game" and as an umpire to interpret and enforce the rules decided on. What the market does is to reduce greatly the range of issues that must be decided through political means, and thereby to minimize the extent to which government need participate directly in the game. The characteristic feature of action through political channels is that it tends to require or enforce substantial conformity. The great advantage of the market, on the other hand, is that it permits wide diversity. It is, in political terms, a system of proportional representation. Each man can vote, as it were, for the color of tie he wants and get it; he does not have to see what color the majority wants and then, if he is in the minority, submit.

It is this feature of the market that we refer to when we say that the market provides economic freedom. But this characteristic also has implications that go far beyond the narrowly economic. Political freedom means the absence of coercion of a man by his fellow men. The fundamental threat to freedom is power to coerce, be it in the hands of a monarch, a dictator, an oligarchy, or a momentary majority. The preservation of freedom requires the elimination of such concentration of power to the fullest possible extent and the dispersal and distribution of whatever power cannot be eliminated—a system of checks and balances. By removing the organization of economic activity from the control of political authority, the market eliminates this source of coercive power. It enables economic strength to be a check to political power rather than a reinforcement.

Economic power can be widely dispersed. There is no law of conservation which forces the growth of new centers of economic strength to be at the expense of existing centers. Political power, on the other hand, is more difficult to decentralize. There can be numerous small independent governments. But it is far more difficult to maintain numerous equipotent small centers of political power in a single large government than it is to have numerous centers of economic strength in a single large economy. There can be many millionaires in one large economy. But can there be more than one really outstanding leader, one person on whom the energies and enthusiasms of his countrymen are centered? If the central government gains power, it is likely to be at the expense of local governments. There seems to be something like a fixed total of political power to be distributed. Consequently, if economic power is joined to political power, concentration seems almost inevitable. On the other hand, if economic power is kept in separate hands from political power, it can serve as a check and a counter to political power.

The force of this abstract argument can perhaps best be demonstrated by example. Let us consider first, a hypothetical example that may help to bring out the principles involved, and then some actual examples from recent experience that illustrate the way in which the market works to preserve political freedom.

One feature of a free society is surely the freedom of individuals to advocate and propagandize openly for a radical change in the structure of the society—so long as the advocacy is restricted to persuasion and does not include force or other forms of coercion. It is a mark of the political freedom of a capitalist society that men can openly advocate and work for socialism. Equally, political freedom in a socialist society would require that men be free to advocate the introduction of capitalism. How could the freedom to advocate capitalism be preserved and protected in a socialist society?

In order for men to advocate anything, they must in the first place be able to earn a living. This already raises a problem in a socialist society, since all jobs are under the direct control of political authorities. It would take an act of self-denial whose difficulty is underlined by experience in the United States after World War II with the problem of "security" among Federal employees, for a socialist government to permit its employees to advocate policies directly contrary to official doctrine.

But let us suppose this act of self-denial to be achieved. For advocacy of capitalism to mean anything, the proponents must be able to finance their cause—to hold public meetings, publish pamphlets, buy radio time, issue newspapers and magazines, and so on. How could they raise the funds? There might and probably would be men in the socialist society with large incomes, perhaps even large capital sums in the form of government bonds and the like, but these would of necessity be high public officials. It is possible to conceive of a minor socialist official retaining his job although openly advocating capitalism. It strains credulity to imagine the socialist top brass financing such "subversive" activities.

The only recourse for funds would be to raise small amounts from a large number of minor officials. But this is no real answer. To tap these sources, many people would already have to be persuaded, and our whole problem is how to initiate and finance a campaign to do so. Radical movements in capitalist societies have never been financed this way. They have typically been supported by a few wealthy individuals who have become persuaded—by a Frederick Vanderbilt Field, or an Anita McCormick Blaine, or a Corliss Lamont, to mention a few names recently prominent, or by a Friedrich Engels, to go farther back. This is a role of inequality of wealth in preserving political freedom that is seldom noted— the role of the patron.

In a capitalist society, it is only necessary to convince a few wealthy people to get funds to launch any idea, however strange, and there are many such persons, many independent foci of support. And, indeed, it is not even necessary to persuade people or financial institutions with available funds of the soundness of the ideas to be propagated. It is only necessary to persuade them that the propagation can be financially successful; that the newspaper or magazine or book or other venture will be profitable. The competitive publisher, for example, cannot afford to publish only writing with which he personally agrees; his touchstone must be the likelihood that the market will be large enough to yield a satisfactory return on his investment.

In this way, the market breaks the vicious circle and makes it possible ultimately to finance such ventures by small amounts from many people without first persuading them. There are no such possibilities in the socialist society; there is only the all-powerful state.

Let us stretch our imagination and suppose that a socialist government is aware of this problem and is composed of people anxious to preserve freedom. Could it provide the funds? Perhaps, but it is difficult to see how. It could establish a bureau for subsidizing subversive propaganda. But how could it choose whom to support? If it gave to all who asked, it would shortly find itself out of funds, for socialism cannot repeal the elementary economic law that a sufficiently high price will call forth a large supply. Make the advocacy of radical causes sufficiently remunerative, and the supply of advocates will be unlimited.

Moreover, freedom to advocate unpopular causes does not require that such advocacy be without cost. On the contrary, no society could be stable if advocacy of radical change were costless, much less subsidized. It is entirely appropriate that men make sacrifices to advocate causes in which they deeply believe. Indeed, it is important to preserve freedom only for people who are willing to practice self-denial, for otherwise freedom degenerates into license and irresponsibility. What is essential is that the cost of advocating unpopular causes be tolerable and not pro-hibitive.

But we are not yet through. In a free market society, it is enough to have the funds. The suppliers of paper are as willing to sell it to the *Daily Worker* as to the *Wall Street Journal.* In a socialist society, it would not be enough to have the funds. The hypothetical supporter of capitalism would have to persuade a govern-ment factory making paper to sell to him, the government printing press to print his pamphlets, a government post office to distribute them among the people, a government agency to rent him a hall in which to talk, and so on.

Perhaps there is some way in which one could overcome these difficulties and preserve freedom in a socialist society. One cannot say it is utterly impossible. What is clear, however, is that there are very real difficulties in establishing insti-tutions that will effectively preserve the possibility of dissent. So far as I know, none of the people who have been in favor of socialism and also in favor of free-dom have really faced up to this issue, or made even a respectable start at devel-oping the institutional arrangements that would permit freedom under socialism. By contrast, it is clear how a free market capitalist society fosters freedom. . . .

Another example of the role of the market in preserving political freedom, was revealed in our experience with McCarthyism. Entirely aside from the substantive issues involved, and the merits of the charges made, what protection did individu-als, and in particular government employees, have against irresponsible accusa-tions and probings into matters that it went against their conscience to reveal? Their appeal to the Fifth Amendment would have been a hollow mockery without an alternative to government employment.

Their fundamental protection was the existence of a private-market economy in which they could earn a living. Here again, the protection was not absolute. Many potential private employers were, rightly or wrongly, averse to hiring those pillo-ried. It may well be that there was far less justification for the costs imposed on many of the people involved than for the costs generally imposed on people who advocate unpopular causes. But the important point is that the costs were limited and not prohibitive, as they would have been if government employment had been the only possibility.

It is of interest to note that a disproportionately large fraction of the people involved apparently went into the most competitive sectors of the economy—small business, trade, farming—where the market approaches most closely the ideal free market. No one who buys bread knows whether the wheat from which it is made was grown by a Communist or a Republican, by a constitutionalist or a Fascist, or, for that matter, by a Negro or a white. This illustrates how an imper-sonal market separates economic activities from political views and protects men from being discriminated against in their economic activities for reasons that are irrelevant to their productivity—whether these reasons are associated with their views or their color.

As this example suggests, the groups in our society that have the most at stake in the preservation and strengthening of competitive capitalism are those minority groups which can most easily become the object of the distrust and enmity of the majority—the Negroes, the Jews, the foreign-born, to mention only the most obvious. Yet, paradoxically enough, the enemies of the free market—the Socialists and Communists—have been recruited in disproportionate measure from these groups. Instead of recognizing that the existence of the market has protected them from the attitudes of their fellow countrymen, they mistakenly attribute the residual discrimination to the market.

87
Norman Thomas

Norman Mattoon Thomas (1884–1968) was the outstanding spokesman and advocate of democratic socialism in the United States. Many times a Socialist party candidate for the presidency, Thomas was fearless and trenchant in his criticism of American capitalism. His honest and articulate presentation of the case for socialism, his willingness to admit error and to venture the untried, and above all his devotion to democratic process and to civil liberties endeared him to many Americans and won the respect of all. In the pamphlet *Democratic Socialism* (1953), from which the following passages come, he restates concisely the argument for economic planning in a modern democracy.

[PLANNING AND DEMOCRACY]*

The modern socialist must begin by emphasizing the importance of planning. It is a simple impossibility to support in decency, if at all, the present population of the world on the principle that each man and each group must act as intelligently as it can for itself without any conscious and planned cooperation. We continually recognize this in action. It is one of the amusing paradoxes of American life that the years have heard the loudest outcries against government planning, have been precisely the years when of necessity we have accepted the most planning by government, national, state and city. The long list of subsidies and other aids to all sorts of groups in America which we cited in another connection have required government planning.

. . .

It is no argument against planning to say that some planning has been bad. We are far more likely to get a constructive critical approach to planning when we accept its necessity in terms of the common good. I remember that I was the only presidential candidate in 1948 who openly criticized the outrageous potato subsidy of that year. I believed in planning and therefore I believed in criticizing bad planning without primary consideration of the effect of such criticism upon sections of the farm vote.

*From N. M. Thomas, *Democratic Socialism: A New Appraisal*, New York, 1953; reprinted with the permission of the publishers, the League for Industrial Democracy.

Obviously, economic planning is something different than laying out blueprints for buildings. We are planning for people whose understanding and cooperation must be enlisted. Plans must be flexible and allow for contributions from different levels. Even under our imperfect approach to a planning so many Americans have distrusted, we have proved that this flexible planning is possible.

PLANNING AND LIBERTY

Yet we are hysterically told that all government planning is essentially and necessarily the foe of liberty. That is nonsense unless one is to interpret liberty in the completely unrealistic sense of the right of any individual always to do what he pleases. Unquestionably, modern automobile traffic puts restraints on the whimsical liberty of pedestrians or drivers. Reasonable traffic regulation is a necessity wholly consistent with freedom. So in a more difficult field are the controls necessary in our complex and interdependent community. . . .

SOCIALIST PLANNING FOR AMERICA

Let the reader consider the outline of socialist planning for America which follows and ask himself which valid freedom has been violated.

Socialist planning for America will emphasize the importance of production. The best use of our resources and technology obviously requires planning devoted to an economy of abundance for all. The evil of our acquisitive society is not that in sum total we have too many material possessions but too few. It is scarcity that makes men passionately concerned for possession. It is against a background of general scarcity that conspicuous waste acquires its greatest moral opprobrium and that conspicuous wealth gives dangerous power and prestige. There may be virtue for the individual or some individuals in the embrace of Lady Poverty. The involuntary poverty of mankind in the face of its collective power to acquire abundance is a disgrace to society and a deep injury to men.

Socialist planning for abundant production and fairer distribution would be carried on through controls of machinery of taxation and fiscal control already in operation. It would be exercised through labor, social security, and welfare legislation. . . .

Planning will be simplified by the right kind of social ownership. It is, for instance, much easier to plan for power development under public ownership than to force recalcitrant private companies into line. The government had to take the initiative to get proper action on rural electrification. Moreover, in times of relative depression, the government is in a position to do what private owners cannot, that is, deliberately to expand certain lines of production for the future on terms which will give employment, when employment is desperately needed. At all times it is easier to prevent the shocking wastes of such natural resources as our forests, and our oil, wastes inherent in private ownership and competitive exploitation, if we have social ownership.

. . .

SOCIAL, PRIVATE, AND COOPERATIVE OWNERSHIP

There are some advantages for freedom and enterprise in varieties of ownership. The state under the most democratic theory and practice will become too huge, too cumbersome, if it seeks to control directly all economic activity. There are men with a deep seated desire to work for themselves. They will work harder and be more ingenious in so doing. Ours is not the economy of a beleaguered garrison which has to ration diminishing supplies for everybody and everything. There is room in it for individual ownership and individual effort. Justification of such ownership must always be accompanied by a genuine responsibility for management on terms consistent with the common good.

There is not one perfect formula for what ought to be owned under social legislation. One determining factor is the public attitude, which varies according to time and place. Each generation should be allowed to make its own decisions, but there ought to be assurance that once decisions are made they will stand for a reasonable length of time, whether under public or private ownership.

Heretofore publicly owned enterprises in America have operated under disadvantages that socialism should avoid. We Americans are, or think we are, committed to a theory of private enterprise. The publicly owned enterprises have been a more or less regretted exception. Sometimes it has been a sick industry which has had to be taken over by government which is then blamed for the sickness. Always there has been a conscious or unconscious tendency in the world of industry to discredit and even sabotage public ownership. Witness the attitude of industry generally toward the exceedingly useful TVA. To be truly successful, public ownership and democratic operation must be accepted in principle and extensively practiced in appropriate areas.

For some years, American socialists have been fairly well agreed that social ownership should be extended to the "commanding heights" of our economy, which include our natural resources, our system of money, banking and credit, and certain basic industries and services.

The social ownership of industries should be determined in the light of certain tests: (1) their basic importance to our lives; (2) the degree of their monopolization and the effectiveness of competition in controlling prices; (3) the degree to which absentee ownership is divorced from responsible management. Today, in huge enterprises, managers work for the private stockholders who themselves do little or nothing except to provide working capital. Even that is largely provided out of profits set aside by the managers for expansion. Yet the stockholders expect their working capital to be immortal and always to produce dividends. . . .

What socialists advocate, let me again insist, is not nationalization, but socialization. A thousand times I have said that the virtue of government ownership depends upon who owns the government. It would be more accurate to say that government must be democratic, that it should act only as a trustee of society, and that consumers as a whole and workers in a particular industry should be directly concerned in the management of any publicly owned industry.

88
Friedrich A. Hayek

Friedrich A. Hayek (1899–1992) was, like Milton Friedman, a professor of economics at The University of Chicago. He too believed that when a democracy tries to engage in long-range economic planning on the socialist model, it will destroy itself. This is so, he argues, because an elected assembly is never *capable* of making the decisions such plans require. "Experts" must therefore be appointed to manage the economy; these experts come to wield such great power that eventually they become economic dictators. A planned economy and a democratic society are necessarily incompatible, Hayek contends; centralized economic planning is "the road to serfdom."

PLANNING AND DEMOCRACY*

The common features of all collectivist systems may be described, in a phrase ever dear to socialists of all schools, as the deliberate organization of the labors of society for a definite social goal. That our present society lacks such "conscious" direction toward a single aim, that its activities are guided by the whims and fancies of irresponsible individuals, has always been one of the main complaints of its socialist critics.

In many ways this puts the basic issue very clearly. And it directs us at once to the point where the conflict arises between individual freedom and collectivism. The various kinds of collectivism, communism, fascism, etc., differ among themselves in the nature of the goal toward which they want to direct the efforts of society. But they all differ from liberalism and individualism in wanting to organize the whole of society and all its resources for this unitary end and in refusing to recognize autonomous spheres in which the ends of the individuals are supreme. In short, they are totalitarian in the true sense of this new word which we have adopted to describe the unexpected but nevertheless inseparable manifestations of what in theory we call collectivism.

The "social goal," or "common purpose," for which society is to be organized is usually vaguely described as the "common good," the "general welfare," or the "general interest." It does not need much reflection to see that these terms have no sufficiently definite meaning to determine a particular course of action. The welfare and the happiness of millions cannot be measured on a single scale of less and more. The welfare of a people, like the happiness of a man, depends on a great many things that can be provided in an infinite variety of combinations. It cannot be adequately expressed as a single end, but only as a hierarchy of ends, a comprehensive scale of values in which every need of every person is given its place. To direct all our activities according to a single plan presupposes that every one of

---

*From F. Hayek, *The Road to Serfdom,* 1944. © 1944 by the University of Chicago Press. Reprinted by permission of the University of Chicago Press and of Routledge and Kegan Paul, Ltd.

our needs is given its rank in an order of values which must be complete enough to make it possible to decide among all the different courses which the planner has to choose. It presupposes, in short, the existence of a complete ethical code in which all the different human values are allotted their due place. . . .

The essential point for us is that no such complete ethical code exists. The attempt to direct all economic activity according to a single plan would raise innumerable questions to which the answer could be provided only by a moral rule, but to which existing morals have no answer and where there exists no agreed view on what ought to be done. People will have either no definite views or conflicting views in such questions, because in the free society in which we have lived there has been no occasion to think about them and still less to form common opinions about them.

Not only do we not possess such an all-inclusive scale of values: it would be impossible for any mind to comprehend the infinite variety of different needs of different people which compete for the available resources and to attach a definite weight to each. For our problem it is of minor importance whether the ends for which any person cares comprehend only his own individual needs, or whether they include the needs of his closer or even those of his more distant fellows—that is, whether he is egoistic or altruistic in the ordinary senses of these words. The point which is so important is the basic fact that it is impossible for any man to survey more than a limited field, to be aware of the urgency of more than a limited number of needs. Whether his interests center round his own physical needs, or whether he takes a warm interest in the welfare of every human being he knows, the ends about which he can be concerned will always be only an infinitesimal fraction of the needs of all men.

This is the fundamental fact on which the whole philosophy of individualism is based. It does not assume, as is often asserted, that man is egoistic or selfish or ought to be. It merely starts from the indisputable fact that the limits of our powers of imagination make it impossible to include in our scale of values more than a sector of the needs of the whole society, and that, since, strictly speaking, scales of value can exist only in individual minds, nothing but partial scales of values exist—scales which are inevitably different and often inconsistent with each other. From this the individualist concludes that the individuals should be allowed, within defined limits, to follow their own values and preferences rather than somebody else's; that within these spheres the individual's system of ends should be supreme and not subject to any dictation by others. It is this recognition of the individual as the ultimate judge of his ends, the belief that as far as possible his own views ought to govern his actions, that forms the essence of the individualist position.

This view does not, of course, exclude the recognition of social ends, or rather of a coincidence of individual ends which makes it advisable for men to combine for their pursuit. But it limits such common action to the instances where individual views coincide; what are called "social ends" are for it merely identical ends of many individuals—or ends to the achievement of which individuals are willing to contribute in return for the assistance they receive in the satisfaction of their own desires. Common action is thus limited to the fields where people agree on common ends. Very frequently these common ends will not be ultimate ends to the individuals but means which different persons can use for different purposes. In fact, people are most likely to agree on common action where the common end is not an ultimate end to them but a means capable of serving a great variety of purposes.

When individuals combine in a joint effort to realize ends they have in common, the organizations, like the state, that they form for this purpose are given their own system of ends and their own means. But any organization thus formed remains one "person" among others, in the case of the state much more powerful than any of the others, it is true, yet still with its separate and limited sphere in which alone its ends are supreme. The limits of this sphere are determined by the extent to which the individuals agree on particular ends; and the probability that they will agree on a particular course of action necessarily decreases as the scope of such action extends. There are certain functions of the state on the exercise of which there will be practical unanimity among its citizens; there will be others on which there will be agreement of a substantial majority; and so on, until we come to fields where, although each individual might wish the state to act in some way, there will be almost as many views about what the government should do as there are different people.

We can rely on voluntary agreement to guide the action of the state only so long as it is confined to spheres where agreement exists. But not only when the state undertakes direct control in fields where there is no such agreement is it bound to suppress individual freedom. We can unfortunately not indefinitely extend the sphere of common action and still leave the individual free in his own sphere. Once the communal sector, in which the state controls all the means, exceeds a certain proportion of the whole, the effects of its actions dominate the whole system. Although the state controls directly the use of only a large part of the available resources, the effects of its decisions on the remaining part of the economic system become so great that indirectly it controls almost everything. Where, as was, for example, true in Germany as early as 1928, the central and local authorities directly control the use of more than half the national income (according to an official German estimate then, 53 per cent), they control indirectly almost the whole economic life of the nation. There is, then, scarcely an individual end which is not dependent for its achievement on the action of the state, and the "social scale of values" which guides the state's action must embrace practically all individual ends.

It is not difficult to see what must be the consequences when democracy embarks upon a course of planning which in its execution requires more agreement than in fact exists. The people may have agreed on adopting a system of directed economy because they have been convinced that it will produce great prosperity. In the discussions leading to the decision, the goal of planning will have been described by some such term as "common welfare," which only conceals the absence of real agreement on the ends of planning. Agreement will in fact exist only on the mechanism to be used. But it is a mechanism which can be used only for a common end; and the question of the precise goal toward which all activity is to be directed will arise as soon as the executive power has to translate the demand for a single plan into particular plan. Then it will appear that the agreement on the desirability of planning is not supported by agreement on the ends the plan is to serve. The effect of the people's agreeing that there must be central planning, without agreeing on the ends, will be rather as if a group of people were to commit themselves to take a journey together without agreeing where they want to go: with the result that they may all have to make a journey which most of them do not want at all. That planning creates a situation in which it is necessary for us to agree on a much larger number of topics than we have been used to, and that in a planned system we cannot confine collective action to the tasks on which we can agree but are forced to produce agreement on everything in order that any action can be taken at all, is one of the features which contributes more than most to determining the character of a planned system.

It may be the unanimously expressed will of the people that its parliament should prepare a comprehensive economic plan, yet neither the people nor its representatives need therefore be able to agree on any particular plan. The inability of democratic assemblies to carry out what seems to be a clear mandate of the people will inevitably cause dissatisfaction with democratic institutions. Parliaments come to be regarded as ineffective "talking shops," unable or incompetent to carry out the tasks for which they have been chosen. The conviction grows that if efficient planning is to be done, the direction must be "taken out of politics" and placed in the hands of experts—permanent officials or independent autonomous bodies.

The difficulty is well known to socialists. It will soon be half a century since the Webbs began to complain of "the increased incapacity of the House of Commons to cope with its work."* More recently, Professor Laski has elaborated the argument:

"It is common ground that the present parliamentary machine is quite unsuited to pass rapidly a great body of complicated legislation. The National Government, indeed, has in substance admitted this by implementing its economy and tariff measures not by detailed debate in the House of Commons but by a wholesale system of delegated legislation. A Labour Government would, I presume, build upon the amplitude of this precedent. It would confine the House of Commons to the two functions it can properly perform: the ventilation of grievances and the discussion of general principles of its measures. Its Bills would take the form of general formulae conferring wide powers on the appropriate government departments; and those powers would be exercised by Order in Council which could, if desired, be attacked in the House by means of a vote of no confidence. The necessity and value of delegated legislation has recently been strongly reaffirmed by the Donoughmore Committee; and its extension is inevitable if the process of socialisation is not to be wrecked by the normal methods of obstruction which existing parliamentary procedure sanctions."

And to make it quite clear that a socialist government must not allow itself to be too much fettered by democratic procedure, Professor Laski at the end of the

---

*Sidney and Beatrice Webb, *Industrial Democracy* (1897), p. 800 n.

same article raised the question "whether in a period of transition to Socialism, a Labour Government can risk the overthrow of its measures as a result of the next general election"—and left it significantly unanswered.*

It is important clearly to see the causes of this admitted ineffectiveness of parliaments when it comes to a detailed administration of the economic affairs of a nation. The fault is neither with the individual representatives nor with parliamentary institutions as such but with the contradictions inherent in the task with which they are charged. They are not asked to act where they can agree, but to produce agreement on everything—the whole direction of the resources of the nation. For such a task the system of majority decision is, however, not suited. Majorities will be found where it is a choice between limited alternatives; but it is a superstition to believe that there must be a majority view on everything. There is no reason why there should be a majority in favor of any one of the different possible courses of positive action if their number is legion. Every member of the legislative assembly might prefer some particular plan for the direction of economic activity to no plan, yet no one plan may appear preferable to a majority to no plan at all.

Nor can a coherent plan be achieved by breaking it up into parts and voting on particular issues. A democratic assembly voting and amending a comprehensive economic plan clause by clause, as it deliberates on an ordinary bill, makes nonsense. An economic plan, to deserve the name, must have a unitary conception. Even if a parliament could, proceeding step by step, agree on some scheme, it would certainly in the end satisfy nobody. A complex whole in which all the parts must be most carefully adjusted to each other cannot be achieved through a compromise between conflicting views. To draw up an economic plan in this fashion is even less possible than, for example, successfully to plan a military campaign by democratic procedure. As in strategy it would become inevitable to delegate the task to the experts.

Yet the difference is that, while the general who is put in charge of a campaign is given a single end to which, for the duration of the campaign, all the means under his control have to be exclusively devoted, there can be no such single goal given to the economic planner, and no similar limitation of the means imposed upon him. The general has not got to balance different independent aims against each other; there is for him only one supreme goal. But the ends of an economic plan, or of any part of it, cannot be defined apart from the particular plan. It is the essence of the economic problem that the making of an economic plan involves the choice between conflicting or competing ends—different needs of different

---

*H. J. Laski, "Labour and the Constitution," *New Statesman and Nation,* No. 81 (new ser.), September 10, 1932, p. 277. In a book (*Democracy in Crisis* [1933], particularly p. 87) in which Professor Laski later elaborated these ideas, his determination that parliamentary democracy must not be allowed to form an obstacle to the realization of socialism is even more plainly expressed: not only would a socialist government "take vast powers and legislate under them by ordinance and decree" and "suspend the classic formulae of normal opposition" but the "continuance of parliamentary government would depend on its [i.e., the Labour government's] possession of guarantees from the Conservative Party that its work of transformation would not be disrupted by repeal in the event of its defeat at the polls."

As Professor Laski invokes the authority of the Donoughmore Committee, it may be worth recalling that Professor Laski was a member of that committee and presumably one of the authors of its report.

people. But which ends do so conflict, which will have to be sacrificed if we want to achieve certain others, in short, which are the alternatives between which we must choose, can only be known to those who know all the facts; and only they, the experts, are in a position to decide which of the different ends are to be given preference. It is inevitable that they should impose their scale of preferences on the community for which they plan. . . .

The argument by which the planners usually try to reconcile us with this development is that, so long as democracy retains ultimate control, the essentials of democracy are not affected. Thus Karl Mannheim writes:

"The only [*sic*] way in which a planned society differs from that of the nineteenth century is that more and more spheres of social life, and ultimately each and all of them, are subjected to state control. But if a few controls can be held in check by parliamentary sovereignty, so can many. . . . In a democratic state sovereignty can be boundlessly strengthened by plenary powers without renouncing democratic control."*

This belief overlooks a vital distinction. Parliament can, of course, control the execution of tasks where it can give definite directions, where it has first agreed on the aim and merely delegates the working-out of the detail. The situation is entirely different when the reason for the delegation is that there is no real agreement on the ends, when the body charged with the planning has to choose between ends of whose conflict parliament is not even aware, and when the most that can be done is to present to it a plan which has to be accepted or rejected as a whole. There may and probably will be criticism; but as no majority can agree on an alternative plan, and the parts objected to can almost always be represented as essential parts of the whole, it will remain quite ineffective. Parliamentary discussion may be retained as a useful safety valve and even more as a convenient medium through which the official answers to complaints are disseminated. It may even prevent some flagrant abuses and successfully insist on particular shortcomings being remedied. But it cannot direct. It will at best be reduced to choosing the persons who are to have practically absolute power. The whole system will tend toward that plebiscitarian dictatorship in which the head of the government is from time to time confirmed in his position by popular vote, but where he has all the powers at his command to make certain that the vote will go in the direction he desires.

It is the price of democracy that the possibilities of conscious control are restricted to the fields where true agreement exists and that in some fields things must be left to chance. But in a society which for its functioning depends on central planning this control cannot be made independent on a majority's being able to agree; it will often be necessary that the will of a small minority be imposed upon the people, because this minority will be the largest group able to agree among themselves on the question at issue. Democratic government has worked successfully where, and so long as, the functions of government were, by a widely accepted creed, restricted to fields where agreement among a majority could be

---

Man and Society in an Age of Reconstruction (1940), p. 340.

achieved by free discussion; and it is the great merit of the liberal creed that it reduced the range of subjects on which agreement was necessary to one on which it was likely to exist in a society of free men. It is now often said that democracy will not tolerate "capitalism." If "capitalism" means here a competitive system based on free disposal over private property, it is far more important to realize that only within this system is democracy possible. When it becomes dominated by a collectivist creed, democracy will inevitably destroy itself.

We have no intention, however, of making a fetish of democracy. It may well be true that our generation talks and thinks too much of democracy and too little of the values which it serves. It cannot be said of democracy, as Lord Acton truly said of liberty, that it "is not a means to a higher political end. It is itself the highest political end. It is not for the sake of a good public administration that it is required, but for the security in the pursuit of the highest objects of civil society, and of private life." Democracy is essentially a means, a utilitarian device for safeguarding internal peace and individual freedom. As such it is by no means infallible or certain. Nor must we forget that there has often been much more cultural and spiritual freedom under an autocratic rule than under some democracies—and it is at least conceivable that under the government of a very homogeneous and doctrinaire majority democratic government might be as oppressive as the worst dictatorship. Our point, however, is not that dictatorship must inevitably extirpate freedom but rather than planning leads to dictatorship because dictatorship is the most effective instrument of coercion and the enforcement of ideals and, as such, essential if central planning on a large scale is to be possible. The clash between planning and democracy arises simply from the fact that the latter is an obstacle to the suppression of freedom which the direction of economic activity requires. But in so far as democracy ceases to be a guaranty of individual freedom, it may well persist in some form under a totalitarian regime. A true "dictatorship of the proletariat," even if democratic in form, if it undertook centrally to direct the economic system, would probably destroy personal freedom as completely as any autocracy has ever done.

The fashionable concentration on democracy as the main value threatened is not without danger. It is largely responsible for the misleading and unfounded belief that, so long as the ultimate source of power is the will of the majority, the power cannot be arbitrary. The false assurance which many people derive from this belief is an important cause of the general unawareness of the dangers which we face. There is no justification for the belief that, so long as power is conferred by democratic procedure, it cannot be arbitrary; the contrast suggested by this statement is altogether false: it is not the source but the limitation of power which prevents it from being arbitrary. Democratic control *may* prevent power from becoming arbitrary, but it does not do so by its mere existence. If democracy resolves on a task which necessarily involves the use of power which cannot be guided by fixed rules, it must become arbitrary power.

89
Thomas Hill Green

Thomas Hill Green (1826–1882) was a British Neo-Hegelian philosopher who was troubled by the apparent paradox that, to widen some freedoms in our community, we must narrow others. This may be well justified, Green argued, if we make the very important distinction between *negative* freedom and *positive* freedom, that is, between freedom *from* the hindrances imposed by others and freedom *to* engage in worthwhile activity. Many positive freedoms require the development of human capacities; insuring such development will often entail the sacrifice of some negative freedoms. So, *when* may a democratic central government act restrictively? When the state can, by so doing, remove real obstacles to the self-fulfillment of its individual citizens.

[NEGATIVE AND POSITIVE FREEDOM]*

We shall probably all agree that freedom, rightly understood, is the greatest of blessings; that its attainment is the true end of all our efforts as citizens. But when we thus speak of freedom, we should consider carefully what we mean by it. We do not mean merely freedom from restraint or compulsion. We do not mean merely freedom to do as we like irrespectively of what it is that we like. We do not mean a freedom that can be enjoyed by one man or one set of men at the cost of a loss of freedom to others. When we speak of freedom as something to be so highly prized, we mean a positive power or capacity of doing or enjoying some- thing worth doing or enjoying, and that, too, something that we do or enjoy in common with others. We mean by it a power which each man exercises through the help or security given him by his fellow-men, and which he in turn helps to secure for them. When we measure the progress of a society by its growth in free- dom, we measure it by the increasing development and exercise on the whole of those powers of contributing to social good with which we believe the members of the society to be endowed; in short, by the greater power on the part of the citi- zens as a body to make the most and best of themselves. Thus, though of course there can be no freedom among men who act not willingly but under compulsion, yet on the other hand the mere removal of compulsion, the mere enabling a man to do as he likes, is in itself no contribution to true freedom. In one sense no man is so well able to do as he likes as the wandering savage. He has no master. There is no one to say him nay. Yet we do not count him really free, because the freedom of savagery is not strength, but weakness. The actual powers of the noblest savage do not admit of comparison with those of the humblest citizen of a law-abiding state. He is not the slave of man, but he is the slave of nature. Of compulsion by natural necessity he has plenty of experience, though of restraint by society none

*From T. H. Green, *Liberal Legislation and Freedom of Contract,* 1880. This passage is reprinted from *The Works of Thomas Hill Green,* Volume 3, published by Longmans, Green and Co., London, 1888.

at all. Nor can he deliver himself from that compulsion except by submitting to this restraint. So to submit is the first step in true freedom, because the first step towards the full exercise of the faculties with which man is endowed. But we rightly refuse to recognize the highest development on the part of an exceptional individual or exceptional class, as an advance towards the true freedom of man, if it is founded on a refusal of the same opportunity to other men. The powers of the human mind have probably never attained such force and keenness, the proof of what society can do for the individual has never been so strikingly exhibited, as among the small groups of men who possessed civil privileges in the small republics of antiquity. The whole framework of our political ideas, to say nothing of our philosophy, is derived from them. But in them this extraordinary efflorescence of the privileged class was accompanied by the slavery of the multitude. That slavery was the condition on which it depended, and for that reason it was doomed to decay. There is no clearer ordinance of that supreme reason, often dark to us, which governs the course of men's affairs, than that no body of men should in the long run be able to strengthen itself at the cost of others' weakness. The civilization and freedom of the ancient world were short-lived because they were partial and exceptional. If the ideal of true freedom is the maximum of power for all members of human society alike to make the best of themselves, we are right in refusing to ascribe the glory of freedom to a state in which the apparent elevation of the few is founded on the degradation of the many, and in ranking modern society, founded as it is on free industry, with all its confusion and ignorant licence and waste of effort, above the most splendid of ancient republics.

If I have given a true account of that freedom which forms the goal of social effort, we shall see that freedom of contract, freedom of all the forms of doing what one will with one's own, is valuable only as a means to an end. That end is what I call freedom in the positive sense: in other words, like liberation of the powers of all men equally for contributions to a common good. No one has a right to do what he will with his own in such a way as to contravene this end. It is only through the guarantee which society gives him that he has property at all, or, strictly speaking, any right to his possessions. This guarantee is founded on a sense of common interest. Every one has an interest in securing to every one else the free use and enjoyment and disposal of his possessions, so long as that freedom on the part of one does not interfere with a like freedom on the part of others, because such freedom contributes to that equal development of the faculties of all which is the highest good for all. This is the true and the only justification of rights of property. Rights of property, however, have been and are claimed which cannot thus be justified. We are all now agreed that men cannot rightly be the property of men. The institution of property being only justifiable as a means to the free exercise of the social capabilities of all, there can be no true right to property of a kind which debars one class of men from such free exercise altogether. We condemn slavery no less when it arises out of a voluntary agreement on the part of the enslaved person. A contract by which anyone agreed for a certain consideration to become the slave of another we should reckon a void contract. Here, then, as a limitation upon freedom of contract which we all recognize as rightful.

No contract is valid in which human persons, willingly or unwillingly, are dealt with as commodities, because such contracts of necessity defeat the end for which alone society enforces contracts at all.

Are there no other contracts which, less obviously perhaps but really, are open to the same objection? In the first place, let us consider contracts affecting labor. Labor, the economist tells us, is a commodity exchangeable like other commodities. This is in a certain sense true, but it is a commodity which attaches in a peculiar manner to the person of man. Hence restrictions may need to be placed on the sale of this commodity which would be unnecessary in other cases, in order to prevent labor from being sold under conditions which make it impossible for the person selling it ever to become a free contributor to social good in any form. This is most plainly the case when a man bargains to work under conditions fatal to health, in an unventilated factory. Every injury to the health of the individual is, so far as it goes, a public injury. It is an impediment to the general freedom; so much deduction from our power, as members of society, to make the best of ourselves. Society is, therefore, plainly within its right when it limits freedom of contract for the sale of labor, so far as is done by our laws for the sanitary regulations of factories, workshops, and mines. It is equally within its right in prohibiting the labor of women and young persons beyond certain hours. If they work beyond those hours, the result is demonstrably physical deterioration; which, as demonstrably, carries with it a lowering of the moral forces of society. For the sake of that general freedom of its members to make the best of themselves, which it is the object of civil society to secure, a prohibition should be put by law, which is the deliberate voice of society, on all such contracts of service as in a general way yield such a result. The purchase or hire of unwholesome dwellings is properly forbidden on the same principle. Its application to compulsory education may not be quite so obvious, but it will appear on a little reflection. Without a command of certain elementary arts and knowledge, the individual in modern society is as effectually crippled as by the loss of a limb or a broken constitution. He is not free to develop his faculties. With a view to securing such freedom among its members it is as certainly within the province of the state to prevent children from growing up in that kind of ignorance which practically excludes them from a free career in life, as it is within its province to require the sort of building and drainage necessary for public health.

Our modern legislation then with reference to labor, and education, and health, involving as it does manifold interference with freedom of contract, is justified on the ground that it is the business of the state, not indeed directly to promote moral goodness, for that, from the very nature of moral goodness, it cannot do, but to maintain the conditions without which a free exercise of the human faculties is impossible. It does not indeed follow that it is advisable for the state to do all which it is justified in doing. We are often warned now-a-days against the danger of overlegislation; or, as I heard it put in a speech of the present home secretary in the days when he was sowing his political wild oats, of "grandmotherly government." There may be good ground for the warning, but at any rate we should be quite clear what we mean by it. The outcry against state interference is often raised by men whose real objection is not to state interference but to centralization, to the constant aggression of the central executive upon local authorities. As I have already pointed out, compulsion at the discretion of some elected municipal board proceeds just as much from the state as does compulsion exercised by a government office in London. No doubt, much needless friction is avoided, much is gained in the way of elasticity and adjustment to circumstances, by the independent local administration of general laws; and most of us would agree that of late there has been a dangerous tendency to override municipal discretion by the hard and fast rules of London "departments." But centralization is one thing: over-legislation, or the improper exercise of the power of the state, quite another. It is one question whether of late the central government has been unduly trenching on local government, and another question whether the law of the state, either as administered by central or by provincial authorities, has been unduly interfering with the discretion of individuals. We may object most strongly to advancing centralization, and yet wish that the law should put rather more than less restraint on those liberties of the individual which are a social nuisance. But there are some political speculators whose objection is not merely to centralization, but to the extended action of the law altogether. They think that the individual ought to be left much more to himself than has of late been the case. Might not our people, they ask, have been trusted to learn in time for themselves to eschew unhealthy dwellings, to refuse dangerous and degrading employment, to get their children the schooling necessary for making their way in the world? Would they not for their own comfort, if not from more chivalrous feeling, keep their wives and daughters from overwork? Or, failing this, ought not women, like men, to learn to protect themselves? Might not all the rules, in short, which legislation of the kind we have been discussing is intended to attain, have been attained without it; not so quickly, perhaps, but without tampering so dangerously with the independence and self-reliance of the people?

Now, we shall probably all agree that a society in which the public health was duly protected, and necessary education duly provided for, by the spontaneous action of individuals, was in a higher condition than one in which the compulsion of law was needed to secure those ends. But we must take men as we find them. Until such a condition of society is reached, it is the business of the state to make the best security it can for the young citizens' growing up in such health and with so much knowledge as is necessary for their real freedom. In so doing it need not at all interfere with the independence and self-reliance of those whom it requires to do what they would otherwise do for themselves. The man who, of his own right feeling, saves his wife from overwork and sends his children to school, suffers no moral degradation from a law which, if he did not do this for himself, would seek to make him do it. Such a man does not feel the law as constraint at all. To him it is simply a powerful friend. It gives him security for that being done efficiently which, with the best wishes, he might have much trouble in getting done efficiently if left to himself. No doubt it relieves him from some of the responsibility which would otherwise fall to him as head of a family, but, if he is what we are supposing him to be, in proportion as he is relieved of responsibilities in one direction he will assume them in another. The security which the state gives him for the safe housing and sufficient schooling of his family will only make him the more careful for their well-being in other respects, which he is left to look after for himself. We need have no fear, then, of such legislation having an ill-effect on those who, without the law, would have seen to that being done, though probably less efficiently, which the law requires to be done. But it was not their case that the laws we are considering were especially meant to meet. It was the overworked women, the ill-housed and untaught families, for whose benefit they were intended. And the question is whether without these laws the suffering classes could have been delivered quickly or slowly from the condition they were in. Could the enlightened self-interest or benevolence of individuals, working under a system of unlimited freedom of contract, have ever brought them into a state compatible with the free development of the human faculties? No one considering the facts can have any doubt as to the answer to this question. Left to itself, or to the operation of casual benevolence, a degraded population perpetuates and increases itself. Read any of the authorized accounts, given before royal or parliamentary commissions, of the state of the laborers, especially of the women and children, as they were in our great industries before the law was first brought to bear on them, and before freedom of contract was first interfered with in them. Ask yourself what chance there was of a generation, born and bred under such conditions, ever contracting itself out of them. Given a certain standard of moral and material well-being, people may be trusted not to sell their labor, or the labor of their children, on terms which would not allow that standard to be maintained. But with large masses of our population, until the laws we have been considering took effect, there was no such standard. There was nothing on their part, in the way either of self-respect or established demand for comforts, to prevent them from working and living, or from putting their children to work and live, in a way in which no one who is to be a healthy and free citizen can work and live. No doubt there were many high-minded employers who did their best for their work-people before the days of state-interference, but they could not prevent less scrupulous hirers of labor from hiring it on the cheapest terms. It is true that cheap labor is in the long run dear labor, but it is so only in the long run, and eager traders do not think of the long run. If labor is to be had under conditions incompatible with the health or decent housing or education of the laborer, there will always be plenty of people to buy it under those conditions, careless of the burden in the shape of rates and taxes which they may be laying up for posterity. Either the standard of well-being on the part of the sellers of labor must prevent them from selling their labor under those conditions, or the law must prevent it. With a population such as ours was forty years ago, and still largely is, the law must prevent it and continue the prevention for some generations, before the sellers will be in a state to prevent it for themselves. . . .

90
John Rawls

John Rawls (1921–   ) presents a unified theory of justice in which each of the ideals of democracy has its appropriate place. A just society will provide a *system* of liberties; to understand that system the distinction between positive and negative liberties is not helpful. Liberty in all its forms can be explained by reference to three items: "the agents who are free, the restrictions or limitations they are free from, and what it is that they are free to do or not to do." The ideal of *equal* liberty when applied to the constitution of the political body, Rawls contends, yields the principle of equal participation, democracy itself. *A Theory of Justice* is one of the most influential contemporary analyses of political ideals; in it Rawls seeks to explain the meaning, and the extent, and the worth of political liberty.

[THE SYSTEM OF LIBERTY]*

The controversy between the proponents of negative and positive liberty as to how freedom should be defined is one I shall leave aside. I believe that for the most part this debate is not concerned with definitions at all, but rather with the relative values of the several liberties when they come into conflict. . . . While both sorts of freedom are deeply rooted in human aspirations, freedom of thought and liberty of conscience, freedom of the person and the civil liberties, ought not to be sacrificed to political liberty, to the freedom to participate equally in political affairs. This question is clearly one of substantive political philosophy, and a theory of right and justice is required to answer it. Questions of definition can have at best but an ancillary role.

Therefore I shall simply assume that liberty can always be explained by a reference to three items: the agents who are free, the restrictions or limitations which they are free from, and what it is that they are free to do or not to do. Complete explanations of liberty provide the relevant information about these three things. Very often certain matters are clear from the context and a full explanation is unnecessary. The general description of liberty, then, has the following form: this or that person (or persons) is free (or not free) from this or that constraint (or set of constraints) to do (or not to do) so and so. Associations as well as natural persons may be free or not free, and constraints may range from duties and prohibitions defined by law to the coercive influences arising from public opinion and social pressure. For the most part I shall discuss liberty in connection with constitutional and legal restrictions. In these cases liberty is a certain structure of institutions, a certain system of public rules defining rights and duties. Set in this background, liberty always has the above three-part form. Moreover, just as there are

---

*From John Rawls, *A Theory of Justice,* Harvard University Press, Cambridge, 1971. Reprinted by permission.

various kinds of agents who may be free—persons, associations, and states—so there are many kinds of conditions that constrain them and innumerable sorts of things that they are or are not free to do. In this sense there are many different liberties which on occasion it may be useful to distinguish. Yet these distinctions can be made without introducing different senses of liberty.

Thus persons are at liberty to do something when they are free from certain constraints either to do it or not to do it and when their doing it or not doing it is protected from interference by other persons. If, for example, we consider liberty of conscience as defined by law, then individuals have this liberty when they are free to pursue their moral, philosophical, or religious interests without legal restrictions requiring them to engage or not to engage in any particular form of religious or other practice, and when other men have a legal duty not to interfere. A rather intricate complex of rights and duties characterizes any particular liberty. Not only must it be permissible for individuals to do or not to do something, but government and other persons must have a legal duty not to obstruct. I shall not delineate these rights and duties in any detail, but shall suppose that we understand their nature well enough for our purposes.

Several brief comments. First of all, it is important to recognize that the basic liberties must be assessed as a whole, as one system. That is, the worth of one liberty normally depends upon the specification of the other liberties, and this must be taken into account in framing a constitution and in legislation generally. While it is by and large true that a greater liberty is preferable, this holds primarily for the system of liberty as a whole, and not for each particular liberty. Clearly when the liberties are left unrestricted they collide with one another. To illustrate by an obvious example, certain rules of order are necessary for intelligent and profitable discussion. Without the acceptance of reasonable procedures of inquiry and debate, freedom of speech loses its value. It is essential in this case to distinguish between rules of order and rules restricting the content of speech. While rules of order limit our freedom, since we cannot speak whenever we please, they are required to gain the benefits of this liberty. Thus the delegates to a constitutional convention, or the members of the legislature, must decide how the various liberties are to be specified so as to yield the best total system of equal liberty. They have to balance one liberty against another. The best arrangement of the several liberties depends upon the totality of limitations to which they are subject, upon how they hang together in the whole scheme by which they are defined. . . .

A final point. The inability to take advantage of one's rights and opportunities as a result of poverty and ignorance, and a lack of means generally, is sometimes counted among the constraints definitive of liberty. I shall not, however, say this, but rather I shall think of these things as affecting the worth of liberty, the value to individuals of the rights that the first principle defines. With this understanding, and assuming that the total system of liberty is drawn up in the manner just explained, we may note that the two-part basic structure allows a reconciliation of liberty and equality. Thus liberty and the worth of liberty are distinguished as follows: liberty is represented by the complete system of the liberties of equal citizenship, while the worth of liberty to persons and groups is proportional to their capacity to advance their ends within the framework the system defines. Freedom as equal liberty is the same for all; the question of compensating for a lesser than equal liberty does not arise. But the worth of liberty is not the same for everyone. Some have greater authority and wealth, and therefore greater means to achieve their aims. The lesser worth of liberty is, however, compensated for, since the capacity of the less fortunate members of society to achieve their aims would be even less were they not to accept the existing inequalities whenever the difference principle is satisfied. But compensating for the lesser worth of freedom is not to be confused with making good an unequal liberty. Taking the two principles together, the basic structure is to be arranged to maximize the worth to the least advantaged of the complete scheme of equal liberty shared by all. This defines the end of social justice. . . .

[THE PRINCIPLE OF EQUAL PARTICIPATION]

The principle of equal liberty, when applied to the political procedure defined by the constitution, I shall refer to as the principle of (equal) participation. It requires that all citizens are to have an equal right to take part in, and to determine the outcome of, the constitutional process that establishes the laws with which they are to comply. Justice as fairness begins with the idea that where common principles are necessary and to everyone's advantage, they are to be worked out from the viewpoint of a suitably defined initial situation of equality in which each person is fairly represented. The principle of participation transfers this notion from the original position to the constitution as the highest-order system of social rules for making rules. If the state is to exercise a final and coercive authority over a certain territory, and if it is in this way to affect permanently men's prospects in life, then the constitutional process should preserve the equal representation of the original position to the degree that this is practicable.

For the time being I assume that a constitutional democracy can be arranged so as to satisfy the principle of participation. But we need to know more exactly what this principle requires under favorable circumstances, when taken to the limit so to speak. These requirements are, of course, familiar.

Nevertheless, it is worthwhile to see how these liberties fall under the principle of participation.

We may begin by recalling certain elements of a constitutional regime. First of all, the authority to determine basic social policies resides in a representative body selected for limited terms by and ultimately accountable to the electorate. This representative body has more than a purely advisory capacity. It is a legislature with lawmaking powers and not simply a forum of delegates from various sectors of society to which the executive explains its actions and discerns the movements of public sentiment. Nor are political parties mere interest groups petitioning the government on their own behalf; instead, to gain enough support to win office, they must advance some conception of the public good. The constitution may, of course, circumscribe the legislature in numerous respects; and constitutional norms define its actions as a parliamentary body. But in due course a firm majority of the electorate is able to achieve its aims, by constitutional amendment if necessary.

All sane adults, with certain generally recognized exceptions, have the right to take part in political affairs, and the precept one elector one vote is honored as far as possible. Elections are fair and free, and regularly held. Sporadic and unpredictable tests of public sentiment by plebiscite or other means, or at such times as may suit the convenience of those in office, do not suffice for a representative regime. There are firm constitutional protections for certain liberties, particularly freedom of speech and assembly, and liberty to form political associations. The principle of loyal opposition is recognized, the clash of political beliefs, and of the interests and attitudes that are likely to influence them, are accepted as a normal condition of human life. A lack of unanimity is part of the circumstances of justice, since disagreement is bound to exist even among honest men who desire to follow much the same political principles. Without the conception of loyal opposition, and an attachment to constitutional rules which express and protect it, the politics of democracy cannot be properly conducted or long endure.

[THE MEANING OF EQUAL POLITICAL LIBERTY]

Three points concerning the equal liberty defined by the principle of participation call for discussion: its meaning, its extent, and the measures that enhance its worth. Starting with the question of meaning, the precept of one elector one vote implies, when strictly adhered to, that each vote has approximately the same weight in determining the outcome of elections. And this in turn requires, assuming single member territorial constituencies, that members of the legislature (with one vote each) represent the same number of electors. I shall also suppose that the precept necessitates that legislative districts be drawn up under the guidance of certain general standards specified in advance by the constitution and applied as far as possible by an impartial procedure. These safeguards are needed to prevent gerrymandering, since the weight of the vote can be as much affected by feats of gerrymander as by districts of disproportionate size. The requisite standards and procedures are to be adopted from the standpoint of the constitutional convention in which no one has the knowledge that is likely to prejudice the design of constituencies. Political parties cannot adjust boundaries to their advantage in the light of voting statistics; districts are defined by means of criteria already agreed to in the absence of this sort of information. Of course, it may be necessary to introduce certain random elements, since the criteria for designing constituencies are no doubt to some extent arbitrary. There may be no other fair way to deal with these contingencies.

The principle of participation also holds that all citizens are to have an equal access, at least in the formal sense, to public office. Each is eligible to join political parties, to run for elective positions, and to hold places of authority. To be sure, there may be qualifications of age, residency, and so on. But these are to be reasonably related to the tasks of office; presumably these restrictions are in the common interest and do not discriminate unfairly among persons or groups in the sense that they fall evenly on everyone in the normal course of life.

[THE EXTENT OF EQUAL POLITICAL LIBERTY]

The second point concerning equal political liberty is its extent. How broadly are these liberties to be defined? Offhand it is not clear what extent means here. Each of the political liberties can be more or less widely defined. Somewhat arbitrarily, but nevertheless in accordance with tradition, I shall assume that the main variation in the extent of equal political liberty lies in the degree to which the constitution is majoritarian. The definition of the other liberties I take to be more or less fixed. Thus the most extensive political liberty is established by a constitution that uses the procedure of so-called bare majority rule (the procedure in which a minority can neither override nor check a majority) for all significant political decisions unimpeded by any constitutional constraints. Whenever the constitution limits the scope and authority of majorities, either by requiring a greater plurality for certain types of measures, or by a bill of rights restricting the powers of the legislature, and the like, equal political liberty is less extensive. The traditional devices of constitutionalism—bicameral legislature, separation of powers mixed with checks and balances, a bill of rights with judicial review—limit the scope of the principle of participation. I assume, however, that these arrangements are consistent with equal political liberty provided that similar restrictions apply to everyone and that the constraints introduced are likely over time to fall evenly upon all sectors of society.

[THE WORTH OF POLITICAL LIBERTY]

Turning now to the worth of political liberty, the constitution must take steps to enhance the value of the equal rights of participation for all members of society. It must underwrite a fair opportunity to take part in and to influence the political process. The distinction here is analogous to that made before: ideally, those similarly endowed and motivated should have roughly the same chance of attaining positions of political authority irrespective of their economic and social class. But how is this fair value of these liberties to be secured?

We may take for granted that a democratic regime presupposes freedom of speech and assembly, and liberty of thought and conscience. These institutions are not only required by the first principle of justice but, as Mill argued, they are necessary if political affairs are to be conducted in a rational fashion. While rationality is not guaranteed by these arrangements, in their absence the more reasonable course seems sure to be rejected in favor of policies sought by special interests. If the public forum is to be free and open to all, and in continuous session, everyone should be able to make use of it. All citizens should have the means to be informed about political issues. They should be in a position to assess how proposals affect their well-being and which policies advance their conception of the public good. Moreover, they should have a fair chance to add alternative proposals to the agenda for political discussion. The liberties protected by the principle of participation lose much of their value whenever those who have greater private means are permitted to use their advantages to control the course of public debate. For eventually these inequalities will enable those better situated to exercise a larger influence over the development of legislation. In due time they are likely to acquire a preponderant weight in settling social questions, at least in regard to those matters upon which they normally agree, which is to say in regard to those things that support their favored circumstances.

Compensating steps must, then, be taken to preserve the fair value for all of the equal political liberties. A variety of devices can be used. For example, in a society allowing private ownership of the means of production, property and wealth must be kept widely distributed and government monies provided on a regular basis to encourage free public discussion. In addition, political parties are to be made independent from private economic interests by allotting them sufficient tax revenues to play their part in the constitutional scheme. (Their subventions might, for example, be based by some rule on the number of votes received in the last several elections, and the like.) What is necessary is that political parties be autonomous with respect to private demands, that is, demands not expressed in the public forum and argued for openly by reference to a conception of the public good. If society does not bear the costs of organization, and party funds need to be solicited from the more advantaged social and economic interests, the pleadings of these groups are bound to receive excessive attention. And this is all the more likely when the less favored members of society, having been effectively prevented by their lack of means from exercising their fair degree of influence, withdraw into apathy and resentment.

Historically one of the main defects of constitutional government has been the failure to insure the fair value of political liberty. The necessary corrective steps have not been taken, indeed, they never seem to have been seriously entertained. Disparities in the distribution of property and wealth that far exceed what is compatible with political equality have generally been tolerated by the legal system. Public resources have not been devoted to maintaining the institutions required for the fair value of political liberty. Essentially the fault lies in the fact that the democratic political process is at best regulated rivalry; it does not even in theory have the desirable properties that price theory ascribes to truly competitive markets. Moreover, the effects of injustices in the political system are much more grave and long lasting than market imperfections. Political power rapidly accumulates and becomes unequal; and making use of the coercive apparatus of the state and its law, those who gain the advantage can often assure themselves of a favored position. Thus inequities in the economic and social system may soon undermine whatever political equality might have existed under fortunate historical conditions. Universal suffrage is an insufficient counterpoise; for when parties and elections are financed not by public funds but by private contributions, the political forum is so constrained by the wishes of the dominant interests that the basic measures needed to establish just constitutional rule are seldom properly presented. These questions, however, belong to political sociology. I mention them here as a way of emphasizing that our discussion is part of the theory of justice and must not be mistaken for a theory of the political system. We are in the way of describing an ideal arrangement, comparison with which defines a standard for judging actual institutions, and indicates what must be maintained to justify departures from it.

[THE IDEALLY JUST CONSTITUTION]

By way of summing up the account of the principle of participation, we can say that a just constitution sets up a form of fair rivalry for political office and authority. By presenting conceptions of the public good and policies designed to promote social ends, rival parties seek the citizens' approval in accordance with just procedural rules against a background of freedom of thought and assembly in which the fair value of political liberty is assured. The principle of participation compels those in authority to be responsive to the felt interests of the electorate. Representatives are not, to be sure, mere agents of their constituents, since they have a certain discretion and they are expected to exercise their judgment in enacting legislation. In a well-ordered society they must, nevertheless, represent their constituents in the substantive sense: they must seek first to pass just and effective legislation, since this is a citizen's first interest in government, and secondly, they must further their constituents' other interests insofar as these are consistent with justice. The principles of justice are among the main criteria to be used in judging a representative's record and the reasons he gives in defense of it. Since the constitution is the foundation of the social structure, the highest-order system of rules that regulates and controls other institutions, everyone has the same access to the political procedure that it sets up. When the principle of participation is satisfied, all have the common status of equal citizen.

Finally, to avoid misunderstanding, it should be kept in mind that the principle of participation applies to institutions. It does not define an ideal of citizenship; nor does it lay down a duty requiring all to take an active part in political affairs. The duties and obligations of individuals are a separate question that I shall discuss later. What is essential is that the constitution should establish equal rights to engage in public affairs and that measures be taken to maintain the fair value of these liberties. In a well-governed state only a small fraction of persons may devote much of their time to politics. There are many other forms of human good. But this fraction, whatever its size, will most likely be drawn more or less equally from all sectors of society. The many communities of interests and centers of political life will have their active members who look after their concerns.

EQUALITY

Approaches to the ideal of equality have differed greatly, from the metaphysical to the mundane. The burden of democrats, never yet fully sustained, has been to realize in the life of the community that equalitarian ideal so ardently professed. Inequalities of wealth and talent have always been theoretically problematic, and are likely to remain so. Achieving political equality between the sexes, and among the races, would appear in principle to be less problematic—yet these plainly unjust inequalities have been among the greatest challenges for contemporary democracies. This subsection begins with several formulations of the moral ideal; it concludes with a series of great cases from American constitutional history.

91
Immanuel Kant

Immanuel Kant (1724–1804), one of the greatest of all philosophers, sought to explain how the categorical imperative—the fundamental principle of all morality—can be correctly formulated in different ways. One of its formulations— act in such a way that your action treats all humanity as an end, and never as a means only—is a consequence of the nature of humanity. This formulation is defensible, Kant argues, because every rational will has absolute worth in itself; the possession of this absolute, intrinsic worth provides the ground for holding that, in a very deep sense, all human beings are and must be equal.

[ALL HUMANS ARE EQUAL IN BEING ENDS IN THEMSELVES]*

Supposing, however, that there were something *whose existence* has *in itself* an absolute worth, something which, being *an end in itself,* could be a source of definite laws, then in this and this alone would lie the source of a possible categorical imperative, i.e., a practical law.

Now I say: man and generally any rational being *exists* as an end in himself, *not merely as a means* to be arbitrarily used by this or that will, but in all his actions, whether they concern himself or other rational beings, must be always regarded at the same time as an end. All objects of the inclinations have only a conditional worth, for if the inclinations and the wants founded on them did not exist, then their object would be without value. But the inclinations themselves being sources of want, are so far from having an absolute worth for which they should be desired, that on the contrary it must be the universal wish of every rational being to be wholly free from them. Thus the worth of any object which is *to be acquired* by our action is always conditional. Beings whose existence depends not on our will but on Nature's, have nevertheless, if they are irrational beings, only a relative value as means, and are therefore called *things;* rational beings, on the contrary, are called *persons,* because their very nature points them out as ends in themselves, that is as something which must not be used merely as means, and so far therefore restricts freedom of action (and is an object of respect). These, therefore, are not merely subjective ends whose existence has a worth *for us* as an effect of our action, but *objective ends,* that is, things whose existence is an end in itself: an end moreover for which no other can be substituted, which they should subserve *merely* as means, for otherwise nothing whatever would possess *absolute worth;* but if all worth were conditioned and therefore contingent, then there would be no supreme practical principle of reason whatever.

If then there is a supreme practical principle or, in respect of the human will, a categorical imperative, it must be one which, being drawn from the conception of

*From Immanuel Kant, *Foundations of the Metaphysics of Morals,* 1785.

that which is necessarily an end for every one because it is *an end in itself,* constitutes an *objective* principle of will, and can therefore serve as a universal practical law. The foundation of this principle is: *rational nature exists as an end in itself.* Man necessarily conceives his own existence as being so: so far then this is a *subjective* principle of human actions. But every other rational being regards its existence similarly, just on the same rational principle that holds for me: so that it is at the same time an objective principle, from which as a supreme practical law all laws of the will must be capable of being deduced. Accordingly the practical imperative will be as follows: *So act as to treat humanity, whether in thine own person or in that of any other, in every case as an end withal, never as means only.*

92
Thomas Paine

Thomas Paine (1737–1809) believed that natural rights, possessed by all men and by all in the same sense, justify equal participation in government and are therefore central for democratic theory, as Thomas Jefferson had also argued in the Declaration of Independence. These natural rights, which may in some cases be converted by members of a civil community into civil rights, explain the natural unity of mankind.

THE UNITY OF MAN*

Every history of the creation, and every traditionary account, whether from the lettered or unlettered world, however they may vary in their opinion or belief of certain particulars, all agree in establishing one point, *the unity of man;* by which I mean that men are all of *one degree,* and consequently that all men are born equal, and with equal natural right, in the same manner as if posterity had been continued by *creation* instead of *generation,* the latter being the only mode by which the former is carried forward; and consequently every child born into the world must be considered as deriving its existence from God. The world is as new to him as it was to the first man that existed, and his natural right in it is of the same kind.

The Mosaic account of the creation, whether taken as divine authority or merely historical, is full to this point, *the unity or equality of man.* The expression admits of no controversy. "And God said, Let us make man in our own image. In the image of God created he him; male and female created he them." The distinction of sexes is pointed out, but no other distinction is even implied. If this be not divine authority, it is at least historical authority, and shews that the equality of man, so far from being a modern doctrine, is the oldest upon record.

*From Thomas Paine, *The Rights of Man,* 1792.

It is also to be observed that all the religions known in the world are founded, so far as they relate to man, on the *unity of man,* as being all of one degree. Whether in heaven or in hell, or in whatever state man may be supposed to exist hereafter, the good and the bad are the only distinctions. Nay, even the laws of governments are obliged to slide into this principle, by making degrees to consist in crimes and not in persons.

It is one of the greatest of all truths, and of the highest advantage to cultivate. By considering man in this light, and by instructing him to consider himself in this light, it places him in a close connection with all his duties, whether to his Creator or to the creation, of which he is a part; and it is only when he forgets his origin, or, to use a more fashionable phrase, his *birth and family,* that he becomes dissolute. It is not among the least of the evils of the present existing governments in all parts of Europe that man, considered as man, is thrown back to a vast distance from his Maker, and the artificial chasm filled up with a succession of barriers, or sort of turnpike gates, through which he has to pass. I will quote Mr. Burke's catalogue of barriers that he has set up between man and his Maker. Putting himself in the character of a herald, he says: "We fear God—we look with *awe* to kings— with affection to Parliaments—with duty to magistrates—with reverence to priests, and with respect to nobility." Mr. Burke has forgotten to put in "chivalry." He has also forgotten to put in Peter.

The duty of man is not a wilderness of turnpike gates, through which he is to pass by tickets from one to the other. It is plain and simple, and consists but of two points. His duty to God, which every man must feel; and with respect to his neighbor, to do as he would be done by. If those to whom power is delegated do well, they will be respected: if not, they will be despised; and with regard to those to whom no power is delegated, but who assume it, the rational world can know nothing of them.

Hitherto we have spoken only (and that but in part) of the natural rights of man. We have now to consider the civil rights of man, and to show how the one originates from the other. Man did not enter into society to become *worse* than he was before, nor to have fewer rights than he had before, but to have those rights better secured. His natural rights are the foundation of all his civil rights. But in order to pursue this distinction with more precision, it will be necessary to mark the different qualities of natural and civil rights.

A few words will explain this. Natural rights are those which appertain to man in right of his existence. Of this kind are all the intellectual rights, or rights of the mind, and also all those rights of acting as an individual for his own comfort and happiness, which are not injurious to the natural rights of others. Civil rights are those which appertain to man in right of his being a member of society. Every civil right has for its foundation some natural right pre-existing in the individual, but to the enjoyment of which his individual power is not, in all cases, sufficiently competent. Of this kind are all those which relate to security and protection.

From this short review it will be easy to distinguish between that class of natural rights which man retains after entering into society and those which he throws into the common stock as a member of society.

The natural rights which he retains are all those in which the *power* to execute is as perfect in the individual as the right itself. Among this class, as is before mentioned, are all the intellectual rights, or rights of the mind; consequently religion is one of those rights. The natural rights which are not retained, are all those in which, though the right is perfect in the individual, the power to execute them is defective. They answer not his purpose. A man, by natural right, has a right to judge in his own cause; and so far as the right of the mind is concerned, he never surrenders it. But what availeth it him to judge, if he has not power to redress? He therefore deposits this right in the common stock of society, and takes the arm of society, of which he is a part, in preference and in addition to his own. Society *grants* him nothing. Every man is a proprietor in society, and draws on the capital as a matter of right.

From these premises two or three certain conclusions will follow:

First, That every civil right grows out of a natural right; or, in other words, is a natural right exchanged.

Secondly, That civil power properly considered as such is made up of the aggregate of that class of the natural rights of man, which becomes defective in the individual in point of power, and answers not his purpose, but when collected to a focus becomes competent to the purpose of every one.

Thirdly, That the power produced from the aggregate of natural rights, imperfect in power in the individual, cannot be applied to invade the natural rights which are retained in the individual, and in which the power to execute is as perfect as the right itself.

We have now, in a few words, traced man from a natural individual to a member of society, and shewn, or endeavoured to shew, the quality of the natural rights retained, and of those which are exchanged for civil rights. . . .

93
Alexis de Tocqueville

His study of the American democracy led de Tocqueville to conclude that in a democracy equality is the "peculiar and preponderant fact with which all others are connected." Democrats have a taste for freedom, to be sure; but their passion for equality is ardent and overwhelming, and it never can be fully satisfied because there is always to be found some other dimension upon which inequalities arise that the democrat will strive to overcome.

[EQUALITY AND LIBERTY COMPARED]*

It is possible to imagine an extreme point at which freedom and equality would meet and blend. Let us suppose that all the people take a part in the government, and that each one of them has an equal right to take a part in it. As no one is different from

*From Alexis de Tocqueville, *Democracy in America,* 1835.

his fellows, none can exercise a tyrannical power; men will be perfectly free because they will all be entirely equal; and they will all be perfectly equal because they are entirely free. To this ideal state democratic nations tend. This is the only complete form that equality can assume upon earth; but there are a thousand others which, without being equally perfect, are not less cherished by those nations.

The principle of equality may be established in civil society without prevailing in the political world. There may be equal rights of indulging in the same pleasures, of entering the same professions, of frequenting the same places; in a word, of living in the same manner and seeking wealth by the same means, although all men do not take an equal share in the government. A kind of equality may even be established in the political world though there should be no political freedom there. A man may be the equal of all his countrymen save one, who is the master of all without distinction and who selects equally from among them all the agents of his power. Several other combinations might be easily imagined by which very great equality would be united to institutions more or less free or even to institutions wholly without freedom.

Although men cannot become absolutely equal unless they are entirely free, and consequently equality, pushed to its furthest extent, may be confounded with freedom, yet there is good reason for distinguishing the one from the other. The taste which men have for liberty and that which they feel for equality are, in fact, two different things; and I am not afraid to add that among democratic nations they are two unequal things.

Upon close inspection it will be seen that there is in every age some peculiar and preponderant fact with which all others are connected, this fact almost always gives birth to some pregnant idea or some ruling passion, which attracts to itself and bears away in its course all the feelings and opinions of the time; it is like a great stream towards which each of the neighboring rivulets seems to flow.

Freedom has appeared in the world at different times and under various forms; it has not been exclusively bound to any social condition, and it is not confined to democracies. Freedom cannot, therefore, form the distinguishing characteristic of democratic ages. The peculiar and preponderant fact that marks those ages as its own is the equality of conditions; the ruling passion of men in those periods is the love of this equality. Do not ask what singular charm the men of democratic ages find in being equal, or what special reasons they may have for clinging so tenaciously to equality rather than to the other advantages that society holds out to them: equality is the distinguishing characteristic of the age they live in; that of itself is enough to explain that they prefer it to all the rest.

But independently of this reason there are several others which will at all times habitually lead men to prefer equality to freedom.

If a people could ever succeed in destroying, or even in diminishing, the equality that prevails in its own body, they could do so only by long and laborious efforts. Their social condition must be modified, their laws abolished, their opinions superseded, their habits changed, their manners corrupted. But political liberty is more easily lost; to neglect to hold it fast is to allow it to escape. Therefore not only do men cling to equality because it is dear to them; they also adhere to it because they think it will last forever.

That political freedom in its excesses may compromise the tranquillity, the property, the lives of individuals is obvious even to narrow and unthinking minds. On the contrary, none but attentive and clear-sighted men perceive the perils with which equality threatens us, and they commonly avoid pointing them out. They know that the calamities they apprehend are remote and flatter themselves that they will only fall upon future generations, for which the present generation takes but little thought. The evils that freedom sometimes brings with it are immediate; they are apparent to all, and all are more or less affected by them. The evils that extreme equality may produce are slowly disclosed; they creep gradually into the social frame: they are seen only at intervals, and at the moment at which they become most violent, habit already causes them to be no longer felt.

The advantages that freedom brings are shown only by the lapse of time, and it is always easy to mistake the cause in which they originate. The advantages of equality are immediate, and they may always be traced from their source.

Political liberty bestows exalted pleasures from time to time upon a certain number of citizens. Equality every day confers a number of small enjoyments on every man. The charms of equality are every instant felt and are within the reach of all; the noblest hearts are not insensible to them, and the most vulgar souls exult in them. The passion that equality creates must therefore be at once strong and general. Men cannot enjoy political liberty unpurchased by some sacrifices, and they never obtain it without great exertions. But the pleasures of equality are self-proffered; each of the petty incidents of life seems to occasion them, and in order to taste them nothing is required but to live.

Democratic nations are at all times fond of equality, but there are certain epochs at which the passion they entertain for it swells to the height of fury. This occurs at the moment when the old social system, long menaced, is overthrown after a severe internal struggle, and the barriers of rank are at length thrown down. At such times men pounce upon equality as their booty, and they cling to it as to some precious treasure which they fear to lose. The passion for equality penetrates on every side into men's hearts, expands there, and fills them entirely. Tell them not that by this blind surrender of themselves to an exclusive passion they risk their dearest interests; they are deaf. Show them not freedom escaping from their grasp while they are looking another way; they are blind, or rather they can discern but one object to be desired in the universe. . . .

I think that democratic communities have a natural taste for freedom; left to themselves, they will seek it, cherish it, and view any privation of it with regret. But for equality their passion is ardent, insatiable, incessant, invincible; they call for equality in freedom; and if they cannot obtain that, they still call for equality in slavery. They will endure poverty, servitude, barbarism, but they will not endure aristocracy.

This is true at all times, and especially in our own day. All men and all powers seeking to cope with this irresistible passion will be overthrown and destroyed by it. In our age freedom cannot be established without it, and despotism itself cannot reign without its support. . . .

It is possible to conceive of men arrived at a degree of freedom that should completely content them: they would then enjoy their independence without anxiety and without impatience. But men will never establish any equality with which they can be contented. Whatever efforts a people may make, they will never succeed in reducing all the conditions of society to a perfect level; and even if they unhappily attained that absolute and complete equality of position, the inequality of minds would still remain, which, coming directly from the hand of God, will forever escape the laws of man. However democratic, then, the social state and the political constitution of a people may be, it is certain that every member of the community will always find out several points about him which overlook his own position; and we may foresee that his looks will be doggedly fixed in that direction. When inequality of conditions is the common law of society, the most marked inequalities do not strike the eye; when everything is nearly on the same level, the slightest are marked enough to hurt it. Hence the desire of equality always becomes more insatiable in proportion as equality is more complete.

Among democratic nations, men easily attain a certain equality of condition, but they can never attain as much as they desire. It perpetually retires from before them, yet without hiding itself from their sight, and in retiring draws them on. At every moment they think they are about to grasp it; it escapes at every moment from their hold. They are near enough to see its charms, but too far off to enjoy them; and before they have fully tasted its delights, they die.

94
The Seneca Falls Declaration
of Sentiments

The first great convention to advance and protect the rights of women in America was held in Seneca Falls, New York, in 1848. Any inequality of rights between men and women, the delegates to that convention argued, needs *rational justification.* But no such justification can be given for the subsidiary position into which women had long been supposed to fall by nature. The convention adopted The Seneca Falls Declaration of Sentiments, and pledged themselves to work tirelessly for the emancipation of women in the American democracy. The intellectual power and rhetorical effectiveness of Jefferson's ringing phrases in The Declaration of Independence was before their minds. They copied the shape of his argument there, borrowed many of his words and phrases, brought them to bear upon the ideal of sexual equality. Inequality of right between men and women could no longer be defended.

In 1972 the Equal Rights Amendment to the Constitution of the United States was proposed by our national Congress; the deadline for its ratification by three-fourths of the State legislatures was June 30, 1982. The proposed amendment read in whole: "Equality of rights under the law shall not be denied or abridged by The United States or any State on account of sex." A majority of State legislatures did ratify this amendment, but the needed three-fourths had not been reached by the deadline date; the Equal Rights Amendment failed.

[THE HISTORY OF REPEATED INJURIES AND USURPATIONS ON THE PART OF MAN TOWARD WOMAN]*

When, in the course of human events, it becomes necessary for one portion of the family of man to assume among the people of the earth a position different from that which they have hitherto occupied, but one to which the laws of nature and of nature's God entitle them, a decent respect to the opinions of mankind requires that they should declare the causes that impel them to such a course.

We hold these truths to be self-evident: that all men and women are created equal; that they are endowed by their Creator with certain inalienable rights; that among these are life, liberty, and the pursuit of happiness; that to secure these rights governments are instituted, deriving their just powers from the consent of the governed. Whenever any form of government becomes destructive of these ends, it is the right of those who suffer from it to refuse allegiance to it, and to insist upon the institution of a new government, laying its foundation on such principles, and organizing its powers in such form, as to them shall seem most likely to effect their safety and happiness. Prudence, indeed, will dictate that governments long established should not be changed for light and transient causes; and accordingly all experience hath shown that mankind are more disposed to suffer while evils are sufferable, than to right themselves by abolishing the forms to which they are accustomed. But when a long train of abuses and usurpations, pursuing invariably the same object, evinces a design to reduce them under absolute despotism, it is their duty to throw off such government, and to provide new guards for their future security. Such has been the patient sufferance of the women under this government, and such is now the necessity which constrains them to demand the equal station to which they are entitled.

The history of mankind is a history of repeated injuries and usurpations on the part of man toward woman, having in direct object the establishment of an absolute tyranny over her. To prove this, let facts be submitted to a candid world.

He has never permitted her to exercise her inalienable right to the elective franchise.

He has compelled her to submit to laws, in the formation of which she had no voice.

He has withheld from her rights which are given to the most ignorant and degraded men—both natives and foreigners.

Having deprived her of this first right of a citizen, the elective franchise, thereby leaving her without representation in the halls of legislation, he has oppressed her on all sides.

He has made her, if married, in the eye of the law, civilly dead.

He has taken from her all right in property, even to the wages she earns.

*The Seneca Falls Declaration of Sentiments, 1848.

He has made her, morally, an irresponsible being, as she can commit many crimes with impunity, provided they be done in the presence of her husband. In the covenant of marriage, she is compelled to promise obedience to her husband, he becoming, to all intents and purposes, her master—the law giving him power to deprive her of her liberty, and to administer chastisement.

He has so framed the laws of divorce, as to what shall be the proper causes, and in case of separation, to whom the guardianship of the children shall be given, as to be wholly regardless of the happiness of women—the law, in all cases, going upon a false supposition of the supremacy of man, and giving all power into his hands.

After depriving her of all rights as a married woman, if single, and the owner of property, he has taxed her to support a government which recognizes her only when her property can be made profitable to it.

He has monopolized nearly all the profitable employments, and from those she is permitted to follow, she receives but a scanty remuneration. He closes against her all the avenues to wealth and distinction which he considers most honorable to himself. As a teacher of theology, medicine, or law, she is not known.

He has denied her the facilities for obtaining a thorough education, all colleges being closed against her.

He allows her in Church, as well as State, but a subordinate position, claiming Apostolic authority for her exclusion from the ministry, and, with some exceptions, from any public participation in the affairs of the Church.

He has created a false public sentiment by giving to the world a different code of morals for men and women, by which moral delinquencies which exclude women from society, are not only tolerated, but deemed of little account in man.

He has usurped the prerogative of Jehovah himself, claiming it as his right to assign for her a sphere of action, when that belongs to her conscience and to her God.

He has endeavored, in every way that he could, to destroy her confidence in her own powers, to lessen her self-respect and to make her willing to lead a dependent and abject life.

Now, in view of this entire disfranchisement of one-half the people of this country, their social and religious degradation—in view of the unjust laws above mentioned, and because women do feel themselves aggrieved, oppressed, and fraudulently deprived of their most sacred rights, we insist that they have immediate admission to all the rights and privileges which belong to them as citizens of the United States.

In entering upon the great work before us, we anticipate no small amount of misconception, misrepresentation, and ridicule; but we shall use every instrumentality within our power to effect our object. We shall employ agents, circulate tracts, petition the State and National legislatures, and endeavor to enlist the pulpit and the press in our behalf. We hope this Convention will be followed by a series of Conventions embracing every part of the country.

95
Harold J. Laski

Harold J. Laski (1893–1950) was a leading Socialist theoretician (and Chairman of the British Labour Party) who understood that absolute equality of treatment of all citizens by the state could not be defended, but that equality of opportunity must be assured. Democratic equality, he held, entails the abolition of the hereditary House of Lords. It also entails that "we cannot justify the existences of gross economic differences until the point is reached when the primary claims of men win a full response. . . . I have no right to cake if my neighbor, because of that right, is compelled to go without bread. . . . I am urging that great inequalities of wealth make impossible the attainment of freedom."

[HOW IS EQUALITY TO BE UNDERSTOOD?]*

. . . To minds so ardent for liberty as de Tocqueville and Lord Acton liberty and equality were antithetic things. It is a drastic conclusion. But it turns, in the case of both men, upon a misunderstanding of what equality implies. Equality does not mean identity of treatment. There can be no ultimate identity of treatment so long as men are different in want and capacity and need. The purpose of society would be frustrated at the outset if the nature of a mathematician met an identical response with that to the nature of a bricklayer. Equality does not even imply identity of reward for effort so long as the difference in reward does not enable me, by its magnitude, to invade the rights of others.

Equality, broadly, is a coherence of ideas each one of which needs special examination. Undoubtedly, it implies fundamentally a certain levelling process. It means that no man shall be so placed in society that he can overreach his neighbour to the extent which constitutes a denial of the latter's citizenship. It means that my realisation of my best self must involve as its logical result the realisation by others of their best selves. It means such an ordering of social forces as will balance a share in the toil of living with a share in its gain also. It means that my share in that gain must be adequate for the purposes of citizenship. It implies that even if my voice be weighed as less weighty than that of another, it must yet receive consideration in the decisions that are made. The meaning, ultimately, of equality surely lies in the fact that the very differences in the nature of men require mechanisms for the expression of their wills that give to each its due hearing. The power, in fact, of the ideal of equality lies in the historical evidence that so far in the record of the State the wills of men have been unequally answered. Their freedom, where it has been gained, has accordingly been built upon the unfreedom of others. Inequality, in a word, means the rule of limited numbers because it secures freedom only to those whose will is secure of respect.

---

*From Harold J. Laski, *A Grammar of Politics,* 1925.

They will dominate the State and use its power for their own purposes. They will make the fulfilment of their private desires the criterion of public good.

Equality, therefore, means first of all the absence of special privilege. . . . In the penumbra of equality, it means, in the political sphere, that my will, as a factor in the counting of heads, is equal to the will of any other. It means that I can move forward to any office in the State for which men are prepared to choose me. It means that I am not to find that there are persons in the State whose authority is qualitatively different from my own. Whatever rights inhere in another by virtue of his being a citizen must inhere, and to the same extent, in me also. There is no justification in such a view for the existence of an hereditary second chamber. For, obviously, in the second generation of such an assembly men exercise political authority not in virtue of their own qualities, but by reason of parental accident. So, also, no office that carries with it power can ever be rightly regarded as an incorporeal hereditament, for that is to associate important functions with qualities other than fitness for their performance. The exclusion of any man, or body of men, from access to the avenues of authority is always, that is to say, a denial of their freedom.

Equality means, in the second place, that adequate opportunities are laid open to all. By adequate opportunities we cannot imply equal opportunities in a sense that implies identity of original chance. The native endowments of men are by no means equal. Children who are brought up in an atmosphere where things of the mind are accounted highly are bound to start the race of life with advantages no legislation can secure. Parental character will inevitably affect profoundly the quality of the children whom it touches. So long, therefore, as the family endures—and there seems little reason to anticipate or to desire its disappearance—the varying environments it will create make the notion of equal opportunities a fantastic one.

But that is not to say that the opportunities created may not be adequate. We can at least see first that all men are given such training as seems, in the light of experience, most likely to develop their faculties to the full. We can at least surround those circumstances with the physical media without which the training of the mind can hardly be successful. We can, where we discover talent, at least make it certain that it does not perish for want of encouragement. These conditions do not exist today. Children who come hungry to school cannot, on the average, profit by education in like degree to those who are well fed. The student who is trying to do his work in a room which serves for the various tasks of life cannot find that essential isolation without which the habit of thought can rarely be cultivated. The boy or girl who has to assume that at fourteen they are bound to pass into the industrial world rarely acquires that frame of mind which searches with eagerness for the cultivation of intelligence. In the modern world, broadly speaking, opportunity is a matter of parental circumstance. Boys of a certain social status may assume that they will pass from the secondary school to the university. Boys whose parents are, broadly, manual workers will in the vast majority of cases be inevitably destined to manual work also. There is no reason to decry either the value or the dignity of manual work; but there is every reason to examine the social adequacy of a system which does not at every point associate the best training available with those whose qualities most fit them to benefit by that training. We do not want— possibly we cannot afford—to prolong the period of education unduly. But no State has established conditions of reasonable adequacy until the period of education is sufficiently long, first, to ensure that the citizen knows how to use his mind, and second, that those of special capacity are given that further training which prevents the wastage of their talent.

No one can deny that this wastage to-day is enormous. Any student of the results of adult education in Europe will have realised how great is the reservoir of talent we leave unused until it is too late. The sacrifices to-day involved when the average manual worker seeks the adequate education of his children are sacrifices we have no right to demand. Often enough, the training of one child is built upon the conviction of others to a life of unremitting toil. The circumstances which those who live by intellectual work know to be essential to its performance are, as a matter of definition almost, denied to the vast majority of the population. And since citizenship is largely a matter of the use of trained intelligence, it is obvious, accordingly, that its substance is denied to all save a fraction of the community. Our business, therefore, is to assure such an education to all as will make every vocation, however humble, one that does not debar those who follow it from the life of intelligence. That certainly means an extension of the period within which the earning of one's living is impossible. It means also that even after the earning period has commenced there are full opportunities for the devotion of leisure to intellectual ends. It means, thirdly, that those who devote themselves to the business of teaching represent the best minds at the service of the community. In the modern State the teacher has a responsibility far greater than that which devolves upon any other citizen; and unless he teaches from a full mind and a full heart he cannot release the forces which education has in leash.

Nothing in all this denies the probability that mental qualities are inherited and that, other things being equal, the children of able parents will be abler than the children of average parents. But it does deny the equation, characteristic of the modern State, between ability and material position. The average trade-union leader cannot afford to send his sons to the university; but the ability of the average trade-union leader is probably not inferior to that of the average banker or the average bishop. Where, that is to say, the inequalities of our system are not due to natural causes, there is a clear case for their remedy. Nor can we hope to discover the existence of capacity unless our system provides for its discovery. It may do so to-day in the case of the rich; assuredly it does not do so in the case of the poor. And it is urgent to remember that, important as nature may be, it requires an adequate nurture if it is to function satisfactorily. The present inequalities are not referable to principle. We have therefore to define the outlines of such a system as build the inequalities we admit upon the needs of society. At present they most largely arise from the impact of the property system upon the structure of the State. But what is reflected by the property system is less ability to serve the community than ability to gain economic power without reference to the quality of wants supplied.

The provision of adequate opportunity is, therefore, one of the basic conditions of equality, and it is mainly founded upon the training we offer to citizens. For the power that ultimately counts in society is the power to utilise knowledge; and disparities of education result, above all, in disparities in the ability to use that power. I am not pleading for equality of function. I am pleading only for the obvious truth that without education a man is not so circumstanced that he knows how to make the best of himself and that therefore, for him, the purpose of society is, *ab initio,* frustrated. Once men are in that situation where they can know themselves, the use they make of their opportunities becomes subject to principles of which equality is only one.

But if we agree, as I have argued earlier, that a democratic State regards its members as equally entitled to happiness, it follows that such differences as exist must not be differences inexplicable in terms of reason. Distinctions of wealth or status must be distinctions to which all men can attain and they must be required by the common welfare. If a State permits the existence of an hereditary aristocracy it must be because it is capable of proof that an hereditary aristocracy multiplies the chances of each man's realising his best self. If we are to have an economic system in which the luxury of a few is paralleled by the misery of the many, it must be because the common welfare requires that luxury. In each case the proposition is open to historical disproof. An hereditary aristocracy is bound, sooner or later, to use its political power to general disadvantage, unless, like the peerage of France, it has ceased to be anything but a faded memory. A State divided into a small number of rich and a large number of poor will always develop a government manipulated by the rich to protect the amenities represented by their property. It therefore follows that the inequalities or any social system are justified only as it can be demonstrated that the level of service they procure is obviously higher because of their existence. . . . . It is obvious that a statesman in office must be so remunerated that he is not oppressed by narrow material cares; and that might well involve placing him in a higher financial rank than a bootmaker or a shop assistant. In each case the measure of difference is conceived in social terms. It is set in a principle which is demonstrably rational. It is fitting the circumstances of function to the environment of which it has need.

Such a view admits, at least as a matter of theory, of fairly simple statement in institutional terms. The urgent claims of all must be met before we can meet the particular claims of some. The differences in the social or economic position of men can only be admitted after a minimum basis of civilisation is attained by the community as a whole. That minimum basis must admit of my realising the implications of personality. Above that level, the advantages of the situation I occupy must be advantages necessary to the performance of a social function. The advantages I enjoy must be the result of my own effort, because they are the return to me for my own services, and I am clearly not entitled to enjoy them as the result of someone else's services. One man is not entitled to a house of twenty rooms until all people are adequately housed; and one man, even in that environment, is not entitled to a house of twenty rooms because his father was a great advocate or a large industrialist. The things that are due to me are the rights I must enjoy in order to be a citizen, and the differential advantages which society adjudges inherent in the particular occupation I follow. . . .

The answer involved in this attitude is far less simple than it seems. If the State exists for social good, "capacity" can only mean capacity to add to social good. It is not in the least certain that the exercise of talent in a society like our own does in fact result in social benefit. Capacity, in short, must run in the leading-strings of principle. It must be excited to the end our institutions have in view. And since that end is the achievement of happiness for each individual, it seems obvious that we must, if the margin be insufficient, suffer equally by its insufficiencies. We can never, therefore, as a matter of principle, justify the existence of differences until the point is reached when the primary claims of men win a full response. I have no right to cake if my neighbour, because of that right, is compelled to go without bread. Any social organisation from which this basis is absent by denying equality denies all that gives meaning to the personality of men.

Equality, therefore, involves up to the margin of sufficiency identity of response to primary needs. And that is what is meant by justice. We are rendering to each man his own by giving him what enables him to be a man. We are, of course, therein protecting the weak and limiting the power of the strong. We so act because the common welfare includes the welfare of the weak as well as of the strong. . . .

Broadly, I am urging that great inequalities of wealth make impossible the attainment of freedom. It means the dictation of the physical and mental circumstances which surround the less fortunate. It means the control of the engines of government to their detriment. The influence of the great corporations upon the legislative system of the United States is only a supreme example of that control. Hardly less deleterious is the way in which it controls the intellectual environment it encounters. It is able to weight the educational system in its interest. It is able, by the rewards it offers, to affect the propertyless brain-worker to its service. Since the judiciary will be largely selected from its paid advocates, legal decisions will largely reflect the lessons of its experience. Even the Churches will preach a gospel which is permeated by their dependence upon the support of the wealthy.

Political equality, therefore, is never real unless it is accompanied by virtual economic equality; political power, otherwise, is bound to be the handmaid of economic power. The recognition of this dependence is in the main due to the explanation of historic evolution, and it is, indeed, almost as old as the birth of scientific politics. Aristotle pointed out the equation between democracy and the rule of the poor, between oligarchy and the rule of the rich. The struggle to remedy economic disparity is the key to Roman history; it is at the root of English agrarian discontent. It underlies the sermons of John Ball, the *Utopia* of More, the *Oceana* of Harrington. The early history of socialism is most largely the record of a perception that the concentration of property other than labour-power in a few hands is fatal to the purpose of the State. It was that perception which Marx, in the *Communist Manifesto,* made the foundation of the most formidable political philosophy in the modern world. For though the materialistic interpretation of history is an over-emphasis of one link in the chain of causation, it is the link most intimately related to the experience of ordinary men. It is overwhelmingly right in its insistence that either the State must dominate property, or property will dominate the State.

For, as Madison wrote, "the only durable source of faction is property." But it is obvious that to base the differences between men on a contest for economic wealth is to destroy the possibility of a well-ordered commonwealth. It is to excite all the qualities in men—envy, arrogance, hatred, vanity—which prevent the emergence of social unity. It is to emphasise a competition based on their separation, instead of a competition based upon their mutual interest. As soon as we postulate approximate equality of wealth, our methods of social organisation enable us to respond to men's needs in terms of the substance of those needs. We are the more bound to this effort immediately we admit the logic of universal suffrage. For to confide to the mass of men the control of ultimate political power is broadly to admit that the agencies of the State must be utilised to respond to their needs. They involve, if they are to be satisfied, such a distribution of influence over authority as will balance fairly the incidence of its results among the members of society. It means, that is, that I must adjust my scale of wants to social welfare as that is organised in terms of a valuation which equally weights the primary needs of citizens; and that valuation remains ineffective if my power is a function not of my personality, but of my property.

But virtual equality in economic power means more than approximate equality of wealth. It means that the authority which exerts that power must be subject to the rules of democratic governance. It means the abrogation of unlettered and irresponsible will in the industrial world. It involves building decisions on principles which can be explained. . . . There is, that is to say, all the difference in the world between an authority which grows naturally out of functions which are set consistently in a public context, and an authority which, equally consistently, is the outcome of private and irresponsible will.

The existence of this latter type is fatal to the civic implications of equality. It poisons industrial relations. It makes the position of master and servant one of waiting upon the threshold of war. Above all, it is intolerable wherever the function involved is one where continuity of service is essential to the life of the community. That industries like coal and electric power, transport and banking, the supply of meat and the provision of houses, should be left to the hazards of private enterprise will appear as unthinkable to a future generation as it is unthinkable to our own that the army of the State should be left to private hands. They must be subject to rules as rigorous as those which govern medicine, simply because they are not less vital to the national life. That does not mean direct operation by government as the inevitable alternative. It means the planning of constitutions for essential industries; and the possible types of constitutions are as various in industry as elsewhere.

96
Ralph Barton Perry

Ralph Barton Perry (1876–1957), an American philosopher and historian of democracy, has captured more perfectly than any other thinker the central role of equality as a democratic ideal. Believing that all persons are endowed with approximately the same faculties of reason and conscience, democrats have adopted the "maxim of equal opportunity"—but, he points out, this is not so much a judgment of fact as it is an expression of sentiment about human beings. Recognizing the inevitable competition encouraged by the maxim of equal opportunity, democracies naturally seek to limit the damage such competition does to those who are in fact not equally endowed. "It never has been and never will be possible for a democratic state to avoid bestowing gratuities on its people with a view to promoting the equality of their competitive positions."

[HUMAN EQUALITY AND THE MAXIM OF EQUAL OPPORTUNITY]*

The eighteenth-century exponents of equality knew as well as Calhoun and Adams or more modern critics that men are endowed by nature with unequal capacity, as they are endowed with unequal stature, strength, fingerprints, or cephalic indices. The equality of which they spoke drew its meaning, not from a mere disregard of facts, but from a group of ideas which had their roots in Greek and Hebrew antiquity and their proof in the moral, political, and religious philosophy of the age.

The equalitarian doctrine can be summarily expounded. It was not an assertion that the several individual members of the human race are *as a matter of fact in all respects* alike; but that they *are and ought to be* alike in *certain* respects; and that these likenesses have a great deal to do with the aims of organized society.

In the first place, all men are equally men—which means not that they possess human attributes in the same degree, but that they possess the same attributes in some degree. All members of an audience, whether they sit in boxes or in the pit, possess the same type of skeleton, the same organs, and the same physiological functions. Whether a man is born in a hovel or in a palace, the reproductive process is the same; whether a man works in a private office on Wall Street or in a coal mine in Pennsylvania, he draws his energy from the combustion of food, and gives off carbon dioxide. But the generic sameness of men is not confined to these baser anatomical and physiological levels; they possess the same psychological traits, from the simpler reflexes of coughing and sneezing to the so-called higher processes of memory and thought. All men experience pleasure and pain, hunger and thirst, fear and anger, love and hate, joy and despair. All men recollect their past, anticipate their future, and perceive their present. All men exercise in some degree the activities of generalization and inference. This fact may be sum-

*Ralph Barton Perry, *Puritanism and Democracy,* 1944, The Vanguard Press.

marily expressed either in naturalistic or in religious terms. All men belong to the same species in the hierarchy of evolution; or all men are created in the same image of God.

What is true of the constitution of man is true also of his life-cycle, and his fundamental relationships to his fellow men and to his physical environment. All men are born, grow old, and die. They traverse the same ardors of youth, the same sobrieties of middle age, and the same scleroses of senescence. All men inhabit the same planet, are exposed to its alternations of season and weather, and are dependent on its resources. All men have parents, and most men have brothers and sisters and children. All men have neighbors, with whom they must establish terms of reasonable accord. All men suffer from the necessity, or enjoy the opportunity, of living with their fellows. They all have one life to live, face the same inevitable death, and hear the same crack of doom.

Owing to many causes, men are disposed to forget or ignore these indisputable facts. Generic sameness tends to be eclipsed by differences of individual and class. Equalitarianism exhorts us to reverse this tendency: to be reverently disposed toward the commonplace, and to be astonished by what is taken for granted. . . .

According to the way of thinking characteristic of the eighteenth century, the notable differences between man and man, such as that between king and subject, noble and commoner, priest and layman, or rich and poor, are products of organized society. This idea led to the habit of abstracting from organized society, and from the differences which it has created. Men were imaginatively divested of institutional accretions—their trappings, powers, and privileges; and when thus denuded and reduced to the ranks they looked strangely alike. The doctrine that equality is "natural" was a way of saying that the more palpable and invidious inequalities are artificial.

That which is artificial can be unmade, and the purpose of social change was thus conceived as the restoration of a primitive equality. But, as was the case with the conception of "nature" in all its applications, this retrospective manner of speaking concealed the essence of the matter. Fundamentally, nature signified what men *could* be and *ought* to be, rather than what they *had* been. When man's past came to be better known, the state of nature was transferred from the past to the future, and conceived as an attainable and valid ideal rather than as a historical beginning.

Man's equality of endowment came thus to be conceived in terms of a sameness of potentiality rather than of attainment, and faith in human nature assumed the form of a belief in his educability. This faith was still extravagant, but the locus of its extravagance was shifted. It became an excessively optimistic view, not of what men are or have been, but of what they are capable of becoming when the frustrations and malformations due to human institutions are corrected. Given the air and the sun and the moisture which they require, all individuals of the species are capable, it was believed, of the same flowering. The error now lay in underestimating the inborn differences which predetermine the limits of growth.

The biological emphasis on inherited traits and the psychological emphasis on inherited aptitude and intelligence belong to a later age from that in which American democracy was born, and their acceptance modifies one of its premises. But democracy accepts innate limitations reluctantly. It gives to every man the benefit of the doubt, and the doubt is so far justified as to make the gift significant. The rival claims of heredity and environment are still disputed, and no final adjudication of them is yet in sight.

Anti-democratic social philosophies justify inequalitarian institutions, as Aristotle once justified slavery. It is claimed that the inequalities of power and privilege in organized society are a mere projection of the native and ineradicable inequalities of its members. Men get what they are fit for, and what they are fit for will in the long run determine their happiness. This theory affords a suspiciously convenient justification for those who are most favored by the existing system, as did the puritan theory that power and privilege are the just earnings of virtue. Reformers are accused of making humble people discontented with a lot which corresponds to their inborn capacity and provides the only kind of happiness of which they are capable.

The democratic social philosophy, on the other hand, emphasizes the degree to which mental and moral traits are an effect of the social environment, and proposes that this environment shall be made as auspicious as possible. The extreme hereditarian position is, in the present state of the question, as dogmatic as the doctrine of equal potentiality. Even the commonly accepted opinion of the relative superiority of races is a product of pride and vested interest rather than of science. The least that can be said for the equalitarian view is that it is the more generous and fruitful of two dogmatisms between which science allows an option.

Insofar as native differences of capacity are admitted, there is a tendency in democracy to conceive them as differences of vocation rather than of merit or dignity. And if the idea of generic equality tends to be superseded by the idea of equal opportunity, which affirms only that each man shall be enabled to raise his attainment to the limit of his capacity, this is still accompanied by the belief that such capacity is high. Democracy retains, if only as a regulative principle of social organization, an elixir of hopefulness. For what men attain is, in part, an effect of their belief in themselves and of the confident expectation of others.

Generic equality, then, is the idea that beneath the clothes they wear, and the status or occupation which organized society has bestowed upon them, all men are men, with the same faculties, the same needs and aspirations, the same destiny, and similar potentialities of development. Granting that the reservations are more evident to ourselves than to our fathers, this is still true. No one will deny it, once the question is raised in this form.

Why is this unquestionable fact so neglected that it has to be proclaimed? The founders of democracy were right not only in affirming the fact, but in their explanation of its neglect. The generic sameness of men is overlaid with surface differences. Men wear clothes and insignia, and they wear them on the outside of their persons where they are most in evidence. Every man has a station in life into which he is born, or to which he attains. This station is in part a matter of space and time. A man's spatio-temporal location distributes other men along radii of proximity; his neighbors are near, and others are distant. Those who are near can be seen easily, while those at a distance require the straining of the eye or an unnatural exercise of the faculty of imagination. But his station is also functional, consisting in the role he plays in the drama of life, and determining the relations in which he stands to his fellow actors.

These differences of station are not only more palpable but more interesting. Attention is fastened, not upon the common physiognomy of man, but upon those differences of feature, emphasis, and expression which distinguish the individual face with which one may claim acquaintance. And the functional differences that divide men are of commanding importance, in the sense of practical urgency. One's transactions are not with mankind, but with distinct individuals, or limited groups of individuals. Having an aching tooth, it is more important to consider a dentist as such than to reflect that he is a man, like oneself. The worker's struggle for existence forces upon his attention the difference between those who own capital and those who, like himself, depend upon the wages which the capitalist dispenses.

Man's generic sameness tending thus to be ignored, what is the means of heightening it and investing it with feeling? It might be supposed that modern science in its application to man would have provided such a means. Biology, anthropology, and psychology concern themselves with structures, functions, and laws common to all men. But the scientist, while he is interested in man, is not in his scientific capacity interested in men. Nor is it sufficient merely to acquire perspective. It is true that distance tends to render individual differences unnoticeable. To the European, all Chinese or even Orientals tend to 'look alike.' From an astronomical distance all men, as earth-dwellers, present an aspect of sameness that subordinates the uniqueness of genius and the significance of historic events. But it is also true that distance extinguishes interest in individuals. If human suffering occurs at a sufficient distance, it produces apathy; the suffering or the death of a few thousand, more or less, signifies little.

Neither science nor distance will create equalitarianism, which is an interest in individual men, combined with a recognition of their sameness. It is an appreciation of their common value. It is not a perception or a judgment, but a sentiment. . . .

The maxim of equal opportunity owes its place in the American creed not only to the alleged personal and social benefits of competition, but also to the assumption that, since all men are endowed with the same faculties of reason and conscience, and since natural resources are abundant, the effect of equal opportunity will be to raise all men to *approximately* the same high level of attainment. The fact is that equality of opportunity is at best a secondary principle, subordinate to the principle of the maximum possible benefit to all individuals. There is no ethical axiom to the effect that individuals are entitled only to what they have earned or achieved for themselves. As between the maxims "Each man should be rewarded in proportion to his service" and "To each according to his needs," the ethics of universalistic individualism is clearly on the side of the latter. Ethically speaking, there is no limit to the benefit which the state should confer on its members save its power to confer such benefits.

The competitive system in its ordinary economic sense has its own peculiar limitations. Even though it be admitted that economic goods are promoted by the system of laissez faire, it does not follow that this system is equally favorable to the so-called creative goods of art and science, "where to divide is not to take away." To covet excellence in art and science does not imply that one shall outstrip or deprive others, but that one shall judge oneself by some standard of perfection. It may well be that the state can best promote goods of this sort by furnishing qualified individuals with the requisite means, education, and leisure, thus relieving them from the pressure and the preoccupations of competitive struggle. Whatever in this sphere of life it can do is what it ought to do, without respect to any prejudice in favor of independent livelihood.

But the secondary character of equal opportunity is best demonstrated by stressing the fact that any free competitive struggle predetermines the attributes of the successful contestant. Its freedom is relative to the rules, the rules define the form of the achievement, and the form of the achievement favors those who possess the corresponding form of capacity. All orderly competitions encourage something. Competition for wealth puts a premium upon the qualities of acquisitiveness. This may or may not be desirable; in any case, it is important to recognize its negative as well as its positive implications. Insofar as society as a whole is cast into the form of the traditional laissez-faire capitalism, it sanctions greed and guile as well as industry and invention.

It is important, furthermore, that if the race is to be "fair," the contestants should be at all times free from handicaps other than the ineradicable handicaps of native aptitude. But since the economic struggle is a continuing struggle of families and groups, the individual in some measure inherits the gains or losses of his antecedents; and he finds himself not at the start of a race where all are abreast, but at some later stage where the contestants are already spread in a column of advancement.

Public education is an attempt to remove this handicap of birth. It does so only to a limited degree. It may provide the individual of the younger generation with free "tuition," or even give him "room and board," but it cannot discount the effects of the domestic environment. It cannot free the son of poor parents from the pressure of livelihood, or the lack of "spending money," or the social ignominy of caste. So long as there are marked differences which surround the individual during his early years and create advantages and disadvantages of "background," it cannot be said that the contestants in the economic struggle are equal. The individual also finds himself competing, not with other individuals, but with durable and centrally controlled aggregations of corporate wealth. It is this which is fundamentally accountable for the socialistic strain in modern social thought. Professor Tawney says:

> In the absence of measures which prevent the exploitation of groups in a weak economic position by those in a strong, and make the external conditions of health and civilization a common possession, the phrase equality of opportunity is obviously a jest, to be described as amusing or heartless according to taste. It is the impertinent courtesy of an invitation offered to unwelcome guests, in the certainty that circumstances will prevent them from accepting it.

At any stage of the contest, furthermore, the individual finds himself permanently favored or handicapped by his gains or losses up to that time. He runs only one race. Suppose him to be a man whose powers mature late, or who is the victim of accidental misfortune, or whose aptitudes lie elsewhere than in the economic struggle for existence. He enters the race at an early age, and being outdistanced, can never from henceforth compete on equal terms with his fellows.

Much has been said of the value of struggle as a school of character. But this school is commonly judged by those who succeed in graduating—little is heard of those who fail. The experience of adversity is benign to those who triumph over adversity. To those who fail, especially if they believe that their failure has been due to no fault of their own, adversity is often a cause of bitterness and moral dissolution. As the struggle for existence becomes more desperate, the number of moral casualties increases and the number of victors declines.

It never has been and never will be possible for a democratic state to avoid bestowing gratuities on its people with a view to promoting the equality of their competitive positions. It owes to all individuals as much of further positive good as it can dispense. It owes this in the sense that this is the reason for its being. In setting the terms of competition it assumes responsibility for the effect of those terms on the individuals who compete. It is obliged to make the terms of the race fair in substance and not merely in name; but it is no less obliged to consider the effect of the race upon the contestants, both upon those who win and upon those who lose. It has a duty, furthermore, toward the creation and distribution of those goods which flourish best under non-competitive conditions. These considerations amply justify measures which democratic states have in fact undertaken: to provide facilities for individual development, to correct the abuses of competition, to foster the arts and sciences, to protect the standard of living, to succor the ill, the poor, or the unemployed, and to redistribute wealth.

Gross inequalities of wealth tend, furthermore, to destroy that spirit of fraternity and of mutual respect which we have yet to consider, and which constitutes the spirit and flavor of a democratic society. "Where conditions are such," as Professor Tawney says, "that two-thirds of the wealth is owned by one per cent of the population, the ownership of property is more properly regarded as the badge of a class than as the attribute of a society." Democracy defeats its own purpose if it merely substitutes for a hierarchy of birth, or of ecclesiastical or political privilege, a hierarchy based on the advantages and the disadvantages of accumulated wealth, or the degree of economic opportunity which its members enjoy. Said James Fitzjames Stephen:

> Equality, like liberty, appears to me to be a big name for a small thing . . . Upon the whole, I think that what little can be truly said of equality is that as a fact human beings are not equal; that in their dealings with each other they ought to recognize real inequalities where they exist as much as substantial equality where it exists. That they are equally prone to exaggerate real distinctions, which is vanity, and to deny their existence, which is envy.

But this is not "a small thing." The writer of these words commits the opposite and more serious error of making little of much—of making nothing of what is in a sense everything. For from these mixed equalities and inequalities and from the attitude taken toward them is compounded the very essence of social life.

97
The Supreme Court of the United States: Cases on Equality

The Fourteenth Amendment to the Constitution of the United States sought to make concrete the country's commitment to the equality of its citizens under the law. That Amendment says, in part: "No State shall . . . deny to any person within its jurisdiction the equal protection of the laws." This "equal protection clause" had of course to be interpreted in deciding actual cases—and those cases have exhibited the torturous development of the meaning of equality in America.

In the landmark case of *Plessy v. Ferguson* (1896) the doctrine of "separate but equal" was held constitutional; so long as equal facilities were provided the races, their being dealt with *separately* was not to be forbidden. Justice Harlan, in a dissent that has reverberated through our history, condemns that view and predicts the race hatred it was likely to foster. "Our Constitution is colorblind," he wrote, "and neither knows nor tolerates classes among citizens. In respect of civil rights, all citizens are equal before the law."

The "separate but equal" doctrine was overturned at last in the monumental decision in *Brown v. Board of Education* (1954), ordering the racial integration of the public schools: ". . . in the field of public education the doctrine of 'separate but equal' has no place. Separate educational facilities are inherently unequal."

Twenty-five years after *Brown* the enrollment of minority students in medical schools and law schools, as in universities generally, remained disproportionately low. Institutions seeking to correct this imbalance, and certainly not intending to discriminate invidiously, devised admission systems that gave some preference to minority applicants. Such preferences were believed by many white applicants to deny *them* the equal protection of the laws. In *University of California v. Bakke,* the Court struck down one such preferential program, yet insisted that race could be one among many considerations in a college admissions system. Only considerations having constitutional weight may justify the uses of such racial classifications, said the Court; racial preference given to any group for less weighty reasons would indeed violate the equal protection clause of the Constitution.

PLESSY v. FERGUSON   163 U.S. 537 (1896)

A statute of the State of Louisiana obliged railroad companies to "provide equal but separate accommodations for the white, and colored races," and ordering that no persons "shall be admitted to occupy seats in coaches, other than the ones assigned to them on account of the race they belong to." Plessy, "of mixed descent, in the proportion of seven-eighths Caucasian and one-eighth African blood," refused to comply with the order to vacate his seat in a coach reserved for whites, and was thereupon ejected and jailed for the violation of that statute. The opinion of the Supreme Court, delivered by Justice Brown, upheld his conviction. A statute which implies merely a legal distinction between the white and colored races—a distinction which is founded in the color of the two races, and which must always exist so long as white men are distinguished from the other race by color—has no tendency to destroy the legal equality of the two races, or reestablish a state of involuntary servitude. . . .

We think the enforced separation of the races, as applied to the internal commerce of the State, neither abridges the privileges or immunities of the colored man, deprives him of his property without due process of law, nor denies him the equal protection of the laws, within the meaning of the Fourteenth Amendment. . . .

So far, then, as a conflict with the Fourteenth Amendment is concerned, the case reduces itself to the question whether the statute of Louisiana is a reasonable regulation, and with respect to this there must necessarily be a large discretion on the part of the legislature. In determining the question of reasonableness it is at liberty to act with reference to the established usages, customs and traditions of the people, and with a view to the promotion of their comfort, and the preservation of the public peace and good order. Gauged by this standard, we cannot say that a law which authorizes or even requires the separation of the two races in public conveyances is unreasonable, or more obnoxious to the Fourteenth Amendment than the acts of Congress requiring separate schools for colored children in the District of Columbia, the constitutionality of which does not seem to have been questioned, or the corresponding acts of state legislatures.

Justice Harlan, Dissenting:

In respect of civil rights, common to all citizens, the Constitution of the United States does not, I think, permit any public authority to know the race of those entitled to be protected in the enjoyment of such rights. Every true man has pride of race, and under appropriate circumstances when the rights of others, his equals before the law, are not to be affected, it is his privilege to express such pride and to take such action based upon it as to him seems proper. But I deny that any legislative body or judicial tribunal may have regard to the race of citizens when the civil rights of those citizens are involved. Indeed, such legislation, as that here in question, is inconsistent not only with that equality of rights which pertains to citizenship, National and State, but with the personal liberty enjoyed by every one within the United States. . . .

These notable additions to the fundamental law [The Thirteenth and Fourteenth Amendments to the U.S. Constitution] were welcomed by the friends of liberty throughout the world. They removed the race line from our governmental systems. They had, as this court has said, a common purpose, namely, to secure "to a race recently emancipated, a race that through many generations have been held in slavery, all the civil rights that the superior race enjoy." They declared, in legal effect, this court has further said, "that the law in the States shall be the same for the black as for the white; that all persons, whether colored or white, shall stand equal before the laws of the States, and, in regard to the colored race, for whose protection the amendment was primarily designed, that no discrimination shall be made against them by law because of their color." . . .

In view of the Constitution, in the eye of the law, there is in this country no superior, dominant, ruling class of citizens. There is no caste here. Our Constitution is color-blind, and neither knows nor tolerates classes among citizens. In respect of civil rights, all citizens are equal before the law. The humblest is the peer of the most powerful. The law regards man as man, and takes no account of his surroundings or of his color when his civil rights as guaranteed by the supreme law of the land are involved. It is, therefore, to be regretted that this high tribunal, the final expositor of the fundamental law of the land, has reached the conclusion that it is competent for a State to regulate the enjoyment by citizens of their civil rights solely upon the basis of race. . . .

The destinies of the two races, in this country, are indissolubly linked together, and the interests of both require that the common government of all shall not permit the seeds of race hate to be planted under the sanction of law. What can more certainly arouse race hate, what more certainly create and perpetuate a feeling of distrust between these races, than state enactments, which, in fact, proceed on the ground that colored citizens are so inferior and degraded that they cannot be allowed to sit in public coaches occupied by white citizens? That, as all will admit, is the real meaning of such legislation as was enacted in Louisiana.

The sure guarantee of the peace and security of each race is the clear, distinct, unconditional recognition by our governments, National and State, of every right that inheres in civil freedom, and of the equality before the law of all citizens of the United States without regard to race. State enactments, regulating the enjoyment of civil rights, upon the basis of race, and cunningly devised to defeat legitimate results of the war, under the pretence of recognizing equality of rights, can have no other result than to render permanent peace impossible, and to keep alive a conflict of races, the continuance of which must do harm to all concerned. . . .

The arbitrary separation of citizens, on the basis of race, while they are on a public highway, is a badge of servitude wholly inconsistent with the civil freedom and the equality before the law established by the Constitution. It cannot be justified upon any legal grounds.

If evils will result from the commingling of the two races upon public highways established for the benefit of all, they will be infinitely less than those that will surely come from state legislation regulating the enjoyment of civil rights upon the basis of race. We boast of the freedom enjoyed by our people above all other peoples. But it is difficult to reconcile that boast with a state of the law which, practically, puts the brand of servitude and degradation upon a large class of our fellow-citizens, our equals before the law. The thin disguise of "equal" accommodations for passengers in railroad coaches will not mislead any one, nor atone for the wrong this day done.

BROWN v. BOARD OF EDUCATION   347 U.S. 483 (1954)

Chief Justice Warren delivered the unanimous opinion of the Court: The children of minority families of all colors and conditions, through their lawyers, long urged the courts to outlaw the racial segregation that did serious and lasting damage to their education. This required the outright reversal of *Plessy* and its "separate but equal" doctrine. Cases from South Carolina, Virginia, and Delaware were joined in 1954 with a case from Topeka, Kansas, all having the same central objective: admission to the public schools on a nonsegregated basis, all persons to be treated as equals without regard to their race. The Legal Defense Fund of the NAACP, (whose Director, Thurgood Marshall, was later to become a justice of the Supreme Court) argued in its brief that "race is an irrational basis for governmental action under our Constitution" and that "as a matter of law, race is not an allowable basis of differentiation in governmental action." Half a century after *Plessy* the civil rights movement prevailed at last. Chief Justice Warren delivered the unanimous opinion of the Supreme Court, in what will certainly remain one of the great landmarks in the interpretation of the ideal of equality.

In the first cases in this Court construing the Fourteenth Amendment, decided shortly after its adoption, the Court interpreted it as proscribing all state-imposed discriminations against the Negro race. The doctrine of "separate but equal" did not make its appearance in this Court until 1896 in the case of *Plessy v. Ferguson, supra,* involving not education but transportation. American courts have since labored with the doctrine for over half a century. In this Court, there have been six cases involving the "separate but equal" doctrine in the field of public education. . . .

In none of these cases was it necessary to re-examine the doctrine to grant relief to the Negro plaintiff. And in *Sweatt v. Painter, supra,* the Court expressly reserved decision on the question whether *Plessy v. Ferguson* should be held inapplicable to public education.

In the instant cases, that question is directly presented. Here, unlike *Sweatt v. Painter,* there are findings below that the Negro and white schools involved have been equalized, or are being equalized, with respect to buildings, curricula, qualifications and salaries of teachers, and other "tangible" factors. Our decision, therefore, cannot turn on merely a comparison of these tangible factors in the Negro and white schools involved in each of the cases. We must look instead to the effect of segregation itself on public education.

In approaching this problem, we cannot turn the clock back to 1868 when the Amendment was adopted, or even to 1896 when *Plessy v. Ferguson* was written. We must consider public education in the light of its full development and its present place in American life throughout the Nation. Only in this way can it be determined if segregation in public schools deprives these plaintiffs of the equal protection of the laws.

Today, education is perhaps the most important function of state and local governments. Compulsory school attendance laws and the great expenditures for education both demonstrate our recognition of the importance of education to our democratic society. It is required in the performance of our most basic public responsibilities, even service in the armed forces. It is the very foundation of good citizenship. Today it is a principal instrument in awakening the child to cultural values, in preparing him for later professional training, and in helping him to adjust normally to his environment. In these days, it is doubtful that any child may reasonably be expected to succeed in life if he is denied the opportunity of an education. Such an opportunity, where the state has undertaken to provide it, is a right which must be made available to all on equal terms.

We come then to the question presented: Does segregation of children in public schools solely on the basis of race, even though the physical facilities and other "tangible" factors may be equal, deprive the children of the minority group of equal educational opportunities? We believe that it does.

In *Sweatt v. Painter, supra,* in finding that a segregated law school for Negroes could not provide them equal educational opportunities, this Court relied in large part on "those qualities which are incapable of objective measurement but which make for greatness in a law school." In *McLaurin v. Oklahoma State Regents, supra,* the Court, in requiring that a Negro admitted to a white graduate school be treated like all other students, again resorted to intangible considerations: ". . . his ability to study, to engage in discussions and exchange views with other students, and, in general, to learn his profession." Such considerations apply with added force to children in grade and high schools. To separate them from others of similar age and qualifications solely because of their race generates a feeling of inferiority as to their status in the community that may affect their hearts and minds in a way unlikely ever to be undone. The effect of this separation on their educational opportunities was well stated by a finding in the Kansas case by a court which nevertheless felt compelled to rule against the Negro plaintiffs:

> Segregation of white and colored children in public schools has a detrimental effect upon the colored children. The impact is greater when it has the sanction of the law; for the policy of separating the races is usually interpreted as denoting the inferiority of the negro group. A sense of inferiority affects the motivation of a child to learn. Segregation with the sanction of law, therefore, has a tendency to [retard] the educational and mental development of negro children and to deprive them of some of the benefits they would receive in a racial[ly] integrated school system.

Whatever may have been the extent of psychological knowledge at the time of *Plessy v. Ferguson,* this finding is amply supported by modern authority. Any language in *Plessy v. Ferguson* contrary to this finding is rejected.

We conclude that in the field of public education the doctrine of "separate but equal" has no place. Separate educational facilities are inherently unequal. Therefore, we hold that the plaintiffs and others similarly situated for whom the actions have been brought are, by reason of the segregation complained of, deprived of the equal protection of the laws guaranteed by the Fourteenth Amendment.

UNIVERSITY OF CALIFORNIA REGENTS v. BAKKE
438 U.S. 265 (1978)

Justice Powell delivered the opinion of the Court: Allan Bakke was twice denied admission to the Medical School of the University of California at Davis while an affirmative action program in effect there reserved a percentage of the seats in each entering class for minority applicants who competed only against one another. After lengthy proceedings before the Supreme Court, a complicated set of opinions were delivered by six justices, their combined outcome being this: Bakke prevailed and was ordered admitted to the Medical School, although the University was not forbidden to accord *any* consideration to race in its admission process. The preferential program in question was struck down. Some justices rejected it because it was a violation of the Civil Rights Act of 1964 prohibiting institutions receiving Federal funds from discriminating against any individual "because of such individual's race, color, religion, sex, or national origin." Justice Powell, who delivered the judgment of the Court, agreed that the California program violated the law, but held that, more fundamentally, its racial preference violated the equal protection clause of the Fourteenth Amendment.

This case presents a challenge to the special admissions program of the petitioner, the Medical School of the University of California at Davis, which is designed to assure the admission of a specified number of students from certain minority groups. . . . The parties fight a sharp preliminary action over the proper characterization of the special admissions program. Petitioner prefers to view it as establishing a "goal" of minority representation in the Medical School. Respondent, echoing the courts below, labels it a racial quota.

This semantic distinction is beside the point: The special admissions program is undeniably a classification based on race and ethnic background. To the extent that there existed a pool of at least minimally qualified minority applicants to fill the 16 special admissions seats, white applicants could compete only for 84 seats in the entering class, rather than the 100 open to minority applicants. Whether this limitation is described as a quota or a goal, it is a line drawn on the basis of race and ethnic status.

The guarantees of the Fourteenth Amendment extend to all persons. Its language is explicit: "No State shall . . . deny to any person within its jurisdiction the equal protection of the laws." It is settled beyond question that the "rights created by the first section of the Fourteenth Amendment are, by its terms, guaranteed to the individual. The rights established are personal rights." The guarantee of equal protection cannot mean one thing when applied to one individual and something else when applied to a person of another color. If both are not accorded the same protection, then it is not equal. . . .

> Distinctions between citizens solely because of their ancestry are by their very nature odious to a free people whose institutions are founded upon the doctrine of equality." *Hirabayashi,* 320 U.S., at 100.
>
> "[A]ll legal restrictions which curtail the civil rights of a single racial group are immediately suspect. That is not to say that all such restrictions are unconstitutional. It is to say that courts must subject them to the most rigid scrutiny. *Korematsu,* 323 U.S., at 216.

The Court has never questioned the validity of those pronouncements. Racial and ethnic distinctions of any sort are inherently suspect and thus call for the most exacting judicial examination. . . .

We have held that in "order to justify the use of a suspect classification, a State must show that its purpose or interest is both constitutionally permissible and substantial, and that its use of the classification is 'necessary . . . to the accomplishment' of its purpose or the safeguarding of its interest."

. . . The special admissions program purports to serve the purposes of: (i) "reducing the historic deficit of traditionally disfavored minorities in medical schools and in the medical profession"; (ii) countering the effects of societal discrimination; (iii) increasing the number of physicians who will practice in communities currently underserved; and (iv) obtaining the educational benefits that flow from an ethnically diverse student body. It is necessary to decide which, if any, of these purposes is substantial enough to support the use of a suspect classification.

A

If petitioner's purpose is to assure within its student body some specified percentage of a particular group merely because of its race or ethnic origin, such a preferential purpose must be rejected not as insubstantial but as facially invalid. Preferring members of any one group for no reason other than race or ethnic origin is discrimination for its own sake. This the Constitution forbids.

B

The State certainly has a legitimate and substantial interest in ameliorating, or eliminating where feasible, the disabling effects of identified discrimination. The line of school desegregation cases, commencing with *Brown,* attests to the importance of this state goal and the commitment of the judiciary to affirm all lawful means toward its attainment. In the school cases, the States were required by court order to redress the wrongs worked by specific instances of racial discrimination. That goal was far more focused than the remedying of the effects of "societal discrimination," an amorphous concept of injury that may be ageless in its reach into the past.

We have never approved a classification that aids persons perceived as members of relatively victimized groups at the expense of other innocent individuals in the absence of judicial, legislative, or administrative findings of constitutional or statutory violations. . . . Without such findings of constitutional or statutory violations, it cannot be said that the government has any greater interest in helping one individual than in refraining from harming another. Thus, the government has no compelling justification for inflicting such harm.

Petitioner does not purport to have made, and is in no position to make, such findings. Its broad mission is education, not the formulation of any legislative policy or the adjudication of particular claims of illegality. For reasons similar to those stated in Part III of this opinion, isolated segments of our vast governmental structures are not competent to make those decisions, at least in the absence of legislative mandates and legislatively determined criteria. Before relying upon these sorts of findings in establishing a racial classification, a governmental body must have the authority and capability to establish, in the record, that the classification is responsive to identified discrimination. Lacking this capability, petitioner has not carried its burden of justification on this issue.

Hence, the purpose of helping certain groups whom the faculty of the Davis Medical School perceived as victims of "societal discrimination" does not justify a classification that imposes disadvantages upon persons like respondent, who bear no responsibility for whatever harm the beneficiaries of the special admissions program are thought to have suffered. To hold otherwise would be to convert a remedy heretofore reserved for violations of legal rights into a privilege that all institutions throughout the Nation could grant at their pleasure to whatever groups are perceived as victims of societal discrimination. That is a step we have never approved.

C

Petitioner identifies, as another purpose of its program, improving the delivery of health-care services to communities currently underserved. It may be assumed that in some situations a State's interest in facilitating the health care of its citizens is sufficiently compelling to support the use of a suspect classification. But there is virtually no evidence in the record indicating that petitioner's special admissions program is either needed or geared to promote that goal. . . .

Petitioner simply has not carried its burden of demonstrating that it must prefer members of particular ethnic groups over all other individuals in order to promote better health-care delivery to deprived citizens. Indeed, petitioner has not shown that its preferential classification is likely to have any significant effect on the problem.

D

The fourth goal asserted by petitioner is the attainment of a diverse student body. This clearly is a constitutionally permissible goal for an institution of higher education. . . . The atmosphere of "speculation, experiment. and creation"—so essential to the quality of higher education—is widely believed to be promoted by a diverse student body.

Thus, in arguing that its universities must be accorded the right to select those students who will contribute the most to the "robust exchange of ideas," petitioner invokes a countervailing constitutional interest, that of the First Amendment. In this light, petitioner must be viewed as seeking to achieve a goal that is of paramount importance in the fulfillment of its mission. . . .

Physicians serve a heterogeneous population. An otherwise qualified medical student with a particular background—whether it be ethnic, geographic, culturally advantaged or disadvantaged—may bring to a professional school of medicine experiences, outlooks, and ideas that enrich the training of its student body and better equip its graduates to render with understanding their vital service to humanity.

Ethnic diversity, however, is only one element in a range of factors a university properly may consider in attaining the goal of a heterogeneous student body. Although a university must have wide discretion in making the sensitive judgments as to who should be admitted, constitutional limitations protecting individual rights may not be disregarded. Respondent urges—and the courts below have held—that petitioner's dual admissions program is a racial classification that impermissibly infringes his rights under the Fourteenth Amendment. As the interest of diversity is compelling in the context of a university's admissions program, the question remains whether the program's racial classification is necessary to promote this interest.

It may be assumed that the reservation of a specified number of seats in each class for individuals from the preferred ethnic groups would contribute to the attainment of considerable ethnic diversity in the student body. But petitioner's argument that this is the only effective means of serving the interest of diversity is seriously flawed. In a most fundamental sense the argument misconceives the nature of the state interest that would justify consideration of race or ethnic background. It is not an interest in simple ethnic diversity, in which a specified percentage of the student body is in effect guaranteed to be members of selected ethnic groups, with the remaining percentage an undifferentiated aggregation of students. The diversity that furthers a compelling state interest encompasses a far broader array of qualifications and characteristics of which racial or ethnic origin is but a single though important element. Petitioner's special admissions program, focused *solely* on ethnic diversity, would hinder rather than further attainment of genuine diversity. . . .

It has been suggested that an admissions program which considers race only as one factor is simply a subtle and more sophisticated—but no less effective—means of according racial preference than the Davis program. A facial intent to discriminate, however, is evident in petitioner's preference program and not denied in this case. No such facial infirmity exists in an admissions program where race or ethnic background is simply one element—to be weighed fairly against other elements—in the selection process. "A boundary line," as Mr. Justice Frankfurter remarked in another connection, "is none the worse for being narrow." And a court would not assume that a university, professing to employ a facially nondiscriminatory admissions policy, would operate it as a cover for the functional equivalent of a quota system. In short, good faith would be presumed in the absence of a showing to the contrary in the manner permitted by our cases. . . .

In summary, it is evident that the Davis special admissions program involves the use of an explicit racial classification never before countenanced by this Court. . . .

The fatal flaw in petitioner's preferential program is its disregard of individual rights as guaranteed by the Fourteenth Amendment. Such rights are not absolute. But when a State's distribution of benefits or imposition of burdens hinges on ancestry or the color of a person's skin, that individual is entitled to a demonstration that the challenged classification is necessary to promote a substantial state interest. Petitioner has failed to carry this burden. For this reason, that portion of the California court's judgment holding petitioner's special admissions program invalid under the Fourteenth Amendment must be affirmed.

In enjoining petitioner from ever considering the race of any applicant, however, the courts below failed to recognize that the State has a substantial interest that legitimately may be served by a properly devised admissions program involving the competitive consideration of race and ethnic origin. For this reason, so much of the California court's judgment as enjoins petitioner from any consideration of the race of any applicant must be reversed.

98
Martin Luther King, Jr.

Martin Luther King, Jr. (1929–1968), the greatest American hero in the fight for racial equality, was a devout Christian who urged that unjust laws oppressing minorities or segregating the races *ought* not be obeyed. He was arrested and imprisoned on numerous occasions; in 1963, responding to fellow clergymen who had criticized the civil disobedience he led in Birmingham as unwise and untimely, he wrote from jail the letter from which the passage below is taken. King was confident that deliberate self-sacrifice in behalf of racial justice would ultimately provoke the nation to moral reflection and to legal reform. A year after this letter was written, the U.S. Congress passed the Civil Rights Act of 1964, which forbids discrimination, in most settings, on the basis of race, color, religion, sex, or national origin. Martin Luther King, Jr.—assassinated in 1968— did more than any other single person to goad the American nation to live up to the ideal of universal human equality it had so long professed, but so imperfectly realized.

[CIVIL DISOBEDIENCE IN DEFENSE OF GOD-GIVEN RIGHTS]*

We know through painful experience that freedom is never voluntarily given by the oppressor; it must be demanded by the oppressed. Frankly, I have yet to engage in a direct-action campaign that was "well timed" in the view of those who have not suffered unduly from the disease of segregation. For years now I have heard the word "Wait!" It rings in the ear of every Negro with piercing familiarity. This "Wait" has almost always meant "Never." We must come to see, with one of our distinguished jurists, that "justice too long delayed is justice denied."

We have waited for more than 340 years for our constitutional and God-given rights. The nations of Asia and Africa are moving with jet-like speed toward gaining political independence, but we still creep at horse-and-buggy pace toward gaining a cup of coffee at a lunch counter. Perhaps it is easy for those who have

*From *Letter from Birmingham City Jail*, 1963.

never felt the stinging darts of segregation to say, "Wait." But when you have seen vicious mobs lynch your mothers and fathers at will and drown your sisters and brothers at whim; when you have seen hate-filled policemen curse, kick and even kill your black brothers and sisters; when you see the vast majority of your twenty million Negro brothers smothering in an airtight cage of poverty in the midst of an affluent society; when you suddenly find your tongue twisted and your speech stammering as you seek to explain to your six-year-old daughter why she can't go to the public amusement park that has just been advertised on television, and see tears welling up in her eyes when she is told that Funtown is closed to colored children, and see ominous clouds of inferiority beginning to form in her little mental sky, and see her beginning to distort her personality by developing an unconscious bitterness toward white people; when you have to concoct an answer for a five-year-old son who is asking: "Daddy, why do white people treat colored people so mean?"; when you take a cross country drive and find it necessary to sleep night after night in the uncomfortable corners of your automobile because no motel will accept you; when you are humiliated day in and day out by nagging signs reading "white" and "colored"; when your first name becomes "nigger," your middle name becomes "boy" (however old you are) and your last name becomes "John," and your wife and mother are never given the respected title "Mrs."; when you are harried by day and haunted by night by the fact that you are a Negro, living constantly at tiptoe stance, never quite knowing what to expect next, and are plagued with inner fears and outer resentments; when you are forever fighting a degenerating sense of "nobodiness"—then you will understand why we find it difficult to wait. There comes a time when the cup of endurance runs over, and men are no longer willing to be plunged into the abyss of despair. I hope, sirs, you can understand our legitimate and unavoidable impatience.

You express a great deal of anxiety over our willingness to break laws. This is certainly a legitimate concern. Since we so diligently urge people to obey the Supreme Court's decision of 1954 outlawing segregation in the public schools, at first glance it may seem rather paradoxical for us consciously to break laws. One may well ask: "How can you advocate breaking some laws and obeying others?" The answer lies in the fact that there are two types of laws: just and unjust. I would be the first to advocate obeying just laws. One has not only a legal but a moral responsibility to obey just laws. Conversely, one has a moral responsibility to disobey unjust laws. I would agree with St. Augustine that "an unjust law is no law at all."

Now, what is the difference between the two? How does one determine whether a law is just or unjust? A just law is a man-made code that squares with the moral law or the law of God. An unjust law is a code that is out of harmony with the moral law. To put it in the terms of St. Thomas Aquinas: An unjust law is a human law that is not rooted in eternal law and natural law. Any law that uplifts human personality is just. Any law that degrades human personality is unjust. All segregation statutes are unjust because segregation distorts the soul and damages the personality. It gives the segregator a false sense of superiority and the segregated a false sense of inferiority. Segregation, to use the terminology of the Jewish philosopher Martin Buber, substitutes an "I—it" relationship for an "I—thou" relationship and ends up relegating persons to the status of things. Hence segregation is not only politically, economically and sociologically unsound, it is morally wrong and sinful. Paul Tillich has said that sin is separation. Is not segregation an existential expression of man's tragic separation, his awful estrangement, his terrible sinfulness? Thus it is that I can urge men to obey the 1954 decision of the Supreme Court, for it is morally right; and I can urge them to disobey segregation ordinances, for they are morally wrong.

Let us consider a more concrete example of just and unjust laws. An unjust law is a code that a numerical or power majority group compels a minority group to obey but does not make binding on itself. This is *difference* made legal. By the same token, a just law is a code that a majority compels a minority to follow and that it is willing to follow itself. This is *sameness* made legal.

Let me give another explanation. A law is unjust if it is inflicted on a minority that, as a result of being denied the right to vote, had no part in enacting or devising the law. Who can say that the legislature of Alabama which set up that state's segregation laws was democratically elected? Throughout Alabama all sorts of devious methods are used to prevent Negroes from becoming registered voters, and there are some counties in which, even though Negroes constitute a majority of the population, not a single Negro is registered. Can any law enacted under such circumstances be considered democratically structured?

Sometimes a law is just on its face and unjust in its application. For instance, I have been arrested on a charge of parading without a permit. Now, there is nothing wrong in having an ordinance which requires a permit for a parade. But such an ordinance becomes unjust when it is used to maintain segregation and to deny citizens the First-Amendment privilege of peaceful assembly and protest.

I hope you are able to see the distinction I am trying to point out. In no sense do I advocate evading or defying the law, as would the rabid segregationist. That would lead to anarchy. One who breaks an unjust law must do so openly, lovingly, and with a willingness to accept the penalty. I submit that an individual who breaks a law that conscience tells him is unjust, and who willingly accepts the penalty of imprisonment in order to arouse the conscience of the community over its injustice, is in reality expressing the highest respect for law.

Of course, there is nothing new about this kind of civil disobedience. It was evidenced sublimely in the refusal of Shadrach, Meshach and Abednego to obey the laws of Nebuchadnezzar, on the ground that a higher moral law was at stake. It was practiced superbly by the early Christians, who were willing to face hungry lions and the excruciating pain of chopping blocks rather than submit to certain unjust laws of the Roman Empire. To a degree, academic freedom is a reality today because Socrates practiced civil disobedience. In our own nation, the Boston Tea Party represented a massive act of civil disobedience.

We should never forget that everything Adolf Hitler did in Germany was "legal" and everything the Hungarian freedom fighters did in Hungary was "illegal." It was "illegal" to aid and comfort a Jew in Hitler's Germany. Even so, I am sure that, had I lived in Germany at the time, I would have aided and comforted

my Jewish brothers. If today I lived in a Communist country where certain principles dear to the Christian faith are suppressed, I would openly advocate disobey-
ing that country's antireligious laws. . . .

Like a boil that can never be cured so long as it is covered up but must be
opened with all its ugliness to the natural medicines of air and light, injustice must
be exposed, with all the tension its exposure creates, to the light of human conscience and the air of national opinion before it can be cured.

In your statement you assert that our actions, even though peaceful, must be
condemned because they precipitate violence. But is this a logical assertion? Isn't
this like condemning a robbed man because his possession of money precipitated
the evil act of robbery? Isn't this like condemning Socrates because his unswerv-
ing commitment to truth and his philosophical inquiries precipitated the act by the
misguided populace in which they made him drink hemlock? Isn't this like condemning Jesus because his unique God-consciousness and never-ceasing devotion
to God's will precipitated the evil act of crucifixion? We must come to see that, as
the federal courts have consistently affirmed, it is wrong to urge an individual to
cease his efforts to gain his basic constitutional rights because the quest may precipitate violence. Society must protect the robbed and punish the robber. . . .

Oppressed people cannot remain oppressed forever. The yearning for freedom
eventually manifests itself, and that is what has happened to the American Negro.
Something within has reminded him of his birthright of freedom, and something
without has reminded him that it can be gained. Consciously or unconsciously, he
has been caught up by the *Zeitgeist,* and with his black brothers of Africa and his
brown and yellow brothers of Asia, South America and the Caribbean, the United
States Negro is moving with a sense of great urgency toward the promised land of
racial justice. If one recognizes this vital urge that has engulfed the Negro community, one should readily understand why public demonstrations are taking
place. The Negro has many pent-up resentments and latent frustrations, and he
must release them. So let him march; let him make prayer pilgrimages to the city
hall; let him go on freedom rides—and try to understand why he must do so. If his
repressed emotions are not released in nonviolent ways, they will seek expression
through violence; this is not a threat but a fact of history. So I have not said to my
people: "Get rid of your discontent." Rather, I have tried to say that this normal
and healthy discontent can be channeled into the creative outlet of nonviolent
direct action. And now this approach is being termed extremist.

But though I was initially disappointed at being categorized as an extremist, as
I continued to think about the matter I gradually gained a measure of satisfaction
from the label. Was not Jesus an extremist for love. "Love your enemies, bless
them that curse you, do good to them that hate you, and pray for them which
despitefully use you, and persecute you." Was not Amos an extremist for justice:
"Let justice roll down like waters and righteousness like an ever-flowing stream."
Was not Paul an extremist for the Christian gospel: "I bear in my body the marks
of the Lord Jesus." Was not Martin Luther an extremist: "Here I stand; I cannot do
otherwise, so help me God." And John Bunyan: "I will stay in jail to the end of
my days before I make a butchery of my conscience." And Abraham Lincoln:

"This nation cannot survive half slave and half free." And Thomas Jefferson: "We hold these truths to be self-evident, that all men are created equal . . ." So the question is not whether we will be extremists, but what kind of extremists we will be. Will we be extremists for hate or for love? Will we be extremists for the preservation of injustice or for the extension of justice? In that dramatic scene on Calvary's hill three men were crucified. We must never forget that all three were crucified for the same crime—the crime of extremism. Two were extremists for immorality, and thus fell below their environment. The other, Jesus Christ, was an extremist for love, truth and goodness, and thereby rose above his environment. Perhaps the South, the nation and the world are in dire need of creative extremists. . . .

I have no fear about the outcome of our struggle in Birmingham, even if our motives are at present misunderstood. We will reach the goal of freedom in Birmingham and all over the nation, because the goal of America is freedom. Abused and scorned though we may be, our destiny is tied up with America's destiny. Before the pilgrims landed at Plymouth, we were here. Before the pen of Jefferson etched the majestic words of the Declaration of Independence across the pages of history, we were here. For more than two centuries our forebears labored in this country without wages; they made cotton king; they built the homes of their masters while suffering gross injustice and shameful humiliation—and yet out of a bottomless vitality they continued to thrive and develop. If the inexpressible cruelties of slavery could not stop us, the opposition we now face will surely fail. We will win our freedom because the sacred heritage of our nation and the eternal will of God are embodied in our echoing demands. . . .

Over the past few years I have consistently preached that nonviolence demands that the means we use must be as pure as the ends we seek. I have tried to make clear that it is wrong to use immoral means to attain moral ends. But now I must affirm that it is just as wrong, or perhaps even more so, to use moral means to preserve immoral ends. . . .

I wish you had commended the Negro sit-inners and demonstrators of Birmingham for their sublime courage, their willingness to suffer and their amazing discipline in the midst of great provocation. One day the South will recognize its real heroes. They will be the James Merediths, with the noble sense of purpose that enables them to face jeering and hostile mobs, and with the agonizing loneliness that characterizes the life of the pioneer. They will be old, oppressed, battered Negro women, symbolized in a seventy-two-year-old woman in Montgomery, Alabama, who rose up with a sense of dignity and with her people decided not to ride segregated buses, and who responded with ungrammatical profundity to one who inquired about her weariness: "My feets is tired, but my soul is at rest." They will be the young high school and college students, the young ministers of the gospel and a host of their elders, courageously and nonviolently sitting in at lunch counters and willingly going to jail for conscience' sake. One day the South will know that when these disinherited children of God sat down at lunch counters, they were in reality standing up for what is best in the American dream and for the most sacred values in our Judaeo-Christian heritage, thereby bringing our nation back to those great wells of democracy which were dug deep by the founding fathers in their formulation of the Constitution and the Declaration of Independence. . . .

If I have said anything in this letter that overstates the truth and indicates an unreasonable impatience, I beg you to forgive me. If I have said anything that understates the truth and indicates my having a patience that allows me to settle for anything less than brotherhood, I beg God to forgive me.

I hope this letter finds you strong in the faith. I also hope that circumstances will soon make it possible for me to meet each of you, not as an integrationist or a civil-rights leader but as a fellow clergyman and a Christian brother. Let us all hope that the dark clouds of racial prejudice will soon pass away and the deep fog of misunderstanding will be lifted from our fear-drenched communities, and in some not too distant tomorrow the radiant stars of love and brotherhood will shine over our great nation with all their scintillating beauty.

99
Nelson Mandela

Nelson Mandela (1918–   ), leader of the African National Congress (ANC), was tried in 1964 for sabotage and conspiracy to overthrow the government of South Africa; he was convicted and sentenced to imprisonment for life. That government's policy of legally enforced racial segregation in all spheres of life—*apartheid*—evoked bitter opposition from peoples around the globe; under great international pressure the government offered, after 27 years of imprisonment, to release Mandela—but he refused to accept release until apartheid had been formally ended and blacks in South Africa had been formally granted full political equality. In 1990 the government met his terms; he left prison to receive the acclaim of all the world. Immediately after the adoption of the new Constitution in 1994, democratic elections were held in which the votes of blacks and whites are treated equally; Nelson Mandela was elected first President of the new Republic of South Africa.

[POLITICAL DIVISION BASED ON COLOR
IS ENTIRELY ARTIFICIAL]*

From my reading of Marxist literature and from conversations with Marxists, I have gained the impression that Communists regard the parliamentary system of the West as undemocratic and reactionary. But on the contrary, I am an admirer of such a system.

Magna Carta, the Petition of Rights and the Bill of Rights are documents held in veneration by democrats throughout the world.

*From Nelson Mandela, Statement at Trial, Rivonia, South Africa, 1964.

I have great respect for British political institutions, and for the country's system of justice. I regard the British Parliament as the most democratic institution in the world, and the independence and impartiality of its judiciary never fail to arouse my admiration.

The American Congress, that country's doctrine of separation of powers, as well as the independence of its judiciary, arouse in me similar sentiments.

I have been influenced in my thinking by both West and East. All this has led me to feel that in my search for a political formula, I should be absolutely impartial and objective. I should tie myself to no particular system of society other than that of socialism. I must leave myself free to borrow the best from the West and from the East. . . .

The Government often answers its critics by saying that Africans in South Africa are economically better off than the inhabitants of the other countries in Africa. I do not know whether this statement is true and doubt whether any comparison can be made without having regard to the cost-of-living index in such countries.

But even if it is true, as far as the African people are concerned it is irrelevant. Our complaint is not that we are poor by comparison with people in other countries, but that we are poor by comparison with the white people in our own country, and that we are prevented by legislation from altering this imbalance.

The lack of human dignity experienced by Africans is the direct result of the policy of white supremacy. White supremacy implies black inferiority. Legislation designed to preserve white supremacy entrenches this notion.

Menial tasks in South Africa are invariably performed by Africans. When anything has to be carried or cleaned the white man will look around for an African to do it for him, whether the African is employed by him or not.

Because of this sort of attitude, whites tend to regard Africans as a separate breed. They do not look upon them as people with families of their own; they do not realize that they have emotions, that they fall in love like white people do, that they want to be with their wives and children like white people want to be with theirs, that they want to earn enough money to support their families properly, to feed and clothe them and send them to school. . . .

Africans want to be paid a living wage. Africans want to perform work they are capable of doing, and not work the Government declares them to be capable of. Africans want to be allowed to live where they obtain work, and not be endorsed out of an area because they were not born there.

Africans want to be allowed to own land in places where they work, and not be obliged to live in rented houses they can never call their own. Africans want to be part of the general population, and not confined to living in their own ghettos. . . .

Above all, we want equal political rights, because without them our disabilities will be permanent. I know this sounds revolutionary to the whites in this country, because the majority of voters will be Africans. This makes the white man fear democracy.

But this fear cannot be allowed to stand in the way of the only solution which will guarantee racial harmony and freedom for all. It is not true that the enfranchisement of all will result in racial domination. Political division, based on color, is entirely artificial, and when it disappears, so will the domination of one color group by another. The ANC has spent half a century fighting against racialism. When it triumphs it will not change that policy.

This then is what ANC is fighting. Their struggle is a truly national one. It is a struggle of the African people, inspired by their own suffering and their own experience. It is a struggle for the right to live.

During my lifetime I have dedicated myself to this struggle of the African people. I have fought against white domination, and I have fought against black domination. I have cherished the ideal of a democratic and free society in which all persons live together in harmony and with equal opportunities. It is an ideal I hope to live for and to achieve. But if needs be, it is an ideal for which I am prepared to die.

AUTONOMY

100
Carl Cohen

Autonomy is that ideal condition in which an individual moral agent is *self*-governed, goals and rules of conduct *self*-imposed. A community that is truly self-governed, one whose goals and whose laws are jointly self-imposed, may likewise deserve being described as autonomous. Fully moral conduct requires autonomy, but autonomy alone is no guarantee that acts will be right. Democracy, Carl Cohen argues, is moral autonomy written large.

DEMOCRACY AS AUTONOMY*

Democracy may be prized for its own sake, because it has intrinsic value. Exhibiting this intrinsic value does not serve, strictly, as an argument in support of democracy. It does not vindicate democracy by showing its good consequences, nor does it justify democracy by showing it founded upon true principles. It serves only to call attention to certain necessary features of democracy, features worthy of being prized not for their consequences or origins, but for themselves alone.

The essence of democracy is participation in the government of a community by the members of that community; it is *self*-government. No one doubts that in the smaller scale of individual life and conduct self-government is a great and

*From Carl Cohen, *Democracy,* New York, The Free Press, 1972.

intrinsic value; for its own sake each person prizes his freedom and capacity to govern his own life, to pursue his own ends in his own ways. This experience of personal self-government is writ large in the process of democracy. In the two cases—an individual controlling his own life and a community controlling its own affairs—the same principle is being realized; it is the principle of autonomy.

Autonomy is the expression of self-government as a moral ideal. *Autos,* self; *nomos,* law; auto-nomy is that ideal condition under which any rational agent gives law to itself. Among the ideals of morality it has long been one of the highest. Kant wrote:

> Looking back now on all previous attempts to discover the principle of morality, we need not wonder why they all failed. It was seen that man was bound to laws by duty, but it was not observed that the laws to which he is subject are *only those of his own giving,* though at the same time they are *universal,* and that he is only bound to act in conformity to his own will; a will, however, which is designed by nature to give universal laws. For when one has conceived man only as subject to a law (no matter what), then this law required some interest, either by way of attraction of constraint, since it did not originate as a law from *his own* will, but this will was according to a law obliged by *something else* to act in a certain manner. Now by this necessary consequence all the labor spent in finding a supreme principle of duty was irrevocably lost. For men never elicited duty, but only a necessity of acting from certain interest. Whether this interest was private or otherwise, in any case the imperative must be conditional, and could not by any means be capable of being a moral command. I will therefore call this the principle of *Autonomy* of the will, in contrast with every other which I accordingly reckon as *Heteronomy. (Fundamental Principles of the Metaphysics of Morals,* 1785, Second Section)

Democrats are not necessarily committed to a Kantian position in moral philosophy; but anyone who respects and treasures what Kant called the "supreme principle of morality," the autonomy of the will, will find democracy intrinsically valuable. In it, as in no other system of government, this principle is clearly and fully embodied.

The truly moral agent imposes rules of right conduct upon himself. The proper content of these rules may be a matter of dispute, and the fact that the rules are self-imposed gives no guarantee that the agent has chosen the correct rule, or that he has applied it so as to render his act objectively right. But whatever our judgment of the act, the moral character of the actor depends upon his autonomy; only that person's character is good whose right acts flow from his own will, voluntarily, not from compulsion or constraint. Moral autonomy is the direction and control of action by the agent from within. It is not sufficient, but it is necessary for the most praiseworthy conduct.

Community autonomy—the inter-personal correlate of autonomy in the life of the individual—is fully realized only when the community is democratically governed. Only under democracy do the members of the community at large develop their own rules governing joint affairs, and impose these rules upon themselves. As in the case of individual conduct, the fact that the rules are self-imposed gives no guarantee that the members have acted wisely or justly in choosing their rules or in applying them. However, if the rules governing the members of the community do not arise from their own participation, but are imposed from without or by some despotic element within, the moral character of the community must suffer, even if the decisions imposed are good ones. Individual and community are analogues in this matter; the appraisal of the morality of their conduct depends not only upon what is done, but also upon the source of the decision to do it. Ideally that source of direction and control will be within, autonomous. In the social sphere this autonomy is realizable only when government is carried on through the participation of the governed.

Autonomy is not a consequence of democracy; it does not arise after or because of democracy. In the life of the community autonomy *is* democracy; from a purely moral perspective the autonomous character of democratic government is its most fundamental and perhaps most important feature. It is an intrinsic value of democracy, prized directly for its own sake.

AUTONOMY AND HETERONOMY CONTRASTED

The great merit of autonomy in community life is clearly seen when autonomous and heteronomous governments are contrasted in several respects. The *first* is their conflicting conceptions of the *source of the laws.* Heteronomous (*hetero,* other) communities are governed by laws arising from a source other than the members of the community themselves. Authority there rests in some person or body external to the citizens at large, the resultant system properly being called authoritarian. The relation of citizens to governors is that of subordinates to superiors; laws are proclaimed to the people, coming from above and from outside of the people themselves. Government under such systems is necessarily external; even when the laws are good, they must then prove an intrusion into the life of the citizen.

Superficially it may appear that the relation of the citizen to the laws will be external whatever the system of government. The laws command that so-and-so be done; the citizen must obey or be punished. Below the surface, however, the origin of the laws makes a great deal of difference to the citizen commanded. That difference may not be evident in the process of law enforcement—although even on this level there is likely to be more respect shown by the law enforcement officer for the citizen when the former really sees himself as a servant of the public. The great difference lies rather in the convictions of the citizens, their attitudes toward the laws, and in the consequent motivation of their law-abiding conduct.

Where government is autonomous respect for law has a more moral as well as more rational foundation. It is more moral because one's participation in the law-making process commits one to abide by the outcome; it is more rational because the laws are the servants of the citizens themselves, serving their own purposes and not those of others. If the laws here prove intrusive, or otherwise bad, they do so because of their particular content, not because of their external source. The laws of a democracy may serve the community poorly, but they are necessarily its servants, not its masters.

Moreover, the moral quality of the public acts of a citizen—his deliberate obedience or disobedience of the laws—is intensified by his recognition of the autonomy of the community of which he is a participating member. Whatever the sanctions with which obedience might be compelled, it also becomes, because of this recognition, an act of voluntary self-regulation. Not only is the autonomous community itself a moral agent; it elevates the moral agency of its individual members.

Second: with respect to the *source of the objectives of the community,* the contrast between autonomous and heteronomous systems is fundamental. Here also the basic alternatives are two, however many their variants in practice: the objectives of a community may be selected by its members for themselves, or objectives may be imposed upon them by others, whether by one person or a few.

Heteronomy manifests itself in command relationships, depends essentially upon the recognition by citizens of their subordinate status and of the ruling authority of their superiors. The clearest example of heteronomy in the selection of goals is military organization. The explicit reason for the being of every military unit is the accomplishment of some antecedently determined mission, one that is assigned from above, imposed upon each person or unit by some higher authority in the chain of command.

Such command relationships are intensely antithetical to democracy. The members of a democracy recognize no superiors in deciding what, as a community, they should do or be. A democratically governed community performs no "mission" assigned by others, but attends to its own business in its own way. Being autonomous government, democracy entails that the choice of goals, as well as the enactment of laws, be determined by the general participation of the membership. Autonomy requires that ends as well as means be developed from within, not imposed from without.

Third: perhaps the deepest antipathy between autonomous and heteronomous systems lies in their opposing conceptions of the *nature and proper role of the individual.* Community autonomy goes hand in hand with the recognition of dignity in each participating member, a dignity whose universality is central to justificatory arguments in defense of democracy in the body politic. No heteronomous government can do justice to this dignity, however wise or benevolent its rule. This is because the citizen, in a heteronomous government, is most fundamentally the instrument of another, a tool for the accomplishment of some higher purpose imposed from without. Every unit in a hierarchical system (excepting only the apex itself) is essentially *sub*ordinate; the role of every person and group is service to superiors, the accomplishment of assigned objectives. The spirit of subordination is exhibited by the language used in its practice. Citizens become, strictly, *subjects;* in the military as in hierarchically organized private businesses human constituents are conceived not as persons but as *personnel;* public pronouncements by leaders are commonly framed in the imperative mood. Where community autonomy is denied, the autonomy of the individual members of the community must also be in good measure denied.

Authoritarian systems will, of course, profess great concern for the welfare of their citizens. Even where that concern is genuine, however, the welfare sought is determined not by the citizens but by their rulers, who claim to know better than they what is really best for them. What is benefit in the rulers' eyes may be injury in theirs; and even if not the subjects are necessarily insulted and demeaned by being compelled to do what others believe is right or good for them. In using human beings as means to the ends of others, heteronomous systems cannot recognize or honor in practice the universal possession of human dignity. Such recognition and honor, however, is a necessary feature of democracy, its essence being the participation of persons in decisions that affect their own lives.

Finally: it is autonomous systems only that can do full justice to *human rationality.* Autonomy requires of the moral agent—whether individual person or community—a special respect for the power of reason in government. In imposing rules or laws upon itself, the autonomous community presupposes the capacity of its citizens to recognize their need for rules and their understanding of the self-imposed obligation to apply them and obey them consistently. Further, autonomous government presupposes that this rationality will be deep enough and widespread enough to permit the citizens to devise and formulate rules of their own, not merely to adhere to rules set down by others. Human rationality is thus honored in practice by permitting that rationality to be effective in the government of common life. If rationality be a distinctive human characteristic, deserving a central place in the decision-making process of human beings, then democratic, autonomous government is distinctively and deeply humane.

NAME AND
TITLE INDEX